The Eastern Orthodox Churches

The Eastern Orthodox Churches

Concise Histories with Chronological Checklists of Their Primates

MICHAEL BURGESS

McFarland & Company, Inc., Publishers
Jefferson, North Carolina, and London

The present work is a reprint of the library bound edition of The Eastern Orthodox Churches: Concise Histories with Chronological Checklists of Their Primates, *first published in 2005 by McFarland.*

LIBRARY OF CONGRESS CATALOGUING-IN-PUBLICATION DATA

Burgess, Michael, 1948–
    The Eastern Orthodox churches : concise histories with chronological checklists of their primates / Michael Burgess.
        p.   cm.
    Includes bibliographical references and index.

    ISBN 978-0-7864-6081-6
    softcover : 50# alkaline paper ∞

    1. Orthodox Eastern Church — History. 2. Patriarchs and patriarchate — History. 3. Patriarchs and patriarchate — Registers. I. Title.
BX290.B87   2011
281'.5 — dc22   2005010582

British Library cataloguing data are available

© 2005 Michael Burgess. All rights reserved

No part of this book may be reproduced or transmitted in any form or by any means, electronic or mechanical, including photocopying or recording, or by any information storage and retrieval system, without permission in writing from the publisher.

Front cover image © 2011 Shutterstock

Manufactured in the United States of America

McFarland & Company, Inc., Publishers
  Box 611, Jefferson, North Carolina 28640
  www.mcfarlandpub.com

In memory of
DICK MARCHAND AND TED DIKTY

In friendship for
KARL PRUTER AND DAVE BOURQUIN

And, as always, for
BLESSÈD MARY

Contents

Preface ... 1

I.	Church of Aght'amar	5
II.	Church of Aghunie	8
III.	Church of Albania	12
IV.	Coptic Church of Alexandria	14
V.	Coptic Catholic Church of Alexandria	20
VI.	Greek Church of Alexandria	22
VII.	Latin Church of Alexandria	27
VIII.	Churches of America	29
IX.	Greek Church of Antioch	33
X.	Greek Melkite Catholic Church of Antioch	39
XI.	Latin Church of Antioch	45
XII.	Maronite Church of Antioch	48
XIII.	Syrian Catholic Church of Antioch	52
XIV.	Syrian Orthodox "Jacobite" Church of Antioch	57
XV.	Church of Armenia	63
XVI.	Church of Assyria (Church of the East)	69
XVII.	Churches of Austria-Hungary (Cernovci, Karlovci, Sibiu)	76
XVIII.	Chaldean Church of Babylon	83
XIX.	Church of Belarus	89
XX.	Church of Bulgaria	91
XXI.	Church of China	97
XXII.	Armenian Apostolic Church of Cilicia	98
XXIII.	Armenian Catholic Church of Cilicia	101
XXIV.	Armenian Church of Constantinople	103
XXV.	Greek Church of Constantinople (Ecumenical Patriarchate)	107

XXVI.	Latin Church of Constantinople	119
XXVII.	Church of Crete	123
XXVIII.	Church of Cyprus	126
XXIX.	Church of Czechoslovakia	132
XXX.	Church of Eritrea	134
XXXI.	Church of Estonia	135
XXXII.	Church of Ethiopia	138
XXXIII.	Church of Finland	145
XXXIV.	Church of Georgia	147
XXXV.	Church of Greece	154
XXXVI.	Churches of India	160
XXXVII.	Church of Japan	177
XXXVIII.	Armenian Church of Jerusalem	179
XXXIX.	Greek Church of Jerusalem	183
XL.	Latin Church of Jerusalem	188
XLI.	Church of Latvia	190
XLII.	Church of Macedonia (Ohrid)	193
XLIII.	Church of Moldova	198
XLIV.	Church of Montenegro	200
XLV.	Church of Poland	203
XLVI.	Church of Romania	205
XLVII.	Church of Rome	209
XLVIII.	Church of Russia	218
XLIX.	Church of Serbia (Peć)	225
L.	Church of the Sinai	230
LI.	Churches of Ukraine	233

Appendix 1.	Name Variants	243
Appendix 2.	Statistical Comparisons	251
Appendix 3.	Current Hierarchs by Church	253
Appendix 4.	Current Hierarchs by Date of Accession	257
Appendix 5.	Current Hierarchs by Date of Birth	259

Selected Bibliography — 261
Index of Primates — 267

Preface

The Eastern Orthodox Churches attempts to record as authoritatively as possible the primates and brief histories of every Eastern church that claims autocephaly or autonomy and has some reasonable historical or national claim to recognition as an independent church group; or, while lacking such universal recognition from other groups, nonetheless possesses a significant body of communicants. The several small splinter groups that claim ecclesiastical descent from the various attempts between the wars to erect national American churches are not included. Exceptions have been made for entities (such as the Church of Macedonia) whose claims of autocephaly are little recognized but who meet all the other criteria; these are included. Also included are those Latin churches which correspond to the ancient Eastern sees, even though most became no more than titular honors following the departure of the crusaders who had erected them; but such Western patriarchates as Venice, Lisbon, and the East and West Indies have been omitted, since they have never followed the pattern of the other churches.

Other features include source citations, a comprehensive index, and diacritical marks to distinguish the Greek letters *ēta* and *ōmega* from *epsilon* and *omicron*.

Each list of primates has been verified by mailing copies to the heads of the ecclesiastical bodies in question; I have been much gratified by the generous level of response.

The churches themselves have been regarded as the final arbiters of their officially sanctioned lists of primates. Where two or more churches claim the same basic patriarchal list prior to a certain date, but differ on exact names and dates, each list has been run separately, without any attempt to sort out claims and counterclaims, and without making any effort to rectify the lists one against another. I have never actually found any two such lists that completely agreed with one another; also, in every case where I received an "official" list from a church, its records disagreed with all the others in my possession, sometimes widely.

The reasons for adopting such guidelines are obvious. The official lists determine the postnominal numbering of both past and future church leaders; to vary from them, even slightly, is to invite ever-increasing discrepancies, in a world where such variations are already pervasive. Historians may quibble over the reality or even the name of this or that patriarch, as they do with certain rulers of secular states; in the end, however, we must agree to call Louis XVIII of France by that name, and not Louis

XVII (who never reigned), in order to establish some common ground for discussion. This book is my attempt at finding that common ground. Only in the case of the Ethiopian Orthodox Church, where the "official" church list varies enormously from the known historical record, have I felt compelled to provide two lists, the second derived from independent research. In other official lists, where evidence exists of additional primates not recorded by the church, I have sometimes interpolated such additions with appropriate notes in brackets.

The patriarchs' names have been transliterated as closely and consistently as possible from the languages actually used in each of the churches today. It was A. M. H. J. Stokvis who, in his monumental work *Manuel d'histoire, de généalogie, et de chronologie de touts les états du globe*, first established the principle of reproducing the names of rulers in the forms approximating as closely as possible those actually used in the vernaculars of their countries. Although the Eastern churches are, as a group, often referred to as "Greek Orthodox" by the uninformed, many of the churches that once used Greek as their official tongue now employ Arabic or some other native language. The transliterations are based on the systems established by the Library of Congress and the American Library Association for the romanization of non–English alphabets (see the Library of Congress's *Cataloging Bulletin*, nos. 118 and following, collected in *LC Romanization Tables and Cataloging Policies* [Tseng]), with occasional minor variations to standardize usage between similar languages. Since there is, as yet, no universally accepted method of transliterating the Syriac language into English, the system used by Arthur John MacLean in his *A Dictionary of the Dialects of Vernacular Syriac* (Oxford University Press, 1901) has been followed, with minor variations.

In those instances where there is some legitimate question as to which language is considered official by a particular church, in every case the language in common use among the people covered by its jurisdiction has been chosen first, with alternate versions where known. For example, the Coptic Church uses both Coptic and Arabic for official purposes; however, Coptic has long since ceased to be spoken except for liturgical functions, and so the Arabic versions of the patriarchs' names are listed first, followed by the Coptic versions in parentheses. Similarly, Arabic has been preferred over Syriac for the two Syrian patriarchates of Antioch.

The primary source for each church's history and leadership is, finally, the church itself. I contacted each of these bodies directly, and sent them copies of the lists and histories I had already compiled, requesting facsimile copies of their official records in the languages used by them for everyday church purposes. Eighty percent of the churches responded to my queries, either by providing copies of their official lists, or by referring me to published records they accepted as accurate and authoritative. A handful accepted the lists I sent them as genuine. All of the lists were buttressed by further research in the sources cited at the bottom of the history of each church, plus other research. These citations are not intended to be exhaustive, but merely reflect those books or periodical articles I personally found most useful. Official websites maintained by the churches have also been cited as sources, without addresses, however, since these tend to change fairly frequently.

On the subject of doctrine I remain mute. My purpose here is to record the chronology of each church as it perceives itself. I make no judgments about the correctness or legitimacy of any jurisdictional or theological beliefs or claims or counterclaims. Churches are listed in no other priority than alphabetical order. The fragmentation of the churches of Eastern Christendom is a fact of history which cannot be denied by the impartial observer; however, the reasons behind the balkanization of Orthodoxy are complex and not easily understood, having more perhaps to do with the cultural and historical backgrounds of each region than with any real or perceived differences in doctrine. These frequent feuds and jealousies have resulted, for example, in five different churches claiming the title of Patriarch of Antioch, three of them acknowledging the supremacy of the Pope of Rome.

To avoid this maze I have included here any established Eastern church that claims autocephaly (complete canonical independence from its brothers) or autonomy (complete self-governance except for the consecration of its primate), that elects a patriarch or an equivalent monarchical figure as its primate, and that possesses at least a patina of ecclesiastical legitimacy (a structure recognized by other autocephalous churches, or one that corresponds to a national boundary, or one that possesses a certain size and organizational structure). Also included are those uniate Eastern churches which correspond to one of the ancient patriarchal sees but acknowledge the supremacy of the Roman Church; plus the Church of Rome itself, since it was one of the original patriarchates of early christianity. The autocephaly of some of these churches is not recognized by others, and the mere inclusion of a church, however large or small, should not be regarded as an endorsement of the claims it makes for itself. For those few churches that did not respond to my queries, I have produced as accurate an amalgamation of current scholarly opinion as possible, taking into account the known chronology of recent patriarchs to standardize their numbering.

The churches are arranged in alphabetical order by their chief sees or national boundaries. Each entry includes a brief summary of the church's history, some indication of the location and size and language of its flock, the official title of the primate, the chief see of the church, a note on the language used in each church, primary sources cited, and a chronological checklist of its primates.

When known, surnames are listed for the primates recorded, in italics following their reign name. Alternate names are sometimes given in parentheses for primates when the official appellation in use today appears to vary from the language in use at the time the primate actually reigned. Second, third, and subsequent reigns are noted in brackets after each name.

The word "interregnum" designates any intermediate period, however brief, between the death, resignation, or deposition of one primate and the succession of another. For the purposes of this book, I have arbitrarily chosen to note only those interregna which have lasted three years or longer, on the grounds that these represent a significant interrruption in the normal sequence of governance.

Primates regarded by official church histories as interlopers are noted with the words "anti-patriarch," "anti-pope," or some similar appellation. The words "coadjutor" or "suffragan" signify prelates elected or appointed to assist the primate; such individuals may or may not have succeeded in their own right, and may or may not be numbered with the rest of their church's leaders. "Unconsecrated" denotes a primate who was properly elected or appointed, but never actually consecrated to his new post, and therefore may or may not be included on the offical list of primates of that church.

A "locum tenens" ("topotērētēs" or "τοποτηρητης" in Greek) designates a prelate who may never have served as primate of his church, but who acted as chief administrative officer of the primatial office until a new primate could be elected. He may have succeeded as locum tenens automatically, as the senior member of the hierarchy, or may have himself been elected or appointed by a holy synod or temporal or ecclesiastical authority.

Appendices to the text include a list of name variants, some statistical comparisons, and lists of current (as of 2005) hierarchs arranged by church, by date of ascension, and by date of birth. A bibliography and index are also provided.

I wish to thank each of the churches and churchmen who responded to my many letters of inquiry, and also those other individuals who assisted in various ways, especially Mar Aprem; Mary A. Burgess; Araxie Charukian, cousin of the late Armenian Catholicos Garegin I; Dr. Jeffrey M. Elliot; Father Gareth M. Evans; Rev. Antony Gabriel; Kenneth A. Gakus; Chakir al-Hamwi; Dr. Robert H. Hewsen; Rev. Demetrius J. King; Father Patrick McReynolds; Rev. Nenos S. Michael; the late Dr. Fran J. Polek; the late Archbishop Andrew Prazsky; Bishop Karl Pruter; Bishop Thomas Mar Makarios; Rev. Father Alexey Young. Thanks also to my predecessors in compilation, Anthony Stokvis, the Assemanis, Bertold Spuler, Otto Meinardus, Michel Le Quien, and others, whose pioneering efforts to record accurately the facts of both secular and religious chronology provided much inspiration to an aspiring college student.

Thanks also to the following libraries and organizations who provided varying levels of assistance: the staff of the Interlibrary Loan Department of the John M. Pfau Library, California State University, San Bernardino Library, who obtained many rare books for me; Le Centre Orthodoxe de Patriarcat Oecuménique, Chambésy, Genève, Switzerland; the Crosby Library, Gonzaga University, Spokane; the Doheny Library, University of Southern California, Los Angeles; Dr. Elizabeth Briere and the Fellowship of St. Alban and St. Sergius; the Library of Congress; the Tomás Rivera Library, University of California, Riverside; the Libraries of the University of California at Los Angeles; the LaVerne University Library.

Additions and corrections are welcome, and should be sent to the author in the care of McFarland & Company, Inc., Publishers.

Michael Burgess
September 2005

I.

Church of Aght'amar

The Armenian Catholicate of Aght'amar was founded in 1113, the result of a schism with the mother church that was not mended until 1409. Aght'amar was essentially a local church, located on an island in, and on the shores surrounding, Lake Van in Eastern Turkey, southwest of Armenia proper. Although able to maintain itself for many centuries as an autonomous church, it became increasingly dependent on Etchmiadzin for clergy and support.

The terrible massacres of Armenians conducted by the Turks between 1890 and 1915, and the subsequent expulsion from Turkey of most the survivors, decimated the Aght'amar Church; when the last Catholicos died in 1895, in the middle of the upheaval, a successor could not be elected; by the time the situation had stabilized, after World War I, so few Armenians remained in Eastern Turkey that restoration of the Catholicosate was impractical. Aght'amar was then reduced in status to a diocese under the direct control of the Church at Etchmiadzin.

SOURCES: *The Church of Armenia* (Ormanian); *Dictionnaire d'Histoire et de Géographie Ecclésiastique*; *The History of the Armenian People* (Morgan).

CATHOLICOS-PATRIARCHS OF AGT'AMAR

1.	Dawit' I *T'ornikian*	1113–1165?
	Grigor [coadjutor?]	1140?
	Hovhannês [coadjutor?]	1155?
2.	Step'anos I	1165?–1185?

INTERREGNUM

3.	Step'anos II	–1272
4.	Step'anos III *Sefedinian*	1272–1296?
	Khach'atur [coadjutor?]	1287?
	Step'anos (IV) *Tghay* [anti-catholicos?]	1288–1292
	Eghishê [anti-catholicos?]	1292–1300

5.	Zak'aria I *Sefedinian*	1296–1336
	Nersês [coadjutor]	1312
	Dawit' *Sefedinian* [coadjutor?]	1326?
6.	Step'anos IV *Ardzruni*	1336?–1346
7.	Dawit' II *Sefedinian*	1346–1368?
	Nersês *Bolat* [anti-catholicos]	1368?–1369?
8.	Zak'aria II *Nahatak*	1369–1393
	Nersês [anti-catholicos]	1393?
9.	Dawit' III	1393–1433
10.	Zak'aria III	1434–1464
11.	Step'anos V *Kurdjibeguyan*	1464–1489
	Nersês *Kurdjibeguyan* [anti-catholicos]	1489?
12.	Zak'aria IV	1489–1496
13.	Atom	1496–1510
14.	Hovhannês I	1510–1512
15.	Grigoris I	1512–1544?
16.	Grigoris II	1544?–1586?
17.	Grigoris III	1586?–1612?
	Step'anos (VI) [anti-catholicos]	1612?
	Baghdasar [anti-catholicos]	1630?

INTERREGNUM

18.	Martiros *Gurji*	1660–1662
	Karapet *Krdshadz* [anti-catholicos]	1661?
19.	Petros I	1662?–1670
20.	Step'anos VI	1671?
21.	P'ilippos	1671?
22.	Karapet I	1677–1679?
23.	Hovhannês II *T'iwt'iwnji*	1679–1681?
24.	T'ovma I *Toghlabeghian*	1681–1698
25.	Awetis	1697
26.	Sahak *Artskets'i*	1698
27.	Hovhannês III *Kêtsuk*	1699–1704
28.	Hayrapet *P'aykhets'i*	1705–1707
29.	Grigor IV *Gawahets'i*	1707–1711

INTERREGNUM

30.	Hovhannês IV *Hayots'-Zobets'i*	1720
	T'ovma [locum tenens]	1722?
	Ghazar [locum tenens]	1723?
31.	Grigor V *Hizants'i*	1725
32.	Baghdasar	1735?–1736
	Sahak (II) [anti-catholicos]	1736

I. Church of Aght'amar

	Hakob [anti-catholicos]	1736
33.	Nikoghayos	1736–1751
34.	Grigor VI	1751–1761
35.	T'ovma II	1761–1783
36.	Karapet II	1783–1787
37.	Markos	1788–1791
	Hovhannês (V) [anti-catholicos]	1791?
38.	T'êodoros	1792–1794
39.	Mik'ayêl	1796–1810
40.	Karapet III	1810?–1813?
41.	Khach'atur I	1813–1814
42.	Karapet IV	1814?–1816?
43.	Harut'iwn	1816?–1823
44.	Hovhannês V *Shatakhets'i*	1823–1843
45.	Khach'atur II *Mokats'i*	1844–1851
46.	Gabriêl *Shiroyan*	1851–1857
47.	Petros II *Pilpilian*	1858–1864
48.	Khach'atur III *Shiroyan*	1864–1895

CATHOLICOSATE DISESTABLISHED *1895*

II.

Church of Aghunie
(Caucasian Albania)

Located on the western shores of the Caspian Sea, directly east of Armenia, the sovereign state of Albania or Aghunie was an independent Armenian principality which bordered on both Armenia proper and on the Kingdom of Georgia. As with Georgia, Aghunie soon developed its own Church, independent of Armenia by the fifth century, if not sooner. For more than a thousand years the Albanian Church maintained a semi-autonomous existence, sometimes acting as an autocephalous body, on other occasions depending upon the Church of Armenia to supply new patriarchs or bishops. With the disappearance of the secular state of Albania, circa 1100, the Catholicosate gradually lost its separate status. The last patriarch, who bore the title of Catholicos of Aghunie, Lpink, and Choga, was deposed in 1815 and died in 1828, the Church thereupon being demoted to the status of a diocese under Etchmiadzin.

SOURCES: "The Albanian Chronicle of Mxit'ar Gos" (Dowsett); *Dictionnaire d'Histoire et de Géographie Ecclésiastique*; *The History of the Armenian People* (Morgan); *A History of the Caucasian Albanians* (Movsês); "A Neglected Passage in the History of the Caucasian Albanians" (Dowsett); *O Literature Kavkazskoĭ Albaniĭ* (Mnats'akanyan).

CATHOLICOS-PATRIARCHS OF CAUCASIAN ALBANIA

1. Eghishê — −79

INTERREGNUM

2. name unknown — 302–325

INTERREGNUM

3. Grigoris I — 340–342
4. Matt'êos I — 342–
5. Sahak I
6. Movsês I

II. Church of Aghunie

7. Pant
8. Ghazar
9. Zak'aria I
10. Dawit' I — −399
11. Hovhan(nes) I — 400−

INTERREGNUM

12. Shup'aghishoy — 500−
13. Eremia I — −552
14. Abas — 552–596
15. Viroy — 596–630
16. Zak'aria II — 630–646
17. Hovhan(nes) II — 646–670
18. Ukhtanês — 670–681?
19. Eghiazar — 681?–687?
20. Nersês I — 687?–704
21. Simêon I — 704–706
22. Mik'ayêl — 706–741
23. Anastas — 741–745
24. Hovsêp' I — 745–762
25. Dawit' II — 762–766
26. Dawit' III — 766–775
27. Matt'ê (or Matt'êos) II — 775–777
28. Movsês II — 777–779
29. Aharon — 779–781
30. Soghomon I — 782
31. T'êodoros — 782–786
32. Soghomon II — 786–797
33. Hovhannês III — 797–822
34. Movsês III — 822
35. Dawit' IV — 822–849
36. Hovsêp' II — 849–874
37. Samuêl — 874–891
38. Hovhan IV — 892–901
39. Simêon II — 902–923
40. Dawit' V — 923–929
41. Sahak II — 929–947
42. Gagik I — 947–961
43. Dawit' VI — 961–968
44. Dawit' VII — 968–974
45. Petros I — 974–992
46. Movsês IV — 992–997
47. Markos I — 997–
48. Hovsêp' III — 1038?
49. Markos II — −1077

50.	Step'anos I	1077–1103
51.	Hovhannês V	1103–1130
52.	Step'anos II	1130–1132

INTERREGNUM

53.	Grigoris II (or Gagik II)	1139–
54.	Babkên	1147?
55.	Step'anos III	1155?–1195
56.	Nersês II [coadjutor?]	1171?
57.	Hovhannês VI	1195–1235
58.	Nersês III	1235–1262
59.	Step'anos IV	1262–1323
60.	Suk'ias	1323
61.	Petros II	1323–
62.	Hovhannês VII	
63.	Hovhannês VIII	
64.	Petros III	–1406
65.	Karapet	1406–1411
66.	Dawit' VIII	1411
67.	Matt'êos III	1412–1440
68.	At'anasios	1440–1441
69.	Grigor III	1441–
70.	Hovhannês IX	–1470
71.	Matt'êos IV	1470–
72.	Aristakês I	–1478
73.	Nersês IV	1478–1481
74.	Chmavon I	1481–
75.	T'ovma	–1495
76.	Arakel	1495–1511
77.	Aristakês II	1511–1521
78.	Sargis I	1521–1555
79.	Grigor IV	1556–1563
80.	P'ilippos	1563–
81.	Dawit' IX	1573–1574
82.	Hovhannês X	–1586
83.	Chmavon II	1586–1611
84.	Aristakês III	1588–1593
85.	Melk'iset'	1593–1596
86.	Simêon III	1596–
87.	Hovhannês XI	1633–1634
88.	Grigor V	1634–1653
89.	Petros IV	1653–1675
	Simêon IV [anti-catholicos]	1675–1701
90.	Eremia II	1676–1700
91.	Esayi	1701–1727

II. Church of Aghunie

	Nersês V [anti-catholicos]	1706–1727
92.	Nersês V	1727–1763
	Israyêl [anti-catholicos]	1763–1765
93.	Hovhannês XII	1763–1786
94.	Simêon V	1794–1810
95.	Sargis II *Hassan-Jalaliants'*	1794–1815

III.

Church of Albania

Albania was placed under the ecclesiastical jurisdiction of the Patriarchate of Peć in 1346. With the abolition of the Serbian patriarchate in 1766, the administration of the Church was transferred to the Ecumenical Patriarch in Constantinople. During the centuries of Ottoman occupation, most of the population converted to Islam, approximately one-fourth remaining Christian; two-thirds of the latter are Orthodox, the rest being Catholic or other denominations.

When Albania became independent in 1914, the Orthodox Church there asserted itself, unilaterally declaring its autocephaly in September 1922. In January 1924, three priests, including Theofan "Fan" Noli (an Albanian-American), Hierotheos (a Greek), and Chrysostomos (also Greek), were consecrated as bishops of the new church, and formed themselves into a synod, with Noli being named the first Archbishop of Albania. Questions were raised by other Orthodox churches over these consecrations, and the Ecumenical Patriarch refused his recognition. Noli became Prime Minister of Albania later that same year, but lost a political struggle to President Ahmed Zogu (later King Zog), and was forced to leave the country in December.

Five years later, Visarion Xhuvani gained the recognition of the government of King Zog I, and was consecrated Archbishop on 12 February 1929; he reconstituted the synod and reasserted Albanian autocephaly on 18 February.

Constantinople still withheld recognition, until an agreement was reached with Kristofor Kisi, a member of the Albanian Holy Synod, on 12 April 1937. Visarion was forced to resign by the King, and Kisi installed as Metropolitan Archbishop. The Communist regime deposed Kisi in 1948 and installed Païsi Voditsa, putting great pressure on the Church during the next two decades. The government finally abolished the practice of religion altogether in 1967; every place of worship was closed, public and private worship being forbidden. Archbishop Damian was arrested after serving less than a year; he died under house arrest in 1973.

In late 1990 and early 1991 the Communist government agreed to allow free elections, and restored freedom of religion to the population; mass was openly celebrated in an Orthodox church for the first time in twenty-three years. The Ecumenical Patriarch promptly announced a program of assistance to re-establish the Albanian Church, appointing in 1990 a Greek Exarch, Anastasios Janullatos, to ordain new Albanian clergy and reconstitute the shattered Church resources. Anastasios was promoted to

Archbishop on 2 August 1992, amid protests from some of his communicants, who felt that the post ought to go to an Albanian.

By 1994 dissident members had formed a protest group lobbying for the restoration of autocephalous status to the Church of Albania and the banishment of all foreign nationals from the hierarchy; two newly-appointed Greek bishops were denied entrance visas by the government. However, a compromise was finally reached with the church in the mid–1990s, allowing Anastasios to continue serving as head of the reconstituted Autocephalous Church of Albania, but permitting just one other Greek prelate to remain on the Holy Synod.

The head of the Albanian Church bears the title Metropolitan of Tiranë and Durresi, Archbishop of All Albania. The official language is Albanian. There were roughly 160,000 communicants in Albania (according to *Eastern Christianity and Politics*) prior to 1967; the number of those belonging to the church today is unknown.

SOURCES: *Eastern Christianity and Politics in the Twentieth Century* (Ramet, ed.); *Échos d'Orient*; *Episkepsis*; *Europa World Yearbook*; *Gegenwartslage der Ostkirchen* (Spuler); *History of the Church* (Jedin, ed.); *Orthodoxia*; *Profiles in Belief* (Piepkorn); official church website.

METROPOLITAN ARCHBISHOPS OF ALBANIA

1.	Theofan "Fan" *Noli*	1923–1924
	Jerotheu *Vllaho* (Hierotheos *Blachos*) [locum tenens]	1924–1929
2.	Visarion *Xhuvani*	1929–1936
3.	Kristofor *Kisi*	1937–1948
4.	Païsi *Vodica*	1949–1966
5.	Damian *Kokoneši*	1966–1973
	Sofron *Borova* [locum tenens]	1967–1973

INTERREGNUM

	Anastasios *Janullatos* [as exarch]	1990–1992
6.	Anastasios *Janullatos*	1992–

IV.

Coptic Church of Alexandria

The ancient Patriarchate of Alexandria was one of the original seats of early Christianity, having been founded, according to legend, by St. Mark the Evangelist. Although renowned as an early center of monasticism, the Egyptian Church was also plagued with schisms and controversy from its earliest centuries. The supporters of Arianism erected a separate patriarchate in the year 336; it survived, with breaks, until 378. Less than a century later, the patriarch Dioskoros (Di[u]squrus) I embraced monophysitism, precipitating a major doctrinal struggle at the Council of Chalcedon in 451. Dioskoros was subsequently declared a heretic, deposed, and banished, with the full support of Eastern Emperor Marcian. The Greek ruling class of Egypt elected Proterios to fill the now-vacant see; the native population, however, most of whom spoke Coptic (a degenerate form of ancient Egyptian), rallied around Dioskoros, sending him a delegation to assure him of their loyalty. He died in 454, before he could return from exile.

Thus began the great split in the Alexandrian Church. At the death of Dioskoros, the populace demanded a new patriarch, but the government refused; when the Emperor died, however, an Egyptian mob murdered Proterios, and installed their own leader, Timotheos Ailouros ("The Cat") in his place. Constantinople was unable to reestablish civil control over Egypt for three years, at which point Timotheos was exiled, and a supporter of Chalcedon, Timotheos Salophakiolos ("Wobbling Hat," or, in other words, "vacillating"), was put in his place. Ailouros was restored by the Emperor Basiliskos in 475, deposed again in 476, and died in 477. The Byzantine Emperor Zeno, determined to put an end to the civil and religious strife in Egypt, banished the Greek patriarch in 489, leaving the Coptic line without rivals for fifty years. In 536, the Copts split again, one faction following Gaïanos; the Roman pope used the occasion to establish Paulos as Melkite Patriarch of Egypt. Despite periods of success, the Copts were never really secure from the depredations of the Greeks until the Arab conquest of 642; from this point forward, except for a seventy-six year gap between 651–727, there are two separate lines of patriarchs.

The Coptic line, representing the common people, has always been by far the larger church, encompassing perhaps 80 percent of the Christian population in Egypt. Coptic is the official language of the Church, but Arabic is used for everyday purposes (and the patriarchs below are listed with the Arabic versions of their names). A month before his assassination in 1981, Egyptian President Anwar al-Sadat tried to placate

Muslim extremists by exiling Coptic Pope Shanudah III to a monastery in the Egyptian desert. He was kept there under house arrest until 1 January 1985, when President Hosni Mubarak restored him to his position.

The primate bears the title "Pope and Patriarch of the Great City of Alexandria and of All the Land of Egypt, of Jerusalem the Holy City, of Nubia, Abyssinia, and Pentapolis, and All the Preaching of St. Mark." Although the chief see of the Church is technically Alexandria, its administrative offices are actually located in Cairo. Eight to ten million communicants are spread throughout Northern Africa (particularly Egypt), with major overseas populations in the United States and other countries.

SOURCES: *Christian Egypt Ancient and Modern* (Meinardus); *Die Christlich-Koptische Ägypten Einst und Heute* (Cramer); *Coptic Egypt* (Kamil); *The Coptic Encyclopedia* (Atiya); *Dictionnaire d'Histoire et de Géographie Ecclésiastiques*; *Episkepsis*; *Gegenwartslage der Ostkirchen* (Spuler); *Histoire de L'Église Copte* (Roncaglia); *Historia tēs Ekklēsias Alexandreias (62–1934)* (Papadopoulos); *History of the Church* (Jedin, ed.); *The History of the Coptic Church* (Yuhanna); *A History of the Patriarchs of the Egyptian Church* (Atiya; regarded as official by the church); *A History of the Patriarchs of the See of Alexandria* (Tawudrus); *A Lonely Minority: The Middle East and North Africa*; *The Modern Story of Egypt's Copts* (Wakin); *Monks and Monasteries of the Egyptian Desert* (Meinardus); *Die Morgenlandischen Kirchen* (Spuler); *Mujaz Tarikh Batarikat al-Iskandariyah* (Nabib); *Oriens Christianus* (Le Quien); *Orthodoxia*; personal communication; *Précis de l'Histoire d'Egypte* (Munier); *Profiles in Belief* (Piepkorn); *Qissat al-Khanisah al-Qibtiyah* (al-Misri); official church website.

COPTIC POPES AND PATRIARCHS OF ALEXANDRIA
(Coptic forms of the names are in parentheses)

1.	Murqus I (Markos)	43?–68
2.	Aniyanus (Anianos)	68–85
3.	Miliyus (Milios)	83–98
4.	Kurdunus (Kerdōn)	98–109
5.	Abrimus (Primos)	109–122
6.	Yustus (Ioustos)	122–130
7.	Awminiyus (Eumenios)	130–142
8.	Markiyanus (Markianos)	143–154

INTERREGNUM

9.	Kallawtiyanus (Kallauthianos)	157–167
10.	Aghribbinus (Agrippinos)	167–180
11.	Yuliyanus (Ioulianos)	180–189
12.	Dimitriyus I (Dēmētrios)	189–231
13.	Yaraklas (Hieraklas)	231–247
14.	Diyunisiyus (Dionysios)	247–264
15.	Maksimus (Maximos)	264–282

16.	Thawna (Theōnas)	282–300
17.	Butrus I (Petros)	300–311
18.	Arshalawus (Archelaos or Achillas)	311–312
19.	Aliksandarus I (Alexandros)	312–326
20.	Athanasiyus I (Athanasios)	326–373
21.	Butrus II (Petros) [brother of #22]	373–380
22.	Timuthawus I (Timotheos) [brother of #21]	380–385
23.	T(h)awfilus (Theophilos)	385–412
24.	Kirillus I (Kyrillos) [nephew of #23]	412–444
25.	Disqurus I (Dioskoros)	444–458
26.	Timuthawus II (Timotheos) *Ailouros* "The Cat"	458–460?
	Timuthawus *Salophakialos* [anti-pope]	460–475
	Timuthawus II (Timotheos) [2nd time]	475–480
27.	Butrus III (Petros) *Mongos*	480–488
28.	Athanasiyus II (Athanasios)	488–494
29.	Yuhannis I (Ioannēs) *Hemula*	495–503
30.	Yuhannis II (Ioannēs) *Nikiotēs*	503–515
31.	Disqurus II (Dioskoros) [nephew of #26]	515–517
32.	Timuthawus III (Timotheos)	517–535
33.	Thawdusiyus I (Theodosios)	535–567
34.	Butrus IV (Petros)	567–569
35.	Damiyanus (Damianos)	569–605
36.	Anastasiyus (Anastasios)	605–616
37.	Andruniqus (Andronikos)	616–622
38.	Banyamin I (Beniamin)	622–661
39.	Aghathu(n) (Agathōn)	661–677
40.	Yuhannis III (Ioannēs)	677–686
41.	Isaaq (Isaak)	686–689
42.	Simawun I (Symeōn)	689–701

INTERREGNUM

43.	Aliksandarus II (Alexandros)	705–730
44.	Qusma(n) I (Kosmas)	730–731
45.	Thawdurus (Theodōros)	731–743
46.	Kha'il (or Mikha'il) I (Chaēl)	744–767
47.	Mina I (Minas)	767–774
48.	Yuhannis IV (Ioannēs)	775–799
49.	Murqus II (Markos)	799–819
50.	Ya'qub (Iakōbos)	819–830
51.	Simawun II (Symeōn)	830
52.	Yusab I (Iosēph)	830–849
53.	Kha'il (or Mikha'il) II (Chaēl)	849–851
54.	Qusma(n) II (Kosmas)	851–858
55.	Sanutiyus (or Shanudah) I (Senouthios)	858–880
56.	Mikha'il III (Michaēl)	880–907

IV. Coptic Church of Alexandria

57.	Ghubriyal I (Gabriēl)	909–920
58.	Qusma(n) III (or Quzman) (Kosmas)	920–932
59.	Makariyus I (Makarios)	932–952
60.	Thawfaniyus (Theophanios or Theophanēs)	952–956
61.	Mina II (Minas)	956–974
62.	Abram (or Afram) *ibn Zar'ah* (Abraam)	975–978
63.	Filut(h)awus (Philotheos)	979–1003
64.	Zakhariya(s) (Zakharias)	1004–1032
65.	Sanutiyus (or Shanudah) II (Senouthios)	1032–1046
66.	Akhristudulus (Christodoulos)	1047–1077
67.	Kirillus II (Kyrillos)	1078–1092
68.	Mikha'il IV (Michaēl)	1092–1102
69.	Makariyus II (Makarios)	1102–1128

Interregnum

70.	Ghubriyal II *ibn Turaik* (Gabriēl)	1131–1145
71.	Mikha'il V (Michaēl)	1145–1146
72.	Yuhannis V *ibn Abi'l-Fath* (Iōannēs)	1147–1167
73.	Murqus III *ibn Zur'a* (Markos)	1167–1189
74.	Yuhannis VI *ibn Abi Ghali* (Iōannēs)	1189–1216

Interregnum

75.	Kirillus III *Dawud ibn Laqlaq* (Kyrillos)	1235–1243

Interregnum

76.	Athanasiyus III *ibn Kalil* (Athanasios)	1250–1261
77.	Yuhannis VII *ibn Abi Sa'id* (Iōannēs)	1262–1268
78.	Ghubriyal III (Gabriēl)	1268–1271
	Yuhannis VII [2nd time]	1271–1293
79.	Thawdusiyus II (Theodosios)	1294–1300
80.	Yuhannis VIII (Iōannēs)	1300–1320
81.	Yuhannis IX (Iōannēs)	1320–1327
82.	Banyamin II (Beniamin)	1327–1339
83.	Butrus V (Petros)	1340–1348
84.	Murqus IV (Markos)	1349–1363
85.	Yuhannis X *al-Mu'taman* (Iōannēs)	1363–1369
86.	Ghubriyal IV (Gabriēl)	1370–1378
87.	Mattawus (or Matta) I (Mattheos)	1378–1409
88.	Ghubriyal V (Gabriēl)	1409–1427
89.	Yuhannis XI *Abu'l-Farag* (Iōannēs)	1427–1452
90.	Mattawus II (Mattheos)	1452–1465
91.	Ghubriyal (or Ghabrial) VI (Gabriēl)	1466–1475

92.	Mikha'il VI (Michaēl)	1476–1478
93.	Yuhannis XII (Iōannēs)	1479–1482
94.	Yuhannis XIII (Iōannēs)	1484–1524
95.	Ghubriyal VII (Gabriēl)	1525–1568
96.	Yuhannis XIV *al-Manfaluti* (Iōannēs)	1570–1585
97.	Ghubriyal VIII (Gabriēl)	1586–1601
98.	Murqus V (Markos)	1602–1618
99.	Yuhannis XV (Iōannēs)	1619–1634
100.	Mattawus III (Mattheos)	1634–1649
101.	Murqus VI (Markos)	1650–1660
102.	Mattawus IV *al-Miri* (Mattheos)	1660–1675
103.	Yuhannis XVI *al-Maghribi* (Iōannēs)	1676–1718
104.	Butrus VI (Petros)	1718–1726
105.	Yuhannis XVII *al-Malawi* (Iōannēs)	1726–1745
106.	Murqus VII (Markos)	1745–1769
107.	Yuhannis XVIII *al-Fayumi* (Iōannēs)	1769–1796
108.	Murqus VIII (Markos)	1796–1809
109.	Butrus VII *al-Gawli* (Petros)	1809–1852
110.	Kirillus IV *Dawud Tuma Bashut* (Kyrillos)	1854–1861
111.	Dimitriyus II (Dēmētrios)	1862–1870

Interregnum

	Murqus [locum tenens]	1870–1874
112.	Kirillus V *ibn Ibrahim Sa'ad Matar al-Nasikh* (Kyrillos)	1874–1927
	Yuhannis [locum tenens]	1927–1928
113.	Yuhannis XIX (Iōannēs)	1928–1942
	Yusab *Filibbus* [locum tenens]	1942–1944
114.	Makariyus III (Makarios)	1944–1945
	Athanasiyus [locum tenens]	1945–1946
115.	Yusab II *Filibbus* (Iōsēph)	1946–1954

Interregnum

	Athanasiyus [locum tenens]	1954–1959
116.	Kirillus VI *Azir Yusuf 'Ata* (Kyrillos)	1959–1971
	Antuniyus [locum tenens]	1971
117.	Shanudah III *Gayid Rafail* (Senouthios)	1971–

Gaïanite or Julianist Patriarchs of Alexandria
(Not considered valid by the Coptic Church)

33.	Gaïanos (or Gaïnas or Kayanus)	536–565
34.	Elpidios (or Helpidios)	565–567

IV. Coptic Church of Alexandria

35.	Dōrotheos	567–
36.	Iōannes (III) [anti-pope]	567–

INTERREGNUM

| 37. | Mēnas | 634? |

INTERREGNUM

| 38. | Theodōros | 695? |

V.

Coptic Catholic Church of Alexandria

The Church of Rome regarded Patriarch Dioskoros (Disqurus) and his successors as heretics; and although attempts were made by both churches at various times to resolve their differences, these had ceased by the middle ages. In 1675 Catholic missionaries entered Egypt, and gradually managed to convert some of the Coptic population during the ensuing sixty-six years. In 1741, when the Coptic Bishop Athanasiyus of Jerusalem recognized the supremacy of Rome, he was made Apostolic Administrator of the Catholic Copts, and was confirmed in his rank by the Pope.

A Coptic Patriarchate was established by Pope Leo XII in 1824, but no patriarch was appointed until 1899, in the person of Kirillus Makariyus. Kirillus was forced to resign in 1908, when he lapsed into heresy and rejoined the original Coptic Church; thereafter, the patriarchal office remained vacant until 1947.

The primate bears the title "Patriarch of Alexandria of the Copts and of All the Preaching of St. Mark." The official language of this small church is Coptic, but Arabic is used on most occasions (and the patriarchs listed below are given in the Arabic versions of their names). Administrative offices are located at Cairo. There are some 200,000 communicants located in Egypt and in the United States.

SOURCES: *The Catholic Eastern Churches* (Attwater); *Catholic Encyclopedia*; *The Christian Churches of the East* (Attwater); *Dictionnaire d'Histoire et de Géographie Ecclésiastiques*; *Gegenwartslage der Ostkirchen* (Spuler); *The Middle East and North Africa*; *Die Morgenländischen Kirchen* (Spuler); *New Catholic Encyclopedia*; "Pope Calls for Broad Mideast Peace" (Montalbano); official church website.

COPTIC CATHOLIC PATRIARCHS OF ALEXANDRIA
(Patriarchs of the Old Church Recognized As Legitimate)

1.	Murqus I (Markos)	50?–68
2.	Aniyanus (Anianos)	68–83
3.	Abiliyus (or Miliyus) (Abilios)	83–95
4.	Kurdunus (Kerdōn)	95–106

V. Coptic Catholic Church of Alexandria

5.	Abrimus (Primos)	106–118
6.	Yustus (Ioustos)	118–129
7.	Awminiyus (Eumenēs)	129–141
8.	Markiyanus (Markianos)	141–152
9.	Kallawtiyanus (Keladiōn)	152–166
10.	Aghribbinus (Agrippinos)	166–178
11.	Yuliyanus (Ioulianos)	178–188
12.	Dimitriyus (Dēmētrios)	188–230
13.	Yaraklas (Hēraklas)	230–246
14.	Diyunisiyus (Dionysios)	246–264
15.	Maksimus (I) (Maximos)	264–282
16.	Thawna (Theōnas)	282–300
17.	Butrus I (Petros)	300–310
18.	Arshalawus (Archelaos)	310–311
19.	Aliksandarus (Alexandros)	312–328
20.	Athanasiyus (I) (Athanasios)	328–373
21.	Butrus II (Petros)	373–378
22.	Timuthawus (Timotheos)	378–384
23.	Thawfilus (Theophilos)	384–412
24.	Kirillus I (Kyrillos) [nephew of #23]	412–444

THE CATHOLIC PATRIARCHATE RESTORED
(Apostolic Administrators 1741–1899, 1908–1947)

1.	Athanasiyus (II) (Athanasios)	1741–1781
2.	Yuhannis *Faragi* (Iōannēs)	1781–1788
3.	Mattawus *Righat* (Mattheos)	1788–1822
4.	Maksimus (II) *Jayid* (Maximos)	1824–1831
5.	Thawdurus *Abu Karim* (Theodōros)	1832–1854
6.	Athanasiyus (III) *Khuzam* (Athanasios)	1854–1864
7.	Aghabiyus *Bishai* (Agapios)	1866–1887

INTERREGNUM

8.	Kirillus *Makariyus* (Kyrillos) [as apostolic administrator]	1895–1899
25.	Kirillus II *Makariyus* (Kyrillos)	1899–1908
9.	Maksimus (III) *Sidfawi* (Maximos)	1908–1927
10.	Murqus *Khuzam* (as administrator)	1927–1947
26.	Murqus II *Khuzam* (Markos)	1947–1958
	Ishaq *Ghattas* [coadjutor]	1955–1958
27.	Istifanus I *Sidarus* (Stephanos)	1958–1986
11.	Andrawus *Ghattas* (*i.e.*, Istifanus II) [apostolic administrator]	1984–1986
28.	Istifanus II *Ghattas* (Stephanos)	1986–

VI.

Greek Church of Alexandria

Greek was the *lingua franca* in the ancient Near East, so it was only natural that the educated class, including the hierarchies of the early Christian churches, often wrote and spoke in Greek. Before the Arab conquests of the seventh century, Egypt was ruled from Byzantium; court and governmental officials also spoke Greek, reinforcing the pattern. The common people, however, spoke a degenerate form of old Egyptian called Coptic. The split between these two classes became evident during the reign of Patriarch Dioskoros, who embraced monophysitism, thereby causing a permanent split in the Alexandrian Church.

Dioskoros was replaced by a Greek-speaking, government-sponsored candidate, Proterios, who had acceded to the mandates of the Council of Chalcedon. The patriarchate was supplanted by the Emperor Zeno in 489, and not restored until 537; it again lapsed between 651–727, in the aftermath of the Arab invasion. The Greek Church has always been much smaller than its Coptic brother, essentially serving only the Greek-speaking populations of North Africa, which declined dramatically during the twentieth century. However, in recent decades efforts have been made to establish missionary colonies south of the Sahara, with some success.

The official language of the Church is Greek. The primate bears the title (recognized in 325) of "Pope and Patriarch of Alexandria and All Africa," and ranks first in primacy behind the Ecumenical Patriarch. The Church has approximately 350,000 members, 20,000 in Egypt, the rest located in Africa south of the Sahara.

SOURCES: *Dictionnaire d'Histoire et de Géographie Ecclésiastiques*; *Échos d'Orient*; *Episkepsis*; *Gegenwartslage der Ostkirchen* (Spuler); *Historia tēs Ekklēsias Alexandreias (62–1934)* (Papadopoulos; regarded as official by the Church); *History of the Church* (Jedin, ed.); *Jahrbuch der Orthodoxie* (Proc); *The Middle East and North Africa*; *Die Morgenlandischen Kirchen* (Spuler); *Oriens Christianus* (Le Quien); "Pinakes Patriarchōn"; *Profiles in Belief* (Piepkorn); official church website.

POPES AND PATRIARCHS OF ALEXANDRIA

1.	Markos I *Euangelistēs*	42–62
2.	Anianos	62–84

VI. Greek Church of Alexandria

3.	Abilios	84–98
4.	Kerdōn	98–110
5.	Primos	110–121
6.	Ioustos	121–131
7.	Eumenēs (or Hymenaios)	131–144
8.	Markos II (or Markianos)	144–154
9.	Keladiōn	154–167
10.	Agrippinos	167–179
11.	Ioulianos	179–189
12.	Dēmētrios	189–232
13.	Hēraklas	232–247
14.	Dionysios	248–265
15.	Maximos	265–282
	Paphnytios [anti-pope]	282–
16.	Theōnas	282–300
17.	Petros I	300–311
18.	Achillas	311–312
19.	Alexandros I	313–328
20.	Athanasios I	328–373
	Pistos [Arian anti-pope]	336–338?
	Grēgorios [Arian anti-pope]	339–341
	Grēgorios [Arian anti-pope] [2nd time]	344–348
	Geōrgios [Arian anti-pope]	357–361
	Loukas [Arian anti-pope]	365–
21.	Petros II [brother of #22]	373–380
	Loukas [Arian anti-pope] [2nd time]	375–378
22.	Timotheos I *Aktēmōn* [brother of #21]	380–384
23.	Theophilos I	384–412
24.	Kyrillos I [nephew of #23]	412–444
25.	Dioskoros I	444–451
26.	Proterios	451–460
27.	Timotheos II *Ailouros*	457–460
28.	Timotheos III *Salophakialos*	460–475
	Timotheos II *Ailouros* [2nd time]	475–477
29.	Petros III *Mongos*	477
	Timotheos III *Salophakialos* [2nd time]	477–482
30.	Iōannēs I *Talaïas*	482
	Petros III *Mongos* [2nd time]	482–489
31.	Athanasios II *Keletēs*	489–496
32.	Iōannēs II	496–505
33.	Iōannēs III	505–516
34.	Dioskoros II	516–517
35.	Timotheos IV	517–535
36.	Theodosios I	537?
37.	Gaïnas	537?
38.	Paulos *of Tabennensi*	537–540

39.	Zōilos (or Zoïlos)	541–551
40.	Apollinarios	551–570
41.	Iōannēs IV *Theopeithēs*	570–580
42.	Eulogios I	581–608
43.	Theodōros *Skribōn*	608–609
44.	Iōannēs V *Eleēmōn*	610–619
45.	Geōrgios I	620–630
46.	Kyros *of Phasis*	630–643?
47.	Petros IV	643–651
48.	Eutychios I	654–
49.	Theodōros I	655?
50.	Iōannēs VI	670?
51.	Petros V	680?
52.	Petros VI	690–
53.	Theophylaktos	695?
54.	Onopsos	711?
55.	Eusebios	720?

INTERREGNUM

56.	Kosmas I *"The Needle-Maker"*	727–768
57.	Politianos	768–813
58.	Eustathios	813–817
59.	Christophoros I	817–848
60.	Sōphronios I	848–860
61.	Michaēl I	860–870
62.	Michaēl II	870–903

INTERREGNUM

63.	Christodoulos	907–932
64.	Eutychios II	933–940
65.	Sōphronios II	941?
66.	Isaak	941–954
67.	Iōb (or Iakōbos I)	954–960

INTERREGNUM

68.	Ēlias I	963–1000
69.	Arsenios	1000–1010
70.	Theophilos II	1010–1020
71.	Geōrgios II	1021–1052
72.	Philotheos I	1045–
73.	Leontios	1052–1059
74.	Alexandros II	1059–1062

VI. Greek Church of Alexandria

75.	Iōannēs VII *Kōdōnatos*	1062–1100
76.	Eulogios II	1110?
77.	Kyrillos II	1115?
78.	Sab(b)as	1117?
79.	Theodosios II	1130?
80.	Sōphronios III	1166?
81.	Ēlias II *Alphtheras*	1170?
82.	Eleutherios	1180?
83.	Markos III	1195?
84.	Nikolaos I	1210?–1243
85.	Grēgorios I	1243–1263
86.	Nikolaos II	1263–1276
87.	Athanasios III	1276–1316
88.	Grēgorios II	1316–1354
89.	Grēgorios III	1354–1366
90.	Nēphōn	1366–1385
91.	Markos IV	1385–1389
92.	Nikolaos III	1389–1398
93.	Grēgorios IV	1398–1412
94.	Nikolaos IV	1412–1417
95.	Athanasios IV	1417–1425
96.	Markos V	1425–1435
97.	Philotheos II	1435–1459
98.	Markos VI	1459–1484
99.	Grēgorios V	1484–1486
100.	Athanasios V [not on official list]	1500?
101.	Philotheos III [not on official list]	1523–
102.	Iōakeim I *ho "Panu"*	–1567
103.	Silbestros	1569–1590
104.	Meletios I *Pēgas* [#184 of Constantinople]	1590–1601
105.	Kyrillos III *Loukaris* [#187 of Constantinople]	1601–1620
106.	Gerasimos I *Spartaliōtēs Krēs*	1620–1636
107.	Mētrophanēs *Kritopoulos*	1636–1639
108.	Nikēphoros *Klarontzanēs*	1639–1645
109.	Iōannikios *Diodios ho Berrhoias*	1645–1664
110.	Iōakeim II *Kōs*	1665?–1671
111.	Païsios	1671–1678
112.	Parthenios I *Prochoros*	1678–1688
113.	Gerasimos II *Palidas*	1688–1710
114.	Samouēl *Kapasoulēs*	1712
115.	Kosmas II *Byzantios* [#218 of Constantinople; #6 of Sinai]	1712–1714
	Samouēl *Kapasoulēs* [2nd time]	1714–1723
	Kosmas II *Byzantios* [2nd time]	1723–1736
116.	Kosmas III *Kalokagathos*	1737–1746
117.	Matthaios *Psaltēs*	1746–1765

118.	Kyprianos [anti-archbishop of Cyprus]	1766–1783
119.	Gerasimos III *Gēmarēs* (*Kaliklas*)	1783–1788
120.	Parthenios II *Pankōstas*	1788–1805
121.	Theophilos III *Pankōstas*	1805–1825
122.	Hierotheos I	1825–1845
123.	Artemios	1845–1847
124.	Hierotheos II *Staphylopatēs*	1847–1858
125.	Kallinikos *Olympios*	1858–1861
126.	Iakōbos II *Pankōstas*	1861–1865
127.	Nikanōr	1866–1870
	Neilos [anti-patriarch]	1869–1870
128.	Sōphronios IV *Meidintzoğlou* [#254 of Constantinople]	1870–1899
	Meletios *Apostolopoulos* [locum tenens]	1899–1900
129.	Phōtios *Peroğlou*	1900–1925
	Theophanēs [locum tenens]	1925–1926
130.	Meletios II *Metaxakēs* [#262 of Constantinople; #114 of Greece]	1926–1935
	Theophanēs [locum tenens]	1935–1936
131.	Nikolaos V *Euangelidēs*	1936–1939
	Theophanēs [locum tenens]	1939
132.	Christophoros II *Daniēlidēs*	1939–1966
	Kōnstantinos *Katsarakēs* [locum tenens]	1966–1968
133.	Nikolaos VI *Barelopoulos*	1968–1986
	Barnabas *Phōtaras* [locum tenens]	1986–1987
134.	Parthenios III *Koïnidēs*	1987–1996
	Paulos *Lingrēs* [locum tenens]	1996–1997
135.	Petros VII *Papapetrou*	1997–2004
	Petros *Iakoumelos* [locum tenens]	2004
136.	Theodōros II *Choreutakēs*	2004–

VII.

Latin Church of Alexandria

The Latin Patriarchate of Alexandria was established in the year 1215 by Pope Innocentius III, being one of four such creations made during the time of the crusades to correspond to the patriarchates of the ancient world, and to provide rival jurisdictions to the Greek churches and primates already established at each see. The Alexandrian Church survived in actuality for no more than one hundred years, after which time it became a purely titular honor, with the patriarchs being based in Rome. The title was abolished by Pope Paul VI in 1964.

SOURCES: *The Catholic Encyclopedia*; *De Patriarchis Alexandrinis* (Sollerius); *Dictionnaire d'Histoire et de Géographie Ecclésiastiques*; *The New Catholic Encyclopedia*; *Oriens Christianus* (Le Quien).

LATIN PATRIARCHS OF ALEXANDRIA

1.	Athanasius *de Clermont*	1219–
2.	Ægidius *de Ferrare*	1295–1310
3.	Otto *de Sala*	1322–1323
4.	Ioannes I *de Aragón*	1328–1334
5.	Guillelmus *de Chanac*	1342–1348
6.	Humbertus *de Vienne*	1351–1355
7.	Arnaldus Bernardus *du Pouget*	1361?–1369
8.	Ioannes II *de Cardaillac*	1372–
9.	Petrus I *Amiel de Brenac*	1388?–
10.	Simon *de Cramaud*	1391?
11.	Leonardus *Delfino*	1401–1402?
12.	Ugo *de Robertis*	1402–
13.	Petrus II *Amaury de Lordat*	1409?
14.	Ioannes III *Vitelleschi*	1435?
15.	Marcus *Condolmer*	1445?
16.	Ioannes IV *d'Harcourt*	1451?
17.	Bernardinus *Caraffa*	1505?
18.	Alphonsus *de Fonseca*	1506?

19.	Christophorus *del Monte*	1550?
20.	Ferdinandus *de Loazes* [#31 of Antioch]	1566?
21.	Alexander I *Riario*	1570?
22.	Henricus *Cajétan*	1585?
23.	Michael *Bonelli*	1587?
24.	Seraphinus Oliverus *Razalio*	1602?
25.	Fredericus *Borromée* [#60 of Constantinople]	1655?
26.	Alexander II *Crescenzi* [#36 of Antioch]	1675?
27.	Carolus Ambrosius *Mezzabarba*	1719?
28.	Hieronymus *Crispi*	1740?
29.	Iosephus Antonius *Davanzati*	1746?

INTERREGNUM

30.	Paulus I Augustus *Foscolo*	1847–1867
31.	Paulus II *Ballerini*	1867–1897
32.	Dominicus *Marinangeli*	1898–1921
33.	Paulus III *de Huyn*	1921–1946

INTERREGNUM

34.	Lucas Ermenegildus *Pasetto*	1950–1954

PATRIARCHATE DISESTABLISHED 1964

VIII.

Churches of America

In the twentieth century, America has become the refuge of last resort for churches exiled from their original jurisdictions. Many of the major national churches have established separate branches in North America. Only one of these, the Orthodox Church in America, has officially been granted autocephaly by the Russian Orthodox Church, and even this grant of independence is not universally acknowledged by the rest of Orthodoxy. Other churchmen have attempted to erect independent Orthodox jurisdictions to provide blanket havens for all of their Orthodox brethren, of whatever nationality or ethnic background. The lists below are by no means complete, including only those bodies with significant histories and/or congregations.

SOURCES: *Bishops Extraordinary* (Pruter); *Directory of Autocephalous Bishops* (Pruter); *Eastern Christianity and Politics in the Twentieth Century* (Ramet, ed.); *The Encyclopedia of American Religions* (Melton); *Europa World Yearbook*; *History of the Church* (Jedin, ed.); *Gegenwartslage der Ostkirchen* (Spuler); *Jahrbuch der Orthodoxie* (Proc); *The Old Catholic Sourcebook* (Pruter & Melton); *Orthodox America: 1794–1976* (Tarasar); *Profiles in Belief* (Piepkorn); *Year Book and Church Directory of the Orthodox Church in America*; *Year Book of the Greek Orthodox Diocese of North and South America*; official church websites.

THE GREEK ORTHODOX CHURCH IN AMERICA (ECUMENICAL PATRIARCHATE)

The Ecumenical Patriarchate established a separate archdiocese for its American parishes on 11 May 1922, appointing Archbishop Alexandros as its first primate. Two years later, following the republican revolution in Greece, Archbishop Basileios Kompopoulos, the royalist Metropolitan of Chaldeia, came to the United States and proclaimed a completely independent American church on 18 March 1924; at a synod held on 26 November of that year, the delegates ratified his decision, calling the new body the Autocephalous Greek Orthodox Church of America. Basileios was subsequently elected Metropolitan of American and Canada, in opposition to Archbishop Alexandros. The schism was not healed for six years, until the appointment by the Ecumenical Patriarch Phōtios II of Archbishop Athēnagoras as Archbishop. Basileios returned to Turkey on 20 June 1930, abandoning his claims of ecclesiastical independence.

Archbishop Athēnagoras, perhaps the most remarkable Orthodox churchman of the twentieth century, was a personal friend of President Harry S. Truman; he resigned his position early in 1949 to accept election as Ecumenical Patriarch, and later become known for his efforts to bridge the differences between Eastern Orthdoxy and Roman Catholicism.

The Archdiocese of North and South America (as it was originally called) was reduced in the 1990s to encompass just the United States. This is the largest Orthodox body in the West, comprising two and one-half million communicants, under the jurisdiction of a primate who operates virtually independently, but acknowledges the Patriarch of Constantinople as his superior. The head of the church bears the title Archbishop and Primate of the Greek Orthodox Church in America, Exarch of the Atlantic and Pacific Oceans. The official Church language is Greek, although English and other languages are also used in some parishes. In recent decades several other American branches or groups of parishes of national churches have put themselves under the administration of the Archbishop, including Ukrainian, Carpathian, and Albanian dioceses.

ARCHBISHOPS OF AMERICA
(Under the Ecumenical Patriarch)

1.	Alexandros *of Rodostolon*	1922–1930
	Damaskēnos [locum tenens]	1930
2.	Athēnagoras *Spyrou* [#269 of Constantinople]	1930–1949
3.	Timotheos *Euangelidēs*	1949
4.	Michaēl *Kōnstantinidēs*	1949–1958
5.	Iakōbos *Kykysēs*	1958–1996
6.	Spyridōn *Papageōrgiou*	1996–1999
7.	Dēmētrios *Trakatellēs*	1999–

METROPOLITANS OF AMERICA AND CANADA

1.	Basileios *Kompopoulos*	1924–1930

THE ORTHODOX CHURCH IN AMERICA

The Orthodox Church in America originated as the Alaskan diocese of the Russian Orthodox Church; it later expanded its mission to the continental United States. The chaos of the Russian Revolution hindered communications between the mother church and its overseas branches, causing a split in loyalties. Some believers adhered to the Soviet-dominated Russian Patriarchate which emerged from World War I; others favored the Russian Orthodox Church Outside Russia. The American branch of the Russian Orthodox Church resisted attempts by both churches to re-establish control, finally asserting its independence in 1919 by electing its own leader, Archbishop Aleksandr.

In 1924 the Fourth Sobor of the Church met in Detroit, declaring "temporary autonomy," and naming Archbishop Platon "Metropolitan of All America and Canada." Two years later Platon rejected the claims of the Russian Orthodox Church Outside Russia, and in 1931 further rejected attempts by the Patriarchate of Russia to reassert direct control, although Moscow was acknowledged as theoretically paramount. The name of the Church was changed in 1955 to the Russian Orthodox Greek Catholic Church in America.

The parent church finally accepted the inevitable, and granted the Americans autocephaly on 10 April 1970; a year later, the church was renamed The Orthodox Church in America. Most of the other Orthodox churches have not recognized the canonical independence of the American church. Several other Orthodox denominations, including Albanians and Romanians, later joined the new church as semi-autonomous dioceses. The church is the second largest Orthodox ecclesiastical body in America, comprising some one million communicants. The head of the Church bears the title Metropolitan of All America and Canada. The official Church language is English, although some parishes continue to use Russian (as well as other national languages).

METROPOLITAN ARCHBISHOPS OF THE ORTHODOX CHURCH IN AMERICA
(Bishops 1798, Archbishops 1905, Metropolitans 1924)

1.	Ioasaf *Bolotov*	1798–1799

INTERREGNUM

2.	Innokentiĭ *Veniaminov* [#30 of Russia]	1840–1858
	Pëtr *Ekaterinovskiĭ* [locum tenens]	1859–1866
	Pavel *Popov* [locum tenens]	1866–1870
3.	Ioann *Mitropolskiĭ*	1870–1877
4.	Nestor *Zass*	1878–1882

INTERREGNUM

5.	Vladimir *Sokolovskiĭ-Autonomov*	1887–1891
6.	Nikolaĭ I *Adoratskiĭ*	1891
7.	Nikolaĭ II *Ziorov* [#9 of Poland]	1891–1898
8.	Tikhon *Belavin* [#11 of Russia]	1898–1907
9.	Platon *Rozhdestvenskiĭ* [#19 of exarchs of Georgia]	1907–1914
10.	Evdokim *Meshcherskiĭ*	1914–1918
11.	Aleksandr *Nemolovskiĭ*	1919–1922
	Platon [2nd time]	1922–1934

12.	Theophilus (Feofil) *Pashkovskiĭ*	1934–1950
13.	Leonty (Leontiĭ) *Turkevich*	1950–1965
	Ireney (Irineĭ) *Bekish* [locum tenens]	1965
14.	Ireney (Irineĭ) *Bekish* [#4 of Japan]	1965–1977
	Sylvester *Haruns* [locum tenens]	1974–1977
15.	Theodosius (Feodosiĭ) *Lazor*	1977–2002
16.	Herman (German) *Swaiko*	2002–

THE AMERICAN ORTHODOX CATHOLIC CHURCH

In 1905 Russian Archbishop (later Patriarch) Tikhon Belavin recommended that a separate exarchate be created for "the National Orthodox Churches with their own bishops." Subsequently, several foreign bishops were ordained, but no separate church structure was organized until 2 February 1927, when Metropolitan Platon erected the Holy Eastern Orthodox Catholic Apostolic Church as an autonomous body under the Russian Orthodox Church in America; Archbishop Aftimios, head of the Syrian diocese of New York, was named Primate. The name of the church was changed to the American Orthodox Catholic Church on 1 December 1927. Disagreements between the two primates appeared almost immediately. In October 1929 Aftimios denounced Platon, causing a permanent split. He retired on 19 April 1933, and died on 24 July 1966.

Following his departure, the structure of the Church rapidly disintegrated. One of his four bishops returned to Platon's jurisdiction, and two died in 1934, leaving only Ignatius Nichols. Nichols divided the Church into Eastern and Western rites, retaining the latter for himself, and naming Bishop Sophronius Bishara head of the Eastern rite. He also ordained new bishops, the first of which was consecrated alone, in violation of canon law, due to lack of higher clergy. By this time, however, most of the congregations had fallen away, and the history of this Church thereafter is one of continued splintering and disputes. Therefore, just Archbishop Aftimios is listed below, being the only leader of this Church to have controlled any significant body of communicants.

PRIMATES OF THE AMERICAN ORTHODOX CATHOLIC CHURCH

1.	Aftimios *Ofiesh*	1927–1933

IX.

Greek Church of Antioch

The ancient Church of Antioch ranks third in primacy among the original patriarchal sees of the Near East, behind Constantinople and Alexandria. Founded by St. Peter, the Church grew rapidly in the third greatest city of the Roman Empire, led by a series of learned and illustrious primates. However, like the Church of Alexandria, Antioch was soon to be plagued by a series of heresies, controversies, and misfortunes.

The Patriarch Sebēros (Severus) espoused monophysitism, under the protection of Byzantine Emperor Anastasius. When the Emperor died in 518, his successor, Justin I, forced Sebēros to flee to Alexandria, although the bishop maintained his position in exile. At Antioch, Paulos was consecrated as Sebēros's successor, thereby creating a dual patriarchate similar to that of Alexandria. Each party maintained it was the rightful heir to the patriarchal throne, but neither was able to overthrow the other. The Melkite faction, so-called because it had the support of the Empire, catered mainly to the Greek population; the Jacobite faction, as it came to be known, had the support of a majority of the common people. This disparity only increased after the Muslim invasion of the seventh century.

Unlike its brother churches of Alexandria and Jerusalem, however, the Orthodox Patriarchate of Antioch gradually moved away from its Greek origins, ordaining its first native-speaking clergy in the sixteenth century. The process was accelerated by a further split in the Church that occurred in 1724. At the death of Patriarch Athanasiyus, two factions emerged: one group of bishops elected Kirillus, who acknowledged the supremacy of the Pope of Rome, the other chose Silfistrus, who claimed autocephaly; the Ecumenical Patriarch supported the latter candidate, who remained ensconced at Constantinople.

Since 1724 there have been two separate churches, the Catholic faction being called Melkite, the other group Orthodox. The former continued to appoint native priests and bishops; the price paid by the Orthodox faction for having their candidate consecrated primate by the Ecumenical Patriarch was 180 years of interference by Constantinople in Antioch's patriarchal elections; only previously-approved Greeks were allowed to succeed. The election of the first native-born patriarch in two hundred years was engineered by a faction of the Holy Synod in 1898, who chose Malatiyus II; he in turn replaced the last of the Greek higher clergy with Syrians, thereby insuring native successions in the future.

A third schism took place when Orthodox Patriarch Ghrighuriyus died in 1928. A majority of the Synod elected Arsaniyus as his replacement either in late 1930 or on 7 February 1931; a minority faction elected Aliksandarus several days later. The breach was not healed until the death of Arsaniyus on 9 January 1933. In recent decades the Church has consistently supported the right of the Palestinians to their own state; the funeral of Ilyas IV in 1979 was attended by high-ranking officials of the Syrian government, in an unusual display of solidarity between Christians and Muslims.

The primate of the Orthodox Church bears the title Patriarch of Great Antioch and of all the East. His chief see is located at Damascus, Syria. The official Church language is Arabic. Roughly 65,000 communicants are scattered throughout the Middle East (primarily in Southern Syria and Lebanon), plus a thriving overseas community in North and South America and in Australia.

SOURCES: *Dictionnaire d'Histoire et de Géographie Ecclésiastiques*; *Échos d'Orient*; *Episkepsis*; *Gegenwartslage der Ostkirchen* (Spuler); *History of the Church* (Jedin, ed.); *Jahrbuch der Orthodoxie* (Proc); *Die Morgenländischen Kirchen* (Spuler); *Oriens Christianus* (Le Quien); *Orthodoxia*; "Pinakes Patriarchōn"; *Profiles in Belief* (Piepkorn); *Syrian Christians in Muslim Society* (Haddad); *The Ancient Church on New Shores* (Gabriel); official church website.

ORTHODOX PATRIARCHS OF ANTIOCH
(Greek names are listed in parentheses)

1.	Butrus I (Petros) *Apostolos* [#1 of Rome]	45–53
2.	Afudiyus (Euodios)	53–68
3.	Ighnatiyus I (Ignatios)	68–100
4.	Hirus I (Hērōs)	100–127
5.	Kurniliyus (Kornēlios)	127–151
6.	Hirus II (Hērōs)	151–169
7.	Thiyufilus (Theophilos)	169–182

INTERREGNUM

8.	Maksimiyanus (Maximianos)	188–191?
9.	Sirabiyun (Serapiōn)	191–212
10.	Asqlibiyadhis (Asklēpiadēs)	212–218
11.	Filitus (Philētos)	218–231
12.	Zibinus (Zebinos)	232–240
13.	Babilas (Babylas)	240–253
14.	Fabiyus (Phabios)	253–256
15.	Dimitriyanus (Dēmētrianos)	256–263
16.	Amfilukhiyus (Amphilochios)	263–267
17.	Bulus I (Paulos) *Samosateus*	267–270
18.	Dumnus I (Domnos)	270–273
19.	Timayus (Timaios)	273–277
20.	Kirillus I (Kyrillos)	277–299

IX. Greek Church of Antioch

21.	Tiraniyun (Tyraniōn)	299–308
22.	Fitaliyus I (Bitali[o]s)	308–314
23.	Filughunus (Philogonios)	314–324
24.	Baflinus I (Paulinos) *of Tyre*	324–325
25.	Afstatiyus (Eustathios)	325–332
	Baflinus I (Paulinos) [2nd time]	332
26.	Aflaliyus (Eulalios)	332
27.	Afruniyus (Euphronios)	333–334
28.	Flakentiyus (Plakentios)	334–341
29.	Istifanus I (Stephanos)	341–345
30.	Lawndiyus (Leontios) *"The Eunuch"*	345–350
31.	Afdhuksiyus (Eudoxios) [#31 of Constantinople]	350–354
32.	Malatiyus I (Meletios)	354
	Afdhuksiyus (Eudoxios) [2nd time]	354–357
33.	Aniyanus (Annias or Ammianos)	357–360
34.	Afzuyus (Euzōïos)	360–370
35.	Duruthiyus I (Dōrotheos)	370–371
36.	Baflinus II (Paulinos)	371–376
37.	Fitaliyus II (Bitali[o]s)	376–384
38.	Flafiyanus I (Phlabianos)	384–404
39.	Burfirus (Porphyrios)	404–408
40.	Aliksandarus I (Alexandros)	408–418
41.	Thiyudutus (Theodotos)	418–427
42.	Yuhanna I (Iōannēs)	427–443
43.	Dumnus II (Domnos)	443–450
44.	Maksimus (Maximos)	450–459
45.	Basiliyus I (Basileios)	459
46.	Akakiyus (Akakios)	459–461
47.	Martiriyus (Martyrios)	461–465
48.	Butrus II (Petros) *Knapeus ("The Fuller")*	465–466
49.	Yuliyanus (Ioulianos)	466–474
	Butrus II [2nd time]	474–475
50.	Yuhanna II (Iōannēs)	475–490
51.	Istifanus II (Stephanos)	490–493
52.	Istifanus III (Stephanos)	493–495
53.	Kalandhiyun (Kallandiōn)	495
54.	Yuhanna III (Iōannēs) *Kōdōnatos*	495–497
55.	Baladhiyus (Palladios)	497–505
56.	Flafiyanus II (Phlabianos)	505–513
57.	Subrus (Sebēros) *al-Antakhah*	513–518
58.	Bulus II (Paulos) *Xēnodokos*	518–521
59.	Afrasiyus (Euphrasios) *ibn Malaha*	521–526
60.	Afram (Ephraim) *of Amida*	526–546
61.	Dumnus III (Domnos)	546–561
62.	Anastasiyus I (Anastasios) *al-Sinaïtah*	561–571

63.	Ghrighuriyus I (Grēgorios) *al-Sinaïtah*	571–594
	Anastasiyus I [2nd time]	594–599
64.	Anastasiyus II (Anastasios) *al-Sinaïtah*	599–610
65.	Ghrighuriyus II (Grēgorios)	610–620
66.	Anastasiyus III (Anastasios)	620–628
67.	Maqiduniyus (Makedonios)	628–631
68.	Athanasiyus I (Athanasios) *al-Jama'il*	631
	Maqiduniyus [2nd time]	632–640
69.	Jawrjiyus I (Geōrgios)	640–656
70.	Makariyus I (Makarios)	656–681
71.	Thiyufanis (Theophanēs)	681–687
72.	Sibastianus (Sebastianos)	687–690
73.	Jawrjiyus II (Geōrgios)	690–695
74.	Aliksandarus II (Alexandros)	695–742?
75.	Istifanus IV (Stephanos)	742–748
76.	Thiyufilaktus (Theophylaktos) *ibn Qanbara*	748–767
77.	Thiyudhurus I (Theodōros)	767–797?
78.	Yuhanna IV (Iōannēs)	797–810
79.	Ayyub I (Iōb)	810–826
80.	Niqulawus I (Nikolaos)	826–834
81.	Sim'an I (Symeōn)	834–840
82.	Ilyas I (Ēlias)	840–852
83.	Thiyudusiyus I (Theodosios)	852–860
84.	Niqulawus II (Nikolaos)	860–871
85.	Istifanus V (Stephanos)	871
	Niqulawus II [2nd time]	871–879
86.	Mikha'il I (Michaēl)	879–890
87.	Zakhariya (Zacharias)	890–902?
88.	Jawrjiyus III (Geōrgios)	902–917
89.	Ayyub II (Iōb)	917–939
90.	Afstratiyus (Eustratios)	939–960
91.	Khristufurus I (Christophoros)	960–966
92.	Thiyudhurus II (Theodōros)	966–977
93.	Aghabiyus (Agapios)	977–995
94.	Yuhanna V (Iōannēs) *Politēs*	995–1000
95.	Niqulawus III (Nikolaos) *Stouditēs*	1000–1003
96.	Ilyas II (Ēlias)	1003–1010
97.	Jawrjiyus IV (Geōrgios) *Laskaris* (or Thiyudhurus [Theodōros] III)	1010–1015
98.	Makariyus II (Makarios) "the Virtuous"	1015–1023
99.	Alafthariyus (Eleutherios)	1023–1028
100.	Basiliyus II (Basileios)	1028
101.	Butrus III (Petros)	1028–1051
102.	Yuhanna VI (Iōannēs)	1051–1062
103.	Amiliyanus (Aimilianos)	1062–1075

IX. Greek Church of Antioch

104.	Thiyudusiyus II (Theodosios) *Chrysobergēs*	1075–1084
105.	Niqifurus (Nikēphoros) *"The Black"*	1084–1090
106.	Yuhanna VII (Iōannēs) *Oxeitēs*	1090–1106
107.	Yuhanna VIII (Iōannēs)	1106–1137
108.	Luqa (Loukas)	1137–1155
109.	Yuhanna IX (Iōannēs)	1155–1159
110.	Aftimiyus I (Euthymios)	1159–1164
111.	Makariyus III (Makarios)	1164–1166
112.	Athanasiyus II (Athanasios)	1166–1180
113.	Thiyudusiyus III (Theodosios)	1180–1182
114.	Ilyas III (Ēlias)	1182–1184
115.	Khristufurus II (Christophoros)	1184–1185
116.	Thiyudhurus IV (Theodōros) *Balsamōn*	1185–1199
117.	Yuwakim I (Iōakeim)	1199–1219
118.	Duruthiyus II (Dōrotheos)	1219–1245
119.	Sim'an II (Symeōn) *ibn Abu Sa'ib*	1245–1268
120.	Aftimiyus II (Euthymios)	1268–1269
121.	Thiyudusiyus IV (Theodosios)	1269–1276
122.	Thiyudusiyus V (Théodose) *de Villehardouin*	1276–1285
123.	Arsaniyus I (Arsenios)	1285–1293
	Kirillus II (Kyrillos) [anti-patriarch]	1287–1308?
124.	Dhiyunisiyus (Dionysios)	1293–1308
125.	Murqus I (Markos)	1308–1342
126.	Ighnatiyus II (Ignatios)	1342–1353
127.	Mikha'il II (Michaēl)	1353–1376
128.	Bakhumiyus I (Pachomios)	1376–1393
129.	Nilus (Neilos)	1393–1401
130.	Mikha'il III (Michaēl)	1401–1410
131.	Bakhumiyus II *al-Hawrani*	1410–1411
132.	Yuwakim II (Iōakeim)	1411–1426
133.	Murqus II (Markos)	1426–1436
134.	Dhuruthiyus III (Dōrotheos) *ibn al-Sabbuni*	1436–1454
135.	Mikha'il IV (Michaēl) *ibn al-Mawardi*	1454–1462
136.	Murqus III (Markos)	1462–1476
137.	Yuwakim III (Iōakeim)	1476–1483
138.	Ghrighuriyus III (Grēgorios)	1483–1497
139.	Dhuruthiyus IV (Dōrotheos) *ibn al-Sabbuni*	1497–1523
140.	Mikha'il V (Michaēl) *ibn al-Mawardi*	1523–1541
141.	Duruthiyus V (Dōrotheos)	1541–1543
142.	Yuwakim IV (Iōakeim) *ibn Jumma*	1543–1576
143.	Mikha'il VI *Sabbagh al-Hamawi*	1577–1581
144.	Yuwakim V *ibn Daww*	1581–1592

145.	Yuwakim VI *Ziyada*	1593–1604
146.	Duruthiyus V *ibn al-Ahmar*	1604–1611
147.	Athanasiyus III *al-Dabbas*	1611–1619
148.	Ighnatiyus III *'Atiyah*	1619–1634
149.	Aftimiyus III *al-Karmah*	1635–1636
150.	Aftimiyus IV (Euthymios) *apo Chiou*	1636–1648
151.	Makariyus IV *al-Za'im*	1648–1672
152.	Niyufutus (Neophytos) *apo Chiou*	1674–1684
153.	Athanasiyus IV *al-Dabbas* [#45 of Cyprus]	1686–1694
154.	Kirillus III *al-Za'im* [grandson of #143]	1694–1720
	Athanasiyus IV [2nd time]	1720–1724
	Yuwakim VII [anti-patriarch]	1724
155.	Silfistrus (Silbestros) *apo Kyprou* [cousin of #145]	1724–1766
156.	Filimun (Philēmōn) *apo Aleppo*	1766–1767
157.	Daniyal (Daniēl) *apo Chiou*	1767–1791
158.	Antimiyus (Anthemios) *of Helenopolis*	1792–1813
159.	Sirafim (Serapheim) *apo Kōnstantinopoleōs*	1813–1823
160.	Mithudiyus (Methodios) *apo Naxou*	1823–1850
161.	Ayruthiyus (Hierotheos) *Hagiotaphitēs*	1850–1885
162.	Jirasimus (Gerasimos) *Propapas* [#135 of Jerusalem]	1885–1891
163.	Asbiridun (Spyridōn) *apo Kyprou*	1892–1898
	Jarmanus (Germanos) [locum tenens]	1898–1899
	Malatiyus [locum tenens]	1899
164.	Malatiyus II *al-Dumani*	1899–1906
	Athanasiuys *of Homs* [locum tenens]	1906
165.	Ghrighuriyus IV *Haddad*	1906–1928
166.	Arsaniyus II *Haddad*	1930–1931
167.	Aliksandarus III *Tah(h)an*	1931–1958
	Arsaniyus II *Haddad* [as anti-patriarch]	1931–1933
	Apifaniyus [anti-patriarch]	1935–
	Thiyudusiyus *Abu Rajaili* [locum tenens]	1958
168.	Thiyudusiyus VI *Abu Rajaili*	1958–1970
169.	Ilyas IV *Muawad*	1970–1979
	Ilyas *Kurban* [locum tenens]	1979
170.	Ighnatiyus IV *Hazim*	1979–

X.

Greek Melkite Catholic Church of Antioch

The history of the Melkite Church of Antioch is closely tied to that of the Greek Orthodox Church. A number of patriarchs during the Middle Ages made formal professions of allegiance to Rome, or sent other ambassadors to the Popes; within the Melkite Church itself, two factions gradually emerged, one favoring continued contacts with Rome, the other preferring complete autocephaly. The controversy came to a head in 1724, when each of the factions elected its own Patriarch. A part of the synod chose Kirillus Tanas, an advocate of autonomy under the Pope, as their new primate; a smaller faction simultaneously elected as rival patriarch Silbestros, a Greek bishop who favored autocephaly under the tutelage of the Ecumenical Patriarch.

The primates of this Church have long been known for their erudition and learning, and have been native Syrians from before the beginning of the split. Both Maksimus IV Sa'igh and Maksimus V Hakim were also prominent in ecumenical efforts.

The primate bears the title Patriarch of Antioch and all the East, of Alexandria and of Jerusalem (the latter two cities being added to his title under Maksimus III); his jurisdiction includes all Greek Melkite uniates in the Near East and the Americas, totalling roughly one million communicants. The Patriarch alternates his residence between the cities of Cairo and Beirut. The official Church language is Arabic. Although the term "Melkite" was applied in ancient times to many of the Chalcedonian Greek Orthodox churches, the word has now come to refer only to the Greek Catholic Church of Antioch.

SOURCES: *The Almanac of the Melkite Greek Catholic Church 1986* (regarded as official); *The Catholic Eastern Churches* (Attwater); *Catholic Encyclopedia*; *The Christian Churches of the East* (Attwater); *Chronologie des Patriarches Melchites d'Antioche de 1250 à 1500* (Nasrallah); *Dictionnaire d'Histoire et de Géographie Ecclésiastiques*; *Gegenwartslage der Ostkirchen* (Spuler); *The Middle East and North Africa*; *Die Morgenlandischen Kirchen* (Spuler); *New Catholic Encyclopedia*; *Notes et Documents pour Servir a L'Histoire du Patriarchat Melchite d'Antioche* (Nasrallah); *Oriens Christianus* (Le Quien); "Pope Calls for Broad Mideast Peace" (Montalbano); *Sa Béatitude Maximos IV et la Succession Apostolique du Siège d'Antioche* (Nasrallah); *Syrian Christians in Muslim Society* (Haddad); *Vie de la Chrétiente Melkite sous la Domination Turque* (Nasrallah); official church website.

Greek Melkite Catholic Patriarchs of Antioch

1. Butrus I (Petros) *Apostolos* [#1 of Rome]   36–43
2. Afudiyus (Euodios)   43–70?
3. Ighnatiyus I (Ignatios)   70?–107
4. Hirun (Hērōn)   107?–130?
5. Kurniliyus (Kornēlios)   130?–150?
6. Hirus (Heros)   150?–170?
7. Thiyufilus (Theophilos)   170?–182
8. Maksimiyanus (Maximianos)   182–191
9. Sirabiyun (Serapiōn)   191–212
10. Asqlibiyadhis (Asklēpiadēs)   212–218
11. Filitus (Philētos)   218–231
12. Zibinus (Zebinos)   231–240?
13. Babilas (Babylas)   240–250
14. Fabiyus (Phabios)   250–253
15. Dimitriyanus (Dēmētrianos)   253
16. Bulus I (Paulos) *Samosateus*   253–260
17. Dumnus I (Domnos)   260–266
18. Timayus (Timaios)   266–271
19. Kirillus I (Kyrillos)   271–306
20. Tiranus (Tyrannos)   306–314
21. Fitalis (Bitalis)   306–314
22. Filughunus (Philogonios)   320–325
23. Afstatiyus (Eustathios)   325–331
24. Baflinus (Paulinos) *of Tyre*   331
25. Aflaliyus (Eulalios)   331–333
26. Afruniyus (Euphronios)   333–334
27. Flakilus (Phlakilos)   334–343
28. Istifanus I (Stephanos)   343–344
29. Lawndiyus (Leontios) *"The Eunuch"*   344–358
    Aniyas (Annias) [anti-patriarch]   357–360
30. Afdhuksiyus (Eudoxios) [#31 of Constantinople]   358–359
31. Malatiyus (Meletios)   359?–381
    Afzuyus (Euzōïos) [anti-patriarch]   360–370
    Duruthiyus (Dōrotheos) [anti-patriarch]   370–371
    Baflinus (Paulinos) II [anti-patriarch]   371–376
32. Flafiyanus I (Phlabianos)   381–404
33. Burfirus (Porphyrios)   404–416
34. Aliksandarus (Alexandros)   416–417
35. Thiyudutus (Theodotos)   417–429?
36. Yuhanna I (Iōannēs)   429?–442?
37. Dumnus II (Domnos)   442?–449
38. Maksimus I (Maximos)   449?–455
39. Basiliyus I (Basileios)   456–458

X. Greek Melkite Catholic Church of Antioch

40.	Akakiyus (Akakios)	458–459
41.	Martiriyus (Martyrios)	459–470?
42.	Butrus II (Petros) *Knapeus "The Fuller"*	470?–471?
43.	Yuliyanus (Ioulianos)	471–476?
	Butrus II [2nd time]	476?–477?
44.	Yuhanna II (Iōannēs) *Kōdōnatos*	477?–478?
45.	Istifanus II (Stephanos)	478–481
46.	Kalandhiyun (Kallandiōn)	481–485
	Butrus II [3rd time]	485–488
47.	Baladus (Palladios)	488?–498
48.	Flafiyanus II (Phlabianos)	498–512
49.	Subrus (Sebēros) *al-Antakhah*	512–518
50.	Bulus II (Paulos) *Xēnodokos*	519–521
51.	Afrasiyus (Euphrasiōn) *ibn Malaha*	521–526
52.	Afram (Ephraim) *of Amida*	526–545
53.	Dumnus III (Domnos)	545–559
54.	Anastasiyus I (Anastasios) *al-Sinaïtah*	559–570
55.	Ghrighuriyus I (Grēgorios) *al-Sinaïtah*	570–593
	Anastasiyus I [2nd time]	593–598
56.	Anastasiyus II (Anastasios) *al-Sinaïtah*	599–609

INTERREGNUM

57.	Maqiduniyus (Makedonios)	639?–649?
58.	Jawrjiyus I (Geōrgios)	649?–660?
59.	Makariyus I (Makarios)	660?–681
60.	Thiyufanis (Theophanēs)	681–683?
61.	Tuma (Thōmas)	683?–685?
62.	Jawrjiyus II (Geōrgios)	685?–702?
	Sabastiyanus (Sebastianos) [anti-patriarch]	687–690

INTERREGNUM

63.	Istifanus III (Stephanos)	742?–745?
64.	Thiyufilaktus (Theophylaktos) *ibn Qanbara*	745?–768?
65.	Thiyuduritus (Theodōritos)	787?
66.	Ayyub (Iōb)	813?–845?
67.	Niqulawus I (Nikolaos)	847–866?
68.	Istifanus IV (Stephanos)	866–870
69.	Thiyudusiyus I (Theodosios)	870–890
70.	Sim'an I (Symeōn) *ibn Zarnaq*	892–907
71.	Ilyas I (Ēlias)	907–934
72.	Thiyudusiyus II (Theodosios)	936–943
73.	Thiyukharistus (Theocharistos)	944–948

INTERREGNUM

74.	Khristufurus (Christophoros)	960–969
75.	Thiyudurus I (Theodōros)	970–976
76.	Aghabiyus I (Agapios)	978–996
77.	Yuhanna III (Iōannēs) *Politēs*	997–1022
78.	Niqulawus II (Nikolaos) *Stouditēs*	1022–1030
79.	Ilyas II (Ēlias)	1031–1032
80.	Thiyudurus II (Theodōros) *Laskaris*	1033–1041
81.	Basiliyus II (Basileios)	1041?–1051?
82.	Butrus III (Petros)	1052–1057
83.	Thiyudusiyus III (Theodosios) *Chrysobergēs*	1057–
84.	Amiliyanus (Aimilianos)	1074?–1090?
85.	Niqifurus (Nikēphoros) *"The Black"*	1090–
86.	Yuhanna IV (Iōannēs) *Oxeitēs*	1098–1100

INTERREGNUM

87.	name unknown	1137–1155
88.	Athanasiyus I (Athananios)	1157?–1171

INTERREGNUM

89.	Thiyudurus III (Theodōros) *Balsamōn*	1185?–1195?

INTERREGNUM

90.	Sim'an II (Symeōn) *ibn Abi Sa'ib*	1206?–1235?

INTERREGNUM

91.	Dawud (Dabid)	1242?–1247?

INTERREGNUM

92.	Aftimiyus I (Euthymios)	1258?–1273?
93.	Thiyudusiyus IV (Théodose) *de Villehardouin*	1275–1284?
94.	Arsaniyus (Arsenios)	1284?–1290?
95.	Kirillus II (Kyrillos)	1290?–1308?
96.	Diyunisiyus I (Dionysios)	1308?–1316?
97.	Kirillus III (Kyrillos)	1316–
98.	Diyunisiyus II (Dionysios)	1325?

X. Greek Melkite Catholic Church of Antioch

99.	Sufruniyus (Sōphronios)	1335?
100.	Ighnatiyus II (Ignatios)	1344?–1359?
101.	Bakhumiyus I (Pachomios)	1359?–1368
102.	Mikha'il I (Michaēl)	1368–1375
	Bakhumiyus I [2nd time]	1375–1377
103.	Murqus I (Markos)	1377–1378
	Bakhumiyus I [3rd time]	1378–1386
104.	Niqun (Nikōn)	1387?–1395
105.	Mikha'il II (Michaēl)	1395–1412
106.	Bakhumiyus II (Pachomios) *al-Hawrani*	1412
107.	Yuwakim I (Iōakeim)	1412?–1425?
108.	Murqus II (Markos)	1425?–1434?
109.	Duruthiyus I *ibn al-Sabbuni*	1434?–1451
110.	Mikha'il III *ibn al-Mawardi*	1451?–1456?
111.	Murqus III (Markos)	1456?–1458?
112.	Yuwakim II (Iōakeim)	1458?–1459?

INTERREGNUM

113.	Mikha'il IV (Michaēl)	1470?–1484?
114.	Duruthiyus II *ibn al-Sabbuni*	1484?–1500?

INTERREGNUM

115.	Mikha'il V *ibn al-Mawardi*	1523?–1529
	Yuwakim III [anti-patriarch]	1527
116.	Duruthiyus III (Dōrotheos)	1529?–1531
117.	Yuwakim III (Iōakeim) [2nd time]	1531–1534?
118.	Mikha'il VI *Sabbagh*	1534–1543
	Yuwakim IV *ibn Jumma* [anti-patriarch]	1540
119.	Yuwakim IV *ibn Jumma* [2nd time]	1543?–1575
	Makariyus II *ibn Khilal* [anti-patriarch]	1543?–1550?
120.	Mikha'il VII *al-Hamawi*	1576–1593
	Yuwakim V *ibn Daww* [anti-patriarch]	1581–1592
121.	Yuwakim VI *Ziyada*	1593–1604
122.	Duruthiyus IV *ibn al-Ahmar*	1604–1612
123.	Athanasiyus II *al-Dabbas*	1612–1620
124.	Ighnatiyus III *'Atiyah*	1620–1634
	Kirillus IV *al-Dabbas* [anti-patriarch]	1620–1627
125.	Aftimiyus II *al-Karmah*	1634
126.	Aftimiyus III (Euthymios) *apo Chiou*	1634–1647
127.	Makariyus III *al-Za'im*	1647–1672
128.	Kirillus V *al-Za'im* [grandson of #127]	1672
129.	Niyufutus (Neophytos) *apo Chiou*	1672–1682
	Kirillus V [2nd time]	1682–1720

	Athanasiyus III *al-Dabbas* [anti-patriarch]	1685–1694
130.	Athanasiyus III [2nd time] [#45 of Cyprus]	1720–1724
	Yuwakim VII [anti-patriarch]	1724
131.	Kirillus VI *al-Tanas*	1724–1759
132.	Athanasiyus IV *Jawhar* [great-nephew of #131]	1759–1760
133.	Maksimus II *Hakim*	1760–1761
134.	Thiyudusiyus V *Dahan*	1761–1788
	Athanasiyus IV [anti-patriarch]	1765–1768
	Athanasiyus IV [3rd time]	1788–1794
135.	Kirillus VII *Siyaj*	1794–1796
136.	Aghabiyus II *Matar*	1796–1812
137.	Ighnatiyus IV *Sarruf*	1812
138.	Athanasiyus V *Matar*	1813
139.	Makariyus IV *Tawil*	1813–1815
140.	Ighnatiyus V *Qattan*	1816–1833
141.	Maksimus III *Mazlum*	1833–1855
142.	Aklimandus *Bahuth*	1856–1864
143.	Ghrighuriyus II *Yusuf-Sayur*	1864–1897
144.	Butrus IV *Jirayjiri*	1898–1902
145.	Kirillus VIII *Jiha*	1902–1916

INTERREGNUM

146.	Dimitriyus *Qadi*	1919–1925
147.	Kirillus IX *Mughabghab*	1925–1947
148.	Maksimus IV *al-Sa'igh*	1947–1967
149.	Maksimus V *Hakim*	1967–2000
	Yuhanna *Haddad* [apostolic administrator]	2000
150.	Ghrighuriyus III *Laham*	2000–

XI.

Latin Church of Antioch

The Latin Patriarchate of Antioch was established in the year 1100 at the time of the first crusade, shortly after the conquest of Jerusalem. This was one of four such creations made during the period of the crusades to correspond to the patriarchates of the ancient world, and to provide rival jurisdictions to the Greek churches and prelates. The Antiochian Church survived until the fall of Acre in 1291, after which time it became a purely titular honor, with the patriarchs being based in Rome. During the renaissance the rank of "patriarch" in the Latin church became a kind of intermediate level between archbishop and cardinal, many patriarchs relinquishing their titles when promoted to the College of Cardinals. The title was officially abolished by Pope Paul VI in 1964.

SOURCES: *The Catholic Encyclopedia*; *Dictionnaire d'Histoire et de Géographie Ecclésiastiques*; *The New Catholic Encyclopedia*; *Oriens Christianus* (Le Quien).

LATIN PATRIARCHS OF ANTIOCH

1.	Bernardus	1100–1134
2.	Radulphus I (Ralph *of Domfront*)	1135–1140

INTERREGNUM

3.	Aymericus (Aimery) *de Limoges*	1142–1187
4.	Radulphus II	1187–1201
5.	Petrus I *d'Angoulême*	1201–1208
6.	Petrus II *d'Amalfi*	1209–1217
7.	Petrus III *Capoue* [nephew of #6]	1219
8.	Raynerius *de Tuscia*	1219–1225
9.	Albertus I *de Robertis*	1226–1246
10.	Elias	1246?–1250

INTERREGNUM

11.	Opizio I	1254–1255

12.	Christianus	1256–1268
13.	Opizio II *Fieschi*	1270?–1292

INTERREGNUM

14.	Isnardus *Tacconi*	1311–1329

INTERREGNUM

15.	Geraldus Odo *de Camboulit*	1342–1348

INTERREGNUM

16.	Raymundus *de Saigues*	1364–1374
17.	Petrus IV *Clasquerin*	1375–
18.	Ioannes I *de Maguellone*	1408–
19.	Ioannes II *de Vico*	1410?
20.	Venceslaus *Králik*	1410?–1416

INTERREGNUM

21.	Dionysius *du Moulin*	1439–1447
22.	Iacobus Juvenalis *des Ursins*	1449–1457
23.	Guillelmus I *de La Tour*	1457?–1470
24.	Guillelmus II	1471
25.	Gerardus *de Crussol*	1471–1472
26.	Laurentius I *Zane*	1473–1485
27.	Iordanus *de' Caetani*	1485–
28.	Sebastianus	1495?
29.	Alphonsus I *Carafa*	1504–
30.	Alphonsus II	–1529

INTERREGNUM

31.	Ferdinandus *de Loazes* [#20 of Alexandria]	1566–1568
32.	Ioannes III *de Ribera*	1568–1611

INTERREGNUM

33.	Ludovicus I Caetanus *di Sermoneta*	1622–1626?
34.	Ioannes IV Baptistus *Pamfili* [#234 of Rome]	1626?–1629
35.	Cæsar *Monti*	1629?–1650

INTERREGNUM

36.	Alexander *Crescenzi* [#26 of Alexandria]	1675?–1688

XI. Latin Church of Antioch

INTERREGNUM

37.	Michael Angelus *Mattei*	1693–
38.	Carolus I Thomas *Maillard de Tournon*	1701–1710
39.	Gilbertus *Borromeo*	1711–1717

INTERREGNUM

40.	Philippus *Anastasi*	1724–1735
41.	Ioaquim Ferdinandus *Puerto Carrero*	1735–1743
42.	Antonius I Maria *Pallavicino*	1743–1749
43.	Ludovicus II *Calini*	1751–1766
44.	Domenicus *Giordani*	1766–1780
45.	Carolus II *Camuzio*	1781–
46.	Iulius Maria *della Somaglia*	1788–1795
47.	Ioannes V Franciscus Guidus *di Bagno dei Talenti*	1795–1796
48.	Antonius II *Despuig y Dameto*	1799–1810

INTERREGNUM

49.	Laurentius II *Mattei*	1822–1833
50.	Antonius III *Piatti*	1837–1841
51.	Nicolaus *Tanara*	1845–1853
52.	Albertus II *Barbolani*	1856–1857
53.	Iosephus Melchiades *Ferlisi* [#78 of Constantinople]	1858–1860
54.	Carolus III *Belgrado*	1862–1866
55.	Paulus *Brunoni*	1869–1877
56.	Petrus V *Villanova Castellacci*	1879–1881
57.	Placidus *Ralli*	1882–1884
58.	Vincentius *Tizzani*	1886–1892
59.	Franciscus de Pauli *Cassetta*	1895–1899
60.	Carolus IV Antonius *Nocella* [#84 of Constantinople]	1899–1901
61.	Laurentius III *Passerini*	1901–1915
62.	Ladislaus Michael *Zaleski*	1916–1925
63.	Robertus *Vicentini*	1925–1953

PATRIARCHATE DISESTABLISHED 1964

XII.

Maronite Church of Antioch

The Maronite Church is unique among the uniate Eastern churches in having a history unmarred by significant internal schism. Its origins can be traced to the monastery of Bait-Marun, built around the shrine of St. Marun (or Maro) on the bank of the Orontes River east of Antioch. The abbey was closely allied with the Byzantine Emperors, and when the Emperor Heraclius professed monothelitism, Bait-Marun followed suit. In 681, according to unconfirmed tradition, during a period when the Greek Patriarchs of Antioch were living in exile in Constantinople, the monks elected their first primate, whose successors eventually began calling themselves Patriarchs of Antioch; the first documented use of the title was a grant by Pope Alexander IV. Maronite history claims that this first Patriarch was Yuhanna Marun (or John Maro; he is not, however, the same man as the earlier saint of the same name); in reality, however, the early history of the Maronites before 1100 is almost totally veiled in obscurity, and no verifiable list of its early patriarchs can now be compiled. Most scholars now regard the traditional list of primates between Maro and Yusuf al-Jirjisi as semi-mythical.

When the original monastery was destroyed about the year 900, the monks and their flock moved *en masse* into the protection of the Lebanese mountains, where they remained virtually impregnable against the surrounding Muslim population. The West first made contact with the Maronites about the year 1100, shortly after their conquest of Jerusalem during the First Crusade. The Maronites acknowledged the ecclesiastical supremacy of the Pope of Rome about 1182, and have remained a part of the Catholic Church ever since, becoming increasingly Latinized as the centuries have passed.

In 1860 the Druze began massacring the unarmed Maronites, provoking conflicts between Christian and Muslim that have continued to this day. As the strongest Christian faction in Lebanon, the Maronites have traditionally held the balance of political and economic power there; an article of the Lebanese Constitution provides that the office of the presidency can only be occupied by a Maronite. In recent decades the Lebanese Civil War served to isolate even further the Maronites from their Muslim neighbors, and to question their long-term viability.

The primate bears the title Patriarch of Antioch (of the Maronites) and All the East; he resides at Bkerkeh and Dimaneh. Although there are some two to five million Maronites living within Lebanon (estimates vary), there are also a significant number of adherents dwelling in neighboring Middle Eastern countries, as well as in the Americas. The official Church language is Arabic. For several centuries, the Patriarchs of the Maronites have traditionally taken the second name "Butrus" (Peter) in honor of the apostle who, according to legend, founded the Patriarchate of Antioch.

SOURCES: *The Catholic Eastern Churches* (Attwater); *Catholic Encyclopedia*; *The Christian Churches of the East* (Attwater); *L'Église Maronite* (Dib; regarded as official by the Church); *Gegenwartslage der Ostkirchen* (Spuler); *Histoire de l'Église Syriaque Maronite d'Antioch* (Ghabra'il); "Les Listes Patriarcales de L'Église Maronite: Étude Critique et Historique" (Chabot); *The Maronites in History* (Moosa); *The Middle East and North Africa*; *Die Morgenländischen Kirchen* (Spuler); *Murder, Mayhem, Pillage, and Plunder* (Mishaqa); *Politics and Change in a Traditional Society: Lebanon, 1711–1845* (Harik); *Politics in Lebanon* (Binder); *New Catholic Encyclopedia*; *Oriens Christianus* (Le Quien); "Pope Calls for Broad Mideast Peace" (Montalbano); *Series Chronologica Patriarchum Antiochiae* (Assemani); *Who's Who in Lebanon*; official church website.

MARONITE PATRIARCHS OF ANTIOCH

1.	Yuhanna I *Marun*	681–707
2.	Kurush [nephew of #1]	707–
3.	Jibra'il I	
4.	Yuhanna II *Marun*	
5.	Yuhanna III	
6.	Ghrighuriyus I	
7.	Istifanus I	
8.	Murqus	
9.	Awsabiyus	
10.	Yuhanna IV	
11.	Ishu' I	
12.	Dawud I	
13.	Ghrighuriyus II	
14.	Tiyufilaqtus	
15.	Ishu' II	
16.	Dumitiyus	
17.	Ishaq	
18.	Yuhanna V	
19.	Sim'an I	
20.	Aramiya I	
21.	Yuhanna VI	
22.	Sim'an II	
23.	Sim'an III	
24.	Yusuf I *al-Jirjisi*	1100?–1120?
25.	Butrus I	1121?–1130?
26.	Ghrighuriyus III *of Halat*	1130?–1141
27.	Ya'qub I *Butrus of Ramat*	1141?–1151
28.	Yuhanna VII *of Lahfad*	1151–1154

29.	Butrus II	1154–1173
30.	Butrus III	1188?
31.	Butrus IV *of Lahfad*	–1199?
32.	Aramiya II (or Irmiya) *al-Amshiti*	1199?–1230
33.	Danil I *Biblesis*	1230–1236
34.	Yuhanna VIII *Butrus al-Jaji*	1239?–1244?
35.	Sim'an IV	1244?–1268?
36.	Ya'qub II	1268?–
37.	Butrus V	1269?
38.	Danil II *al-Amshiti*	1270?–1272?
39.	Aramiya III *al-Dimlisawi*	1272–1297
40.	Luqa *al-Banhrani* [rival patriarch]	1272–1300
41.	Sim'an V	1300?–1322?
42.	Yuhanna IX	1322?–1357?
43.	Jibra'il II (or Jabra'il) *al-Hajjula*	1357?–1367?
44.	Dawud II *Yuhanna*	1367?–1402
45.	Yuhanna X *al-Jaji*	1404–1445
46.	Ya'qub III *ibn Hid al-Hadathi*	1445–1458
47.	Butrus VI *ibn Yusuf al-Hadathi* [brother of #46]	1458–1492
48.	Sim'an VI (or Shim'un) *ibn Dawud al-Hadathi* [nephew of #47]	1492–1524
49.	Musi (or Musa) *ibn Sa'adi al-'Aquri*	1524–1567
50.	Mikha'il I *ibn Yuhanna al-Ruzzi*	1567–1581
51.	Sarkis *ibn Yuhanna al-Ruzzi* [brother of #50]	1581–1596

Interregnum

52.	Yusuf II *ibn Musa al-Ruzzi* [nephew of #51]	1599–1608
53.	Yuhanna XI *ibn Makhluf*	1608–1633
54.	Jirjis I *ibn 'Amayrah*	1633–1644
55.	Yusuf III *ibn Halib al-'Aquri*	1644–1647
56.	Yuhanna XII *al-Safrawi*	1648–1656
57.	Jirjis II *Habakuk al-Bashalani*	1657–1670
58.	Istifan(us) II *ibn Mikha'il al-Duwayhi*	1670–1704
59.	Jibra'il III *al-Blawzawi*	1704–1705
60.	Ya'qub IV Butrus *Awwad*	1705–1733
61.	Yusuf IV Butrus *Dirgham al-Khazin*	1733–1742
	Tubiyya Butrus *al-Khazin* [anti-patriarch]	1733
62.	Sim'an VII Butrus *Awwad*	1743–1756
63.	Tubiyya Butrus *al-Khazin* [2nd time]	1756–1766
64.	Yusuf V Butrus *Istifan*	1766–1793
65.	Mikha'il II Butrus *Fadl*	1793–1795
66.	Filibbus Butrus *al-Jumayyil*	1795–1796
67.	Yusuf VI Butrus *al-Tiyyan*	1796–1807
68.	Yuhanna XIII Butrus *al-Hilu*	1809–1823
69.	Yusuf VII Butrus *Hubaysh*	1823–1845

XII. Maronite Church of Antioch

70.	Yusuf VIII Butrus *al-Khazin*	1845–1854
71.	Bulus I Butrus *Mas'ad al-Tarsi*	1854–1890
72.	Yuhanna XIV Butrus *Hajj*	1890–1898
73.	Ilyas Butrus *al-Huwayyik*	1899–1931
74.	Antun I Butrus *'Aridah*	1932–1955
75.	Bulus II Butrus *al-Ma'ushi*	1955–1975
76.	Antun(iyus) II Butrus *Khraish*	1975–1985
77.	Nasr Allah Butrus *Sfayr*	1986–

XIII.

Syrian Catholic Church of Antioch

The history of the Syrian Catholic Patriarchate of Antioch is directly tied to that of the Jacobite Church. Catholic missionaries were sent to Syria as early as 1552, seeking to convert both the people and their prelates. About 1650, their efforts resulted in the conversion of one 'Abd al-Ghal Akhijan, who was sent to the Maronites for instruction. The Maronite Patriarch of Antioch consecrated him Syrian Catholic Bishop of Aleppo in 1656 under the name Andrawus. He was able to build a following, and to use his influence to capture the patriarchal throne in the election of 1661. This created a split in the Syrian Church, when a dissident faction elected their own patriarch, with both claiming to be the legitimate primate. Andrawus was followed by Butrus, who was imprisoned in 1701, thereby ending the schism.

In 1783 the reigning Syrian patriarch named as his successor Mar Mikha'il Jarwah, who had recently converted to Catholicism. A dissident faction immediately elected a non–Catholic patriarch, thereby creating a permanent split in the West Syrian Church, one faction acknowledging the supremacy of the Pope of Rome, the other claiming complete autocephaly.

The primate bears the title Patriarch of Antioch of the Syrians. The Church uses both Syriac and Arabic as official languages, but the latter is in common use. The chief see of the Church is Beirut (since 1899), although the roughly 150,000 communicants are spread throughout the Middle East (particularly Syria and Lebanon) and in the Americas. Like his Jacobite counterpart, the Patriarch always takes the name Ighnatiyus as his first name, in honor of the saint who served as third Patriarch of Antioch; to this he adds a second saint's name.

SOURCES: *The Catholic Eastern Churches* (Attwater); *Catholic Encyclopedia*; *The Christian Churches of the East* (Attwater); *Chronique de Michel le Syrien* (Michael I); *Eastern Christianity and Politics in the Twentieth Century* (Ramet, ed.); *Europa World Yearbook*; *Gegenwartslage der Ostkirchen* (Spuler); *The Middle East and North Africa*; *Die Morgenlandischen Kirchen* (Spuler); *New Catholic Encyclopedia*; *Oriens Christianus* (Le Quien); "Pope Calls for Broad Mideast Peace" (Montalbano); *Al-Salasil al-Tarikhiyah fi Asaqifat al Abrashiyat al-Suryaniyah* (Tarrazi; regarded as official by the Church); *A Short History of Syriac Christianity to the Rise of Islam* (McCullough); *Syrian Christians in Muslim Society* (Haddad); official church website.

XIII. Syrian Catholic Church of Antioch

SYRIAN CATHOLIC PATRIARCHS OF ANTIOCH

1. Butrus I (Petros) [#1 of Rome]   35–42
2. Awdiyus (Euodios)   42–68
3. Ighnatiyus I (Ignatios)   68–107
4. Irun (Hērōn)   107–127
5. Qurnil (Kornēlios)   127–154
6. Irus (Erōs)   154–170
7. Thiyufilus (Theophilos)   170–172
8. Maksimus I (Maximos)   172–190
9. Sirabiyun (Serapiōn)   190–211
10. Asqlibiyad (Asklēpiadēs)   211–223
11. Filitus (Philētos)   223–226
12. Azibina (Zebinos)   226–236
13. Babula (Babylas)   236–244
14. Fabiyus (Phabios)   244–255
15. Dimitriyus (Dēmētrios)   255–263
16. Bulus I (Paulos) *ho Samosateus*   263–271
17. Dumnus I (Domnos)   271–274
18. Timathiyus (Timotheos)   274–283
19. Qurillus (Kyrillos)   283–299
20. Turanus (Tyrannos)   299–313
21. Bitalis (Bitalis)   313–315
22. Bilujin (Philogonos)   315–320
23. Awstathiyus (Eustathios)   320–332
24. Fulin (Paulinos) *of Tyre*   332–337
25. Awlaliyus (Eulalios)   337–338
26. Afrun (Euphronios)   338–342
27. Filaqas (Phlakilos)   342–346
28. Istifan I (Stephanos)   346–351
29. Aluntiyus (Leontios) *"The Eunuch"*   351–357
30. Awduksiyus (Eudoxios) [#31 of Constantinople]   357–360
31. Aniyanus (Anianos)   360–362
32. Malatiyus (Meletios)   362–381
33. Flabiyanus I (Phlabianos)   381–404
34. Awghris (Euagrios)   404
35. Burfuriyus (Porphyrios)   404–414
36. Iskandar (Alexandros)   414–424
37. Thiyudut (Theodotos)   424–427
38. Yuhanna I (Iōannēs)   427–440
39. Dumnus II (Domnos)   440–449
40. Maksimus II (Maximos)   449–456
41. Basiliyus I (Basileios)   456–458
42. Aqaq (Akakios)   458–460
43. Martur (Martyrios)   460–470
44. Butrus II (Petros) *Knapheus*   470–471

	Martur [2nd time]	471–473
45.	Yulyan I (Ioulianos)	473–477
	Butrus II [2nd time]	477–480
46.	Yuhanna II (Iōannēs) *Kōdōnatos*	480
47.	Istifan II (Stephanos)	480–481
48.	Istifan III (Stephanos)	481–482
49.	Qalandun (Kallandiōn)	482–483
	Butrus II [3rd time]	483–484
	Yuhanna II [2nd time]	484–485
	Butrus II [4th time]	485–488
50.	Baladiyus (Palladios)	488–495
51.	Flabiyanus II (Phlabianos)	495–512
52.	Sawira I (Sebēros) *al-Antakhah*	512–518
53.	Bulus II (Paulos) *Xēnodokos*	518–521
54.	Afrasiyus (Euphrosios) *ibn Malaha*	521–528
55.	Afram I *of Amida*	528–546
56.	Sirkis *of Tella*	539–541
57.	Bulus III *"The Black"*	541–571
58.	Butrus III (Petros) *of Kallinikos*	571–591
59.	Yulyan II	592–595
60.	Athanasiyus I *Gammala*	595–631
61.	Yuhanna III	631–649
62.	Thiyudur	649–667
63.	Sawira II *ibn Mashqa*	667–680

INTERREGNUM

64.	Athanasiyus II *of Baladh*	684–688
65.	Yulyan III (Julianus) *"The Roman"*	688–709
66.	Ayliya	709–723
67.	Athanasiyus III	724–740
68.	Yuhanna IV	740–755
69.	Ishaq I	755–756
70.	Athanasiyus IV *Sandaliyus*	756–758
71.	Jirjis I	758–790
	Yuhanna [anti-patriarch]	758–763?
	Dawud [anti-patriarch]	763–
72.	Yusuf	790–792
73.	Quriyaqus	793–817
74.	Diyunisiyus I *of Tell Mahar*	818–845
75.	Yuhanna V	847–874

INTERREGNUM

76.	Ighnatiyus II	878–883

XIII. Syrian Catholic Church of Antioch

INTERREGNUM

77.	Thiyudusiyus	887–895
78.	Diyunisiyus II	896–909
79.	Yuhanna VI	910–922
80.	Basiliyus II	923–935
81.	Yuhanna VII	936–953
82.	Yuhanna VIII	954–957
83.	Diyunisiyus III	958–961
84.	Ibrahim I	962–963
85.	Yuhanna IX *Sarighta*	965–986
86.	Athanasiyus V *Salikha*	987–1003
87.	Yuhanna X *of Abhdun*	1004–1030
88.	Diyunisiyus IV *Khihi*	1032–1042
89.	Yuhanna XI [nephew of #87]	1042–1057
90.	Athanasiyus VI *Khayya*	1058–1063
91.	Yuhanna XII *Ishu' ibn Shushan*	1063–1073
92.	Basiliyus III *Sinnadus*	1074–1075
93.	Yuhanna XIII *Shinudah*	1075–1077
94.	Diyunisiyus V *Lazarus*	1077–1079
95.	Yuhanna XIV	1079–1087
96.	Diyunisiyus VI	1088–1090
97.	Athanasiyus VII *Abu'l-Faraj*	1091–1129
98.	Yuhanna XV *Mawdyani*	1129–1137
99.	Athanasiyus VIII *Ishu' ibn Qatrah*	1139–1166
100.	Mikha'il I *al-Kabir*	1167–1200
101.	Athanasiyus IX *Saliba Qarakha*	1200–1207
102.	Mikha'il II *Ishu' Siftana*	1207–1208
103.	Yuhanna XVI *Ishu'*	1208–1220
104.	Ighnatiyus III *Dawud*	1222–1252
105.	Diyunisiyus VII *Aharon Angur*	1252–1253
106.	Yuhanna XVII *ibn Ma'dani*	1253–1263
107.	Ighnatiyus IV *Ishu'*	1264–1283
108.	(Ighnatiyus) Filuksinus *Nimrud*	1283–1292
109.	Ighnatiyus V *ibn Wahib ibn Zakha*	1293–1333
110.	Ighnatiyus Ismil *Yuhanna*	1333–1366
111.	Ighnatiyus Shihab	1366–1381
112.	Ighnatiyus Ibrahim II *ibn Gharib*	1381–1412
113.	Ighnatiyus Bihnam I *Hajlaya*	1412–1455
114.	Ighnatiyus Khalaf	1455–1484
115.	Ighnatiyus Yuhanna XVIII *Akhsinaya Bar Shilla*	1484–1494
116.	Ighnatiyus Nuh [#77 of India]	1494–1509
117.	Ighnatiyus Ishu' I	1509–1510
118.	Ighnatiyus Ya'qub	1510–1519
119.	Ighnatiyus Dawud	1519–1520
120.	Ighnatiyus 'Abd Allah	1520–1557

121.	Ighnatiyus Ni'mat Allah	1557–1576
122.	Ighnatiyus Butrus IV Dawud	1577–1591
123.	Ighnatiyus Bilatus	1591–1597
124.	Ighnatiyus 'Abd al-Ghani	1597–1598
125.	Ighnatiyus Butrus V	1598–1639
126.	Ighnatiyus Shukr Allah I	1640–
127.	Ighnatiyus Shim'un I *of Tur-Abdin* [rival]	1640–1659
128.	Ighnatiyus Ishu' II *Qamah*	1655–1661
129.	Ighnatiyus Andrawus *Akhijan Murabbi*	1662–1677
	Ighnatiyus Habib *al-Mazziyati* [anti-patriarch]	1674–1686
130.	Ighnatiyus Butrus VI *Shahbadin*	1677–1702
131.	Ighnatiyus Jirjis II	1690–1709
132.	Ighnatiyus Ishaq II *Azar*	1709–1723
133.	Ighnatiyus Shukr Allah II	1723–1745
134.	Ighnatiyus Jirjis III	1746–1768
135.	Ighnatiyus Jirjis IV	1768–1781
136.	Ighnatiyus Mikha'il III *Jarwah*	1782–1800
137.	Ighnatiyus Mikha'il IV *Dahir*	1802–1810
138.	Ighnatiyus Sim'an II *Hindi Zora*	1811–1818
139.	Ighnatiyus Butrus VII *Jarwah*	1820–1851
140.	Ighnatiyus Antun I *Samhiri*	1853–1864
141.	Ighnatiyus Filibbus *Arkus*	1866–1874
142.	Ighnatiyus Jirjis V *Shilhut*	1874–1891
143.	Ighnatiyus Bihnam II *Banni*	1893–1897
144.	Ighnatiyus Afram II *Rahmani*	1898–1929
145.	Ighnatiyus Jibra'il *Tabbuni*	1929–1968
146.	Ighnatiyus Antun II *Huwayyik* (or *Hayek*)	1968–1998
147.	Ighnatiyus Musa *Dawud*	1998–2001
148.	Ighnatiyus Butrus VIII *Abd al-Ahad*	2001–

XIV.

Syrian Orthodox "Jacobite" Church of Antioch

When the Antiochian Patriarch, Sebēros (Severus), embraced monophysitism, certain members of his Church dissented, finally forcing him into exile at Alexandria in 518. The split, as with the Copts in Egypt, had more to do with temporal politics than spiritual values, the opponents of Sebēros supporting the Greek power structure. When he died in 538, his followers elected Sergios as his successor, thereby perpetuating a dual patriarchate.

In 542 Ya'qub al-Barda'i (Jacob Baradæus), a Syrian priest, began a thirty-six-year-long series of travels throughout the Near East, during which time he ordained thousands of priests, and everywhere extolled the virtues of monophysitism. His efforts solidified the Church's support among the people, and left such a lasting impression that his followers are still called "Jacobites" even today.

The "Jacobites" flourished under the early centuries of Muslim rule, but later entered a long decline. In 1313 and again in 1364 the Patriarchate split into several factions. Since that time the Syrian prelates of Antioch have taken the name Ighnatiyus as their prename, in honor of St. Ignatius, the third Patriarch of Antioch; to this is added a second saint's name and numeral. In 1662 the Church split again, as several uniate factions rallied to Patriarch Andrawus. This schism was put down, but a second Catholic break took place in 1783; and since this time there have been two Syrian Patriarchs.

The primate bears the title Patriarch of Antioch and of All the Domain of the Apostolic Throne. He has resided at Homs in Syria since the 1930s, with administrative offices in Damascus. The official languages of the Church are Syriac and Arabic, but the latter is in common use. Roughly three million adherents of the Church are spread throughout the Middle East, Asia, and the Americas, about half of them located in Southeastern India (Malabar).

SOURCES: "Christian Sect Slips Toward Extinction" (Pope); *Chronique de Michel le Syrien* (Michael I); *Episkepsis*; *Europa World Yearbook*; *Gegenwartslage der Ostkirchen* (Spuler); *History of the Church* (Jedin, ed.); *The Middle East and North Africa*; *Die Morgenländischen Kirchen* (Spuler); *Oriens Christianus* (Le Quien); *Orthodoxia*; *Profiles in Belief* (Piepkorn); *A Short History of Syriac Christianity to the Rise of Islam* (McCullough); *Syrian Christians in Muslim Society* (Haddad); official church website.

Syrian Patriarchs of Antioch

1.	Butrus I (Petros) [#1 of Rome]	37–67
2.	Afudiyus (Euodios)	67–68
3.	Ighnatiyus I (Ignatios) *Nurono*	68–107
4.	Hirun (or Hirus) (Hērōn or Hērōs)	107–127
5.	Qurniliyus (Kornēlios)	127–154
6.	Awrus (or Ayrus) (Erōs)	154–169
7.	Thawfilus (Theophilos)	169–182
8.	Maksimus I (Maximos)	182–191
9.	Sirabiyun (Serapiōn)	191–211
10.	Asqlibiyadis (Asklēpiadēs) the Confessor	211–220
11.	Filitus (Philētos)	220–231
12.	Zabina (Zebinos)	231–237
13.	Babula (Babylas)	237–251
14.	Fabiyus (Phabios)	251–254
15.	Dimitriyanus (Dēmētrianos)	254–260
16.	Bulus I (Paulos) *ho Samosateus*	260–268
17.	Dumnus I (Domnos)	268–273
18.	Timiyus (Timaios or Timos)	273–282
19.	Qurillus (Kyrillos)	283–303
20.	Turanus (Tyrannos)	304–314
21.	Fitalis (Bitalios)	314–320
22.	Filujuniyus (Philogonios)	320–323
23.	Bulinus (Paulinos) *of Tyre*	323–324
24.	Awstathiyus (Eustathios)	324–337
	Awlaliyus (Eulalios) [anti-patriarch]	331–333
	Awfruniyus (Euphronios) [anti-patriarch]	333–334
	Filaqilus (Phlakilos) [anti-patriarch]	334–344
	Istifanus (Stephanos) [anti-patriarch]	342–344
	Lawntiyus (Leontios) *"The Eunuch"* [anti-patriarch]	344–357
	Awduksiyus (Eudoxios) [anti-patriarch] [#31 of Constantinople]	358–359
	Aniyanus (Anianos) [anti-patriarch]	359
	Afzuyus (Euzōïos) [anti-patriarch]	360
25.	Militus (Meletios)	360–381
	Bulinus (Paulinos) [anti-patriarch]	362–388
26.	Flabiyanus I (Phlabianos)	381–404
	Awighriyus (Euagrios) [anti-patriarch]	388–393
27.	Burfuriyus (Porphyrios)	404–412
28.	Aliksandarus (Alexandros)	412–417
29.	Thawdutus (Theodotos)	417–428
30.	Yuhanna I (Iōannēs)	428–442
31.	Dumnus II (Domnos)	442–449
32.	Maksimus II (Maximos)	449–455
	Basiliyus (Basileios) [anti-patriarch]	456–458

XIV. Syrian Orthodox "Jacobite" Church of Antioch

	Aqaq (Akakios) [anti-patriarch]	458–459
33.	Marturiyus (Martyrios)	459–468
34.	Butrus II (Petros) *Knapheus*	468–488
	Yuliyanus (Ioulianos) [anti-patriarch]	471–476
	Yuhanna (Iōannēs) *Kōdōnatos* [anti-patriarch]	476–478
	Istifanus (Stephanos) [anti-patriarch]	478–481
	Istifanus (Stephanos) [anti-patriarch]	481–482
	Qalandiyun (Kallandiōn) [anti-patriarch]	482–485
35.	Baladiyus (Palladios)	488–498
36.	Flabiyanus II (Phlabianos)	498–512
37.	Sawiriyus I (Sebēros) *al-Antakhah*	512–538
	Bulus (Paulos) *the Jew* [anti-patriarch]	518–521
	Afrasiyus (Euphrosios) *ibn Malaha* [anti-patriarch]	521–528
	Afram (Ephraim) *of Amida* [anti-patriarch]	528–546
38.	Sirjiyus (Sergios) *of Tella*	544–546

Interregnum

39.	Bulus II *"The Black"*	550–575

Interregnum

40.	Butrus III (Petros) *of Kallinikos*	581–591
41.	Yulyan I	591–595
42.	Athanasiyus I *Gammala*	595–631
43.	Yuhanna II *of the Sedre*	631–648
44.	Thiyudurus	649–667
45.	Sawiriyus II *ibn Mashqa*	667–681
46.	Athanasiyus II *of Baladh*	683–686
47.	Yulyan II (Julianus) *"The Roman"*	686–708
48.	Ayliya I	709–723
49.	Athanasiyus III *Sandaliyus*	724–740
50.	Iwannis I	740–754
	Awannis [anti-patriarch]	754–
	Isaaq [anti-patriarch]	755–756
	Athanasiyus *al-Sandali* [anti-patriarch]	–758
51.	Jawrji I	758–790
	Yuhanna [anti-patriarch]	758–763?
	Dawud [anti-patriarch]	763–
52.	Yusuf	790–792
53.	Quriyaqus *of Takrit*	793–817
54.	Diyunisiyus I *of Tell Mahar*	817–845
55.	Yuhanna III	846–873

Interregnum

56.	Ighnatiyus II	878–883

INTERREGNUM

57.	Thawdusiyus *Rumanus of Takrit*	887–896
58.	Diyunisiyus II	897–909
59.	Yuhanna IV *Qurzahli*	910–922
60.	Basiliyus I	923–935
61.	Yuhanna V	936–953
62.	Iwannis II	954–957
63.	Diyunisiyus III	958–961
64.	Ibrahim	962–963
65.	Yuhanna VI *Sarighta al-Ma'tuk*	965–985
66.	Athanasiyus IV *Salikha*	986–1002
67.	Yuhanna VII *ibn Abhduni*	1004–1033
68.	Diyunisiyus IV *Yahya Khihi*	1033–1044

INTERREGNUM

69.	Yuhanna VIII [nephew of #67]	1049–1057
70.	Athanasiyus V *Hajji*	1058–1063
71.	Yuhanna IX *Ishu' ibn Shushan*	1063–1073
72.	Basiliyus II *Sinnadus*	1074–1075
	Yuhanna *Abdun* [anti-patriarch]	1075–1091?
73.	Diyunisiyus V *Lazarus*	1077–1078
74.	Iwannis III	1080–1082

INTERREGNUM

75.	Diyunisiyus VI	1088–1090
76.	Athanasiyus VI *ibn Khamuru Abu'l-Faraj*	1091–1129
77.	Yuhanna X *Mawdyani*	1129–1137
78.	Athanasiyus VII *Ishu' ibn Qatrah*	1138–1166
79.	Mikha'il I *al-Kabir "The Great"*	1166–1199
80.	Athanasiyus VIII *Saliba Qarakha*	1200–1207
81.	Yuhanna XI *Ishu'*	1208–1220
82.	Ighnatiyus III *Dawud* [#65 of Malankara Orthodox of India, #48 of Malankara Jacobite of India]	1222–1252
	Diyunisiyus *Aharon Angur* [anti-patriarch]	1252–1261
83.	Yuhanna XII *ibn al-Ma'dani* [#67 of Malankara Orthodox of India, #50 of Malankara Jacobite of India]	1252–1263
84.	Ighnatiyus IV *Ishu'*	1264–1282
85.	Filuksinus I *Nimrud*	1283–1292
86.	Mikha'il II *ibn Sawma*	1292–1312
	Qustantinus [anti-patriarch]	1292–

XIV. Syrian Orthodox "Jacobite" Church of Antioch

87.	Mikha'il III *Ishu' ibn Shushan*	1312–1349
	Ighnatiyus Qustantinus [anti-patriarch]	1312–1313
	Ighnatiyus *ibn Wahib ibn Zakha* [anti-patriarch]	1313–1333
	Ighnatiyus Isma'il *Yuhanna* [anti-patriarch]	1333–1365
88.	Basiliyus III *Ghubriyal*	1349–1387
	Ighnatiyus Shihab [anti-patriarch]	1365–1381
	Ighnatiyus Ibrahim *ibn Gharib* [anti-patriarch]	1381–1412
89.	Filuksinus II *"The Scribe"*	1387–1421
	Ighnatiyus Bihnam *Hajlaya* [anti-patriarch]	1412–1445
90.	Basiliyus IV *Shim'un Man'Amaya*	1421–1444
91.	Ighnatiyus Bihnam *Hajlaya* [#91 of Malankara Orthodox of India, #56 of Malankara Jacobite of India]	1445–1454
92.	Ighnatiyus Khalaf	1455–1483
93.	Ighnatiyus Yuhanna XIII *Akhsinaya Bar Shilla*	1483–1493
94.	Ighnatiyus Nuh [#60 of Malankara Jacobite of India]	1493–1509
95.	Ighnatiyus Ishu' I	1509–1512
96.	Ighnatiyus Ya'qub I	1512–1517
97.	Ighnatiyus Dawud I	1517–1520
98.	Ighnatiyus 'Abd Allah I	1520–1557
99.	Ighnatiyus Ni'mat Allah [#65 of Malankara Jacobite of India]	1557–1576
100.	Ighnatiyus Dawud II Shah *Butrus ibn Nur ad-Din* [#67 of Malankara Jacobite of India]	1576–1591
101.	Ighnatiyus Bilatus [#68 of Malankara Jacobite of India]	1591–1597
102.	Ighnatiyus Hidayat Allah [#70 of Malankara Jacobite of India]	1597–1639
103.	Ighnatiyus Shim'un *of Tur-Abdin*	1640–1659
104.	Ighnatiyus Ishu' II *Qamah*	1659–1662
105.	Ighnatiyus 'Abd al-Masih I *al-Rawhi* [#73 of Malankara Jacobite of India]	1662–1686
	Ighnatiyus Habib *al-Mazziyati* [anti-patriarch]	1674–1686
106.	Ighnatiyus Jirjis II [#75 of Malankara Jacobite of India]	1687–1708
107.	Ighnatiyus Ishaq *Azar* [#77 of Malankara Jacobite of India]	1709–1723
108.	Ighnatiyus Shukr Allah [#81 of Malankara Jacobite of India]	1723–1745
109.	Ighnatiyus Jirjis III	1745–1768

110.	Ighnatiyus Jirjis IV [#84 of Malankara Jacobite of India]	1768–1781
111.	Ighnatiyus Matiyus *ibn 'Abd Allah*	1782–1817
112.	Ighnatiyus Yunan	1817–1818
113.	Ighnatiyus Jirjis V *Sayyar*	1819–1837
114.	Ighnatiyus Ilyas II *Ankaz* [#82 of Malankara Orthodox Church, #91 of Malankara Jacobite of India]	1838–1847
115.	Ighnatiyus Ya'qub II	1847–1871
116.	Ighnatiyus Butrus IV *al-Ma'usili*	1872–1894
117.	Ighnatiyus 'Abd al-Masih II	1895–1905
118.	Ighnatiyus 'Abd Allah II *al-Saddi* (*Sattuf*)	1906–1915
119.	Ighnatiyus Ilyas III *Shakar*	1917–1932
120.	Ighnatiyus Afram *Barsum*	1933–1957
121.	Ighnatiyus Ya'qub III *Tuma*	1957–1980
122.	Ighnatiyus Zakka '*Iwas*	1980–

SYRIAN PATRIARCHS OF ANTIOCH AT TUR ABHDIN
(Not recognized as valid by the Church)

1.	Ighnatiyus Sabbas *ibn Wahib*	1364–1389
2.	Ighnatiyus Ishu' I *ibn Muta*	1390–1418?
3.	Ighnatiyus Mas'ud I *Slakhaya*	1418–1420
4.	Ighnatiyus Hinukh *Inwardaya*	1421–1445
5.	Ighnatiyus Quma *ibn Gafil*	1446–1455
6.	Ighnatiyus Ishu' II *Inwardaya*	1455–1466
7.	Ighnatiyus 'Aziz *ibn Shabhta*	1466–1488
8.	Ighnatiyus Yuhanna *ibn Qufar*	1488–1493
	Ighnatiyus Shaba *Arbaya* [anti-patriarch]	1488–
9.	Ighnatiyus Mas'ud II	1490?–1495

XV.

Church of Armenia

Although the Armenian Church claims to have been founded by the apostles Thaddeus and Bartholomew, most traditions point to St. Gregory as the original organizer of the Church, about the year 300. Gregory was made Bishop of Armenia shortly thereafter. The political isolation of the Armenian kingdom quickly led to its ecclesiastical isolation as well; this was reinforced by the Church's decision (circa 500) to repudiate the Council of Chalcedon, and embrace monophysitism.

The Patriarch of Armenia was the first to use the title "Catholicos" (Greek "Katholikos") a distinction which has since been adopted by many neighboring churches in the Near East. About the year 1100, the Patriarch moved his residence from Ashtishat in Armenia to the city of Sis, in Cilicia, then the center of a thriving Armenian/Latin monarchy.

After the fall of the kingdom in 1375, the chief see of the Church was moved to Etchmiadzin (1441), in Armenia proper, where it remains to this day. Several subsidiary Armenian patriarchates gradually emerged over the centuries. These included Aght'amar (the result of a schism in 1113), Jerusalem (1311), Caucasian Albania (semi-independent from earliest times), Sis (1441), Constantinople (1461), and the Catholic Patriarchate of Cilicia (1742). Two of these, Aght'amar and Albania, have lapsed; of the others, all but Sis and Cilicia acknowledge Etchmiadzin as first among equals of the Armenian primates; the churches at Constantinople and Jerusalem accept some guidance in their affairs from the mother church.

The Turkish massacres of Armenian nationals in 1890–1915 decimated the Armenian population in Eastern Turkey, resulting in the abandonment of the Aght'amarian Patriarchate, and changing the balance of power in the Armenian Church. The Catholicosate of Sis moved south into Lebanon, where it found renewed strength; at the same time, Etchmiadzin withdrew behind the borders of Armenia proper, which became a Soviet republic in 1921.

The Soviet invasion resulted in suppression of the Church during the two decades between the wars; at the death of Patriarch Khorên, in 1938, no election was allowed for a successor. The *Locum Tenens*, Georg, greatly aided the Soviet war effort during World War II, organizing and financing an Armenian regiment; in return, Stalin permitted new patriarchal elections in 1945. Most overseas members of the Armenian Church are governed by bishops appointed from Etchmiadzin, although both the Jerusalem and Cilician patriarchates are represented in America.

The primate bears the title Patriarch and Catholicos of All the Armenians. The official Church language is Armenian. Roughly four million communicants are located in Armenia, the Middle East, and the Americas.

SOURCES: *Armenia: The Survival of a Nation* (Walker); *The Church of Armenia* (Ormanian); *Dictionnaire de Théologie Catholique*; *Dictionnaire d'Histoire et de Géographie Ecclésiastique*; *Eastern Christianity and Politics in the Twentieth Century* (Ramet, ed.); *Europa World Yearbook*; *Gegenwartslage der Ostkirchen* (Spuler); *The History of the Armenian People* (Morgan); *History of the Church* (Jedin, ed.); *Die Morgenlandischen Kirchen* (Spuler); *Orthodoxia*; *Profiles in Belief* (Piepkorn); *Religion in the Soviet Union* (Kolarz); *Chosen of God* (Maksoudian); official church website.

TRADITIONAL PATRIARCHS OF THE OLD CHURCH

1.	T'adêos	43–66
2.	Bart'oghimêos	60–68
3.	Zak'aria	68–72
4.	Zementos	72–76
5.	Atrnerseh	77–92
6.	Mushê I	93–123
7.	Shahên	124–150
8.	Shawarsh	151–171
9.	Ghewondios	172–190

INTERREGNUM

10.	Mehruzhan	240–270

INTERREGNUM

CATHOLICOSES OF ARMENIA

1.	Grigor I "The Illuminator" *Lusaworich'*	302–325
2.	Aristakês I *Part'e* [son of #11]	325–333
3.	Vrt'anês *Part'e* [brother of #12]	333–341
4.	Husik I *Part'e* [son of #13]	341–347
	Daniêl [unconsecrated]	347
5.	P'arhên of *Ashtishat* [cousin of #14]	348–352
	Shahak [locum tenens]	352–353
6.	Nersês I "The Great" [grandson of #14]	353–373
	Shahak [locum tenens]	359–363
7.	Shahak (or Husik II)	373–377
8.	Zawên [cousin of #17]	377–381
9.	Aspurakês [brother of #18]	381–386

XV. Church of Armenia

10.	Sahak I "The Great" *Part'e*	387–436
	Surmak [anti-catholicos]	428–429
	Brguisho [anti-catholicos]	429–432
	Shmuel [anti-catholicos]	432–437
	Surmak [2nd time]	437–444
	Mesrop [locum tenens]	439–440
	Hovsêp' I [locum tenens]	440–444
11.	Hovsêp' I	444–452
12.	Melitê	452–456
13.	Movsês I	456–461
14.	Giwt	461–478
	Kristap'or *Ardzruni* [anti-catholicos]	478
15.	Hovhannês I *Mandakuni*	478–490
16.	Babkên	490–516
17.	Samuêl	516–526
18.	Mushê II	526–534
19.	Sahak II	534–539
20.	K'ristap'or I	539–545
21.	Ghewond	545–548
22.	Nersês II	548–557
23.	Hovhannês II	557–574
24.	Movsês II	574–604

Interregnum

	Hovhannês [anti-catholicos]	590–611
	Vrt'anês *Kert'ogh* [locum tenens]	604–607
25.	Abraham I	607–615
26.	Komitas	615–628
27.	K'ristap'or II	628–630
28.	Ezr	630–641
29.	Nersês III *Shinogh*	641–661
30.	Anastas	661–667
31.	Israyêl	667–677
32.	Sahak III	677–703
33.	Eghia	703–717
34.	Hovhannês III *Imastaser*	717–728
35.	Dawit' I	728–741
36.	Trdat I	741–764
37.	Trdat II	764–767
38.	Sion	767–775
39.	Esayi	775–788
40.	Step'anos I	788–790
41.	Hovab	790–791
42.	Soghomon	791–792
43.	Gêorg I *Hailorbuk*	792–795

44.	Hovsêp' II *Karidj*	795–806
45.	Dawit' II	806–833
46.	Hovhannês IV	833–855
47.	Zak'aria I	855–876
48.	Gêorg II	877–897
49.	Mashtots'	897–898
50.	Hovhannês V "The Historian" *Patmaban*	898–929
51.	Step'anos II *Rshtuni*	929–930
52.	T'êodoros I *Rshtuni*	930–941
53.	Eghishê *Rshtuni*	941–946
54.	Anania	946–968
55.	Vahan *Siuni*	968–969
56.	Step'anos III	969–972
57.	Khach'ik I *Arsharuni*	973–992
58.	Sargis I	992–1019
59.	Petros *Getadardz*	1019–1058
	Dioskoros [anti-catholicos]	1036–1038
60.	Khach'ik II [coadjutor 1049]	1058–1065
61.	Grigor II *Vkayasêr*	1066–1105
	Gêorg [coadjutor]	1067–1072
	Sargis [anti-catholicos]	1076–1077
	T'êodoros *Alakhosik* [anti-catholicos]	1077–1090
	Poghos [anti-catholicos]	1086–1087
62.	Barsegh [coadjutor 1081]	1105–1113
63.	Grigor III *Pahlawuni*	1113–1166
	Dawit' *T'ornikian* [anti-catholicos]	1114–
64.	Nersês IV *Shnorhali*	1166–1173
65.	Grigor IV *Tghay*	1173–1193
66.	Grigor V *K'aravêzh*	1193–1194
67.	Grigor VI *Apirat*	1194–1203
	Barsegh [anti-catholicos]	1195–1206?
68.	Hovhannês VI *Medzabaro*	1203–1221
	Anania [anti-catholicos]	1204–1208?
	Dawit' [coadjutor]	1204–1207
69.	Kostandin I	1221–1267
70.	Hakob I *Guitnakan*	1268–1286
71.	Kostandin II *Pronogordz*	1286–1289
72.	Step'anos IV	1290–1293
73.	Grigor VII	1293–1307
74.	Kostandin III	1307–1322
75.	Kostandin IV	1323–1326
76.	Hakob II	1327–1341
77.	Mkhit'ar	1341–1355
	Hakob II [2nd time]	1355–1359
78.	Mesrop	1359–1372
79.	Kostandin V	1372–1374

XV. Church of Armenia

80.	Poghos I	1374–1382
81.	T'êodoros II	1382–1392
82.	Karapet I *Bobik*	1392–1404
83.	Hakob III	1404–1411
84.	Grigor VIII *K'antsoghat*	1411–1418
85.	Poghos II	1418–1430
86.	Kostandin VI	1430–1439
	Hovsêp' [anti-catholicos]	1430?
87.	Grigor IX *Musabêgiants'* [#1 of Cilicia]	1439–1441
88.	Kirakos	1441–1443
89.	Gêorg III *Jalalbêgiants'*	1443–1465
	Karapet [anti-catholicos]	1446–
	Zak'aria [anti-catholicos]	1461–1462
90.	Aristakês II *At'orakal* [coadjutor 1448]	1465–1469
91.	Sargis II *Ajatar* [coadjutor 1462]	1469–1474
92.	Hovhannês VII *Ajakir* [coadjutor 1470]	1474–1484
93.	Sargis III *Miwsayl* [coadjutor 1474]	1484–1515
	Aristakês [coadjutor]	1484–1499
	T'adêos [coadjutor]	1499–1504
	Eghishê [coadjutor]	1504–1505
	Hovhannês [coadjutor]	1505–1506
	Nersês [coadjutor]	1506–1507
94.	Zak'aria II [coadjutor 1507]	1515–1520
95.	Sargis IV [coadjutor 1515]	1520–1536
96.	Grigor X	1536–1545
97.	Step'anos V	1545–1567
	Barsegh [coadjutor]	1549–1552
	Aristakês [coadjutor]	1555–
98.	Mik'ayêl [coadjutor 1545]	1567–1576
	Step'anos [coadjutor]	1567–
99.	Grigor XI [coadjutor 1552]	1576–1590
	T'adêos [coadjutor]	1577–
	Arakel [coadjutor]	1577–
100.	Dawit' III [coadjutor 1579]	1590–1629
	Melk'isedek [coadjutor]	1593–1603
	Grigor *Serapion* [coadjutor]	1603–1624
	Sahak [coadjutor]	1624–1629?
101.	Movsês III	1629–1632
102.	P'ilippos	1632–1655
103.	Hakob IV	1655–1680
	Eghiazar [anti-catholicos]	1663–1682
104.	Eghiazar	1682–1691
105.	Nahapet	1691–1705
106.	Aghek'sandr I	1706–1714
107.	Astuatsatur	1715–1725
108.	Karapet II	1726–1729

109.	Abraham II	1730–1734
110.	Abraham III	1734–1737
111.	Ghazar	1737–1748
	Hovhannês [anti-catholicos]	1740–
	Petros *Kutur* [locum tenens]	1748
	Ghazar [2nd time]	1748–1751
112.	Minas	1751–1753
113.	Aghek'sandr II *Karakashian*	1753–1755
	Sahak *Ahagwin* [unconsecrated]	1755–1760
	Hakob (V) [locum tenens]	1755–1759
114.	Hakob V	1759–1763
115.	Simêon	1763–1780
116.	Ghukas	1780–1799
	Hovsêp' *Arghutian* [unconsecrated]	1800–1801
117.	Dawit' IV *Gorghanian*	1801–1807
118.	Daniêl [elected 1801]	1807–1808
119.	Ep'rem	1809–1830
120.	Hovhannês VIII	1831–1842
121.	Nersês V *Ashtaraketsi*	1843–1857
122.	Matt'êos I *Ch'ukhachian* [#66 of Constantinople]	1858–1865
123.	Gêorg IV *K'êrêst'êchian* [#67 of Constantinople]	1866–1882

Interregnum

	Nersês *Vartsapetian* [unconsecrated; #72 of Constantinople]	1884
124.	Makar *Ter-Petrosian*	1885–1891
125.	Mkrtich' *Khrimian* [#71 of Constantinople]	1892–1907
126.	Matt'êos II *Izmirlian* [#75 of Constantinople]	1908–1910
	Gêorg *Surênian* [locum tenens]	1910–1911
127.	Gêorg V *Surênian*	1911–1930
	Khorên *Muradbêgian* [locum tenens]	1930–1932
128.	Khorên *Muradbêgian*	1932–1938

Interregnum

	Gêorg *Ch'êôrêk'chian* [locum tenens]	1938–1945
129.	Gêorg VI *Ch'êôrêk'chian*	1945–1954
	Vahan *Kostanian* [locum tenens]	1954
	Eghishê *Derderian* [locum tenens]	1954–1955
130.	Vazgên *Palchian*	1955–1994
	T'orgom *Manugian* [locum tenens] [#96 of Jerusalem]	1994–1995
131.	Garegin I *Sargisian* [#44 of Cilicia]	1995–1999
	Nersês *Pozapalian* [locum tenens]	1999
132.	Garegin II *Nersêsian*	1999–

XVI.

Church of Assyria (Church of the East)

The Church of Assyria, also called the Church of the East and (erroneously) the Nestorian Church, traces its history to a small Christian community founded by the apostles in the kingdom of Edessa, during the first century after Christ. The list of bishops (with their years of rule) claimed by the Church during these early years cannot be verified; its tradition of apostolic succession has never been challenged, however.

About the year 280 Mar Papa organized the Church into a Metropolitanate centered around the city of Seleucia, about thirty miles from the modern city of Baghdad. The title of Catholicos was assumed in 410 A.D. The Church grew rapidly, reaching its peak of cultural development and influence during the reign of Catholicos Yabhalaha III. By this time, Assyrian missionaries had established major branches of the Church throughout China and the Far East, and seemed destined to make the Assyrian Church the sole source of Christian instruction for the oriental world. The rise of the Mongols slowed this missionary effort, and nearly destroyed the Church itself.

By the mid-fifteenth century, the remnants of the Assyrian Church had sought refuge in the mountains of Kurdistan. The widespread destruction of churches and the wholesale slaughter of Church leaders led to the election (with Shim'un V [or VI]) of the nephew of the previous patriarch; the new patriarch had been raised in his uncle's house, and trained from birth for the high position which he now occupied. Thus the patriarchate became hereditary in the Bar Mama family, with succession from uncle to nephew or sometimes brother.

When the crisis subsided, a hundred years later, a significant faction of bishops and secular leaders attempted to restore the ancient electoral process on the death of Ishu'yabh Shim'un VII (or VIII) in 1551. They chose as patriarch a monk, Sa'ud bar Dani'il, who took the religious name of Yukhannan Shim'un IX Sulaqa (one of the churches inserts an extra "Shim'un" into their official list of patriarchs, hence the discrepancy in numbering). Dinkha Shim'un VIII bar Mama was named by his family as successor to his uncle, Ishu'yabh, thereby splitting the Church into two factions.

To complicate matters, Sulaqa immediately sought the backing of Rome to legitimize his position; the Pope confirmed Sulaqa's election and named him Patriarch.

Yukhannan Shim'un IX was arrested and executed by his rival, Dinkha Shim'un VIII bar Mama, in 1555, and was immediately succeeded by Marun 'Abdishu' IV.

The history of the next ten years is obscure. Dinkha Shim'un VIII bar Mama died in 1558, and was succeeded by his relative, Iliya VI. Marun 'Abdishu' IV died in 1567 (or 1571), and was succeeded after some delay by Yabhalaha IV (also called Shim'un X). A third faction, headed by the Metropolitan of Gelu, Dinkha Shim'un (XI), rejected the authority of the Bar Mama family, and submitted to Catholicos Yabhalaha; on the latter's death in 1580, Dinkha Shim'un XI was elected his successor, the first patriarch of the Shim'un family. Thus was established a second hereditary line of patriarchs, in opposition to the Bar Mama family.

Throughout the next three hundred years, the Catholicoses of the Shim'un family remained isolated in the mountains of Kurdistan, gradually losing contact with Rome. The last hereditary Catholicos, Ishai Shim'un XXIII, succeeded his uncle in 1920 at the age of twelve. In 1933, after returning to Iraq from his British school, he attempted to restore the old civil authority of the Patriarch. His supporters then took up arms, and were massacred by Iraqi government soldiers. Shim'un spent the rest of his life in exile, much of it in San Francisco.

He resigned his office in 1973, without any obvious successor, immediately throwing his Church into turmoil. Church leaders from Iraq pleaded with the Patriarch to withdraw his resignation, at least until some provision could be made for the succession; Shim'un agreed to return for a six-month period, at which point a Synod of three bishops was appointed to govern the Church during the interregnum. When Shim'un was assassinated by a disgruntled communicant in November 1975, the bishops restored the ancient electoral process, and a new patriarch, Mar Dinkha IV, was chosen in October 1976. Dinkha and Pope John Paul II issued a joint declaration of faith on 11 November 1994, stating that their accord represented "a fundamental step on the way to full communion."

The official language of the Church is Syriac. The primate, who uses the title "Catholicos-Patriarch of the Church of the East," currently resides in Chicago. The roughly 400,000 communicants are located primarily in the United States, with a few communities remaining in Iraq and Iran.

SOURCES: *The Catholic Eastern Churches* (Attwater); *Catholic Encyclopedia*; *The Christian Churches of the East* (Attwater); *De Catholicis seu Patriarchis Chaldæorum et Nestorianorum* (Assemani); *Dictionnaire de Théologie Catholique*; *Europa World Yearbook*; *Gegenwartslage der Ostkirchen* (Spuler); *Historia tēs Assyraikēs Nestorianikēs Ekklēsias* (Arbanitēs); *History of the Church* (Jedin, ed.); *The Middle East and North Africa*; *Die Morgenlandischen Kirchen* (Spuler); *New Catholic Encyclopedia*; *Oriens Christianus* (Le Quien); *Orthodoxia*; *Profiles in Belief* (Piepkorn); "The Patriarchs of the Church of the East from the Fifteenth to Eighteenth Centuries" (Murre-Van den Berg); Rev. Nenos Michael (personal communication); Mar Aprem (personal communication); official church website.

CATHOLICOS-PATRIARCHS OF ASSYRIA

1. Shim'un I *Kipa*   33

XVI. Church of Assyria (Church of the East)

2.	T'uma I *Shlikha* [#1 of Malankara Orthodox of India]	33
3.	Bar T'ulmai	33
4.	Addai (or T'addai) I *Shlikha* [#2 of Malankara Orthodox of India]	33–45
5.	Agai [#3 of Malankara Orthodox of India]	45–48
6.	Mari I [#4 of Malankara Orthodox of India]	48–81

Interregnum

	Abris [#5 of Malankara Orthodox of India]	90–107

Interregnum

	Abraham I [#6 of Malankara Orthodox of India]	130–152

Interregnum

9.	Ya'qub I [#7 of Malankara Orthodox of India]	172–190
10.	Abad *M'shikha*	191–203
11.	Akha *d'Awuhi* [#8 of Malankara Orthodox of India]	205–220

Interregnum

12.	Shakhlupa *of Kashkar* [#9 of Malankara Orthodox of India]	224–244

Interregnum

13.	Papa *bar Gaggai* [#10 of Malankara Orthodox of India, #1 of Malankara Jacobite of India]	247–326
14.	Shim'un II *bar Sabba'i* [#11 of Malankara Orthodox of India, #2 of Malankara Jacobite of India]	328–341

Interregnum

15.	Shahdust [#12 of Malankara Orthodox of India, #3 of Malankara Jacobite of India]	345–347

Interregnum

16.	Bar Ba'shmin [#13 of Malankara Orthodox of

	India, #4 of Malankara Jacobite of India]	350–358

INTERREGNUM

17.	T'umarsa [#14 of Malankara Orthodox of India, #5 of Malankara Jacobite of India]	383–393
18.	Qayuma [#15 of Malankara Orthodox of India, #6 of Malankara Jacobite of India]	393–399
19.	Iskhaq [#16 of Malankara Orthodox of India, #7 of Malankara Jacobite of India]	399–411
20.	Akhkhi [#17 of Malankara Orthodox of India, #8 of Malankara Jacobite of India]	411–415
21.	Yabhalaha I [#18 of Malankara Orthodox of India, #9 of Malankara Jacobite of India]	415–420
22.	Ma'na [#19 of Malankara Orthodox of India, #10 of Malankara Jacobite of India]	420
23.	Qarabukt [#20 of Malankara Orthodox of India]	421
24.	Dadishu' [#21 of Malankara Orthodox of India, #11 of Malankara Jacobite of India]	421–456
25.	Babai (or Babwi) I [#22 of Malankara Orthodox of India, #12 of Malankara Jacobite of India]	457–484
26.	Aqaq [#23 of Malankara Orthodox of India]	484–496
27.	Babai II [#24 of Malankara Orthodox of India]	496–502
28.	Shila [#25 of Malankara Orthodox of India]	505–523
29.	Narsai	524–535
30.	Ilisha' [rival catholicos] [#26 of Malankara Orthodox of India]	524–538
31.	Pulus [#27 of Malankara Orthodox of India]	539–540
32.	Mari Aba I *Raba* [#28 of Malankara Orthodox of India]	540–552
33.	Yusip [#29 of Malankara Orthodox of India]	552–567

INTERREGNUM

34.	Khazqi'il	570–581
35.	Ishu'yabh I *Arzunaya*	581–595
36.	Sabrishu' I *Garmaqaya*	596–604
37.	Grigur *Partaya*	605–608

INTERREGNUM

38.	Ishu'yabh II *Gdalaya*	628–644

INTERREGNUM

39.	Mari Immih	647–650

XVI. Church of Assyria (Church of the East)

40.	Ishu'yabh III *Khdayabaya*	650–660
41.	Giwargis I	661–680
42.	Yukhannan I *bar Marta*	680–682

INTERREGNUM

43.	Khnanishu' I *"The Lame"*	686–693
44.	Yukhannan II *Garba* *"The Leper"*	693–694

INTERREGNUM

45.	Slibazka	714–728

INTERREGNUM

46.	Pit'iun	731–740
47.	Mari Aba II	741–751
48.	Surin	752–754
49.	Ya'qub II	754–773
50.	Khnanishu' II	774–778
51.	Timat'ius I	780–820
52.	Ishu' *bar Nun*	820–824
53.	Giwargis II	825–832
54.	Sabrishu' II	832–836
55.	Abraham II *d'Margaa*	837–850
56.	T'iyadusis I (or T'iyaduris)	850–852

INTERREGNUM

57.	Sargis *Subaya*	860–872
58.	Anush *d'Bit' Garmai*	873–884
59.	Yukhannan III *bar Narsai*	884–892
60.	Yukhannan IV *bar Akhiha*	892–898
61.	Yukhannan V *bar Agbara* (or *Bar'aysa*)	900–905
62.	Abraham III *Abraza*	906–937
63.	'Ummanu'il	937–949

INTERREGNUM

64.	Israyil *Karkaya* [unconsecrated]	961–962
65.	'Abdishu' I *Garmaqaya*	963–986
66.	Mari II *bar Tubi At'uraya*	987–1000
67.	Yukhannan VI *bar Ishu'*	1001–1012
68.	Yukhannan VII *Nazuk*	1013–1022

69.	Ishu'yabh IV *bar Khazqi'il*	1023–1027
70.	Iliya I	1028–1049
71.	Yukhannan VIII *bar Targali*	1049–1057
72.	Sabrishu' III *bar Zanbur*	1057–1072
73.	'Abdishu' II *bar Arus Anraya*	1072–1090
74.	Makkikha I *bar Shlimun*	1092–1109
75.	Iliya II *bar Mulki*	1111–1132
76.	Bar Suma *d'Subi*	1133–1135
77.	Bar Gabbara	1135–1136
78.	'Abdishu' III *bar Mulki* [nephew of #75]	1138–1147
79.	Ishu'yabh V *Baladaya*	1148–1175
80.	Iliya III *Abu Khalim*	1176–1190
81.	Yabhalaha II *bar Qayyuma*	1191–1222
82.	Sabrishu' IV *bar Qayyuma*	1222–1226
83.	Sabrishu' V *bar Masikh*	1226–1256
84.	Makkikha II (or T'iyadusis II)	1257–1265
85.	Dinkha I *Arbilaya*	1265–1281
86.	Yabhalaha III *bar Turkaya*	1281–1318
87.	Timat'ius II	1318–1328
88.	Dinkha II	1329–1359
89.	Dinkha III	1359–1368
90.	Shim'un III	1369–1392

INTERREGNUM

91.	Shim'un IV	1403–1407
92.	Iliya IV	1407–1420
93.	Shim'un V	1420–1447
94.	Shim'un VI *d'Bat' Sadi*	1448–1490
95.	Iliya V	1491–1504
96.	Shim'un VII	1505–1538
97.	Ishu'yabh Shim'un VIII *bar Mama* [brother of #96]	1538–1551
98.	Dinkha Shim'un IX *bar Mama* [nephew of #97]	1552–1558
99.	Yabhalaha IV Shim'un X	1558–1580
100.	Dinkha Shim'un XI	1580–1600
101.	Iliya Shim'un XII	1600–1653
102.	Ishu'yabh Shim'un XIII	1653–1690
103.	Yabhalaha Shim'un XIV	1690–1692
104.	Dinkha Shim'un XV	1692–1700
105.	Shlimun Shim'un XVI [nephew of #104?]	1700–1740?
106.	Mikha'il Shim'un XVII *Mukhatas* [nephew?]	1740?–1780?
107.	Yunan Shim'un XVIII [nephew?]	1780?–1820?
108.	Abraham Shim'un XIX [nephew?]	1820?–1861
109.	Rubil Shim'un XX [nephew?]	1861–1903
110.	Binyamin Shim'un XXI [nephew of #109]	1903–1918
111.	Pulus Shim'un XXII [brother of #110]	1918–1920

XVI. Church of Assyria (Church of the East)

	Yusip Khnanishu' [locum tenens]	1918–1927
	Abimaleck Timotheos [joint locum tenens] [#24 of India — Chaldean]	1920s
112.	Ishai Shim'un XXIII [nephew of #111]	1920–1975
113.	Dinkha IV *Khnanishu'*	1976–

ANCIENT HOLY APOSTOLIC AND CATHOLIC CHURCH OF THE EAST

On 25 September 1968, Mar Thoma Darmo, Metropolitan of the Chaldean Syrian Church of India, and a longtime opponent of the hereditary patriarchate and the use of the Gregorian calendar, was elected Catholicos-Patriarch of the newly-organized Ancient Apostolic and Catholic Church of the East, with its seat at Baghdad. He was consecrated on 10 October. The dissidents, including both laity and clergy, were able to persuade the Iraqi government to cede them many of the churches and properties previously owned by the followers of Shim'un XXIII.

Darmo died a year later, on 9 September 1969, and was eventually succeeded by Mar Addai II on 20 February 1972. Efforts by the two rival patriarchs to unite the churches, or to agree on mutually-recognized eastern and western patriarchates, have thus far failed. A major liturgical difference between the two denominations is the use of the Julian Calendar by the Ancient Apostolic Church (its rival employs the Gregorian Calendar). Roughly 30,000 communicants reside in Iraq and the United States.

SOURCES: news reports; *Orthodoxia*; Mar Aprem (personal communication); official church website.

CATHOLICOS-PATRIARCHS OF THE CHURCH OF THE EAST

112.	T'uma II *Darmu* [#25 of India — Chaldean]	1968–1969

INTERREGNUM

	Addai *Giwargis* [locum tenens]	1969–1972
113.	Addai II *Giwargis*	1972–

XVII.

Churches of Austria-Hungary (Cernovci, Karlovci, Sibiu)

The Church of Sremski Karlovci (or Srijemski Karlovac) was autonomous from at least 1690, when the Holy Roman Emperors granted former Serbian Patriarch Arsenije III and thousands of his followers refuge from Turkish depredations. The archdiocese of Karlovci was located in the southern part of the Kingdom of Hungary (then part of the Holy Roman Empire, later an autonomous section of the Austrian-Hungarian Empire). The Austrians deliberately used the Orthodox denominations within the boundaries of their expanding state to bolster their political and economic claims to southeastern Europe, and to provide ecclesiastical counterpoints against the rising tide of nationalism in the Balkans, particularly among the Serbians.

Thus, among the many consequences of the two Austrian revolutions of 1848 were the naming of a new and vigorous Emperor, Franz Josef I, the erection of the Hungarian half of his realm into a second cultural and political center of the Empire, and the unilateral granting of the title "Patriarch" to Josif Rajačić, then Metropolitan of Sremski Karlovci, on 15 December 1848.

Although the Ecumenical Patriarch protested this non-ecclesiastical lifting of Karlovci into the patriarchal ranks (and the assumption of autocephaly that went with it), the title remained in use until 1918. This creation of a newly independent rival church just forty miles up the Danube from Belgrade (Beograd), the capital of the rising state of Serbia, was no accident, since it supported the government policy of stopping Serbian expansionism at any cost.

Similarly, the Church of Sibiu was taken from Karlovci, and erected on 24 December 1864 into an autonomous church to service the Romanians in northeastern Hungary, and to act as a direct challenge to the newly independent state of Romania and its soon-to-be-proclaimed autocephalous church. The third church, Cernovci (now Chernovtsy in the independent ex–Soviet state of Ukraine), was made autonomous on 23 January 1873 in the northeastern section of the Empire.

All three churches were under the direct supervision of the Austro-Hungarian government, which interferred blatantly in more than one ecclesiastical "election," all higher-level appointments requiring confirmation from the Emperor before the primates could be consecrated. In 1908, for example, the leading candidate for Patriarch of

Karlovci, Gavrilo Zmajević, although elected, was never consecrated due to government opposition, and a second nominated candidate then declined election when it became obvious that the Emperor would not agree.

Finally, the government-sponsored prelate, Bogdanović, was forced upon the assemblage; in a bizarre twist, he apparently committed suicide five years later by driving his car off a cliff. The see remained vacant until the end of World War I. Unusually, many of the primates of this church were better known under their surnames (*e.g.*, Patriarch Rajačić) than their given names.

The Church of Karlovci, which had some 800,000 communicants prior to World War I, merged into the new Serbian Patriarchate in the aftermath of World War I (1920), the Serbian leader subsuming the title of Metropolitan of Karlovci. The Church of Sibiu, which included roughly 220,000 members, became a metropolitanate in the Church of Romania in 1918. The Church of Cernovci (or Cernauti or Chernovtsy) in Bukovina, with some half million communicants, became part of the Church of Romania in 1918, some parishes being given to Poland and Russia. When the Soviets occupied the city in 1940, the Church was transferred to Russia, and with the disintegration of the Soviet Union, it now falls under the jurisdiction of Ukraine.

SOURCES: *Biographisches Lexikon zur Geschichte Südosteuropas* (Bernath & Nehring); *Dictionnaire de Théologie Catholique*; *Échos d'Orient*; *The Habsburg Empire, 1790–1918* (Macartney); *A History of Modern Serbia, 1804–1918* (Petrovich); *History of the Church* (Jedin, ed.); *Istoria Bisericii Ortodoxe Române*; *Karlovačko Vladičanstvo* (Grbic).

METROPOLITAN ARCHBISHOPS OF CERNOVCI (BUKOVINA)

1.	Nicolae	
2.	Stefan I	
3.	Iosif	
4.	Meletie	
5.	Lavrentie I	
6.	Grigorie	
7.	Sava I	
8.	Ghelasie	
9.	Ioanichie	1472–1504
10.	Pahomie	1504–1522

INTERREGNUM

11.	Teofan I	1528–1530
12.	Teodosie I	1530–1550?
13.	Mitrofan	1550?–1552
14.	Gheorghe I	1552–1558
15.	Eftimie	1558–1561?
16.	Dimitrie	1561?–1564?
17.	Isaia I	1564?–1577
18.	Gheorghe II *Moghila* (or *Movila*)	1577–1588
19.	Ghedeon I	1588–1591?

20.	Mardarie	1591?–1595
21.	Amfilohie	1595–1598
22.	Teodosie II *Barbovschi*	1598–1600
23.	Anastasie I *Crimca*	1600
	Teodosie II [2nd time]	1600–1605
24.	Ioan	1605–1608
25.	Efrem	1608–1613
26.	Atanasie II	1613–1616?
	Efrem [2nd time]	1616?–1623?
27.	Evloghie	1623–1627
28.	Dionisie	1627–1629
	Evloghie [2nd time]	1628–1639?
29.	Anastasie III	1639?–1644?
30.	Stefan II	1644?–1646?
31.	Teofan II	1646?–1651
32.	Iorest	1651?–1656
33.	Sava II	1656–1658
34.	Teofan III	1658–1666
35.	Serafim	1667–1669
36.	Teodosie III	1669?–1671
	Serafim [2nd time]	1671–1685?
37.	Misail I	1685?–1689
38.	Lavrentie II	1689–1702
	Nicolae *Vasilevici* [anti-archbishop]	1691–
39.	Ghedeon II	1701?–1708
40.	Calistru	1708–1728
41.	Antonie	1728–1729
42.	Misail II	1729–1735
43.	Varlaam	1735–1745
44.	Iacob *Putneanul*	1745–1750
45.	Dosoftei *Herescu*	1750–1789
46.	Daniïl *Vlahovići*	1789–1822
47.	Isaia II *Baloşescu*	1823–1834
48.	Eugenie (or Evghenie) *Hacman*	1835–1873
49.	Teofil *Bendela*	1873–1875
50.	Teoctist *Blajevici*	1877–1879
51.	Silvestru *Morariu-Andrievici*	1880–1895
52.	Arcadie *Ciupercovici*	1896–1902
53.	Vladimir *Repta*	1902–1924
54.	Nectarie *Cotlarciuc*	1924–1935
55.	Visarion *Puiu*	1935–1940
56.	Tit *Simedrea*	1940–1945
	Emilian *Antal Târgovişteanul* [locum tenens]	1945–1948
57.	Sebastian *Rusan* [titular archbishop]	1948–1950

METROPOLITANATE DISESTABLISHED 1950

PATRIARCHS OF SREMSKI KARLOVCI
(Metropolitans 1690, Patriarchs 1848)

1.	Arsenije I *Crnojević* (or *Čarnojević*) [#24 of Serbia]	1690–1706
2.	Isaija I *Đaković*	1708
3.	Stevan I *Metohijac*	1708–1709
4.	Sofronije *Podgoričanin*	1710–1711
	Atanasije *Ljubojević* [locum tenens]	1711–1712
5.	Vićentije I *Popović*	1713–1725
6.	Mojsej(e) I *Petrović*	1726–1730
	Nikolaj *Dmitrijević* [locum tenens]	1730–1731
7.	Vićentije II *Jovanović*	1731–1737

INTERREGNUM

8.	Arsenije II *Jovanović Šakabenta* [#28 of Serbia]	1741–1748
9.	Isaija II *Antonović*	1748–1749
10.	Pavle *Nenadović*	1749–1768
	Jovan *Đorđević* [locum tenens]	1768–1769
11.	Jovan *Đorđević* [#32 of Sibiu]	1769–1773
12.	Vićentije III *Jovanović-Vidak*	1774–1780
13.	Mojsej II *Putnik*	1781–1790
14.	Stevan II (or Stefan) *Stratimirović*	1790–1836
15.	Stevan III *Stanković*	1837–1841
	Georgije (I) *Hranislav* [locum tenens]	1841–1842
16.	Josif *Rajačić*	1842–1861

INTERREGNUM

	Samuïlo *Maširević* [locum tenens]	1861–1864
17.	Samuïlo *Maširević*	1864–1870

INTERREGNUM

	Arsenije (III) *Stojković* [locum tenens]	1870–1872
	Nikanor *Grujić* [locum tenens]	1872–1874
	Arsenije (III) *Stojković* [unconsecrated]	1874
18.	Prokopije *Ivačković* [#38 of Sibiu]	1874–1880
	Teofan *Živković* [locum tenens]	1880

	German *Anđelić* [locum tenens]	1880–1882
	Arsenije (III) *Stojković* [unconsecrated]	1881
	Teofan *Živković* [unconsecrated]	1881
19.	German *Anđelić*	1882–1888
20.	Georgije (II) *Branković*	1890–1907
	Lukijan *Bogdanović* [locum tenens]	1907–1908
	Gavrilo *Zmajević* [unconsecrated]	1908
	Mitrofan *Šević* [refused election]	1908
21.	Lukijan *Bogdanović*	1908–1913

Interregnum

	Miron *Nikolić* [locum tenens]	1913
	Mihaïlo *Grujić* [locum tenens]	1913–1914
	Miron *Nikolić* [locum tenens]	1914–1919
	Georgije (III) *Letić* [locum tenens]	1919–1922

Merged into the Church of Serbia

Metropolitan Archbishops of Sibiu
(now Ardealului)

1.	Ghelasie	1376?
2.	Ioan I	1456?
3.	Ioanichie	1479?
4.	Daniïl I	1488–1500?

Interregnum

| 5. | Marcu | 1516– |
| 6. | Danciu (Stefan?) | 1516–1534 |

Interregnum

| 7. | Petru | 1538–1550 |

Interregnum

8.	Ioan II	1553–1557?
9.	Hristofor I	1557–1559?
10.	Sava I	1559–
11.	Gheorghe	1561?–1562
	Sava I [2nd time]	1562–1570

XVII. Churches of Austria-Hungary (Cernovci, Karlovci, Sibiu)

12.	Eftimie	1571?–1574
13.	Hristofor II	1574–1579
14.	Ghenadie I	1579–1585
15.	Ioan III	1585–1605?
16.	Teoctist	1606–1622
17.	Dosoftei	1624–1627
18.	Ghenadie II	1627–1640
19.	Ilie *Iorest*	1640–1643
20.	Simion *Stefan*	1643–1656
21.	Sava II *Brancovici*	1656
22.	Ghenadie III	1659–1660
23.	Daniïl II	1660?–1662
	Sava II [2nd time]	1662–1680
24.	Iosif *Budal*	1680–1682
25.	Ioasaf	1682–1683
26.	Sava III	1684–1685
27.	Varlaam	1685–1692
28.	Teofil	1692–1697
29.	Atanasie *Anghel*	1697–1701

INTERREGNUM

30.	Iov *Tirca* (or Ioan)	1706?–1707

INTERREGNUM

31.	Dionisie *Novacovici*	1761–1767
32.	Ioan IV *Gheorghievici* [#11 of Carlovci]	1768–1769
33.	Sofronie *Chirilovici*	1769–1774

INTERREGNUM

	Ioan *Popovici* [locum tenens]	1774–1784
34.	Ghedeon *Nichitici*	1783–1788
	Ioan *Popovici* [locum tenens]	1788–1789
35.	Gherasim *Adamovici*	1789–1796

INTERREGNUM

	Ioan *Popovici* [locum tenens]	1796–1805
	Nicolae *Hutovici* [locum tenens]	1805–1811
36.	Vasile I *Moga*	1810–1845
	Andrei *Saguna* [locum tenens]	1846–1847
37.	Andrei *Saguna*	1847–1873

38.	Procopie *Ivaşcovici* [#18 of Carlovci]	1873–1874
	Ioan *Popasu* [unconsecrated]	1874
39.	Miron *Romanul*	1874–1898
40.	Ioan V *Metianu*	1898–1916
41.	Vasile II *Mangra*	1916–1918
	Ioan *Papp* [locum tenens]	1918–1920
42.	Nicolae I *Balan*	1920–1955
	Justinian *Marina* [#3 of Romania; locum tenens]	1955–1956
43.	Iustin *Moïsescu* [#4 of Romania]	1956–1957
44.	Nicolae II *Colan*	1957–1967
	Nicolae *Corneanu* [locum tenens]	1967
45.	Nicolae III *Mladin*	1967–1981
	Teoctist *Arăpaşu* [#5 of Romania; locum tenens]	1980–1982
46.	Antonie *Plamadeala*	1982–

XVIII.

Chaldean Church of Babylon

The history of the Chaldean Church through 1551, when the great schism occurred, has been given in the chapter on Assyria. Yukhannan Sulaqa, the nominee of the anti–Bar Mama faction, was sent to Rome, where his election was ratified by Pope Iulius III. Sulaqa was given the official title of "Patriarch of the Chaldeans." When he returned to Iraq, Sulaqa's rival had him arrested and executed, thereby thinking to end the division. But Sulaqa's supporters elected 'Abdishu' IV as his successor, and then Yabhalaha IV when 'Abdishu' died. Yabhalaha was succeeded in 1580 by the Metropolitan of Gehu, Dinkha Shim'un XI, who founded a second hereditary patriarchate to oppose the Bar Mama faction.

Ironically, the doctrinal positions of the two factions, once so clearly defined, slowly blurred with the centuries. The Shim'uns were forced through political pressure to move their see into the mountains of Kurdistan, thereby isolating their church from outside contact. By the year 1670 their contact with Rome had dwindled to nothing.

The Bar Mamas, on the other hand, had begun exchanging letters with the Roman Popes in 1586, and formally submitted to papal authority in 1616 at Djarbakir, although this profession had lapsed by 1669. Subsequently, the Metropolitan Yusip of Djarbakir withdrew his allegiance from both parties in 1672, fleeing to Rome by 1675. Pope Innocent XI granted him the title of Patriarch in 1681, thereby creating a third Assyrian patriarchate.

Yusip's successor, Yusip III (or II), was erroneously named Patriarch of Babylon in 1701, apparently the result of confusion in Rome over the identity of the city of Baghdad. On the death of Yusip V in 1779, his nephew, Yusip Agustinus Khindi, succeeded his uncle only as Apostolic Administrator and Metropolitan of Djarbakir; he was never able to obtain official recognition from Rome as the new patriarch.

Iliya XIII bar Mama, the last hereditary catholicos of his family, died in 1804. His Catholic cousin, Yukhannan (VIII) Khurmiz, claimed the title, and again sought official recognition from the pope. With two Catholic rivals to the patriarchal throne, the Roman Church declined to recognize either claimant until the death of Yusip Khindi in 1828. Khurmiz was thereupon acknowledged as Patriarch in 1830. To forestall the possibility of a new hereditary patriarchate, a coadjutor Patriarch with the right of succession was appointed in 1838.

The Chaldean Church nearly broke with Rome again in 1869 over the imposition by the Pope of the bull *Reversurus*, which deprived the Patriarch of his prerogative to ordain Chaldean bishops, and which caused similar unrest in Armenian Cilicia. Yusip VI was threatened with excommunication in 1876, but managed to smooth over his difficulties with Rome before dying two years later.

Recently the 2003 patriarchal election exacerbated the recent split between the more traditionalist clergy (mostly bearded), who hearken back to the Church's Assyrian roots, and a second faction (mostly clean-shaven) hoping to increase the Church's ties with the West. A transitional primate, the retired Archbishop 'Ummanu'il Karim Delly, was finally chosen in November after an initial synod held some months earlier had failed to agree upon a candidate.

The official language of the Church is Syriac. The primate bears the title Patriarch of Babylon of the Chaldeans, and resides at Baghdad, Iraq. Roughly 560,000 communicants are scattered throughout the Middle East, particularly in Iraq and Iran, with a strong (50,000+ member) overseas contingent in North America, mostly in Detroit and Chicago. This is the largest of the three Chaldean churches.

SOURCES: *The Catholic Eastern Churches* (Attwater); *Catholic Encyclopedia*; *The Christian Churches of the East* (Attwater); *De Catholicis seu Patriarchis Chaldæorum et Nestorianorum* (Assemani); *Dictionnaire de Théologie Catholique*; *Eastern Christianity and Politics in the Twentieth Century* (Ramet, ed.); *Gegenwartslage der Ostkirchen* (Spuler); *The Middle East and North Africa*; *Die Morgenlandischen Kirchen* (Spuler); *New Catholic Encyclopedia*; "Pope Calls for Broad Mideast Peace" (Montalbano); *Oriens Christianus* (Le Quien); "The Patriarchs of the Church of the East from the Fifteenth to Eighteenth Centuries" (Murre-Van den Berg); official church website.

CHALDEAN PATRIARCHS OF ASSYRIA

1. T'uma *Shlikha* [#1 of Malankara Orthodox of India]   –33
2. Addai *Shlikha* [#2 of Malankara Orthodox of India]   33–
3. Agai [#3 of Malankara Orthodox of India]
4. Mari I [#4 of Malankara Orthodox of India]
5. Abris [#5 of Malankara Orthodox of India]
6. Abraham I [#6 of Malankara Orthodox of India]
7. Ya'qub I [#7 of Malankara Orthodox of India]
8. Akha *d'Awuhi* [#8 of Malankara Orthodox of India]
9. Shakhlupa *of Kashkar* [#9 of Malankara Orthodox of India]
10. Papa *bar Gaggai* [#10 of Malankara Orthodox of India, #1 of Malankara Jacobite of India]   300?
11. Shim'un I *bar Sabbai* [#11 of Malankara Orthodox of India, #2 of Malankara Jacobite of India]   –341
12. Shahdust [#12 of Malankara Orthodox of India, #3 of Malankara Jacobite of India]   341?–342
13. Bar Ba'shmin [#13 of Malankara Orthodox of India, #4 of Malankara Jacobite of India]   342?–348

XVIII. Chaldean Church of Babylon

INTERREGNUM

14.	T'umarsa [#14 of Malankara Orthodox of India, #5 of Malankara Jacobite of India]	388?–
15.	Qayuma [#15 of Malankara Orthodox of India, #6 of Malankara Jacobite of India]	–399
16.	Iskhaq [#16 of Malankara Orthodox of India, #7 of Malankara Jacobite of India]	399–410
17.	Akhkhi [#17 of Malankara Orthodox of India, #8 of Malankara Jacobite of India]	411–414
18.	Yabhalaha I [#18 of Malankara Orthodox of India, #9 of Malankara Jacobite of India]	415–420
19.	Ma'na [#19 of Malankara Orthodox of India, #10 of Malankara Jacobite of India]	420
20.	Qarabukt [#20 of Malankara Orthodox of India]	420
21.	Dadishu' [#21 of Malankara Orthodox of India, #11 of Malankara Jacobite of India]	421?–456
22.	Babwi [#22 of Malankara Orthodox of India, #12 of Malankara Jacobite of India]	457–484
23.	Aqaq [#23 of Malankara Orthodox of India]	485–496?
24.	Babai [#24 of Malankara Orthodox of India]	497–503?
25.	Shila [#25 of Malankara Orthodox of India]	505–522?
26.	Narsai	524–537?
27.	Ilisha' [#26 of Malankara Orthodox of India]	524–537?
28.	Pulus I [#27 of Malankara Orthodox of India]	537?–539?
29.	Aba I *Raba* [#28 of Malankara Orthodox of India]	540–552
30.	Yusip I [#29 of Malankara Orthodox of India]	551–567?
31.	Khazqi'il	567–581
32.	Ishu'yabh I *Arzunaya*	582–595
33.	Sabrishu' I *Garmaqaya*	596–604
34.	Grigur *Partaya*	605–609

INTERREGNUM

35.	Ishu'yabh II *Gdalaya*	628–646?
36.	Mari Immih	647–650
37.	Ishu'yabh III *Khdayabaya*	650–658?

INTERREGNUM

38.	Giwargis I	661–681?
39.	Yukhannan I *bar Marta*	681?–683
40.	Khnanishu' I *"The Lame"*	685?–700?
	Yukhannan *Garba* "The Leper" [anti-catholicos]	691–693?

INTERREGNUM

41.	Slibazka	714–728

INTERREGNUM

42.	Pit'iun	731–740
43.	Aba II	741–751

INTERREGNUM

44.	Surin	754
45.	Ya'qub II	754–773
46.	Khnanishu' II	773–780
47.	Timat'ius I	780–823
48.	Ishu' *bar Nun*	823–828
49.	Giwargis II	828–831?
50.	Sabrishu' II	831–835
51.	Abraham II *d'Margaa*	837–850

INTERREGNUM

52.	T'iyadusis (Solomon)	853–858
53.	Sargis *Subaya*	860–872

INTERREGNUM

54.	Israyil I *of Kashkar* [unconsecrated]	877
55.	Anush *d'Bit' Garmai*	877–884
56.	Yukhannan II *bar Akhiha*	884–891
57.	Yukhannan III *bar Narsai*	893–899
58.	Yukhannan IV *bar Agbara*	900–905
59.	Abraham III *Abraza*	905–936
60.	'Ummanu'il I	937–960
61.	Israyil II *Karkaya*	961
62.	'Abdishu' I	963–986
63.	Mari II *bar Tubi At'uraya*	987–999
64.	Yukhannan V *bar Ishu'*	1000–1011
65.	Yukhannan VI *Nazuk*	1012–1016

INTERREGNUM

66.	Ishu'yabh IV *bar Khazqi'il*	1020–1025

XVIII. Chaldean Church of Babylon

INTERREGNUM

67.	Iliya I	1028–1049
68.	Yukhannan VII *bar Targali*	1049–1057

INTERREGNUM

69.	Sabrishu' III *bar Zanbur*	1064–1072

INTERREGNUM

70.	'Abdishu' II *bar Arus Anraya*	1075–1090
71.	Makkikha I *bar Shlimun*	1092–1110
72.	Iliya II *bar Mulki* [uncle of #74]	1111–1132
73.	Bar Suma *d'Subi*	1134–1136
74.	'Abdishu' III *bar Mulki* [nephew of #72]	1139–1148
75.	Ishu'yabh V *Baladaya*	1149–1175
76.	Iliya III *Abu Khalim*	1176–1190
77.	Yabhalaha II *bar Qayyuma*	1190–1222
78.	Sabrishu' IV *bar Qayyuma*	1222–1224
79.	Sabrishu' V *bar Masikh*	1226–1256
80.	Makkikha II	1257–1265
81.	Dinkha I *Arbilaya*	1265–1281
82.	Yabhalaha III *bar Turkaya*	1283–1318
83.	Timat'ius II	1318–1332
84.	Dinkha II	1332–1364
85.	Shim'un II	1364–
86.	Shim'un III	1400?
87.	Iliya IV	–1437
88.	Shim'un IV *d'Bat' Sadi*	1437–1497
89.	Shim'un V	1497–1502?
90.	Iliya V	1502–1503
91.	Shim'un VI [brother of #92]	1504–1538
92.	Ishu'yabh Shim'un VII *bar Mama* [brother of #91]	1538–1551
93.	Dinkha Shim'un VIII *bar Mama* [nephew of #92]	1551–1558
94.	Iliya VI *bar Mama*	1558–1576
97.	Shim'un Iliya VII *bar Mama*	1576–1591
99.	Iliya VIII *bar Mama*	1591–1617
100.	Shim'un Iliya IX *bar Mama*	1617–1660
101.	Yukhannan Iliya X *bar Mama*	1660–1700
104.	Marugin Iliya XI *bar Mama*	1700–1722
106.	Dinkha Iliya XII *bar Mama*	1722–1778
108.	Ishu'yabh Iliya XIII *bar Mama* [nephew of #106; cousin of #109]	1778–1804

INTERREGNUM

Yukhannan *Khurmiz* [locum tenens;
cousin of #108]   1804–1830

Patriarchs of the Chaldeans at Djarbakir (Seert)

95. Yukhannan Shim'un IX *Sulaqa* (*Sa'ud bar Dani'il*) 1551–1555
96. Marun 'Abdishu' IV   1555–1567

INTERREGNUM

98. Shim'un Yabhalaha IV   1578–1580

Patriarchs of Babylon of the Chaldeans at Djarbakir

102. Yusip II (I)   1681–1695
103. Ma'ruf Yusip III (II) *Sliba*   1696–1712
105. Timat'ius Yusip IV (III) *Mushi*   1713–1757
107. Lazar Yusip V (IV) *Khindi*   1757–1781

INTERREGNUM

Agustinus Yusip (V) *Khindi* [nephew
of #107; unconsecrated]   1804–1828

Patriarchs of Babylon of the Chaldeans at Baghdad

109. Yukhannan VIII *Khurmiz* [cousin of #108]   1830–1838
110. Niqula I Ishai Ya'qub *Zaya*   1838–1847
111. Yusip VI *Audu*   1848–1878
112. Pitrus Iliya XIV *Abulyunan*   1879–1894
113. Giwargis 'Abdishu' V *Khayyat'*   1895–1899
114. Yusip 'Ummanu'il II *T'uma*   1900–1947
115. Yusip VII *Ghanima*   1947–1958
116. Pulus II *Shaikhu*   1958–1989
117. Rapa'il *Bidawid*   1989–2003
     Shlimun *Warduni* (apostolic administrator)   2003
118. 'Ummanu'il III *Delly*   2003–

XIX.

Church of Belarus

The White Russians were strong opponents of the Bolsheviks during the Russian Civil War. Following the Soviet victory, the Bishop of Minsk, Melhisedek Paieuskiĭ, proclaimed the independence of the B(y)elorussian Church on 23 July 1922, and assumed the title of Metropolitan, not so much from nationalistic fervor, but to protect his flock from the reform movement then sweeping Russian Orthodoxy. In 1925 he renounced his title in Moscow at the insistence of the Patriarchal Locum Tenens.

Two years later, however, a group of influential communicants met in Minsk to reaffirm their Church's autocephaly, publishing a constitution which proclaimed a Belorussian Autocephalous Orthodox Church. In 1929 the Soviets moved against the nationalists, completely eradicating organized religion in the Republic.

When the German armies invaded in 1941, the movement revived, nominally under Metropolitan Panteleiman, although an actual Church structure was never achieved in the chaos of the Nazi administration. The 1944 German withdrawal forced the Church into exile in West Germany. Panteleiman later rejoined the Russian Patriarchate; other surviving prelates, under the leadership of Metropolitan Archbishop Syrhiey Okhotenko, organized the Byelorussian Autocephalic Orthodox Church on 5 June 1948 at Constanz, Switzerland; Syrhiey himself later settled at Adelaide, Australia.

A second group of exiles formed the Byelorussian Orthodox Church, which later joined the Greek Orthodox Archdiocese of North and South America, under the aegis of the Ecumenical Patriarch. Other prelates, led by Archbishops Benedykt and Filofeĭ, joined the Russian Orthodox Church Outside of Russia on 6 May 1946. None of these churches in exile were ever very large, and after Syrhiey's death on 2 October 1971, they disintegrated into a scattered handful of parishes and communicants.

The Russian Orthodox Church granted the national Belarussian Church autonomy in 1990, and raised Metropolitan Filaret to the rank of Exarch. The Church now operates semi-independently, but the primate must still be confirmed and consecrated by the Patriarch of Moscow.

The primate bears the title Metropolitan Archbishop of Minsk and Slutsk, Patriarchal Exarch of All Belarus. The official language of the Church is Belorussian. The present-day number of communicants is unknown.

Sources: *Échos d'Orient*; *Orthodoxia*; personal communication; *Profiles in Belief* (Piepkorn); *Religion in the Soviet Union* (Kolarz); official church website.

METROPOLITANS OF BELARUS

1. Melhisedek *Paieuskiĭ*   1922–1925

INTERREGNUM

2. Panteleiman *Rozhnovskiĭ*   1942–1946

RUSSIAN METROPOLITANS AND EXARCHS OF BELARUS

1. Nikodim *Rotov*   1963
2. Sergiĭ *Petrov*   1963–1965
3. Antoniĭ *Melnikov*   1965–1978
4. Filaret *Vakhromeev*   1978–

XX.

Church of Bulgaria

The rise of the autocephalous Church of Bulgaria closely coincides with the founding of an independent Bulgarian Empire. Tsar Boris I was converted to Christianity about 865, and asked the Patriarch of Constantinople for a prelate to organize a Bulgarian Church. Fifty years later, Archbishop Leontiĭ was the first Bulgarian Church leader to be called Patriarch. When the Byzantine Emperor conquered Bulgaria in 1018, the Church was reunited to Constantinople, its chief see being moved to Okhrid. Eastern Bulgaria regained independence in 1186, with the patriarchate being re-established at Turnovo, but it was again placed under Okhrid when Bulgaria fell in 1393. The Patriarchate of Okhrid was itself dismantled in 1767, and all of the South Slavic churches were transferred to the direct control of the Ecumenical Patriarch.

The rise of Bulgarian nationalism in the mid–1800s revived interest in a Bulgarian Church. In 1860 Bishop Ilarion (not the same man elected Exarch in 1872) defied the Ecumenical Patriarch by declaring his diocese independent. In 1870 the Ottoman Empire recognized the Bulgarian Church as an autocephalous exarchate; the Patriarchate of Constantinople, however, officially declared the Bulgarian Church schismatic in 1872.

That same year the first Exarch, Ilarion, was elected, but declined to accept, and was replaced after a few days with Exarch Antim I. On the death of Exarch Ĭosif I, in 1915, the government of Tsar Ferdinand (and later Tsar Boris III) set up a synodal council patterned after the Russian model, and dispensed with the office of primate. Following the Soviet occupation, a new Exarch was elected in 1945. He immediately sought reconciliation with Constantinople, which recognized his Church's independence on 22 February 1945.

Exarch Stefan I soon had difficulties with the new government, however, and was forced to resign in 1948. The state issued a new constitution for the Church in 1950, which specified that its head would now be called Patriarch. Metropolitan Kiril I was the first to receive the revived title, on 10 May 1953; the title of Patriarch was recognized by the Ecumenical Patriarch of Constantinople on 1 August 1961.

A major controversy arose in the aftermath of the fall of the Communist regime in the early 1990s. Khristofor Subev, a dissent priest who headed a reformist group of synodalists, mounted a campaign to depose Patriarch Maksim I, on the grounds that he had been uncanonically appointed by the secular Communist government. Maksim was declared illegitimate and removed from office by the Bulgarian Supreme Court, and a rival synod under Metropolitan Pimen was constituted with official government recognition, but Maksim eventually prevailed, and the nonagenarian Pimen and his dissident bishops were reconciled to the mother church in October of 1998.

The primate bears the title Patriarch of Bulgaria, Metropolitan Archbishop of Sofia. The official Church language is Bulgarian. Roughly eight million communicants are located primarily in Bulgaria, with a strong overseas contingent in the United States.

SOURCES: *Deset Godini Bulgarska Patriarshiia*; *Dictionnaire de Théologie Catholique*; *Dictionnaire d'Histoire et de Géographie Ecclésiastique*; *Eastern Christianity and Politics in the Twentieth Century* (Ramet, ed.); *Échos d'Orient*; *Episkepsis*; *Gegenwartslage der Ostkirchen* (Spuler); *A History of Christianity in the Balkans* (Spinka); *History of the Church* (Jedin, ed.); *Istoricheski Pregled' na Bulgarska-ta TSurkva* (Drinov); *Jahrbuch der Orthodoxie* (Proc); *Orthodoxia*; *Profiles in Belief* (Piepkorn); *A History of Bulgaria, 1393–1895* (MacDermott); official church website.

PATRIARCHS OF BULGARIA AT PRESLAV
(Archbishops at Pliska 870; Patriarchs at Preslav 919)

1. Iosif I (or Stefan) — 870–878?
2. Georgi I — 878?–919?
3. Leontiĭ — 919–
4. Dimitriĭ I — 923?
5. Sergiĭ I — 925?
6. Grigoriĭ I — –927
7. Damian — 927?–972?
8. German I — 972?–1000?
9. Filip — 1000?–1015?
10. David — 1015?–1018

ARCHBISHOPS OF OKHRID (OHRID)
(See also the Church of Macedonia and Ohrid)

1. Ioan I — 1018–1037?
2. Luv I (Leōn *ek Rōmaiōn*) — 1037?–1054?
3. Teodul I (Theodoulos *apo Mōkiou*) — 1056?–1065
4. Ioan II *Lakapin* (Iōannēs *Lampēnos*) — 1065–1078?
5. Ioan III *Ainos* (Iōannēs *Aoinos*) — 1079?–1084
6. Teofilakt (Theophylaktos *ex Euripou*) — 1085?–1108?
7. Luv II *Mung* (Leōn *Boungos*) — 1108?–1120?
8. Mikhaïl *Maksim* (Michaēl *Maximos*) — 1120?–
9. Ioan IV *Komnin* (Iōannēs *Komnēnos*) — 1143?–1157?
10. Evstatiĭ (Eustathios) — 1159?
11. Konstantin I — 1160?–1170?
12. name unknown — 1178?–1182?

PATRIARCHS OF BULGARIA AT TURNOVO

11.	Vasiliĭ I	1185–1233
12.	Ioakim I	1233?–1246
13.	Vasiliĭ II	1246–
14.	Ioakim II	–1272
15.	Ignatiĭ I	1272?–1277?
16.	Makariĭ I	–1291
17.	Ioakim III	1291–1300
18.	Visarion	1310?
19.	Doroteĭ I	1320?
20.	Roman	1330?
21.	Teodosiĭ I	1337?
22.	Ioanikiĭ II	1340?
23.	Simeon I	1346?
24.	Teodosiĭ II (or Teodosije)	1363?
25.	Ioanikiĭ III	1370?
26.	Evtimiĭ	1375–1393

ARCHBISHOPS (1018) AND PATRIARCHS (1558) OF OKHRID
(See also the Church of Macedonia and Ohrid)

13.	Ioan V *Kamatir* (Iōannēs *Kamatēros*)	1183?–1215?
14.	Dimitriĭ II *Khomatian* (Dēmētrios *Chōmatianos* [or *Chōmatēnos*])	1216?–1234?
15.	Ioanikiĭ I	1240?
16.	Sergiĭ II	1250?
17.	Konstantin II *Kavasila* (Kōnstantinos *Kabasilas*)	1254?–1259?
18.	IAkov *Proarkhiĭ*	1265?
19.	Adrian	1275?
20.	Gen(n)adiĭ	1285?
21.	Makariĭ II	1295?–1299?
22.	Grigoriĭ II	1317?
23.	Antim *Metokhit* (Anthimos *Metochitēs*)	1341?
24.	Nikolaĭ I	1347?
25.	Grigoriĭ III	1364?–1378?
26.	name unknown	1389?–1394
27.	Mateĭ	1408–1411?
28.	name unknown	1430?
29.	Nikodim	1452?
30.	Doroteĭ II	1466?
31.	Marko *Ksilokarav* (Markos *Xylokarabēs*) [#163 of Constantinople]	1467?–
32.	Nikolaĭ II	1486–1502?
33.	Zakhariĭ	1515?

34.	Prokhor	1528?–1550
35.	Simeon II	1550
36.	Grigoriĭ IV	1551–
37.	Nikanor	–1557
38.	Païsiĭ	1558–1566
39.	Parteniĭ I	1566–1567
40.	Sofroniĭ	1567–1572?
41.	Gavriĭl	1572–1587
42.	Teodul II	1588–1590
43.	Ioakim IV	1590–1593
44.	Atanasiĭ I	1593–1596
45.	Valaam	1596–1598
46.	Nektariĭ I	1598–1604
	Atanasiĭ I [2nd time]	1604–1614
47.	Mitrofan	1614–1616
48.	Georgi II	1616–1617
49.	Nektariĭ II	1617–1622?
50.	Porfiriĭ *Paleolog* (Porphyrios *Palaiologos*)	1624?
51.	Ioasaf I	1628?
52.	Avraamiĭ *Mesapsa* (Abraamios)	1629?–1634?

INTERREGNUM

53.	Meletiĭ I	1637–1643
54.	Khariton	1643–1647?
55.	Daniĭl	1647?–1650
	Khariton [2nd time]	1651–1652
56.	Dionisiĭ I	1652–1653
57.	Atanasiĭ II	1653–1660
58.	Pafnutiĭ	1660
59.	Ignatiĭ II	1660–1662
60.	Arseniĭ I	1662–1663?
61.	Zosima I	1663–1670
62.	Panaret	1671
63.	Nektariĭ III	1673?
64.	Ignatiĭ III	1673–1675?
65.	Grigoriĭ V	1675–1676
66.	Teofan	1676
67.	Meletiĭ II	1676–1677
68.	Parteniĭ II	1677–1683
	Grigoriĭ V [2nd time]	1683–1688
69.	German II	1688–1690
70.	Grigoriĭ VI	1691–1693
71.	Ignatiĭ IV	1693–1695
72.	Zosima II	1695–1699

73.	Rafaïl	1699–1702
	German II [2nd time]	1702–1703
74.	Dionisiĭ II (Dionysios) *of Chios*	1703–1706
	Zosima II [2nd time]	1707–1708
75.	Metodiĭ I	1708
	Zosima II [3rd time]	1708–1709
	Dionisiĭ II [2nd time]	1709–1714
76.	Filoteĭ	1714–1718
77.	Ioasaf II	1719–1745
78.	Ĭosif II	1746–1751
79.	Dionisiĭ III	1751–1756
80.	Metodiĭ II	1757–1758
81.	Kiril	1759–1762
82.	Ieremiia	1762–1763
83.	Ananiĭ	1763
84.	Arseniĭ II	1763–1767

Metropolitans of Tsarigrad and Sofia

1.	Ilarion	–1838
2.	Panaret	1838–1840?
3.	Neofit *Bozveli*	1840?–1850?
4.	Païsiĭ	1850?–1856?
	Neofit [2nd time]	1856?–1857?
	Païsiĭ [2nd time]	1861–

Patriarchs of Bulgaria at Tsarigrad and Sofia
(Exarchs 1872, Patriarchs 1953)

	Ilarion [refused election]	1870–1872
1.	Antim	1872–1877
2.	Ĭosif	1877–1915

Interregnum

	Parteniĭ [locum tenens]	1915–1918
	Vasiliĭ *of Ruse* [locum tenens]	1918–1922
	Stefan *Giorgiev* [locum tenens]	1922–1934
	Neofit [locum tenens]	1934–1944
	Stefan *Giorgiev* [2nd time]	1944–1945
3.	Stefan *Giorgiev*	1945–1948

Interregnum

	Mikhaïl [locum tenens]	1948–1949

	Païsiĭ *of Vratsa* [locum tenens]	1949–1951
	Kiril *Markov* [locum tenens]	1951–1953
4.	Kiril *Markov*	1953–1971
5.	Maksim *Minkov*	1971–
	Pimen *Nedelchev* [anti-patriarch]	1996–1998

XXI.

Church of China

China had no Orthodox population until the aftermath of the Russian Revolution of 1917, when refugees fled across the Siberian-Chinese border into Manchuria. By 1939 an estimated 300,000 Orthodox communicants, almost all of Russian descent, were crowded into Northeastern China, under the tutelage of five Orthodox bishops.

Following World War II, the Russian Orthodox Church placed the dioceses under first an Archbishop (1945) and then an Exarch (1946). The Communist takeover of mainland China in 1949 forced many of the Orthodox believers back into Russia or into permanent foreign exile. In 1950 the government demanded that the higher clergy be nationalized. On 30 May 1957 the Russian Orthodox Church gave the Chinese Orthodox Church its autonomy, but this act was recognized by no other Orthodox jurisdiction.

The last Chinese bishop died in 1965, and no others were allowed by the Chinese government to be elected in his place. An Archdiocese has been established by the Ecumenical Patriarchate in the past decade in Hong Kong, but the Russian Church has again reiterated its right to govern the Chinese faithful.

The last primate bore the title Bishop of Beijing and All China. The official language of the Church is Chinese. About 20,000 communicants remained in 1956.

SOURCES: *Gegenwartslage der Ostkirchen* (Spuler).

BISHOPS OF CHINA
(Archbishops 1945, Exarchs 1946, Bishops 1956)

1.	Nestor *Anisimov*	1945–1948
2.	Viktor *Sviatin*	1950–1956
3.	Vasiliĭ (Basil) *Shuan*	1956–1962
	Simeon *Du* [locum tenens]	1962–1965

INTERREGNUM

XXII.

Armenian Apostolic Church of Cilicia

The official residence of the Armenian Catholicos (see the chapter on Armenia) was moved from Armenia Major (the capital city of Ani) to Cilicia (Lesser Armenia), first to Romkla (1149) and then to Sis (1293), where a thriving Armenian and Latin kingdom had recently been founded. As the kingdom grew and expanded, so the Church also thrived.

By the middle of the fourteenth century, however, the Mamluk Arabs began to exert pressure on Lesser Armenia, eventually conquering it in 1375; the last Armenian king, Ghevon (Leo) VI, was driven into exile, and the Armenian cathedral was destroyed. Nonetheless, the Catholicos remained in Sis until the year 1441, when an Armenian National Church Council elected a Catholicos in Armenia Major, at Etchmiadzin, with Catholicos Grigor IX remaining in Sis as the Catholicos of Cilicia. The line of succession continues unbroken until today.

During the massacres of 1890–1915, the Church of Cilicia was severely affected; many Church members were forced to leave Turkey or be killed, and many of those who fled settled just over the border in Syria and Lebanon. The Catholicos was among those who moved south, finally settling at Antelias, a suburb of Beirut, in 1921. Through an agreement with the Armenian Patriarch of Jerusalem, certain of the latter's churches in Lebanon and Cyria were ceded to Cilicia. In 1956 Catholicos Vazgên I of Etchmiadzin attempted to interfere in the election of the new Catholicos for the Great House of Cilicia, and to subordinate Cilicia to the level of a dependent patriarchate; the electors rejected his moves, and elected a pro-independence Archbishop, Zareh I. In 1995 the popular Cilician Catholicos Garegin II was elected Vazgên's successor as Garegin I, in the hope that the two churches could again be reunited.

The Armenian Apostolic Church, as it is now known, differs from the other Armenian churches in claiming complete autocephaly; it acknowledges the Patriarch at Etchmiadzin as first among equals in Armenian Christianity. The primate bears the title Catholicos of the Great House of Cilicia. The official Church language is Armenian. Roughly one million communicants are located in Lebanon, Syria, and Cyprus, with thriving overseas communities in Greece, Iran, Kuwait, the United Arab Emirates, and the Americas.

XXII. Armenian Apostolic Church of Cilicia

SOURCES: *Dictionnaire d'Histoire et de Géographie Ecclésiastique*; *Eastern Christianity and Politics in the Twentieth Century* (Ramet, ed.); *Europa World Yearbook*; *Gegenwartslage der Ostkirchen* (Spuler); *History of the Church* (Jedin, ed.); *The Middle East and North Africa*; *Orthodoxia*; *Pat'mutium Kat'oghikosats' Kilikoy* (Kiwlesêrêan; regarded as official by the Church); *Profiles in Belief* (Piepkorn); official church website.

ARMENIAN CATHOLICOSES OF CILICIA

1.	Grigor I *Musabêgiants'* [#87 of Armenia]	1441–1451
2.	Karapet	1446–1478
3.	Step'anos	1477?–1483

INTERREGNUM

4.	Hovhannês I	1488–1489
5.	Hovhannês II	1489–1525
6.	Hovhannês III	1525–1539
7.	Simêon I	1539–1545
8.	Ghazar	1545–1547
9.	T'oros I	1548–1550?
10.	Khach'atur I *Chorik*	1550?–1560
11.	Khach'atur II *"The Musician"*	1560–1584
12.	Azaria I	1584–1601
	Tiratur [anti-catholicos; #8 of Constantinople]	1586–1592
13.	Hovhannês IV	1602–1621
	Petros [coadjutor]	1601–1608
14.	Minas	1621–1632
15.	Simêon II	1633–1648
16.	Nersês	1648–1654
17.	T'oros II	1654–1657
18.	Khach'atur III	1657–1674
	Dawit' [anti-catholicos]	1663–1679
19.	Sahak I *Mêykhachêchi*	1674–1686
29.	Azaria II	1683?–1686?
21.	Grigor II	1686–1693?
22.	Astuatsatur	1693–1694?
23.	Matt'êos	1694–1705
24.	Hovhannês V	1705–1721
25.	Petros I [coadjutor]	1708–1710
26.	Grigor III	1721?–1729
27.	Hovhannês VI	1729–1733
28.	Ghukas [brother of #30]	1733–1737
29.	Mik'ayêl I [brother of #27]	1737–1758
30.	Gabriêl [brother of #28]	1757–1770
31.	Ep'rem I [nephew of #30]	1771–1784

48.	Khach'atur III *Shiroyan*	1864–1895
	Eghiazar *Adshapahian* [coadjutor]	1780?
32.	T'oros III *Adshapahian*	1784–1796
33.	Kirakos I *"The Great"*	1797–1822
34.	Ep'rem II	1823–1831
	Hovhannês [coadjutor]	1831–1833
35.	Mik'ayêl II	1832–1855
36.	Kirakos II	1855–1865

Interregnum

	Kirakos [locum tenens]	1866–1871
37.	Mkrtich' *K'êfsizian Marach'ts'i*	1871–1894

Interregnum

	Grigor *Aleadjian* [locum tenens]	1895
38.	Sahak II *Khapayan*	1902–1939
39.	Babkên *Giwlêsêrian* [coadjutor]	1931–1936
	Petros *Sarachian* [vicar general]	1939–1940
40.	Petros II *Sarachian*	1940
	Eghishê [locum tenens]	1940–1942
	Khat *Adjapahian* [locum tenens]	1942–1945
41.	Garegin I *Hovsêp'ian(ts)*	1943–1952

Interregnum

	Khat *Adjapahian* [locum tenens]	1952–1955
	Khorên *Baroyan* [locum tenens]	1955–1956
42.	Zareh *Payaslian*	1956–1963
43.	Khorên *Baroyan*	1963–1983
44.	Garegin II *Sargisian* [coadjutor 1977; #131 of Armenia]	1983–1995
45.	Aram *K'êshishian*	1995–

XXIII.

Armenian Catholic Church of Cilicia

The Armenian Church of Cilicia in Turkey had uniate factions as long ago as the fourteenth century. These were nurtured and developed by Roman Catholic missionaries sent to Asia Minor by the Popes. In 1740 the uniates elected Abraham Ardzivian Patriarch in succession to Armenian Cilician Patriarch Ghukas; he was confirmed by Pope Benedictus XIV in 1742. He established a tradition by appending "Petros" (Peter) to his name, in honor of the founder of the Roman Church; his successors have followed his pattern, and have thereafter numbered themselves consecutively from the first Patriarch.

In 1867 Pope Pius IX caused great controversy by issuing his bull, *Reversurus*, which outlined the powers and rights of the Armenian and Chaldean sees, established a new election law, and gave the Pope the right to appoint or veto all new bishops. A number of the existing bishops blamed the new Patriarch, Anton Hassun, an outsider, for the regulations, and elected their own primate; the schism was not healed until the resignation of Hassun.

Hassun had also been Archbishop-Primate of Constantinople since 1846, and had been named by the Pope specifically to unite the two jurisdictions; he was made a cardinal in 1880, and died in Rome soon after. The official residence of the Catholicos remained at Constantinople until 1928. Among recent patriarchs, Grigor Petros XV Aghajanian was widely known for his efforts to reunite Eastern Christianity.

The primate bears the title Patriarch of the Catholic Armenians and Catholicos of Cilicia. His chief see is located in a suburb of Beirut, Lebanon, with an estimated 143,000 adherents in Lebanon and Southeastern Turkey, as well as several congregations in the Americas. The official Church language is Armenian.

Sources: *The Catholic Eastern Churches* (Attwater); *Catholic Encyclopedia*; *The Christian Churches of the East* (Attwater); *Gegenwartslage der Ostkirchen* (Spuler); *The Middle East and North Africa*; *Die Morgenlandischen Kirchen* (Spuler); *New Catholic Encyclopedia*; "Pope Calls for Broad Mideast Peace" (Montalbano); official church website.

Armenian Catholic Catholicos-Patriarchs of Cilicia

1.	Abraham Petros I *Ardzivian*	1740–1749
2.	Hakob Petros II *Hovsêp'ian*	1749–1753
3.	Mik'ayêl Petros III *Gasparian*	1753–1780
4.	Barsegh Petros IV *Avkadian*	1780–1788
5.	Grigor Petros V *Kupelian*	1788–1812

Interregnum

6.	Grigor Petros VI *Jeranian*	1815–1841
7.	Hakob Petros VII *Holasian*	1842–1843
8.	Grigor Petros VIII *Ter-Astuatsaturian*	1844–1866
9.	Anton Petros IX *Hassun(ian)*	1866–1881
	Hakob Petros IX *Bak'darian* [anti catholicos]	1870–1880?
10.	Step'anos Petros X *Azarian*	1881–1899
11.	Poghos Petros XI *Emmanuelian*	1899–1904
12.	Poghos Petros XII *Sabbaghian*	1904–1910
13.	Poghos Petros XIII *Terzian*	1910–1931
14.	Awetis Petros XIV *Arpiarian*	1931–1937
15.	Grigor Petros XV *Aghajanian*	1937–1962
16.	Ignatios Petros XVI *Batanian*	1962–1976
17.	Hemayag Petros XVII *Ghedighian*	1976–1982
18.	Hovhannês Petros XVIII *Gasparian*	1982–1999
19.	Nersês Petros XIX *Tarmouni*	1999–

XXIV.

Armenian Church of Constantinople

When Ottoman Sultan Mehmet II conquered Constantinople in 1453, he summoned the new Ecumenical Patriarch, and made him responsible for the Greek populations in the empire, with corresponding judicial and administrative powers. Similarly, the Armenian Bishop of Constantinople was given temporal authority over the Armenian subjects of the Ottoman Empire, with the new title of Patriarch, in 1461. Like the Ecumenical Patriarch, the Armenian primate was subjected to intense political pressures and behind-the-scenes machinations; the result was constant Turkish interference in the governance of the Armenian Patriarchate, with individual primates being appointed or removed at the will of the Sultan or his viziers, often as a result of bribes. At the same time, the size and influence of the Patriarchate expanded with the Ottoman Empire, rivaling at times that of the Catholicos at Etchmiadzin.

When the Empire began to fail, however, the Church gradually saw its power diminish; the Armenian massacres of 1890–1915, with the subsequent exile of most of the survivors, reduced it to less than one-tenth of its former size, its territory shrinking to the state of Turkey proper. As in its relations with the Ecumenical Patriarchate, the Turkish republican government has followed a pattern of interference even in the twentieth century, preventing the Church from filling seats on its Council in the 1960s and '70s, and attempting to appoint a rival Locum Tenens in 1990. Tensions have eased somewhat, however, since the election of Mesrop II.

The primate bears the title Patriarch of Constantinople. The official Church language is Armenian. The number of communicants is unknown, but small.

SOURCES: *Dictionnaire d'Histoire et de Géographie Ecclésiastique*; *Gegenwartslage der Ostkirchen* (Spuler); *The History of the Armenian People* (Morgan); *Orthodoxia*; "Zhamanakagrowt'iwn T'oirk'ioy Hayots' Patriark'nerow" (regarded by the Church as official); official church website.

ARMENIAN PATRIARCHS OF CONSTANTINOPLE

1.	Hovakim	1461–1478
2.	Nikoghayos	1478–1489
3.	Karapet I	1489–1509

4.	Martiros I	1509–1526
5.	Grigor I	1526–1537
6.	Astuatsatur I	1537–1550
7.	Step'anos I	1550–1561
8.	Tiratur	1561–1563
9.	Hakob I	1563–1573
10.	Hovhannês I	1573–1581
11.	T'ovmas I	1581–1587
12.	Sargis I	1587–1590
13.	Hovhannês II	1590–1591
14.	Azaria	1591–1592
15.	Sargis II	1592–1596
	Tiratur [2nd time]	1596–1599
16.	Melk'isedek I	1599–1600
17.	Hovhannês III	1600–1601
18.	Grigor II	1601–1608
	Hovhannês III [2nd time]	1609–1611
	Grigor II [2nd time]	1611–1621
	Hovhannês III [3rd time]	1621–1623
	Grigor II [3rd time]	1623–1626
19.	Zak'aria I	1626–1631
	Hovhannês III [4th time]	1631–1636
	Zak'aria I [2nd time]	1636–1640
20.	Dawit'	1640–1641
21.	Kirakos	1641–1642
22.	Khach'atur I	1642–1643
	Dawit' [2nd time]	1643–1644
23.	T'ovma II	1644
	Dawit' [3rd time]	1644–1649
	Dawit' [4th time]	1650–1651
24.	Eghiazar	1651–1652
25.	Hovhannês IV	1652–1655
	T'ovma II [2nd time]	1657–1659
26.	Martiros II	1659–1660
27.	Ghazar	1660–1663
28.	Hovhannês V	1663–1664
29.	Sargis III	1664–1665
	Hovhannês V [2nd time]	1665–1667
	Sargis III [2nd time]	1667–1670
30.	Step'anos II	1670–1674
31.	Hovhannês VI	1674–1675
32.	Andrêas	1675–1676
33.	Karapet II	1676–1679
34.	Sargis IV	1679–1680
	Karapet II [2nd time]	1680–1681
35.	T'oros	1681

XXIV. Armenian Church of Constantinople

	Karapet II [3rd time]	1681–1684
36.	Ep'rem	1684–1686
	Karapet II [4th time]	1686–1687
	T'oros [2nd time]	1687–1688
37.	Khach'atur II	1688
	Karapet II [5th time]	1688–1689

INTERREGNUM

38.	Matt'êos I	1692–1694
	Ep'rem [2nd time]	1694–1698
39.	Melk'isedek II	1698–1699
40.	Mkhit'ar	1699–1700
	Melk'isedek II [2nd time]	1700–1701
	Ep'rem [3rd time]	1701–1702
41.	Awetik'	1702–1703
42.	Galust *Vayzhavk*	1703–1704
43.	Nersês I	1704
	Awetik' [2nd time]	1704–1706
	Matt'êos I [2nd time]	1706
44.	Martiros III	1706
45.	Mik'ayêl	1706–1707
46.	Sahak	1707
47.	Hovhannês VII	1707–1708
	Sahak [2nd time]	1708–1714
48.	Hovhannês VIII	1714–1715
49.	Hovhannês IX *Kolot*	1715–1741
50.	Hakob II *Nalian Zmarats'i*	1741–1748
51.	Prokhoron	1749
52.	Minas	1749–1751
53.	Gêorg I	1751–1752
	Hakob II [2nd time]	1752–1764
54.	Grigor III *Pasmachian*	1764–1773
55.	Zak'aria II	1773–1781
56.	Hovhannês X	1781–1782
	Zak'aria II [2nd time]	1782–1799
57.	Daniêl	1799–1800
58.	Hovhannês XI *Zamach'erchian*	1800–1801
59.	Grigor IV *Khamsets'i*	1801–1802
	Hovhannês XI [2nd time]	1802–1813
60.	Abraham *Gholian*	1813–1815
61.	Poghos I *Grigorian*	1815–1823
62.	Karapet III *Palat'ts'i*	1823–1831
63.	Step'anos III *Zak'arian*	1831–1839
64.	Hakobos III *Serobian*	1839–1840
	Step'anos III [2nd time]	1840–1841

65.	Astuatsatur II	1841–1844
66.	Matt'êos II *Ch'ukhachian* [#122 of Armenia]	1844–1848
	Hakobus III [2nd time]	1848–1858
67.	Gêorg II *K'êrêst'êchian* [#123 of Armenia]	1858–1860
68.	Sargis V *Guyumchian*	1860–1861
	Stêp'an (IV) *Maghak'ian* [locum tenens]	1861–1863
69.	Poghos II *T'agt'agian*	1863–1869
70.	Ignatios *Gagmachian*	1869
71.	Mkrtich' *Khrimian* [#125 of Armenia]	1869–1873
72.	Nersês II *Vartsapetian*	1874–1884
73.	Harut'iwn *Vehapetian* [#90 of Jerusalem]	1885–1888
74.	Khorên *Ashegian*	1888–1894
75.	Matt'êos III *Izmirlian* [#126 of Armenia]	1894–1896
76.	Maghak'ia *Örmanian*	1896–1908
	Matt'êos III *Izmirlian* [2nd time]	1908–1909
77.	Eghishê *Durian* [#91 of Jerusalem]	1909–1911
78.	Hovhannês XII *Arsharuni*	1912–1913
79.	Zawên *Eghiayan*	1913–1915

INTERREGNUM

	Zawên *Eghiayan* [2nd time]	1919–1922

INTERREGNUM

	Gêorg *Arslanian* [locum tenens]	1922–1927
80.	Mesrop I *Naroyan*	1927–1944

INTERREGNUM

	Gêorg *Arslanian* [locum tenens]	1944–1950
81.	Garegin I *Khach'aturian*	1951–1961
82.	Shnorhk' *Galustian*	1961–1990
	Sahan *Sivakian* [locum tenens]	1990
83.	Garegin II Petros *Kazanjian*	1990–1998
	Mesrop *Mutafian* [locum tenens]	1998
	Sahan *Sivakian* [anti-locum tenens]	1998
84.	Mesrop II *Mutafian*	1998–

XXV.

Greek Church of Constantinople (Ecumenical Patriarchate)

The Ecumenical Patriarchate is first in honor among the original Orthodox churches, having been founded, according to tradition, by the apostle Andrew at the small town of Byzantium. Byzantium was transformed by the Emperor Constantine I into the imperial capital, Constantinople, and made the center of a new Christian empire; simultaneously, the Church of Constantinople became the "New Rome," growing rapidly in size and power as the Empire flourished.

By the Council of Chalcedon, in 451, Constantinople was recognized as having precedence over Antioch and Alexandria, and by 590 the primate was calling himself the "Ecumenical Patriarch." Gradually, a split developed between East and West, as Constantinople and Rome both strived to gain absolute primacy over the Christian world. The strains were exacerbated by the intrusion of the temporal authorities and politics into both religious worlds, including interference with the elections of the primates, and manipulation of the hierarchies.

The differences between East and West came into the open in the years 857–878, with the struggle between Patriarchs Ignatios and Phōtios for the Patriarchal throne of Constantinople. The Pope supported Ignatios, while much of the Eastern hierarchy supported Phōtios. In the end, Phōtios outlasted Ignatios; his outspoken opposition to Roman rule proved to be the example which all of the Eastern churches would soon come to follow. The formal breach came during the reign of Michaēl I Kēroularios, when the two churches exchanged mutual excommunications (1054).

Two attempts at reconciliation both failed: in 1274 Emperor Michael VIII ordered his prelates to reach a compromise with Rome, which they did; it was never popular, however, and was repudiated by Andronicus II in 1282. During the last few decades of the Empire, while it was under severe pressure from the Turks, Emperors John VIII and Constantine XI sought aid from the West by again forcing a reunion at the Council of Florence in 1439. The marriage of churches was unsuccessful in gaining any significant military aid for the beleaguered Greeks, and the city fell to the Turks on 29 May 1453. The union was officially repudiated in 1472.

The invasion of the Turks benefited the Patriarchate in curious ways: the new ruler, Sultan Mehmet II, appointed Gennadios II to the empty patriarchal throne, and gave him temporal powers over the Orthodox faithful in the new Empire. Thereafter the Patriarchs served at the pleasure of the Sultans and their Viziers, being deposed or murdered virtually at will, sometimes subverting the election process through bribes.

In partial recompense, however, the Church gained domination over all the other Eastern churches, save only the non–Chalcedonian denominations and the Patriarchate of Russia, which Constantinople was forced to acknowledge as independent in 1589. In 1766–1767 the Patriarch managed to have the Sultan suppress the ancient Patriarchates of Peć (Serbia) and Ohrid (Macedonia), replacing the hierarchies there with Greek prelates. The Church had reached the apex of its power and influence.

In 1833 the Church of Greece set a precedent by demanding ecclesiastical independence from Constantinople, as the forces of nationalism began sweeping Eastern Europe. One by one, as each country achieved independence, the temporal and religious authorities of these states insisted on autocephaly for their own churches. By the end of World War I, the once-great Patriarchate was reduced in size to Turkey proper, and to overseas colonies of Orthodox immigrants in the Americas and elsewhere.

The overthrow of the Ottoman Empire in 1922 did not end Turkish governmental interference in Orthodox affairs; on the contrary, Patriarch Meletios IV was forced into exile in 1923, as was Kōnstantinos VI in 1925. Other direct or indirect pressures, including Turkish support of the independent Turkish Orthodox Church, have continued to this day; in the 1972 patriarchal election, for example, the Turks insisted on excluding several potential candidates from consideration, including the acknowledged frontrunner, Metropolitan Melitōn. As a result, the most junior member of that body, Dēmētrios I, then a virtual unknown, was elected.

At the latter's death in 1991, his assistant, Metropolitan Bartholomaios, was unanimously elected Patriarch without interference from the Turkish officials, the first such instance in modern history.

Noteworthy among recent primates of the Church was Patriarch Athēnagoras I, former Archbishop of North and South America, and a friend of President Harry S Truman, who became Patriarch in 1948. This extraordinary primate was the first Patriarch of Constantinople to meet with the Pope of Rome in 500 years; together, they lifted the excommunications imposed by each church on the other in 1054, and did much to lessen the atmosphere of antagonism that had overshadowed relations between East and West over many centuries. Athēnagoras's two successors have continued his ecumenical work.

The primate bears the title Ecumenical Patriarch, Archbishop of Constantinople and New Rome. The official Church language is Greek. The Patriarch resides in a section of Istanbul (Constantinople) called the Phanar, a name which is sometimes applied to the Church itself, much as the Church of Rome is sometimes called the Vatican. Communicants number in the millions, most located in Turkey, the Americas, Western Europe, Australia, and other points overseas; the Ecumenical Patriarch also has authority over the autonomous Churches of Crete, Finland, and Estonia, Mount Athos, and the Dodecanese islands of the Aegean Sea. Patriarch Bartholomaios I was instrumental in re-establishing the devastated Albanian Orthodox Church beginning in 1990.

SOURCES: *Dictionnaire de Théologie Catholique*; *Dictionnaire d'Histoire et de Géographie Ecclésiastique*; *Eastern Christianity and Politics in the Twentieth Century* (Ramet, ed.); *Échos d'Orient*; *Eleutheroudakē Enkyklopaidikon Lexikon*; *Episkepsis*; *Gegenwart-*

slage der Ostkirchen (Spuler); *History of the Church* (Jedin, ed.); *Jahrbuch der Orthodoxie* (Proc); "Oikoumenikon (Patriarcheion)"; *Oriens Christianus* (Le Quien); *Orthodoxia*; *The Oxford Dictionary of Byzantium* (Kazhdan); *Patriarchikoi Pinakes* (Gedeōn); *The Patriarchs of Constantinople* (Cobham); "Pinakes Patriarchōn"; *Profiles in Belief* (Piepkorn); official church website. The list below is based primarily on Gedeōn (regarded as official at the time of its publication) and Kazhdan.

ECUMENICAL PATRIARCHS OF CONSTANTINOPLE

1.	Andreas *Prōtoklētos*	30?–38
2.	Stachys *Apostolos*	38–54
3.	Onēsimos	54–68

INTERREGNUM

4.	Polykarpos I	71–89
5.	Ploutarchos	89–105
6.	Sedekiōn	105–114
7.	Diogenēs	114–129
8.	Eleutherios	129–136
9.	Phēlix (or Philix)	136–141
10.	Polykarpos II	141–144
11.	Athēnodōros	144–148
12.	Euzōïos	148–154
13.	Laurentios	154–166
14.	Alypios	166–169
15.	Pertinax	169–187
16.	Olympianos	187–198
17.	Markos I	198–211
18.	Philadelphos	211–214
19.	Kyriakos I (or Kyrillianos)	214–230
20.	Kastinos	230–237
21.	Eugenios I	237–242
22.	Titos	242–272
23.	Dometios	272–303
24.	Rhouphinos	303
25.	Probos	303–315
26.	Mētrophanēs I	315–325
27.	Alexandros	325–337?
28.	Paulos I	337?–339
29.	Eusebios *Nikomēdeias*	341–342?
	Paulos I [2nd time]	342–344
30.	Makedonios I	344–346
	Paulos I [3rd time]	346–351
	Makedonios I [2nd time]	350–360

31.	Eudoxios *Antiocheias* [#31 of Antioch]	360–369
32.	Dēmophilos	369–379
33.	Euagrios	379
	Dēmophilos [Arian anti-patriarch; 2nd time]	379–386
34.	Grēgorios I *Nazianzēnos Theologos*	380–381
35.	Maximos I *Kynikos*	381
36.	Nektarios [brother of #38]	381–397
	Marinos [Arian anti-patriarch]	386–
37.	Iōannēs I *Chrysostomos*	398–404
38.	Arsakios [brother of #36]	404–405
39.	Attikos	406–425
	Dōrotheos [Arian anti-patriarch]	–407
	Bardas [Arian anti-patriarch]	407–
40.	Sisinnios I	426–427
41.	Nestorios	428–431
42.	Maximianos	431–434
43.	Proklos	434–446
44.	Phlabianos (Flavianus)	446–449
45.	Anatolios	449–458
46.	Gennadios I	458–471
47.	Akakios	472–489
48.	Phrabitas (Fravitas)	489–490
49.	Euphēmios	490–496
50.	Makedonios II	496–511
51.	Timotheos I *Kēlōn*	511–518
52.	Iōannēs II *Kappadokēs* (or *Kappadokos*)	518–520
53.	Epiphanios	520–535
54.	Anthimos I	536
55.	Mēnas *Sampsōn*	536–552
56.	Eutychios	552–565
57.	Iōannēs III *Scholastikos* (or *Scholastikōn*)	565–577
	Eutychios [2nd time]	577–582
58.	Iōannēs IV *Nēsteutēs*	582–595
59.	Kyriakos II	595?–606
60.	Thōmas I	607–610
61.	Sergios I	610–638
62.	Pyrrhos	638–641
63.	Paulos II	641–653
	Pyrrhos [2nd time]	654
64.	Petros	654–666
65.	Thōmas II	667–669
66.	Iōannēs V	669–675
67.	Kōnstantinos I	675–677
68.	Theodōros I	677–679
69.	Geōrgios I	679–686
	Theodōros I [2nd time]	686–687

XXV. Greek Church of Constantinople (Ecumenical Patriarchate)

70.	Paulos III	688–694
71.	Kallinikos I	694–706
72.	Kyros	706–712
73.	Iōannēs VI	712–715
74.	Germanos I	715–730
75.	Anastasios	730–754
76.	Kōnstantinos II	754–766
77.	Nikētas I	766–780
78.	Paulos IV	780–784
79.	Tarasios [uncle of #86]	784–806
80.	Nikēphoros I	806–815
81.	Theodotos I *Kassitēras Melissēnos*	815–821
82.	Antōnios I *Kassimatas* (or *Kassimatēs* or *Kasymatas*) *Byrsodepsēs*	821–837?
83.	Iōannēs VII *Grammatikos Pankratiou*	837?–843
84.	Methodios I	843–847
85.	Ignatios *Rhangabē*	847–858
86.	Phōtios I [nephew of #79]	858–867
	Ignatios [2nd time]	867–877
	Phōtios I [2nd time]	877–886
87.	Stephanos I	886–893
88.	Antōnios II *Kauleas* (or *Kaulias*)	893–901
89.	Nikolaos I *Mystikos*	901–907
90.	Euthymios I	907–912
	Nikolaos I [2nd time]	912–925
91.	Stephanos II *apo Amaseias*	925–927
92.	Tryphōn	927–931
93.	Theophylaktos *Lekapēnos*	933–956
94.	Polyeuktos	956–970
95.	Basileios I *Skamandrēnos*	970–974
96.	Antōnios III *Stouditēs Pachen*	974–979
97.	Nikolaos II *Chrysobergios* (or *Chrysobergēs*)	979–991

INTERREGNUM

98.	Sisinnios II	996–998

INTERREGNUM

99.	Sergios II	1001–1019
100.	Eustathios *apo Palatiou*	1019–1025
101.	Alexios *Stouditēs*	1025–1043
102.	Michaēl I *Kēroul(l)arios* (or *Kēroularis*)	1043–1058
103.	Kōnstantinos III *Leichoudēs*	1059–1063

104.	Iōannēs VIII *Xiphilinos*	1064–1075
105.	Kosmas I *Hierosolymitēs*	1075–1081
106.	Eustratios *Garidas*	1081–1084
107.	Nikolaos III *Grammatikos Kyrdiniatēs*	1084–1111
108.	Iōannēs IX *Agapētos Hieromnēmōn*	1111–1134
109.	Leōn *Styppēs* (or *Styppeiōtēs*)	1134–1143
110.	Michaēl II *Kourkouas Oxeitēs*	1143–1146
111.	Kosmas II *Attikos*	1146–1147
112.	Nikolaos IV *Mouzalōn* [#26 of Cyprus]	1147–1151
113.	Theodotos II	1151?–1153?
114.	Neophytos I *Enkleistos Klaustrarios*	1153?
115.	Kōnstantinos IV *Chliarēnos*	1154–1157
116.	Loukas *Chrysobergēs*	1157–1169?
117.	Michaēl III *Anchialou*	1170–1178
118.	Charitōn *Eugeneiōtēs*	1178–1179
119.	Theodosios I *Bo(r)rhadiōtēs*	1179–1183
120.	Basileios II *Kamatēros Phylakopoulos*	1183–1186
121.	Nikētas II *Mountanēs*	1186–1189
122.	Dositheos *Hierosolymitēs* [#93 of Jerusalem]	1189
123.	Leontios *Theotokitēs*	1189
	Dositheos *Hierosolymitēs* [2nd time]	1189–1191
124.	Geōrgios II *Xiphilinos*	1191–1198
125.	Iōannēs X *Kamatēros* (or *Kamateros*)	1198–1206
126.	Michaēl IV *Autōreianos* (or *Autoreianos*)	1208–1214
127.	Theodōros II *Eirēnikos Kōpas*	1214–1216
128.	Maximos II *apo Akoimētōn*	1216
129.	Manouēl I *Sarantēnos Charitopoulos*	1216?–1222
130.	Germanos II	1223–1240
131.	Methodios II	1240?–1241?
132.	Manouēl II	1243?–1254
133.	Arsenios *Autōreianos*	1254–1260
134.	Nikēphoros II *apo Ephesou*	1260–1261
	Arsenios [2nd time]	1261–1265
135.	Germanos III	1265–1266
136.	Iōsēph I *Galesiōtēs*	1266–1275
137.	Iōannēs XI *Bekkos*	1275–1282
	Iōsēph I [2nd time]	1282–1283
138.	Grēgorios II *Kyprios*	1283–1289
139.	Athanasios I	1289–1293
140.	Iōannēs XII *Kosmas*	1294–1303
	Athanasios I [2nd time]	1303–1309
141.	Nēphōn I (or Niphōn) *apo Kyzikou*	1310–1314
142.	Iōannēs XIII *Glykys*	1315–1319
143.	Gerasimos I	1320–1321
144.	Hēsaïas	1323–1332
145.	Iōannēs XIV *Kalekas*	1334–1347

XXV. Greek Church of Constantinople (Ecumenical Patriarchate)

146.	Isidōros I *Boucheiras apo Monembasias*	1347–1350
147.	Kallistos I	1350–1353
148.	Philotheos *Kokkinos apo Hērakleias*	1353–1354?
	Kallistos I [2nd time]	1355–1363
	Philotheos [2nd time]	1364–1376
149.	Makarios	1376?–1379
150.	Neilos *Kerameus* (or *Kerameōs*)	1380–1388
151.	Antōnios IV	1389–1390
	Makarios [2nd time]	1390–1391
	Antōnios IV [2nd time]	1391–1397
152.	Kallistos II *Xanthopoulos*	1397
153.	Matthaios I *apo Kyzikou*	1397–1402
	Matthaios I *apo Kyzikou* [2nd time]	1403–1410
154.	Euthymios II	1410–1416
155.	Iōsēph II *apo Ephesou*	1416–1439
156.	Mētrophanēs II *apo Kyzikou*	1440–1443
157.	Grēgorios III *Mammas* (or *Mammēs*) [#33 of Latin Church of Constantinople]	1443–1451?
158.	Athanasios II [locum tenens]	1451–1453

INTERREGNUM

159.	Gennadios II *Scholarios Kourtesēs*	1454–1456
160.	Isidōros II *Xanthopoulos*	1456–1462
	Gennadios II [2nd time]	1462–1463
161.	Sōphronios I *Syropoulos*	1463–1464
	Gennadios II [3rd time]	1464
162.	Iōasaph I *Kokkas*	1464–1466?
163.	Markos II *Xylokarabēs Eugenikos* [#31 of Bulgaria, #34 of Macedonia]	1466
164.	Symeōn *Trapezountios*	1466?–1467
165.	Dionysios I *Symeōnēs apo Philippoupoleōs*	1467–1471
	Symeōn [2nd time]	1471–1475
166.	Raphaēl I *Serbos*	1475–1476
167.	Maximos III *Manassēs*	1476–1482
	Symeōn [3rd time]	1482–1486
	Nēphōn II (or Nyphōn) *apo Thessalonikēs* [#8 of Romania]	1486–1488
	Dionysios I [2nd time]	1488–1490
169.	Maximos IV *apo Serrōn*	1491–1497
	Nēphōn II [2nd time]	1497–1498
170.	Iōakeim I	1498–1502
	Nēphōn II [3rd time]	1502
171.	Pachōmios I *apo Zichnōn*	1503–1504

	Iōakeim I [2nd time]	1504
	Pachōmios I [2nd time]	1504–1513
172.	Theolēptos I *apo Iōanninōn*	1513–1522
173.	Hieremias I *apo Sophias*	1520–1522
174.	Iōannikios I *apo Sōzopoleōs*	1522–1523
	Hieremias I [2nd time]	1523–1537
175.	Dionysios II	1537
	Hieremias I [3rd time]	1537–1546
	Dionysios II [2nd time]	1546–1555
176.	Iōasaph II *Megaloprepēs apo Adrianoupoleōs*	1555–1565
177.	Mētrophanēs III *apo Kaisareias*	1565–1572
178.	Hieremias II *Tranos apo Larissēs*	1572–1579
	Mētrophanēs III [2nd time]	1579–1580
	Hieremias II [2nd time]	1580–1584
179.	Pachōmios II *Patestos apo Kaisareias*	1584–1585
180.	Theolēptos II *apo Philippoupoleōs*	1585–1586?

Interregnum

	Nikēphoros *Hierodiakonos* [locum tenens]	1586?
	Dionysios [locum tenens]	1586?
	Nikēphoros *Hierodiakonos* [2nd time]	1586?–
	Hieremias II [3rd time]	1589–1595
181.	Matthaios II *apo Iōanninōn*	1595
182.	Gabriēl I	1596
183.	Theophanēs I *Karykēs* [#77 of Greece]	1596–1597
184.	Meletios I *Pēgas* [locum tenens; #104 of Alexandria]	1597–1598?
	Matthaios II [2nd time]	1598?–1602?
185.	Neophytos II *Karykēs* [#78 of Greece]	1602–1603
	Matthaios II [3rd time]	1603
186.	Raphaēl II *apo Methymnēs*	1603–1607
	Neophytos II [2nd time]	1607–1612
187.	Kyrillos I *Loukaris* [locum tenens; #105 of Alexandria]	1612
188.	Timotheos II *apo Palaiōn Patrōn*	1612–1620
	Kyrillos I [2nd time]	1620–1623
189.	Grēgorios IV *Straboamaseias*	1623
190.	Anthimos II *apo Adrianoupoleōs*	1623
	Kyrillos I [3rd time]	1623–1630
191.	Isaak	1630
	Kyrillos I [4th time]	1630–1633
192.	Kyrillos II *Kontarēs apo Borrhoias*	1633
	Kyrillos I [5th time]	1633–1634
193.	Athanasios III *Patellarios apo Thessalonikēs*	1634
	Kyrillos I [6th time]	1634–1635
	Kyrillos II [2nd time]	1635–1636

XXV. Greek Church of Constantinople (Ecumenical Patriarchate)

194.	Neophytos III *apo Hērakleias*	1636–1637
	Kyrillos I [7th time]	1637–1638
	Kyrillos II [3rd time]	1638–1639
195.	Parthenios I *Gerōn apo Naupaktou*	1639–1644
196.	Parthenios II *Oxys Keskinēs*	1644–1646
197.	Iōannikios II *Lindios apo Hērakleias*	1646–1648
	Parthenios II [2nd time]	1648–1651
	Iōannikios II [2nd time]	1651–1652
198.	Kyrillos III *Spanos apo Tornobou*	1652
	Athanasios III [2nd time]	1652
199.	Païsios I *apo Larissēs*	1652–1653
	Iōannikios II [3rd time]	1653–1654
	Kyrillos III [2nd time]	1654
	Païsios I [2nd time]	1654–1655
	Iōannikios II [4th time]	1655–1656
200.	Parthenios III *Parthenakēs apo Chiou*	1656–1657
201.	Gabriēl II *apo Ganou kai Chōras*	1657
202.	Theophanēs II *apo Melekinou*	1657
203.	Parthenios IV *Mogilalos Koukoumēs*	1657–1662
204.	Dionysios III *Bardalis Spanos*	1662–1665
	Parthenios IV [2nd time]	1665–1667
205.	Klēmēs *apo Ikoniou*	1667
206.	Methodios III *Morōnēs apo Hērakleias*	1668–1671
	Parthenios IV [3rd time]	1671
207.	Dionysios IV *Mouselimēs Komnēnos*	1671–1673
208.	Gerasimos II *apo Tornobou*	1673–1674
	Parthenios IV [4th time]	1675–1676
	Dionysios IV [2nd time]	1676–1679
209.	Athanasios IV *apo Rhaidestou*	1679
210.	Iakōbos *apo Larissēs*	1679–1682
	Dionysios IV [3rd time]	1682–1684
	Parthenios IV [5th time]	1684–1685
	Iakōbos [2nd time]	1685–1686
	Dionysios IV [4th time]	1686–1687
	Iakōbos [3rd time]	1687–1688
211.	Kallinikos II *Akarnan apo Prousēs*	1688
212.	Neophytos IV *apo Adrianoupoleōs*	1688–1689
	Kallinikos II [2nd time]	1689–1693
	Dionysios IV [5th time]	1693–1694
	Kallinikos II [3rd time]	1694–1702
213.	Gabriēl III *Smyrnaios apo Chalkēdonos*	1702–1707
214.	Neophytos V *apo Hērakleias* [unconsecrated]	1707
215.	Kyprianos *apo Kaisareias Kappadokias*	1707–1709
216.	Athanasios V *Krēs apo Adrianoupoleōs*	1709–1711
217.	Kyrillos IV *apo Kyzikou*	1711–1713
	Kyprianos [2nd time]	1713–1714

218.	Kosmas III *Chalkēdonios* [#115 of Alexandria, #61 of Sinai]	1714–1716
219.	Hieremias III *apo Kaisareias Kappadokias*	1716–1726
	Kyrillos (V) *apo Prousēs* [anti-patriarch]	1720
220.	Kallinikos III *apo Hērakleias* [one day]	1726
221.	Païsios II *Kiomourtzoglous apo Nikomēdeias*	1726–1732
	Hieremias III [2nd time]	1732–1733
222.	Serapheim I *apo Nikomēdeias*	1733–1734
223.	Neophytos VI *apo Kaisareias Kappadokias*	1734–1740
	Païsios II [2nd time]	1740–1743
	Neophytos VI [2nd time]	1743–1744
	Païsios II [3rd time]	1744–1748
224.	Kyrillos V *Karakalos apo Nikomēdeias*	1748–1751
	Païsios II [4th time]	1751–1752
	Kyrillos V [2nd time]	1752–1757
225.	Kallinikos IV *apo Proïlabou*	1757
226.	Serapheim II *apo Philippoupoleōs*	1757–1761
227.	Iōannikios III *Karatzas apo Chalkēdonos*	1761–1763
228.	Samouēl *Chantzerēs apo Derkōn*	1763–1768
229.	Meletios II *apo Larissēs*	1768–1769
230.	Theodosios II *Maridakēs apo Thessalonikēs*	1769–1773
	Samouēl [2nd time]	1773–1774
231.	Sōphronios II [#125 of Jerusalem]	1774–1780
232.	Gabriēl IV *apo Palaiōn Patrōn*	1780–1785
233.	Prokopios *apo Smyrnēs*	1785–1789
234.	Neophytos VII *apo Marōneias*	1789–1794
235.	Gerasimos III *apo Derkōn*	1794–1797
236.	Grēgorios V *Angelopoulos apo Smyrnēs*	1797–1798
	Neophytos VII [2nd time]	1798–1801
237.	Kallinikos V *apo Nikaias*	1801–1806
	Parthenios [locum tenens]	1806
	Grēgorios V [2nd time]	1806–1808
	Hieremias IV *apo Mitylēnēs* [locum tenens]	1808
	Kallinikos V [2nd time]	1808–1809
238.	Hieremias IV *apo Mitylēnēs*	1809–1813
239.	Kyrillos VI *Serbetsoglous apo Adrianoupoleōs*	1813–1818
	Grēgorios V [3rd time]	1818–1821
240.	Eugenios II *apo Pissideias*	1821–1822
241.	Anthimos III *apo Chalkēdonos*	1822–1824
242.	Chrysanthos *apo Serrōn*	1824–1826
243.	Agathangelos *apo Chalkēdonos* [#10 of Serbia — Beograd]	1826–1830
244.	Kōnstantios I *apo Sinaiou* [#68 of Sinai]	1830–1834
245.	Kōnstantios II *Asophos apo Tornobou*	1834–1835

XXV. Greek Church of Constantinople (Ecumenical Patriarchate)

246.	Grēgorios VI *Phortouniadēs apo Serrōn*	1835–1840
247.	Anthimos IV *Tambakēs apo Nikomēdeias*	1840–1841
248.	Anthimos V *Chrysaphidēs apo Kyzikou*	1841–1842
249.	Germanos IV *apo Derkōn*	1842–1845
250.	Meletios III *Pankalos apo Kyzikou*	1845
251.	Anthimos VI *Iōannidēs apo Ephesou*	1845–1848
	Anthimos IV [2nd time]	1848–1852
	Germanos IV [2nd time]	1852–1853
	Anthimos VI [2nd time]	1853–1855
252.	Kyrillos VII *apo Amaseias*	1855–1860
253.	Iōakeim II *Kokkōdēs apo Kyzikou*	1860–1863
254.	Sōphronios III *Meidintzoğlou* [#128 of Alexandria]	1863–1866
	Grēgorios VI [2nd time]	1867–1871
	Anthimos VI [3rd time]	1871–1873
	Iōakeim II [2nd time]	1873–1878
255.	Iōakeim III *Debetzēs* (or *Dēmētriadēs*)	1878–1884
256.	Iōakeim IV *apo Chiou*	1884–1886
257.	Dionysios V *Charitōnidēs* [#75 of Crete]	1887–1891
258.	Neophytos VIII *Papakōnstantinou*	1891–1894
259.	Anthimos VII *Tsatsos*	1895–1896
260.	Kōnstantinos V *Baliadēs*	1897–1901
	Iōakeim III [2nd time]	1901–1912
261.	Germanos V *Kabakopoulos*	1913–1918

Interregnum

	Dōrotheos *apo Prousēs* [locum tenens]	1918–1921
	Nikolaos *apo Kaisareias* [locum tenens]	1921
	Germanos *Karabangelēs* [refused election]	1921
262.	Meletios IV *Metaxakēs* [#130 of Alexandria, #114 of Greece]	1921–1923
	Nikolaos *apo Kaisareias* [locum tenens]	1923
263.	Grēgorios VII *Zerboudakēs* (or *Papastaurianos*)	1923–1924
264.	Kōnstantinos VI *Arboğlu*	1924–1925
265.	Basileios III *Geōrgiadēs*	1925–1929
266.	Phōtios II *Maniatēs*	1929–1935
267.	Beniamin(os) *Christodoulos*	1936–1946
268.	Maximos V *Baportzēs*	1946–1948
	Thōmas [locum tenens]	1948
269.	Athēnagoras *Spyrou* [#2 of America]	1948–1972
	Melitōn [locum tenens]	1972
270.	Dēmētrios *Papadopoulou*	1972–1991
271.	Bartholomaios *Archontōnēs*	1991–

The Church of Turkey

The Turkish Orthodox Church was founded by an Orthodox priest, Paulos Euthymios Karachissaridēs, who called himself Papa Eftim (the Turkish version of Euthymios). Desiring to establish a national church independent of Constantinople for Turkish-speaking Christians, particularly in Anatolia, Eftim began urging Turkish parishes of the Orthodox Church to rally around his standard. On 1 April 1922 he proclaimed the independence of the Turkish Orthodox Church, stating that Patriarch Meletios IV of Constantinople had occupied the throne uncanonically; this was followed by the first Church Congress on 21 September.

The government of the new Republic of Turkey, under the leadership of President Kemal Ataturk, was eager to drive a wedge into the Greek communities, and supported Eftim's claims, ultimately causing the flight of Meletios, and later the exile of his second successor, Kōnstantinos VI. Eftim twice tried unsuccessfully to take over the Holy Synod. Constantinople responded by excommunicating him in 1924.

Undaunted, Eftim established his headquarters in Istanbul, issued a statement that two members of the Synod had lifted the anathema and had then consecrated him as bishop, and in 1926 proclaimed himself Archbishop of the Independent Turkish Orthodox Church of Istanbul and Exarch of All Turkish Orthodox. To provide for the succession, he ordained his son and nephew to the priesthood, and raised a second son to the deaconate.

Eftim resigned his leadership in 1962, dying six years later; he was succeeded by his son, Turgut Erenerol, as Papa Eftim II, and then by another son as Papa Eftim III. In December 1965 the two Turkish churches renounced their mutual excommunications. Although the Turkish government supported its efforts to take over parishes and churches formerly controlled by Constantinople, the church had diminished so severely in size by the death of Eftim III in 2002 that it disintegrated.

Sources: "An Autocephalous Turkish Orthodox Church" (Jacob); *Eastern Christianity and Politics in the Twentieth Century* (Ramet, ed.); *Gegenwartslage der Ostkirchen* (Spuler); "The Political Role of the Turkish Orthodox Patriarchate (So-Called)" (Donef).

Archbishops of the Turkish Orthodox Church

1. Papa Eftim I (Euthymios) *Karachissaridēs* — 1926–1962
2. Papa Eftim II *Erenerol* — 1962–1991
3. Papa Eftim III *Erenerol* — 1991–2002

The Church Disestablished 2002

XXVI.

Latin Church of Constantinople

The Latin Patriarchate of Constantinople was established in the year 1204, as a direct result of the Fourth Crusade, which stopped short of the Holy Land and instead conquered the capital of the Byzantine Empire. When the Greek patriarch fled the city, Bishop Thomas Morosini was named his successor. This church was one of four such creations made during the period of the crusades to correspond to the patriarchates of the ancient world, and to provide rival jurisdictions to the Greek churches and prelates.

The Latin Church of Constantinople survived until the reconquest of that city by the Greeks in 1261, after which time it became a purely titular honor, with the patriarchs being based in Rome. During the renaissance the rank of "Patriarch" in the Latin church became a kind of intermediate level between archbishop and cardinal, many Patriarchs relinquishing their titles when promoted to the College of Cardinals. The title was officially abolished by Pope Paul VI in 1964.

SOURCES: *The Catholic Encyclopedia*; *Dictionnaire d'Histoire et de Géographie Ecclésiastiques*; *The New Catholic Encyclopedia*; *Oriens Christianus* (Le Quien).

LATIN PATRIARCHS OF CONSTANTINOPLE

1.	Thomas I *Morosini*	1204–1211

INTERREGNUM

2.	Gervasius (or Everardus)	1215–1219
3.	Matthæus (or Matthias)	1221–1226
	Ioannes I *Halegrin* [unconsecrated]	1226
4.	Simon	1227–1232
5.	Nicolaus I *de Castro Arquato*	1234–1251
6.	Pantaleon *Giustiniani*	1253–1286
7.	Petrus I *Correr*	1286–1302
8.	Leonardus *Faliero*	1302–1305?

Interregnum

9.	Nicolaus II	1308–1331?
10.	Petrus II *de Bolonesio*	1331?–
11.	Cardinalis (?)	1332–1335
12.	Gotius (or Goctius) *Battaglia*	1335–1339
13.	Rolandus *de Ast*	1339
14.	Stephanus I	1339–1345
15.	Stephanus II	1346
16.	Guillelmus I *de Castello*	1346–1361

Interregnum

17.	Petrus III *Thomas*	1364–1366
18.	Paulus I *Guillelmus*	1366–1370
19.	Hugolinus *de Malabranca*	1371–1375?
20.	Iacobus I *d'Itri*	1376–1378
21.	Guillelmus II	1379
22.	Thomas II *Palaiologos Tagaris* [rival]	1379?–1384?
23.	Paulus II	1379?–
24.	Ludovicus I	1405
25.	Angelus *Correr*	1405
26.	Antonius I *Correr* [nephew of #25]	1405–1408
27.	Alphonsus	1408–
28.	Franciscus I *Landus*	1409
29.	Ioannes II *Contarini*	1409–
30.	Ioannes III *de la Rochetaillée*	1412–1423
	Ioannes II *Contarini* [2nd time]	1424–
31.	Franciscus II *de Conzié*	1430–
32.	Franciscus III *Condulmer*	1438–
33.	Gregorius (Grēgorios) *Mammas* [#157 of Greek Church of Constantinople]	1454?–1459
34.	Isidorus (Isidor) *of Kiev*	1459–1463
35.	Bessarion	1463–1472
36.	Petrus IV *Riario*	1472–1474
37.	Hieronymus *Lando*	1474–1497
38.	Ioannes IV *Michele*	1497–1503
39.	Ioannes V *Borgia*	1503
40.	Franciscus IV *de Lorris*	1503–1506
41.	Marcus *Cornaro*	1506–1507
42.	Thomas III *Bakócz de Erdoed*	1507–1521
	Marcus *Cornaro* [2nd time]	1522–1524
43.	Gillus *Caninio*	1524–1530
44.	Franciscus V *Pesaro*	1530–1544
45.	Marinus *Grimani*	1545–1546
46.	Ranucius *Farnese*	1546–1549

XXVI. Latin Church of Constantinople

47.	Fabius I *Colonna*	1550–1554
	Ranucius *Farnese* [2nd time]	1554–1565
48.	Scipio *Rebiba*	1565–1573
49.	Prosperus *Rebiba* [nephew of #49]	1573–1594
50.	Silvius *Savelli*	1594–1596
51.	Hercules *Tassoni*	1596–1597
52.	Bonifacius *Bevilacqua*	1598–1599
53.	Bonaventurus Secusius *de Caltagirone*	1599–1618?
54.	Ascanius *Gesualdi*	1618–1640
55.	Franciscus VI Maria *Machiavelli*	1640–1641
56.	Ioannes VI Iacobus *Panciroli*	1641–1643
57.	Ioannes VII Baptistus *Spada*	1643–1658
58.	Volunnius *Bandinelli*	1658–1667
59.	Stephanus III *Ugolini*	1667–1670
60.	Fredericus *Borromée* [#25 of Alexandria]	1670–1673

INTERREGNUM

61.	Odoardus *Cybò*	1689–1700

INTERREGNUM

62.	Ludovicus II *Pic de la Mirandole*	1706–1712

INTERREGNUM

63.	Andreas *Riggio*	1716–1717
64.	Camillus *Cybò*	1718–1729
65.	Mondillus *Orsini*	1729–
66.	Ferdinandus Maria *de Rossi*	1751–1759
67.	Philippus Ioshua *Caucci*	1760–1771
68.	Ioannes VIII *de la Puebla*	1771–1779
69.	Franciscus VII Antonius *Marcucci*	1781–1799

INTERREGNUM

70.	Benedictus *Fenoja*	1805–1812

INTERREGNUM

71.	Iosephus I *della Porta Rodiani*	1823–1835
72.	Ioannes IX *Soglia-Ceroni*	1835–1839
73.	Antonius II Maria *Traversi*	1839–1842
74.	Iacobus II *Sinibaldi*	1843–1844?

75.	Fabius II Maria *Asquini*	1844–1845
76.	Ioannes X Ludovicus *Canali*	1845–1851
77.	Dominicus *Lucciardi*	1851

INTERREGNUM

78.	Iosephus II Melchiades *Ferlisi* [#53 of Antioch]	1860–1865
79.	Rogerus Ludovicus Æmilius *Antici-Mattei*	1866–1875

INTERREGNUM

80.	Iacobus III Gregorius *Gallo*	1878–1881

INTERREGNUM

81.	Iulius *Lenti*	1887–1894
82.	Ioannes XI Baptistus *Casali del Drago*	1895–1899
83.	Alexander *Sanminiatelli-Zabarella*	1899–1901
84.	Carolus Antonius *Nocella* [#60 of Antioch]	1901–1903
85.	Iosephus III *Cap[p]etelli*	1903–1917

INTERREGNUM

86.	Michael *Zezza di Zapponeta*	1923–1927
87.	Antonius III Anastasius *Rossi*	1927–1948

PATRIARCHATE DISESTABLISHED 1964

XXVII.

Church of Crete

The autonomous Church of Crete was founded in the year 65 a.d., according to tradition, by the Apostle Paul, the first known bishop being his disciple, Titos (a name which has remained popular among the island's clergy). Although Crete is now a province of the Republic of Greece, the Church resisted being placed under the Archbishop of Athens after the Greek Revolution of the 1820s, and instead maintained itself as an appendage of the Ecumenical Patriarchate. In 1878 the Church was granted self-governance, and in 1961 complete autonomy by Constantinople, now managing all of its own affairs except for the consecration of each new primate.

The primate bears the title Archbishop of Crete and Metropolitan of Herakleion. The official language of the Church is Greek. The number of communicants is almost equal to the population of the island, about a half million.

Sources: *Dictionnaire d'Histoire et de Géographie Ecclésiastiques*; *Échos d'Orient*; *Episkepsis*; *History of the Church* (Jedin, ed.); *Jahrbuch der Orthodoxie* (Proc); "Krētē—Ekklēs." (Beneres; regarded as official by the Church); *Oriens Christianus* (Le Quien); *Orthodoxia*; official church website.

Metropolitan Archbishops of Crete

1.	Paulos I	64?
2.	Titos I *Apostolos*	64?
3.	Philippos	170–190
4.	Dioskoros	
5.	Kyrillos I *Hieromartys*	–304
6.	Myrōn *Thaumatourgos*	–350
7.	Kriskēs	256?
8.	Petros I *Ikonios*	431?
9.	Martyrios	451?
10.	Theodōros	553?
11.	Iōannēs I	597?
12.	Paulos II	667?
13.	Eumenios I *Thaumatourgos*	668?

14.	Basileios I	680?–692?
15.	Andreas I *Krētēs*	712–740
16.	Petros II *Kolybitēs*	761?
17.	Ēlias I	787?
18.	Iōannēs II	
19.	Nikētas I	
20.	Nikētas II	
21.	Kyrillos II	820?
22.	Basileios II	823–828
24.	Basileios III	878?
25.	Ēlias II	920–961
26.	Andreas II	900s
27.	Nikētas III	
28.	Stephanos	1027?–1030?
29.	Iōannēs III	1106?
30.	Leōn	
31.	Michaēl	
32.	Kōnstantinos I	
33.	Ēlias III	
34.	Basileios IV	
35.	Kōnstantinos II	
36.	Nikolaos I	
37.	Iōannēs IV	1166–1177
38.	Manouēl I	
39.	Manouēl II	
40.	Nikolaos II	1195?–1221?

Interregnum

41.	Nikēphoros I *Moschopoulos*	1285–1322
42.	Antōnios *Homologētēs*	1306?
43.	Nikēphoros II	1312?–1318?
44.	Makarios	1357?
45.	Anthimos I *Homologētēs* [#58 of Greece]	1365–1370
46.	Ignatios [locum tenens]	1381?
47.	Prochoros [locum tenens]	1410?
48.	Belisarios [locum tenens]	1499?

Interregnum

49.	Neophytos *Patellaros*	1646–1679
50.	Nikēphoros III *Skōtakēs*	1679–1681?
51.	Kallinikos I	1683–1685?
52.	Arsenios I	1687–1688
53.	Athanasios *Kalliopolitēs*	1688–1697

XXVII. Church of Crete

54.	Kallinikos II	1697–1699
55.	Arsenios II	1699–1701
56.	Iōasaph	1702–1710?
57.	Kōnstantios *Chalkiopoulos*	1711–1716
58.	Gerasimos I *apo Kissamou*	1716–1719
	Kōnstantios *Chalkiopoulos* [2nd time]	1719–1722
59.	Daniēl *apo Rithymnēs*	1722–1725
60.	Gerasimos II *Letitzēs Gerontas*	1725–1755
	Anthimos II [locum tenens?]	1756
61.	Gerasimos III *apo Chiou*	1756–1769
62.	Zacharias *Maridakēs*	1769–1786
63.	Maximos *Progiannakopoulos*	1786–1800
64.	Gerasimos IV *Pardalēs*	1800–1821
65.	Methodios *apo Karpathou*	1823
66.	Kallinikos III *ex Ankialou*	1823–1830
67.	Meletios I *Nikoletakēs*	1831–1839
68.	Porphyrios *Phōtiadēs*	1839
69.	Kallinikos IV *Gargalados*	1839–1842
70.	Kallinikos V *Chougias*	1842–1843
71.	Chrysanthos *Lesbios*	1843–1850
72.	Sōphronios I *apo Ainou*	1850
73.	Dionysios I *Byzantios*	1850–1856
74.	Iōannikios *Xephloudēs Zagorēsios*	1856–1858
75.	Dionysios II *Charitōnidēs* [#257 of Constantinople]	1858–1868
76.	Meletios II *Kalymnios*	1868–1874
77.	Sōphronios II *apo Didumoteichou*	1874–1877
	Meletios II [2nd time]	1877–1882
78.	Timotheos I *Kastrinogiannakēs*	1882–1897
79.	Eumenios II *Xēroudakēs*	1897–1920
80.	Titos II *Zōgraphidēs*	1922–1933
81.	Timotheos II *Benerēs*	1934–1941
82.	Basileios V *Markakēs*	1941–1950
83.	Eugenios *Psalidakēs*	1950–1978
84.	Timotheos III *Papoutsakēs*	1978–

XXVIII.

Church of Cyprus

Tradition states that the Church of Cyprus was founded by St. Barnabas, an early disciple of the apostles. It was recognized as autocephalous in 431, under an independent Archbishop. When the island was captured by the Crusaders in 1191, the Orthodox bishops were put under the authority of the Latin Archbishop of Nikosia, and were systematically suppressed. Finally, when Archbishop Germanos died, about 1275, no elections were allowed for a new primate, although the principal Greek sees continued to have Greek bishops.

Three centuries later, the Ottomans took possession of Cyprus in 1571, and the native population began lobbying for a new primate, whom they received a year later in the person of Timotheos. In 1821 the Turks murdered Archbishop Kyprianos and his three bishops for sending aid to the Greek rebels on the mainland.

In the twentieth century both Church and state have been plagued with continual struggles between the Greek and Turkish populations, and between the British administration and those seeking either independence or union with Greece. The Archbishop's throne remained vacant for nine years between 1900 and 1909, as various factions supporting Kyrillos II and Kyrillos III sought to control the election. The abortive revolution of 1931 resulted in chaos; when Kyrillos III died in 1933, the British administration delayed new elections for fourteen years. Finally, the Locum Tenens, Metropolitan Leontios, was allowed to assume the throne (1947), but died a month after his election.

Archbishop Makarios III was a major figure in the Cypriot struggle for independence; following his election in 1950 at the early age of 37, he led the forces seeking to free Cyprus from British rule. He was subsequently exiled, but returned as first President of Cyprus in 1959. His later years were troubled with a series of unsettling events.

First, three of his Metropolitans attempted to unseat him in 1973, claiming that canon law prevented a church official from also holding a secular political office, and demanding Makarios resign his Presidency; when he refused, they named Gennadios of Paphos as new Archbishop. Makarios convened an extraordinary Synod, presided over by the three Greek Patriarchs of Alexandria, Jerusalem, and Antioch; the Synod condemned the insurrection, and revalidated Makarios's authority, deposing Gennadios and two other members of the Cypriot Holy Synod.

A year later Makarios was again forced into exile, following a political revolution, but returned in 1975, after the Turkish Army had invaded the island and established the separate Turkish state of North Cyprus. This extraordinary churchman died in 1977 at the age of sixty-three, and was succeeded by Archbishop Chrysostomos.

In the early years of the new century, the declining physical and mental health of Archbishop Chrysostomos caused a number of scandals in the Church, including controversies over major financial mismanagement by the Archbishop's relatives, and over the alleged homosexuality of a Cypriot bishop (he was later cleared of all charges).

The primate bears the title Archbishop of Nova Justiniana and All Cyprus, but resides at Nikosia. The official Church language is Greek. The approximately 442,000 members of this island church are all located on Cyprus.

Sources: *Dictionnaire d'Histoire et de Géographie Ecclésiastique*; *Échos d'Orient*; *Hē Ekklēsia tēs Kyprou* (Mitsidēs; regarded by the Church as official); *Episkepsis*; *Europa World Yearbook*; *Gegenwartslage der Ostkirchen* (Spuler); *Hēmerlogion Ekklēsias Kyprou 1992* (regarded as official by the Church); *History of the Church* (Jedin, ed.); *History of the Orthodox Church of Cyprus* (Hackett); *Jahrbuch der Orthodoxie* (Proc); *The Middle East and North Africa*; *Orthodoxia*.

Archbishops of Cyprus

1.	Barnabas I *Apostolos*	45?
	Aristiōn [not officially recognized]	70?
	Hērakleidēs [not officially recognized]	90?
2.	Gelasios	325?
3.	Epiphanios I	368–403
4.	Sabinos I	403–
5.	Trōïlos	–431
	Theodōros [not officially recognized]	431?
6.	Rhēginos	431–
7.	Olympios I	449?–451?
8.	Sabinos II	457?–458?
9.	Anthemios	478?
10.	Olympios II	490?
11.	Philoxenos	510?
12.	Damianos	530?
13.	Sōphronios I	550?
14.	Grēgorios (I)	570?
15.	Arkadios I	600?
16.	Ploutarchos	620?–625?
17.	Arkadios II	630?–641?
18.	Sergios	643?
19.	Epiphanios II	681?–685?
20.	Iōannēs I	691?
21.	Geōrgios I	753?
22.	Kōnstantinos	783?–787?
23.	Epiphanios III	870?

24.	Eustathios	890?
25.	Basileios	1080?
26.	Nikolaos *Mouzalōn* [#112 of Constantinople]	1110?
27.	Iōannēs II *Krētikos*	1151?–1174
28.	Barnabas II	1175–
29.	Sōphronios II	1191?
30.	Hēsaïas	1209?–1218?
	Symeōn (or Hilariōn) [anti-archbishop]	1218?–1220
31.	Neophytos I	1222?–1251
32.	Geōrgios II (or Grēgorios II)	1254?
33.	Germanos I *Pēsimandros*	1260?–1275?

INTERREGNUM

The Greek Church Restored

34.	Timotheos	1572–1588?
35.	Laurentios	1588?
36.	Neophytos II	–1592
37.	Athanasios I	1592–1600
38.	Beniamin	1600–1605
39.	Christodoulos I	1606–1638?
	Timotheos (II) [anti-archbishop]	1622–
	Ignatios [anti-archbishop]	1634–
	Christodoulos (II) [anti-archbishop]	1637–1638
40.	Nikēphoros	1640?–1674
41.	Hilariōn (II) *Tzigalas* (or *Kigalas*)	1674–1682
42.	Christodoulos II	1682–1685?

INTERREGNUM

43.	Iakōbos I	1691?–1692?

INTERREGNUM

44.	Germanos II	1695?–1705
45.	Athanasios II *al-Dabbas* [#153 of Antioch]	1705–1708
46.	Iakōbos II	1709–1718
	Ephraim [anti-archbishop]	1715
47.	Silbestros	1718–1733
48.	Philotheos	1734–1745
	Neophytos (III) [anti-archbishop]	1745
	Philotheos [2nd time]	1745–1759
49.	Païsios	1759–1761

XXVIII. Church of Cyprus

	Kyprianos [anti-archbishop; #118 of Alexandria]	1761
	Païsios [2nd time]	1761–1767
50.	Chrysanthos	1767–1783
	Iōannikios [anti-archbishop]	1783
	Chrysanthos [2nd time]	1783–1810
51.	Kyprianos	1810–1821
52.	Iōakeim	1821–1824
53.	Damaskēnos	1824–1827
54.	Panaretos	1827–1840
55.	Iōannikios	1840–1849
56.	Kyrillos I [cousin of #52]	1849–1854
57.	Makarios I	1854–1865
58.	Sōphronios III	1865–1900

INTERREGNUM

	Kyrillos *Papadopoulos* [locum tenens]	1900–1909
59.	Kyrillos II *Papadopoulos*	1909–1916
60.	Kyrillos III *Basileiou*	1916–1933

INTERREGNUM

	Leontios *Leontiou* [locum tenens]	1933–1947
61.	Leontios *Leontiou*	1947
62.	Makarios II *Myriantheus*	1947–1950
63.	Makarios III *Mouskos*	1950–1973
	Gennadios [anti-archbishop]	1973
	Makarios III [2nd time]	1973–1977
64.	Chrysostomos *Kykkotēs*	1977–

LATIN ARCHBISHOPS OF CYPRUS

1.	Alanus	1196–
2.	Terrius	1206–1211
3.	Albertus	1211–
4.	Durandus [unconsecrated]	1212–1213

INTERREGNUM

5.	Eustorgius *de Montaigu* (or *d'Auvergne*)	1217?–1239
6.	Elias I	1240–1251
7.	Hugo I *de Pise* (or *de Fagiano*)	1251–1260

INTERREGNUM

8.	Raphael	1264–
9.	Ranulphus (or Arnulphus)	1275?–1280

INTERREGNUM

10.	Ioannes I *d'Ancone*	1288–1295
11.	Gerardus *de Langres*	1295–1312?
12.	Ioannes II *de Polo* (or *del Conte*)	1312–1332
13.	Helias II *des Nabinaux*	1332–1342
14.	Philippus I *de Chambarlhac*	1344–1360

INTERREGNUM

15.	Raymundus *de la Pradèle*	1366–
16.	Paloungerus	1370?
17.	Michael	1375?
18.	Andreas I	1380?
19.	Conradus I	1396–
20.	Ioannes III	1400?
21.	Conradus II *Caraccioli*	1402–1405
22.	Stephanus *de Carrare*	1406–1412
23.	Ugo II *de Lusignan*	1413–1442
	Iacobus I *Benoît* [locum tenens]	1442
24.	Galesius *de Montolif*	1445–1447
25.	Andreas II	1447–
26.	Iacobus II *de Lusignan*	1459
27.	Elias III	1460–1463?
28.	Isidorus	1463?–
29.	Antonius *Tuneto*	1464?
30.	Ioannes IV Franciscus *Brusato*	1464?
31.	Fabricius	1464–
32.	Guillelmus *Gonème*	1467–
33.	Ludovicus *Pérez Fabrice*	1471–1483
34.	Victor *Marcello*	1477–
35.	Benedictus *Soranzo*	1484–
36.	Sebastianus *Priuli*	1496–1498?

INTERREGNUM

37.	Aldobrandinus *des Ursins*	1502–1517?
38.	Livius *Podocator*	1524–
39.	Guido *Brunelli*	1530?
40.	Cæsar *Podocator*	1553–

	Philippus II *Mocenigo*	1560–1571?
42.	Iulianus	1571–1577

LATIN ARCHBISHOPRIC DISESTABLISHED 1577

XXIX.

Church of Czechoslovakia

Czechoslovakia, like Poland, is predominately a Catholic nation. The proclamation of Czech independence following World War I led to a resurgence of nationalism in this small Slavic country, including demands by the handful of Orthodox believers in Slovakia (then the eastern half of the country) for their own independent church.

Some of these communicants petitioned the Serbian patriarch for their own bishop; he organized the Church on 8 August 1921, and consecrated Matej Pavlík on 24 September under the religious name of Gorazd II (he assumed the numeral because the successor to St. Methodius as Archbishop of Moravia a thousand years earlier had been named Gorazd). Little more than a year later, on 8 February 1923, the Ecumenical Patriarch consecrated a rival Archbishop in the person of Sabbazd or Savvatij Vrabec; his Church was declared autocephalous a month later, on 8 March, but never attained the following of the Serbian-supported enterprise.

Most of the Czech Church remained under nominal Serbian control until the Second World War, when Gorazd was murdered by the Nazis in 1942 for harboring partisan refugees on church property; his rival, Archbishop Savvatij, was imprisoned at Dachau from 1942–45. Gorazd was later canonized by the Czech Church.

On 8 November 1945, following the Soviet occupation of Czechoslovakia, the Church was put under the authority of the Moscow Patriarchate, and a new (Russian) Exarch was appointed; the Soviets then forcibly attempted (1950) to merge the Byzantine-Rite Catholics in Slovakia into the Orthodox body. On 8 December 1951 Patriarch Aleksiĭ I of Russia granted the Czechs their autocephaly, and on 8 December Exarch Jelevferij was elected Metropolitan. This grant of autocephaly was not recognized by the Ecumenical Patriarch until 27 August 1998. Gradually the Russian prelates were displaced by Czech bishops, until an all-native hierarchy was constituted.

The impending division of Czechoslovakia on 1 January 1993 into the Czech Republic and Slovakia prompted much discussion on the future of the Czech Church. Ultimately, at a synod held on 12 December 1992, Church leaders decided to separate Slovakia into an autonomous metropolitanate under the Archbishop of Presov, with the unity of the overall church still being maintained; he then succeeded as Metropolitan in 2000. The future remains uncertain, however, since neither of the autonomous halves of this small church has sufficient followers to maintain a stable hierarchical structure.

XXIX. Church of Czechoslovakia

The primate bears the title Metropolitan of the Czech Lands and Slovakia (since 1992), having formerly been called Metropolitan of Prague and All Czechoslovakia. The official language is Czech. Of the 71,000 communicants, about three-fifths live in Slovakia, the rest in the Czech Republic.

Sources: *Czechoslovakia* (Büsek and Spulber); *Eastern Christianity and Politics in the Twentieth Century* (Ramet, ed.); *Échos d'Orient*; *Episkepsis*; *Europa World Yearbook*; *Gegenwartslage der Ostkirchen* (Spuler); *History of the Church* (Jedin, ed.); *Jahrbuch der Orthodoxie* (Proc); *Orthodoxia*; personal communication; *Profiles in Belief* (Piepkorn); official church website.

METROPOLITAN ARCHBISHOPS OF CZECHOSLOVAKIA
(Bishops 1921, Exarchs 1946, Metropolitans 1951)

1.	Gorazd II *Pavlík* [rival bishop]	1921–1942
	Sabbazd (or Savvatij or Sawatij) *Vrabec* [rival bishop]	1923–1951

INTERREGNUM

2.	Jelevferij *Voroncov*	1946–1955
3.	Ján *Kuchtin*	1956–1964
4.	Dorotej *Filipp*	1964–1999
	Nikolaj *Kocvár* [locum tenens]	1999–2000
5.	Nikolaj *Kocvár*	2000–

XXX.

Church of Eritrea

The Eritrean Orthodox Church was originally an archdiocese of the Ethiopian Orthodox Church. Following the declaration of Eritrean independence from Ethiopia on 24 May 1993, after a long civil war between the two countries, the Church of Eritrea also separated from its mother church on 28 September 1993, becoming an autonomous ecclesiastical body under the aegis of the Coptic Orthodox Church. The church was elevated to patriarchal status and autocephaly by the Coptic Patriarch in April 1998, and Abuna Filippos was consecrated the first Patriarch of Eritrea on 8 May 1998.

The primate bears the title Patriarch of Asmara and All Eritrea. The principal language is Amharic. The number of communicants is unknown. **Sources**: *Europa World Yearbook*; news reports; *Orthodoxia*.

PATRIARCHS OF ERITREA
(Archbishops [Abunas] 1993, Patriarchs 1998)

1.	Mika'el *Wolde Mika'el*	–1980?
2.	Gabr'el *Iyasu*	1980–1985
3.	Tadewos *Biwonegin*	1985–1988
4.	Nikodimos *Abebe*	1988–1991
5.	Filippos *Berhan*	1991–2002
	Ya'eqob [locum tenens]	2002
6.	Ya'eqob	2002–2003
	Antonios [locum tenens]	2003–2004
7.	Antonios	2004–
	Dioskoros [rival patriarch]	2005–

XXXI.

Church of Estonia

The Church of Estonia fell under the jurisdication of the Russian Orthodox Church prior to World War I, being part of the Diocese (later Archdiocese) of Riga, Latvia (*q.v.*).

Following the declaration of Estonian independence on 12 April 1917, the Estonian Apostolic Orthodox Church was organized, and a bishop elected in the person of Paul Kulbusch (Bishop Plato); he was consecrated on 31 December 1917, and murdered by the Bolsheviks on 14 January 1919.

On 20 May 1920, the Estonian Church was granted autonomy by Russian Patriarch Tikhon. The Estonian Church unilaterally seceded from Russian jurisdiction on 23 September 1922, and on 7 July 1923 the Church's autonomy was officially recognized by Ecumenical Patriarch Meletios IV. Some ethnic Russians living in Estonia refused to accept the Church's jurisdiction, however, preferring to have a Russian primate; the dispute was settled by placing the Estonian parishes under the independent Metropolitan of the Estonian Apostolic Orthodox Church, and the Russian churches under the Russian Archbishop of Narva and Izhborsk.

The Russian invasion of 1940 forced Metropolitan Aleksander to renounce his status in March 1941, but he re-established the Church a few months later when the Nazis occupied the country. The withdrawal of the German armies in 1944 was the beginning of the end; those members of the Church who did not go into exile were forced to submit a second time on 5 March 1945.

Metropolitan Aleksander settled at Stockholm, Sweden, where he organized the Estonian Orthodox Church in Exile, under the overall jurisdiction of the Patriarchate of Constantinople; other émigrés established Church branches in the United States and Canada. Aleksander died in 1954, and was succeeded by a series of Locum Tenentes appointed by the Ecumenical Patriarch. On 1 September 1968 an assembly of exiled Estonians in Stockholm, Sweden, elected Archpriest Sergi Samon to be their bishop, and again pressed for his appointment in 1973, but consecration was refused by the Ecumenical Patriarch.

In September 1991 Estonia once again achieved independence from the Soviet Union; the Estonian Apostolic Orthodox Church was granted autonomy by the Russian Church on 28 April 1993. A second decree awarding the Estonian Church autonomy under the aegis of Constantinople was issued by the Ecumenical Patriarch on 20

February 1996; he then appointed the head of Finnish Orthodox Church, Johannes Rinne, to organize the Estonian Church.

This led to a second confrontation between the two Patriarchates, which threatened at one point to levy mutual excommunications, but the issues were finally resolved amicably on 16 May 1996, with both churches agreeing to allow their Estonian communicants to choose between Russian-organized parishes and those maintained by the Estonian Church under the guidance of Constantinople. However, the Estonian government refused to register the "Estonian Russian Orthodox Church of the Moscow Patriarchate" until 18 April 2002.

Estonia's population is largely Roman Catholic, with perhaps one-fifth of believers professing orthodoxy. The primate bears the title Metropolitan of Tallinn and All Estonia. The official language of the Church is Estonian. There were roughly 212,000 communicants of the Church in 1935, one-third of them of Russian origin; the number of believers today is unknown, but the percentage of those deriving from Russian ancestry exceeds fifty percent.

Sources: *Échos d'Orient*; *Eesti Apostlik Ortodoksne Kirik Eksilis, 1944–1960*; *Episkepsis*; *Europa World Yearbook*; *The Latvian Orthodox Church* (Cherney); *Profiles in Belief* (Piepkorn); *Religion in the Soviet Union* (Kolarz); official church website.

METROPOLITAN ARCHBISHOPS OF ESTONIA

1.	Plato *Kulbusch*	1917–1919
2.	Aleksander *Paulus*	1920–1941
	Aleksander *Paulus* [2nd time]	1941–1944

SUBSUMED BY RUSSIAN ORTHODOX CHURCH 1944

PRIMATES OF THE ESTONIAN CHURCH IN EXILE

	Aleksander *Paulus* [in exile]	1944–1953
	Athēnagoras I *Kabbadas* [locum tenens]	1954–1956
3.	Jüri *Välbe*	1956–1961
	Athēnagoras I *Kabbadas* [2nd time]	1961–1962
	Athēnagoras II *Kokkinakēs* [locum tenens]	1964–1973
4.	Sergi(us) *Samon* [unconsecrated]	1973–1974
	Paul *Menebisoglou* [locum tenens]	1974–1996?

METROPOLITAN ARCHBISHOPS OF ESTONIA

	Johannes *Rinne* [locum tenens] [#7 of Finland]	1996–1999
5.	Stefanus (Stephanos) *Charalambidēs*	1999–

RUSSIAN METROPOLITANS OF ESTONIA
(Bishops 1941, Archbishops 1996, Metropolitans 2000)

1.	Sergiĭ *Voskresenskiĭ*	1941

INTERREGNUM

2.	Pavel *Dimitrovskiĭ*	1944–1946
3.	Grigoriĭ *Chukov*	1946–1947
4.	Isidor *Bogoiavenskiĭ*	1947–1949
	Grigoriĭ *Chukov* [2nd time]	1949–1950
5.	Roman *Tang*	1950–1952

INTERREGNUM

6.	Ioann *Alekseev*	1958–1961
7.	Aleksius (Aleksiĭ) *Ridiger* [#15 of Russia]	1961–1987

INTERREGNUM

8.	Kornelius (Korneliĭ) *Jakobs*	1990–

XXXII.

Church of Ethiopia

Traditionally, the Ethiopian Church was founded by a Coptic monk of the Church of Alexandria, St. Frumentios, who took the name Salama when he became the first Abuna (Father) in 245. However, the early history of the Ethiopian Church is obscure, and the list of Abunas recorded by the Church cannot be confirmed. It is known that the Ethiopians were from the first dependent on the Coptic Church of Alexandria for their primates, and that all of their bishops until recent times were Coptic monks who had to make the arduous journey from Alexandria to take up their duties.

During the medieval period several attempts were made by Catholic missionaries to convert the population, but they were ultimately suppressed. Negus Haile Selassie demanded the independence of the Church when the old Abuna died in 1926. Coptic Pope Yuannis XIX ended three years of negotiations in 1929 by appointing a Copt as Abuna, and by simultaneously consecrating four native bishops to help provide a future Ethiopian hierarchy.

During the Italian occupation, the government deposed the Coptic primate, unilaterally declared the Church autocephalous, and appointed a blind Bishop, Abraha, as first Patriarch; he was followed by Yohannes. When the allies freed Ethiopia, Abuna Qerlos was restored, dying in 1950. Basilyos was elected the first Ethiopian Metropolitan in 1951, and was consecrated as the first Catholicos-Patriarch of Ethiopia on 28 June 1959. His successor, Tewoflos, was deposed in 1976 by the Marxist government, who replaced him with a junior bishop, Takla Haymanot, who died in 1988.

When the Communist president was overthrown in 1991, Patriarch Merkorewos, who had been appointed by the Dergue (the government council), was deposed that same year. A reformer, Paulos Gebre-Yohannes, was elected as his successor on 7 July 1992. Two months later, on 22 September 1992, the head of the American branch of the Church, Archbishop Yes(e)haq, a supporter of Merkorewos, refused to accept the election, declaring that the previous Patriarch had been illegally deposed, and proclaiming his Archdiocese independent of the mother Church. The matter remains unresolved. In September 1993, following the declaration of Eritrea's independence after a long civil war with Ethiopia, the Ethiopian Church recognized the Eritrean Church as an autonomous ecclesiastical jurisdiction.

The Patriarch's official residence is Axum, but he actually resides in the capital, Addis Ababa. His title is Catholicos Patriarch of Addis Ababa and All Ethiopia. The official Church language is Amharic. The official record of Abunas differs so widely from the historical record (so far as it can be determined) that both lists have reproduced here separately. Roughly twenty million communicants are located primarily in Ethiopia, with approximately 80,000 members located in the U.S.

Sources: *Church and State in Ethiopia: 1270–1527* (Tamrat); *The Church of Abyssinia* (Hyatt); *Dictionnaire d'Histoire et de Géographie Ecclésiastique*; *Eastern Christianity and Politics in the Twentieth Century* (Ramet, ed.); *Episkepsis*; *The Ethiopian Church* (O'Leary); *The Ethiopian Orthodox Church* (Molnar); *Ethiopiens Ortodokse Kirke* (Andersen); *Europa World Yearbook*; *Gegenwartslage der Ostkirchen* (Spuler); *History of the Church* (Jedin, ed.); "Le Liste dei Metropoliti d'Abissinia" (Guidi); *Die Morgenlandischen Kirchen* (Spuler); *Orthodoxia*; *Profiles in Belief* (Piepkorn); official church website.

ABUNAS AND CATHOLICOS-PATRIARCHS OF ETHIOPIA
(Official List)

1. Salama I *Fremenatos*   245?
2. Salama II (or Minas I)
3. Petros I
4. Matewos I
5. Marqos I
6. Yohannes I
7. Gabr'el I
8. Yohannes II
9. Gabr'el II
10. Minas II
11. Mika'el I
12. Yes'aq I (or Ishaq)
13. Sem'on I
14. Petros II
15. Mika'el II
16. Gabr'el III
17. Yohannes III
18. Matewos II
19. Mika'el III
20. Sem'on II
21. Yohannes IV
22. Marqos II
23. Abreham I
24. Gerlos I (or Gerillos)
25. Takla Haymanot I
26. Yohannes V
27. Mika'el IV
28. Sem'on III
29. Petros III

30. Matewos III
31. Ya'eqob (or Ewostatewos)
32. Fiqtor I (or Salama III)
33. Qerlos II (or Qerillos)
34. Qozmos I
35. Yostos I
36. Mika'el V
37. Gabr'el IV
38. Mika'el VI
39. Matewos IV
40. Yosab I
41. Yosef
42. Qozmos II
43. Filatawos I
44. Petros IV
45. Yohannes VI
46. Fiqtor II
47. Yostos II
48. Barmeya (or Barmeyu)
49. Mika'el VII
50. Gabr'el V
51. Minas III
52. Yohannes VII
53. Yohannes VIII
54. Abreham II
55. Marqos III
56. Maqares
57. Mika'el VIII
58. Matewos V
59. Marqos IV
60. Mika'el IX
61. Gabr'el VI
62. Yohannes IX
63. Qerlos III
64. Minas IV
65. Matewos VI
66. Mika'el X
67. Gabr'el VII
68. Marqos V
69. Gabr'el VIII
70. Matewos VII
71. Yohannes X
72. Minas V
73. Marqos VI
74. Krestodolo I
75. Zakaryas

XXXIII. Church of Ethiopia

76. Filatawos II
77. Suntyos (or Sentyos)
78. Gabr'el IX
79. Yohannes XI — 1437?
80. Mika'el XI — 1438–1458?
81. Gabr'el X — 1438–1458?
82. Bartalomewos
83. Matewos VIII
84. Yohannes XII
85. Yeshaq II — 1481–1510?
86. Marqos VII — 1481–1530?
87. Kaladyanu
88. Petros V
89. Matewos IX
90. Sem'on IV
91. Yosab II — 1539?–1559?
92. Mika'el XII
93. Matewos X
94. Marqos VIII — 1576?–1588?
95. Petros VI — 1600?–1607
96. Sem'on V — 1600?–1617
    Se'la Krestos [anti-abuna] — 1617?–1633?
97. Marqos IX — 1634?–1648?
98. Mika'el XIII — 1648?
99. Yohannes XIII — 1648?–
100. Krestodolo II — 1663?–1671
101. Sinoda — 1671?–1693?
102. Marqos X — 1693?–1716

INTERREGNUM

103. Krestodolo III — 1720–1735

INTERREGNUM

104. Yohannes XIV — 1743–1761

INTERREGNUM

105. Yosab III — 1770–1803
106. Makaryos — 1804–1808?

INTERREGNUM

107. Qerlos IV — 1815?–1828?

INTERREGNUM

108.	Salama IV Andreyas	1841–1867
109.	Atnatewos	1869–1876

INTERREGNUM

110.	Petros VII	1881–1889
111.	Matewos XI	1889–1926

INTERREGNUM

112.	Qerlos V	1927–1936
	Abraha (III) [anti-abuna]	1936–1939
	Yohannes XV [anti-abuna]	1939–1945
	Qerlos V [2nd time]	1945–1950
113.	Basilyos	1951–1970
114.	Tewoflos *Melaktu*	1971–1976
	Yohannes [locum tenens]	1976
115.	Takla Haymanot II *Wolde Mika'el*	1976–1988
116.	Merkorewos *Fenta*	1988–1991
	Zena Marqos *Bogosew* [locum tenens]	1991–1992
117.	Paulos *Gebre Yohannes*	1992–

ABUNAS AND CATHOLICOS-PATRIARCHS OF ETHIOPIA
(Historical List)

1.	Salama I *Fremenatos*	245?
2.	Minas I	270?
3.	Qerlos I	623?
4.	Yohannes I	820?–840?
5.	Ya'eqob I	848?
6.	Salama II	870?
7.	Petros I	923?
8.	Minas II	923?
9.	Bartalomewos I	950?
10.	Dengel (or Dan'el)	969?
11.	Fiqtor	1050?–1077
12.	Qerlos II *Abdon*	1077–
13.	Sawiros [nephew of #11]	1078?
14.	Giyorgis I	1102?
15.	Mika'el I *Habib al-Atfihi*	1105?–1153
	[alternate dates for reign]:	1130?–1199?
	Qerlos III [anti-abuna]	1144?

XXXIII. Church of Ethiopia

16.	Mika'el II *Kilus ibn al-Mulabbas*	1205–1210?
17.	Yes'aq I (or Yeshaq)	1210?–
18.	Ezra	1215?
19.	Yerda' Mika'el III	1220?
20.	Samu'el	1223?
21.	Giyorgis II	1225
22.	Tomas	1237
23.	Ya'eqob II	1250?
24.	Qerlos IV	1260?–1273
25.	Takla Haymanot I	1280
26.	Salama III	1285?
27.	Yohannes II	1310?
28.	Honoriwos	1315?
29.	Maqares	1320?
30.	Ya'eqob III *Madhinana Egzie*	1337–1344
31.	Gabra Krestos	1344?–1348?
32.	Salama IV	1348–1388
33.	Bartalomewos II	1398?–1436
34.	Yohannes III	1437?
35.	Mika'el IV	1438–1455?
36.	Gabr'el	1438–1458?

Interregnum

37.	Yeshaq II	1481–1505?
38.	Marqos I	1481–1530?
39.	Yohannes IV	1530?
40.	Marqos II	1538–1546?
41.	Yusab I (or Yosab)	1547?–1559?
42.	Petros II	1559?–1570?
43.	Marqos III	1576?–1588?
44.	Krestodolo I	1588?–
45.	Petros III	1600?–1607
46.	Sem'on	1607?–1617
47.	Se'la Krestos (or Rezq Allah)	1617?–1633
48.	Marqos IV	1634–1648?
49.	Mika'el V	1649?
50.	Yohannes V	1649?–

Interregnum

51.	Krestodolo II	1663?–1671?
52.	Marqos V	1671?
53.	Sinoda	1671?–1693?
54.	Marqos VI	1693?–1716

INTERREGNUM

55. Krestodolo III   1720–1735

INTERREGNUM

56. Yohannes VI   1743–1761
57. Salama V   1762–1770?
58. Yusab II   1770–1803
59. Makaryos   1804–1808?

INTERREGNUM

60. Qerlos V   1815?–1828?

INTERREGNUM

61. Andreyas (or Indriyas)   1841
62. Salama VI (same as Andreyas?)   1841–1867
63. Atnatewos   1869–1876

INTERREGNUM

64. Petros IV   1881–1889
65. Matewos   1889–1926

INTERREGNUM

66. Qerlos VI   1927–1936
    Abraha [anti-abuna]   1936–1939
    Yohannes VII [anti-abuna]   1939–1945
    Qerlos VI [2nd time]   1945–1950
67. Basilyos   1951–1970
68. Tewoflos *Melaktu*   1971–1976
    Yohannes [locum tenens]   1976
69. Takla Haymanot II *Wolde Mika'el*   1976–1988
70. Merkorewos *Fenta*   1988–1991
    Zena Marqos *Bogosew* [locum tenens]   1991–1992
71. Paulos *Gebre Yohannes*   1992–

XXXIII.

Church of Finland

The autonomous Church of Finland was originally an adjunct of the Patriarchate of Russia during the years when Finland was a province of the Russian Empire. A separate Archeparchy to govern Vyborg and the Finnish archdiocese was established in 1892 under Antoni Vadkovskiĭ. With the outbreak of the Russian Revolution in 1917, the Finns secured their independence from the Soviets.

The small Finnish Orthodox Church was granted autonomy by the Russians in 1921, and then sent a petition to Constantinople in 1923, requesting autocephaly. The Ecumenical Patriarch Meletios IV responded that the Church was too small to support autocephalous status, but granted autonomy under the aegis of Constantinople on 9 July 1923 (Moscow did not recognize this until 1957).

The Archbishop was granted the status of a Metropolitan on 1 February 1972, but continues to use the title of Archbishop. The Finnish Church is now self-governing in every respect, except that the consecration of a new Archbishop must include a representative of the Ecumenical Patriarch (and thus his approval).

The primate bears the title Archbishop of Karelia and all Finland. The official language of the Church is Finnish. Approximately 57,000 adherents are centered primarily in eastern Finland (Karelia), around Helsinki, the national capital, and near Kuopia.

Sources: *Eastern Christianity and Politics in the Twentieth Century* (Ramet, ed.); *Échos d'Orient*; *Episkepsis*; *Europa World Yearbook*; *Gegenwartslage der Ostkirchen* (Spuler); *History of the Church* (Jedin, ed.); *Jahrbuch der Orthodoxie* (Proc); *The Latvian Orthodox Church* (Cherney); *Orthodoxia*; *Profiles in Belief* (Piepkorn); "Suomen Ortodoksinen Kirkko" (Rossi); official church website.

ARCHBISHOPS OF FINLAND
(Archeparchs 1892, Archbishops 1923)

1.	Antoni *Vadkovski*	1892–1898
2.	Nikolai *Nalimov* [#14 of exarchs of Georgia]	1898–1905
3.	Sergei *Stragorodski* [#12 of Russia]	1906–1917
4.	Serafim *Lukianov* [assistant bishop]	1918–1919
5.	Mikael *Kasanskin* [assistant bishop]	1919–1922

6. Herman *Aav* [assistant bishop] 1922–1925
Herman *Aav* [archbishop] 1925–1960
7. Paavali *Olmari* 1960–1987
8. Johannes *Rinne* 1987–2001
9. Leo *Makkonen* 2001–

XXXIV.

Church of Georgia

The ancient Kingdom of Georgia, located in the Caucasus Mountains between the Black and Caspian Seas, was an autonomous kingdom as early as the first century b.c., but did not convert to Christianity until the 4th century a.d. Its physical isolation from the West promoted the independence of its bishops and archbishops, who gradually became recognized as autonomous and finally autocephalous, by the year 1089 (however, the Church itself dates its autocephaly from the appointment by Constantinople of the first Catholicos-Archbishop, Petre I, in 467).

King Giorgi XII willed his country to Russia on his death in late 1800; the Russian army promptly occupied Georgia in 1801. The last Georgian Patriarch, Anton II, who had been in secular life Prince Teymuraz, younger brother of the King, was deposed from his position in 1811, the Georgian Church being put under the authority of the Synod of the Russian Orthodox Church at Moscow. Russian Exarchs governed the Georgian Orthodox Church from 1811 until the Russian Revolution of 1917, when the breakdown in governmental and ecclesiastical authority allowed the Georgian Church to re-establish its autocephaly (12 March 1917), and elect a new Patriarch, Kirion III, in September 1917; he died a year later under mysterious circumstances, apparently murdered by Soviet agents.

Georgia joined the Transcaucasian Republic in 1917, but proclaimed its independence as a socialist republic a year later. Soviet forces occupied Georgia in February 1921; the Georgian Soviet Socialist Republic became a constituent republic of the U.S.S.R. in 1936. With the arrival of the Soviets, persecution to limit the Church's influence on the political and social life of the Georgian people was harsh and immediate: Patriarch Ambrosi was arrested in February 1923, together with most of the Church hierarchy, and sent to prison.

Following his death in March of 1927, his newly elected successor, K'ristep'ore III, moved toward support of the Soviet state, although official pressure on the Church was maintained, with parishioners being harassed and churches being closed on a continuing basis. The autocephaly of the Georgian Orthodox Apostolic Church was finally acknowledged by Moscow (and the Russian Patriarchate) on 31 October 1943. The Church gradually managed to promote its independence from government control during the post–World War II period, with many setbacks, including one rumor that Catholicos Davit' V was actually chosen for his post by the KGB.

His successor, Ilia II, was just forty-four at his election on 23 December 1977, and has revitalized the Church considerably in recent years, appointing many new bishops, reopening churches, initiating new journals and other publications, and generally exciting the interest of the Georgian youth. Under his firm tutelage, the Church of Georgia seems to have a bright future.

The Church was officially recognized as autocephalous (and the patriarchal title confirmed) by the Ecumenical Patriarch of Constantinople in 1990. Georgia regained its independence on 25 August 1991; civil war broke out within the year, threatening the fragile unity of the new country, and conflict has continued in Abkhazia and other regions.

The official language of the church is Georgian. The primate bears the title Catholicos-Patriarch of All Georgia, Archbishop of Mtshet and Tbilisi, his chief see being the latter city. The roughly five million communicants are mostly located within the confines of the Georgian Republic.

Sources: *Dictionnaire de Théologie Catholique*; *Dictionnaire d'Histoire et de Géographie Ecclésiastique*; *Eastern Christianity and Politics in the Twentieth Century* (Ramet, ed.); *Échos d'Orient*; *Episkepsis*; *Europa World Yearbook*; *History of the Church* (Jedin, ed.); *Jahrbuch der Orthodoxie* (Proc); *Gegenwartslage der Ostkirchen* (Spuler); Catholicos Ilia II (personal communication); *Orthodoxia*; *Profiles in Belief* (Piepkorn); *Religion in the Soviet Union* (Kolarz); official church website.

CATHOLICOS-PATRIARCHS OF GEORGIA
(Bishops 335, Catholicos-Archbishops 467, Catholicos-Patriarchs 1012)

1.	Ioane I	335–363
2.	Iakobi	363–375
3.	Iobi	375–390
4.	Elia I	390–400
5.	Svimeon I	400–410
6.	Mose	410–425
7.	Iona	425–429
8.	Ieremia	429–433
9.	Grigol I	433–434
10.	Basil I	434–436
11.	Mobidani	436–448
12.	Iovel I	448–452
13.	Mik'el I	452–467
14.	Petre I	467–474
15.	Samoel I	474–502
16.	Gabriel I	502–510
17.	T'avp'ech'agh I	510–516
18.	Ch'irmagi *Chigirmane*	516–523
19.	Saba I	523–533
20.	Evlavi	533–544
21.	Samoel II	544–553

XXXIV. Church of Georgia

22.	Makari	553–569
23.	Svimon II	569–575
24.	Samoel III	575–582
25.	Samoel IV	582–591
26.	Bart'lome	591–595
27.	Kirion I (or Svimon Petre)	595–610
28.	Ioan II	610–619
29.	Babila	619–629
30.	T'abori	629–634
31.	Samoel V	634–640
32.	Evnoni	640–649
33.	T'avp'ech'agh II	649–664
34.	Evlale	664–668
35.	Ioveli II	668–670
36.	Samoel VI	670–677
37.	Giorgi I	677–678
38.	Kirion II	678–683
39.	Izid-Bozidi	683–685
40.	T'eodore I	685–689
41.	Petre II	689–720
42.	T'alale	720–731
43.	Mamai	731–744
44.	Ioane III	744–760
45.	Grigol II	760–767
46.	Sarmeane	767–774
47.	Mik'el II	774–780
48.	Samoel VII	780–790
49.	Kirile I	791–802
50.	Grigol III	802–814
51.	Samoel VIII	814–826
52.	Giorgi II	826–838
53.	Gabriel II	838–860
54.	Arsen I	860–887
55.	Evsuk'i	887–908
56.	Klimentos	908–914
57.	Basil II	914–930
58.	Mik'el III	930–944
59.	Davit' I	944–955
60.	Arsen II	955–980
61.	Ok'ropir Ioane I	980–1001
62.	Svimon III	1001–1012
63.	Melk'isedek I	1012–1045
64.	Ok'ropir Ioane II	1045–1049
65.	Ek'vt'ime I	1049–1055
66.	Giorgi III	1055–1065
67.	Gabriel III	1065–1080

68.	Dimitri	1080–1090
69.	Basil III *Karichisdze*	1090–1100
70.	Ioane IV	1100–1142
71.	Svimeon IV *Gulaberidze*	1142–1146
72.	Saba II	1146–1150
73.	Nikoloz I *Gulaberidze*	1150–1178
74.	Mik'el IV	1178–1186
75.	T'eodore II	1186–1206
76.	Basili IV	1206–1208
77.	Ioane V	1208–1210
78.	Epip'ane	1210–1220
79.	Ek'vt'ime II	1220–1222
80.	Arsen III	1222–1225
81.	Giorgi IV	1225–1230
82.	Arsen IV	1230–1240
83.	Nikoloz II	1240–1280
84.	Abram I	1280–1310
85.	Ek'vt'ime III	1310–1325
86.	Mik'el V	1325–1330
87.	Basil V	1330–1350
88.	Dorot'eoz I	1350–1356
89.	Shio I	1356–1364
90.	Nikoloz III	1364–1380
91.	Giorgi V	1380–1397
92.	Eliozi	1399–1411
93.	Mik'el VI	1411–1426
94.	Davit' II *Bagrationi*	1426–1430
95.	T'eodore III	1430–1435
96.	Davit' III *Gobeladze*	1435–1439
97.	Shio II	1440–1443
	Davit' III [2nd time]	1443–1459
98.	Markozi	1460–1466
99.	Davit' IV	1466–1479
100.	Evagre	1480–1492
101.	Abram II *Abalaki*	1492–1497
102.	Ep'rem I	1497–1500
	Evagre [2nd time]	1500–1503
103.	Dorot'eos II	1503–1510
104.	Dionise	1510–1511
	Dorot'eos II [2nd time]	1511–1516
105.	Basil VI	1517–1528
106.	Malak'ia	1528–1538
107.	Melk'isedek II *Bagrationi*	1538–1541
108.	Germane	1541–1547
109.	Svimon V	1547–1550
110.	Zebede I	1550–1557

XXXIV. Church of Georgia

INTERREGNUM

111.	Nikoloz IV *Bagrationi*	1562–1584
112.	Nikoloz V *Bagrationi*	1584–1591
113.	Dorot'eoz III	1592–1599
114.	Domenti I	1599–1603
115.	Zebede II	1603–1610
116.	Ioane VI *Avaliashvili*	1610–1613

INTERREGNUM

117.	K'ristep'ore I	1616–1622
118.	Zak'aria *Jorjadze*	1623–1630
119.	Evdemoz I *Diasamidze*	1630–1637
120.	K'ristep'ore II *Amilak'ori*	1638–1660
121.	Domenti II *Bagrationi*	1660–1676
122.	Nikoloz VI *Amilak'ori*	1678–1688
123.	Ioane VII *Diasamidze*	1688–1691
	Nikoloz VI [2nd time]	1691–1696
	Ioane VII [2nd time]	1696–1700
124.	Evdemoz II *Diasamidze*	1701–1705
125.	Domenti III *Bagrationi*	1705–1725
126.	Besarioni *Orbeliani*	1725–1737
127.	Kirile II	1737–1739
	Domenti III [2nd time]	1739–1741
128.	Nikoloz VII *K'herk'evlidze*	1741–1744
129.	Anton I *Bagrationi*	1744–1755
130.	Iosebi *Jandieri*	1755–1764
	Anton I [2nd time]	1764–1788
131.	Anton II (Teymuraz) *Bagrationi*	1788–1811

CATHOLICATE SUBSUMED BY RUSSIA

RUSSIAN EXARCHS OF GEORGIA

1.	Varlaam *Eristavi*	1811–1817
2.	Feofilakt *Rusanov*	1817–1821
3.	Iona *Vasil'evskiĭ*	1821–1832
4.	Moiseĭ *Bogdanov-Platonov*	1832–1834
5.	Evgeniĭ *Baganov*	1834–1844
6.	Isidor *Nikolskiĭ*	1844–1858
7.	Evseviĭ *Ilinskiĭ*	1858–1877
8.	Ioannikiĭ *Rudnev* [#32 of Russia]	1877–1882
9.	Pavel *Lebedev*	1882–1887

10. Palladiĭ *Raev*	1887–1892
11. Vladimir *Bogoiavlens'kyĭ* [#81 of Ukraine]	1892–1898
12. Flavian *Gorodetskiĭ* [#6 of Poland; #80 of Ukraine]	1898–1901
13. Aleksiĭ I *Opotskiĭ*	1901–1905
14. Nikolaĭ *Nalimov* [#2 of Finland]	1905–1906
15. Nikon *Sofiĭskiĭ*	1906–1908
16. Innokentiĭ *Beliaev*	1909–1913
17. Aleksiĭ II *Mochanov*	1913–1914
18. Pitirim *Oknov*	1914–1915
19. Platon *Rozhdestvenskiĭ* [#9 of America]	1915–1917

Catholicos-Patriarchs of Georgia

Leonide *Okropiridze* [locum tenens]	1917
132. Kirion(i) III *Sadzaglishvili*	1917–1918
133. Leonide *Okropiridze*	1918–1921
134. Ambrosi *K'elaia*	1921–1927

Interregnum

Kalistrate *Tsintsadze* [locum tenens]	1923–1926
135. K'ristep'ore III *Tsitskishvili*	1927–1932
136. Kalistrate *Tsintsadze*	1932–1952
137. Melk'isedek III *Pk'aladze*	1952–1960
138. Ep'rem II *Sidamonidze* [cousin of #133]	1960–1972
139. Davit' V *Devdariani*	1972–1977
Ilia *Shiolashvili* [locum tenens]	1977
140. Ilia II *Shiolashvili*	1977–

The Georgian Church of Abkhazia (Imerati)

The independent Church of Abkhazia developed in the kingdom of the same name, and was extinguished with the Russian occupation in the late eighteenth and early nineteenth centuries. Records of the primates of this church are fragmentary. Both lists are adapted from the official records of the Patriarchate of Georgia at Tbilisi.

Catholicos-Patriarchs of Abkhazia

1. Nikoloz I	1290?
2. Danieli	1375?
3. Arseni	1390

XXXIV. Church of Georgia

4.	Ioane (or Ioakime)	1455–1474
5.	Step'ane	1470–1516

INTERREGNUM

6.	Malak'ia I *Abashidze*	1529–1532

INTERREGNUM

7.	Evdemoz I *Chk'etidze*	1557–1578
8.	Ek'vt'ime I *Sakvarelidze*	1578–1605

INTERREGNUM

9.	Grigol I	1612–1616?
10.	Malak'ia II *Gurieli*	1616–1639
11.	Mak'sime I *Machutadze*	1639–1657
12.	Besarioni I	1647–1656
13.	Nikifore	1657
14.	Zak'aria *K'variani*	1657–1659
15.	Svimon I *Chk'etidze*	1660–1666
16.	Svimon II	1665–1681
17.	Evdemoz II *Sakvarelidze*	1666–1669
18.	Ek'vt'ime II *Sakvarelidze*	1669–1673
19.	Davit'i *Nemsadze*	1673–1676
20.	Giorgi	1681?–
21.	Nikolozi II	1703–1710
22.	Grigoli II *Lortk'ifanidze*	1706–1742
23.	Germane *Tsulukidze*	1742–1754
24.	Besarioni II *Eristavi*	1755–1769
25.	Iosebi *Bagrationi*	1769–1776
26.	Mak'sime II *Abashidze*	1776–1795
27.	Dositeosi	1792–1814

CATHOLICOSATE SUBSUMED BY RUSSIA

XXXV.

Church of Greece

The history of the Orthodox Church of Greece is closely tied to the Greek War of Independence in the early nineteenth century. Many of the clergy had supported the revolutionaries, so it was natural that they should demand ecclesiastical reforms once independence had been won. At two national assemblies, in 1821 and 1829, they pressed the issue, and on 15 July 1833 King Othōn promulgated a charter of autocephaly. The Patriarch of Constantinople refused to acknowledge the break until 1850.

When subsequent events added territory to the kingdom, these areas were absorbed into the Church as well, making it among the largest national Orthodox churches in the world today in population. Beginning in 1917, the government followed a consistent pattern of interference in Church affairs, often deposing or appointing Archbishops virtually at will. Thus, following the military *coup d'état* of 1967, Chrysostomos II was forced to resign, and Hierōnymos took his place; the latter then resigned when the generals were overthrown in 1973, and Archbishop Serapheim took his place. The democratic government which assumed power in 1974 has left the Church in relative peace, and Serapheim enjoyed a stable reign, the longest of any Greek primate in the twentieth century. His successor, Archbishop Christodoulos, was elected in 1998.

The primate bears the title Archbishop of Athens and All Greece. The official Church language is Greek. Roughly nine million members are located primarily within the confines of the Greek Republic. Excluded from Church jurisdiction are Crete and the other islands of the eastern Aegean Sea, and the monasteries of Mount Athos, which fall under the aegis of the Ecumenical Patriarch.

Sources: *Dictionnaire d'Histoire et de Géographie Ecclésiastiques*; *Eastern Christianity and Politics in the Twentieth Century* (Ramet); *Échos d'Orient*; *Episkepsis*; *Episkopikoi Katalogoi Hellados* (Basileios); *Europa World Yearbook*; *Gegenwartslage der Ostkirchen* (Spuler); *Historia tēs Ekklēsias Hellados* (Papadopoulos); *History of the Church* (Jedin, ed.); *Jahrbuch der Orthodoxie* (Proc); *The Orthodox Church and Independent Greece, 1821–1852* (Frazee); *Orthodoxia*; official church website.

ARCHBISHOPS OF GREECE

1.	Dionysios I *Areopagitēs*	93?

XXXV. Church of Greece

2. Narkissos — 117–138
3. Pouplios (Publius) — 161–180
4. Kodratos (Quadratus) — 200?
5. Leōnidēs — 250?
6. Olympios — 300?
7. Pistos — 325?
8. Klēmatios — 400?
9. Modestos — 431?
10. Athanasios I — 451–458
11. Anatolios — 459?
12. Iōannēs I — 550?
13. Grēgorios I — 600?
14. Iōannēs II — 680?
15. Andreas — 692–693?
16. Theocharistos — 694–702
17. Marinos — 702–704
18. Iōannēs III — 704–714
19. Grēgorios II — 780?
20. Theodosios I — 800?
21. Adamantios — 810?
22. Iōannēs IV — 810–819
23. Theodosios II — 820?
24. Hypatios — 827?
25. Dēmētrios I — 835?
26. Germanos I — –841

Interregnum

27. Dēmētrios II — 846–857
28. Gabriēl I — 858–860
29. Grēgorios III — 860–867
30. Kosmas I — 867
31. Nikētas I — 867–877
32. Sabbas I — 877–880
33. Anastasios — 880–889
34. Sabbas II — 889–914
35. Geōrgios I — 914–922
36. Nikētas II — 922–927
37. Kōnstantinos — 965?
38. Philippos — 981?
39. Theodēgios — 985–1007
40. Michaēl I — 1007–1030
41. Leōn I *Synkellos* — 1054?–1061?
42. Leōn II *Synkellos* — 1061?–1069?
43. Iōannēs V *Blachernitēs* — 1069–1087
44. Nikētas III *Kourtēs* — 1086–1103

45.	Nikēphoros	1103–1121
46.	Gerasimos	1127?
47.	Michaēl II	1133?
48.	Theophylaktos	1140?
49.	Geōrgios II	1145–1160

INTERREGNUM

50.	Nikētas IV (or Nikolaos) *Hagiotheodōritēs*	1166–1175
51.	Geōrgios III *Xēros*	1175–1179
52.	Geōrgios IV *Bourtzēs*	1180
53.	Iōannēs VI	1180–1181
54.	Michaēl III *Akominatos Chōniatēs*	1182–1222

INTERREGNUM

55.	Meletios I	1275–1289
56.	Lazaros *apo Sina*	1300?
57.	Kosmas II	1339
58.	Anthimos I *Homologētēs* [#45 of Crete]	1339–1366
59.	Neophytos I	1366
60.	Nikodēmos	1371?
61.	name unknown	1380?
62.	Dōrotheos I	1387–1393?
63.	Makarios I	1394–1404
64.	Gerbasios I	1432?
65.	Theodōros	1438–1453?
66.	Isidōros	1456?
67.	Theophanēs I	1458?
68.	Gerbasios II	1462?
68.	name unknown	1465?–1466?
70.	Dōrotheos II	–1472
71.	Anthimos II	1489?
72.	Neophytos II	1492–1498

INTERREGNUM

73.	Laurentios	1528–1550
74.	Kallistos	1550–1564
75.	Sōphronios I	1565–1570
76.	Nikanōr	1570–1592
77.	Theophanēs II *Karykēs* [#183 of Constantinople]	1592–1597
78.	Neophytos III *Karykēs* [#185 of Constantinople]	1597–1602
79.	Samouēl *Primpetos*	1602

XXXV. Church of Greece

80.	Nathanaēl *Emporos*	1602–1604
81.	Anthimos III *apo Naupliou kai Argous*	1604–1610
82.	Kyrillos I	–1611
83.	Mētrophanēs	–1619
84.	Theophanēs III	1620–1633
85.	Sōphronios II	1633–1636
86.	Daniēl *apo Talantiou*	1636–1655
87.	Anthimos IV *apo Talantiou*	1655–1676
88.	Iakōbos I *apo Mytilēnēs*	1676–1686
89.	Athanasios II	1686–1689
90.	Makarios II *Pelekanos*	1689–1693
91.	Anthimos V	1693–1699
92.	Kyrillos II	1699–1703
93.	Meletios II *Mētrou apo Naupaktou kai Artēs*	1703–1713
94.	Iakōbos II	1713–1734
95.	Zacharias	1734–1741
96.	Anthimos VI	1741–1756
97.	Athanasios III	1756–1760
	Anthimos VI [2nd time]	1760–1764
98.	Bartholomaios *apo Drystras*	1764–1780
99.	Neophytos IV	1774–1776
100.	Gabriēl II	1781
101.	Benediktos *apo Pisidias*	1781–1785
102.	Athanasios IV *Taklikartēs* (or *T[s]alikarēs*)	1785–1787
	Benediktos [2nd time]	1787–1796
	Athanasios IV [2nd time]	1796–1799
103.	Grēgorios IV	1799–1820
104.	Dionysios II	1820–1823
105.	Grēgorios V *Argyrokastritēs apo Euripou*	1827–1828

Interregnum

106.	Anthimos VII *apo Artēs*	1828–1830

Interregnum

107.	Neophytos V *Metaxas apo Talantiou*	1833–1861
108.	Misaēl *Apostolidēs*	1862
109.	Theophilos *Blachopapadopoulos*	1862–1873
110.	Prokopios I *Geōrgiadēs*	1874–1889
111.	Germanos II *Kalligas*	1889–1896
112.	Prokopios II *Oikonomidēs*	1896–1901
113.	Theoklētos I *Mēnopoulos*	1902–1917
114.	Meletios III *Metaxakēs* [#111 of Alexandria; #262 of Constantinople]	1918–1920

	Theoklētos I *Mēnopoulos* [2nd time]	1920–1922
115.	Chrysostomos I *Papadopoulos*	1923–1938
116.	Damaskēnos *Papandreou*	1938
117.	Chrysanthos *Philippidēs*	1938–1941
	Damaskēnos *Papandreou* [2nd time]	1941–1949
118.	Spyridōn *Blachos*	1949–1956
119.	Dōrotheos III *Kottaras*	1956–1957
120.	Theoklētos II *Panagiōtopoulos*	1957–1962
121.	Iakōbos III *Babanatsos*	1962
122.	Chrysostomos II *Chatzēstaurou*	1962–1967
123.	Hierōnymos *Kotsōnēs*	1967–1973
124.	Serapheim *Tikas*	1974–1998
125.	Christodoulos *Paraskevaïdēs*	1998–

OLD CALENDARISTS OF GREECE

In 1924 Greek Archbishop Chrysostomos I introduced a reform of the calendar into his Church, switching from the Julian calendar (now badly out of date) to the Gregorian calendar. The latter was regarded by some local parish priests as a tool of the papacy, and they rebelled against using it. In 1935 three Greek bishops joined the Old Calendarist movement, and began organized the first rival synod to the Archbishop of the Greek Orthodox Church, under the leadership of Metropolitan Chrysostomos of Florina. A second, much smaller group developed two years later under Metropolitan Germanos, and has continued to this date, operating under the name, the True Orthodox Church of Greece.

Although many of the rebel bishops later returned to the mainline Church, Florina continued to develop a separate Church structure until his death in 1955, when the major Old Calendar Church body suddenly found itself without any bishops. A new hierarchy was constituted in the early 1960s, thanks to the intervention of the Russian Orthodox Church Outside Russia. In the 1970s and '80s, however, the Church began following an all-too-familiar pattern in Orthodoxy, splintering itself among a number of rival synods.

The successor Synod to that of Chrysostomos of Florina remains the governing body of the largest group of Greek Orthodox Old Calendarists, following closely by that of Metropolitan Kyprianos. The size of these churches is exceedingly difficult to determine. Only the larger structures and major leaders of these factions have been listed below. The overlap in dates indicates the splitting of synods.

Sources: official church websites.

METROPOLITANS OF THE OLD CALENDARIST ORTHODOX CHURCHES OF GREECE

1.	Chrysostomos I *of Florina*	1935–1955

XXXV. Church of Greece

INTERREGNUM

2.	Akakios	1962–1963
3.	Auxentios	1963–1994
4.	Chrysostomos II	1985–
5.	Kyprianos	1986–

ARCHBISHOPS OF THE TRUE ORTHODOX CHURCH OF GREECE

	Germanos (I) [locum tenens]	1935–1937
	Germanos (II) *Barykopoulos* [locum tenens]	1937–1943
	Matthaios [locum tenens]	1943–1949
1.	Matthaios [as archbishop]	1949–1950
	Dēmētrios [locum tenens]	1950–1958
2.	Agathangelos	1958–1972
3.	Andreas	1972–

XXXVI.

Churches of India

The St. Thomas Christians are located primarily in Kerala, along the southwest coast of India. According to legend, some of the natives were converted by St. Thomas the Apostle in the decades following the death of Christ; real historical evidence is scarce, however, until the coming of European missionaries in the sixteenth century, when a flourishing Eastern Church was found. The existing communities were governed by bishops appointed by the Catholicos-Patriarch of Assyria (East Syria); when Roman Catholic missionaries began making inroads into the established churches, some of the local parishes, feeling that strong local leadership was needed to resist this threat, revolted against their Patriarch, and on 22 May 1643 consecrated one of their archdeacons as Metropolitan, under the title Mar Thoma I. Thus begins the independent existence of the Syrian churches of Malabar.

From the first the churches were plagued by schisms and disputes, a trend which continues to this day. Succession was often hereditary, from brother to brother or uncle to nephew; thus, Mar Thoma I was followed by his brother, Mar Thoma II, also a member of the Pakalomarram family. Since the original Mar Thoma was consecrated only by a laying-on of hands, and not by two other bishops, his successors have striven through the centuries to obtain recognition either from Rome or from the West Syrian Patriarch of Antioch.

Mar Thoma VI approached both Churches, offering to join either if new bishops were sent to India; the Jacobite Patriarch was the first to respond, sending three prelates in the late 1760s; Mar Thoma was reconsecrated in 1772, taking the new name of Dionysios I. Consecrated with him was Mar Koorilose, whom Dionysios feared as a potential rival. He promptly exiled Koorilose to Thozhiyoor (Toliyur), where the latter founded the first of the splinter churches, which has continued to this day; it remains the smallest of the Malabar Orthodox groups. Curiously, the Church of Toliyur eventually developed during the nineteenth century a kind of symbiotic relationship with the Mar Thoma family, each line providing properly-consecrated bishops for the other when their respective sees fell vacant.

By the mid-nineteenth century, dissidents in the Mar Thoma Church had begun pressing for reforms in the liturgy and clergy. They placed their hopes on Mathews Mar Athanasios, who was consecrated bishop by the West Syrian patriarch in 1843. After a period of struggle, Mar Dionysios IV was forced to retire, and Mar Athanasios was recognized as sole Metropolitan of the Malabar Church.

But a dissident priest, Joseph, was consecrated as Mar Dionysios V in 1865, causing a new split, each Metropolitan claiming to be the rightful heir to the church properties. Ultimately, the secular courts of Travancore State ruled in favor of Athanasios. This did not end the controversy, however, for Dionysios then appealed to the Syrian patriarch, Ighnatiyus Butrus IV, to adjudicate the argument in person; this he did in 1875, excommunicating Athanasios and proclaiming Dionysios the only true leader of the Malabar Church. The result of these difficulties was the increasing polarization of the Malankara communities, a further split in the churches, and the establishment of an unfortunate precedent whereby ecclesiastical disputes would now be settled by the temporal authorities.

The price of Dionysios's recognition as head of the Syrian Church in Malabar was his acknowledgement of the supremacy of the West Syrian patriarch, whose aid he had sought. When Dionysios V died in 1909, the Syrian Patriarch consecrated Geevarghese Dionysios VI in his place. Later that year the new Syrian Patriarch (Ighnatiyus 'Abd Allah II), came to India, where he became embroiled in a jurisdictional dispute with his supposed agent. 'Abd Allah excommunicated Dionysios in 1911, and appointed Mar Koorilose the new Metropolitan. Dionysios refused to accept the Patriarch's actions, and each side again went to court.

The matter was further complicated by the arrival in 1912 of the deposed Syrian Patriarch, Ighnatiyus 'Abd al-Masih II, who immediately consecrated Paulose Mar Ivanios as Catholicos of Malankara, thus in effect creating (with the best of intentions) a third church. When Dionysios died in 1934, the Catholicos was named his successor, thereby reducing the churches to two factions, one supporting the Syrian Patriarch, one claiming ecclesiastical independence.

The split was finally healed in 1958, and reinforced with the installation of Baselios Mar Augen I as Catholicos in 1964; Syrian Patriarch Ighnatiyus Afram I travelled to India to participate in the ceremony. Ten years later, the dispute flared anew, with Augen claiming equality with his Syrian counterpart. Augen was suspended by Afram from his ecclesiastical functions, an action Augen angrily refused to recognize. Augen died at an advanced age a few months later in 1975. At his death, the Syrian Patriarch appointed Paulose Mar Philoksenos the new Catholicos, even though Mathews Mar Athanasios had already been named Augen's designated successor. Once more the churches went to court.

The autocephalous Malankara Orthodox Syrian Church is located at Kottayam, Kerala; its primate uses the title Catholicos of Malankara. Approximately 1.6 million communicants are located primarily in southwestern India, with a few members overseas (mostly in the United States).

The autonomous Malankara Jacobite Syrian Church is located at Moovattupuzha, Kerala; its primate bears the title Catholicos Metropolitan of Malabar, and acknowledges the supremacy of the Syrian Patriarch of Antioch, to which it contributes 1.5 million of that church's communicants.

Sources: *Catholicate Sapthathi Souvenir*; *Eastern Christianity in India* (Tisserant); *Eastern Churches Review*; *Gegenwartslage der Ostkirchen* (Spuler); *History of the Church* (Jedin, ed.); *The Indian Christians of St Thomas* (Brown); *The Malabar Church and Other Orthodox Churches* (Daniel); *The Orthodox Church of India* (Daniel); *Orthodoxia*; *Profiles in Belief* (Piepkorn); *The St. Thomas Christian Encyclopedia of India* (Menachery); *The Syrian Christians of Kerala* (Pothan); *The Syrian Church of Malabar* (Daniel); *Die Syrischen Kirchen in Indien* (Verghese); *The Thomas Christians* (Podipara); Bishop Thomas Mar Makarios (personal communication); official church websites.

METRANS OF THE MALANKARA SYRIAN CHURCH
(Bishops 1665 and 1772, Metrans 1876)

1.	Mar Thoma I *Pakalomarram*	1652–1670
	Mar Gregorios (I)	1665–1672
2.	Mar Thoma II [nephew of #1]	1670–1686
	Mar Thoma	1674
	Mar Baselios (I)	1685
	Mar Yuhanna	1685–1693
3.	Mar Thoma III	1686–1688
4.	Mar Thoma IV	1688–1728
5.	Mar Thoma V	1728–1765
	Mar Baselios (II)	1751–1763
	Mar Gregorios (II)	1751–1772
	Mar Ivanios	1751–1794
6.	Mar Thoma VI [suffragan 1761; nephew of #5]	1765–1772
	[under the title Mar Dionysios I]:	1772–1808
7.	Mathew Mar Thoma VII [suffragan 1796; nephew of #6]	1808–1809
8.	Mar Thoma VIII [suffragan 1806]	1809–1816
9.	Pulikkottil Mar Dionysios II	1815–1816
10.	Mar Thoma IX [uncle of #8]	1816
11.	Geevarghese Mar Phileksinose [#4 of Thozhiyoor]	1816–1817
12.	Punnathra Mar Dionysios III *Ittoop*	1817–1825
	Geevarghese Mar Phileksinose [2nd time]	1825–1829
13.	Cheepat Mar Dionysios IV *Kattanar*	1829–1852
14.	Yoyakin Mar Koorilose (or Yoakim) [rival]	1846–1852
15.	Mathews Mar Athanasios *Palakunnath* [suffragan 1842; #1 of Mar Thoma]	1852–1875
16.	Joseph Mar Dionysios V *Putikkottil*	1865–1909
17.	Geevarghese Mar Dionysios VI *Vattasseril* [suffragan 1908]	1909–1934

MERGED WITH THE MALANKARA ORTHODOX SYRIAN CHURCH

MAPHRIANS AND CATHOLICOSES OF THE EAST
(UNDER SYRIAN ORTHODOX CHURCH)

1.	Thomas I [#2 of Assyria]	35–72

XXXV. Churches of India

2.	Addai [#4 of Assyria]	72–120
3.	Aggai [#5 of Assyria]	120–152
4.	Mari [#6 of Assyria]	152–185
5.	Abrosios [#7 of Assyria]	185–201
6.	Abraham I [#8 of Assyria]	201–213
7.	Yakoub [#9 of Assyria]	213–231
8.	Ahod Abuci [#10 of Assyria]	231–246
9.	Shahluppa [#12 of Assyria]	246–266
10.	Pappa [#13 of Assyria]	267–336
11.	Simun I *Bar Sheba* [#14 of Assyria]	337–350
12.	Shahoudoth [#15 of Assyria]	350–352
13.	Bar Bosomin [#16 of Assyria]	352–360
14.	Thomuso [#17 of Assyria]	360–368
15.	Quoyumo [#18 of Assyria]	370–375
16.	Ishaq [#19 of Assyria]	375–386
17.	Oah [#20 of Assyria]	386–393
18.	Yahb Allaho [#21 of Assyria]	393–398
19.	Magina [#22 of Assyria]	398–400
20.	Merbukhat [#23 of Assyria]	401–420
21.	Daudesh [#24 of Assyria]	421–456
22.	Babuyah [#25 of Assyria]	457–484
23.	Acasios [#26 of Assyria]	485–498
24.	Babi [#27 of Assyria]	499–502
25.	Shilo [#28 of Assyria]	502–504
26.	Elisho [#30 of Assyria]	504–536
27.	Paulose I [#31 of Assyria]	537–539
28.	Aabo [#32 of Assyria]	540–552
29.	Joseph I [#33 of Assyria]	552–556

INTERREGNUM

30.	Ahoudemme	559–577
31.	Qoum Yesu	578–579

INTERREGNUM

32.	Samuel	614–624

INTERREGNUM

33.	Morooso	628–649
34.	Denha I	650–659

INTERREGNUM

35.	Bar Yesu	669–684

36.	Abraham II	686–687
37.	David	687
38.	Youhanon I *Soubo*	687–688
39.	Denha II	688–728
40.	Paulose II	728–757
41.	Youhanon II *Keeyunoyo*	758–788
42.	Joseph II	789–793
43.	Sharbeel	794–810
44.	Simun II	812–828
45.	Baselios I *Bar Baldoyo*	828–838
46.	Daniel	838–847
47.	Thoma II *of Tigris*	848–856
48.	Lo Asar	856–869

INTERREGNUM

49.	Sargis	872–883

INTERREGNUM

50.	Athanasios I	887–904

INTERREGNUM

51.	Thoma III *Asthunoro*	912–913
52.	Denha III	915–935

INTERREGNUM

53.	Baselios II	938–962
54.	Kooriakose	964–982

INTERREGNUM

55.	Youhanan III *Damascus*	991–997
56.	Ignatios I *Barkiki*	997–1022

INTERREGNUM

57.	Athanasios II *of Edessa*	1027–1041

INTERREGNUM

58.	Baselios III *of Tigris*	1046–1069

XXXV. Churches of India

INTERREGNUM

59.	Youhanan IV *Sleeba*	1075–1106

INTERREGNUM

60.	Dionysios I *Moosa*	1112–1142
61.	Ignatios II *Lo Asar*	1143–1164
62.	Youhanan V *Srugayo*	1165–1188
63.	Dionysios II *Bar Msah*	1188–1204
64.	Gregorios I *Yakoub*	1204–1215
65.	Ignatios III *David* [#82 of Syrian Orthodox of Antioch]	1215–1222
66.	Dionysios III *Sleeba*	1222–1231
67.	Youhanan VI *Bar Madan* [# 83 of Syrian Orthodox of Antioch]	1232–1253
68.	Ignatios IV *Sleeba of Edessa*	1253–1258

INTERREGNUM

69.	Gregorios II *Bar Hebraeus*	1266–1286

INTERREGNUM

70.	Gregorios III *Bar Sauma*	1289–1308

INTERREGNUM

71.	Gregorios IV *Mathai*	1317–1360

INTERREGNUM

72.	Athanasios Mar Abraham III	1365–1379

INTERREGNUM

73.	Baselios Mar Bahnam I [#91 of Syrian Orthodox of Antioch]	1404–1412

INTERREGNUM

74.	Dioscoros Mar Bahnam II	1415–1417

INTERREGNUM

75.	Baselios Mar Barsauma	1422–1455

INTERREGNUM

76.	Baselios Mar Asiz	1471–1487

INTERREGNUM

77.	Ignatios Mar Nuh *of Homs* [#94 of Syrian Orthodox Church of Antioch]	1490–1494
78.	Baselios Mar Abraham IV	1494–1496

INTERREGNUM

79.	Baselios IV	1560–1589

INTERREGNUM

80.	Baselios Mar Yalda	1634–1685

INTERREGNUM

81.	Baselios Mar Shakrulla	1751–1764

INTERREGNUM

82.	Baselios Mar Elias [#114 of Syrian Orthodox of Antioch]	1838–1840

INTERREGNUM

83.	Baselios Mar Bahnam III	1850–1860

OFFICE ABOLISHED BY SYNOD IN 1860

CATHOLICOSES OF THE EAST AND MALANKARA METROPOLITANS OF THE MALANKARA ORTHODOX SYRIAN CHURCH ("CATHOLICOS FACTION")

84.	Baselios Mar Paulose *Kathanar*	1912–1913

XXXV. Churches of India

Interregnum

	Geevarghese Mar Dionysios VI [locum tenens]	1913–1925
85.	Baselios Mar Geevarghese I *Karuchira*	1925–1928
	Geevarghese Mar Dionysios VI [locum tenens]	1928–1929
86.	Baselios Mar Geevarghese II *Kallacheril*	1929–1964
	Alexios Mar Theodosios [suffragan]	1934–1962
87.	Baselios Mar Augen (or Ougen) *Turuthi* [suffragan 1962]	1964–1975
88.	Baselios Mar Thoma Mathews I *Vattakunnel* [suffragan 1970]	1975–1991
89.	Baselios Mar Thoma Mathews II [suffragan 1980]	1991–
	Thomas Mar Timotheos [suffragan 1992]	

Maphrians and Catholicoses of the East
(Under the Syrian "Jacobite" Church of Antioch)
(Metropolitans of Seleucia 285, Catholicoses of Seleucia 399, Great Metropolitans of the East 559, Maphrians of the East 629)

1.	Papa bar Aggai [#13 of Assyria]	285–326?
2.	Shimun bar Sabbae [#14 of Assyria]	326?–344
3.	Shahdost [#15 of Assyria]	344–345
4.	Barbashmin [#16 of Assyria]	345–346
5.	Thomooso [#17 of Assyria]	364?–372?
6.	Qayuma [#18 of Assyria]	372?–380

Interregnum

7.	Ishaq I [#19 of Assyria]	399–410?
8.	Ahai [#20 of Assyria]	410?–414?
9.	Yaballaha [#21 of Assyria]	414?–420
10.	Mana [#22 of Assyria]	420
11.	Dadyeshu [#24 of Assyria]	421–450
12.	Babowai [#25 of Assyria]	450–484

Interregnum

13.	Ahudemeh	559–575

Interregnum

14.	Khameeso	578–609

INTERREGNUM

15. Samuel   614–624

INTERREGNUM

16. Marutha   629–649
17. Denha I   649–659

INTERREGNUM

18. Easo   669–683
19. Abraham I   685–686
20. David I   686
21. Yuhannan I   686–688
22. Denha II   688–728
23. Paulose I   728–757
24. Yuhannan II   758–785
25. Joseph   785–786

INTERREGNUM

26. Sarbiel   794–810
27. Shemavun   811–
28. Baselios I   –830
29. Daniel   829–834
30. Thoma I   834–847
31. Baselios II   848–868
32. Malkeesadek   857–869

INTERREGNUM

33. Sargis   872–883

INTERREGNUM

34. Athanasius I   887–903

INTERREGNUM

35. Thoma II   910–911
36. Denha III   912–932

INTERREGNUM

37. Baselios III   936–960

XXXV. Churches of India

38.	Kuriakose	962–979
39.	Yuhannan III	980?–988

INTERREGNUM

40.	Ignatius bar Keekke	991–1016

INTERREGNUM

41.	Athanasius II *of Edessa*	1027–1041

INTERREGNUM

42.	Baselios IV *of Tigrith*	1046–1069

INTERREGNUM

43.	Yuhannan Sleeba I	1075–1106

INTERREGNUM

44.	Dionysius Mosa	1112–1134

INTERREGNUM

45.	Ignatius Lazar I	1142?–1164
46.	Yuhannan Sarugoyo	1164–1188
	Dionysius [anti-maphrian]	1189–1203
47.	Gregorios Yakub	1189–1214
48.	Ignatius David II [#82 of Syrian Orthodox of Antioch]	1215–1222
49.	Dionysius Sleeba II	1222–1231
50.	Yuhannan bar Ma'dani [#83 of Syrian Orthodox of Antioch]	1232–1252
51.	Ignatius Sleeba III	1252–1258

INTERREGNUM

52.	Gregorios bar Ebrayo	1264–1286
53.	Gregorios bar Souma [brother of #52]	1288–1308

INTERREGNUM

54.	Gregorios Mathai I	1317–1345
	Gregorios bar Kainaya [anti-maphrian]	1361?

55.	Athanasius Abraham II	1364–1379

INTERREGNUM

56.	Baselios Behnam I *al-Hadli* [#91 of Syrian Orthodox of Antioch]	1404–1412

INTERREGNUM

57.	Behnam II Araboyo	1415–1417

INTERREGNUM

58.	Bar Souma Moudyano	1422–1455

INTERREGNUM

59.	Baselios Azeez	1471–1487
60.	Nuh *the Lebanese* [#94 of Syrian Orthodox of Antioch]	1489–1493

INTERREGNUM

61.	Abraham III	1496–1508
62.	Baselios Elias I	–1523

INTERREGNUM

63.	Athanasius Habeeb I	1528–1533
64.	Baselios Elias II	1533–1552

INTERREGNUM

65.	Baselios Nemet Allah [#99 of Syrian Orthodox of Antioch]	1555–1557
66.	Baselios Abd al-Ghani I	1557–1575
67.	Baselios David Shah *ibn Nur 'Adin* [#100 of Syrian Orthodox of Antioch]	1575–1576
68.	Baselios Philathose [#101 of Syrian Orthodox of Antioch]	1576–1591
69.	Baselios Abd al-Ghani II	1591–1597
70.	Pathros Hadaya [#102 of Syrian Orthodox of Antioch]	1597

XXXV. Churches of India

INTERREGNUM

71.	Baselios Isaya	1626

INTERREGNUM

72.	Baselios Sakralla I	1639–1652

INTERREGNUM

73.	Baselios Abd al-Masih [#105 of Syrian Orthodox of Antioch]	1655–1662

INTERREGNUM

74.	Baselios Habeeb II	1665–1674
75.	Baselios Geevarghese I [#106 of Syrian Orthodox of Antioch]	1674–1687
76.	Baselios Yeldho	1678–1685
77.	Baselios Ishaq II [#107 of Syrian Orthodox of Antioch]	1687–1709
78.	Baselios Mathai II	1709

INTERREGNUM

79.	Baselios Lazar II	1713
80.	Baselios Mathai III	1714–
81.	Baselios Sakralla II [#108 of Syrian Orthodox of Antioch]	–1722

INTERREGNUM

82.	Gregorios Lazar III	1730–1742

INTERREGNUM

83.	Baselios Sakralla III	1748–1764
84.	Baselios Geevarghese II [#110 of Syrian Orthodox of Antioch]	1760–1768

INTERREGNUM

85.	Baselios Sleeba IV	1773–

86.	Baselios Bishara	1782–1811
87.	Baselios Yavanan	1803
88.	Baselios Kurillos *Abd al-Azeez*	1811–1816

INTERREGNUM

89.	Baselios Mathew IV	1820

INTERREGNUM

90.	Baselios Elias III	1825–1827
91.	Baselios Elias IV [#114 of Syrian Orthodox of Antioch]	1827–1838

INTERREGNUM

92.	Baselios Behnam III	1852–1859

OFFICE ABOLISHED BY SYNOD IN 1860

METROPOLITANS OF THE MALANKARA JACOBITE SYRIAN CHURCH

1.	Paulose Mar Koorilose	1911–1917

INTERREGNUM

	Paulose Mar Athanasios [locum tenens]	1918–1935
2.	Paulose Mar Athanasios	1935–1953

INTERREGNUM

3.	Abraham Mar Climis	1957–1958
4.	Baselios Mar Geevarghese *Kallacheril*	1958–1964

CATHOLICOS METROPOLITANS OF THE MALANKARA JACOBITE SYRIAN CHURCH ("PATRIARCH FACTION")
(UNDER THE SYRIAN CHURCH OF ANTIOCH)

93.	Baselios Mar Augen *Turuthi*	1964–1975
94.	Baselios Mar Paulose II	1975–1996
	Gregorios Mar Geevarghese [locum tenens]	1996–1999

	Dionysios/Divannasios Mar Thomas [locum tenens]	1999–2002
95.	Baselios Mar Thomas I	2002–

MALANKARA MAR THOMA SYRIAN CHURCH

On the death of Mathews Mar Athanasios, Metran of the Malankara Syrian Church, in 1877, he was succeeded by Thomas Mar Athanasios, who lost control over most of his parishes and church buildings in a series of lawsuits filed during his sixteen-year reign by rival Metran Dionysios V. Subsequently, his movement was renamed the Malankara Mar Thoma Syrian Church, and gradually absorbed elements of both Anglicanism and evangelism, as new parishes were established and reforms effected. It remains today the most Protestant of all the Malabar Syrian churches.

At the death or resignation of the primate, the most senior bishop automatically succeeds. The official language of the Church (and of its brother churches) is Malayalam. The primate, who since Titos I has always taken the additional surname Mar Thoma, bears the title Metropolitan (Metran), and resides at Tiruvalla, Kerala. Roughly 700,000 communicants are located mostly in southwestern India.

Sources: *Eastern Christianity in India* (Tisserant); *Europa World Yearbook*; *History of the Church* (Jedin, ed.); *The Indian Christians of St Thomas* (Brown); *The Malabar Church and Other Orthodox Churches* (Daniel); *The Malabar Independent Syrian Church* (Fenwick); *The Orthodox Church of India* (Daniel); *The St. Thomas Christian Encyclopedia of India*; *The Syrian Church of Malabar* (Daniel); official church website.

METRANS OF THE MAR THOMA SYRIAN CHURCH

1.	Mathews Mar Athanasios *Palakunnath* [#16 of Malankara]	1843–1877
2.	Thomas Mar Athanasios [suffragan 1868; cousin of #1]	1877–1893
3.	Titos I *Mar Thoma*	1894–1910
4.	Titos II *Mar Thoma* [suffragan 1899]	1910–1944
5.	Abraham *Mar Thoma* [suffragan 1917]	1944–1947
6.	Juhanon *Mar Thoma* [suffragan 1937]	1947–1976
7.	Aleksander *Mar Thoma* [suffragan 1954]	1976–1999
8.	Philipose Mar Chrysostom *Mar Thoma* Thomas Mar Athanasios [suffragan 1982] Joseph Mar Irenaeus [suffragan]	1999–

CHALDEAN SYRIAN (MELLUSIAN) CHURCH
(UNDER THE JURISDICTION OF THE CHURCH OF THE EAST)

The Chaldean Syrian Church, which patterns some of its liturgy after the Assyrian (East Syrian) Church, originally acknowledged the supremacy of the Catholic Chaldean Patriarchate of Babylon. The church switched allegiance to the Church of the East in the 1890s, when Mar Abdisho made himself an autonomous Metropolitan. Mar Thoma Darmo, who had for years opposed the principle of heredity succession used by the Assyrian Church, was elected Patriarch of an anti–Shim'un faction in 1968; his successor in India, Mar Aprem, continued to acknowledge Darmo's church as paramount until 1995, when he reunited his church with that of Mar Dinkha IV. The church's headquarters are located at Trichur, Kerala, where most of the church's 15,000 communicants reside.

Sources: *Eastern Christianity in India* (Tisserant); *History of the Church* (Jedin, ed.); *The Indian Christians of St Thomas* (Brown); *The Malabar Church and Other Orthodox Churches* (Daniel); *The Orthodox Church of India* (Daniel); *The St. Thomas Christian Encyclopedia of India*; *The Syrian Church of Malabar* (Daniel); Mar Aprem (private communication).

Metropolitans of the Chaldean Syrian Church

1.	Yusip I *of Edessa*	345?
2.	T'uma I	795?–824?
3.	Sabrishu'	880?
4.	Piruz	880?
5.	Yukhannan I	1000?
6.	T'uma II	1056?
7.	Yukhannan II	1110?
8.	Yukhannan III	1122?–1129?
9.	Yusip II	1231
10.	Da'ud	1285?
11.	Pulus	1295?
12.	Ya'qub I	1328?
13.	Yabhalaha I	1407?
14.	T'uma III	1490?
15.	Yukhannan IV	1490?
16.	Yabhalaha II	1503?
17.	Dinkha	1503?
18.	Ya'qub II	1503–1549?
19.	Yusip III	1556–1569
20.	Abraham	1568–1597

Interregnum

21.	Mar Thoma (IV) *Rocos*	1861–1862
22.	Mar Abdisho *Thondanatta*	1864–1874
23.	Mar Yohannon (V) Elia *Mellus*	1874–1882
	Mar Abdisho *Thondanatta* [2nd time]	1882–1900
	Mar Michael Augustine [locum tenens]	1900–1911

XXXV. Churches of India

INTERREGNUM

24. Mar Abimaleck Timotheus 1908–1945

INTERREGNUM

Poulos *Konikara* [locum tenens] 1945–1952
25. Mar Thoma (V) *Darmo* [#1 of Church of the East] 1952–1968
26. Mar Aprem 1968–1995

MERGED WITH THE ASSYRIAN CHURCH 1995

MALABAR INDEPENDENT SYRIAN CHURCH OF THOZHIYOOR (TOLIYUR)

The small Independent Syrian Church of Thozhiyoor was founded by Mar Koorilose, who fled the jurisdiction of Mar Dionysios I in 1772, and established a small independent church body. Since the Church can usually support only one or two bishops at a time, when the Metropolitan dies or resigns, the new primate is elected by representatives of each of the congregations from a list of eligible priests, and the candidate is then consecrated by the Metran of the Malankara Mar Thoma Syrian Church.

As is often the case with the other Keralan churches, a successor may be chosen before the death of the previous occupant of the Metropolitan office, and consecrated by both the old Metropolitan and the Metran; two of these suffragans did not live long enough to become undisputed Metropolitan. In 1977 Paulose Mar Phileksinose III joined the Catholic Church, resigning without leaving a successor, and taking some of his communicants with him; the remaining members of the Church then elected a new successor. The primate bears the title of Metropolitan of Thozhiyoor, his chief see. The Church is the smallest of the Kerala dioceses, with roughly 10,000 communicants. The official language of the Church is Malayalam.

Sources: *Eastern Christianity in India* (Tisserant); *History of the Church* (Jedin, ed.); *The Indian Christians of St Thomas* (Brown); *The Malabar Church and Other Orthodox Churches* (Daniel); *The Malabar Independent Syrian Church* (Fenwick; regarded as official by the Church); *The Orthodox Church of India* (Daniel); *The St. Thomas Christian Encyclopedia of India*; *The Syrian Church of Malabar* (Daniel); official church website.

METROPOLITANS OF THE MALABAR INDEPENDENT SYRIAN CHURCH OF THOZHIYOOR

1. Abraham Mar Koorilose I *Kattumangat* 1771–1802
2. Geevarghese Mar Koorilose II [brother of #1; suffragan 1794] 1802–1808

	Joseph Mar Ivanios *Kasseesa* [suffragan]	1807
3.	Skaria Mar Phileksinose I *Kasseesa* [suffragan 1807]	1808–1811
4.	Geevarghese Mar Phileksinose II [#11 of Malankara Syrian Church]	1811–1829
5.	Geevarghese Mar Koorilose III *Koothoor*	1829–1856
6.	Joseph Mar Koorilose IV *Kasseesa*	1856–1888
7.	Joseph Mar Athanasios I [suffragan 1883]	1888–1898
8.	Geevarghese Mar Koorilose V *Pulikottil* [suffragan 1892]	1898–1935
	Paulose Mar Athanasios II *Panakal* [suffragan]	1917–1927
9.	Kooriakose Mar Koorilose VI	1936–1947
10.	Geevarghese Mar Koorilose VII *Kasseesa*	1948–1967
11.	Paulose Mar Phileksinose III [suffragan 1967]	1967–1977
12.	Mathews Mar Koorilose VIII	1978–1986
13.	Joseph Mar Koorilose IX *Panakal* [suffragan 1981]	1986–

XXXVII.

Church of Japan

The autonomous Church of Japan was an adjunct for many years of the Patriarchate of Moscow and All Russia, Nikolaï Kassatkin having been consecrated as the first Bishop in 1880. He was advanced in rank to Metropolitan in 1906.

On the outbreak of World War II, the Japanese government insisted that the Russians leave Japan, and that an independent Japanese primate, Nikolaï Ono, be elected to administer the Church. After the war, the Church split into two factions, one supported by the Russian patriarchate, the other by the former Russian Archdiocese of North America. Both churches were given independence by the Russian Patriarch on the same day in 1970, and merged into one small Church; the Russian-consecrated Bishop returned to the Soviet Union. This grant of autonomy has not been recognized by any other Orthodox church save the Orthodox Church in America.

The autonomous Japanese Church remains too small to consecrate its own primates, relying on the Russian Orthodox Church to provide those services. Native-born Archbishop Theodosius Nagashima assumed authority over the Church on 19 March 1972; he died in 1999, and was temporarily replaced (in the absence of any other higher clergy) by a Russian-appointed Bishop. Archpriest Peter Arihara was elected the new Archbishop in 2000, but had to resign when he became terminally ill; he was replaced by another Japanese archpriest, Archbishop Daniel Nashiro.

The primate bears the title Archbishop of Tokyo, Primate and Metropolitan of All Japan. The official language of the Church is Japanese. Roughly 25,000 communicants are spread throughout Japan, heavily concentrated in the major cities.

Sources: *Europa World Yearbook*; *Gegenwartslage der Ostkirchen* (Spuler); *History of the Church* (Jedin, ed.); "Holy Orthodox Church" (Onami); *Jahrbuch der Orthodoxie* (Proc); *Orthodoxia*; official church website.

METROPOLITAN ARCHBISHOPS OF JAPAN
(Bishops 1880, Metropolitans 1906, Archbishops 1947, Metropolitans 1970)

1.	Nikolaï I *Kassatkin*	1880–1912
2.	Sergiï *Tykhomirov*	1912–1940

Japanese/Russian Jurisdiction

	Arsen *Tsakawa* [locum tenens]	1940–1941
3.	Nikolaĭ II *Ono*	1941–1967?
4.	Nikolaĭ III *Sayama*	1967–1970

Merged with the Autonomous Church

American Jurisdiction

3.	Benjamin *Basalyga*	1946–1952
4.	Ireney *Bekish* [#14 of America]	1953–1960
5.	Nikon *de Greve*	1960–1962
6.	Amvrosiĭ	1962
7.	Vladimir *Nagoskiĭ*	1962–1972

Autonomous Holy Orthodox Church

8.	Theodosius *Nagashima*	1972–1999
	Innokentiĭ *Vasil'ev* [locum tenens]	1999–2000
	Peter *Arihara* [unconsecrated]	2000
9.	Daniel *Nashiro*	2000–

XXXVIII.

Armenian Church of Jerusalem

The Armenian Church of Jerusalem has traditionally claimed the title of Patriarch since the year 638, as the keeper of the sacred sites of Palestine. It does not appear to have been recognized elsewhere, however, until 1311, when the Patriarch Sargis obtained permission from the Mamluk Sultan to assume the title. The title was then regranted by the Armenian Patriarch of Constantinople about 1720.

The Church acknowledges the supremacy of the mother Armenian Church at Etchmiadzin, which ordains new bishops and prepares new chrism. Its territory includes Israel and Jordan, and a small overseas contingent in California. On 20 March 1957 Tiran Nersoyan (who later was chosen primate of the American branch of the Church) was elected Patriarch of Jerusalem, but the Jordanian government, which controlled eastern Jerusalem at the time, did not recognize the new primate, and forcibly deported him on 30 August 1958.

The primate bears the title Patriarch of Jerusalem. The official Church language is Armenian. The Patriarch of this small group of roughly 900 communicants resides at the monastery of St. James on Mount Zion in Jerusalem, and is elected by the General Clerical Assembly there.

Sources: *Dictionnaire d'Histoire et de Géographie Ecclésiastique*; *Gegenwartslage der Ostkirchen* (Spuler); *Hay Erowsaghême Darerow Mêjên* (Kêok'chian); *The History of the Armenian People* (Morgan); *Jerusalem and the Armenians* (Antreassian); *Orthodoxia*; official church website.

Armenian Patriarchs of Jerusalem

1.	Abraham I	638–669
2.	Grigor I *Ezekielian*	669–696
3.	Gêorg	696–708
4.	Mkrtich' I	708–730
5.	Hovhannês I	730–758
6.	Step'anos	758–774
7.	Eghia	774–797

INTERREGNUM

8. Abraham II   885–909

INTERREGNUM

9. Grigor II   981–1006
10. Arsen   1006–1038
11. Mesrop I [coadjutor]   1008

INTERREGNUM

12. Simêon I   1090–1109
13. Movsês   1109–1133
14. Esayi I   1133–1152
15. Sahak I   1152–1180
16. Abraham III *of Jerusalem*   1180–1191
17. Minas I   1191–1205
18. Abraham IV   1205–1218
19. Arakel   1218–1230
20. Hovhannês II *of Garin*   1230–1238
21. Karapet I *of Jerusalem*   1238–1254
22. Hakobus I   1254–1281
23. Sargis I   1281–1313
24. Astuatsatur I   1313–1316
25. Dawit' I   1316–1321
26. Poghos I   1321–1323
27. Vrt'anês I   1323–1332
28. Hovhannês III *Joslin*   1332–1341
29. Barsegh   1341–1356
30. Karapet II [locum tenens]   1356
31. Grigor III   1356–1363
32. Kirakos I [coadjutor]   1363
33. Mkrtich' II   1363–1378
34. Hovhannês IV   1378–1386
35. Grigor IV *of Egypt*   1386–1391
36. Esayi II   1391–1394
37. Sargis II   1394–1415
38. Martiros I [coadjutor]   1399
39. Mesrop II [coadjutor]   1402
40. Poghos II *of Karni*   1415–1419
41. Martiros II *of Egypt*   1419–1430
42. Minas II [coadjutor]   1426
43. Esayi III   1430–1431
44. Hovhannês V   1431–1441

XXXVIII. Armenian Church of Jerusalem

45.	Muron [coadjutor]	1436–1437
46.	Abraham V *of Egypt*	1441–1454
47.	Mesrop III	1454–1461
48.	Petros I	1461–1476
49.	Mkrtich' III	1476–1479
50.	Abraham VI *of Aleppo*	1479–1485
51.	Hovhannês VI *of Egypt*	1485–1491
52.	Martiros III *of Broussa*	1491–1501
53.	Petros II	1501–1507
54.	Sargis III	1507–1517
55.	Hovhannês VII	1517–1522
56.	Astuatsatur II *of Melitene*	1522–1542
57.	P'ilippos	1542–1550
58.	Astuatsatur II [2nd time]	1550–1551
59.	Andrêas *of Melitene*	1551–1583
60.	Dawit' II *of Melitene*	1583–1613
61.	Grigor V *Baron-Ter*	1613–1645
62.	Astuatsatur III *of Daron*	1645–1664
63.	Eghiazar *of Hromkla*	1664–1665
64.	Astuatsatur III [2nd time]	1665–1666
65.	Eghiazar [2nd time]	1666–1668
66.	Astuatsatur III [3rd time]	1668–1670
67.	Eghiazar [3rd time]	1670–1677
68.	Martiros IV	1677–1680
69.	Hovhannês VIII *of Amasia*	1680–1681
70.	Martiros IV [2nd time]	1681–1683
71.	Hovhannês IX *of Constantinople*	1684–1697
72.	Simêon II [coadjutor]	1688–1691
73.	Minas III	1697–1704
74.	Galust [coadjutor]	1697–1704
75.	Grigor VI [coadjutor]	1697–1704
	Awetik' [#41 of Constantinople]	1704–1706
	Matt'êos [#38 of Constantinople]	1706
	Martiros V [#44 of Constantinople]	1706
	Mik'ayêl [#45 of Constantinople]	1706–1707
	Sahak II [#46 of Constantinople]	1707
	Hovhannês X [#47 of Constantinople]	1707–1708
	Sahak II [2nd time]	1708–1714
	Hovhannês XI [#48 of Constantinople]	1714–1715
76.	Grigor VII *"The Chain-Bearer"*	1715–1749
77.	Hakob II *Nalian Zmarats'i* [#50 of Constantinople]	1749–1752
78.	T'êodoros I *of Khorên*	1752–1761
79.	Karapet III *of Kantsag*	1761–1768
80.	Poghos III *of Van*	1768–1775
81.	Hovakim (or Hovhannês) *of Kanaker*	1775–1793

82.	Petros III	1794–1800
83.	T'êodoros II *of Van*	1800–1818
84.	Gabriêl	1818–1840
85.	Poghos IV [vicar general]	1824–1847
86.	Zak'aria *Ter-Grigorian of Gop*	1841–1846
87.	Kirakos II *Mnats'akanian of Jerusalem*	1847–1850
88.	Hovhannês XII *Movsêsian of Zmurnia*	1850–1860

INTERREGNUM

	Vrt'anês (II) [locum tenens]	1860–1864
89.	Esayi IV *Karapetian*	1864–1885

INTERREGNUM

	Eremia *Sahagian* [locum tenens]	1885–1889
90.	Harut'iwn *Vehapetian* [#73 of Constantinople]	1889–1910

INTERREGNUM

	Ghewond *Maksoutian* [locum tenens]	1910?–1914
	Maghak'ia *Örmanian* [locum tenens]	1914–1916
	Sahak *Khapayan* [locum tenens]	1916–1917
91.	Eghishê I *Durian* [#77 of Constantinople]	1921–1930
	Mesrop *Nishanian* [locum tenens]	1930–1931
92.	T'orgom I *Gushakian*	1931–1939
93.	Mesrop IV *Nishanian*	1939–1944
94.	Kuregh *Israelian*	1944–1949

INTERREGNUM

	Eghishê II *Derderian* [locum tenens]	1949–1957
	Tiran *Nersoyan* [patriarch-elect; unconsecrated]	1957–1958
	Eghishê II *Derderian* [locum tenens]	1958–1960
95.	Eghishê II *Derderian*	1960–1990
96.	T'orgom II *Manugian*	1990–

XXXIX.

Greek Church of Jerusalem

Of the ancient Orthodox patriarchates, Jerusalem ranks fourth in honor. Having been founded, according to tradition, by the apostle James, it has always been a small church, being confined in territory to the current states of Israel and Jordan; it was recognized as a Patriarchate in 451, as keeper of the holy places in Palestine. During the Ottoman period, the Church became heavily dependent on the Ecumenical Patriarch, who consecrated (and often chose) the new patriarchs.

In 1872, for example, Patriarch Kyrillos II was deposed for refusing to condemn the secession of the Bulgarian Church. In 1908 the revolution of the Young Turks prompted the Palestinian Orthodox faithful, who comprised a majority of believers in the Church, to demand concessions from the hierarchy, which had been completely comprised of Greeks, many of them foreigners, for at least 400 years.

When Patriarch Damianos died in 1931, the struggle went public, causing a four-year delay in the patriarchal election. The new Patriarch, Timotheos, was another Greek, but he promised reforms, which were duly enacted in 1938, to provide a voice in Church matters to the native Christians. Further changes were made by his successor, Benediktos, who in 1958 provided for the election of two Arab bishops. The Patriarch of Jerusalem also consecrates the Abbot-Archbishop of the Sinai (*q.v.*).

The primate bears the title Patriarch of the Holy City of Jerusalem and of All Palestine. The official Church language is Greek. The roughly 260,000 communicants are located primarily in Israel, Jordan, and the Sinai peninsula.

Sources: *Échos d'Orient*; *Episkepsis*; *Europa World Yearbook*; *Gegenwartslage der Ostkirchen* (Spuler); *Historia tēs Ekklēsias Hierosolymōn* (Papadopoulos; regarded as official by the Church); *History of the Church* (Jedin, ed.); *Jahrbuch der Orthodoxie* (Proc); *The Middle East and North Africa*; *Oriens Christianus* (Le Quien); *Orthodoxia*; "Pinakes Patriarchōn"; *La Question de Palestine et Le Patriarcat de Jerusalem* (Moschopoulos); official church website.

Greek Patriarchs of Jerusalem

1.	Iakōbos I *Adelphotheos*	50?–62
2.	Symeōn I *Kleōpa*	62?–107?

3.	Ioustos I (or Ioudas) I	107?–111
4.	Zakchaios	111?–
5.	Tōbias	
6.	Beniamin *Philippos*	
7.	Iōannēs I	
8.	Matthias	
9.	Philippos	
10.	Senekas	
11.	Ioustos II	
12.	Leuïs	
13.	Ephraim I	
14.	Iōsēph I	
15.	Ioudas II	–134?
16.	Markos I	134?–
17.	Kassianos	
18.	Pouplios	
19.	Maximos I	
20.	Ioulianos I	
21.	Gaïos I (or Gaïanos)	
22.	Gaïos II	
23.	Symmachos	
24.	Ioulianos II (or Oualēs I)	
25.	Kapiōn	
26.	Maximos II	
27.	Antōnios	
28.	Oualēs II (or Oēalēs)	
29.	Dolichianos	–185?
30.	Narkissos	185–211
31.	Dios (or Ailios)	213
32.	Germaniōn	213
33.	Gordios	213
34.	Alexandros	213–251
35.	Mazabanēs	251–260
36.	Hymenaios	260–298
37.	Zambdas	298–300
38.	Hermōn	300–314
39.	Makarios I	314–333
40.	Maximos III	333–348
41.	Kyrillos I	350–357
	Kyrillos I [2nd time]	358–360
	Kyrillos I [3rd time]	362–367

INTERREGNUM

	Kyrillos I [4th time]	378–386?
42.	Iōannēs II	386–417

XXXIX. Greek Church of Jerusalem

43.	Praülios	417–422
44.	Ioubenalios	422–458
45.	Anastasios I	458–478
46.	Martyrios	478–486
47.	Salloustios	486–494
48.	Ēlias I	494–516
49.	Iōannēs III	516–524
50.	Petros	524–552
51.	Makarios II	552
52.	Eustochios	552–564
	Makarios II [2nd time]	564–575
53.	Iōannēs IV	575–594
54.	Amōs	594–601
55.	Isaakios	601–609
56.	Zacharias	609–632
57.	Modestos	632–634
58.	Sōphronios I	634–638

Interregnum

59.	Anastasios II	–706
60.	Iōannēs V	706–735
61.	Theodōros	735–770
62.	Ēlias II	770–797
63.	Geōrgios	797–807
64.	Thōmas I	807–820
65.	Basileios	820–838
66.	Iōannēs VI	838–842
67.	Sergios I	842–844

Interregnum

68.	Solomōn	855–860
69.	Theodosios	862–878
70.	Ēlias III	878–907
71.	Sergios II	908–911
72.	Leontios I	912–929
73.	Athanasios I	929–937
74.	Christodoulos I	937–
75.	Agathōn	950–964
76.	Iōannēs VII	964–966
77.	Christodoulos II	966–969
78.	Thōmas II	969–978
79.	Iōsēph II	980–983
80.	Orestēs (or Hieremias)	983–1005

INTERREGNUM

81.	Theophilos I	1012–1020
82.	Nikēphoros I	1020
83.	Iōannikios	1020–1040
84.	Sōphronios II	1040–1059
85.	Euthymios I	–1084
86.	Symeōn II	1084–1106
87.	Sab(b)as	1106
88.	Iōannēs VIII *Chrysostomitēs Merkouropōlos*	1106–

INTERREGNUM

89.	Nikolaos	1156
90.	Iōannēs IX	1156–1166
91.	Nikēphoros II	1166–1170
92.	Leontios II	1170–1190
93.	Dositheos I [#122 of Constantinople]	–1191
94.	Markos II	1191–
95.	Euthymios II	–1223
96.	Anastasios II	1224–1236
97.	Sōphronios III	1236–

INTERREGNUM

98.	Grēgorios I	–1298
99.	Thaddaios	1298

INTERREGNUM

100.	Athanasios III	1313?–1334
101.	Grēgorios II	1332
102.	Lazaros	1334?–1368
	Gerasimos [anti-patriarch]	1334?–1349
103.	Arsenios	1344

INTERREGNUM

104.	Dōrotheos I	1376–1417
105.	Theophilos II	1417–1424
106.	Theophanēs I	1424–1431
107.	Iōakeim	1431–
108.	Theophanēs II	–1450
109.	Athanasios IV	1452–1460?

XXXIX. Greek Church of Jerusalem

110.	Iakōbos II	1460–
111.	Abraam	–1468
112.	Grēgorios III	1468–1493

Interregnum

113.	Markos III	–1503
114.	Dōrotheos II	1503?–1537
115.	Germanos *Peloponnesios*	1537–1579
116.	Sōphronios IV	1579–1608
117.	Theophanēs III	1608–1644
118.	Païsios	1645–1660
119.	Nektarios [#58 of Sinai]	1660–1669
120.	Dositheos II	1669–1707
121.	Chrysanthos *Notaras*	1707–1731
122.	Meletios *apo Kaisareias*	1731–1737
123.	Parthenios	1737–1766
124.	Ephraim II	1766–1771
125.	Sōphronios V [#231 of Constantinople]	1771–1775
126.	Abramios	1775–1788
127.	Prokopios I	1788
128.	Anthimos	1788–1808
129.	Polykarpos	1808–1827
130.	Athanasios V	1827–1845
131.	Kyrillos II	1845–1872
132.	Prokopios II	1873–1875
133.	Hierotheos	1875–1882
	Phōtios [anti-patriarch]	1882–1883
134.	Nikodēmos	1883–1890
135.	Gerasimos *Propapas* [#162 of Antioch]	1891–1896
136.	Damianos *Kassiōtēs*	1897–1931
	Keladiōn *of Ptolemaïs* [locum tenens]	1931–1934
	Melitōn *of Madabon* [locum tenens]	1934–1935

Interregnum

	Keladiōn *of Ptolemaïs* [locum tenens]	1931–1935
137.	Timotheos *Themelēs*	1935–1955
	Athēnagoras *apo Sebasteias* [locum tenens]	1955–1957
138.	Benediktos *Papadopoulos*	1957–1980
	Germanos *Mamaladēs* [locum tenens]	1980–1981
139.	Diodōros *Karibalēs*	1981–2000
	Kornēlios *Rodoussakēs* [locum tenens]	2000–2001
140.	Eirēnaios *Skopelitēs*	2001–2005
	Kornēlios *Rodoussakēs* [locum tenens]	2005
141.	Theophilos III *Giannopoulos*	2005–

XL.

Latin Church of Jerusalem

The Latin Patriarchate of Jerusalem was established in the year 1099 as a direct result of the First Crusade, which resulted in a Latin kingdom being established at Jerusalem. This Church was one of four such creations made during the period of the crusades to correspond to the patriarchates of the ancient world, and to provide rival jurisdictions to the Greek churches and prelates. The Church of Jerusalem survived in actuality until the conquest of Acre by the Muslims in 1291, after which time it became a purely titular honor, with the Patriarchs being based in Rome. The title was suspended between 1374–1830.

When the honor was restored, the patriarch eventually came actually to reside (1847) at his primatial see of Jerusalem, unlike the three titular Latin patriarchs of Constantinople, Alexandria, and Antioch, who continued to remain in Rome. Thus, when the ancient Latin titles were abolished by Pope Paul VI in 1964 to promote ecumenism, that of Jerusalem was retained. The first native-born Palestinian leader, Michael Sabbah, was elected in 1987 on the resignation of his predecessor. The primate bears the title Patriarch of Jerusalem of the Latins. Some 63,000 communicants are located primarily in Israel and Jordan. The official church language is Arabic.

Sources: *The Catholic Encyclopedia*; *Dictionnaire d'Histoire et de Géographie Ecclésiastiques*; *The New Catholic Encyclopedia*; *Oriens Christianus* (Le Quien); "Pope Calls for Broad Mideast Peace"; official church website.

LATIN PATRIARCHS OF JERUSALEM

1.	Arnulphus	1099–1100
2.	Dai(m)bertus (or Dagobertus) *of Pisa*	1100–1107
	Ehremarus [anti-patriarch]	1105?
3.	Gibelinus *of Arles*	1107–1111
	Arnulphus [2nd time]	1111–1118
4.	Gormundus (Warmund *of Picquigny*)	1118–1128
5.	Stephanus *of Chartres*	1128–1130
6.	Willemus (or Guillemus) I *of Messines*	1130–1145
7.	Fulcherus	1146–1157

XL. Latin Church of Jerusalem

8.	Amalricus *of Nesle*	1157–1180
9.	Eraclius (or Eracleus or Heraclius)	1180–1191
10.	Sulpitius	1191–
11.	Michael I	1194
12.	Monachus	1194–
13.	Soffredus	1203–
14.	Albertus I	1204–1214
15.	Gualterus (or Lotharius)	1214?–
16.	Radulphus I (Ralph *of Merencourt*)	1217?–1225
17.	Giroldus (or Geraldus)	1225–1239
18.	Robertus *of Nantes*	1240–1254
19.	Iacobus I *Pantaléon* [#180 of Rome]	1255–1261
20.	Bartholomæus *de Braganza*	1261–
21.	Humbertus *de Romanis*	1262?
22.	Guillelmus II *of Agen*	1263–1270
23.	Thomas *Agni de Lentino*	1272–1277
24.	Aiglerius (or Angelus)	1275?
25.	Ioannes *de Vercellis*	1278–
26.	Elias I	1279–1287
27.	Nicolaus *de Hanapis*	1288–1294
28.	Radulphus II	1294–1304
29.	Antonius *Beccus*	1305–1310

Interregnum

30.	Petrus I *de Plana-Cassano*	1314–1322
31.	Petrus II *Nicosiensis*	1322–1324
32.	Raymundus *Bequin*	1324–1328
33.	Petrus III *de Palude*	1329–1342
34.	Elias II *de Nabinallis*	1342–
35.	Guillelmus III	1351–
36.	Philippus I *de Cabassole*	1361–1368
37.	Guillelmus IV	1369–1374

Interregnum

38.	Augustus *Foscolo*	1830–1847
39.	Iosephus *Valerga*	1847–1872
40.	Vincentius *Bracco*	1873–1889
41.	Aloysius I *Piavi*	1889–1905
42.	Philippus II *Camassei*	1906–1919
43.	Aloysius II *Barlassina* [auxiliary 1918]	1920–1947
44.	Albertus II *Gori*	1949–1970
45.	Iacobus II Iosephus *Beltritti* [coadjutor 1965]	1970–1987
46.	Michael II *Sabbah*	1987–

XLI.

Church of Latvia

Latvia, which existed as an independent Republic between the world wars, is largely Roman Catholic, with just nine percent of the faithful being Orthodox. Nonetheless, the same nationalistic forces that led to the founding of separate Orthodox Churches in Poland and Czechoslovakia also prompted demands by the clergy and populace in Latvia for their own Church. The Latvian Church was originally part of the Russian Orthodox Church, which had first erected a separate diocese governing both Latvia and Estonia (but centered at Riga) in 1836.

Following World War I, Latvia and the other Baltic states declared their independence of Russia, and the churches located therein soon followed suit. The Latvian parishes announced their autonomy from Russia on 26 February 1920, which was confirmed by Russian Patriarch Tikhon on 19 July 1921.

The Latvian Church transferred its autonomous jurisdiction to the Ecumenical Patriarch of Constantinople on 4 February 1936, when the new Archbishop, Augustins Petersons, was created a Metropolitan. Petersons was forced to renounce independence on 17 June 1940, during the Soviet occupation of the Baltic republics, and the Church was returned to the direct jurisdiction of the Russian Church on 4 January 1941.

No independent, organized Latvian Church structure survived the Russian suppression, either in Latvia or in the West, although scattered Latvian parishes still exist in the United States and in Europe. They continued to acknowledge Metropolitan Augustins until his death in 1955. Thereafter, the Ecumenical Patriarch placed the Latvian Church under the guardianship of the Metropolitans of Thyateira and Great Britain. Between 1941–90 Russian primates were appointed by the Patriarch to govern the mostly Russian communicants remaining in Latvia.

Latvia seceded from the Soviet Union in March 1990. On 4 January 1993 the Latvian Church declared that it would return to an autonomous status under the overall jurisdiction of Constantinople, based on the ruling of the Ecumenical Patriarch in 1936. Russian Patriarch Aleksiĭ II confirmed the Latvian Church's autonomy two days later, but insisted that it remain under the overall jurisdiction of the Russian Orthodox Church.

The primate bears the title Metropolitan of Riga and All Latvia. The official language of the Church is Latvian. Roughly 240,000 communicants belonged to the Church in 1936; current membership is unknown.

XLI. Church of Latvia

Sources: *Échos d'Orient*; *Episkepsis*; *The Latvian Orthodox Church* (Cherney); *Orthodoxia*; *Profiles in Belief* (Piepkorn); *Religion in the Soviet Union* (Kolarz); official church website.

RUSSIAN METROPOLITANS OF LATVIA
(Eparchs 1836, Bishops 1870, Archbishops 1893)

1.	Irinarkh *Popov*	1836–1841
2.	Filaret I *Gumilevskiĭ*	1842–1848
3.	Platon *Gorodetskiĭ* [#77 of Ukraine]	1848–1867
4.	Veniamin *Karelin*	1867–1874
5.	Serafim *Protopopov*	1874–1877
6.	Filaret II *Filaretov*	1877–1882
7.	Donat *Babinskiĭ-Sokolov*	1882–1887
8.	Arseniĭ *Briantsev*	1887–1897
9.	Agafangel *Preobrazhenskiĭ*	1897–1910
10.	Ioann *Smirnov*	1910–1918

AUTONOMOUS LATVIAN ORTHODOX CHURCH
(Metropolitans 1936)

1.	Jānis I *Pommers*	1920–1934
2.	Augustins *Petersons*	1936–1941

LATVIAN ORTHODOX CHURCH IN EXILE

2.	Augustins *Petersons*	1941–1955
	Athēnagoras I *Kabbadas* [locum tenens]	1955–1962
	Athēnagoras II *Kokkinakēs* [locum tenens]	1964–1979
	Methodios *Fougas* [locum tenens]	1979–1988
	Grēgorios *Hadgitophēs* [locum tenens]	1988–1993

RUSSIAN METROPOLITANS OF LATVIA
(Bishops 1941, Archbishops 1994, Metropolitans 2002)

8.	Sergiĭ *Voskresensky*	1941–1943
9.	Jānis II *Garklavs*	1943–1944

INTERREGNUM

unknown primates	1947–1962

	Nikon *Fomichev* [locum tenens]	1962–1963
10.	Nikon *Fomichev*	1963–1966
11.	Aleksiĭ *Konoplev*	1966
12.	Leonids *Poljakov*	1966–1989
13.	Aleksandrs *Kudrjašovs*	1989–

XLII.

Church of Macedonia (Ohrid)

The Orthodox Church of Macedonia is unique among the old Slavic churches in not being tied directly to one of the great Slavic states that arose in the early middle ages. The first Archbishop of Ohrid, Filip, was head of the Bulgarian Church; and for almost two hundred years, the two jurisdictions were synonymous. When the second Bulgarian patriarchate was established in 1186, Ohrid managed to maintain its independence, its primate eventually assuming the title of Patriarch.

The territory comprising the Patriarchate of Ohrid varied over the centuries, but generally included present-day Macedonia, and parts of what are now northern Albania, western Bulgaria, and northwestern Greece. Ohrid itself is located in the former Yugoslavia on Lake Ohrid, near its current border with Albania. At the behest of the Ecumenical Patriarch Samouēl, Ottoman Sultan Mustafa III issued a decree in 1766 subordinating Ohrid and Peć under the jurisdiction of Constantinople; when Serbia attained its independence, the Ohrid Metropolitanate was transferred to Peć, the modern Patriarchate of Serbia.

After World War II, the new Soviet state of Yugoslavia divided the country into six constituent republics, one of which was Macedonia. The large Orthodox population there began petitioning the state for re-establishment of a church separate from the Patriarchate of Serbia. When Serbian Patriarch Vikentije died on 5 July 1958, the leading churchmen in Macedonia called for a general assembly of clergy and lay people. These met at Ohrid on 5 October 1958. The assembly declared the ancient Church of Ohrid restored, and elected Vicar-Bishop Dositej unilaterally as the new Metropolitan Archbishop of the restored see. These actions were immediately attacked by the Serbian patriarch, who asked the government to deny the new Church recognition. President Tito, however, supported the move, and the new Serbian Patriarch, German, apparently recognized the Macedonian Church's "autonomy" on 18 July 1959, under the overall guidance of the Serbian Church.

German later assisted Metropolitan Dositej in consecrating a second Macedonian bishop, Kliment. This enabled Dositej canonically to create a new Macedonian Synod which would be self-perpetuating. The new church continued to press for complete independence, but when the Serbians refused to agree, an assembly of the Macedonian Church and people declared the Church autocephalous on 19 July 1967.

Thus far, no other Orthodox churches have recognized the Macedonian Church's claim to autocephaly (as few nations have recognized the Macedonian state's independence), but, given the history of Eastern Orthodoxy since 1800, such recognition seems likely over the long term.

On 15 December 1992, in the midst of the Yugoslavian Civil War, the Serbian Church declared the hierarchy of the Macedonian Church to be schismatic, and appointed an administrator of the Macedonian Metropolitanate; the new Republic of Macedonia refused to grant the Serbian administrator, Jovan Mladenović, a visa, and he was transferred to the United States a year later; he was replaced by Pahomije Gačić, and later by a dissident Macedonian Metropolitan, Jovan Vraniskovski.

Archbishop Gavril resigned his office for reasons of ill health on 9 June 1993, and was replaced by Archbishop Mihail on 5 December 1993. On 22 June 1994 the Church of Serbia threatened to excommunicate the entire hierarchy of the Macedonian Church. Archbishop Stefan succeeded in 1999.

The primate bears the title Metropolitan Archbishop of Ohrid and Macedonia; he resides at Skopje, the capital of Macedonia. The official Church language is Macedonian. There are eight bishops (including the ruling Archbishop and four metropolitans), with roughly one million communicants in the Republic of Macedonia, and another 400,000 in the Americas, Western Europe, and Australia.

Sources: *Church and State in Yugoslavia Since 1945* (Alexander); *Eastern Christianity and Politics in the Twentieth Century* (Ramet, ed.); *Europa World Yearbook*; *Gegenwartslage der Ostkirchen* (Spuler); *History of the Church* (Jedin, ed.); *Jahrbuch der Orthodoxie* (Proc); "The Orthodox Church in Yugoslavia: The Problem of the Macedonian Church" (Pavlowitch); *Orthodoxia*; *Profiles in Belief* (Piepkorn); official church website.

PATRIARCHS OF OHRID
(Archbishops 1018, Patriarchs 1000, 1558)
(See also the CHURCH OF BULGARIA)

1.	Filip	1000?–1015
2.	David	1015–1018
3.	Jovan I	1018–1027
4.	Lev I (Leōn *ek Rōmaiōn*)	1027–1056
5.	Teodul I (Theodoulos *apo Mōkiou*)	1056–1065
6.	Jovan II *Lampin* (Iōannēs *Lampēnos*)	1065–1078
7.	Jovan III (Iōannēs *Aoinos*) "The Sober"	1079–1081?
8.	Teofilakt (Theophylaktos *ex Euripou*)	1081–1112?
9.	Lev II (Leōn *Boungos*)	–1120
10.	Mihail I *Maksim* (Michaēl *Maximos*)	1120–
11.	Jevstatij (Eustathios)	1134?
12.	Jovan IV *Komnen* (Iōannēs *Komnēnos*)	1143–1157
13.	Konstantin I	1157–1166

INTERREGNUM

14.	name unknown	1180–1183

XLII. Church of Macedonia

15.	Jovan V *Kamatir* (Iōannēs *Kamatēros*)	1183–1215
16.	Dimitrij *Homatian* (Dēmētrios *Chōmatianos* [or *Chōmatēnos*])	1216–1235
17.	Joanikij	1238?
18.	Sergej	1241?
19.	Konstantin II (Kōnstantinos *Kabasilas*)	1250–1261
20.	Hefajst (Hephaistos)	1265?
21.	Jakov *Proarhij*	1275?
22.	Adrian	1285?
23.	Genadij	1289?
24.	Makarij	1294–1299
25.	Grigorij I	1316?
26.	Antim *Metohit* (Anthimos *Metochitēs*)	1328?
27.	Nikolaj I	1345–1348?
28.	Grigorij II	1348–1378
29.	name unknown	1383–1394

INTERREGNUM

30.	Matej	1408–1410

INTERREGNUM

31.	Nikodim	1452?
32.	Dorotej	1456–1466
33.	Dositej I	1466
34.	Mark *Ksilocarf* (Markos *Xylokarabēs*) [#163 of Constantinople]	1466–1467
35.	Dionisij I	1467–
36.	Maksim	1477–1481
37.	Nikolaj II	1481?–1487?
38.	Zaharij (Zacharias)	1487?–
39.	Prohor	1523–1550
40.	Simeon I	1550
41.	Neofit	1551
42.	Grigorij III	1553?
43.	Nikanor	1555?–1557
44.	Akakij	1557?–1564?
45.	Pajsij	1565–1566
46.	Partenij I	1566?–1567?
47.	Sofronij	1567–1572
48.	Gavril I	1572?–1588
49.	Teodul II	1588
50.	Joahim	1588?–1593
	Gavril I [2nd time]	1593

51.	Atanasij I	1593–1596
52.	Valaam	1597–1598
53.	Nektarij I	1598–
	Atanasij I [2nd time]	1606–
54.	Mitrofan	1610?–1614
	Atanasij I [3rd time]	1614–1615
55.	Nektarij II	1616–1623?
56.	Porfirij *Paleolog* (Porphyrios *Palaiologos*)	1623–1624
57.	Georgij	1627?
58.	Joasav I	1628?
59.	Avram	1629–1634
60.	Simeon II	1634–
61.	Meletij I	1637–1641
62.	Hariton	1641–1646

Interregnum

63.	Danil	1650?
64.	Dionsij II	1651–1656
65.	Arsenij I	1656–1657
66.	Atanasij II	1657
	Arsenij I [2nd time]	1658–1659?
67.	Ignatij I	1659
	Arsenij I [3rd time]	1659
	Ignatij I [2nd time]	1659–1662
68.	Zosim I	1662–1669
69.	Grigorij IV	1669–1670
70.	Panaret	1671
71.	Nektarij III	1671–1673
72.	Ignatij II	1673?
73.	Teofan	1675?–1676
74.	Meletij II	1677–1679
75.	Partenij II	1679–1683
76.	Grigorij V	1683–1687
77.	German I *of Voden*	1688–1691
	Grigorij V [2nd time]	1691–1693
78.	Ignatij III	1693–1695
79.	Zosim II	1695–1699
80.	Rafaïl	1699–1702
	German I [2nd time]	1702–1703
	Ignatij III [2nd time]	1703?–
81.	Dionisij III (Dionysios *apo Chiou*)	1706–1707
	Zosim II [2nd time]	1707?–1708?
82.	Metodij I	1708
	Zosim II [3rd time]	1708–1709
83.	Ermenus	1709–1710?

XLII. Church of Macedonia

	Dionisij III [2nd time]	1710–1714
84.	Filotej	1714–1718
85.	Joasav II	1719–1745
86.	Josif	1746–1752
87.	Dionisij IV	1752–1757
88.	Metodij II	1757–1758
89.	German II	1758–1759
90.	Kiril	1759–1762
91.	Eremij	1761–1763
92.	Ananij	1763
93.	Arsenij II	1764–1767

ARCHBISHOPRIC DISESTABLISHED 1767

METROPOLITAN ARCHBISHOPS OF OHRID AND MACEDONIA

94.	Dositej II *Stojković*	1958–1981
95.	Angelarij *Krstevski*	1981–1986
96.	Gavril II *Miloševski*	1986–1993
	Timotej *Jovanovski* [joint administrator]	1993
	Mihail *Gogov* [joint administrator]	1993
	Stefan *Veljanovski* [joint administrator]	1993
97.	Mihail II *Gogov*	1993–1999
98.	Stefan *Veljanovski*	1999–

SERBIAN EXARCHS OF AUTONOMOUS ARCHDIOCESE OF OHRID
(*Administrators 1993, Exarchs 2002*)

1.	Jovan I *Mladenović*	1993–1994
2.	Pahomije *Gačić*	1994–2002?
3.	Jovan II *Vraniskovski*	2002–

XLIII.

Church of Moldova

Prior to World War II, Moldova was part of Bessarabia in Romania, but this narrow strip of land was annexed by the Soviet Union in June 1940, merged with other territory, and renamed the Moldavian Soviet Socialist Republic. Following the breakup of the Soviet Union in 1991, Moldavia declared its independence under the name of Moldova. Although there was speculation that Moldova might reunite with Romania, since much of the population speaks Romanian, the government has resisted any such ideas.

The Church of Moldova was originally part of the Church of Romania, and then forcibly incorporated into the Russian Orthodox Church in 1940. On 24 December 1992 Russian Patriarch Aleksiĭ II declared the Eparchy of Molodova autonomous under its own self-governing synod; the Eparch received a new title, Metropolitan.

At the same time a number of priests broke away from the Russian Church and received recognition from Patriarch Teoctist of Romania as the Bessarabian Orthodox Metropolia (its original name), but the Moldovan government blocked the move, and Patriarch Aleksiĭ II reaffirmed the Russian Church's paramountcy. The Romanian Church was not officially registered by the government until 31 July 2002. The Moldovan state is said to favor the eventual creation of an autocephalous religious body independent of both the Russian and Romanian churches.

The head of the Church bears the title Metropolitan of Kishinev and All Moldova. The Church uses both Russian and Romanian as languages. The current number of communicants is unknown, but the official Moldovan Church claims 839 active parishes under its jurisdiction, while the Romanian branch claims 68 parishes.

Sources: current news reports; *Orthodoxia*.

METROPOLITANS OF MOLDOVA
(Bishops 1989, Archbishops 1990, Metropolitans 1992)

1.	Varfolomeĭ *Gondarovskiĭ*	1969–1972
2.	Ionafan *Kopolovich*	1972–1986
3.	Serapion *Fadeev*	1986–1989
4.	Vladimir *Cantareanu*	1989–

Metropolitans of Bessarabia

	Petru *Păduraru* [locum tenens]	1992–1995
1.	Petru *Păduraru*	1995–

XLIV.

Church of Montenegro

The autonomous Church of Montenegro (Crna Gora) was independent from at least 1491, when Vladika Vavyla assumed temporal as well as spiritual authority. Vladika Danilo I, who succeeded in 1697, restricted future candidates for the office to members of his own family, erecting an hereditary succession similar to that of the Catholicos-Patriarchs of Assyria (*q.v.*). For the next 150 years, each Vladika was followed at his death or deposition by his nephew or cousin.

Ironically, it was the second Danilo, in 1852, who broke the string, renouncing his religious authority, and assuming the temporal title of "Prince," while simultaneously announcing his intention to marry. Thereafter, until the end of the Montenegrin state in the aftermath of World War I, the Vladikas maintained religious authority only.

In 1920, following the unification of the South Serbs into the new state of Yugoslavia, Metropolitan Mitrofan helped lead the integration of the five autocephalous and autonomous Serbian churches (Serbia, Montenegro, Sremski Karlovci, Bukovina Dalmatia, and the remaining provinces of southeastern Yugoslavia then under the direct control of the Ecumenical Patriarch) into one body. On 12 November 1920, Metropolitan Dimitrij of Serbia was elected Patriarch of the unified Church; Metropolitan Gavrilo, Mitrofan's successor in Montenegro, himself was elected Patriarch of Serbia in 1937.

Earlier primates bore the title Vladika or Metropolitan of Cetinje and All Montenegro; current church leaders use the title Metropolitan of Montenegro and Primorje (or The Littoral). The Church had roughly 220,000 communicants in 1906.

Following the disintegration of Yugoslavia in the early 1990s, there was much local agitation for the re-establishment of an autocephalous church. On 31 October 1993 the "Committee of the Restoration of the Autocephaly of the Montenegrin Orthodox Church" demonstrated in Cetinje during a Serbian Church synod, and chose an exiled bishop, Antonije Abramović, as the first "Patriarch of Montenegro." He has not been recognized by Serbia or the other orthodox churches. The Serbian Church continues to maintain its own hierarchical structure. The present-day membership of both churches is unknown.

Sources: *Biographisches Lexikon zur Geschichte Südosteuropas* (Bernath & Nehring); *Eastern Europe and the Commonwealth States*; *Échos d'Orient*; *The Falcon & the Eagle* (Treadway); *Manuel d'Histoire, de Généalogie et de Chronologie* (Stokvis); *Rodoslovne Tablice i Grbovi*; official church website.

Vladikas and Metropolitans of Montenegro
(*Hereditary Prince-Bishops "Vladikas" of the House of Petrović-Njegoš, 1697–1852; Metropolitans of Cetinje, 1858–1920*)

1.	Ilarion I	1220–1242
2.	German I	1245?
3.	Neofit	1250–1270
4.	Jevstatije	1270–1278
5.	Mihaïlo I	1280?
6.	Andrija	1290?
7.	Jovan	1293–1305
8.	Mihaïlo II	1305–1319

Interregnum

9.	Jevtimije	1405
10.	Arsenije I	1405–1417
11.	David	1424?
12.	Teodosije	1446?
13.	Josif	1453?
14.	Visarion I	1482–1485
15.	Pahomije I	1491?
16.	Vavyla	1491–1520
17.	German II	1520–
18.	Pavle	1530?
19.	Vasilije I	1532?
20.	Nikodim	1540?
21.	Romul (or Romil)	1540–1559
22.	Makarije	1560
23.	Ruvim I	1561?
24.	Pahomije II *Komanin*	1569?
25.	Gerasim	1575?
26.	Venijamin	1582–1591
27.	Nikanor I	1591?
28.	Stevan	1591?
29.	Ruvim II *Boljević Njegoš*	1593–1636

Interregnum

30.	Mardarije I *Kornećanin*	1639?–1649?
31.	Visarion II *Kolinović*	1649?
32.	Mardarije II *Kornećanin*	1659?
33.	Ruvim III *Boljević*	1673–1685
34.	Vasilije II *Veljekraïski*	1685?
35.	Visarion III *Borilović Bajica*	1685–1692

36.	Sava(tije) I *Kaluđerović*	1694–1697
37.	Danilo I *Šćepčev Petrović* [cousin of #38]	1697–1735
38.	Sava II *Petrović* [coadjutor 1719; cousin of #37]	1735–1750
39.	Vasilije III *Petrović* [coadjutor 1744; nephew of #37]	1750–1766
	Sava II [2nd time]	1766–1767
	Arsenije II *Plamenac* [anti-vladika]	1767–1773
	Sava II [3rd time]	1773–1781
40.	Arsenije II *Plamenac* [2nd time]	1781–1782
41.	Petar I *Petrović Njegoš* [cousin of #39]	1782–1830
42.	Petar II *Petrović Njegoš* [nephew of #41]	1830–1851
	Pero *Petrović Njegoš* [locum tenens]	1851–1852
43.	Danilo II *Petrović Njegoš* [unconsecrated; nephew of #42]	1852

Interregnum

	Nikanor *Ivanović-Njeguš* [locum tenens]	1853–1858
44.	Nikanor II *Ivanović-Njeguš*	1858–1860
	Ilari(j)on *Roganović* [locum tenens]	1860–1863
45.	Ilari(j)on II *Roganović*	1863–1882
46.	Visarion IV *Ljubiša*	1882–1884
	Mitrofan *Ban* [locum tenens]	1884–1885
47.	Mitrofan *Ban*	1885–1920

Serbian Metropolitans of Montenegro

	Mitrofan Ban [as local metropolitan]	1920
48.	Gavrilo *Dožić* [#41 of Serbia]	1920–1938
49.	Joanikije *Lipovac*	1940–1945
50.	Arsenije III *Bradvarević*	1947–1960
51.	Danilo III *Dajković*	1961–1990
52.	Amfilohije *Radović*	1990–

Vladikas and Metropolitans of the Montenegrin Orthodox Church

48.	Antonije *Abramović*	1993–1996
49.	Mihailo III *Dede(j)ić*	1998–

XLV.

Church of Poland

Poland has historically been an anomaly among the Eastern European states, the Polish kings having been converted at an early date to Roman Catholicism; most of the population remains Catholic to this day. However, an Orthodox Church diocese was established as early as the year 1087 in Przemysl, in eastern Poland, under the direct control of the Patriarchate of Russia. During the seventeenth century, Polish Orthodoxy was subject to persecution at the hands of the state, many believers being forced to acknowledge Catholic Eastern Rite bishops. Following the partitions of the late 1700s, Russia occupied the eastern half of Poland, and encouraged the re-establishment of the Orthodox hierarchy, against much resistance from the populace. A separate Polish archdiocese was erected by 1834, but no Archbishop of Warsaw actually resided there until 1840.

The Russian Revolution of 1917 resulted in the eventual independence of the Polish state, with administration of the Orthodox Church of Poland being transferred to the Ecumenical Patriarch at Constantinople. Following the lead of the other Slavic churches, the Polish Orthodox Church promptly sought autocephaly, a general synod unilaterally declaring the church's independence in 1922. The Patriarch of Russia refused recognition, and the controversy led to the assassination of Archbishop Jerzy by a Russian monk a year later.

Nonetheless, autocephaly was recognized by the Ecumenical Patriarch on 13 November 1924. When the Soviets occupied the country during World War II, they immediately re-established control over the Church, finally deposing Metropolitan Dionizy in 1947, and replacing him with a Russian administrator. Autocephaly was then regranted by the Moscow Patriarchate on 15 June 1951, with a new Ukrainian-born Metropolitan, Makary Oksijuk, being elected a month later.

The primate bears the title Metropolitan Archbishop of Warsaw and All Poland. The official Church language is Polish. The Polish Orthodox Church remains small in comparison with the powerful Polish Catholic Church, having 870,000 communicants; most Orthodox believers live in the eastern sections of Poland, near the Russian border.

Sources: *Eastern Christianity and Politics in the Twentieth Century* (Ramet, ed.); *Échos d'Orient*; *Episkepsis*; *Europa World Yearbook*; *Gegenwartslage der Ostkirchen* (Spuler); *History of the Church* (Jedin, ed.); *Jahrbuch der Orthodoxie* (Proc); *Orthodoxia*;

Profiles in Belief (Piepkorn); "Cerkiew Prawosławna w Polsce po Zakończeniu II Wojny Światowej" (Gerent); "Historia Diecezji Warszawsko-Bielskiej"; official church website.

METROPOLITAN ARCHBISHOPS OF POLAND
(Archbishops 1840, Exarchs 1921, Metropolitans 1922)

1.	Antonij *Rafalskij*	1840–1843
2.	Nikanor I *Klemientiewskij*	1843–1848
3.	Arsenij *Moskwin*	1848–1860
4.	Joannikij *Gorskij*	1860–1875
5.	Leontij *Lebjedinskij*	1875–1891
6.	Fławian *Gorodieckij* [#12 of exarchs of Georgia]	1891–1898
7.	Ijeronim *Ekzemplarskij*	1898–1905
8.	Nikanor II *Kamienskij*	1905–1908
9.	Nikolaj *Ziorow* [#7 of America]	1908–1915
10.	Iosaf *Kałłistow*	1915–1918
11.	Serafin *Cziczagow* [unconsecrated]	1918–1921
12.	Jerzy *Jaroszewski*	1921–1923
13.	Dionizy *Waledyński*	1923–1948

INTERREGNUM

	Tymoteusz *Szretter* [locum tenens]	1947–1951
14.	Makary *Oksijuk*	1951–1959
	Tymoteusz *Szretter* [locum tenens]	1959–1961
15.	Tymoteusz *Szretter*	1961–1962

INTERREGNUM

	Jerzy *Korenistow* [locum tenens]	1962–1965
16.	Stefan *Rudyk*	1965–1969
	Jerzy *Korenistow* [locum tenens]	1969–1970
17.	Bazyli *Doroszkiewicz*	1970–1998
	Sawa *Hrycuniak* [locum tenens]	1998
18.	Sawa *Hrycuniak*	1998–

XLVI.

Church of Romania

The Orthodox Church of Romania developed in tandem with the secular Romanian state. The princes of Moldavia and Wallachia sought ecclesiastical autonomy as a means of furthering the growth of their realms. Thus, the Voievode of Wallachia petitioned the Patriarch of Constantinople for the establishment of a separate Metropolitanate at Currea de Argeş, a request which was granted in 1359. Similarly, Moldavia secured its own Metropolitan in 1401, in the person of Iosif Muşat.

The union of the two Romanian states in 1861, and the international recognition of its independence in 1878, led to demands for an autocephalous church. These were granted by Constantinople on 13 April 1885, with the Metropolitan of Ungro-Vlachia (Wallachia) being acknowledged as Metropolitan Primate of Romania. The patriarchate was established on 4 February 1925, and recognized by Constantinople on 30 July 1925.

The Soviet occupation in 1944, and the subsequent establishment of a communist government, imposed many hardships on the Church; it became, as in Russia, the semi-official religion for believers. The harshness of the Ceauşescu regime resulted in further setbacks for an already besieged church. The civil chaos which resulted from the latter's fall at the end of 1989 resulted in the resignation of Patriarch Teoctist in January 1990, but he was restored to his position three months later.

However, many of the Romanian Church's hierarchs continue to be criticized for having cooperated with the Communist regime. The church of the neighboring newly-independent state of Moldova, a territory which had been a part of Romania prior to World War II (when it was annexed to the Soviet Union), was declared autonomous by the Patriarch of Russia on 24 December 1992. In 1993 Patriarch Teoctist attempted to reassert the authority of the Romanian Church over Moldova, but the government of Moldova adamantly opposed what it regarded as interference by a foreign power, as did Patriarch Aleksiĭ II of Russia.

The primate bears the title Patriarch of All Romania, Locum Tenens of Caesarea in Cappadocia, Metropolitan of Ungro-Vlachia (*i.e.*, Wallachia), Archbishop of Bucuresti. The official language is Romanian. Roughly eighteen million communicants reside in Romania and the United States.

Sources: *Eastern Christianity and Politics in the Twentieth Century* (Ramet, ed.); *Échos d'Orient*; *Episkepsis*; *Europa World Yearbook*; *Gegenwartslage der Ostkirchen* (Spuler); *History of the Church* (Jedin, ed.); *Istoria Bisericii Ortodoxe Române* (Păcurariu; regarded as official by the Church); *Jahrbuch der Orthodoxie* (Proc); *Orthodoxia*; *Profiles in Belief* (Piepkorn); *The Romanian Orthodox Church, Yesterday and Today*; *Dicționarul Teologilor Români* (Păcurariu); official church website.

METROPOLITANS OF ROMANIA
(Metropolitans of Ungro-Vlachia 1359, Metropolitan Primates 1865)

1.	Iachint	1359–1372
2.	Hariton	1372–1380?
3.	Antim I *Critopol*	1380?–1401
4.	Teodor I	1400s
5.	Iosif I	1464–1477?
6.	Macarie I	1477–1487?
7.	Ilarion I	1487?–1502?
8.	Nifon I [#168 of Constantinople]	1503?–1505
9.	Maxim *Brancovici*	1505–1508

INTERREGNUM

10.	Macarie II	1512–1521?
11.	Teodor II	1521?–1523
12.	Ilarion II	1523–1526?
13.	Mitrofan I	1526?–1534?
14.	Varlaam I	1534?–1544
15.	Anania	1544–1558
16.	Efrem	1558?–1566?
17.	Daniïl I	1566?–1568
18.	Eftimie I	1568–1576
19.	Serafim	1576–1585
20.	Mihail I	1585?–1589
21.	Nichifor	1589–1592
22.	Mihail II	1592–1594
23.	Eftimie II	1594–1602
24.	Luca	1602–1629
25.	Grigorie I	1629–1636
26.	Teofil	1636–1648
27.	Stefan I	1648–1653
28.	Ignatie I	1653–1655
	Stefan I [2nd time]	1655–1668
29.	Teodosie	1668–1672
30.	Dionisie I	1672
31.	Varlaam II	1672–1679
	Teodosie [2nd time]	1679–1708
32.	Antim II *Ivireanul*	1708–1716
33.	Mitrofan II	1716–1719

XLVI. Church of Romania

34.	Daniïl II	1719–1731
35.	Stefan II	1732–1738
36.	Neofit I *Cretanul*	1738–1753
37.	Filaret I *Mihalitzis*	1753–1760
38.	Grigorie II	1760–1787
39.	Grigorie III *Socoteanu* [locum tenens]	1770–1771
40.	Cosma *Popescu*	1787–1792
41.	Filaret II	1792–1793
42.	Dositei *Filitti*	1793–1810
43.	Gavriïl *Bănulescu* [exarch]	1808–1812
44.	Ignatie II	1810–1812
	Iosif *al Argeşului* [locum tenens]	1812
45.	Nectarie	1812–1819
46.	Dionisie II *Lupu*	1819–1821
	Dionisie [locum tenens]	1821–1822
	Benedict *Troadas* [locum tenens]	1822
	Gherasim *al Buzaului* [locum tenens]	1822
	Benedict *Troadas* [locum tenens]	1822
47.	Grigorie IV *Dascălul*	1823–1829

Interregnum

Neofit [locum tenens]	1829–1833
Grigorie IV *Dascălul* [2nd time]	1833–1834

Interregnum

	Neofit [locum tenens]	1833–1840
	Chesarie [locum tenens]	1833–1840
	Ilarion [locum tenens]	1833–1840
48.	Neofit II	1840–1849
	Nifon [locum tenens]	1849–1850
49.	Nifon II	1850–1875
50.	Calinic *Miclescu*	1875–1886
	Inochentie *Moisiu* [locum tenens]	1886
51.	Iosif II *Gheorghian*	1886–1893
	Gherasim *Timus* [locum tenens]	1893
52.	Ghenadie *Petrescu*	1893–1896
	Iosif *Naniescu* [locum tenens]	1896
	Gherasim *Timus* [locum tenens]	1896
	Partenie *Clinceni* [locum tenens]	1896
	Iosif II *Gheorghian* [2nd time]	1896–1908
53.	Atanasie *Mironescu*	1909–1911
	Teodosie *Aţanasiu* [locum tenens]	1911–1912
54.	Conon *Aramescu-Donici*	1912–1919

	Platon *Ciosu* [locum tenens]	1919
55.	Miron *Cristea*	1919–1925

Patriarchs of Romania

1.	Miron *Cristea*	1925–1939
	Nicodim *Munteanu* [locum tenens]	1939
2.	Nicodim *Munteanu*	1939–1948
	Justinian *Marina* [locum tenens]	1948
3.	Justinian *Marina*	1948–1977
	Iustin *Moïsescu* [locum tenens]	1977
4.	Iustin *Moïsescu* [#43 of Austria — Sibiu]	1977–1986
	Teoctist *Arăpaşu* [locum tenens]	1986
5.	Teoctist *Arăpaşu*	1986–

Old Calendarists
(Genuine Orthodox Church of Romania)

In 1924 the Romanian Metropolitan Primate Miron introduced the Gregorian calendar into his Church. As also happened almost simultaneously in Greece, some of the old-line parish clergy rebelled against the idea of any such developments. The opposition coalesced around the Hieromonk Glicherie Tanase, Abbot of the Monastery of Prokrov in Moldova. Persecuted by the authorities, Glicherie was eventually arrested and imprisoned. He was freed during the chaos of the Second World War, and eventually began rebuilding the structure of his new Church at Slatioara Monastery.

Since the church had no higher clergy, retired Bishop Galaction Codrun was invited to become the first Metropolitan of the Church in 1955. He in turn consecrated the first bishops of the Genuine Orthodox Church, including Father Glicherie, who succeeded him as primate at Galaction's death in 1957.

The official language of the Church is Romanian. The Old Calendarists claim a following of a half million celebrants in Romania, although the real number is judged by some observers to be perhaps a tenth of that figure. The Metropolitan continues to reside at Slatioara.

Sources: official church website.

Metropolitans of the Genuine Orthodox Church of Romania

1.	Glicherie *Tanase* [as first hierarch]	1924–1955
2.	Galaction *Codrun*	1955–1957
	Glicherie *Tanase* [as metropolitan]	1957–1985
3.	Silvestru *Onofrei*	1985–1992
4.	Vlasie *Mogârzan*	1992–

XLVII.

Church of Rome

The Roman Catholic Church is the largest of the ancient Christian patriarchates, the Pope of Rome having been regarded as either first among equals or first in primacy during the early centuries of Christianity. The traditions, language, and history of the Catholic Church gradually moved it away from its Eastern brethren, particularly during the decline of the Roman Empire, to which it was so closely tied. As the temporal center of the Empire shifted to Byzantium (Constantinople), the Byzantine emperors sought to make the latter church pre-eminent among the five original patriarchates. The collapse of the Western Empire, ironically, forced the Popes to become more self-sufficient, and injected them directly into local and international politics.

In 754 the Vatican acquired the first pieces of land in what would eventually become the "Papal States," the temporal domains of the pontiffs in central Italy. After a succession of weak Popes in the ninth and tenth centuries, the continuing political struggle between East and West came to a head in 1054, when the Pope and the Patriarch of Constantinople exchanged excommunications. The other major patriarchates gradually followed Constantinople's lead, although Rome continues to have supporters in the East to the present day. These loyalists have often split away from their Orthodox counterparts to form rival patriarchates which acknowledge the supremacy of the Pope.

The Church went through a period of reform and reorganization during the early Middle Ages. By the year 1200 the Pope had more feudal vassals than any other ruler in Europe, and could impose his will upon the most intransigent of monarchs. In the fourteenth century political turmoil at Rome forced the Pope to move his seat of power to Avignon, in France, under the protection of the French king. In 1378 the newly-elected Pontiff, Urbanus VI, was persuaded to return to Rome, thereby precipating the Great Schism. Disgruntled French cardinals immediately elected their own Pope at Avignon, and all of Europe began dividing itself into two equal camps. Neither side would renounce its claims, and as Pope succeeded Pope, men of good will began to despair that the breach would ever be healed. Finally, a great Council was called at Pisa in 1409 to resolve the issue; it deposed both claimants, and elected its own Pope. Neither of the other pontiffs recognized the actions of the Council, so there were now three papal courts.

In 1415, two of the Popes were persuaded to resign, and a new leader was elected in 1417, whereupon the third line of pontiffs, although it continued until 1430, rapidly lost its legitimacy and supporters. A second great schism occurred with the Protestant Revolution of the sixteenth century; this was met with the reforming Council of Trent in 1545. The Church's temporal powers were directly affected by the rise of nationalism in Europe in the mid-nineteenth century; in 1870 the last remnants of the Papal States were occupied by revolutionary forces, and the Pope withdrew to the Vatican, vowing never to venture forth until his lands were restored. This dispute was settled in 1929 by the Lateran Treaty, through which Italy ceded to the Pope 300 acres of land surrounding the Vatican in Rome. The Pope remains the only patriarch to possess temporal authority, as Head of Vatican City State; this status gives him an international authority and voice shared by no other religious leader in the world.

The Roman Catholic Church remains the most successful of all Christian denominations, with the greatest number of followers worldwide, the largest number of parishes, the largest and most pervasive infrastructure, the greatest financial resources. The primate bears the title Pope, Bishop of Rome, Vicar of Jesus Christ, Successor of the Prince of the Apostles, Supreme Pontiff of the Universal Church, Patriarch of the West, Primate of Italy, Sovereign of Vatican City State. The official language of the Church is Latin, which is used for many official publications; however, Italian is spoken in Vatican City State.

Sources: *Annuario Pontificio per l'Annò...* (regarded as official by the Church); *Échos d'Orient*; *Manuel d'Histoire, de Généalogie et de Chronologie* (Stokvis); *The Oxford Dictionary of Popes* (Kelly); official church website.

POPES OF ROME

1.	Petrus	40?–67?
2.	Linus	67?–76?
3.	Anacletus (I) (or Cletus)	76?–88?
4.	Clemens I	88?–97?
5.	Evaristus	97?–105?
6.	Alexander I	105?–115?
7.	Sixtus I	115?–125?
8.	Telesphorus	125?–136?
9.	Hyginus	136?–140?
10.	Pius I	140?–155?
11.	Anicetus	155?–166?
12.	Soter	166?–175?
13.	Eleutherius	175?–189
14.	Victor I	189–199
15.	Zephyrinus	199–217
16.	Calixtus I	217–222
	Hippolytus [anti-pope]	217–235
17.	Urbanus I	222–230
18.	Pontianus	230–235
19.	Anterus	235–236

XLVII. Church of Rome

20.	Fabianus	236–250
21.	Cornelius	251–253
	Novatianus [anti-pope]	251
22.	Lucius I	253–254
23.	Stephanus I	254–257
24.	Sixtus II	257–258
25.	Dionysius	259–268
26.	Felix I	269–274
27.	Eutychianus	275–283
28.	Gaius	283–296
29.	Marcellinus	296–304

INTERREGNUM

30.	Marcellus I	308–309
31.	Eusebius	309
32.	Miltiades (or Melchiades)	311–314
33.	Sylvester I	314–335
34.	Marcus	336
35.	Iulius I	337–352
36.	Liberius	352–366
	Felix II [anti-pope]	355–365
37.	Damasus I	366–384
	Ursinus [anti-pope]	366–367
38.	Siricius	384–399
39.	Anastasius I	399–401
40.	Innocentius I	401–417
41.	Zosimus	417–418
42.	Bonifacius I	418–422
	Eulalius [anti-pope]	418–419
43.	Coelestinus I	422–432
44.	Sixtus III	432–440
45.	Leo I *Magnus* "The Great"	440–461
46.	Hilarius	461–468
47.	Simplicius	468–483
48.	Felix III	483–492
49.	Gelasius I	492–496
50.	Anastasius II	496–498
51.	Symmachus	498–514
	Laurentius [anti-pope]	498
	Laurentius [anti-pope; 2nd time]	501–505
52.	Hormisdas	514–523
53.	Ioannes I	523–526
54.	Felix IV	526–530
55.	Bonifacius II	530–532
	Dioscorus [anti-pope]	530

56.	Ioannes II (Mercurius)	533–535
57.	Agapetus I	535–536
58.	Silverius	536–537
59.	Vigilius	537–555
60.	Pelagius I	556–561
61.	Ioannes III	561–574
62.	Benedictus I	575–579
63.	Pelagius II	579–590
64.	Gregorius I *Magnus* "The Great"	590–604
65.	Sabinianus	604–606
66.	Bonifacius III	607
67.	Bonifacius IV	608–615
68.	Deusdedit (or Adeodatus I)	615–618
69.	Bonifacius V	619–625
70.	Honorius I	625–638
71.	Severinus	640
72.	Ioannes IV	640–642
73.	Theodorus I	642–649
74.	Martinus I	649–655
75.	Eugenius I	654–657
76.	Vitalianus	657–672
77.	Adeodatus II	672–676
78.	Donus	676–678
79.	Agatho	678–681
80.	Leo II	682–683
81.	Benedictus II	684–685
82.	Ioannes V	685–686
83.	Conon	686–687
	Theodorus II [anti-pope]	687
	Paschalis I [anti-pope]	687
84.	Sergius I	687–701
85.	Ioannes VI	701–705
86.	Ioannes VII	705–707
87.	Sisinnius	708
88.	Constantinus (I)	708–715
89.	Gregorius II	715–731
90.	Gregorius III	731–741
91.	Zacharias	741–752
	Stephanus (II) [unconsecrated]	752
92.	Stephanus II (III)	752–757
93.	Paulus I	757–767
	Constantinus II [anti-pope]	767–769
	Philippus [anti-pope]	768
94.	Stephanus III (IV)	768–772
95.	Adrianus I	772–795
96.	Leo III	795–816

XLVII. Church of Rome

97.	Stephanus IV (V)	816–817
98.	Paschalis I	817–824
99.	Eugenius II	824–827
100.	Valentinus	827
101.	Gregorius IV	827–844
	Ioannes VIII [anti-pope]	844
102.	Sergius II	844–847
103.	Leo IV	847–855
104.	Benedictus III	855–858
	Anastasius III [anti-pope]	855
105.	Nicolaus I *Magnus* "The Great"	858–867
106.	Adrianus II	867–872
107.	Ioannes VIII	872–882
108.	Marinus I	882–884
109.	Adrianus III	884–885
110.	Stephanus V (VI)	885–891
111.	Formosus	891–896
112.	Bonifacius VI	896
113.	Stephanus VI (VII)	896–897
114.	Romanus	897
115.	Theodorus II	897
116.	Ioannes IX	898–900
117.	Benedictus IV	900–903
118.	Leo V	903
	Christophorus [anti-pope]	903–904
119.	Sergius III	904–911
120.	Anastasius III	911–913
121.	Lando (or Landus)	913–914
122.	Ioannes X	914–928
123.	Leo VI	928
124.	Stephanus VII (VIII)	928–931
125.	Ioannes XI	931–935
126.	Leo VII	936–939
127.	Stephanus VIII (IX)	939–942
128.	Marinus II	942–946
129.	Agapetus II	946–955
130.	Ioannes XII (Octavianus)	955–964
131.	Leo VIII	963–965
132.	Benedictus V	964–966
133.	Ioannes XIII	965–972
134.	Benedictus VI	973–974
	Bonifacius VII (Franco) [anti-pope]	974
135.	Benedictus VII	974–983
136.	Ioannes XIV *Canepanova*	983–984
	Bonifacius VII [2nd time]	984–985
137.	Ioannes XV	985–996

138.	Gregorius V (Bruno)	996–999
	Ioannes XVI *Philagathos* [anti-pope]	997–998
139.	Sylvester II (Gerbert)	999–1003
140.	Ioannes XVII *Sicco*	1003
141.	Ioannes XVIII *Fasanus*	1004–1009
142.	Sergius IV (Petrus)	1009–1012
143.	Benedictus VIII (Theophylactus)	1012–1024
	Gregorius VI [anti-pope]	1012
144.	Ioannes XIX (Romanus)	1024–1032
145.	Benedictus IX (Theophylactus)	1032–1044
146.	Sylvester III (Ioannes) *of Sabina*	1045
	Benedictus IX [2nd time]	1045
147.	Gregorius VI *Gratianus*	1045–1046
148.	Clemens II (Suidger)	1046–1047
	Benedictus IX [3rd time]	1047–1048
149.	Damasus II (Poppo)	1048
150.	Leo IX *von Egisheim*	1049–1054
151.	Victor II *von Dollnstein-Hirschberg*	1055–1057
152.	Stephanus IX (X) (Frederick)	1057–1058
	Benedictus X *Mincius* [anti-pope]	1058–1059
153.	Nicolaus II (Gérard)	1059–1061
154.	Alexander II *da Baggio*	1061–1073
	Honorius II *Cadalus* [anti-pope]	1061–1072
155.	Gregorius VII (Hildebrand)	1073–1085
	Clemens III (Guibert) [anti-pope]	1080
	Clemens III (Guibert) [anti-pope; 2nd time]	1084–1100
156.	Victor III (Desiderius)	1086–1087
157.	Urbanus II (Odo)	1088–1099
158.	Paschalis II (Rainerius)	1099–1118
	Theodoricus [anti-pope]	1100
	Albertus [anti-pope]	1102
	Sylvester IV (Maginulf) [anti-pope]	1105–1111
159.	Gelasius II *Caetani*	1118–1119
	Gregorius VIII *Burdinus* [anti-pope]	1118–1121
160.	Calixtus II *di Borgogna*	1119–1124
161.	Honorius II (Lamberto)	1124–1130
	Coelestinus II *Buccapecus* [anti-pope]	1124
162.	Innocentius II *Papareschi*	1130–1143
	Anacletus II *Leonis* [anti-pope]	1130–1138
	Victor IV *Conti* [anti-pope]	1138
163.	Coelestinus II (Guido)	1143–1144
164.	Lucius II *Caccianemici*	1144–1145
165.	Eugenius III *Pignatelli* (or *Paganelli*)	1145–1153
166.	Anastasius IV (Corrado)	1153–1154
167.	Adrianus IV *Breakspear*	1154–1159

XLVII. Church of Rome

168.	Alexander III *Bandinelli*	1159–1181
	Victor IV *de Monticelli* [anti-pope]	1159–1164
	Paschalis III *da Crema* [anti-pope]	1164–1168
	Calixtus III (Giovanni) [anti-pope]	1168–1178
	Innocentius III (Lando) [anti-pope]	1179–1180
169.	Lucius III *Allucingoli*	1181–1185
170.	Urbanus III *Crivelli*	1185–1187
171.	Gregorius VIII *de Morra*	1187
172.	Clemens III *Scolari*	1187–1191
173.	Coelestinus III *Bobone*	1191–1198
174.	Innocentius III *di Segni*	1198–1216
175.	Honorius III *Savelli*	1216–1227
176.	Gregorius IX *di Segni* [nephew of #174]	1227–1241
177.	Coelestinus IV *da Castiglione*	1241
178.	Innocentius IV *Fieschi*	1243–1254
179.	Alexander IV *Segni* [nephew of #176]	1254–1261
180.	Urbanus IV *Pantaléon* [#19 of Jerusalem]	1261–1264
181.	Clemens IV *Foulques*	1265–1268

Interregnum

182.	Gregorius X *Visconti*	1271–1276
183.	Innocentius V *de Tarentaise*	1276
184.	Adrianus V *Fieschi* [nephew of #178]	1276
185.	Ioannes XXI *Juliao*	1276–1277
186.	Nicolaus III *Orsini*	1277–1280
187.	Martinus IV *de Brie*	1281–1285
188.	Honorius IV *Savelli* [great-nephew of #175]	1285–1287
189.	Nicolaus IV *Masci*	1288–1292
190.	Coelestinus V *del Morrone*	1294
191.	Bonifacius VIII *Caetani*	1294–1303
192.	Benedictus XI *Boccasini*	1303–1304
193.	Clemens V *de Got*	1305–1314
194.	Ioannes XXII *Duèse*	1316–1334
	Nicolaus V *Rainalducci* [anti-pope]	1328–1330
195.	Benedictus XII *Fournier*	1334–1342
196.	Clemens VI *Roger*	1342–1352
197.	Innocentius VI *Aubert*	1352–1362
198.	Urbanus V *de Grimoard*	1362–1370
199.	Gregorius XI *de Beaufort*	1370–1378
200.	Urbanus VI *Prignano*	1378–1389
	Clemens VII *de Boulogne* [anti-pope]	1378–1394
201.	Bonifacius IX *Tomacelli*	1389–1404
	Benedictus XIII *de Luna* [anti-pope]	1394–1423
202.	Innocentius VII *de' Migliorati*	1404–1406
203.	Gregorius XII *Correr*	1406–1415

	Alexander V *Philarghi* (or *Filargo*) [anti-pope]	1409–1410
	Ioannes XXIII *Cossa* [anti-pope]	1410–1415
204.	Martinus V *Colonna*	1417–1431
	Clemens VIII *Sánchez Muñoz* [anti-pope]	1423–1429
	Benedictus XIV *Garnier* [anti-pope]	1425–1430
205.	Eugenius IV *Condulmaro*	1431–1447
	Felix V *di Savoia* [anti-pope]	1439–1449
206.	Nicolaus V *Parentucelli*	1447–1455
207.	Calixtus III *de Borja* [uncle of #212]	1455–1458
208.	Pius II *Piccolomini* [uncle of #213]	1458–1464
209.	Paulus II *Barbo*	1464–1471
210.	Sixtus IV *della Rovere*	1471–1484
211.	Innocentius VIII *Cibò*	1484–1492
212.	Alexander VI *de Borja* [nephew of #207]	1492–1503
213.	Pius III *Todeschini-Piccolomini* [nephew of #208]	1503
214.	Iulius II *della Rovere* [nephew of #210]	1503–1513
215.	Leo X *de' Medici*	1513–1521
216.	Adrianus VI *Florensz*	1522–1523
217.	Clemens VII *de' Medici* [cousin of #215]	1523–1534
218.	Paulus III *Farnese*	1534–1549
219.	Iulius III *Ciocchi del Monte*	1550–1555
220.	Marcellus II *Cervini*	1555
221.	Paulus IV *Carafa*	1555–1559
222.	Pius IV *de' Medici*	1559–1565
223.	Pius V *Ghislieri*	1566–1572
224.	Gregorius XIII *Boncompagni*	1572–1585
225.	Sixtus V *Peretti*	1585–1590
226.	Urbanus VII *Castagna*	1590
227.	Gregorius XIV *Sfondrati*	1590–1591
228.	Innocentius IX *Facchinetti*	1591
229.	Clemens VIII *Aldobrandini*	1592–1605
230.	Leo XI *de' Medici* [nephew of #215]	1605
231.	Paulus V *Borghese*	1605–1621
232.	Gregorius XV *Ludovisi*	1621–1623
233.	Urbanus VIII *Barberini*	1623–1644
234.	Innocentius X *Pamfili* (or *Pamphilj*) [#34 of Antioch]	1644–1655
235.	Alexander VII *Chigi*	1655–1667
236.	Clemens IX *Rospigliosi*	1667–1669
237.	Clemens X *Altieri*	1670–1676
238.	Innocentius XI *Odescalchi*	1676–1689
239.	Alexander VIII *Ottoboni*	1689–1691
240.	Innocentius XII *Pignatelli*	1691–1700
241.	Clemens XI *Albani*	1700–1721
242.	Innocentius XIII *dei Conti*	1721–1724
243.	Benedictus XIII *Orsini*	1724–1730

XLVII. Church of Rome

244.	Clemens XII *Corsini*	1730–1740
245.	Benedictus XIV *Lambertini*	1740–1758
246.	Clemens XIII *della Torre Rezzonico*	1758–1769
247.	Clemens XIV *Ganganelli*	1769–1774
248.	Pius VI *Braschi*	1775–1799
249.	Pius VII *Chiaramonti*	1800–1823
250.	Leo XII *della Genga*	1823–1829
251.	Pius VIII *Castiglione*	1829–1830
252.	Gregorius XVI *Cappellari*	1831–1846
253.	Pius IX *Mastai-Ferretti*	1846–1878
254.	Leo XIII *Pecci*	1878–1903
255.	Pius X *Sarto*	1903–1914
256.	Benedictus XV *della Chiesa*	1914–1922
257.	Pius XI *Ratti*	1922–1939
258.	Pius XII *Pacelli*	1939–1958
259.	Ioannes XXIII *Roncalli*	1958–1963
260.	Paulus VI *Montini*	1963–1978
261.	Ioannes Paulus I *Luciani*	1978
262.	Ioannes Paulus II *Wojtyła*	1978–2005
263.	Benedictus XVI *Ratzinger*	2005–

XLVIII.

Church of Russia

The establishment of an independent Russian Church coincided with the decline of the Byzantine Empire, and the simultaneous rise of the Russian Empire. When Emperor Ivan III married the niece of the last Emperor of Constantinople, the claim of succession passed to the Russian state, the princes of which began calling themselves "tsars" (*i.e.*, "caesars"). It was natural that they would seek the independence of their church to bolster their temporal claims.

Although the Russian Church claimed autocephaly from 1448, the recognition of Constantinople and the other ancient patriarchates was not secured until 1589, when Patriarch Hieremias II invested Metropolitan Iov as the first Russian Patriarch. The Civil War which ensued sixteen years later, at the death of Tsar Boris Godunov, increased the patriarchs' political influence; this reached its height under Patriarch Filaret Romanov, whose son Mikhaïl became the first Tsar of the Romanov Dynasty.

When Patriarch Adrian died in 1700, Peter the Great refused to allow the election of a new Patriarch, leaving Stefan IAvorskiĭ (Yavorsky) as Locum Tenens for 21 years. In 1721 Peter promulgated a new constitution for the Church, which abolished the office of Patriarch, and placed its governance under a Holy Synod administered by a lay official appointed by the Tsar.

Thus was established the precedent of direct governmental interference in, and control of, the Russian Orthodox Church, a practice which was later continued by the Soviet state; the new constitution made the Tsar the head of the Church, and provided for a procurator, a minister of the crown, to administer its day-to-day affairs. When Tsar Nikolaĭ II was overthrown in March of 1917, the Russian Orthodox Church convened a national sobor to elect a new Patriarch; Metropolitan Tikhon assumed office in November of that year, almost simultaneously with the outbreak of the Bolshevik Revolution.

The Soviets placed severe restrictions on the revitalized Church, finally imprisoning Tikhon in 1922, and refusing to allow an election for his successor when he died in 1925. Metropolitan Pëtr became Locum Tenens, but was almost immediately arrested; the Metropolitan of Nizhni-Novgorod, Sergiĭ (previously Metropolitan of Finland), succeeded him later that year as Deputy Locum Tenens.

Sergiĭ issued a declaration in July 1927 in which he altered the Church's official stance toward the Moscow government from one of hostility to outright praise and cooperation. Outside observers have called this statement either the great betrayal or the great salvation of the Russian Church. With the invasion of the German armies in 1941, the political climate in Moscow changed, as every segment of society unified behind the Russian war effort.

Sergiĭ himself gathered funds, issued calls to arms, organized rallies, and did everything possible to hasten the Nazi defeat. His many contributions gained him the favorable attention of Iosif Stalin, who granted his request for new patriarchal elections. Sergiĭ assumed office in late 1943, and died within six months. During the next forty years the government permitted subsequent elections within a year of each vacancy, and made the Church one of the few officially-recognized Christian organizations in the Soviet Union, thereby setting a precedent for the other Eastern block countries to follow.

All other potential "national" Orthodox churches within the USSR, with the exception of the ancient, well-established patriarchates of Armenia and Georgia, were merged into the Moscow Patriarchate, as were some Eastern-rite Catholics (particularly the Ukrainians), and many other Christian denominations and sects. The Church became increasingly active in international Orthodox and ecumenical affairs in the 1970s–1980s, and has been particularly vocal before the World Council of Churches and elsewhere in encouraging anti-nuclear and antiwar movements throughout the world.

During the "glasnost" period of the late 1980s and early '90s, governmental restrictions on the practice of religion in the Soviet Union were gradually lifted, permitting the reopening of old churches, monasteries, cathedrals, and seminaries. At the death of Patriarch Pimen in 1990, the Russian Orthodox Church was able to conduct relatively free, immediate elections for the first time since 1917, resulting in the selection of a vigorous patriarch, Aleksiĭ II.

The relaxation of controls has also, however, seen demands from outlying Soviet republics for the reinstitution of national churches as each of these states has declared its independence, and seems certain to result in the same kind of proliferation of religious groups and sects as has already occurred in the West. By the new century the Russian Church had been forced to agree to the autonomy of several jurisdictions in the newly independent ex–Soviet republics, but had successfully fought for the right to control several other churches.

The primate bears the title Patriarch of Moscow and All Russia. The official language of the Church is Russian. The number of believers in Russia is unknown, but certainly numbers in the many millions.

Sources: *Eastern Christianity and Politics in the Twentieth Century* (Ramet, ed.); *Échos d'Orient*; *Episkepsis*; *Gegenwartslage der Ostkirchen* (Spuler); *History of the Church* (Jedin, ed.); *Jahrbuch der Orthodoxie* (Proc); "Patriarkh" (Buganov); *Orthodoxia*; "50-Letie Vosstanovleniia Patriarshestva"; *Profiles in Belief* (Piepkorn); *Religion in the Soviet Union* (Kolarz); *The Russian Orthodox Church* (Ellis); official church website.

Metropolitans of Moscow

1. Pëtr [#27 of Ukraine]   1305–1325

Interregnum

2.	Feognost [#28 of Ukraine]	1328–1352
3.	Aleksiĭ *Pleshcheev* [#29 of Ukraine]	1354–1378
4.	Kiprian [#30 of Ukraine]	1378–1410
5.	Fotiĭ [#34 of Ukraine]	1410–1436
6.	Isidor [#36 of Ukraine]	1436–1448
7.	Iona [#37 of Ukraine]	1448–1462
8.	Feodor	1462–1467
9.	Filipp I	1467–1472
10.	Gerontiĭ	1472–1491
11.	Zosima	1491–1496
12.	Simeon	1496–1511
13.	Varlaam	1511–1521
14.	Porfiriĭ	1521–1522
15.	Daniïl	1522–1539

Interregnum

16.	Makariĭ (I)	1542–1563
17.	German	1563–1565

Interregnum

18.	Filipp II	1568–1572
19.	Antoniĭ	1572–1582
20.	Dionisiĭ	1582–1587
21.	Iov	1587–1589

Patriarchs of Russia
(*The Tsarist Patriarchate*)

1.	Iov	1589–1605
	Ignatiĭ [anti-patriarch]	1605–1606
2.	Germogen	1606–1612

Interregnum

3.	Filaret Romanov [father of Tsar Mikhaml]	1619–1633
4.	Ioasaf I	1634–1641
5.	Iosif	1642–1652
6.	Nikon	1652–1658

Interregnum

7.	Ioasaf II	1667–1672

8.	Pitirim	1672–1673
9.	Ioakim *Savelov*	1674–1690
10.	Adrian	1690–1700
	Stefan *IAvorskiĭ* [locum tenens]	1700–1721

PATRIARCHATE SUSPENDED 1721

Archbishops and Metropolitans of Moscow

| 22. | Iosif (II) *Volchanskiĭ* | 1742–1745 |
| 23. | Platon I *Malinovskiĭ* | 1748–1754 |

INTERREGNUM

| 24. | Timofeĭ *Sacherbatskiĭ* | 1764–1767 |
| 25. | Amvrosiĭ *Zertis-Kamenskiĭ* | 1768–1771 |

INTERREGNUM

| 26. | Platon II *Levshin* | 1775–1812 |

INTERREGNUM

27.	Avgustin *Vinogradskiĭ*	1818–1819
28.	Serafim *Glagolevskiĭ*	1819–1821
29.	Filaret *Drozdov*	1821–1867
30.	Innokentiĭ *Veniaminov* [#2 of America]	1868–1879
31.	Makariĭ (II) *Bulgakov*	1879–1882
32.	Ioannikiĭ *Rudnev* [#8 of exarchs of Georgia]	1882–1891
33.	Leontiĭ *Lebedinskiĭ*	1891–1893
34.	Sergiĭ *Liapidevksiĭ*	1893–1898

INTERREGNUM

| 35. | Makariĭ (III) *Nevskiĭ* | 1912–1917 |

Patriarchs of Russia

| 11. | Tikhon *Belavin* [#8 of America] | 1917–1925 |
| | Agafangel [locum tenens] | 1922 |

INTERREGNUM

| | Pëtr *Polianskiĭ* [locum tenens] | 1925 |

	Sergiĭ *Stragorodskiĭ* [deputy locum tenens]	1925–1926
	Iosif *Petrovykh* [deputy locum tenens]	1926
	Serafim *Samoĭlovich* [deputy locum tenens]	1926–1927
	Sergiĭ *Stragorodskiĭ* [deputy locum tenens]	1927–1937
	Sergiĭ *Stragorodskiĭ* [locum tenens]	1937–1943
12.	Sergiĭ *Stragorodskiĭ* [#3 of Finland]	1943–1944
	Aleksiĭ *Simanskiĭ* [locum tenens]	1944–1945
13.	Aleksiĭ I *Simanskiĭ*	1945–1970
	Pimen *Izvekov* [locum tenens]	1970–1971
14.	Pimen *Izvekov*	1971–1990
	Filaret *Denysenko* [locum tenens]	1990
15.	Aleksiĭ II *Ridiger* [#7 of Estonia]	1990–

THE OLD BELIEVERS

When the Russian Orthodox Patriarch Nikon attempted to reform his church, beginning in 1652, adopting the liturgical practices of the Greek churches, a number of priests from the Moscow parishes rebelled, and eventually split from the Russian Church in 1666. Their leader was the priest Avvakum Petrovich, who was burned at the stake for heresy in 1682. Thereafter, the Old Believers were greatly persecuted and driven underground. The anathemas levied by the Russian Church in 1666 were finally lifted in 1971.

Two basic groups evolved. One, the so-called "Popovtsy" branch, maintained the continued use of clergy (priests) and the sacraments, although lacking any higher prelates; while the other, the "Bezpopovtsy" faction, dispensed with ministers and all of the sacraments, save only baptism. As the Old Believers developed over the centuries, they splintered into at least a dozen different organizations, several of them quite large.

In 1847 one group of the Old Believers implemented a more formal Church structure. Bishop Amvrosiĭ Popovich, a Serbian refugee, was named the first Archbishop; he consecrated the original group of bishops. The "Belokrinitsia" hierarchy, as this branch of the Old Believers came to be called, or more formally, the Russkaia Pravoslavnaia Staroobriadcheskaia TSerkov', split temporarily into two factions in 1863, each with its own primate, although the groups were reunited in 1912. This is by the far largest of the surviving Old Believers organizations. The primate uses the title (since 1988) of Metropolitan Archbishop of Moscow and All Russia.

A second major church, the so-called "Novzybkov" hierarchy, or Russkaia Drevlepravoslavnaia TSerkov', was organized in 1923 under Archbishop Nikola Pozdnev. Its primate uses the title (since 2002) of Patriarch of Moscow and All Russia. The Novzybkov Church has about one-third of the parishes of the older hierarchy.

The official language of both Churches is Russian. The number of communicants for all Old Believers groups exceeds two million.

Sources: official church websites.

Metropolitan Archbishops of Moscow of the "Belokrinitsia" Hierarchy
(Archbishops 1847, Metropolitans 1988)

1.	Amvrosiĭ *Popovich*	1847–1863
2.	Antoniĭ *Shutov*	1863–1881
3.	Savvatiĭ *Levshin*	1882–1898
4.	Ioann *Kartushin*	1898–1915
5.	Meletiĭ *Kartushin*	1915–1934
	Vikentiĭ *Nikitin* [locum tenens]	1934–1938
6.	Irinarkh *Parfenov*	1940–1952
7.	Flavian *Slesarev*	1952–1960
8.	Iosif *Morzhakov*	1961–1970
9.	Nikodim *Latyshev*	1971–1986
	Anastasiĭ *Kononov* [locum tenens]	1986
	Alimpiĭ *Gusev* [locum tenens]	1986
10.	Alimpiĭ *Gusev*	1986–2003
	Ioann *Vitushkin* [locum tenens]	2004
11.	Andrian *Chetvergov*	2004–2005
	Ioann *Vitushkin* [locum tenens]	2005

Second Branch

2.	Antoniĭ *Guslitskiĭ*	1863–1870
3.	Iov *Borisov*	1871–1912

Merged with the Belokrinitsia Church

Patriarchs of the "Novzybkov" Hierarchy
(Archbishops 1923, Patriarchs 2002)

1.	Nikola *Pozdnev*	1923–1934
	Stefan *Rastorguev* [locum tenens]	1934–1935
2.	Stefan *Rastorguev*	1935–1937
3.	Mikhaïl *Kochetov*	1938–1944
4.	Ioann *Kalinin*	1944–1955
5.	Epifaniĭ *Abramov*	1955–1963
6.	Ieremiia *Matveevich*	1963–1969
7.	Pavel *Mashinin*	1969–1979
8.	Gennadiĭ *Antonov*	1979–1996
	Aristarkh *Kalinin* [locum tenens]	1996
9.	Aristarkh *Kalinin*	1996–2000
10.	Aleksandr *Kalinin*	2000–

The Russian Orthodox Church Outside Russia

Patriarch Tikhon issued a statement in 1917 urging the faithful to act independently to preserve the Russian Church; subsequently, a group of exiled, pro-tsarist church members and prelates organized a sobor at Sremski Karlovci, Yugoslavia, on 21 November–2 December, 1921, under the presidency of Metropolitan Antoniĭ of Kiev. The result of this meeting was the organization of the Russian Orthodox Church Outside Russia, sometimes called the Synodal Church.

The Church disapproves of the cooperation between the Patriarchal Church and the Russian government, as embodied in the letters issued by Deputy Locum Tenens (later Patriarch) Sergiĭ Stragodorskiĭ in 1926 and 1927. Antoniĭ became the first head of the Church, with his see at Geneva, Switzerland. He was succeeded in 1936 by Metropolitan Anastasiĭ (who died in 1965), who was followed on his retirement by Metropolitan Filaret in 1964. The chief see of the Metropolitan was moved during the Second World War to Munich, Germany, and in 1952 to New York.

Since then the Church has attracted dissident factions from other exiled churches, particularly those with origins in Eastern Europe. The membership of the Church (roughly 150,000 communicants) is centered primarily in the United States, Western Europe, and Australia, although several dioceses have also been established within the former Soviet Union since 1990.

In 1994 the Russian parishes split into their own independent church, the Free Russian Orthodox Church (called The Russian Orthodox Autonomous Church from 1998). In 2001 Metropolitan Vitaliĭ retired, but then abruptly rescinded his abdication several days later, on October 24, eventually establishing a third church, The Russian Orthodox Church in Exile, centered in Canada.

Sources: *Eastern Christianity and Politics in the Twentieth Century* (Ramet, ed.); *Episkepsis*; "The First Council of the Russian Church Abroad in Sremski Karlovtsi (21 November–2 December 1921)" (Zernov); *History of the Church* (Jedin, ed.); *Jahrbuch der Orthodoxie* (Proc); *Orthodoxia*; *The Russian Orthodox Church Outside Russia* (Young); *Profiles in Belief* (Piepkorn); official church websites.

Metropolitans and First Hierarchs of the Russian Orthodox Church Outside Russia

1.	Antoniĭ *Khrapovitskiĭ* [#82 of Ukraine]	1921–1936
2.	Anastasiĭ *Gribanovskiĭ*	1936–1964
3.	Filaret *Voznesenskiĭ*	1964–1985
	Vitaliĭ *Ustinov* [locum tenens]	1985–1986
4.	Vitaliĭ *Ustinov*	1986–
5.	Laurus (Lavr) *Skurla*	2001–

Russian Orthodox Autonomous Church

1.	Valentin *Rusantsov*	1994–

XLIX.

Church of Serbia (Peć)

As in the other Slavic countries of Eastern Europe, the fate of the Serbian Orthodox Church has been closely tied to the rise and fall of the Serbian state. The first King of Serbia, Stefan II, made his brother, Sava, the first Metropolitan of the Church, in 1219; Sava organized the Church, crowned his brother, and established his see at Peć (also called Pech or Ipek). In 1346 a synod proclaimed the Church autocephalous, awarding the primate the title of Patriarch. Except for a brief period from about 1463–1557, during which the Church was ruled by Ohrid, it remained independent until the suppression of the South Slav patriarchates in 1766–67, when, at the behest of the Ecumenical Patriarch Samouēl, Ottoman Sultan Mustafa III placed Peć and Ohrid under the aegis of Constantinople.

The Serbs revolted against their Turkish overlords beginning in 1806, finally attaining autonomy in 1829 and independence in 1878. Correspondingly, the Serbian Church was given autonomy by Constantinople in 1832 and autocephaly in 1879, the primates using the title Metropolitan Archbishops of Serbia. After World War I, when Serbia became the nucleus of the new state of Yugoslavia, the five autonomous South Slav churches agreed on 26 May 1919 to the unification of the Serbian Churches, and on 30 August 1920 unified their administrations under a common Patriarch.

Serbian Metropolitan Dimitrije was elected first head of the revived Church on 12 November 1920. Constantinople did not recognize the autocephaly of the new Serbian Church until 1922. The Nazi invasion of 1941 severely disrupted the Church administration, forcing the Patriarch into exile; he was eventually imprisoned at Dachau. In addition, the newly-organized Nazi puppet state of Croatia insisted that the Orthodox population within its jurisdiction be erected into an autocephalous church of its own; those members of the Serbian Church who refused to submit were systematically arrested, beaten, and/or murdered. This Croatian Church was immediately suppressed by the government of Marshal Tito in 1945.

The primate bears the title Archbishop of Peć, Metropolitan of Belgrade and Karlovci, and Patriarch of Serbia. The official Church language is Serbian. The chief see is located at Belgrade (Beograd). Roughly eleven million communicants are located primarily in Serbia and Montenegro, plus parts of Bosnic-Hercegovina and Croatia, with a strong overseas contingent in the United States.

Sources: *Biographisches Lexikon zur Geschichte Südosteuropas* (Bernath & Nehring);

The Bosnian Church (Fine); *Church and State in Yugoslavia Since 1945* (Alexander); *Eastern Christianity and Politics in the Twentieth Century* (Ramet, ed.); *Échos d'Orient*; *Episkepis*; *Europa World Yearbook*; *Gegenwartslage der Ostkirchen* (Spuler); *The Habsburg Empire, 1790–1918* (Macartney); *A History of Christianity in the Balkans* (Spinka); *A History of Modern Serbia, 1804–1918* (Petrovich); *History of the Church* (Jedin, ed.); *Jahrbuch der Orthodoxie* (Proc); *Orthodoxia*; "Pećska Patrijarsija" (Grujić); *Profiles in Belief* (Piepkorn); *Srpska Pravoslavna Crkva, 1219–1969* (Lavrentije); official church website.

[For information on the former autocephalous Serbian Church of Karlovci, see the chapter on The Churches of Austria-Hungary.]

METROPOLITAN ARCHBISHOPS OF PEĆ
(Metropolitan Archbishops, 1219–1346)
[*Greek names are listed in parentheses*]

1.	Sava I *Nemanjić*	1219–1233
2.	Arsenije I *Sremac*	1233–1263
3.	Sava II *Nemanjić* [nephew of #1]	1263–1271
4.	Danilo I	1271–1272
5.	Joanikije I	1272–1276
6.	Jevstatije I	1279–1286
7.	Jakov	1286–1292
8.	Jevstatije II	1292–1309
9.	Sava III	1309–1316
10.	Nikodim I	1317–1324
11.	Danilo II	1324–1337
12.	Joanikije II	1338–1346

PATRIARCHS OF PEĆ

1.	Joanikije II	1346–1354
2.	Sava IV	1354–1375
3.	Jefrem	1375–1379
4.	Spiridon	1379–1389
	Jefrem [2nd time]	1389–1392
5.	Danilo III	1392–1398
6.	Sava V	1398–1406
7.	Danilo IV	1406
8.	Kirilo I	1407–1419
9.	Nikon	1420–1435

INTERREGNUM

10.	Teofan	1446

XLIX. Church of Serbia

11.	Nikodim II	1446–1453
12.	Arsenije II	1453–1463

Metropolitan Archbishops of Peć

13.	Joanikije	1506?
14.	Jovan	1508?–1509?
15.	Teodosije	1520?
16.	Marko	1524?
17.	Simeon	1528–1532?
18.	Pavle	1530?–1541?
19.	Teofan	1544?
20.	Josif	1544?

Interregnum

Patriarchs of Peć

13.	Makarije *Sokolović*	1557–1571
14.	Antonije *Sokolović*	1571–1575
15.	Gerasim (or Đerasim) *Sokolović*	1575–1586
16.	Savatije *Sokolović*	1587
17.	Nikanor	1589?
18.	Jerotej	1589–1591
19.	Filip	1591–1592
20.	Jovan *Kantul*	1592–1614
21.	Pajsije I *Janjevac*	1614–1648
22.	Gavrilo I *Rajić*	1648–1655
23.	Maksim *Skopljanac*	1655–1674
24.	Arsenije III *Crnojević* [#1 of Karlovci]	1674–1690
25.	Kalinik I *Skopljanac*	1691–1710
26.	Atanasije I *Ljubojević*	1711–1712
27.	Mojsije *Rajović*	1712–1726
28.	Arsenije IV *Jovanović Šakabenda* [#8 of Karlovci]	1725–1737
29.	Joanikije III (Iōannikios) *Karadža*	1739–1746
30.	Atanasije II *Gavrilović*	1747–1752
31.	Gavrilo II *Mihailović Sarajevac*	1752
32.	Gavrilo III (Gabriēl) *Nikolin*	1752–
33.	Vikentije I *Stefanović*	1756?
34.	Pajsije II (Païsios)	1757?
35.	Gavrilo IV (Gabriēl)	1757?–1758
36.	Kirilo II	1758–1763
37.	Vasilije *Jovanović Brkić* (died 1772)	1763–1765
38.	Kalinik II (Kallinikos)	1765–1766

Patriarchate Disestablished 1766

METROPOLITANS OF BEOGRAD
(*Metropolitan Archbishops 1831*)

1. Antim I (Anthimos)
2. Danilo (Daniēl)
3. Jeremije (Hieremias) *Papazoğlou* — 1766–1784
4. Dionisije I (Dionysios) *Papazoğlou* — 1785–1791
5. Metodije (Methodios) — 1791–1801
6. Leontije (Leontios) *Lambrović* — 1801–1810
7. Melentije I *Stefanović* [unconsecrated] — 1809–1811
   Leontije [2nd time] — 1811–1813
8. Dionisije II (Dionysios) *Nislija* — 1813–1815
9. Melentije II *Pavlović* — 1815–1816
10. Agatangel (Agathangelos) [#243 of Constantinople] — 1816–1825
11. Kirilo (Kyrillos) — 1825–1826
12. Antim II (Anthimos) — 1828–1830
    Melentije II *Pavlović* [2nd time] — 1830–1833
13. Petar *Jovanović* — 1833–1858
14. Mihaïlo *Jovanović* — 1859–1881
    Mojsije *Veresić* [locum tenens] — 1881–1883
15. Teodosije *Mraović* — 1883–1889
    Mihaïlo [2nd time] — 1889–1898
16. Inokentije *Pavlović* — 1898–1905
17. Dimitrije *Pavlović* — 1905–1920

PATRIARCHS OF SERBIA AND PEĆ

39. Dimitrije *Pavlović* — 1920–1930
40. Varnava *Rosić* — 1930–1937
    Dositej *Vasić* [locum tenens] — 1937–1938
41. Gavrilo V *Dožić* [#48 of Montenegro] — 1938–1950
    Josif *Cvijović* [locum tenens] — 1941–1946
    Arsenije *Bradvarević* [locum tenens] — 1950
42. Vikentije II *Prodanov* — 1950–1958
    Hrizostom *Vojinović* [locum tenens] — 1958
43. German *Đorić* — 1958–1990
    Jovan *Pavlović* [locum tenens] — 1989–1990
44. Pavle *Stojčević* — 1990–

THE ORTHODOX CHURCH OF CROATIA

The independent state of Croatia was founded by Nazi-supported partisans on 31 March 1942. Within months the new regime had decided to erect its own autocephalous church to serve the Orthodox communicants within the boundaries of the new republic. This unilateral declaration of independence was not recognized by any other Orthodox church. A Russian prelate living in exiled retirement in Yugoslavia, Bishop Germogen, was chosen and enthroned on 7 June 1942. He was originally offered the title of Patriarch, but decided to use that of Metropolitan instead. Within days of the fall of the Nazi regime in May of 1945, Metropolitan Germogen was arrested and summarily executed by the forces of Marshal Tito. He was 85 years old.

METROPOLITANS OF CROATIA

1. Germogen   1942–1945

L.

Church of the Sinai

The smallest of the universally-recognized autonomous Orthodox churches is the Church of the Sinai, consisting of the monastery of Saint Catherine in the Southern Sinai Desert, and the small neighboring dioceses of Pharan and Raithu. One of the oldest continually-occupied abbeys in the world, it was founded by Emperor Justinian I in 530. Saint Catherine's Monastery was autonomous from an early date, as both the Greek Patriarchates of Alexandria and Jerusalem tried to bring it under their jurisdiction; the recognition of its independent status was finally granted by Constantinople in 1575, and by the other Orthodox churches in 1782.

In the last hundred years the monastery has become known to the outside world for its enormous treasure of original manuscripts dating from early Christian times. The abbot is elected by a council (*synaxis*) of senior monks, and then consecrated by the Greek Orthodox Patriarch of Jerusalem. A church office is also maintained in Cairo, Egypt.

The primate bears the title Archbishop of Sinai, Pharan, and Raithu. The official Church language is Greek. Approximately one hundred communicants worship at the several parishes controlled by the Church of the Sinai, plus the central community of twenty to fifty monks.

Sources: "Les Archevêques du Sinaï" (Cheikho); "Die Autokephale Kirche des Berges Sinai" (Lubeck); *Échos d'Orient*; *Episkepis*; *History of the Church* (Jedin, ed.); *A History of Sinai* (Eckenstein); *Jahrbuch der Orthodoxie* (Proc); *Hē Monē tou Horous Sina* (Papamichalopoulos); *Oriens Christianus* (Le Quien); *Orthodoxia*; *Syntomos Historia tēs Hieras Monēs tou Sina* (Amantos).

ABBOTS AND ARCHBISHOPS OF THE SINAI
(*Bishops of Pharan 530, Bishops of Sinai 869, Archbishops 1203?*)

1.	Geōrgios I	
2.	Netras (or Natēras)	
3.	Mōüsēs	
4.	Martyrios	400?
5.	Makarios I	454?

L. Church of the Sinai

6.	Phōtios	544?–546?
7.	Theodōros	649?–680?
8.	Kōnstantinos	–869?
9.	Markos I	869–
10.	Ēlias	900?
11.	Makarios II	967?
12.	Petros	985?
13.	Symeōn I	1003–1035
14.	Iōrios	1035–
15.	Iōannēs I *Athēnaios*	1081–1091
16.	Markos II	1100?
17.	Zacharias	1103–1114

Interregnum

18.	Geōrgios II	1130–1149

Interregnum

19.	Gabriēl I	1154–1160
20.	Iōannēs II	1164?
21.	Germanos I	1177?
22.	Markos III	1181?
23.	Symeōn II	1203–1223
24.	Euthymios	1223–1224
25.	Makarios III	1224–
26.	Germanos II	1228?
27.	Theodosios	1239?
28.	Symeōn III	1258?
29.	Iōannēs III	1265–1290
30.	Arsenios I	1290–1299?
31.	Iōannēs IV	1299?–
32.	Symeōn IV	1306–1324
33.	Dōrotheos I	1324–1333
34.	Germanos III	1333–
35.	Arsenios II	1338?
36.	Markos IV	1375?
37.	Iōb	1395?
38.	Athanasios I	1410?
39.	Sabbas	1429?
40.	Abraamios (or Abramios)	1435?
41.	Gabriēl II	1445?
42.	Michaēl	1455?
43.	Silouanos	1465?
44.	Kyrillos I	1470?

45.	Solomōn	1480?
46.	Makarios IV	1486?
47.	Lazaros	1491?
48.	Markos V	1496?
49.	Daniēl	1507?
50.	Klēmēs	1514?
51.	Sōphronios	1540?–1545
52.	Makarios V *Kyprios*	1547–
53.	Neilos *Kouerinos*	1555?
54.	Eugenios	1567–1583
55.	Anastasios	1583–1592
56.	Laurentios	1592–1617
57.	Iōasaph *apo Rhodou*	1617–1660
58.	Nektarios [#119 of Jerusalem]	1660–1661
59.	Ananias	1661–1671
60.	Iōannikios I *Laskaris*	1671–1702
61.	Kosmas *Byzantios* [#115 of Alexandria; #218 of Constantinople]	1703–1706
62.	Athanasios II *apo Naousēs tēs Makedonias*	1708–1720
63.	Iōannikios II *Lesbios*	1721–1728
64.	Nikēphoros *Marthalēs Glykys*	1728–1747
65.	Kōnstantios I	1748–1759
66.	Kyrillos II *Krēs*	1759–1790

INTERREGNUM

67.	Dōrotheos II *Byzantios*	1794–1797

INTERREGNUM

68.	Kōnstantios II [#244 of Constantinople]	1804?–1859
69.	Kyrillos III *Byzantios*	1859–1867
70.	Kallistratos	1867–1884
71.	Porphyrios I *apo Zakynthou*	1885–1904
72.	Porphyrios II *Logothetēs*	1904–1926
73.	Porphyrios III *Paulinos*	1926–1968
74.	Grēgorios	1969–1973
75.	Damianos *Samartsēs*	1973–

LI.

Churches of Ukraine

The Russian Revolution of 1917 revitalized the long-dormant movement for Ukrainian independence, and simultaneously led to demands for a separate Ukrainian Orthodox Church. A series of sobors during the height of the Russian Civil War resulted in a split in the Church, with the hierarchy unanimously supporting the Moscow patriarchate, and many laymen and lesser clergy calling for autocephaly. The Ukrainian government issued the "Law on the Supreme Authority of the Ukrainian Church" on 1 January 1919, establishing an autonomous Ukrainian Church, but was unable to implement it, due to the ensuing Soviet invasion of Ukraine.

The reform movement organized the All-Ukrainian Orthodox Church Council in 1919–20, taking over a number of parishes previously controlled by Moscow. The Russian bishop of Kiev then suspended the priestly functions of any clergy supporting the movement; the Council responded by declaring unilateral autocephaly on 5 May 1920. Having no bishops, the movement elected Archpriest Vasyl' Lypkivs'kiĭ Metropolitan of Kiev and All Ukraine on 23 October 1921, making him bishop through a laying-on of hands by the members of the sobor. He in turn ordained other bishops.

Many of the other Orthodox churches refused to recognize the validity of Lypkivs'kiĭ's election or consecration, or the validity of the consecrations made unilaterally by him, in violation of usual Orthodox practice; and he also faced increasingly harsh repression from the Soviets, finally being deposed by them in October 1927. The sobor then elected Mykolaĭ Borets'kiĭ as his successor. The government forcibly convened an extraordinary sobor in January 1930 for the sole purpose of dissolving the Church; its leaders were then imprisoned or exiled.

The German occupation of Ukraine led to a revitalization of Orthodox religious life there, and the establishment of two churches: the Autonomous Orthodox Church in Ukraine was founded in August 1941, under the leadership of Metropolitan Aleksiĭ Hromads'kiĭ; it acknowledged the supremacy of the Moscow Patriarchate, but refused its authority while the Soviets controlled Russia; the Ukrainian Autocephalous Orthodox Church was founded in 1942 by Metropolitan Dionizy of Poland, who consecrated Polykarp Sikors'kiĭ Metropolitan.

Attempts to unite the two churches failed in 1942. Metropolitan Aleksiĭ was assassinated by partisans in 1943. When the Germans withdrew from Ukraine in 1943–44, most of the clergy followed them into exile; those who remained were arrested or deposed, their parishes being reincorporated against their will into the Patriarchate of Russia, which established its own metropolitanate at Kiev.

Metropolitan Polykarp and his followers settled in western Europe. At a sobor in 1947 the Church split into two factions, the larger following Polykarp, and a much smaller group Archbishop Hryhoriĭ. Polykarp died in Paris in 1953, when he was succeeded by Nikanor Abramovych, whose seat was located at Karlsruhe, West Germany. Nikanor established communion with the Canadian Ukrainian Church and the UOC-USA in 1957; at his death in 1969, he was succeeded by Mstyslav Skrypnyk, who became head of the UOC-USA in 1971. The administrative offices of the Church were then transferred to South Bound Brook, New Jersey, although the two churches remain legally and canonically independent.

Following the election of Russian Patriarch Aleksiĭ II in 1990, the Synod of the Russian Church announced that it had granted the metropolitanate Ukrainian Orthodox Church (hereafter known as the Ukrainian Orthodox Church — Moscow) complete autonomy, and that the latter body would henceforth be allowed to be self-governing, with its own Synod. However, nonagenarian Metropolitan Mstyslav Skrypnyk of the Ukrainian Autocephalous Orthodox Church, head of one of the largest independent jurisdictions outside the former Soviet Union, and himself one of the last survivors of the remnants of the original Ukrainian hierarchy, returned to Kiev and was proclaimed Patriarch Mstyslav I on 18 November 1990.

Russian-appointed Metropolitan Filaret Denysenko at first opposed Mstyslav, but when scandals in the former's personal life resulted in him being stripped of all authority by Russian Patriarch Aleksiĭ II in May 1992, he abruptly recognized Mstyslav and tried to subsume his Church, eventually proclaiming the deposition of the elderly primate on 16 December 1992.

Meanwhile, the Holy Synod of the Church of Russia elected on 27 May 1992 a new Metropolitan (soon elevated to the title of Exarch), Volodymyr Slobodan, leaving three distinct factions in Kiev, neither of them recognizing the others' jurisdictions, and all fighting over legal and actual possession of the church parishes and properties. Patriarch Mstyslav died on 11 June 1993.

One faction (the Ukrainian Orthodox Church — Kiev) elected Volodymyr Romaniuk as its new Patriarch, with Metropolitan Filaret as Deputy Head; the other (the Ukrainian Autocephalous Orthodox Church) named Dymytriĭ IArema as Patriarch. The two rival patriarchs were consecrated within ten days of each other in October 1993. The Ukrainian government has variously supported the factions of all three churches, depending on the political winds. At IArema's death, the UAOC declined to elect a successor called "Patriarch"; Archbishop Mefodiĭ became Acting Primate. Volodymyr Romaniuk was succeeded at his death in 1995 by Filaret Denysenko.

The Russian primate bears the title Metropolitan Archbishop of Kiev and All Ukraine. Denysenko's church claims 15 million communicants and 3,000 parishes under its control; Kudriakov's church claims 1,500 parishes; Slobodan's church claims 5,000 parishes; all of these figures may be exaggerated. The official language of these churches is Ukrainian.

Sources: *Échos d'Orient*; *The Encyclopedia of American Religions* (Melton); *Episkepsis*; *Gegenwartslage der Ostkirchen* (Spuler); *History of the Church* (Jedin, ed.); *Jahrbuch der Orthodoxie* (Proc); *The Old Catholic Sourcebook* (Pruter & Melton); *Narys Istoriĭ*

Ukraïns'koï Pravoslavnoï Tserkvy (An Outline of the History of the Ukrainian Orthodox Church) (Vlasovs'kyĭ); *Die Orthodoxe Kirche in der Ukraine von 1917 bis 1945* (Heyer); *Orthodoxia*; *Profiles in Belief* (Piepkorn); *Religion in the Soviet Union* (Kolarz); *Ukraine: A Concise Encyclopaedia* (Nubijovyc); official church websites.

METROPOLITAN ARCHBISHOPS OF UKRAINE
(Metropolitans of Kiev 988, Metropolitans of Kiev and All Rus' 1243, Metropolitans of Kiev and Halych 1507)

1.	Mykhaïlo I	988–992
2.	Leon(tiĭ)	992–1008
3.	Ioann I	1008–1038
4.	Feopempt	1039–
5.	Kyrylo I	1045?
6.	Ilarion	1051–1055?
7.	IEfrem	1055?–1061
8.	Heorhiĭ I	1062?–1073
9.	Ioann II	1077?–1089
10.	Ioann III	1090–1091
11.	Mykola I	1097?–1101
12.	Nykyfor I	1104–1121
13.	Mykyta	1122–1126

INTERREGNUM

14.	Mykhaïlo II	1130–1145?
15.	Klyment *Smoliatych*	1147–1159
16.	Konstiantyn I	1155–1159
17.	Feodor	1160–1162?
18.	Ioann IV	1163–1166
19.	Konstiantyn II	1167–1169
20.	Mykhaïlo III	1171

INTERREGNUM

21.	Nykyfor II	1183–1198

INTERREGNUM

22.	Matfeĭ	1201–1220

INTERREGNUM

23.	Kyrylo II	1224–1233

Interregnum

24.	Iosyp I	1236?–1240?

Interregnum

25.	Kyrylo III	1243?–1281
26.	Maksym *Hrek "The Greek"* (Maximos)	1283–1305

Interregnum

27.	Petro I [#1 of Russia]	1308–1326
28.	Feognost I (Theognostos) [#2 of Russia]	1328–1353
29.	Aleksiĭ *Pleshchieiev* [#3 of Russia]	1354–1378
30.	Kupriian [#4 of Russia]	1375?–1381
31.	Mykhaïlo IV (or Mytiaĭ)	1378?–1379
32.	Pymin	1380–1384
33.	Dionysiĭ I	1384–1385

Interregnum

34.	Fotiĭ (Phōtios) [#5 of Russia]	1408–1431
35.	Herasym	1433–1435
36.	Isydor I (Isidōros) [#6 of Russia]	1436–1441
37.	Iona I *Odnoüshev* [#7 of Russia]	1442?–1461
38.	Hryhoriĭ *Bolharyn*	1458–1472

Interregnum

39.	Spyrydon	1475–1482
40.	Symeon	1481–1488

Interregnum

41.	Iona II *Hlezna*	1492–1494
42.	Makariĭ I	1495–1497
43.	Iosyp II *Bolharynovych*	1498–1501
44.	Iona III	1503–1507
45.	Iosyp III *Soltan*	1508–1521
46.	Iosyp IV	1522–1533
47.	Makariĭ II	1534–1555
48.	Syl'vestr I *Bel'kevych*	1556–1567
49.	Iona IV *Protachevych-Ostrovs'kiĭ*	1568–1577
50.	Iliia *Kucha*	1577–1579

LI. Churches of Ukraine

51.	Onysyfir *Petrovych-Devochka*	1579–1589
52.	Mykhaïlo V *Rahoza*	1589–1596

INTERREGNUM

Greek Exarchs of Ukraine

53.	Iov *Borets'kyĭ*	1620–1631
54.	Isaiia *Kopyns'kyĭ*	1631–1640
55.	Petro II *Mohyla*	1633–1646
56.	Syl'vestr II *Kosov*	1647–1657
57.	Dionysiĭ II *Balaban*	1658–1663
58.	Iosyp V *Neliubovych-Tukal's'kyĭ*	1663–1676
59.	Antoniĭ I *Vinnyts'kyĭ*	1676–1679

INTERREGNUM

Russian Metropolitans of Ukraine

60.	Hedeon *Chetvertyns'kyĭ*	1685–1690
61.	Varlaam I *IAsyns'kyĭ*	1690–1707
62.	Ioasaf I *Krakovs'kyĭ*	1708–1718

INTERREGNUM

63.	Varlaam II *Vanatovych*	1722–1730
64.	Rafaïl *Zborovs'kyĭ*	1731–1747
65.	Tymofiĭ *Shcherbats'kiĭ*	1748–1757
66.	Arseniĭ I *Mohylians'kyĭ*	1757–1770
67.	Havryïl I *Kremenets'kyĭ*	1770–1783
68.	Samuïl *Myslavs'kyĭ*	1783–1796
69.	Iierofeĭ *Malyts'kyĭ*	1796–1799
70.	Havryïl II *Bodoni-Banulesko*	1799–1803
71.	Serapion *Aleksandrovs'kyĭ*	1803–1822
72.	IEvgen *Bolkhovitinov*	1822–1837
73.	Filaret I *Amfiteatrov*	1837–1857
74.	Isydor II *Nykol's'kyĭ*	1858–1860
75.	Arseniĭ II *Moskvyn*	1860–1876
76.	Filofeĭ *Uspens'kyĭ*	1876–1882
77.	Platon *Horogets'kyĭ* [#3 of Latvia]	1882–1891
78.	Ioanikiĭ *Rydniev*	1891–1900
79.	Feognost II *Lebediev*	1900–1903
80.	Flavian *Horodets'kyĭ* [#12 of exarchs of Georgia, #6 of Poland]	1903–1915

81.	Volodymyr I *Bohoiavlens'kyĭ* [#11 of Georgia]	1915–1918
82.	Antoniĭ II *Khrapovyts'kyĭ* [#1 of Russia—Church Outside Russia]	1918–1919
83.	Nazariĭ *Blynov*	1919–1921
84.	Mykhaïlo VI *IEpmakov*	1921–1929
85.	Heorhiĭ II *Deliiev*	1923–1926
86.	Makariĭ III *Karmazin*	1924–1925
87.	Sergiĭ I *Kumyns'kyĭ*	1925–1930
88.	Dymytriĭ *Verbyts'kyĭ*	1930–1932
89.	Sergiĭ II *Hryshyn*	1932–1934
90.	Konstiantyn III *D'iakov*	1934–1937
91.	Oleksandr *Petrovs'kyĭ*	1937–1940
92.	Mykola II *IArushevych*	1941–1944
93.	Panteleimon *Rudyk*	1941–1943
94.	Ioann V *Sokolov*	1944–1964
95.	Ioasaf II *Leliukhin*	1964–1966
96.	Filaret II *Denysenko* [#3 of UAOC-KP]	1966–1992
97.	Volodymyr II *Sabodan*	1992–

UKRAINIAN AUTOCEPHALOUS ORTHODOX CHURCH
(Metropolitans 1921, Archbishops 1942, Patriarchs 1990)

1.	Vasyl'(iĭ) *Lypkivs'kyĭ*	1921–1927
2.	Mykola *Borets'kyĭ*	1927–1930

INTERREGNUM

3.	Polykarp *Sikors'kyĭ*	1942–1953
4.	Nikanor *Burshak-Abramovych*	1953–1969
5.	Mstyslav *Skrypnyk* [#3 of Canada; #2 of USA]	1969–1993
6.	Dymytriĭ *IArema*	1993–2000
	Ihor *Isichenko* [locum tenens]	2000
7.	Mefodiĭ *Kudriakov* [acting primate]	2000–

PATRIARCHS OF THE UKRAINIAN ORTHODOX CHURCH—KIEVAN PATRIARCHATE

1.	Mstyslav *Skrypnyk* [#3 of Canada; #2 of USA]	1990–1993
	Mykola *Hrokh* [locum tenens]	1990–1991
	Antoniĭ *Masendych* [locum tenens]	1991–1993
2.	Volodymyr *Romaniuk*	1993–1995
3.	Filaret *Denysenko* [#96 of Ukraine]	1995–

Metropolitans of the Ukrainian Autonomous Church

1. Aleksiĭ *Hromads'kyĭ* 1942–1943

Metropolitans of the Ukrainian Church of Halych

1. Aleksiĭ   1140?
2. Kuz'ma   1156?
3. Nifont   1303–1305
4. Havryïl   1331?
5. Feodor   1337–1347
6. Antoniĭ   1371–1391

Merged with the Metropolitanate of Kiev

Ukrainian Churches in Exile

The Ukrainian Greek Orthodox Church of Canada

The Ukrainian Greek Orthodox Church in Canada was first organized in 1918 as an autocephalous church under a Syrian bishop, Germanos. In 1924 Ioan Teodorovych came to America, and became head of both the Canadian and American churches. Ilarion Ohiĭenko was consecrated as the first Metropolitan Archbishop of the Canadian Church in 1951. Communion was established in 1957 with the UOC-USA and with the church in Europe.

After the election of Ukrainian Patriarch Mstyslav I in 1990, Metropolitan Vasylyĭ severed his connections with the American autocephalous church, and joined the Greek Orthodox Archdiocese of America, thereby acknowledging the supremacy of the Ecumenical Patriarch and giving up any claims of autocephaly.

The chief see of the Church is located at Winnipeg, Manitoba. The primate uses the title Metropolitan of Winnipeg and of All Canada. The roughly 150,000 communicants are located mostly in the large cities of central Canada.

Sources: *Eastern Christianity and Politics in the Twentieth Century* (Ramet, ed.); *The Encyclopedia of American Religions* (Melton); *History of the Church* (Jedin, ed.); *Jahrbuch der Orthodoxie* (Proc); *The Old Catholic Sourcebook* (Pruter & Melton); *Profiles in Belief* (Piepkorn); official church website.

Metropolitan Archbishops of the Ukrainian Greek Orthodox Church of Canada

(Bishops 1918, Metropolitans 1951)

1. Herman (Germanos)   1918–1924

2.	Ioann *Teodorovych* [#1 of USA]	1924–1947
3.	Mstyslav *Skrypnyk* [#2 of USA; #1 of Autocephalous]	1947–1950
4.	Ilarion *Ohiĭenko*	1951–1972
5.	Mykhaïl *Horoshyĭ*	1972–1975
6.	Andreĭ *Metiiuk*	1975–1985
7.	Vasylyĭ *Fedak*	1985–1990

MERGED WITH GREEK ARCHDIOCESE OF NORTH AMERICA

THE UKRAINIAN ORTHODOX CHURCH OF THE UNITED STATES

The Ukrainian Orthodox Church of the United States of America (Autocephalous) was organized in 1919 by Ukrainian immigrants, receiving its first Metropolitan, Ioan Teodorovych, in 1924. Since questions were raised concerning the validity of his consecration, he was provisionally reconsecrated by two Ukrainian bishops in 1949. At his death on 3 March 1971, he was succeeded by Metropolitan Archbishop Mstyslav Skrypnyk, head of the Ukrainian Autocephalous Orthodox Church (of Europe), who made himself Patriarch of the newly independent Church in Ukraine in 1990.

When Mstyslav died in 1993, the mother church split, and the American branch declined to support either of the new patriarchs, maintaining its independence by electing its own metropolitan, Konstantyn Buggan. Following the lead of its Canadian counterpart, the Church joined the Greek Orthodox Archdiocese of America on 14 March 1995, thereby acknowledging the supremacy of the Ecumenical Patriarch, and thus giving up any claims to autocephaly.

The chief see of the church is located in South Holland, Illinois. The church has branches in Great Britain, Franch, and South America, with about 87,000 communicants. The primate now uses the title Metropolitan of Chicago and of the Ukrainian Orthodox Church in the Diaspora.

Sources: *The Encyclopedia of American Religions* (Melton); *History of the Church* (Jedin, ed.); *Jahrbuch der Orthodoxie* (Proc); *The Old Catholic Sourcebook* (Pruter & Melton); *Profiles in Belief* (Piepkorn); official church website.

METROPOLITAN ARCHBISHOPS OF THE UKRAINIAN ORTHODOX CHURCH OF THE USA

1.	Ioann *Teodorovych* [#2 of Canada]	1924–1971
2.	Mstyslav *Skrypnyk* [#3 of Canada; #1 of Autocephalous]	1971–1993
3.	Konstantyn *Buggan*	1993–1995

MERGED WITH GREEK ARCHDIOCESE OF NORTH AMERICA

The Ukrainian Orthodox Church of America

Other exiles organized the Ukrainian Autocephalic Orthodox Church in Exile in 1954 at Brooklyn, under the leadership of Archbishops Palladiĭ Vydybida-Rudenko and Ihor Huba. After Palladiĭ's death on 1 September 1971, the Church broke into factions, the largest of which merged with the Ukrainian Orthodox Church of America and Canada.

The latter had been founded in 1931 under the leadership of Iosyp Zuk and the aegis of the Greek Orthodox Archdiocese of North and South America of the Ecumenical Patriarchate. Bishop Andreĭ Kushchak succeeded Bohdan Shpylka in 1967, and was named Metropolitan in 1983 by the Ecumenical Patriarch; his successor dropped the Canadian affiliation when the Ukrainian Greek Orthodox Church of Canada joined with Constantinople in 1990.

Archbishop Vsevolod merged his church with that of Metropolitan Konstantyn in 1997. This church had about 25,000 members in North America.

Sources: *The Encyclopedia of American Religions* (Melton); *History of the Church* (Jedin, ed.); *Jahrbuch der Orthodoxie* (Proc); *The Old Catholic Sourcebook* (Pruter & Melton); *Profiles in Belief* (Piepkorn).

Archbishop of the Ukrainian Autocephalous Orthodox Church in Exile

1.	Palladiĭ *Vydybida-Rudenko*	1954–1971

Merged with Ukrainian Orthodox Church of America

Metropolitans of the Ukrainian Orthodox Church of America (and Canada)

1.	Iosyp *Zuk*	1928–1934
2.	Bohdan *Shpylka*	1937–1965
3.	Andreĭ *Kushchak*	1966–1986
4.	Vsevolod *Kolomiĭchev-Maĭdanskiĭ*	1987–1997

Merged with Ukrainian Orthodox Church of USA

Appendix 1.

Name Variants

The names listed below are given in their best-known English-language or Latin-language versions first, with other variants following in alphabetical order.

AARON: Aharon (Arabic, Armenian)
ABILIUS: Abilios (Greek), Abiliyus (Arabic)
ABIMELECH: Abimaleck (Malayalam),
ABRAHAM: Abraam(ios) (Greek), Abraha (Amharic), Abraham (Armenian, Malayalam), Abram (Arabic, Georgian), Abramios (Greek), Abreham (Amharic), Avraamiĭ (Bulgarian), Avram (Macedonian), Avramiĭ (Bulgarian), Ibrahim (Arabic)
ACACIUS: Akakios (Greek), Akakij (Macedonian), Akakiyus (Arabic), Aqaq (Arabic, Syriac)
ADAM: Atom (Armenian)
ADRIAN: Adrian (Bulgarian), Adrianus (Latin), Andrian (Russian), Hadrianus (Latin)
AGAPIUS: Agapios (Greek), Aghabiyus (Arabic)
AGATHANGELUS: Agafangel (Russian)
AGATHO: Agathōn (Greek), Aghathun (Arabic)
AGRIPPINUS: Agrippinos (Greek), Aghribbinus (Arabic)
ALAN: Alanus (Latin)
ALBERT: Albertus (Latin)
ALEXANDER: Aghek'sandr (Armenian), Aleksander (Malayalam), Aleksandr (Russian), Aleksandrs (Latvian), Alexander (Latin), Alexandros (Greek), Aliksandarus (Arabic), Iskandar (Arabic), Oleksandr (Ukrainian)
ALEXIUS: Aleksiĭ (Russian, Ukrainian), Alexios (Greek, Malayalam), Oleksiĭ (Ukrainian)
ALPHONSE: Alphonsus (Latin)
AMBROSE: Ambrosi (Georgian), Amvrosiĭ (Russian)
AMOS: Amōs (Greek)
AMPHILOCHIUS: Amfilohie (Romanian), Amfilohije (Serbian), Amfilokhiyus (Arabic), Amphilochios (Greek)
ANANIAS: Anania (Armenian, Romanian), Ananiĭ (Bulgarian), Ananij (Macedonian)

ANASTASIUS: Anastasie (Romanian), Anastasiĭ (Russian), Anastasios (Albanian, Greek), Anastasius (Latin), Anastasiyus (Arabic)
ANATOLIUS: Anatolios (Greek)
ANDREW: Andrawus (Arabic), Andreas (Greek, Latin), Andrêas (Armenian), Andreĭ (Romanian, Ukrainian), Andreyas (Amharic), Indriyas (Amharic)
ANDRONICUS: Andruniqus (Arabic)
ANGEL: Angelus (Latin)
ANGELARIUS: Angelarij (Macedonian)
ANIANUS: Anianos (Greek), Aniyanus (Arabic)
ANTHEMIUS: Anthemios (Greek), Antimiyus (Arabic)
ANTHIMUS: Anthimos (Greek), Antim (Bulgarian, Macedonian, Romanian)
ANTHONY: Anton (Armenian, Georgian, Ukrainian), Antoni (Finnish), Antonie (Romanian), Antoniĭ (Russian, Ukrainian), Antonij (Polish), Antonije (Montenegrin, Serbian), Antonios (Amharic, Greek), Antonius (Latin), Antun (Arabic)
APOLLINARIUS: Apollinarios (Greek)
ARAM: Aram (Armenian)
ARCADIUS: Arcadie (Romanian), Arkadios (Greek)
ARISTARCHUS: Aristakês (Armenian), Aristarkh (Russian)
ARNOLD: Arnaldus (Latin)
ARSENIUS: Arsaniyus (Arabic), Arsen (Armenian, Georgian), Arseni (Georgian), Arseniĭ (Bulgarian, Russian, Ukrainian), Arsenij (Macedonian, Polish), Arsenije (Montenegrin, Serbian), Arsenios (Greek)
ARTEMUS: Artemios (Greek)
ASCLEPIADES: Asklēpiadēs (Greek), Asqlibiyad(h)(is) (Arabic)

ATHANASIUS: Atanasie (Romanian), Atanasiĭ (Bulgarian), Atanasij (Macedonian), Atanasije (Serbian), At'anasios (Armenian), Athanasios (Greek, Malayalam), Athanasius (Latin, Malayalam), Athanasiyus (Arabic), Atnatewos (Amharic)
ATHENAGORAS: Athēnagoras (Greek)
ATHENODORUS: Athēnodōros (Greek)
ATTICUS: Attikos (Greek)
AUGUSTINE: Augustine (Malayalam), Augustins (Latvian), Avgustin (Russian)
AUGUST: Augustus (Latin)
AUXENTIUS: Auxentios (Greek)
AYMERIC: Aymericus (Latin)
AZARIAH: Azaria (Armenian)
BABYLAS: Babila (Georgian), Babilas (Arabic), Babylas (Greek), Vavyla (Montenegrin)
BALTHAZAR: Baghdasar (Armenian)
BARLAAM: Valaam (Bulgarian, Macedonian), Varlaam (Romanian, Russian, Ukrainian)
BARNABAS: Barnabas (Greek), Varnava (Serbian)
BARTHOLOMEW: Bartalomewos (Amharic), Bartholomæus (Latin), Bartholomaios (Greek), Bart'lome (Georgian), Bart'oghimêos (Armenian), Bar T'ulmai (Syriac), Varfolomeĭ (Russian)
BASIL: Barsegh (Armenian), Baselios (Malayalam), Basileios (Greek), Basili (Georgian), Basiliyus (Arabic), Basilyos (Amharic), Bazyli (Polish), Vasil (Bulgarian), Vasile (Romanian), Vasiliĭ (Bulgarian, Russian), Vasilije (Montenegrin, Serbian), Vasyl'(iĭ) (Ukrainian)
BENEDICT: Benedict (Romanian), Benedictus (Latin), Benediktos (Greek)
BENJAMIN: Banyamin (Arabic), Beniamin(os) (Greek), Veniamin (Russian), Venijamin (Montenegrin)
BERNARD: Bernardus (Latin)
BERNARDINE: Bernardinus (Latin)
BESSARION: Besarioni (Georgian), Visarion (Albanian, Bulgarian, Montenegrin, Romanian)
BOGDAN: Bohdan (Ukrainian)
BONAVENTURE: Bonaventurus (Latin)
BONIFACE: Bonifacius (Latin)
CAESAR: Cæsar (Latin), Chesarie (Romanian)
CALLANDION: Kalandhiyun (Arabic), Kallandiōn (Greek), Qalandiyun (Arabic), Qalandun (Arabic)
CALLINICUS: Calinic (Romanian), Kalinik (Serbian), Kallinikos (Greek)
CALLISTRATUS: Calistru (Romanian), Kalistrate (Georgian), Kallistratos (Greek)
CALLISTUS: Calixtus (Latin), Kallistos (Greek)
CASSIAN: Kassianos (Greek)
CELADION: Kaladyanu (Amharic), Keladiōn (Greek)
CERDON: Kerdōn (Greek)
CHARITON: Charitōn (Greek), Hariton (Macedonian, Romanian), Khariton (Bulgaria)
CHARLES: Carolus (Latin)
CHRISTIAN: Christianus (Latin)
CHRISTODULUS: Akhristudulus (Arabic), Christodoulos (Greek), Krestodolo (Amharic)
CHRISTOPHER: Christophoros (Greek), Christophorus (Latin), Hristofor (Romanian), Kristufurus (Arabic), K'ristap'or (Armenian), K'ristep'ore (Georgian), Kristofor (Albanian)
CHRYSANTHUS: Chrysanthos (Greek)
CHRYSOSTOM: Chrysostom (Malayalam), Chrysostomos (Greek), Hrizostom (Serbian)
CLEMATIUS: Klēmatios (Greek)
CLEMENT: Aklimandus (Arabic), Clemens (Latin), Climis (Malayalam), Klēmēs (Greek), Klimentos (Georgian), Klyment (Ukrainian)
CONON: Conon (Latin, Romanian), Konōn (Greek)
CONSTANT: Kōnstantios (Greek)
CONSTANTINE: Constantinus (Latin), Konstantin (Bulgarian, Macedonian), Kōnstantinos (Greek), Konstantyn (Ukrainian), Konstiantyn (Ukrainian), Kostandin (Armenian), Qustantinus (Arabic)
CORNELIUS: Kornēlios (Greek), Kurniliyus (Arabic), Qurnil(iyus) (Arabic)
COSMAS: Cosma (Romanian), Kosmas (Greek), Kuz'ma (Ukrainian), Qosmos (Amharic), Qusma(n) (Arabic)
CYPRIAN: Kiprian (Russian), Kupriian (Ukrainian), Kyprianos (Greek)
CYRIACUS: Kirakos (Armenian), Kooriakose (Malayalam), Kyriakos (Greek), Quriyaqus (Arabic)
CYRIL: Gerlos (Amharic), Kiril (Bulgarian, Macedonian, Serbian), Kirile (Georgian), Kirillus (Arabic), Kirilo (Serbian), Koorilose (Malayalam), Kuregh (Armenian), Kuril(l)os (Malayalam), Kyrillos (Greek), Kyrylo (Ukrainian), Qer(i)los (Amharic), Qurillus (Arabic)
CYRUS: Kurush (Arabic), Kyros (Greek)
DAMASCENUS: Damaskēnos (Greek)
DAMIAN: Damian (Albanian, Bulgarian), Damianos (Greek), Damiyanus (Arabic)
DANIEL: Dan'el (Amharic), Daniel (Malayalam), Daniêl (Armenian), Danieli (Georgian), Daniĭl (Bulgarian, Romanian, Russian), Danil (Arabic, Macedonian), Danilo (Montenegrin, Serbian), Daniyal (Arabic)
DAVID: David (Bulgarian, Malayalam), Davit'(i) (Georgian), Dawit' (Armenian), Dawud (Arabic)
DEMETRIAN: Dēmētrianos (Greek), Dimitriyanus (Arabic)

DEMETRIUS: Dēmētrios (Greek), Dimitri (Georgian), Dimitrie (Romanian), Dimitriĭ (Bulgarian), Dimitrij (Macedonian), Dimitrije (Serbian), Dimitriyus (Arabic), Dymytriĭ (Ukrainian)
DEMOPHILUS: Dēmophilos (Greek)
DENNIS: Dengel (Amharic), Dhiyunisiyus (Arabic), Dionise (Georgian), Dionisie (Romanian), Dionisiĭ (Bulgarian, Russian), Dionisij (Macedonian), Dionizy (Polish), Dionysiĭ (Ukrainian), Dionysios (Greek, Malayalam), Dionysius (Latin), Divannasios (Malayalam), Diyunisiyus (Arabic)
DIODORUS: Diodōros (Greek)
DIOSCORUS: Dioskoros (Malayalam), Dioskoros (Armenian, Greek), Disqurus (Arabic)
DOMETIUS: Domenti (Georgian), Dometios (Greek), Dumitiyus (Arabic)
DOMINIC: Domenicus (Latin)
DOMNUS: Domnos (Greek), Dumnus (Arabic)
DONATUS: Donat (Russian)
DOROTHEUS: Doroteĭ (Bulgarian), Dorotej (Macedonian), Dorot'eos (Georgian), Dorot'eoz (Georgian), Dōrotheos (Greek), Duruthiyus (Arabic)
DOSITHEUS: Dositei (Romanian), Dositej (Macedonian, Serbian), Dositeosi (Georgian), Dositheos (Greek), Dosoftei (Romanian)
ELEUTHERIUS/LUTHER: Alafthariyus (Arabic), Eleutherios (Greek), Jelevferij (Czech)
ELIAZAR: Eghiazar (Armenian)
ELIJAH/ELIAS: Eghia (Armenian), Elia (Georgian), Elias (Latin, Malayalam), Ēlias (Greek), Eliozi (Georgian), Helias (Latin), Ilia (Georgian), Ilie (Romanian), Iliia (Ukrainian), Iliya (Syriac), Ilyas (Arabic)
ELISHA: Eghishê (Armenian), Ilisha' (Syriac)
EMILIAN: Aimilianos (Greek), Amiliyanus (Arabic), Emilian (Romanian)
EMMANUEL: Manouēl (Greek), 'Ummanu'il (Syriac)
ENOCH: Hinukh (Arabic)
ENOS: Anush (Syriac)
EPHREM/EPHRAIM: Afram (Arabic), Aprem (Malayalam, Syriac), Efrem (Romanian), Ep'rem (Armenian, Georgian), Ephraim (Greek), IEfrem (Ukrainian), Jefrem (Serbian)
EPIPHANY: Apifaniyus (Arabic), Epifaniĭ (Russian), Epip'ane (Georgian), Epiphanios (Greek)
EROS: Awrus (Arabic), Ayrus (Arabic), Erōs (Greek), Irus (Arabic)
EUDOCIMUS: Evdokim (Russian)
EUDOXIUS: Afduksiyus (Arabic), Awduksiyus (Arabic), Eudoxios (Greek)
EUGENE: Augen (Malayalam), Eugenie (Romanian), Eugenios (Greek), Eugenius (Latin), Evgeniĭ (Russian), Evghenie (Romanian), IEvgen (Ukrainian), Ougen (Malayalam)
EULALIUS: Aflaliyus (Arabic), Awlaliyus (Arabic), Eulalios (Greek), Evlale (Georgian)
EULOGIUS: Eulogios (Greek), Evloghie (Romanian)
EUMENIUS: Awminiyus (Arabic), Eumenēs (Greek), Eumenios (Greek)
EUPHEMIUS: Euphemios (Greek)
EUPHRASIUS: Afrasiyus (Arabic)
EUPHRONIUS: Afrun(iyus) (Arabic), Awfruniyus (Arabic), Euphronios (Greek)
EUSEBIUS: Awsabiyus (Arabic), Eusebios (Greek), Evseviĭ (Russian)
EUSTACE: Astatiyus (Arabic), Awstathiyus (Arabic), Eustathios (Greek), Evstatiĭ (Bulgarian), Ewostatewos (Amharic), Jevstatij (Macedonian), Jevstatije (Serbian)
EUSTOCHIUS: Eustochios (Greek)
EUSTRATIUS: Afstratiyus (Arabic), Eustratios (Greek)
EUTHYMIUS: Aftimios (American), Aftimiyus (Arabic), Eftim (Turkish), Eftimie (Romanian), Ek'vt'ime (Georgian), Euthymios (Greek), Evtimiĭ (Bulgarian)
EUTYCHIUS: Eutychios (Greek)
EUZOIUS: Afzuyus (Arabic), Euzōïos (Greek)
EVAGRIUS: Awghris (Arabic), Awighriyus (Arabic), Euagrios (Greek), Evagre (Georgian)
EVODIUS: Afudiyus (Arabic), Awdiyus (Arabic), Euodios (Greek)
EZEKIEL: Iezekiēl (Greek), Kazqi'il (Syriac)
EZRA: Ezr (Armenian)
FABIAN: Fabianus (Latin)
FABIUS: Fabiyus (Arabic), Phabios (Greek)
FELIX: Phēlix (Greek), Philix (Greek)
FERDINAND: Ferdinandus (Latin)
FLACILLUS: Filaqas (Arabic), Phlakilos (Greek)
FLAVIAN: Flabiyanus (Arabic), Flafiyanus (Arabic), Flavian (Russian, Ukrainian), Fławian (Polish), Phlabianos (Greek)
FRANCIS: Franciscus (Latin)
FRAVITAS: Phrabitas (Greek)
FREDERICK: Fredericus (Latin)
GABRIEL: Gabr'el (Amharic), Gabriêl (Armenian), Gavriĭl (Bulgarian, Romanian), Gavril (Macedonian), Gavrilo (Montenegrin, Serbian), Ghubriyal (Arabic), Havryĭl (Ukrainian), Jibra'il (Arabic)
GAIANUS: Gaïanos (Greek), Kayanus (Arabic)
GAIUS/CAIUS: Gaïos (Greek)
GALACTION: Galaction (Romanian)
GEDEON: Ghedeon (Romanian), Hedeon (Ukrainian)
GELASIUS: Gelasios (Greek), Ghelasie (Romanian)
GENNADIUS: Genadiĭ (Bulgarian), Genadij

(Macedonian), Gennadiĭ (Bulgarian, Russian), Gennadios (Greek), Ghenadie (Romanian)
GEORGE: Geevarghese (Malayalam), Gêorg (Armenian), Georgi (Bulgarian), Georgij (Macedonian), Georgije (Serbian), Geōrgios (Greek), Georgius (Latin), Gheorghe (Romanian), Giorgi (Georgian), Giwargis (Syriac), Giyorgis (Amharic), Heorhiĭ (Ukrainian), Jawrji(yus) (Arabic), Jerzy (Polish), Jirjis (Arabic), Jüri (Estonian)
GERALD: Geraldus (Latin)
GERARD: Gerardus (Latin)
GERASIMUS: Gherasim (Romanian, Serbian), Gerasimos (Greek), Herasym (Ukrainian), Jirasimus (Arabic)
GERMAN/HERMAN: German (Bulgarian, Montenegrin, Russian, Serbian), Germane (Georgian), Germanos (Greek), Gherman (Serbian), Herman (Finnish, Ukrainian), Jarmanus (Arabic)
GERMANION: Germaniōn (Greek)
GERONTIUS: Gerontiĭ (Russian)
GERVASE: Gerbasios (Greek), Gervasius (Latin)
GILBERT: Gilbertus (Latin)
GILES: Gillus (Latin)
GLYCERIUS: Glicherie (Romanian)
GORDIUS: Gordios (Greek)
GREGORY: Ghrighuriyus (Arabic), Gregorios (Malayalam), Grēgorios (Greek), Gregorius (Latin), Grigol(i) (Georgian), Grigor (Armenian), Grigorie (Romanian), Grigoriĭ (Bulgarian), Grigorij (Macedonian), Grigoris (Armenian), Grigur (Syriac), Hryhoriĭ (Ukrainian)
HENRY: Henricus (Latin)
HEPHÆSTUS: Hefajst (Macedonian), Hephaistos (Greek)
HERACLAS: Hēraklas (Greek), Yaraklas (Arabic)
HERMOGENES: Germogen (Croatian, Russian)
HERO: Irun (Arabic), Hērōn (Greek)
HIEROTHEUS: Ayruthiyus (Arabic), Hierotheos (Greek), Iierofei (Ukrainian), Jerotej (Serbian), Jerotheu (Albanian)
HILARY: Hilariōn (Greek), Hilarius (Latin), Ilarion (Bulgarian, Romanian, Ukrainian), Ilarijon (Montenegrin)
HIPPOLYTE: Hippolytus (Latin)
HONOR: Honorius (Latin)
HUMBERT: Humbertus (Latin)
HYACINTH: Iachint (Romanian)
HYMENÆUS: Hymenaios (Greek)
HYPATIUS: Hypatios (Greek), Ipatiĭ (Ukrainian)
IGNATIUS: Ighnatiyus (Arabic), Ignatie (Romanian), Ignatiĭ (Bulgarian, Russian), Ignatij (Macedonian), Ignatios (Armenian, Greek, Malayalam), Ignatius (Malayalam)
IGOR: Ihor (Ukrainian)

INNOCENT: Inochentie (Romanian), Innocentius (Latin), Innokentiĭ (Russian), Inokentije (Serbian)
IRENÆUS: Eirēnaios (Greek), Irenæus (Malayalam), Ireneĭ (Russian), Ireney (Russian)
IRENARCHUS: Irinarkh (Russian)
ISAAC: Husik (Armenian), Isaak (Ukrainian), Isaak(ios) (Greek), Ishaq (Arabic, Malayalam), Iskhaq (Syriac), Sahak (Armenian), Yes'aq (Amharic), Yeshaq (Amharic)
ISAIAH: Esayi (Armenian), Hēsaïas (Greek), Isaia (Romanian), Isaiia (Ukrainian), Isaija (Serbian), Isaya (Malayalam),
ISHMAEL: Isma'il (Arabic), Ismil (Arabic)
ISIDOR: Isidor (Russian), Isidōros (Greek), Isidorus (Latin), Isydor (Ukrainian)
ISRAEL: Israyêl (Armenian), Israyil (Syriac)
JACOB/JAMES: Hakob(us) (Armenian), Iacob (Romanian), Iacobus (Latin), Iakobi (Georgian), Iakobos (Greek), IAkov (Bulgarian), Jakov (Macedonian, Serbian), Ya'eqob (Amharic), Yakoub (Malayalam), Ya'qub (Arabic)
JEREMY/JEREMIAH: Aramiya (Arabic), Eremia (Armenian), Eremij (Macedonian), Hieremias (Greek), Ieremia (Georgian), Ieremiia (Bulgarian, Russian)
JEROME: Hierōnymos (Greek), Hieronymus (Latin), Ijeronim (Polish)
JESUS/JOSHUA: Ishu' (Arabic, Syriac)
JOAB: Hovab (Armenian)
JOACHIM: Hovakim (Armenian), Iōakeim (Greek), Ioakim (Bulgarian, Russian), Ioakime (Georgian), Ioaquim (Latin), Joahim (Macedonian), Yuwakim (Arabic)
JOANNICIUS: Ioanichie (Romanian), Ioanikiĭ (Bulgarian, Ukrainian), Ioannikiĭ (Russian), Iōannikios (Greek), Joanikij (Macedonian), Joanikije (Montenegrin, Serbian), Joannikij (Polish)
JOASAPH: Ioasaf (Bulgarian, Romanian, Russian, Ukrainian), Iōasaph (Greek), Iosaf (Polish), Joasav (Macedonian), Yosab (Amharic), Yusab (Arabic)
JOB: Ayyub (Arabic), Iōb (Greek), Iobi (Georgian), Iov (Romanian, Russian, Ukrainian)
JOHN: Hovhan(nes) (Armenian), Ioan (Bulgarian, Romanian), Ioane (Georgian), Ioann (Latvian, Russian, Ukrainian), Ioannes (Latin), Iōannes (Greek), Ivanios (Malayalam), Iwannis (Arabic), Iyunnis (Arabic), Ján (Czech), Jānis (Latvian), Johannes (Finnish), Jovan (Macedonian, Serbian), Juhanon (Malayalam), Yohannes (Amharic), Yohannon (Malayalam), Youhanan (Malayalam), Yuhanna (Arabic), Yuhannan (Malayalam), Yuhannis (Arabic), Yukhannan (Syriac)

JONAH: Iona (Georgian, Russian, Ukrainian), Iōnas (Greek), Yunan (Arabic, Syriac)
JONATHAN: Ionafan (Russian)
JORDAN: Iordanus (Latin)
JORY: Iōrios (Greek)
JOSEPH: Hovsêp' (Armenian), Iosebi (Georgian), Iosēph (Greek), Iosephus (Latin), Iosif (Bulgarian, Romanian, Russian), Iosyp (Ukrainian), Joseph (Malayalam), Josif (Macedonian, Serbian), Yosef (Amharic), Yusip (Syriac), Yusuf (Arabic)
JOSHUA—SEE: Jesus
JUDE: Ioudas (Greek)
JULIAN: Ioulianos (Greek), Iulianus (Latin), Yuliyanus (Arabic), Yulyan (Arabic)
JULIUS: Iulius (Latin)
JUSTIN: Ioustinos (Greek), Iustin (Romanian)
JUSTINIAN: Ioustinianos (Greek), Justinian (Romanian)
JUSTUS: Ioustos (Greek), Yostos (Amharic), Yustus (Arabic)
JUVENAL: Ioubenalios (Greek)
LAURUS: Lavr (Russian)
LAWRENCE: Laurentios (Greek), Laurentius (Latin), Lavrentie (Romanian)
LAZARUS: Ghazar (Armenian), Lazar (Malayalam), Lazaros (Greek)
LEO(N): Ghevond (Armenian), Leo (Finnish), Leōn (Greek), Lev (Macedonian), Luv (Bulgarian)
LEONARD: Leonardus (Latin)
LEONIDAS: Leonide (Georgian), Leōnidēs (Greek), Leonids (Latvian)
LEONTIUS: Ghevondius (Armenian), Leontiĭ (Bulgarian, Russian, Ukrainian), Leontij (Polish), Leontios (Greek)
LEVI: Leuis (Greek)
LEWIS: Ludovicus (Latin)
LIVY: Livius (Latin)
LUCIAN: Loukianos (Greek), Lukijan (Serbian)
LUKE/LUCAS: Ghukas (Armenian), Loukas (Greek), Luca (Romanian), Lucas (Latin), Lucius (Latin), Luqa (Arabic)
MACARIUS: Macarie (Romanian), Makar (Armenian), Makari (Georgian), Makariĭ (Bulgarian, Russian, Ukrainian), Makarij (Macedonian), Makarije (Montenegrin, Serbian), Makarios (Greek), Makariyus (Arabic), Makary (Polish), Makaryos (Amharic), Maqares (Amharic)
MACEDONIUS: Makedonios (Greek), Maqiduniyus (Arabic)
MALACHI: Maghak'ia (Armenian), Malak'ia (Georgian)
MARCIAN: Markianos (Greek), Markiyanus (Arabic)
MARINUS: Marinos (Greek)

MARK: Marcu (Romanian), Marcus (Latin), Marko (Bulgarian, Serbian), Markos (Armenian, Greek), Markozi (Georgian), Marqos (Amharic), Murqus (Arabic)
MARTIN: Martinos (Greek), Martinus (Latin)
MARTYR(IUS): Mardarie (Romanian), Martiriyus (Arabic), Martiros (Armenian), Martur(iyus) (Arabic), Martyrios (Greek)
MARY/MARION: Maria (Greek, Latin)
MATTHEW/MATTHIAS: Mateĭ (Bulgarian), Matej (Macedonian), Matewos (Amharic), Matfeĭ (Ukrainian), Mathai (Malayalam), Mathew (Malayalam), Mathews (Malayalam), Matiyus (Arabic), Matta(wus) (Arabic), Matt'e(os) (Armenian), Matthæus (Latin), Matthaios (Greek)
MAXIM: Maksim (Bulgarian, Macedonian, Serbian), Mak'sime (Georgian), Maksimus (Arabic), Maksym (Ukrainian), Maxim (Romanian), Maximos (Greek)
MAXIMIAN: Maksimiyanus (Arabic), Maximianos (Greek)
MAXIMIN: Maksiminus (Arabic), Maximinos (Greek)
MELCHIZEDEK: Malkeesadek (Malayalam), Melhisedek (Belorussian), Melkhisedek (Bulgarian), Melk'isedek (Armenian, Georgian)
MELETIUS: Malatiyus (Arabic), Melentije (Serbian), Meletie (Romanian), Meletiĭ (Bulgarian, Russian), Meletij (Macedonian), Meletios (Greek), Melitê (Armenian)
MENAS: Mēnas (Greek), Mina (Arabic), Minas (Amharic, Armenian)
MERCURY: Mercurius (Latin), Merkorewos (Amharic)
METHODIUS: Mefodiĭ (Ukrainian), Methodios (Greek), Metodiĭ (Bulgarian), Metodij (Macedonian), Mithudiyus (Arabic)
METROPHANES: Mētrophanēs (Greek), Mitrofan (Bulgarian, Macedonian, Montenegrin, Romanian, Serbian)
MICHAEL: Khaēl (Coptic), Kha'il (Arabic), Michael (Latin, Malayalam), Michaēl (Greek), Mihail (Macedonian, Romanian), Mihaïlo (Serbian), Mikael (Finnish), Mika'el (Amharic), Mik'ayêl (Armenian), Mik'el (Georgian), Mikhaïl (Bulgarian, Russian, Ukrainian), Mikha'il (Arabic), Mykhaïlo (Ukrainian)
MISAEL: Misaēl (Greek), Misail (Romanian), Mysaïl (Ukrainian)
MODESTUS: Modestos (Greek)
MOSES: Mōēsēs (Greek), Moïseĭ (Russian), Mojsej(e) (Serbian), Mojsije (Serbian), Mosa (Malayalam), Mose (Georgian), Mōusēs (Greek), Movsês (Armenian), Mowshe (Armenian), Musa (Arabic), Musi (Arabic)

MYRON: Miron (Romanian, Serbian), Muron (Armenian), Myrōn (Greek)
NARCISSUS: Narsai (Syriac), Narkissos (Greek), Nersês (Armenian)
NATHANIEL: Nathanaël (Greek)
NAZARIUS: Nazariĭ (Ukrainian)
NECTAR: Nectarie (Romanian), Nektariĭ (Bulgarian), Nektarij (Macedonian), Nektarios (Greek)
NEIL: Neilos (Greek), Nilus (Arabic)
NEOPHYTUS: Neofit (Bulgarian, Macedonian, Romanian), Neophytos (Greek), Niyufutus (Arabic)
NESTOR(IUS): Nestorios (Greek), Nestor (Russian)
NICANOR: Nikanor (Bulgarian, Montenegrin, Polish, Serbian, Ukrainian), Nikanōr (Greek)
NICEPHORUS: Nichifor (Romanian), Nikēphoros (Greek), Nikifore (Georgian), Niqifurus (Arabic), Nykyfor (Ukrainian)
NICETAS: Mykyta (Ukrainian), Nikētas (Greek)
NICHOLAS: Mykola (Ukrainian), Nicolae (Romanian), Nicolaus (Latin), Nikoghayos (Armenian), Nikola (Russian), Nikolaĭ (Bulgarian, Finnish, Russian), Nikolaj (Macedonian, Polish, Slovak), Nikolaos (Greek), Nikoloz(i) (Georgian), Niqula (Syriac), Niqulawus (Arabic)
NICODEMUS: Nicodim (Romanian), Nikodēmos (Greek), Nikodim (Bulgarian, Montenegrin, Russian), Nikodimos (Amharic)
NICON: Nikon (Russian), Nikōn (Greek), Niqun (Arabic)
NIMROD: Nimrud (Arabic)
NIPHON: Nēphōn (Greek), Nifon (Romanian), Nifont (Ukrainian), Niphōn (Greek)
NOAH: Nuh (Arabic, Malayalam)
OLYMPIUS: Alimpiĭ (Russian), Olympios (Greek)
ONESIPHORUS: Onysyfir (Ukrainian)
ORESTES: Iorest (Romanian), Orestēs (Greek)
PACHOMIUS: Bakhumiyus (Arabic), Pachomios (Greek), Pahomie (Romanian), Pahomije (Serbian)
PAISIUS: Païsi (Albanian), Païsiĭ (Bulgarian), Païsios (Greek), Pajsij (Macedonian), Pajsije (Serbian)
PALLADIUS: Baladhiyus (Arabic), Baladiyun (Arabic), Baladiyus (Arabic), Baladus (Arabic), Palladiĭ (Russian, Ukrainian)
PANARETUS: Panaret (Bulgarian, Macedonian), Panaretos (Greek)
PANTELEIMON: Pantaleon (Latin), Panteleēmōn (Greek), Panteleiman (Belorussian), Panteleimon (Ukrainian)
PAONIUS: Paonije (Montenegrin)
PAPHNYTIUS: Pafnutiĭ (Bulgarian), Paphnytios (Greek)

PARTHENIUS: Partenie (Romanian), Parteniĭ (Bulgarian), Partenij (Macedonian), Parthenios (Greek)
PASCHAL: Paschalis (Latin)
PAUL: Bulus (Arabic), Paavali (Finnish), Paulos (Amharic, Greek, Malayalam), Paulose (Malayalam), Paulus (Latin), Pavel (Montenegrin, Russian), Pavle (Serbian), Poghos (Armenian), Pulus (Syriac)
PAULIN(US): Baflinus (Arabic), Bulinus (Arabic), Fulin (Arabic), Paulinos (Greek)
PETER: Butrus (Arabic), Pathros (Malayalam), Petar (Montenegrin, Serbian), Pëtr (Russian, Ukrainian), Petre (Georgian), Petro (Ukrainian), Petros (Amharic, Armenian, Greek), Petru (Romanian), Petrus (Latin)
PHILARET: Filaret (Romanian, Russian, Ukrainian)
PHILEMON: Filimun (Arabic), Philēmōn (Greek)
PHILETUS: Filitus (Arabic), Philētos (Greek)
PHILIP: Filibbus (Arabic), Filip (Bulgarian, Macedonian, Serbian), Filipp (Russian), Filippos (Amharic), Philipose (Malayalam), Philippos (Greek), Philippus (Latin), P'ilippos (Armenian)
PHILOGON: Bilujin (Arabic), Filughunus (Arabic), Filujuniyus (Arabic), Philogon(i)os (Greek)
PHILOTHEUS: Filatawos (Amharic), Filofeĭ (Ukrainian), Filoteĭ (Bulgarian), Filuthawus (Arabic), Philotheos (Greek), Tilotej (Macedonian)
PHILOXENUS: Filuksinus (Arabic), Phileksinose (Malayalam), Philoxenos (Greek)
PHOTIUS: Fotiĭ (Russian, Ukrainian), Phōtios (Greek)
PILATE: Bilatus (Arabic), Philathose (Malayalam), Pilatos (Greek)
PISTUS: Pistos (Greek)
PLACID: Placidus (Latin)
PLATO: Plato (Estonian), Platon (Romanian, Russian, Ukrainian), Platōn (Greek)
PLUTARCH: Ploutarchos (Greek)
POIMEN: Pimen (Russian), Poimēn (Greek), Pymin (Ukrainian)
POLITIAN: Politianos (Greek)
POLYCARP: Polykarp (Ukrainian), Polykarpos (Greek)
PORPHYRIUS: Burfirus (Arabic), Burfuriyus (Arabic), Porfiriĭ (Bulgarian, Russian), Porfirij (Macedonian), Porphyrios (Greek)
PRIMUS: Abrimus (Arabic), Primos (Greek)
PROBUS: Probos (Greek)
PROCHORUS: Prohor (Macedonian), Prokhor (Bulgarian), Prokhoron (Armenian)
PROCLUS: Proklos (Greek)
PROCOPIUS: Procopie (Romanian), Prokopije (Serbian), Prokopios (Greek)

PROSPER: Prosperus (Latin)
PROTERIUS: Proterios (Greek)
PUBLIUS: Pouplios (Greek)
PYRRHUS: Pyrrhos (Greek)
QUADRATUS: Kodratos (Greek)
RAPHAEL: Rafaïl (Bulgarian, Macedonian, Ukrainian), Rapa'il (Syriac), Raphael (Latin), Raphaēl (Greek)
RAYMOND: Raymundus (Latin)
REUBEN: Rupil (Syriac)
ROBERT: Robertus (Latin)
ROGER: Rogerus (Latin)
ROLAND: Rolandus (Latin)
ROMAN: Roman (Bulgarian, Russian), Rōmanos (Greek), Romanus (Latin)
RUFINUS: Rhouphinos (Greek), Rufim (Montenegrin)
ROMULUS: Romul (Montenegrin)
SABBAS: Saba (Georgian), Sabbas (Arabic), Sava (Montenegrin, Romanian, Serbian), Sawa (Polish)
SABBATIUS: Sabbazd (Czech), Savatije (Serbian), Savvatiĭ (Russian), Savvatij (Czech)
SABINE: Sabinos (Greek)
SALLUST: Salloustios (Greek)
SAMPSON: Sampsōn (Greek)
SAMUEL: Samoel (Georgian), Samouēl (Greek), Samuel (Armenian, Malayalam), Samu'el (Amharic), Samuïl (Ukrainian), Samuïlo (Serbian)
SEBASTIAN: Sebastian (Romanian), Sebastianos (Greek), Sebastianus (Latin), Sibastiyanus (Arabic)
SENOUTHIUS: Sanutiyus (Arabic), Shanudah (Arabic), Shinudah (Arabic), Sinoda (Amharic), Suntyos (Amharic)
SENECA: Senekas (Greek)
SERAPHIM: Serafim (Finnish, Romanian, Russian), Serafin (Polish), Serapheim (Greek), Seraphinus (Latin), Sirafim (Arabic)
SERAPION: Serapion (Russian, Ukrainian), Serapiōn (Greek), Sirabiyun (Arabic)
SERGIUS: Sargis (Armenian, Malayalam, Syriac), Sergei (Finnish), Sergej (Macedonian), Sergi (Estonian), Sergiĭ (Bulgarian, Russian, Ukrainian), Sergios (Greek), Sergius (Latin), Sirjiyus (Arabic), Sirkis (Arabic)
SEVERIN: Severinus (Latin)
SEVERUS: Sawira (Arabic), Sawiriyus (Arabic), Sawiros (Amharic), Sebēros (Greek), Subrus (Arabic)
SILVAN: Silouanos (Greek)
SIMON/SIMEON: Sem'on (Amharic), Shim'un (Arabic, Malayalam, Syriac), Sim'an (Arabic), Simawun (Arabic), Simeon (Bulgarian, Macedonian), Siméon (Armenian), Simion (Romanian), Simon (Latin, Malayalam),
Svim(e)on (Georgian), Symeon (Ukrainian), Symeōn (Greek)
SISINNIUS: Sisinnios (Greek)
SOLOMON: Shlimun (Syriac), Soghomon (Armenian), Solomōn (Greek)
SOPHRONIUS: Sofron (Albanian), Sofronie (Romanian), Sofroniĭ (Bulgarian), Sofronij (Macedonian), Sofronije (Serbian), Sōphronios (Greek), Sufruniyus (Arabic)
SPYRIDON: Asbiridun (Arabic), Spiridon (Serbian), Spyridōn (Greek), Spyrydon (Ukrainian)
STEPHEN: Istifan(us) (Arabic), Stefan (Bulgarian, Polish, Romanian, Russian), Stefanus (Estonian), Step'ane (Georgian), Step'an(os) (Armenian), Stephanos (Greek), Stephanus (Latin), Stevan (Serbian)
SYLVESTER: Silbestros (Greek), Silfistrus (Arabic), Silvestru (Romanian), Syl'vestr (Ukrainian)
SYMMACHUS: Symmachos (Greek)
TARASIUS: Tarasios (Greek)
THADDEUS: Addai (Syriac), T'addai (Syriac), T'adêos (Armenian), Tadewos (Amharic), Thaddaios (Greek)
THEOCHARISTUS: Theocharistos (Greek), Thiyukharistus (Arabic)
THEOCLETUS: Theoklētos (Greek)
THEOCTISTUS: Teoctist (Romanian)
THEODEGIUS: Theodēgios (Greek)
THEODORE: Feodor (Russian, Ukrainian), Teodor (Romanian), T'eodore (Georgian), T'êodoros (Armenian), Thawdurus (Arabic), Theodoros (Greek), Theodorus (Latin), Thiyudhurus (Arabic), Thiyudur(us) (Arabic), T'iyadurus (Syriac), T'oros (Armenian)
THEODORIC: Theodoricus (Latin)
THEODORITUS: Thiyuduritus (Arabic)
THEODOSIUS: Feodosiĭ (Russian), Teodosie (Romanian), Teodosiĭ (Bulgarian), Teodosije (Serbian), Thawdusiyus (Arabic), Theodosios (Greek, Malayalam), Thiyudusiyus (Arabic), T'iyadusis (Syriac)
THEODOTUS: Thawdutus (Arabic), Theodotos (Greek), Thiyudut(us) (Arabic)
THEODULUS: Teodul (Bulgarian, Macedonian)
THEOGNOSTUS: Feognost (Ukrainian)
THEOLEPTUS: Theoleptos (Greek)
THEONAS: Thawna (Arabic), Theōnas (Greek)
THEOPEMPTUS: Feopempt (Ukrainian)
THEOPHANES: Teofan (Bulgarian, Macedonian, Romanian, Serbian), Thawfaniyus (Arabic), Theofan (Albanian), Theophanēs (Greek), Thiyufanis (Arabic)
THEOPHILUS: Feofil (Russian), Teofil (Romanian), Tewoflos (Amharic), Thawfilus (Arabic), Theophilos (Greek), Thiyufilus (Arabic)

Theophylactus: Feofilakt (Bulgarian, Russian), Theophylaktos (Greek), Thiyufilaktus (Arabic), Tufilaqtus (Arabic)

Thomas: Thoma (Malayalam), Thomas (Latin, Malayalam), Thōmas (Greek), Tomas (Amharic), T'ovma(s) (Armenian), Tuma (Arabic), T'uma (Syriac)

Timæus: Timaios (Greek), Timayus (Arabic), Timiyus (Arabic)

Timothy: Timat'ius (Syriac), Timithiyus (Arabic), Timofeĭ (Russian), Timotej (Macedonian), Timotheos (Greek, Malayalam), Timuthawus (Arabic), Tymofiĭ (Ukrainian), Tymoteusz (Polish)

Tiridates: Trdat (Armenian)

Titus: Tit (Romanian), Titos (Greek, Malayalam)

Tobias: Tōbias (Greek), Tubiyya (Arabic)

Tychon: Tikhon (Russian), Tychōn (Greek)

Tyrranus: Turanus (Arabic), Tyrannos (Greek)

Urban: Urbanus (Latin)

Valens: Oualēs (Greek)

Valentine: Valentin (Russian), Valentinus (Latin)

Victor: Fiqtor (Amharic), Victor (Latin), Viktor (Russian)

Vincent: Vićentije (Serbian), Vikentiĭ (Russian), Vikentije (Serbian), Vincentus (Latin)

Vitalian: Vitalianus (Latin)

Vitalis: Bitalis (Arabic, Greek), Fitalis (Arabic), Fitaliyus (Arabic), Vitaliĭ (Russian)

Vladimir: Vladimir (Romanian, Russian), Volodymyr (Ukrainian)

Walter: Gualterus (Latin)

William: Guillelmus (Latin), Willelmus (Latin)

Zachary: Skaria (Malayalam), Zacharias (Greek, Latin), Zaharij (Macedonian), Zak'aria (Armenian, Georgian), Zakaryas (Amharic), Zakhariĭ (Bulgarian), Zakhariya(s) (Arabic), Zakka (Arabic)

Zebedee: Zebede (Georgian)

Zion: Sion (Armenian)

Zoilus: Zōïlos (Greek)

Zosimus: Zosim (Macedonian), Zosima (Bulgarian, Russian), Zosimus (Latin)

Appendix 2.

Statistical Comparisons

HIGHEST POST-NOMINAL NUMBER (two): Ishai Shim'un XXIII (Assyria), Ioannes XXIII (Rome). Two of the Shim'uns are disputed, as are two of the Johns, so both should probably be numbered as XXI.

HIGHEST POST-NOMINAL NUMBER CURRENTLY BEING USED: Nersês Petros XIX (Armenian Catholic Church of Cilicia); since every Patriarch uses the name Petros, the number increases with each reign.

LONGEST CURRENTLY REIGNING PRIMATE (2005): Patriarch Maksim I (Bulgaria), 33+ years.

SHORTEST REIGN: One day (1726): Kallinikos III (Ecumenical Patriarchate of Constantinople). It should be noted that all of the very short reigns of this and other churches are disputed by scholars and church historians, and may or may not be valid.

THE LONGEST REIGNS

Verifiable reigns exceeding 45 years are exceedingly rare. It is significant that the best-attested church lists, those delineating the Popes of Rome and the Ecumenical Patriarchs of Constantinople, demonstrate maximum reigns no longer than 33 and 31 years, respectively. Iōakeim I of Alexandria is listed in some sources as having ruled 81 years (from 1486–1567), but since he would have had to have been at least 117 years old at his death, even by the most generous accounts, this seems highly unlikely, and certainly unproven. Similarly, the Assyrian Church lists an early Catholicos, Papa bar Gaggai, as having ruled 79 years (247–326), but again, there is no supporting documentation for this claim, and it seems improbable. Step'anos IV of Caucasian Albania is listed with 61 years, Shim'un IV of Babylon with 60 years in one source, and Dinkha Iliya XII of Babylon with 56 years, but none of these spans can be validated, although they are certainly possible. The longest reign that can be regarded as proven is 55 years, 4 months, and 16 days for Ishai Shim'un XXIII (Assyria), followed very closely by Kōnstantios II of the Sinai (Kōnstantios I as Ecumenical Patriarch), with 54 or 55 years, whose exact date of election in 1804 or 1805 as Abbot-Archbishop of the Sinai is unknown. The longest verifiable reigns of the primates of each major church are listed below, as rounded up to the next highest whole year:

Albania: 17 years: Païsi I (1949–1966)
Alexandria (Coptic): 53 years: Kirillus V (1874–1927)
Alexandria (Coptic Catholic): 45 years: Athanasiyus I (328–373)
Alexandria (Greek): 45 years: Athanasios I (328–373)
America: 38 years: Iakōbos I (1958–1996)
Antioch (Greek): 42 years: Silfistrus I (Silbestros) (1724–1766)
Antioch (Greek Melkite): 39 years: Kirillus V (1672, 1682–1720)
Antioch (Maronite): 43 years: Musi I (1524–1567)
Antioch (Syrian Catholic): 43 years: Ighnatiyus Bihnam I (1412–1455)
Antioch (Syrian Orthodox): 42 years: Ighnatiyus Bihnam I (1412–1454)
Armenia: 53 years: Grigor III (1113–1166)
Assyria: 55 years: Ishai Shim'un XXIII (1920–1975)
Austria-Hungary (Karlovci): 46 years: Stevan II (1790–1836)
Babylon: 47 years: Yusip 'Ummanu'il II (1900–1947); Dinkha Iliya XII is listed with 56 years (1722–1778) and Shim'un IV with 60 years (1437–1497), but none of these are verifiable, although certainly possible, given the hereditary nature of this catholicosate
Bulgaria: 48 years: Vasilii I (1185–1233)
Cilicia (Armenian Apostolic): 37 years: Sahak II (1902–1939)
Cilicia (Armenian Catholic): 27 years: Mik'ayêl Petros III (1753–1780)
Constantinople (Armenian): 29 years: Shnorhk' I (1961–1990)
Constantinople (Greek): 31 years: Dometios I (272–303)
Crete: 34 years: Neophytos I (1645?–1679)
Cyprus: 43 years: Chrysanthos I (1767–1810)
Czechoslovakia: 35 years: Dorotej I (1964–1999)
Ethiopia: 37 years: Matewos (1889–1926); Marqos I is listed with 49 years (1481–1530?) and Salama IV with 40 years (1348–1388), but none of these are verifiable, although possible
Finland: 35 years: Herman I (1925–1960)
Georgia: 42 years: Ioane IV (1100–1142)
Greece: 40 years: Michaēl III (1182–1222)
India: 44 years: Joseph Mar Dionysios V (1865–1909)
Japan: 32 years: Nikolaï I (1880–1912)
Jerusalem (Armenian): 34 years: Grigor VII (1715–1749)
Jerusalem (Greek): 42 years: Germanos I (1537–1579)
Jerusalem (Latin): 27 years: Aloysius II (1920–1947)
Macedonia: 32 years: Jovan V (1183–1215)
Montenegro: 48 years: Petar I (1782–1830)
Poland: 28 years: Bazyli I (1970–1998)
Romania: 29 years: Justinian I (1948–1977)
Rome: 32 years: Pius IX (1846–1878)
Russia: 25 years: Aleksiï I (1945–1970)
Serbia: 33 years: Pajsije I (1614–1647)
Sinai: 54/55 years: Kōnstantios II (1804/05–1859)
Ukraine: 34 years: Ioann I (1004–1038)

Appendix 3.

Current Hierarchs by Church

(As of 2005.)

Name	Accession Date	Whole Years Served	Year Born	Age
ALBANIA (ARCHBISHOPRIC):				
Anastasios I	24.VI.1992	13+	1929	76+
ALEXANDRIA (COPTIC PAPACY):				
Shanudah III	31.X.1971	34+	1923	82+
ALEXANDRIA (COPTIC CATHOLIC PATRIARCHATE):				
Istifanus II	9.VI.1986	19+	1920	85+
ALEXANDRIA (GREEK PAPACY):				
Theodōros II	9.X.2004	1+	1954	51+
AMERICA (AUTOCEPHALOUS ORTHODOX CHURCH):				
Herman I	22.VII.2002	3+	1932	73+
AMERICA (GREEK ARCHDIOCESE):				
Dēmētrios I	19.VIII.1999	6+	1928	77+
ANTIOCH (GREEK PATRIARCHATE):				
Ighnatiyus IV	2.VII.1979	26+	1920	85+
ANTIOCH (MARONITE PATRIARCHATE):				
Nasr Allah Butrus I	19.IV.1986	19+	1920	85+
ANTIOCH (MELKITE PATRIARCHATE):				
Ghrighuriyus III	29.XI.2000	5+	1933	72+
ANTIOCH (SYRIAN CATHOLIC PATRIARCHATE):				
Ighnatiyus Butrus VIII	16.II.2001	4+	1930	75+
ANTIOCH (SYRIAN ORTHODOX PATRIARCHATE):				
Ighnatiyus Zakka I	14.IX.1980	25+	1932	73+

Appendix 3.

ARMENIA (CATHOLICOSATE):
Garegin II　　4.XI.1999　　6+　　1951　　54+

ASSYRIA (CHURCH OF THE EAST—CATHOLICOSATE):
Dinkha IV　　17.X.1976　　29+　　1935　　70+

ASSYRIA (ANCIENT APOSTOLIC—CATHOLICOSATE):
Addai II　　20.II.1972　　33+　　1946　　59+

BABYLON (CHALDEAN CATHOLIC PATRIARCHATE):
'Ummanu'il III　　3.XII.2003　　2+　　1927　　78+

BELARUS (EXARCHATE):
Filaret I　　10.X.1978　　27+　　1935　　70+

BULGARIA (PATRIARCHATE):
Maksim I　　4.VII.1971　　34+　　1914　　91+

CHINA (ARCHBISHOPRIC):
vacant

CILICIA (ARMENIAN CATHOLICOSATE):
Aram I　　28.VI.1995　　10+　　1947　　58+

CILICIA (CATHOLIC PATRIARCHATE):
Nersês Petros XIX　　7.X.1999　　6+　　1940　　65+

CONSTANTINOPLE (ARMENIAN PATRIARCHATE):
Mesrop II　　14.X.1998　　7+　　1956　　49+

CONSTANTINOPLE (GREEK ECUMENICAL PATRIARCHATE):
Bartholomaios I　　22.X.1991　　14+　　1940　　65+

CRETE (ARCHBISHOPRIC):
Timotheos III　　10.III.1978　　27+　　1915　　90+

CYPRUS (ARCHBISHOPRIC):
Chrysostomos I　　12.XI.1977　　28+　　1927　　78+

CZECHIA AND SLOVAKIA (METROPOLITANATE):
Nikolaj I　　14.VI.2000　　5+　　1927　　78+

ERITREA (PATRIARCHATE):
Antonios I　　2.III.2004　　1+　　1927　　78+
Dioskoros I　　25.VIII.2005　　0+

ESTONIA (METROPOLITANATE):
Stefanus I　　16.III.1999　　6+　　1940　　65+

ETHIOPIA (PATRIARCHATE):
Paulos I	5.VII.1992	13+	1935	70+

FINLAND (ARCHBISHOPRIC):
Leo I	25.X.2001	4+	1948	57+

GEORGIA (CATHOLICOSATE):
Ilia II	23.XII.1977	28+	1933	72+

GREECE (ARCHBISHOPRIC):
Christodoulos I	28.IV.1998	7+	1939	66+

GREECE (OLD CALENDARISTS):
Chrysostomos II	1985	20+
Kyprianos I	1986	19+
Andreas	1972	33+

INDIA (MALABAR INDEPENDENT SYRIAN CHURCH):
Joseph Koorilose IX	27.VIII.1986	19+	1951	54+

INDIA (MALANKARA JACOBITE SYRIAN CHURCH):
Baselios Thomas I	26.VII.2002	3+	1929	76+

INDIA (MALANKARA ORTHODOX SYRIAN CHURCH):
Baselios Mathews II	29.IV.1991	14+	1915	90+

INDIA (MAR THOMA SYRIAN CHURCH):
Philipose Chrysostom	24.X.1999	6+	1918	87+

JAPAN (METROPOLITANATE):
Daniel I	6.V.2000	5+	1938	67+

JERUSALEM (ARMENIAN PATRIARCHATE):
T'orgom II	22.III.1990	15+	1919	86+

JERUSALEM (GREEK PATRIARCHATE):
Theophilos III	22.VIII.2005	0+	1952	53+

JERUSALEM (LATIN PATRIARCHATE):
Michael II	11.XII.1987	18+	1933	72+

LATVIA (METROPOLITANATE):
Aleksandrs I	23.VIII.1989	16+	1939	66+

MACEDONIA (OHRID) (METROPOLITANATE):
Stefan I	10.X.1999	6+	1955	50+

Appendix 3.

MOLDOVA (EXARCHATE):

Vladimir I   21.VII.1989   16+   1952   53+

MONTENEGRO (ARCHBISHOPRIC):

Mihaïlo III   6.I.1997   8+   1938   67+

POLAND (METROPOLITANATE):

Sawa I   12.V.1998   7+   1938   67+

ROMANIA (OLD CALENDARISTS):

Vlasie I   1992   13+

ROMANIA (PATRIARCHATE):

Teoctist I   9.XI.1986   19+   1915   90+

ROME (PAPACY):

Benedictus XVI   19.IV.2005   0+   1927   78+

RUSSIA (CHURCH OUTSIDE RUSSIA):

Vitaliĭ I   22.I.1986   19+   1910   95+
Laurus I   24.X.2001   4+   1928   77+

RUSSIA (OLD BELIEVERS: BELOKRINITISIA):

vacant

RUSSIA (OLD BELIEVERS: NOVOSYBKOV PATRIARCHATE):

Aleksandr I   9.V.2000   5+   1957   48+

RUSSIA (PATRIARCHATE):

Aleksiĭ II   7.VI.1990   15+   1929   76+

SERBIA (PEC) (PATRIARCHATE):

Pavle I   1.XII.1990   15+   1914   91+

SINAI (ARCHBISHOPRIC):

Damianos I   10.XII.1973   32+   1935   70+

UKRAINE (AUTOCEPHALOUS CHURCH) (PATRIARCHATE):

Mefodiĭ I   15.IX.2000   5+   1949   56+

UKRAINE (KIEVAN PATRIARCHATE):

Filaret I   22.X.1995   10+   1929   76+

UKRAINE (RUSSIAN EXARCHATE):

Volodymyr II   27.V.1992   13+   1935   70+

Appendix 4.

Current Hierarchs by Date of Accession

(As of 2005.)

Accession date/Whole years of rule *Name/See*

1971-07-04 (34+) Maksim I (Bulgaria)
1971-10-31 (34+) Shanudah III (Alexandria — Coptic)
1972-02-20 (33+) Addai II (Assyria — Ancient Church)
1972-00-00 (33+) Andreas I (Greece — Old Calendar)
1973-12-10 (32+) Damianos I (Sinai)
1976-10-17 (29+) Dinkha IV (Assyria — Church of East)
1977-11-12 (28+) Chrysostomos I (Cyprus)
1977-12-13 (28+) Ilia II (Georgia)
1978-03-10 (27+) Timotheos III (Crete)
1978-10-10 (27+) Filaret I (Belarus)
1979-07-02 (26+) Ighnatiyus IV (Antioch — Greek)
1980-11-14 (25+) Ighnatiyus Zakka I (Antioch — Syria)
1985-00-00 (20+) Chrysostomos II (Greece — Old Calendar)
1986-01-22 (19+) Vitaliĭ I (Russia — Church Outside)
1986-04-19 (19+) Nasr Allah Butrus I (Antioch — Maronite)
1986-06-09 (19+) Istifanus II (Alexandria — Catholic)
1986-08-27 (19+) Joseph Koorilose IX (India — Malabar)
1986-11-09 (19+) Teoctist I (Romania — Patriarch)
1986-00-00 (19+) Kyprianos I (Greece — Old Calendar)
1987-12-11 (18+) Michael II (Jerusalem — Latin)
1989-07-21 (16+) Vladimir I (Moldova)
1989-08-23 (16+) Aleksandrs I (Latvia)
1990-03-22 (15+) T'orgom II (Jerusalem — Armenian)
1990-06-07 (15+) Aleksiĭ II (Russia — Patriarch)
1990-12-01 (15+) Pavle I (Serbia)
1991-04-29 (14+) Baselios Mathews II (India — Mar Thoma Syrian)
1991-10-22 (14+) Bartholomaios I (Constantinople)
1992-05-27 (13+) Volodymyr II (Ukraine — Russian)
1992-06-24 (13+) Anastasios I (Albania)
1992-07-05 (13+) Paulos I (Ethiopia)
1992-00-00 (13+) Vlasie I (Romania — Old Calendarists)
1995-06-28 (10+) Aram I (Cilicia — Armenian)
1995-10-22 (10+) Filaret I (Ukraine — Kievan)

Appendix 4.

1997-01-06 (8+)	Mihaïlo III (Montenegro)
1998-04-28 (7+)	Christodoulos I (Greece)
1998-05-12 (7+)	Sawa I (Poland)
1998-10-14 (7+)	Mesrop II (Constantinople — Armenian)
1999-03-16 (6+)	Stefanus I (Estonia)
1999-08-19 (6+)	Dēmētrios I (America)
1999-10-07 (6+)	Nersês Petros XIX (Cilicia — Catholic)
1999-10-10 (6+)	Stefan I (Macedonia)
1999-10-24 (6+)	Philipose Chrysostom (India — Mar Thoma)
1999-11-04 (6+)	Garegin II (Armenia)
2000-05-06 (5+)	Daniel I (Japan)
2000-05-09 (5+)	Aleksandr I (Russia — Novosybkov)
2000-06-14 (5+)	Nikolaj I (Czechoslovakia)
2000-09-15 (5+)	Mefodiĭ I (Ukraine — Autocephalous)
2000-11-29 (5+)	Ghrighuriyus III (Antioch — Melkite)
2001-02-16 (4+)	Ighnatiyus Butrus VIII (Antioch — Syrian Catholic)
2001-10-24 (4+)	Laurus I (Russia — Church Outside)
2001-10-25 (4+)	Leo I (Finland)
2002-07-22 (3+)	Herman I (America — Autocephalous)
2002-07-26 (3+)	Baselios Thomas I (India — Malankara)
2003-12-03 (2+)	'Ummanu'il III (Babylon)
2004-03-02 (1+)	Antonios I (Eritrea)
2004-10-09 (1+)	Theodōros II (Alexandria — Greek)
2005-04-19 (0+)	Benedictus XVI (Rome)
2005-08-22 (0+)	Theophilos III (Jerusalem — Greek)
2005-08-25 (0+)	Dioskoros I (Eritrea; rival patriarch)

Appendix 5.

Current Hierarchs by Date of Birth

Date of birth/Age in whole years *Name/See*

1910-03-18 (95+)	Vitaliĭ I (Russia — Church Outside)
1914-09-11 (91+)	Pavle I (Serbia)
1914-10-29 (91+)	Maksim I (Bulgaria)
1915-00-00 (90+)	Timotheos III (Crete)
1915-01-30 (90+)	Baselios Mathews II (India — Mar Thoma Syrian)
1915-02-07 (90+)	Teoctist I (Romania — Patriarch)
1918-04-27 (87+)	Philipose Chrysostom (India — Mar Thoma)
1919-02-16 (86+)	T'orgom II (Jerusalem — Armenian)
1920-01-16 (85+)	Istifanus II (Alexandria — Catholic)
1920-04-01 (85+)	Ighnatiyus IV (Antioch — Greek)
1920-05-15 (85+)	Nasr Allah Butrus I (Antioch — Maronite)
1923-08-03 (82+)	Shanudah III (Alexandria — Coptic)
1927-00-00 (78+)	Antonios I (Eritrea)
1927-04-16 (78+)	Benedictus XVI (Rome)
1927-09-27 (78+)	Chrysostomos I (Cyprus)
1927-10-06 (78+)	'Ummanu'il III (Babylon)
1927-12-19 (78+)	Nikolaj I (Czechoslovakia)
1928-01-01 (77+)	Laurus I (Russia — Church Outside)
1928-02-01 (77+)	Dēmētrios I (America)
1929-01-28 (76+)	Filaret I (Ukraine — Kievan)
1929-02-23 (76+)	Aleksiĭ II (Russia — Patriarch)
1929-07-22 (76+)	Baselios Thomas I (India — Malankara)
1929-11-09 (76+)	Anastasios I (Albania)
1930-06-28 (75+)	Ighnatiyus Butrus VIII (Antioch — Syrian Catholic)
1932-02-01 (73+)	Herman I (America — Autocephalous)
1932-04-21 (73+)	Ighnatiyus Zakka I (Antioch — Syria)
1933-01-04 (72+)	Ilia II (Georgia)
1933-03-19 (72+)	Michael II (Jerusalem — Latin)
1933-12-15 (72+)	Ghrighuriyus III (Antioch — Melkite)
1935-00-00 (70+)	Paulos I (Ethiopia)
1935-03-21 (70+)	Filaret I (Belarus)
1935-04-04 (70+)	Damianos I (Sinai)
1935-09-15 (70+)	Dinkha IV (Assyria — Church of East)
1935-11-23 (70+)	Volodymyr II (Ukraine — Russian)
1938-04-15 (67+)	Sawa I (Poland)
1938-09-05 (67+)	Daniel I (Japan)
1938-11-08 (67+)	Mihaïlo III (Montenegro)
1939-00-00 (66+)	Christodoulos I (Greece)

Appendix 5.

1939-10-03 (66+)	Aleksandrs I (Latvia)
1940-01-17 (65+)	Nersês Petros XIX (Cilicia — Catholic)
1940-02-29 (65+)	Bartholomaios I (Constantinople)
1940-04-29 (65+)	Stefanus I (Estonia)
1946-08-01 (59+)	Addai II (Assyria — Ancient Church)
1947-00-00 (58+)	Aram I (Cilicia — Armenian)
1948-06-04 (57+)	Leo I (Finland)
1949-03-01 (56+)	Mefodiĭ I (Ukraine — Autocephalous)
1951-00-00 (54+)	Joseph Koorilose IX (India — Malabar)
1951-08-21 (54+)	Garegin II (Armenia)
1952-00-00 (53+)	Theophilos III (Jerusalem — Greek)
1952-08-18 (53+)	Vladimir I (Moldova)
1954-11-25 (51+)	Theodōros II (Alexandria — Greek)
1955-05-01 (50+)	Stefan I (Macedonia)
1956-06-16 (49+)	Mesrop II (Constantinople — Armenian)
1957-11-25 (48+)	Aleksandr I (Russia — Novosybkov)
unknown	Andreas I (Greece — Old Calendar)
unknown	Chrysostomos II (Greece — Old Calendar)
unknown	Dioskoros (Eritrea; rival patriarch)
unknown	Kyprianos I (Greece — Old Calendar)
unknown	Vlasie I (Romania — Old Calendarists)

Selected Bibliography

This bibliography makes no attempt to provide a comprehensive listing of resources on the Eastern churches; rather, it reflects the materials which I personally found useful in compiling this book. I have also listed complete runs of those journals which were consulted for their news and obituary sections over a long span of years.

Alexander, Stella. *Church and State in Yugoslavia Since 1945*. Cambridge: Cambridge University Press, 1979.
Almanach of the Melkite-Greek Catholic Church 1986. Journieh, Lebanon: Le Lien, 1986.
Amantos, Kōnstantinos. *Syntomos Historia tēs Hieras Monēs tou Sina*. Thessalonikē: [s.n.], 1953.
Andersen, Knud Tage. *Ethiopiens Ortodokse Kirke*. København: Savane, Udg. af Dansk Ethioper Mission, 1971.
*Annuario Pontificio per l'Annò 1982- *. Città del Vaticano: Libreria Editrice Vaticana, 1982- .
Antreassian, Assadour. *Jerusalem and the Armenians*. Jerusalem: St. James Press, 1968.
Arbanitēs, Athanasios K. *Historia tēs Assyraikēs Nestorianikēs Ekklēsias*. Athēnai: Athēnais Philekpaideutikēs Etaireias, 1968.
Assemani, Giuseppi Luigi [*i.e.*, Yusuf al-Sim'ani]. *De Catholicis Seu Patriarchis Chaldaeorum et Nestorianorum: Commentarius Historico-Chronologicus*. Romae: Monaldini, 1775. Reprinted: Farnborough, England: Gregg International Publishers, 1969.
Assemani, Giuseppi Simone [i.e., Yusuf Sim'an al-Sim'ani]. *Series Chronologica Patriarcharum Antiochiae*. Romae: Ex Typographia Polyglotta, 1881. Reprinted: Farnborough, England: Gregg International Publishers, 1969.
Atiya, Aziz Suryal, ed. *The Coptic Encyclopedia*. New York: Macmillan Publishing Co., 1991, 8 v.
Atiya, Aziz Suryal. *History of Eastern Christianity*. Notre Dame, IN: University of Notre Dame Press, 1968.
Atiya, Aziz Suryal. *History of the Patriarchs of the Egyptian Church*. Cairo: [s.n.], 1943–59, 3 v.
Attwater, Donald. *The Catholic Eastern Churches*. Milwaukee, WI: Bruce Publishing Co., 1935. Revised and expanded as: *The Christian Churches of the East*. Milwaukee, WI: Bruce Publishing Co., 1947–48, 2 v.
Babgên Kiwlêsêrean, Catholicos of Armenian Cilicia. *Pat'mutiun Kat'oghikosats' Kilikoy: 1441-ên Minchew Merôrer*. Antelias, Lebanon: Tparan Tbrevanuts Katoghikosutean Kilikoy, 1939.
Barrett, David B. *World Christian Encyclopedia: A Comparative Survey of Churches and Religions in the Modern World*. Oxford: Oxford University Press, 1982. 2nd ed., 2001.
Basileios, Bishop of Lēmnos. *Episkopikoi Katalogoi Hellados*. Athēnai: [s.n.], 1972.
Batalden, Stephen K., ed. *Seeking God: The Recovery of Religious Identity in Orthodox Russia, Ukraine, and Georgia*. DeKalb, IL: Northern Illinois University Press, 1993.
Bernath, Mathias, and Karl Nehring, eds. *Biographisches Lexikon zur Geschichte Südosteuropas*. München: R. Oldenbourg Verlag, 1974–81, 4 v.
Binder, Leonard, ed. *Politics in Lebanon*. New York: John Wiley & Sons, 1966.
Brown, Leslie. *The Indian Christians of St Thomas: An Account of the Ancient Syrian Church of Malabar*. Cambridge: Cambridge University Press, 1982.

Buganov, V. I. "Patriarkh," in *Bol'shaia Sovetskaia Entsiklopediia*, Vol. 19, p. 281. Moskva: Bol'shaia Sovetskaia Entsiklopediia, 197–.

Büsek, Vratislav, and Nicolas Spulber, eds. *Czechoslovakia*. New York: Published for the Mid-European Studies Center of the Free Europe Committee by Frederick A. Praeger, 1957.

The Catholic Encyclopedia. New York: Encyclopedia Press, 1908, 15 v.

Catholicate Sapthathi Souvenir. Kottayam, India: Malankara Orthodox Syrian Church, 1982.

Chabot, J. B. "Les Listes Patriarcales de l'Église Maronite: Étude Critique et Historique," in *Mémoires de L'Academie des Inscriptions et Belles-Lettres* 43 (1951): 21–43.

Cheikho, Louis. "Les Archevêques du Sinai," in *Mélanges de la Faculté Orientale de St. Joseph* 2 (1907): 408.

Cherney, Alexander. *The Latvian Orthodox Church*. Welshpool, Powys, Wales: Stylite Publishing Ltd., 1985.

Chrysostomos Papadopoulos, Archbishop of Greece. *Historia tēs Ekklēsias Alexandreias (62–1934)*. Alexandreia: Patriarchikon Typographeion, 1935.

Chrysostomos Papadopoulos, Archbishop of Greece. *Historia tēs Ekklēsias Antiocheias*. Alexandreia: [Patriarchikon Typographeion], 1951.

Chrysostomos Papadopoulos, Archbishop of Greece. *Historia tēs Ekklēsias Hellados*. Athēnai: P. A. Petrakos, 1920.

Chrysostomos Papadopoulos, Archbishop of Greece. *Historia tēs Ekklēsias Hierosolymōn*. Alexandreia: Patriarchikon Typographeion, 1910.

Cobham, Claude Delaval. *The Patriarchs of Constantinople*. London: Ares Publishers, 1911.

Cramer, Maria. *Das Christlich-Koptische Ägypten Einst und Heute*. Wiesbaden: Otto Harrassowitz, 1959.

Daniel, David. *The Orthodox Church of India: History and Faith*. New Delhi: Rachel Daniel, 1972. 2nd ed., 1986.

Daniel, I. *The Malabar Church and Other Orthodox Churches*. Haripad, India: Suvarna Bharathi Press, 1950.

Daniel, I. *The Syrian Church of Malabar*. Madras: Diocesan Press, 1945.

Deset Godini Bulgarska Patriarshiia. Sofia: Sinodalno Izd-vo., 1963.

Dib, Pierre. *L'Église Maronite*. Beyrouth: Édition de la Sagesse, 1962–1973, 3 v.

Dictionnaire d'Archéologie Chrétienne et de Liturgie. Paris: Letouzey et Ané, 1907–1953, 15 v.

Dictionnaire de Théologie Catholique. Paris: Letouzey et Ané, 1909–1950, 15 v.

Dictionnaire d'Histoire et de Géographie Ecclésiastique. Paris: Letouzey et Ané, 1912– (in progress), 28+ v.

Directory of Orthodox Parishes and Institutions in North America, 1998. Torrance, CA: Orthodox Christian Communications Network, 1998.

Donef, Racho. "The Political Role of the Turkish Orthodox Patriarchate (So-Called)." 2003.

Dowsett, C. J. F. "The Albanian Chronicle of Mxit'ar Gos," in *Bulletin of the School of Oriental and African Studies* 21: 472–490.

Dowsett, C. J. F. "A Neglected Passage in the History of the Caucasian Albanians," in *Bulletin of the School of Oriental and African Studies* 19: 456–468.

Drinov, Marin. *Isturicheski Pregled' na Bulgarska-ta Tsurkva ot' Samo-to i Hachalo i do Dnes'*. Vienzh: L. Sommepovzh, 1869.

Eastern Churches News Letter. London: Anglican and Eastern Churches Association, n.s. Nos. 9–, 1979–. News sections.

Eastern Churches Review. London: Oxford University Press (and others), 1966–1978, 10 v. News and Comments, Appointments, and Obituaries sections.

Eastern Europe and the Commonwealth States. London: Europa Publications, 1993–. 2nd ed., 1994.

Échos d'Orient. Paris: échoes d'Orient, Vols. 1–40, 1897–1942. News sections.

Eckenstein, Lina. *A History of Sinai*. New York: Macmillan, 1921. New York: AMS Press, 1980.

Eesti Apostlik Ortodoksne Kirik Eksiilis, 1944–1960. Stockholm: Eesti Apostliku Ortodoksne Kiriku Kultuurfond, 1961.

Ellis, Jane. *The Russian Orthodox Church: A Contemporary History*. Bloomington & Indianapolis: Indiana University Press, 1986.

Episkepsis. Chambésy, Switzerland: Le Centre Orthodoxe du Patriarcat Oecuménique, 1982–. News and obituaries.

The Europa World Year Book. London: Europa Publications, 1947–.

Fenwick, John R. K. *The Malabar Independent Syrian Church*. Nottingham, England: Grove Books, 1992.
Fine, John V. A., Jr. *The Bosnian Church: A New Interpretation: A Study of the Bosnian Church and Its Place in State and Society from the 13th to the 15th Centuries*. Boulder, CO: East European Quarterly, 1975.
Fortescue, Adrian. *The Lesser Eastern Churches*. London: Catholic Truth Society, 1913. New York: AMS Press, 1972.
Frazee, Charles A. *The Orthodox Church and Independent Greece, 1821–1852*. Cambridge: Cambridge University Press, 1969.
Gabriel, Antony, Archpriest. *The Ancient Church on New Shores: Antioch in North America*. San Bernardino, CA: St. Willibrord's Press, 1996.
Gedeōn, Manouēl I. *Patriarchikoi Pinakes*. Kōnstantinopoleōs: Lorenz & Keil, 1890.
Gennadios, Metropolitan of Hēlioupoleōs and Thierōn, ed. *Historia tou Oikoumenikou Patriarcheiou*. Athēnai: Kon. Theolokikēs Scholēs, 1953.
Gerent, Piotr. "Cerkiew Prawosławna w Polsce Zakończeniu II Wojny Światowej." 1998.
Ghabra'il, Mikha'il Abd Allah. *Histoire de L'Église Syriaque Maronite d'Antioche*. 1900. Translation of *Kittab al-Kanisah al-Antakiyah al-Suryaniyah al-Maruniyah*. 1900.
Grbić, Manojlo. *Karlovačko Vladičanstvo: Prilog k Istoriji Srpske Pravoslavne Crkve*. Karlovac: Stamparija Karla Hauptfelda, 1891, 3 v.
Grujić, R. "Pećska Patrijarsija," in *Narodna Enciklopedija Srpsko-Hrvatsko-Slovenačka*, Vol. III, p. 389–399. Zagreb: 1928.
Guidi, I. "Le Liste dei Metropoliti d'Abissinia," in *Bessarione* 4 (Luglio-Agosto, 1899): 1–16.
Hackett, John. *A History of the Orthodox Church of Cyprus from the Coming of the Apostles Paul and Barnabas to the Commencement of the British Occupation (A.D. 45–A.D.1878)*. London: Methuen, 1901.
Haddad, Robert M. *Syrian Christians in Muslim Society: An Interpretation*. Princeton, NJ: Princeton University Press, 1970.
Hagiotaphitikon Hēmerlologion. Hierosolyma: Ekdosis Hierou Koinou tou Panagiou Taphou, 1975?–.
Harik, Iliya F. *Politics and Change in a Traditional Society: Lebanon, 1711–1845*. Princeton, NJ: Princeton University Press, 1968.
Heyer, Friedrich. *Die Orthodoxe Kirche in der Ukraine von 1917 bis 1945*. Köln-Braunsfeld: Rudolf Müller, 1953.
"Historia Diecezji Warszawsko-Bielskiej." Dekanalny Instytut Kultury Prawosławnei w Hainówce, 2000.
Hussey, J. M. *The Orthodox Church in the Byzantine Empire*. Oxford: Clarendon Press, 1986.
Hyatt, Harry Middleton. *The Church of Abyssinia*. London: Luzac & Co., 1928.
Jacob, Xavier. "An Autocephalous Turkish Orthodox Church," in *Eastern Churches Review* 3 (Spring, 1970): 59–71.
Jedin, Hubert. *History of the Church*. New York: Crossroad, 1980–81, 10 v.
Kamil, Jill. *Coptic Egypt: History and Guide*. Cairo: American University in Cairo Press, 1987.
Kazhdan, Alexander P., ed. *The Oxford Dictionary of Byzantium*. New York, Oxford: Oxford University Press, 1991, 3 v.
Kêok'chian, Vahram. *Hay Erowsaghême Darerow Mêjên*. Erowsaghêm: Tp. Srbots' Yakoreants', 1965.
Kidd, B. J. *The Churches of Eastern Christendom from A.D. 451 to the Present Time*. London: Faith Press, 1927. New York: B. Franklin, 1974
King, Archdale A. *The Rites of Eastern Christendom*. Rome: Catholic Book Agency, 1947, 2 v. New York: AMS Press, 1972.
King, Rev. Demetrius J. *A History of the American Orthodox Catholic Church*. Unpublished manuscript used by permission of the author.
Kolarz, Walter. *Religion in the Soviet Union*. London: Macmillan & Co., 1962.
Lavrentije, Bishop, et al., eds. *Srpska Pravoslavna Crkva, 1219–1969: Spomenica o 750-Godishnjici Autokefalnosti*. Beograd: Izdanje Svetog Arhijerejskog Cinoda, Srpske Pravoslavne Crkve, 1969.
Le Quien, Michel. *Oriens Christianus*. Graz: Akademische Druck u. Verlagsanstalt, 1958, 3 v. First published 1740.
Lubeck, Konrad. "Die Autokephale Kirche des Berges Sinai," in *Wissenschaft Liche Beilage zur Germania* no. 16 (1911).
Macartney, C. A. *The Habsburg Empire, 1790–1918*. New York: Macmillan Co., 1969.

MacDermott, Mercia. *A History of Bulgaria, 1393–1895*. London: George Allen & Unwin, 1962.

MacLean, Arthur John. *A Dictionary of the Dialects of Vernacular Syriac*. Oxford: Clarendon Press, 1901.

Maghak'ia Örmanean, Armenian Patriarch of Constantinople. *The Church of Armenia: Her History, Doctrine, Rule, Discipline, Liturgy, Literature, and Existing Condition*, translated by G. Marcar Gregory from *L'Église Arménienne*, edited by Terenig Poladian. 2nd ed. London: A. R. Mowbray, 1955.

Maksoudian, Krikor H., Father. *Chosen of God: The Election of the Catholicos of All Armenians from the Fourth Century to the Present*. New York: St. Vartan Press, 1995.

Marshall, Richard H. Jr., editor. *Aspects of Religion in the Soviet Union, 1917–1967*. Chicago and London: University of Chicago Press, 1971.

Maximos, Metropolitan of Sardēs. *The Oecumenical Patriarchate in the Orthodox Church: A Study in the History and Canons of the Church*. Thessaloniki, Greece: Patriarchal Institute for Patristic Studies, 1976.

McCullough, W. Stewart. *A Short History of Syriac Christianity to the Rise of Islam*. Chico, CA: Scholars Press, 1982.

Meinardus, Otto F. A. *Christian Egypt Ancient and Modern*. Cairo: American University at Cairo Press, 1977.

Meinardus, Otto F. A. *Monks and Monasteries of the Egyptian Desert*. Cairo: American University at Cairo Press, 1961. Expanded 2nd ed., 1989.

Melton, J. Gordon. *The Encyclopedia of American Religions*. Wilmington, NC: McGrath Publishing Co., 1978, 2 v. 6th ed. Detroit: Gale Research Co., 1999.

Menachery, Thomas, ed. *The St. Thomas Christian Encyclopedia of India*. Trichur, India: St. Thomas Christian Encyclopedia of India, 1970, 3 v.

Michael I, Syrian Orthodox Patriarch of Antioch. *Chronique de Michel le Syrien, Patriarche Jacobite d'Antioche (1166–1199)*, edited by J. B. Chabot. Paris: Culture et Civilisation, 1963, 4 v. Originally published 1899.

The Middle East and North Africa. London: Unesco Publications, 195–. Annual.

Mishaqa, Mikhayil, translated by W. M. Thackston Jr. *Murder, Mayhem, Pillage, and Plunder: The History of Lebanon in the 18th and 19th Centuries*. Albany, NY: State University of New York Press, 1988.

al-Misri, Iris Habib. *Qissat al-Khanisah al-Qibtiyah*. Cairo: 196–, 4 v.

Mitsidēs, Andreas N. *Hē Ekklēsia tēs Kyprou*. Leukōsia: Anagennēsē, 1980.

Mnats'akanyan, A. Sh. *O Literature Kavkazskoĭ Albaniĭ*. Erevan: Izdatel'stvo Akademiĭ Nauk Armianskoĭ SSR, 1969.

Molnar, Enricot S. *The Ethiopian Orthodox Church*. Pasadena, CA: Bloy House Theological School, 1969.

Montalbano, William D. "Pope Calls for Broad Mideast Peace," in *Los Angeles Times* (March 5, 1991): A16.

Moosa, Matti. *The Maronites in History*. Syracuse, NY: Syracuse University Press, 1986.

Morgan, Jacques de. *The History of the Armenian People*. Boston: Hairenik Press, 1956. Originally published in 1916 in French.

Movsês Daskhuranci. *The History of the Caucasian Albanians*, translated by C. J. F. Dowsett. London: Oxford University Press, 1961.

Munier, H. *Précis de L'Histoire d'Égypte*. Caire: Institut Français d'Archéologie Orientale du Caire, 1932–35.

Murre-Van den Berg, Heleen H. L. "The Patriarchs of the Church of the East from the Fifteenth to Eighteenth Centuries," in *Hugoye: Journal of Syriac Studies* 2 (July, 1999).

Nasrallah, Joseph. *Chronologie des Patriarches Melchites d'Antioche de 1250 à 1500*. Jerusalem: 1968.

Nasrallah, Joseph. *Notes et Documents pour Servir à l'Histoire du Patriarchat Melchite d'Antioche*. Jerusalem: 1965.

Nasrallah, Joseph. *Sa Béatitude Maximos IV et la Succession Apostolique du Siège d'Antioche*. Paris: 1963.

Nasrallah, Joseph. *Vie de la Chrétiente Melkite sous la Domination Turque*. Paris: Geuthner, 1949.

Neale, J. *A History of the Holy Eastern Church*. London: J. Masters, 1850.

The New Catholic Encyclopedia. New York: McGraw-Hill, 1967–79, 17 v. 2nd ed., Detroit: Gale Group; Washington, DC: Catholic University of America, 2003, 15 v.

Nicol, Donald M. *The Last Centuries of Byzantium, 1261–1453*. 2nd ed. Cambridge: Cambridge University Press, 1993.

Nubijovyc, Volodymyr. *Ukraine: A Concise Encyclopaedia.* Toronto: University of Toronto Press, 1963.
Official Catholic Directory. Chicago: P. J. Kenedy & Sons, 1910–.
"Oikoumenikon (Patriarcheion)," in *Megalē Hellēnikē Enkyklopaideia,* Vol. 18, p. 766–775. Athēnai: Pyrsos, 1932.
O'Leary, De Lacy. *The Ethiopian Church: Historical Notes on the Church of Abyssinia.* London: SPCK, 1936.
Onami, Yuji. "Holy Orthodox Church," in *Kodansha Encyclopedia of Japan,* Vol. 3. Tokyo: Kodansha, 1983.
Orthodox News. London: St. George Orthodox Information Service, Vol. 2–, 1984–. News and obituaries.
Orthodoxia, ed. by Dr. Nikolaus Wyrwoll. Regensburg, Germany: Ostkirchliches Institut, 1982–. Annual directory.
The Oxford Dictionary of Byzantium. New York, Oxford: Oxford University Press, 1991, 3 v.
Păcurariu, Mircea. *Dicționarul Teologilor Români.* București: Univers Enciclopedic, 1996.
Păcurariu, Mircea. *Istoria Bisericii Ortodoxe Române.* București: Editura Institutului Biblic si de Misiune al Bisericii Ortodoxe Române, 1980–81, 3 v.
Papamichalopoulos, Kōnstantinos N. *Hē Monē tou Horous Sina.* Athēnai: E. D. Papas, 1932.
Pavlowitch, Stevan K. "The Orthodox Church in Yugoslavia: The Problem of the Macedonian Church," in *Eastern Churches Review* 1 (Winter 1967/68): 374–388.
Petrovich, Michael Boro. *A History of Modern Serbia, 1804–1918.* New York: Harcourt Brace Jovanovich, 1976, 2 v.
Petrovskiĭ, N. A. *Slovar' Russkikh Lichnykh Imën.* Moskva: Izdatel'stva "Sovetskaia Entsiklopediia," 1966.
"50-Letie Vosstanovleniia Patriarshestva," in *Zhurnal Moskovskoi Patriarkhii* (1971).
Piepkorn, Arthur Carl. *Profiles in Belief: The Religious Bodies of the United States and Canada.* New York: Harper & Row, 1977–79, 4 v. in 3.
"Pinakes Patriarchōn," in *Eleutheroudakē Enkyklopaidikon Lexikon,* Vol. 10, p. 521–523, plus four-page insert between p. 520–521, and p. 487 of the Supplement. Athēnai: Ekdotikos Oikos "Eleutheroudakes," 1930.
Podipara, Placid J. *The Thomas Christians.* London: Darton, Longman & Todd; Bombay: St. Paul Publications, 1970.
Pothan, S. G. *The Syrian Christians of Kerala.* New York: Asia Publishing House, 1963.
Proc, Alex. *Jahrbuch der Orthodoxie: Schematismus 1976/77.* West Germany: Athos-Verlag, 1976? Only year published.
Pruter, Karl, Bishop. *Bishops Extraordinary.* Highlandville, MO: St. Willibrord Press, 1985.
Pruter, Karl, Bishop. *A Directory of Autocephalous Bishops of the Apostolic Succession.* 7th ed. San Bernardino, CA: St. Willibrord's Press, 1995. New editions published every eighteen months.
Pruter, Karl, Bishop. *The Strange Partnership of George Alexander McGuire and Marcus Garvey.* Highlandville, MO: St. Willibrord Press, 1986.
Pruter, Karl, Bishop, and J. Gordon Melton. *The Old Catholic Sourcebook.* New York: Garland Publishing, 1983.
Ramet, Pedro, ed. *Eastern Christianity and Politics in the Twentieth Century.* Christianity Under Stress, Volume I. Durham & London: Duke University Press, 1988.
Rodoslovhe Tablice i Grbovi: Srpskih Dinastijai Vlastele. Beograd: Nova Knjiga, 1987.
The Romanian Orthodox Church, Yesterday and Today, translated by Andrei Bantas. Bucharest: Publishing House of the Bible and Mission Institute of the Romanian Orthodox Church, 1979.
Roncaglia, Martiniano. *Histoire de L'Église Copte.* Beirut: Dar al-Kalima, 1966. 2nd ed., Beirut: Libr. St. Paul, 1985–87, 2 v.
Rossi, Jyrki. "Suomen Ortodoksinen Kirkko." 1990?
Runciman, Steven. *The Orthodox Churches and the Secular State.* The Sir Douglas Robb Lectures, 1970. Auckland: Auckland University Press, 1971.
Sergeĭ Voskresenskiĭ, Metropolitan. "The Orthodox Church Under German Occupation: An Unpublished Memorandum by the Exarch of the Baltic Area, Metropolitan Sergeĭ," in *Eastern Churches Review* 6 (Autumn 1971): 131–161.
Smith, J. Payne (and R. Payne). *A Compendious Syriac Dictionary, Founded upon the Thesaurus Syriacus of R. Payne Smith.* Oxford: Clarendon Press, 1979. Originally published in 1903.
Sobornost. London: Fellowship of St. Alban & St. Sergius, Series 7, 1975–1978; N.S. no. 1, 1979–. News sections.

Spinka, Matthew. *A History of Christianity in the Balkans: A Study in the Spread of Byzantine Culture Among the Slavs*. Chicago: American Society of Church History, 1933. Archon Books, 1968.

Spuler, Bertold. *Gegenwartslage der Ostkirchen in Ihrer Volkishen und Staatlichen Umwelt*. Wiesbaden: Metopen Verlag, 1948. 2nd ed., 1968.

Spuler, Bertold. *Die Morgenlandischen Kirchen*. Leiden: E. J. Brill, 1964.

Stokvis, A. M. H. J. *Manuel d'Histoire, de Généalogie et de Chronologie de Touts les États du Globe*. Leiden: E. J. Brill, 1888–93, 3 v. Reprinted: Leiden: B. M. Israël, 1966, 3 v. in 4.

Taddesse Tamrat. *Church and State in Ethiopia: 1270–1527*. Oxford: Clarendon Press, 1972.

Tarasar, Constance J., ed. *Orthodox America: 1794–1976: Development of the Orthodox Church in America*. Syosset, NY: Orthodox Church in America, Dept. of History and Archives, 1975.

Tarrazi, Philippe de. *Al-Salasil al-Tarikhiyah fi Asaqifat al-Abrashiyat al-Suryaniyah*. Bayrut: 1910.

Timotheos Benerēs, Archbishop of Crete. "Krētē— Ekklēs.," in *Megalē Hellēnikē Enkyklopaideia*, Vol. 15. Athēnai: Ekdotikos Organismos, 1950?

Tisserant, Eugène, Cardinal. *Eastern Christianity in India: A History of the Syro-Malabar Church from the Earliest Times to the Present Day*. Westminster, MD: Newman Press, 1957.

Treadway, John D. *The Falcon & the Eagle: Montenegro and Austria-Hungary, 1908–1914*. West Lafayette, IN: Purdue University Press, 1983.

Tseng, Sally C., with David C. Tseng and Linda C. Tseng. *LC Romanization Tables and Cataloging Policies*. Metuchen, NJ: Scarecrow Press, 1990.

al-Unaysi, Tubiyya. *Silsilah Tarikhiyah lil-Batarikah al-Antakiyin al-Mawarinah*. Rome: 1927.

Ursal, George R. "From Political Freedom to Religious Independence: The Romanian Orthodox Church, 1877–1925," in *Romania Between East and West: Historical Essays in Memory of Constantin C. Giurescu*, edited by Stephen Fischer-Galati, Radu R. Florescu, and George R. Ursal. Boulder, CO: East European Monographs, 1982.

Verghese, Paulos Gregorios. *Die Syrischen Kirchen in Indien*. Stuttgart: Evangelisches Verlagswerk, 1974.

Vlasovs'kyĭ, Ivan. *An Outline of the History of the Ukrainian Orthodox Church = Narys Istoriĭi Ukraïns'koĭ Pravoslavnoĭ TSerkvy*. New York: Ukrainian Orthodox Church of U.S.A., 1957, 3 v. 2nd ed. 1974.

Wakin, Edward. *A Lonely Minority: The Modern Story of Egypt's Copts*. New York: William Morrow, 1963.

Walker, Christopher J. *Armenia: The Survival of a Nation*. New York: St. Martin's Press, 1980. Rev. ed. 1990.

Watha'iq-Tarikhiyah lil-Kursi al-Malaki al-Antaki. Bayrut: Al-Masrah, 1932–33, 3 v. in 5.

Who's Who in Lebanon. Beyrouth: Éditions Publictec, 1963–.

Year Book and Church Directory of the Russian Orthodox Greek Catholic Church of America [later the *... Orthodox Church in America*]. 1968–.

Young, Rev. Father Alexey. *The Russian Orthodox Church Outside Russia: A History and Chronology*. San Bernardino, CA: St. Willibrord's Press, 1993.

Zernov, Nicolas. "The First Council of the Russian Church Abroad in Sremski Karlovtsi (21 November–2 December 1921): The Notes of One of the Participants," in *Eastern Churches Review* 7 (1975): 164–185.

"Zhamanakagrowt'iwn T'oirk'ioy Hayots' Patriark'nerow," in *Shoghakat'* (Autumn, 1961): 59–73.

Index of Primates

This index is arranged alphabetically by the first name of the primate, then alphabetically by church (primary see and denomination), then by dates of reign. A typical entry includes name, other given name(s) or nickname(s), surname(s) (in italics), years of reign, church name. If the same individual is recorded on two or more separate lists, he is sometimes listed completely separately under each church, unless his reign styles and dates are exactly identical, even when it is obvious that the same prelate is involved.

Aabo : 540–552 (India — Malankara Orthodox) 163
Aba I *Raba*, Mari : 540–552 (Assyria), and 540–552 (Babylon) 72, 85
Aba II, Mari : 741–751 (Assyria), and 741–751 (Babylon) 73, 86
Abad *M'shikha* : 191–203 (Assyria) 71
Abas : 552–596 (Aghunie) 9
'Abd al-Ghani, Ighnatiyus : 1597–1598 (Antioch — Syrian Catholic) 56
Abd al-Ghani I, Baselios : 1557–1575 (India — Malankara Jacobite) 170
Abd al-Ghani II, Baselios : 1591–1597 (India — Malankara Jacobite) 170
Abd al-Masih, Baselios : 1655–1662 (India — Malankara Jacobite) 171
'Abd Allah, Ighnatiyus : 1520–1557 (Antioch — Syrian Catholic) 55
'Abd Allah I, Ighnatiyus : 1520–1557 (Antioch — Syrian Orthodox) 61
'Abd Allah II *al-Saddi*, Ighnatiyus : 1906–1915 (Antioch — Syrian Orthodox) 62, 161
'Abd al-Masih I *al-Rawhi*, Ighnatiyus : 1662–1686 (Antioch — Syrian Orthodox) 61
'Abd al-Masih II, Ighnatiyus : 1895–1905 (Antioch — Syrian Orthodox) 62, 161

Abdisho *Thondanatta*, Mar : 1864–1874, 1882–1900 (India — Chaldean) 174
'Abdishu' I *Garmaqaya* : 963–986 (Assyria) 73
'Abdishu' II *bar Arus Anraya* : 1072–1090 (Assyria) 74
'Abdishu' III *bar Mulki* : 1138–1147 (Assyria) 74
'Abdishu' I : 963–986 (Babylon) 86
'Abdishu' II *bar Arus Anraya* : 1075–1090 (Babylon) 87
'Abdishu' III *bar Mulki* : 1139–1148 (Babylon) 87
'Abdishu' IV, Marun : 1555–1567 (Babylon) 70, 83, 88
'Abdishu' V *Khayyat,*' Giwargis : 1894–1899 (Babylon) 88
Abilios : 84–98 (Alexandria — Greek) 23
Abiliyus : 83–95 (Alexandria — Coptic Catholic) 20
Abimaleck Timotheus, Mar : 1920s [locum tenens] (Assyria), 1908–1945 (India — Chaldean) 75, 175
Abraam : -1468 (Jerusalem — Greek) 187
Abraha —*see also*: Abreham
Abraha III : 1936–1939 [anti-abuna] (Ethiopia — Historical), and (Ethiopia — Official) 138, 142, 144
Abraham I : 607–615 (Armenia) 65
Abraham II : 1730–1734 (Armenia) 68

Abraham III : 1734–1737 (Armenia) 68
Abraham I : 130–152 (Assyria), and 2nd cent. (Babylon) 71, 84
Abraham II *d'Margaa* : 837–850 (Assyria), and (Babylon) 73, 86
Abraham III *Abraza* : 906–937 (Assyria), and 905–936 (Babylon) 73, 86
Abraham *Gholian* : 1813–1815 (Constantinople — Armenian) 105
Abraham : 1568–1597 (India — Chaldean) 174
Abraham I : 685–686 (India — Malankara Jacobite) 168
Abraham II, Athanasius : 1364–1379 (India — Malankara Jacobite) 170
Abraham III : 1496–1508 (India — Malankara Jacobite) 170
Abraham I : 201–213 (India — Malankara Orthodox) 163
Abraham II : 686–687 (India — Malankara Orthodox) 164
Abraham III, Athanasios Mar : 1365–1379 (India — Malankara Orthodox) 165
Abraham IV, Baselios Mar : 1494–1496 (India — Malankara Orthodox) 166
Abraham I : 638–669 (Jerusalem — Armenian) 179
Abraham II : 885–909 (Jerusalem — Armenian) 180

Index of Primates

Abraham III *of Jerusalem* : 1180–1191 (Jerusalem — Armenian) 180

Abraham IV : 1205–1218 (Jerusalem — Armenian) 180

Abraham V *of Egypt* : 1441–1454 (Jerusalem — Armenian) 181

Abraham VI *of Aleppo* : 1479–1485 (Jerusalem — Armenian) 181

Abraham Mar Climis : 1957–1958 (India — Malankara Jacobite) 172

Abraham Mar Koorilose I *Kattumangat* : 1771–1802 (India — Thozhiyoor) 175

Abraham *Mar Thoma* : 1917–1944 [suffragan], 1944–1947 (India — Mar Thoma Syrian) 173

Abraham Petros I *Ardzivian* : 1740–1749 (Cilicia — Armenian Catholic) 101–102

Abraham Shim'un XIX : 1820?–1861 (Assyria) 74

Abram : 975–978 (Alexandria — Coptic) 17

Abram I : 1280–1310 (Georgia) 150

Abram II *Abalaki* : 1492–1497 (Georgia) 150

Abramios : 1775–1788 (Jerusalem — Greek) 187

Abramios : 1435? (Sinai) 231

Abreham — *see also*: Abraha

Abreham I : unknown (Ethiopia — Official) 139

Abreham II : unknown (Ethiopia — Official) 140

Abrimus : 106–118 (Alexandria — Coptic), and (Alexandria — Coptic Catholic) 15, 21

Abris : 90–107 (Assyria), and 2nd cent. (Babylon) 71, 84

Abrosios : 185–201 (India — Malankara Orthodox) 163

Acasios : 485–498 (India — Malankara Orthodox) 163

Achillas : 311–312 (Alexandria — Greek) 23

Adamantios : 810? (Greece) 155

Addai I *Shlikha* : 33–45 (Assyria) 71

Addai II *Giwargis* : 1969–1972 [locum tenens], 1972- (Assyria — Ancient Church of the East) 75, 254, 257, 260

Addai *Shlikha* : 33- (Babylon), and 72–120 (India — Malankara Orthodox) 84, 163

Adeodatus I : 615–618 (Rome) 212

Adeodatus II : 672–676 (Rome) 212

Adrian : 1275? (Bulgaria), and 1285? (Macedonia) 93, 195

Adrian : 1690–1700 (Russia) 218, 221

Adrianus I : 772–795 (Rome) 212

Adrianus II : 867–872 (Rome) 213

Adrianus III : 884–885 (Rome) 213

Adrianus IV *Breakspear* : 1154–1159 (Rome) 214

Adrianus V *Fieschi* : 1276 [unconsecrated] (Rome) 215

Adrianus VI *Florensz* : 1522–1523 (Rome) 216

Ægidius *de Ferrare* : 1295–1310 (Alexandria — Latin) 27

Afdhuksiyus : 350–354, 354–357 (Antioch — Greek), and 358–359 (Antioch — Greek Melkite) 35, 40

Aflaliyus : 332 (Antioch — Greek), and 331–333 (Antioch — Greek Melkite) 35, 40

Afram — *see also*: Abram

Afram *of Amida* : 526–546 (Antioch — Greek), and 526–545 (Antioch — Greek Melkite), and 528–546 [anti-patriarch] (Antioch — Syrian Orthodox) 35, 41, 59

Afram *Barsum*, Ighnatiyus : 1933–1957 (Antioch — Syrian Orthodox) 62, 161

Afram I *of Amida* : 528–546 (Antioch — Syrian Catholic) 54

Afram II *Rahmani*, Ighnatiyus : 1898–1929 (Antioch — Syrian Catholic) 56

Afrasiyus *ibn Malaha* : 521–526 (Antioch — Greek), and (Antioch — Greek Melkite), and 521–528 (Antioch — Syrian Catholic), and 521–528 [anti-patriarch] (Antioch — Syrian Orthodox) 35, 41, 54, 59

Afrun : 338–342 (Antioch — Syrian Catholic) 53

Afruniyus : 333–334 (Antioch — Greek), and (Antioch — Greek Melkite) 35, 40

Afstatiyus : 325–332 (Antioch — Greek), and 325–331 (Antioch — Greek Melkite) 35, 40

Afstratiyus : 939–960 (Antioch — Greek) 36

Aftimios *Ofiesh* : 1927–1933 (America — American Orthodox Catholic Church) 32

Aftimiyus I : 1159–1164 (Antioch — Greek) 37

Aftimiyus II : 1268–1269 (Antioch — Greek) 37

Aftimiyus III *al-Karmah* : 1635–1636 (Antioch — Greek) 38

Aftimiyus IV *apo Chiou* : 1636–1648 (Antioch — Greek) 38

Aftimiyus I : 1258?–1273? (Antioch — Greek Melkite) 42

Aftimiyus II *al-Karmah* : 1634 (Antioch — Greek Melkite) 43

Aftimiyus III *apo Chiou* : 1634–1647 (Antioch — Greek Melkite) 43

Afudiyus : 53–68 (Antioch — Greek), and 43–70? (Antioch — Greek Melkite), and 67–68 (Antioch — Syrian Orthodox) 34, 40, 58

Afzuyus : 360–370 (Antioch — Greek), and 360–370 [anti-patriarch] (Antioch — Greek Melkite), and 360 [anti-patriarch] (Antioch — Syrian Orthodox) 35, 40, 58

Agafangel *Preobrazhenskiĭ* : 1897–1910 (Latvia) 191

Agafangel : 1922 [locum tenens] (Russia) 221

Agai : 45–48 (Assyria), and 1st cent. (Babylon) 71, 84

Agapetus I : 535–536 (Rome) 212

Agapetus II : 946–955 (Rome) 213

Agatangel *apo Chalkēdonos* : 1816–1825 (Serbia — Beograd) 228

Agathangelos *apo Chalkēdonos* : 1826–1830 (Constantinople — Greek) 116

Agathangelos : 1958–1972 (Greece — Old Calendarists) 159

Agatho : 678–681 (Rome) 212

Agathōn : 950–964 (Jerusalem — Greek) 185

Aggai : 120–152 (India — Malankara Orthodox) 163

Aghabiyus *Bishai* : 1866–1887 (Alexandria — Coptic Catholic) 21

Aghabiyus : 977–995 (Antioch — Greek) 36

Aghabiyus I : 978–996 (Antioch — Greek Melkite) 42

Aghabiyus II *Matar* : 1796–1812 (Antioch — Greek Melkite) 44

Aghathu(n) : 662–680 (Alexandria — Coptic) 16

Aghek'sandr I : 1706–1714 (Armenia) 67

Aghek'sandr II *Karakashian* : 1753–1755 (Armenia) 68

Aghribbinus : 166–178 (Alexandria — Coptic and Alexandria — Coptic Catholic) 15, 21

Agrippinos : 167–179 (Alexandria — Greek) 23

Agustinus Yusip (V) *Khindi* : 1804–1828 [unconsecrated] (Babylon) 83, 88

Ahai : 410?–414? (India — Malankara Jacobite) 167

Aharon : 779–781 (Aghunie) 9
Ahod Abuci : 231–246 (India — Malankara Orthodox) 163
Ahoudemme : 559–577 (India — Malankara Orthodox) 163
Ahudemeh : 559–575 (India — Malankara Jacobite) 167
Aiglerius : 1275? (Jerusalem — Latin) 189
Ailios : 213 (Jerusalem — Greek) 184
Akakij : 1557?–1564? (Macedonia) 195
Akakios : 472–489 (Constantinople — Greek) 110
Akakios : 1962–1963 (Greece — Old Calendarists) 159
Akakiyus : 459–461 (Antioch — Greek), and 458–459 (Antioch — Greek Melkite) 35, 41
Akha d'Abuhi : 205–220 (Assyria), and 3rd cent. (Babylon) 71, 84
Akhkhi : 411–415 (Assyria), and 411–414 (Babylon) 72, 85
Akhristudulus : 1047–1077 (Alexandria — Coptic) 17
Aklimandus *Bahuth* : 1856–1864 (Antioch — Greek Melkite) 44
Alafthariyus : 1023–1028 (Antioch — Greek) 36
Alanus : 1196- (Cyprus — Latin) 129
Albertus I *de Robertis* : 1226–1246 (Antioch — Latin) 45
Albertus II *Barbolani* : 1856–1857 (Antioch — Latin) 47
Albertus : 1211- (Cyprus — Latin) 129
Albertus I : 1204–1214 (Jerusalem — Latin) 189
Albertus II *Gori* : 1949–1970 (Jerusalem — Latin) 189
Albertus : 1102 [anti-pope] (Rome) 214
Aldobrandinus *des Ursins* : 1500–1517? (Cyprus — Latin) 130
Aleksander *Mar Thoma* : 1954–1976 [suffragan], 1976–1999 (India — Mar Thoma Syrian) 173
Aleksander *Paulus* : 1920–1941, 1941–1944, 1944–1953 [in exile] (Estonia) 135–136
Aleksandr *Nemolovskiĭ* : 1919–1922 (America — Orthodox Church) 31
Aleksandr *Kalinin* : 2000–2002 [archbishop], 2002- [patriarch] (Russia-Novozybkov) 223, 256, 258, 260
Aleksandrs *Kudrjašovs* : 1993- (Latvia) 192, 255, 257, 260
Aleksiĭ *Ridiger* : 1961–1987 (Estonia) 137, 190, 198, 205, 219, 222, 234, 256–257, 259

Aleksiĭ I *Opotskiĭ* : 1901–1905 [exarch] (Georgia) 152
Aleksiĭ II *Molchanov* : 1913–1914 [exarch] (Georgia) 152
Aleksiĭ *Konoplev* : 1966 (Latvia) 192
Aleksiĭ I *Simanskiĭ* : 1944–1945 [locum tenens], 1945–1970 (Russia) 132, 222, 252
Aleksiĭ II *Ridiger* : 1990- (Russia) 137, 190, 198, 205, 219, 222, 234, 256–257, 259
Aleksiĭ *Pleshcheev* : 1354–1378 (Russia — Moscow) 135, 236
Aleksiĭ *Pleshchieiev* : 1354–1378 (Ukraine) 135, 236
Aleksiĭ : 1140? (Ukraine — Halych) 239
Aleksiĭ *Hromads'kyĭ* : 1942–1943 (Ukraine — Autonomous Church) 233, 239
Aleksius *Ridiger* : 1961–1987 (Estonia) 137, 190, 198, 205, 219, 222, 234, 256–257, 259
Alexander I *Riario* : 1570? (Alexandria — Latin) 28
Alexander II *Crescenzi* : 1675? (Alexandria — Latin), and 1675?–1688 (Antioch — Latin) 28, 46
Alexander *Sanminiatelli-Zabarella* : 1899–1901 (Constantinople — Latin) 122
Alexander I : 105?–115? (Rome) 210
Alexander II *da Baggio* : 1061–1073 (Rome) 214
Alexander III *Bandinelli* : 1159–1181 (Rome) 215
Alexander IV *Segni* : 1254–1261 (Rome) 48, 215
Alexander V *Philarghi* : 1409–1410 [anti-pope] (Rome) 216
Alexander VI *de Borja* : 1492–1503 (Rome) 216
Alexander VII *Chigi* : 1655–1667 (Rome) 216
Alexander VIII *Ottoboni* : 1689–1691 (Rome) 216
Alexandros I : 313–328 (Alexandria — Greek) 23
Alexandros II : 1059–1062 (Alexandria — Greek) 24
Alexandros *of Rodostolon* : 1922–1930 (America — Greek) 29–30
Alexandros : 325–337? (Constantinople — Greek) 109
Alexandros : 213–251 (Jerusalem — Greek) 184
Alexios *Stoudites* : 1025–1043 (Constantinople — Greek) 111
Alexios Mar Theodosios : 1934–1962 [suffragan] (India — Malankara Orthodox, 167
Aliksandarus I : 312–326 (Alexandria — Coptic) 16

Aliksandarus II : 705–730 (Alexandria — Coptic) 16
Aliksandarus : 312–328 (Alexandria — Coptic Catholic) 21
Aliksandarus I : 408–418 (Antioch — Greek) 35
Aliksandarus II : 695–742? (Antioch — Greek) 36
Aliksandarus III *Tahhan* : 1931–1958 (Antioch — Greek) 34, 38
Aliksandarus : 416–417 (Antioch — Greek Melkite), and 412–417 (Antioch — Syrian Orthodox) 40, 58
Alimpiĭ *Gusev* : 1986 [locum tenens], 1986–1988 [archbishop], 1988–2003 [metropolitan] (Russia — Belokrinitsia) 223
Aloysius I *Piavi* : 1889–1905 (Jerusalem — Latin) 189
Aloysius II *Barlassina* : 1918–1920 [auxiliary patriarch], 1920–1947 (Jerusalem — Latin) 189, 252
Alphonsus *de Fonseca* : 1506? (Alexandria — Latin) 27
Alphonsus I *Carafa* : 1504- (Antioch — Latin) 46
Alphonsus II : -1529 (Antioch — Latin) 46
Alphonsus : 1408- (Constantinople — Latin) 120
Aluntiyus : 351–357 (Antioch — Syrian Catholic) 53
Alypios : 166–169 (Constantinople — Greek) 109
Amalricus : 1157–1180 (Jerusalem — Latin) 189
Ambrosi *K'elava* : 1921–1927 (Georgia) 147, 152
Amfilohie : 1595–1598 (Austria — Cernovci) 78
Amfilohije *Radović* : 1990- (Montenegro) 202
Amfilokhiyus : 263–267 (Antioch — Greek) 34
Amiliyanus : 1062–1075 (Antioch — Greek), and 1074?–1090? (Antioch — Greek Melkite) 36, 42
Amōs : 594–601 (Jerusalem — Greek) 185
Amvrosiĭ : 1962 (Japan) 178
Amvrosiĭ *Popovich* : 1847–1863 (Russia — Belokrinitsia) 222–223
Amvrosiĭ *Zertis-Kamenskiĭ* : 1768–1771 (Russia — Moscow) 221
Anacletus (I) : 76?–88? (Rome) 210
Anacletus II *Leonis* : 1130–1138 [anti-pope] (Rome) 214
Anania : 946–968 (Armenia) 66
Anania : 1204–1208? [anti-catholicos] (Armenia) 66

Anania : 1544–1558 (Romania) 206
Ananias : 1661–1671 (Sinai) 232
Ananiĭ : 1763 (Bulgaria) 95
Ananij : 1763 (Macedonia) 197
Anastas : 741–745 (Aghunie) 9
Anastas : 661–667 (Armenia) 65
Anastasie I *Crimca* : 1600 (Austria—Cernovci) 78
Anastasie II : 1613–1616? (Austria—Cernovci) 78
Anastasie III : 1639?–1644? (Austria—Cernovci) 78
Anastasiĭ *Kononov* : 1986 [locum tenens] (Russia—Belokrinitsia) 223
Anastasiĭ *Gribanovskiĭ* : 1936–1964 (Russia—Church Outside Russia) 224
Anastasios *Janullatos* : 1990–1992 [exarch], 1992- [archbishop] (Albania) 12–13, 253, 257, 259
Anastasios : 730–754 (Constantinople—Greek) 111
Anastasios : 880–889 (Greece) 155
Anastasios I : 458–478 (Jerusalem—Greek) 185
Anastasios II : -706 (Jerusalem—Greek) 185
Anastasios : 1583–1592 (Sinai) 232
Anastasius I : 399–401 (Rome) 211
Anastasius II : 496–498 (Rome) 211
Anastasius III : 855 [anti-pope] (Rome) 213
Anastasius III : 911–913 (Rome) 213
Anastasius IV : 1153–1154 (Rome) 214
Anastasiyus : 605–616 (Alexandria—Coptic) 16
Anastasiyus I *al-Sinaïtah* : 561–571, 594–599 (Antioch—Greek) 35–36
Anastasiyus II *al-Sinaïtah* : 599–610 (Antioch—Greek) 36
Anastasiyus III : 620–628 (Antioch—Greek) 36
Anastasiyus I *al-Sinaïtah* : 559–570, 593–598 (Antioch—Greek Melkite) 41
Anastasiyus II *al-Sinaïtah* : 599–609 (Antioch—Greek Melkite) 41
Anatolios : 449–458 (Constantinople—Greek) 110
Anatolios : 459? (Greece) 155
Andrawus *Ghattas* : 1984–1984 [apostolic administrator] (Alexandria—Coptic Catholic) 21
Andrawus *Akhijan Murabbi*, Ighnatiyus : 1662–1677 (Antioch—Syrian Catholic) 52, 56–57

Andrêas : 1675–1676 (Constantinople—Armenian) 104
Andreas *Prōtoklētos* : 30?–38 (Constantinople—Greek) 107, 109
Andreas *Riggio* : 1716–1717 (Constantinople—Latin) 121
Andreas I *Krētēs* : 712–740 (Crete) 124
Andreas II : 900s (Crete) 124
Andreas I : 1380? (Cyprus—Latin) 130
Andreas II : 1447- (Cyprus—Latin) 130
Andreas : 692–693? (Greece) 155
Andreas : 1972- (Greece—Old Calendarists) 159, 255, 257, 260
Andrêas *of Melitene* : 1551–1583 (Jerusalem—Armenian) 181
Andrei *Saguna* : 1846–1847 [locum tenens], 1847–1873 (Austria—Sibiu) 81
Andreĭ *Metiiuk* : 1975–1985 (Ukraine—Canada) 240
Andreĭ *Kushchak* : 1967–1986 (Ukraine—America and Canada) 241
Andreyas : 1841 (Ethiopia—Historical) 144
Andrian *Chetvergov* : 2004–2005 (Russia—Belokrinitsia) 223
Andrija : 1290? (Montenegro) 201
Andruniqus : 616–622 (Alexandria—Coptic) 16
Angelarij *Krstevski* : 1981–1986 (Macedonia) 197
Angelus *Correr* : 1405 (Constantinople—Latin) 120
Angelus : 1275? (Jerusalem—Latin) 189
Anianos : 62–84 (Alexandria—Greek) 22
Anicetus : 155?–166? (Rome) 210
Aniyanus : 68–85 (Alexandria—Coptic), and 68–83 (Alexandria—Coptic Catholic) 15, 20
Aniyanus : 355–360 (Antioch—Greek), and 360–362 (Antioch—Syrian Catholic), and 359 [anti-patriarch] (Antioch—Syrian Orthodox) 35, 53, 58
Aniyas : 357–360 [anti-patriarch] (Antioch—Greek Melkite) 40
Anterus : 235–236 (Rome) 210
Anthemios : 478? (Cyprus) 127
Anthimos I : 536 (Constantinople—Greek) 110
Anthimos II *apo Andrianoupoleōs* : 1623 (Constantinople—Greek) 114
Anthimos III *apo Chalkēdonos* : 1822–1824 (Constantinople—Greek) 116
Anthimos IV *Tambakēs apo*

Nikomēdeias : 1840–1841, 1848–1852 (Constantinople—Greek) 117
Anthimos V *Chrysaphidēs* : 1841–1842 (Constantinople—Greek) 117
Anthimos VI *Iōannidēs apo Ephesou* : 1845–1848, 1853–1855, 1871–1873 (Constantinople—Greek) 117
Anthimos VII *Tsatsos* : 1895–1896 (Constantinople—Greek) 117
Anthimos I *Homologētēs* : 1365–1370 (Crete) 124
Anthimos II : 1756 [locum tenens?] (Crete) 125
Anthimos I *Homologētēs* : 1339–1366 (Greece) 156
Anthimos II : 1489? (Greece) 156
Anthimos III *apo Naupliou kai Argous* : 1604–1610 (Greece) 157
Anthimos IV *apo Talantiou* : 1655–1676 (Greece) 157
Anthimos V : 1693–1699 (Greece) 157
Anthimos VI : 1741–1756, 1760–1764 (Greece) 157
Anthimos VII *apo Artēs* : 1828–1830 (Greece) 157
Anthimos : 1788–1808 (Jerusalem—Greek) 187
Antim *Metokhit* : 1341? (Bulgaria) 93
Antim : 1872–1877 [exarch] (Bulgaria) 91, 95
Antim *Metohit* : 1328? (Macedonia) 195
Antim I *Critopol* : 1380?–1401 (Romania) 206
Antim II *Ivireanul* : 1708–1716 (Romania) 206
Antim I : 18th cent. (Serbia—Beograd) 228
Antim II : 1828–1830 (Serbia—Beograd) 228
Antimiyus *of Helenopolis* : 1792–1813 (Antioch—Greek) 38
Anton—*see also*: Antoniĭ
Anton I *Bagrationi* : 1744–1755, 1764–1788 (Georgia) 151
Anton II *Bagrationi* : 1788–1811 (Georgia) 147, 151
Anton Petros IX *Hassun* : 1866–1881 (Cilicia—Armenian Catholic) 101–102
Antoni *Vadkovski* : 1892–1898 (Finland) 145
Antonie : 1728–1729 (Austria—Cernovci) 78
Antonie *Plamadeala* : 1982- (Austria—Sibiu) 82
Antoniĭ—*see also*: Anton, Antoni
Antoniĭ *Melnikov* : 1965–1978 (Belarus) 90
Antoniĭ *Guslitskiĭ* : 1863–1870 (Russia—Belokrinitsia) 223

Antoniĭ *Shutov* : 1863–1881 (Russia — Belokrinitsia) 223
Antoniĭ *Khrapovitskiĭ* : 1921–1936 (Russia — Church Outside Russia) 224
Antoniĭ : 1572–1582 (Russia — Moscow) 220
Antoniĭ I *Vinnyts'kyĭ* : 1676–1679 (Ukraine) 237
Antoniĭ II *Khrapovyts'kyĭ* : 1918–1919 (Ukraine) 238
Antoniĭ *Masendych* : 1991–1993 [locum tenens] (Ukraine — Autocephalous) 238
Antoniĭ : 1371–1391 (Ukraine — Halych) 239
Antonij *Rafalskij* : 1840–1843 (Poland) 204
Antonije *Abramović* : 1993–1996 (Montenegro) 200, 202
Antonije *Sokolović* : 1571–1575 (Serbia) 227
Antōnios I *Kassimatas Byrsodepsēs* : 821–837? (Constantinople — Greek) 111
Antōnios II *Kauleas* : 893–901 (Constantinople — Greek) 111
Antōnios III *Stouditēs Pachen* : 974–979 (Constantinople — Greek) 111
Antōnios IV : 1389–1390, 1391–1397 (Constantinople — Greek) 113
Antōnios *Homologētēs* : 1306? (Crete) 124
Antonios : 2003–2004 [locum tenens], 2004– (Eritrea) 134, 254, 258–259
Antōnios : 2nd cent. (Jerusalem — Greek) 184
Antonius I Maria *Pallavicino* : 1743–1749 (Antioch — Latin) 47
Antonius II *Despuig y Dameto* : 1799–1810 (Antioch — Latin) 47
Antonius III *Piatti* : 1837–1841 (Antioch — Latin) 47
Antonius I *Correr* : 1405–1408 (Constantinople — Latin) 120
Antonius II Maria *Traversi* : 1839–1842 (Constantinople — Latin) 121
Antonius III Anastasius *Rossi* : 1927–1948 (Constantinople — Latin) 122
Antonius *Tuneto* : 1464? (Cyprus — Latin) 130
Antonius *Beccus* : 1305–1310 (Jerusalem — Latin) 189
Antun I Butrus *'Aridah* : 1932–1955 (Antioch — Maronite) 51
Antun II Butrus *Khraish* : 1975–1985 (Antioch — Maronite) 51
Antun I *Samhiri*, Ighnatiyus : 1853–1864 (Antioch — Syrian Catholic) 56

Antun II *Huwayyik*, Ighnatiyus : 1968–1998 (Antioch — Syrian Catholic) 56
Antuniyus : 1971 [locum tenens] (Alexandria — Coptic) 18
Antuniyus II Butrus *Khraish* : 1975–1985 (Antioch — Maronite) 51
Anush *d'Bit' Garmai* : 873–884 (Assyria), and 877–884 (Babylon) 73, 86
Apifaniyus : 1935- [anti-patriarch] (Antioch — Greek) 38
Apollinarios : 551–570 (Alexandria — Greek) 24
Aprem, Mar : 1968–1995 (India — Chaldean) 174–175
Aqaq : 458–460 (Antioch — Syrian Catholic), and 458–459 [anti-patriarch] (Antioch — Syrian Orthodox), and 484–496 (Assyria), and 485–496? (Babylon) 53, 58, 72, 85
Araboyo, Behnam : 1415–1417 (India — Malankara Jacobite) 170
Arakel : 1495–1511 (Aghunie) 10
Arakel : 1577- [coadjutor] (Armenia) 67
Arakel : 1218–1230 (Jerusalem — Armenian) 180
Aram *K'ēshishian* : 1995- (Cilicia — Armenian Apostolic) 100, 254, 257, 260
Aramiya I : unknown (Antioch — Maronite) 49
Aramiya II *al-Amshiti* : 1199?–1230 (Antioch — Maronite) 50
Aramiya III *al-Dimlisawi* : 1272–1297 (Antioch — Maronite) 50
Arcadie *Ciupercovic* : 1896–1902 (Austria — Cernovci) 78
Aristakês I : -1478 (Aghunie) 10
Aristakês II : 1511–1521 (Aghunie) 10
Aristakês III : 1588–1593 (Aghunie) 10
Aristakês I *Part'e* : 325–333 (Armenia) 64
Aristakês II *At'orakal* : 1448–1465 [coadjutor], 1465–1469 [catholicos] (Armenia) 67
Aristakês : 1484–1499 [coadjutor] (Armenia) 67
Aristakês : 1555- [coadjutor] (Armenia) 67
Aristarkh *Kalinin* : 1996 [locum tenens], 1996–2000 (Russia-Novozybkov) 223
Aristiōn : 70? [anti-archbishop] (Cyprus) 127
Arkadios I : 600? (Cyprus) 127
Arkadios II : 630?–641? (Cyprus) 127

Arnaldus Bernardus *du Pouget* : 1361?–1369 (Alexandria — Latin) 27
Arnulphus : 1275?–1280 (Cyprus — Latin) 130
Arnulphus : 1099–1100, 1111–1118 (Jerusalem — Latin) 188
Arsakios : 404–405 (Constantinople — Greek) 110
Arsaniyus I : 1285–1293 (Antioch — Greek) 37
Arsaniyus II *Haddad* : 1930–1933 (Antioch — Greek) 34, 38
Arsaniyus : 1284?–1290? (Antioch — Greek Melkite) 42
Arsen I : 860–887 (Georgia) 149
Arsen II : 995–980 (Georgia) 149
Arsen III : 1222–1225 (Georgia) 150
Arsen IV : 1230–1240 (Georgia) 150
Arsen *Tsakawa* : 1940–1941 [locum tenens] (Japan) 178
Arsen : 1006–1038 (Jerusalem — Armenian) 180
Arseni : 1390 (Georgia — Abkhazia) 152
Arseniĭ I : 1662–1663? (Bulgaria) 94
Arseniĭ II : 1763–1767 (Bulgaria) 95
Arseniĭ *Briantsev* : 1887–1897 (Latvia) 191
Arseniĭ I *Mohylians'kyĭ* : 1757–1770 (Ukraine) 237
Arseniĭ II *Moskvyn* : 1860–1876 (Ukraine) 237
Arsenij I : 1656–1657, 1658–1659?, 1659 (Macedonia) 196
Arsenij II : 1764–1767 (Macedonia) 197
Arsenij *Moskwin* : 1848–1860 (Poland) 204
Arsenije I *Crnojević* : 1690–1706 (Austria — Karlovci) 76, 79
Arsenije II *Jovanović šakabenta* : 1741–1748 (Austria — Karlovci) 79
Arsenije *Stojković* : 1870–1872 [locum tenens], 1874 [unconsecrated], 1881 [unconsecrated] (Austria — Karlovci) 79–80
Arsenije I : 1405–1417 (Montenegro) 201
Arsenije II *Plamenac* : 1767–1773 [anti-vladika], 1781–1782 (Montenegro) 202
Arsenije III *Bradvarević* : 1947–1960 (Montenegro) 202
Arsenije I *Sremac* : 1233–1263 (Serbia) 226
Arsenije II : 1453–1463 (Serbia) 227
Arsenije III *Crnojević* : 1674–1690 (Serbia) 76, 227
Arsenije IV *Jovanović šakabenda* : 1725–1737 (Serbia) 227

272 Index of Primates

Arsenije *Bradvarević* [locum tenens] : 1950 (Serbia) 228
Arsenios : 1000–1010 (Alexandria — Greek) 24
Arsenios *Autōreianos* : 1254–1260, 1261–1265 (Constantinople — Greek) 112
Arsenios I : 1687–1688 (Crete) 124
Arsenios II : 1699–1701 (Crete) 125
Arsenios : 1344 (Jerusalem — Greek) 186
Arsenios I : 1290–1299? (Sinai) 231
Arsenios II : 1338? (Sinai) 231
Arshalawus : 311–312 (Alexandria — Coptic), and 310–311 (Alexandria — Coptic Catholic) 16, 21
Artemios : 1845–1847 (Alexandria — Greek) 26
Asbiridun *of Cyprus* : 1892–1898 (Antioch — Greek) 38
Ascanius *Gesualdi* : 1618–1640 (Constantinople — Latin) 121
Asiz, Baselios Mar : 1471–1487 (India — Malankara Orthodox) 166
Aspurakês : 381–386 (Armenia) 64
Asqlibiyad : 211–223 (Antioch — Syrian Catholic) 53
Asqlibiyadhis *the Confessor* : 212–218 (Antioch — Greek and Antioch — Greek Melkite) 34, 40
Asqlibiyadis *the Confessor* : 211–220 (Antioch — Syrian Orthodox) 58
Astuatsatur : 1715–1725 (Armenia) 67
Astuatsatur : 1693–1694? (Cilicia — Armenian Apostolic) 99
Astuatsatur I : 1537–1550 (Constantinople — Armenian) 104
Astuatsatur II : 1841–1844 (Constantinople — Armenian) 106
Astuatsatur I : 1313–1316 (Jerusalem — Armenian) 180
Astuatsatur II *of Melitene* : 1522–1542, 1550–1551 (Jerusalem — Armenian) 181
Astuatsatur III *of Daron* : 1645–1664, 1665–1666, 1668–1670 (Jerusalem — Armenian) 181
Atanasie *Anghel* : 1697–1701 (Austria — Sibiu) 81
Atanasie *Mironescu* : 1909–1911 (Romania) 207
Atanasiĭ I : 1593–1596, 1604–1614 (Bulgaria) 94
Atanasiĭ II : 1653–1660 (Bulgaria) 94
Atanasij I : 1593–1596, 1606– , 1614–1615 (Macedonia) 196

Atanasij II : 1657 (Macedonia) 196
Atanasije *Ljubojević* : 1711–1712 [locum tenens] (Austria — Karlovci) 79
Atanasije I *Ljubojević* : 1711–1712 (Serbia) 227
Atanasije II *Gavrilović* : 1747–1752 (Serbia) 227
At'anasios : 1440–1441 (Aghunie) 10
Athanasios I : 328–373 (Alexandria — Greek) 23
Athanasios II : 489–496 (Alexandria — Greek) 23
Athanasios III : 1276–1316 (Alexandria — Greek) 25
Athanasios IV : 1417–1425 (Alexandria — Greek) 25
Athanasios V : 1500? (Alexandria — Greek) 25
Athanasios I : 1289–1293, 1303–1309 (Constantinople — Greek) 112
Athanasios II : 1451–1453 [locum tenens] (Constantinople — Greek) 113
Athanasios III *Patellarios apo Thessalonikēs* : 1634, 1652 (Constantinople — Greek) 114–115
Athanasios IV *apo Rhaidestou* : 1679 (Constantinople — Greek) 115
Athanasios V *Krēs apo Adrianoupoleōs* : 1709–1711 (Constantinople — Greek) 115
Athanasios *Kalliopolitēs* : 1688–1697 (Crete) 124
Athanasios I : 1592–1600 (Cyprus) 128
Athanasios II *al-Dabbas* : 1705–1708 (Cyprus) 128
Athanasios I : 451–458 (Greece) 155
Athanasios II : 1686–1689 (Greece) 157
Athanasios III : 1756–1760 (Greece) 157
Athanasios IV *Taklikartēs* : 1785–1787, 1796–1799 (Greece) 157
Athanasios, Paulose Mar : 1917–1935 [locum tenens], 1935–1953 (India — Malankara Jacobite) 172
Athanasios *Palakunnath*, Mathews Mar : 1842–1852 [suffragan], 1852–1875 (India — Malankara Syrian) 160–162, 173
Athanasios I : 887–904 (India — Malankara Orthodox) 164
Athanasios II *of Edessa* : 1027–1041 (India — Malankara Orthodox) 164
Athanasios *Palakunnath*, Mathews Mar : 1843–1877 (India — Mar Thoma Syrian) 173

Athanasios, Thomas Mar : 1868–1877 [suffragan], 1877–1893 (India — Mar Thoma Syrian) 173
Athanasios, Thomas Mar : 1982– [suffragan] (India — Mar Thoma Syrian) 173
Athanasios I, Joseph Mar : 1883–1888 [suffragan], 1888–1898 (India — Thozhiyoor) 176
Athanasios II *Panakal*, Paulose Mar : 1917–1927 [suffragan] (India — Thozhiyoor) 176
Athanasios I : 929–937 (Jerusalem — Greek) 185
Athanasios II : 1224–1236 (Jerusalem — Greek) 186
Athanasios III : 1313?–1334 (Jerusalem — Greek) 186
Athanasios IV : 1452–1460 (Jerusalem — Greek) 186
Athanasios V : 1827–1845 (Jerusalem — Greek) 187
Athanasios I : 1410? (Sinai) 231
Athanasios II *apo Naousēs tēs Makedonias* : 1708–1720 (Sinai) 232
Athanasios Mar Abraham III : 1365–1379 (India — Malankara Orthodox) 165
Athanasius *de Clermont* : 1219– (Alexandria — Latin) 27
Athanasius I : 887–903 (India — Malankara Jacobite) 168
Athanasius II *of Edessa* : 1027–1041 (India — Malankara Jacobite) 169
Athanasius Abraham II : 1364–1379 (India — Malankara Jacobite) 170
Athanasius Habeeb I : 1528–1533 (India — Malankara Jacobite) 170
Athanasiyus I : 326–373 (Alexandria — Coptic) 16, 252
Athanasiyus II : 488–494 (Alexandria — Coptic) 16
Athanasiyus III *ibn Kalil* : 1250–1261 (Alexandria — Coptic) 17
Athanasiyus : 1945–1946, 1954–1959 [locum tenens] (Alexandria — Coptic) 18
Athanasiyus (I) : 328–373 (Alexandria — Coptic Catholic) 21, 252
Athanasiyus (II) : 1741–1781 (Alexandria — Coptic Catholic) 20–21
Athanasiyus (III) *Khuzam* : 1854–1864 (Alexandria — Coptic Catholic) 21
Athanasiyus I *al-Jama'il* : 631 (Antioch — Greek) 36
Athanasiyus II : 1166–1180 (Antioch — Greek) 37
Athanasiyus III *al-Dabbas* :

1611–1619 (Antioch — Greek) 38
Athanasiyus IV *al-Dabbas* : 1686–1694 [anti-patriarch], 1720–1724 (Antioch — Greek) 33, 38
Athanasiyus *of Homs* : 1906 [locum tenens] (Antioch — Greek) 38
Athanasiyus I : 1157?–1171 (Antioch — Greek Melkite) 42
Athanasiyus II *al-Dabbas* : 1612–1620 (Antioch — Greek Melkite) 43
Athanasiyus III *al-Dabbas* : 1685–1694, 1720–1724 (Antioch — Greek Melkite) 33, 44
Athanasiyus IV *Jawhar* : 1759–1760, 1765–1768 [anti-patriarch], 1794–1794 (Antioch — Greek Melkite) 44
Athanasiyus V *Matar* : 1813 (Antioch — Greek Melkite) 44
Athanasiyus I *Gammala* : 595–631 (Antioch — Syrian Catholic) 54
Athanasiyus II *of Baladh* : 684–688 (Antioch — Syrian Catholic) 54
Athanasiyus III : 724–740 (Antioch — Syrian Catholic) 54
Athanasiyus IV *Sandaliyus* : 756–758 (Antioch — Syrian Catholic) 54
Athanasiyus V *Salikha* : 987–1003 (Antioch — Syrian Catholic) 55
Athanasiyus VI *Khayya* : 1058–1063 (Antioch — Syrian Catholic) 55
Athanasiyus VII *Abu'l-Faraj* : 1091–1129 (Antioch — Syrian Catholic) 55
Athanasiyus VIII *Ishu' ibn Qatrah* : 1139–1166 (Antioch — Syrian Catholic) 55
Athanasiyus IX *Saliba Qarakha* : 1200–1207 (Antioch — Syrian Catholic) 55
Athanasiyus I *Gammala* : 595–631 (Antioch — Syrian Orthodox) 59
Athanasiyus II *of Baladh* : 683–686 (Antioch — Syrian Orthodox) 59
Athanasiyus III *Sandaliyus* : 724–740 (Antioch — Syrian Orthodox) 59
Athanasiyus *al-Sandali* : -758 [anti-patriarch] (Antioch — Syrian Orthodox) 59
Athanasiyus IV *Salikha* : 986–1002 (Antioch — Syrian Orthodox) 60
Athanasiyus V *Hajji* : 1058–1063 (Antioch — Syrian Orthodox) 60
Athanasiyus VI *ibn Khamuru Abu'l-Faraj* : 1091–1129 (Antioch — Syrian Orthodox) 60
Athanasiyus VII *Ishu' ibn Qatrah* : 1138–1166 (Antioch — Syrian Orthodox) 60
Athanasiyus VIII *Saliba Qarakha* : 1200–1207 (Antioch — Syrian Orthodox) 60
Athēnagoras *Spyrou* : 1930–1949 (America — Greek), and 1948–1972 (Constantinople — Greek) 29–30, 108, 117
Athēnagoras I *Kabbadas* : 1954–1956, 1961–1962 [locum tenens] (Estonia), and 1955–1962 [locum tenens] (Latvia) 136, 191
Athēnagoras II *Kokkinakēs* : 1964–1973 [locum tenens] (Estonia), and 1964–1979 [locum tenens] (Latvia) 136, 191
Athēnagoras apo Sebasteias : 1955–1957 [locum tenens] (Jerusalem — Greek) 187
Athēnodōros : 144–148 (Constantinople — Greek) 109
Atnatewos : 1869–1876 (Ethiopia — Historical), and (Ethiopia — Official) 142, 144
Atom : 1496–1510 (Aght'amar) 6
Atrnerseh : 77–92 (Armenia) 64
Attikos : 406–425 (Constantinople — Greek) 110
Augen *Turuthi*, Baselios Mar : 1962–1964 [suffragan], 1964–1975 (India — Malankara Orthodox), and (India — Malankara Jacobite) 167, 172
Augustins *Petersons* : 1936–1955 (Latvia) 190–191
Augustus *Foscolo* : 1830–1847 (Jerusalem — Latin) 189
Auxentios : 1963–1994 (Greece — Old Calendarists) 159
Avgustin *Vinogradskiĭ* : 1818–1819 (Russia — Moscow) 221
Avraamiĭ *Mesapsa* : 1629?–1634? (Bulgaria) 94
Avram : 1629–1634 (Macedonia) 196
Awdiyus : 42–68 (Antioch — Syrian Catholic) 53
Awduksiyus : 357–360 (Antioch — Syrian Catholic), and 358–359 [anti-patriarch] (Antioch — Syrian Orthodox) 53, 58
Awetik' : 1702–1703, 1704–1706 (Constantinople — Armenian) 105
Awetik' : 1704–1706 (Jerusalem — Armenian) 181
Awetis : 1697 (Aght'amar) 6
Awetis Petros XIV *Arpiarian* : 1931–1937 (Cilicia — Armenian Catholic) 102
Awannis : 754- [anti-patriarch] (Antioch — Syrian Orthodox) 59
Awfruniyus : 333–334 [anti-patriarch] (Antioch — Syrian Orthodox) 58
Awghris : 404 (Antioch — Syrian Catholic) 53
Awighriyus : 388–393 [anti-patriarch] (Antioch — Syrian Orthodox) 58
Awlaliyus : 337–338 (Antioch — Syrian Catholic), and 331–333 [anti-patriarch] (Antioch — Syrian Orthodox) 53, 58
Awminiyus : 130–142 (Alexandria — Coptic), and 129–141 (Alexandria — Coptic Catholic) 15, 21
Awrus : 154–169 (Antioch — Syrian Orthodox) 58
Awsabiyus : unknown (Antioch — Maronite) 49
Awstathiyus : 320–332 (Antioch — Syrian Catholic), and 324–337 (Antioch — Syrian Orthodox) 53, 58
Ayliya —*see also*: Ilyas
Ayliya : 709–723 (Antioch — Syrian Catholic) 54
Ayliya I : 709–723 (Antioch — Syrian Orthodox) 59
Aymericus *de Limoges* : 1142–1187 (Antioch — Latin) 45
Aymery *de Limoges* : 1142–1187 (Antioch — Latin) 45
Ayrus : 154–169 (Antioch — Syrian Orthodox) 58
Ayruthiyus *Hagiotaphitēs* : 1850–1885 (Antioch — Greek) 38
Ayyub I : 811–826 (Antioch — Greek) 36
Ayyub II : 917–939 (Antioch — Greek) 36
Ayyub : 813?–845? (Antioch — Greek Melkite) 41
Azaria I : 1584–1601 (Cilicia — Armenian Apostolic) 99
Azaria II : 1683?–1686? (Cilicia — Armenian Apostolic) 99
Azaria : 1591–1592 (Constantinople — Armenian) 104
Azibina : 226–236 (Antioch — Syrian Catholic) 53
Azeez, Baselios : 1471–1487 (India — Malankara Jacobite) 170
'Aziz *ibn Shabhta*, Ighnatiyus : 1466–1488 (Antioch — Syrian Orthodox — Tur Abhdin) 62

Babai —*see also*: Babwi
Babai I : 457–484 (Assyria) 72
Babai II : 496–502 (Assyria) 72
Babai : 497–503? (Babylon) 85
Babi : 499–502 (India — Malankara Orthodox) 163

Babila : 619–629 (Georgia) 149
Babilas : 240–243 (Antioch—Greek), and 240–250 (Antioch—Greek Melkite) 34, 40
Babkên : 1147? (Aghunie) 10
Babkên : 516–526 (Armenia) 65
Babkên *Giwlêsêrian* : 1931–1936 [coadjutor] (Cilicia—Armenian Apostolic) 100
Babowai : 450–484 (India—Malankara Jacobite) 167
Babula : 236–244 (Antioch—Syrian Catholic), and 237–251 (Antioch—Syrian Orthodox) 53, 58
Babuya : 457–484 (India—Malankara Orthodox) 163
Babwi—*see also*: Babai
Babwi I : 457–484 (Assyria) 72
Babwi : 457–484 (Babylon) 85
Baflinus I *of Tyre* : 324–325, 332 (Antioch—Greek) 35
Baflinus II : 371–376 (Antioch—Greek) 35
Baflinus *of Tyre* : 331 (Antioch—Greek Melkite) 40
Baflinus : 371–376 [anti-patriarch] (Antioch—Greek Melkite) 40
Baghdasar : 1630? [anti-catholicos] (Aght'amar) 6
Baghdasar : 1735?–1736 (Aght'amar) 6
Bahnam I, Baselios Mar : 1404–1412 (India—Malankara Orthodox) 165
Bahnam II, Dioscoros Mar : 1415–1417 (India—Malankara Orthodox) 165
Bahnam III, Baselios Mar : 1850–1860 (India—Malankara Orthodox) 166
Bakhumiyus I : 1376–1393 (Antioch—Greek), and 1359?–1368, 1375–1377, 1378–1386 (Antioch—Greek Melkite) 37, 43
Bakhumiyus II *al-Hawrani* : 1410–1411 (Antioch—Greek), and 1412 (Antioch—Greek Melkite) 37, 43
Baladhiyus : 497–505 (Antioch—Greek) 35
Baladiyus : 488–495 (Antioch—Syrian Catholic), and 488–498 (Antioch—Syrian Orthodox) 54, 59
Baladus : 488?–498 (Antioch—Greek Melkite) 41
Banyamin I : 622–662 (Alexandria—Coptic) 16
Banyamin II : 1327–1339 (Alexandria—Coptic) 17
Bar Ba'shmin : 350–358 (Assyria), and 342?–348 (Babylon) 71, 84
Bar Bosomin : 352–360 (India—Malankara Orthodox) 163

Bar Gabbara : 1135–1136 (Assyria) 74
Bar Souma Moudyano : 1422–1455 (India—Malankara Jacobite) 170
Bar Suma *d'Subi* : 1133–1135 (Assyria), and 1134–1136 (Babylon) 74, 87
Bar T'ulmai : 33 (Assyria) 71
Bar Yesu : 669–684 (India—Malankara Orthodox) 163
Barbashmin : 345–346 (India—Malankara Jacobite) 167
Bardas : 407- [anti-patriarch] (Constantinople—Greek) 110
Barmeya : unknown (Ethiopia—Official) 140
Barmeyu : unknown (Ethiopia—Official) 140
Barnabas : 1986–1987 [locum tenens] (Alexandria—Greek) 26
Barnabas I *Apostolos* : 45? (Cyprus) 126–127
Barnabas II : 1175- (Cyprus) 128
Barsauma, Baselios Mar : 1422–1455 (India—Malankara Orthodox) 166
Barsegh : 1105–1113 (Armenia) 66
Barsegh (II) : 1195–1206? [anti-catholicos] (Armenia) 66
Barsegh : 1549–1552 [coadjutor] (Armenia) 67
Barsegh : 1341–1356 (Jerusalem—Armenian) 180
Barsegh Petros IV *Avkadian* : 1780–1788 (Cilicia—Armenian Catholic) 102
Bartalomewos I : 950? (Ethiopia—Historical) 142
Bartalomewos II : 1398?–1436 (Ethiopia—Historical) 143
Bartalomewos : unknown (Ethiopia—Official) 141
Bartholomāus *de Braganza* : 1261- (Jerusalem—Latin) 189
Bartholomaios *Archontōnēs* : 1991- (Constantinople—Greek) 108, 117, 254, 257, 260
Bartholomaios *apo Drystras* : 1764–1780 (Greece) 157
Bart'lome : 591–595 (Georgia) 149
Bart'oghimêos : 60–68 (Armenia) 63–64
Baselios I : -830 (India—Malankara Jacobite) 168
Baselios II : 848–868 (India—Malankara Jacobite) 168
Baselios III : 936–960 (India—Malankara Jacobite) 168
Baselios IV *of Tigrith* : 1046–1069 (India—Malankara Jacobite) 169
Baselios I *Bar Baldoyo* : 828–838 (India—Malankara Orthodox) 164

Baselios II : 938–962 (India—Malankara Orthodox) 164
Baselios III *of Tigris* : 1046–1069 (India—Malankara Orthodox) 164
Baselios IV : 1560–1589 (India—Malankara Orthodox) 166
Baselios (I), Mar : 1685 (India—Malankara Syrian) 162
Baselios (II), Mar : 1751–1763 (India—Malankara Syrian) 162
Baselios Abd al-Ghani I : 1557–1575 (India—Malankara Jacobite) 170
Baselios Abd al-Ghani II : 1591–1597 (India—Malankara Jacobite) 170
Baselios Abdul Masih : 1655–1662 (India—Malankara Jacobite) 171
Baselios Azeez : 1471–1487 (India—Malankara Jacobite) 170
Baselios Behnam I *ad-Hadli* : 1404–1412 (India—Malankara Jacobite) 170
Baselios Behnam III : 1852–1859 (India—Malankara Jacobite) 172
Baselios Bishara : 1782–1811 (India—Malankara Jacobite) 172
Baselios David Shah *ibn Nur 'Adin* : 1575–1576 (India—Malankara Jacobite) 170
Baselios Elias I : -1523 (India—Malankara Jacobite) 170
Baselios Elias II : 1533–1552 (India—Malankara Jacobite) 170
Baselios Elias III : 1825–1827 (India—Malankara Jacobite) 172
Baselios Elias IV : 1827–1838 (India—Malankara Jacobite) 172
Baselios Geevarghese I : 1674–1687 (India—Malankara Jacobite) 171
Baselios Geevarghese II : 1760–1768 (India—Malankara Jacobite) 171
Baselios Habeeb II : 1665–1674 (India—Malankara Jacobite) 171
Baselios Isaya : 1626 (India—Malankara Jacobite) 171
Baselios Ishaq II : 1687–1709 (India—Malankara Jacobite) 171
Baselios Kurillos *Abd al-Azeez* : 1811–1816 (India—Malankara Jacobite) 172
Baselios Lazar II : 1713 (India—Malankara Jacobite) 171
Baselios Mar Abraham IV :

1494–1496 (India — Malankara Orthodox) 166
Baselios Mar Asiz : 1471–1487 (India — Malankara Orthodox) 166
Baselios Mar Augen *Turuthi* : 1962–1964 [suffragan], 1964–1975 (India — Malankara Orthodox and Malankara Jacobite) 167, 172
Baselios Mar Bahnam I : 1404–1412 (India — Malankara Orthodox) 165
Baselios Mar Bahnam III : 1850–1860 (India — Malankara Orthodox) 166
Baselios Mar Barsauma : 1422–1455 (India — Malankara Orthodox) 166
Baselios Mar Elias : 1838–1840 (India — Malankara Orthodox) 166
Baselios Mar Geevarghese *Kallacheril* : 1958–1964 (India — Malankara Jacobite) 172
Baselios Mar Geevarghese I *Karuchira* : 1925–1928 (India — Malankara Orthodox) 167
Baselios Mar Geevarghese II *Kallacheril* : 1929–1964 (India — Malankara Orthodox) 167
Baselios Mar Ougen *Turuthi* : 1962–1964 [suffragan], 1964–1975 (India — Malankara Orthodox and Malankara Jacobite) 161, 167
Baselios Mar Paulose II : 1975–1996 (India — Malankara Jacobite) 161, 172
Baselios Mar Paulose *Kathanar* : 1912–1913 (India — Malankara Orthodox) 161, 166
Baselios Mar Shakrulla : 1751–1764 (India — Malankara Orthodox) 166
Baselios Mar Thoma Mathews I *Vattakunnel* : 1970–1975 [suffragan], 1975–1991 (India — Malankara Orthodox) 167
Baselios Mar Thoma Mathews II : 1980–1991 [suffragan], 1991- (India — Malankara Orthodox) 167, 255, 257, 259
Baselios Mar Thomas I : 2002- (India — Malankara Jacobite) 173, 255, 258–259
Baselios Mar Yalda : 1634–1685 (India — Malankara Orthodox) 166
Baselios Mathai II : 1709 (India — Malankara Jacobite) 171
Baselios Mathai III : 1714- (India — Malankara Jacobite) 171
Baselios Mathew IV : 1820 (India — Malankara Jacobite) 172
Baselios Nemet Allah : 1555–1557 (India — Malankara Jacobite) 170
Baselios Philathose : 1576–1591 (India — Malankara Jacobite) 170
Baselios Sakralla I : 1639–1652 (India — Malankara Jacobite) 171
Baselios Sakralla II : -1722 (India — Malankara Jacobite) 171
Baselios Sakralla III : 1748–1764 (India — Malankara Jacobite) 171
Baselios Sleeba IV : 1773- (India — Malankara Jacobite) 171
Baselios Yavanan : 1803 (India — Malankara Jacobite) 172
Baselios Yeldho : 1678–1685 (India — Malankara Jacobite) 171
Basil — *see also*: Basili
Basil I : 434–436 (Georgia) 148
Basil II : 914–930 (Georgia) 149
Basil III *Karichisdze* : 1090–1100 (Georgia) 150
Basil V : 1330–1350 (Georgia) 150
Basil VI : 1517–1528 (Georgia) 150
Basileios *Kompopoulos* : 1924–1930 (America — Greek) 29–30
Basileios I *Skamandrēnos* : 970–974 (Constantinople — Greek) 111
Basileios II *Kamatēros Phylakopoulos* : 1183–1186 (Constantinople — Greek) 112
Basileios III *Geōrgiadēs* : 1925–1929 (Constantinople — Greek) 117
Basileios I : 680?–692? (Crete) 124
Basileios II : 823–828 (Crete) 124
Basileios III : 878? (Crete) 124
Basileios IV : 12th cent. (Crete) 124
Basileios V *Markakēs* : 1941–1950 (Crete) 125
Basileios : 1080? (Cyprus) 128
Basileios : 820–838 (Jerusalem — Greek) 185
Basili — *see also*: Basil
Basili IV : 1206–1208 (Georgia) 150
Basiliyus I : 459 (Antioch — Greek), and 456–458 (Antioch — Greek Melkite) 35, 40
Basiliyus II : 1028 (Antioch — Greek), and 1041?–1051? (Antioch — Greek Melkite) 36, 42
Basiliyus I : 456–458 (Antioch — Syrian Catholic) 53
Basiliyus II : 923–935 (Antioch — Syrian Catholic) 55
Basiliyus III *Sinnadus* : 1074–1075 (Antioch — Syrian Catholic) 55
Basiliyus : 456–458 [anti-patriarch] (Antioch — Syrian Orthodox) 58
Basiliyus I : 923–935 (Antioch — Syrian Orthodox) 60
Basiliyus II *Sinnadus* : 1074–1075 (Antioch — Syrian Orthodox) 60
Basiliyus III *Ghubriyal* : 1349–1387 (Antioch — Syrian Orthodox) 61
Basiliyus IV *Shim'un Man'Amaya* : 1421–1444 (Antioch — Syrian Orthodox) 61
Basilyos : 1951–1970 (Ethiopia — Historical), and (Ethiopia — Official) 138, 142, 144
Bazyli *Doroszkiewicz* : 1970–1998 (Poland) 204, 252
Behnam I, Baselios *al-Hadli* : 1404–1412 (India — Malankara Jacobite) 170
Behnam II Araboyo : 1415–1417 (India — Malankara Jacobite) 170
Behnam III, Baselios : 1852–1859 (India — Malankara Jacobite) 172
Belisarios : 1499? [locum tenens] (Crete) 124
Benedict *Troadas* : 1822, 1822 [locum tenens] (Romania) 207
Benedictus *Fenoja* : 1805–1812 (Constantinople — Latin) 121
Benedictus *Soranzo* : 1484- (Cyprus — Latin) 130
Benedictus I : 575–579 (Rome) 212
Benedictus II : 684–685 (Rome) 212
Benedictus III : 855–858 (Rome) 213
Benedictus IV : 900–903 (Rome) 213
Benedictus V : 964–966 (Rome) 213
Benedictus VI : 973–974 (Rome) 213
Benedictus VII : 974–983 (Rome) 213
Benedictus VIII : 1012–1024 (Rome) 214
Benedictus IX : 1032–1044, 1045, 1047–1048 (Rome) 214
Benedictus X *Mincius* : 1058–1059 [anti-pope] (Rome) 214
Benedictus XI *Boccasini* : 1303–1304 (Rome) 215
Benedictus XII *Fournier* : 1334–1342 (Rome) 215

Benedictus XIII *de Luna* : 1394–1423 [anti-pope] (Rome) 215
Benedictus XIII *Orsini* : 1724–1730 (Rome) 216
Benedictus XIV *Garnier* : 1425–1430 [anti-pope] (Rome) 216
Benedictus XIV *Lambertini* : 1740–1758 (Rome) 101, 217
Benedictus XV *della Chiesa* : 1914–1922 (Rome) 217
Benedictus XVI *Ratzinger* : 2005- (Rome) 217, 256, 258–259
Benediktos *apo Pisidias* : 1781–1785, 1787–1796 (Greece) 157
Benediktos *Papadopoulos* : 1957–1980 (Jerusalem—Greek) 183, 187
Beniamin *Christodoulos* : 1936–1946 (Constantinople—Greek) 117
Beniamin : 1600–1605 (Cyprus) 128
Beniamin *Philippos* : 2nd cent. (Jerusalem—Greek) 184
Beniaminos *Christodoulos* : 1936–1946 (Constantinople—Greek) 117
Benjamin *Basalyga* : 1946–1952 (Japan) 178
Bernardinus *Caraffa* : 1505? (Alexandria—Latin) 27
Bernardus : 1100–1134 (Antioch—Latin) 45
Besarioni : 1725–1737 (Georgia) 151
Besarioni I : 1647–1656 (Georgia—Abkhazia) 153
Besarioni II *Eristavi* : 1755–1766 (Georgia—Abkhazia) 153
Bessarion : 1463–1472 (Constantinople—Latin) 120
Bihnam *Hajlaya*, Ighnatiyus : 1412–1445 [anti-patriarch], 1445–1454 (Antioch—Syrian Orthodox) 55, 61, 252
Bihnam I *Hajlaya*, Ighnatiyus : 1412–1455 (Antioch—Syrian Catholic) 55, 61, 252
Bihnam II *Banni*, Ighnatiyus : 1893–1897 (Antioch—Syrian Catholic) 56
Bilatus, Ighnatiyus : 1591–1597 (Antioch—Syrian Catholic), and (Antioch—Syrian Orthodox) 56, 61
Bilujin : 315–320 (Antioch—Syrian Catholic) 53
Binyamin Shim'un XXI : 1903–1918 (Assyria) 74
Bishara, Baselios : 1782–1811 (India—Malankara Jacobite) 172
Bitalis : 313–315 (Antioch—Syrian Catholic) 53

Bohdan *Shpylka* : 1937–1965 (Ukraine—America and Canada) 241
Bonaventurus Secusius *de Caltagirone* : 1599–1618? (Constantinople—Latin) 121
Bonifacius *Bevilacqua* : 1598–1599 (Constantinople—Latin) 121
Bonifacius I : 418–422 (Rome) 211
Bonifacius II : 530–532 (Rome) 211
Bonifacius III : 607 (Rome) 212
Bonifacius IV : 608–615 (Rome) 212
Bonifacius V : 619–625 (Rome) 212
Bonifacius VI : 896 [unconsecrated] (Rome) 213
Bonifacius VII : 974, 984–985 [anti-pope] (Rome) 213
Bonifacius VIII *Caetani* : 1294–1303 (Rome) 215
Bonifacius IX *Tomacelli* : 1389–1404 (Rome) 215
Brguisho : 429–432 [anti-catholicos] (Armenia) 65
Bulinus *of Tyre* : 323–324 (Antioch—Syrian Orthodox) 58
Bulinus : 362–388 [anti-patriarch] (Antioch—Syrian Orthodox) 58
Bulus I *Samasateus* : 267–270 (Antioch—Greek), and 253–260 (Antioch—Greek Melkite) 34, 40
Bulus II *Xēnodokos* : 518–521 (Antioch—Greek), and 519–521 (Antioch—Greek Melkite) 33, 35, 41
Bulus I Butrus *Mas'ad al-Tarsi* : 1854–1890 (Antioch—Maronite) 51
Bulus II Butrus *al-Ma'ushi* : 1955–1975 (Antioch—Maronite) 51
Bulus I *Samasateus* : 263–271 (Antioch—Syrian Catholic) 53
Bulus II *Xēnodokos* : 518–521 (Antioch—Syrian Catholic) 33, 54
Bulus III *"The Black"* : 541–571 (Antioch—Syrian Catholic) 54
Bulus I *Samasateus* : 260–268 (Antioch—Syrian Orthodox) 58
Bulus *"the Jew"* : 518–521 [anti-patriarch] (Antioch—Syrian Orthodox) 59
Bulus II *"The Black"* : 550–575 (Antioch—Syrian Orthodox) 33, 59
Burfirus : 404–408 (Antioch—Greek), and 404–416 (Antioch—Greek Melkite) 35, 40

Burfuriyus : 404–414 (Antioch—Syrian Catholic), and 404–412 (Antioch—Syrian Orthodox) 53, 58
Butrus I : 300–311 (Alexandria—Coptic) 16
Butrus II : 373–380 (Alexandria—Coptic) 16
Butrus III *Mongos* : 480–488 (Alexandria—Coptic) 16
Butrus IV : 567–569 (Alexandria—Coptic) 16
Butrus V : 1340–1348 (Alexandria—Coptic) 17
Butrus VI : 1718–1726 (Alexandria—Coptic) 18
Butrus VII *al-Gawli* : 1809–1852 (Alexandria—Coptic) 18
Butrus I : 300–310 (Alexandria—Coptic Catholic) 21
Butrus II : 373–378 (Alexandria—Coptic Catholic) 21
Butrus I *Apostolos* : 45–53 (Antioch—Greek) 33–34, 49
Butrus II *Knapeus* : 465–466, 474–475 (Antioch—Greek) 35
Butrus III : 1028–1056 (Antioch—Greek) 36
Butrus I *Apostolos* : 36–43 (Antioch—Greek Melkite) 40, 49
Butrus II *Knapeus* : 470?–471?, 476?–477?, 485–488 (Antioch—Greek Melkite) 41
Butrus III : 1052–1057 (Antioch—Greek Melkite) 42
Butrus IV *Jirayjiri* : 1898–1902 (Antioch—Greek Melkite) 44
Butrus I : 1121?–1130? (Antioch—Maronite) 49
Butrus II : 1154–1173 (Antioch—Maronite) 50
Butrus III : 1188? (Antioch—Maronite) 50
Butrus IV *of Lahfad* : -1199? (Antioch—Maronite) 50
Butrus V : 1269? (Antioch—Maronite) 50
Butrus VI *ibn Yusuf al-Hadathi* : 1458–1492 (Antioch—Maronite) 50
Butrus I : 35–42 (Antioch—Syrian Catholic) 53
Butrus II *Knapheus* : 470–471, 477–480, 483–484, 485–488 (Antioch—Syrian Catholic) 53–54
Butrus III *of Kallinikos* : 571–591 (Antioch—Syrian Catholic) 54
Butrus IV *Dawud*, Ighnatiyus : 1577–1591 (Antioch—Syrian Catholic) 56
Butrus V, Ighnatiyus : 1598–1639 (Antioch—Syrian Catholic) 56
Butrus VI *Shahbadin*, Ighnatiyus :

Index of Primates

1677–1702 (Antioch — Syrian Catholic) 52, 56
Butrus VII *Jarwah*, Ighnatiyus : 1820–1851 (Antioch — Syrian Catholic) 56
Butrus VIII *Abd al-Ahad*, Ighnatiyus : 2001- (Antioch — Syrian Catholic) 56, 253, 258–259
Butrus I : 37–67 (Antioch — Syrian Orthodox) 58
Butrus II *Knapheus* : 468–488 (Antioch — Syrian Orthodox) 59
Butrus III *of Kallinikos* : 581–591 (Antioch — Syrian Orthodox) 59
Butrus IV *al-Ma'usili*, Ighnatiyus : 1872–1894 (Antioch — Syrian Orthodox) 62, 161

Cāsar *Monti* : 1629?–1650 (Antioch — Latin) 46
Cāsar *Podocator* : 1553- (Cyprus — Latin) 130
Calinic *Miclescu* : 1875–1886 (Romania) 207
Calistru : 1708–1728 (Austria — Cernovci) 78
Calixtus I : 217–222 (Rome) 210
Calixtus II *di Borgogna* : 1119–1124 (Rome) 214
Calixtus III : 1168–1178 [anti-pope] (Rome) 215
Calixtus III *de Borja* : 1455–1458 (Rome) 216
Camillus *Cybò* : 1718–1729 (Constantinople — Latin) 121
Cardinalis : 1332–1335 (Constantinople — Latin) 120
Carolus Ambrosius *Mezzabarba* : 1719? (Alexandria — Latin) 28
Carolus I Thomas *Maillard de Tournon* : 1701–1710 (Antioch — Latin) 47
Carolus II *Camuzio* : 1781- (Antioch — Latin) 47
Carolus III *Belgrado* : 1862–1866 (Antioch — Latin) 47
Carolus IV *Nocella* : 1899–1901 (Antioch — Latin) 47
Carolus Antonius *Nocella* : 1901–1903 (Constantinople — Latin) 122
Charitōn *Eugeneiōtēs* : 1178–1179 (Constantinople — Greek) 112
Cheepat Mar Dionysios IV *Kattanar* : 1829–1852 (India — Malankara Syrian) 160, 162
Chesarie : 1833–1840 [locum tenens] (Romania) 207
Ch'irmagi *Chigirmane* : 516–523 (Georgia) 148
Chmavon I : 1481- (Aghunie) 10
Chmavon II : 1586–1611 (Aghunie) 10
Christianus : 1256–1268 (Antioch — Latin) 46

Christodoulos : 907–932 (Alexandria — Greek) 24
Christodoulos I : 1606–1638? (Cyprus) 128
Christodoulos : 1637–1638 [anti-archbishop] (Cyprus) 128
Christodoulos II : 1682–1685? (Cyprus) 128
Christodoulos *Paraskevaïdēs* : 1998- (Greece) 154, 158, 255, 257, 260
Christodoulos I : 937- (Jerusalem — Greek) 185
Christodoulos II : 966–969 (Jerusalem — Greek) 185
Christophoros I : 817–848 (Alexandria — Greek) 24
Christophoros II *Daniēlidēs* : 1939–1966 (Alexandria — Greek) 26
Christophorus *del Monte* : 1550? (Alexandria — Latin) 28
Christophorus : 903–904 [anti-pope] (Rome) 213
Chrysanthos *apo Serrōn* : 1824–1826 (Constantinople — Greek) 116
Chrysanthos *Lesbios* : 1843–1850 (Crete) 125
Chrysanthos : 1767–1783, 1783–1810 (Cyprus) 129, 252
Chrysanthos *Philippidēs* : 1938–1941 (Greece) 158
Chrysanthos *Notaras* : 1707–1731 (Jerusalem — Greek) 187
Chrysostom Mar Thoma, Philipose Mar : 1999- (India — Mar Thoma Syrian) 173, 255, 258–259
Chrysostomos *Kykkotēs* : 1977- (Cyprus) 127, 129, 254, 257, 259
Chrysostomos I *Papadapoulos* : 1923–1938 (Greece) 158
Chrysostomos II *Chatzēstaurou* : 1962–1967 (Greece) 154, 158
Chrysostomos I *of Florina* : 1935–1955 (Greece — Old Calendarists) 158
Chrysostomos II : 1985- (Greece — Old Calendarists) 159, 255, 257, 260
C'irilo — *see also*: Kiril
C'irilo I : 1407–1419 (Serbia)
Clemens I : 88?–97? (Rome) 210
Clemens II : 1046–1047 (Rome) 214
Clemens III : 1080, 1084–1100 [anti-pope] (Rome) 214
Clemens III *Scolari* : 1187–1191 (Rome) 215
Clemens IV *Foulques* : 1265–1268 (Rome) 215
Clemens V *de Got* : 1305–1314 (Rome) 215
Clemens VI *Roger* : 1342–1352 (Rome) 215

Clemens VII *de Boulogne* : 1378–1394 [anti-pope] (Rome) 215
Clemens VII *de' Medici* : 1523–1534 (Rome) 216
Clemens VIII *Sánchez Muñoz* : 1423–1429 [anti-pope] (Rome) 216
Clemens VIII *Aldobrandini* : 1592–1605 (Rome) 216
Clemens IX *Rospigliosi* : 1667–1669 (Rome) 216
Clemens X *Altieri* : 1670–1676 (Rome) 216
Clemens XI *Albani* : 1700–1721 (Rome) 216
Clemens XII *Corsini* : 1730–1740 (Rome) 217
Clemens XIII *della Torre Rezzonico* : 1758–1769 (Rome) 217
Clemens XIV *Ganganelli* : 1769–1774 (Rome) 217
Cletus : 76?–88? (Rome) 210
Climis, Abraham Mar : 1957–1958 (India — Malankara Jacobite) 172
Coelestinus I : 422–423 (Rome) 211
Coelestinus II *Buccapecus* : 1124 [anti-pope] (Rome) 214
Coelestinus II : 1142–1144 (Rome) 214
Coelestinus III *Bobone* : 1191–1198 (Rome) 215
Coelestinus IV *da Castiglione* : 1241 [unconsecrated] (Rome) 215
Coelestinus V *del Morrone* : 1294 (Rome) 215
Conon *Aramescu-Donici* : 1912–1919 (Romania) 207
Conon : 686–687 (Rome) 212
Conradus I : 1396- (Cyprus — Latin) 130
Conradus II *Caraccioli* : 1402–1405 (Cyprus — Latin) 130
Constantinus (I) : 708–715 (Rome) 212
Constantinus II : 767–769 [anti-pope] (Rome) 212
Cornelius : 251–253 (Rome) 211
Cosma *Popescu* : 1787–1792 (Romania) 207

Dadishu' : 421–456 (Assyria), and 421?–456 (Babylon) 72, 85
Dadyeshu : 421–450 (India — Malankara Jacobite) 167
Dagobertus *of Pisa* : 1100–1107 (Jerusalem — Latin) 188
Daimbertus *of Pisa* : 1100–1107 (Jerusalem — Latin) 188
Damaskēnos : 1930 [locum tenens] (America) 30
Damaskēnos : 1824–1827 (Cyprus) 129
Damaskēnos *Papandreou* : 1938, 1941–1949 (Greece) 158

Damasus I : 366–384 (Rome) 211
Damasus II : 1048 (Rome) 214
Damian *Kokoneši* : 1966–1973 (Albania) 12–13
Damian : 927?–972? (Bulgaria) 92
Damianos : 530? (Cyprus) 127
Damianos *Kassiōtēs* : 1897–1931 (Jerusalem — Greek) 183, 187
Damianos *Samartsēs* : 1973- (Sinai) 232, 256–257, 259
Damiyanus : 569–605 (Alexandria — Coptic) 16
Danciu : 1516–1534 (Austria — Sibiu) 80
Dan'el : 969? (Ethiopia — Historical) 142
Daniêl : 347 [unconsecrated] (Armenia) 64
Daniêl : 1807–1808 (Armenia) 68
Daniêl : 1799–1800 (Constantinople — Armenian) 105
Daniêl *apo Rithymnēs* : 1722–1725 (Crete) 125
Daniêl *apo Talantiou* : 1636–1655 (Greece) 157
Daniel : 829–834 (India — Malankara Jacobite), and 838–847 (India — Malankara Orthodox) 164, 168
Daniel *Nashiro* : 2000- (Japan) 177–178, 255, 258–259
Daniêl : 1507? (Sinai) 232
Danieli : 1375? (Georgia — Abkhazia) 152
Daniïl *Vlahović* : 1789–1822 (Austria — Cernovci) 78
Daniïl I : 1488–1500? (Austria — Sibiu) 80
Daniïl II : 1660?–1662 (Austria — Sibiu) 81
Daniïl : 1647?–1650 (Bulgaria) 94
Daniïl I : 1566?–1568 (Romania) 206
Daniïl II : 1719–1731 (Romania) 207
Daniïl : 1522–1539 (Russia — Moscow) 220
Danil I *Biblesis* : 1230–1236 (Antioch — Maronite) 50
Danil II *al-Amshiti* : 1270?–1272? (Antioch — Maronite) 50
Danil : 1650? (Macedonia) 196
Danilo I *šćepčev Petrović* : 1697–1735 (Montenegro) 200, 202
Danilo II *Petrović Njegoš* : 1852 (Montenegro) 200, 202
Danilo III *Dajković* : 1961–1990 (Montenegro) 202
Danilo I : 1271–1272 (Serbia) 226
Danilo II : 1324–1337 (Serbia) 226
Danilo III : 1392–1398 (Serbia) 226

Danilo IV : 1406 (Serbia) 226
Danilo : 18th cent. (Serbia — Beograd) 228
Daniyal *of Chios and Damascus* : 1767–1791 (Antioch — Greek) 38
Da'ud : 1285? (India — Chaldean) 174
Daudesh : 421–456 (India — Malankara Orthodox) 163
David : 1015?–1018 (Bulgaria) 92
David I : 686 (India — Malankara Jacobite) 168
David II, Ignatius : 1215–1222 (India — Malankara Jacobite) 169
David : 687 (India — Malankara Orthodox) 164
David : 1015–1018 (Macedonia) 194
David : 1424? (Montenegro) 201
David Shah, Baselios *ibn Nur 'Adin* : 1575–1576 (India — Malankara Jacobite) 170
Davit' I : 944–955 (Georgia) 149
Davit' II *Bagrationi* : 1426–1430 (Georgia) 150
Davit' III *Gobeladze* : 1435–1439, 1443–1459 (Georgia) 150
Davit' IV : 1466–1479 (Georgia) 150
Davit' V *Devdariani* : 1972–1977 (Georgia) 147, 152
Davit'i *Nemsadze* : 1673–1676 (Georgia — Abkhazia) 153
Dawit' I *T'ornikian* : 1113–1165? (Aght'amar) 5
Dawit' II *Sefedinian* : 1326?, 1346–1368? (Aght'amar) 6
Dawit' III : 1393–1433 (Aght'amar) 6
Dawit' I : -399 (Aghunie) 9
Dawit' II : 762–766 (Aghunie) 9
Dawit' III : 766–775 (Aghunie) 9
Dawit' IV : 822–849 (Aghunie) 9
Dawit' V : 923–929 (Aghunie) 9
Dawit' VI : 961–968 (Aghunie) 9
Dawit' VII : 968–974 (Aghunie) 9
Dawit' VIII : 1411 (Aghunie) 10
Dawit' IX : 1573–1574 (Aghunie) 10
Dawit' I : 728–741 (Armenia) 65
Dawit' II : 806–833 (Armenia) 66
Dawit' *T'ornikian* : 1114- [anticatholicos] (Armenia) 66
Dawit' : 1204–1207 [coadjutor] (Armenia) 66
Dawit' III : 1579–1590 [coadjutor], 1590–1629 [catholicos] (Armenia) 67
Dawit' IV *Gorghanian* : 1801–1807 (Armenia) 68
Dawit' : 1663–1679 [anti-catholicos] (Cilicia — Armenian Apostolic) 99
Dawit' : 1640–1641, 1643–1644, 1644–1649, 1650–1651 (Constantinople — Armenian) 104
Dawit' I : 1316–1321 (Jerusalem — Armenian) 180
Dawit' II *of Melitene* : 1583–1613 (Jerusalem — Armenian) 181
Dawud : 1242?–1247? (Antioch — Greek Melkite) 42
Dawud I : unknown (Antioch — Maronite) 49
Dawud II *Yuhanna* : 1367?–1402 (Antioch — Maronite) 50
Dawud : 763- [anti-patriarch] (Antioch — Syrian Catholic) 54
Dawud, Ighnatiyus : 1519–1520 (Antioch — Syrian Catholic) 55
Dawud : 763- [anti-patriarch] (Antioch — Syrian Orthodox) 59
Dawud I, Ighnatiyus : 1517–1520 (Antioch — Syrian Orthodox) 61
Dawud II Shah *Butrus ibn Nur ad-Din*, Ighnatiyus : 1576–1591 (Antioch — Syrian Orthodox) 61
Dēmētrios : 189–232 (Alexandria — Greek) 23
Dēmētrios *Trakatellēs* : 1999- (America) 30, 253, 258–259
Dēmētrios *Papadopoulou* : 1972–1991 (Constantinople — Greek) 108, 117
Dēmētrios I : 835? (Greece) 155
Dēmētrios II : 846–857 (Greece) 155
Dēmētrios : 1950–1958 [locum tenens] (Greece — Old Calendarists) 159
Dēmophilos : 369–379, 379–386 (Constantinople — Greek) 110
Dengel : 969? (Ethiopia — Historical) 142
Denha I : 649–659 (India — Malankara Jacobite), and 650–659 (India — Malankara Orthodox) 163, 168
Denha II : 688–728 (India — Malankara Jacobite), and (India — Malankara Orthodox) 164, 168
Denha III : 912–932 (India — Malankara Jacobite), and 915–935 (India — Malankara Orthodox) 164, 168
Deusdedit — *see also*: Adeodatus
Deusdedit (I) : 615–618 (Rome) 212
Dhiyunisiyus : 1293–1308 (Antioch — Greek) 37
Dhuruthiyus — *see also*: Duruthiyus

Dhuruthiyus III *ibn al-Sabbuni* : 1436–1454 (Antioch — Greek) 37
Dhuruthiyus IV *ibn al-Sabbuni* : 1497–1523 (Antioch — Greek) 37
Dimitri : 1080–1090 (Georgia) 150
Dimitrie : 1561?–1564? (Austria — Cernovci) 77
Dimitriĭ I : 923? (Bulgaria) 92
Dimitriĭ II *Khomatian* : 1216?–1234? (Bulgaria) 93
Dimitrij *Homatian* : 1216–1235 (Macedonia) 195
Dimitrije *Pavlović* : 1905–1920 [metropolitan], 1920–1930 [patriarch] (Serbia) 200, 225, 228
Dimitriyanus : 256–263 (Antioch — Greek), and 253 (Antioch — Greek Melkite), and 254–260 (Antioch — Syrian Orthodox) 34, 40, 58
Dimitriyus I : 189–231 (Alexandria — Coptic) 15
Dimitriyus II : 1862–1870 (Alexandria — Coptic) 18
Dimitriyus : 188–230 (Alexandria — Coptic Catholic) 21
Dimitriyus *Qadi* : 1919–1925 (Antioch — Greek Melkite) 44
Dimitriyus : 255–263 (Antioch — Syrian Catholic) 53
Dinkha I *Arbilaya* : 1265–1281 (Assyria) 74
Dinkha II : 1329–1359 (Assyria) 74
Dinkha III : 1359–1368 (Assyria) 74
Dinkha IV *Khnanishu'* : 1976- (Assyria) 70, 75, 174, 254, 257, 259
Dinkha I *Arbilaya* : 1265–1281 (Babylon) 87
Dinkha II : 1332–1364 (Babylon) 87
Dinkha : 1503? (India — Chaldean) 174
Dinkha Iliya XII *bar Mama* : 1722–1778 (Babylon) 87, 251–252
Dinkha Shim'un IX *bar Mama* : 1552–1558 (Assyria) 69–70, 74
Dinkha Shim'un XI : 1580–1600 (Assyria) 70, 74, 83
Dinkha Shim'un XV : 1692–1700 (Assyria) 74
Dinkha Shim'un VIII *bar Mama* : 1551–1558 (Babylon) 69–70, 87
Diodōros *Karibalēs* : 1981–2000 (Jerusalem — Greek) 187
Diogenēs : 114–129 (Constantinople — Greek) 109
Dionise : 1510–1511 (Georgia) 150
Dionise : 1627–1629 (Austria — Cernovci) 78

Dionisie *Novacovic* : 1761–1767 (Austria — Sibiu) 81
Dionisie I : 1672 (Romania) 206
Dionisie II *Lupu* : 1819–1821 (Romania) 207
Dionisie : 1821–1822 [locum tenens] (Romania) 207
Dionisiĭ I : 1652–1653 (Bulgaria) 94
Dionisiĭ II *apo Chiou* : 1703–1706, 1709–1714 (Bulgaria) 95
Dionisiĭ III : 1751–1756 (Bulgaria) 95
Dionisiĭ : 1582–1587 (Russia — Moscow) 220
Dionisij I : 1467- (Macedonia) 195
Dionisij II : 1651–1656 (Macedonia) 196
Dionisij III *apo Chiou* : 1706–1707, 1710–1714 (Macedonia) 197
Dionisij IV : 1752–1757 (Macedonia) 197
Dionisije I *Papazoğlou* : 1785–1791 (Serbia — Beograd) 228
Dionisije II *Nislija* : 1813–1815 (Serbia — Beograd) 228
Dionizy *Waledyński* : 1923–1947 (Poland) 203–204, 233
Dionysiĭ I : 1384–1385 (Ukraine) 236
Dionysiĭ II *Balaban* : 1658–1663 (Ukraine) 237
Dionysios : 248–265 (Alexandria — Greek) 23
Dionysios I *Symeōnēs apo Philippoupoleōs* : 1467–1471, 1488–1490 (Constantinople — Greek) 113
Dionysios II : 1537, 1546–1555 (Constantinople — Greek) 114
Dionysios : 1586? [locum tenens] (Constantinople — Greek) 114
Dionysios III *Bardalis Spanos* : 1662–1665 (Constantinople — Greek) 115
Dionysios IV *Mouselimēs Komnēnos* : 1671–1673, 1676–1679, 1682–1684, 1686–1687, 1693–1694 (Constantinople — Greek) 115
Dionysios V *Charitōnidēs* : 1887–1891 (Constantinople — Greek) 117
Dionysios I *Byzantios* : 1850–1856 (Crete) 125
Dionysios II *Charitōnidēs* : 1858–1868 (Crete) 125
Dionysios I *Areopagitēs* : 93? (Greece) 154
Dionysios II : 1820–1823 (Greece) 157
Dionysios Mar Thomas : 1999–2002 [locum tenens]

(India — Malankara Jacobite) 173
Dionysios I *Moosa* : 1112–1142 (India — Malankara Orthodox) 165
Dionysios II *Bar Msah* : 1188–1204 (India — Malankara Orthodox) 165
Dionysios III *Sleeba* : 1222–1231 (India — Malankara Orthodox) 165
Dionysios I, Thomas Mar [i.e., Mar Thoma VI] : 1765–1808 (India — Malankara Syrian) 160, 162, 175
Dionysios II, Pulikkottil Mar : 1815–1816 (India — Malankara Syrian) 162
Dionysios III *Ittoop*, Punnathra Mar : 1817–1825 (India — Malankara Syrian) 162
Dionysios IV *Kattanar*, Cheepat Mar : 1829–1852 (India — Malankara Syrian) 160, 162
Dionysios V *Putikkottil*, Joseph Mar : 1865–1909 (India — Malankara Syrian) 161–162, 173, 252
Dionysios VI *Vattasseril*, Geevarghese Mar : 1908–1909 [suffragan], 1909–1934 (India — Malankara Syrian), and 1913–1925 [locum tenens], 1928–1929 [locum tenens] (India — Malankara Orthodox) 161–162
Dionysius *du Moulin* : 1439–1447 (Antioch — Latin) 46
Dionysius : 1189–1203 [antimaphrian] (India — Malankara Jacobite) 169
Dionysius : 259–268 (Rome) 211
Dionysius Mosa : 1112–1134 (India — Malankara Jacobite) 169
Dionysius Sleeba II : 1222–1231 (India — Malankara Jacobite) 169
Dios : 213 (Jerusalem — Greek) 184
Dioscoros Mar Bahnam II : 1415–1417 (India — Malankara Orthodox) 165
Dioscorus : 530 [anti-pope] (Rome) 211
Dioskoros I : 444–451 (Alexandria — Greek) 23
Dioskoros II : 516–517 (Alexandria — Greek) 23
Dioskoros : 1036–1038 [anti-catholicos] (Armenia) 66
Dioskoros : 3rd cent. (Crete) 123
Dioskoros : 2005- [rival patriarch] (Eritrea) 134, 254, 258, 260
Disqurus I : 444–458 (Alexandria — Coptic) 14, 16, 20, 22

Disqurus II : 515–517 (Alexandria — Coptic) 16
Divannasios Mar Thomas : 1999–2002 [locum tenens] (India — Malankara Jacobite) 173
Diyunisiyus : 247–264 (Alexandria — Coptic), and 246–264 (Alexandria — Coptic Catholic) 15, 21
Diyunisiyus I : 1308?–1316? (Antioch — Greek Melkite) 42
Diyunisiyus II : 1325? (Antioch — Greek Melkite) 42
Diyunisiyus I *of Tell Mahar* : 818–845 (Antioch — Syrian Catholic) 54
Diyunisiyus II : 896–909 (Antioch — Syrian Catholic) 55
Diyunisiyus III : 958–961 (Antioch — Syrian Catholic) 55
Diyunisiyus IV *Khihi* : 1032–1042 (Antioch — Syrian Catholic) 55
Diyunisiyus V *Lazarus* : 1077–1079 (Antioch — Syrian Catholic) 55
Diyunisiyus VI : 1088–1090 (Antioch — Syrian Catholic) 55
Diyunisiyus VII *Aharon Angur* : 1252–1253 (Antioch — Syrian Catholic) 55
Diyunisiyus I *of Tell Mahar* : 817–845 (Antioch — Syrian Orthodox) 59
Diyunisiyus II : 897–909 (Antioch — Syrian Orthodox) 60
Diyunisiyus III : 958–961 (Antioch — Syrian Orthodox) 60
Diyunisiyus IV *Yahya Khihi* : 1033–1044 (Antioch — Syrian Orthodox) 60
Diyunisiyus V *Lazarus* : 1077–1078 (Antioch — Syrian Orthodox) 60
Diyunisiyus VI : 1088–1090 (Antioch — Syrian Orthodox) 60
Diyunisiyus *Aharon Angur* : 1252–1261 [anti-patriarch] (Antioch — Syrian Orthodox) 60
Dolichianos : -185? (Jerusalem — Greek) 184
Domenicus *Marinangeli* : 1898–1921 (Alexandria — Latin) 28
Domenicus *Giordani* : 1766–1780 (Antioch — Latin) 47
Domenti I : 1599–1603 (Georgia) 151
Domenti II *Bagrationi* : 1660–1676 (Georgia) 151
Domenti III *Bagrationi* : 1705–1725, 1739–1741 (Georgia) 151

Dometios : 272–303 (Constantinople — Greek) 109, 252
Dominicus *Lucciardi* : 1851 (Constantinople — Latin) 122
Donat *Babinskiĭ-Sokolov* : 1882–1887 (Latvia) 191
Donus : 676–678 (Rome) 212
Dorotʻeos —*see also*: Dorotʻeoz
Dorotʻeos II : 1503–1510, 1511–1516 (Georgia) 150
Dorotʻeoz —*see also*: Dorotʻeos
Dorotʻeoz I : 1350–1356 (Georgia) 150
Dorotʻeoz III : 1592–1599 (Georgia) 151
Doroteĭ I : 1320? (Bulgaria) 93
Doroteĭ II : 1466? (Bulgaria) 93
Dorotej *Filipp* : 1964–1999 (Czechoslovakia) 133, 252
Dorotej : 1456–1466 (Macedonia) 195
Dōrotheos : 567- (Alexandria — Coptic — Gaianite) 19
Dōrotheos : -407 [anti-patriarch] (Constantinople — Greek) 110
Dōrotheos *apo Prousēs* : 1918–1921 [locum tenens] (Constantinople — Greek) 117
Dōrotheos I : 1387–1393? (Greece) 156
Dōrotheos II : -1472 (Greece) 156
Dōrotheos III *Kottaras* : 1956–1957 (Greece) 158
Dōrotheos I : 1376–1417 (Jerusalem — Greek) 186
Dōrotheos II : 1503?–1537 (Jerusalem — Greek) 187
Dōrotheos I : 1324–1333 (Sinai) 231
Dōrotheos II *Byzantios* : 1794–1797 (Sinai) 232
Dositei *Filitti* : 1793–1810 (Romania) 207
Dositej I : 1466 (Macedonia) 195
Dositej I *Stojković* : 1958–1981 (Macedonia) 193, 197
Dositej *Vasić* [locum tenens] : 1937–1938 (Serbia) 228
Dositeosi : 1792–1814 (Georgia — Abkhazia) 153
Dositheos *Hierosolymitēs* : 1189, 1189–1191 (Constantinople — Greek) 112
Dositheos I : -1191 (Jerusalem — Greek) 186
Dositheos II : 1669–1707 (Jerusalem — Greek) 187
Dosoftei *Herescu* : 1750–1789 (Austria — Cernovci) 78
Dosoftei : 1624–1627 (Austria — Sibiu) 81
Dumitiyus : unknown (Antioch — Maronite) 49
Dumnus I : 270–273 (Antioch — Greek), and 260–266 (Antioch — Greek Melkite) 34, 40

Dumnus II : 443–450 (Antioch — Greek), and 442?–449 (Antioch — Greek Melkite, 35, 40
Dumnus III : 546–561 (Antioch — Greek), and 545–559 (Antioch — Greek Melkite) 35, 41
Dumnus I : 271–274 (Antioch — Syrian Catholic), and 268–273 (Antioch — Syrian Orthodox) 53, 58
Dumnus II : 440–449 (Antioch — Syrian Catholic), and 442–449 (Antioch — Syrian Orthodox) 53, 58
Durandus : 1212–1213 [unconsecrated] (Cyprus — Latin) 129
Duruthiyus —*see also*: Dhuruthiyus
Duruthiyus I : 370–371 (Antioch — Greek) 35
Duruthiyus II : 1219–1245 (Antioch — Greek) 37
Duruthiyus V : 1541–1543 (Antioch — Greek) 37
Duruthiyus VI *ibn al-Ahmar* : 1604–1611 (Antioch — Greek) 38
Duruthiyus (I) : 370–371 [anti-patriarch] (Antioch — Greek Melkite) 40
Duruthiyus I *ibn al-Sabbuni* : 1434?–1451 (Antioch — Greek Melkite) 43
Duruthiyus II *ibn al-Sabbuni* : 1484?–1500? (Antioch — Greek Melkite) 43
Duruthiyus III : 1529?–1531 (Antioch — Greek Melkite) 43
Duruthiyus IV *ibn al-Ahmar* : 1604–1612 (Antioch — Greek Melkite) 43
Dymytriĭ *Verbytsʻkĭ* : 1930–1932 (Ukraine) 238
Dymytriĭ *IArema* : 1993–2000 (Ukraine — Autocephalous) 234, 238

Easo : 669–683 (India — Malankara Jacobite) 168
Efrem : 1608–1613, 1616?–1623? (Austria — Cernovci) 78
Efrem : 1558?–1566? (Romania) 206
Eftim I *Karachissaridēs* : 1926–1962 (Constantinople — Greek — Turkey) 117–118
Eftim II *Erenerol* : 1962–1991 (Constantinople — Greek — Turkey) 118
Eftim III *Erenerol* : 1991–2002 (Constantinople — Greek — Turkey) 118
Eftimie : 1558–1561? (Austria — Cernovci) 77
Eftimie : 1571?–1574 (Austria — Sibiu) 81

Eftimie I : 1568–1576 (Romania) 206
Eftimie II : 1594–1602 (Romania) 206
Eghia : 703–717 (Armenia) 65
Eghia : 774–797 (Jerusalem—Armenian) 179
Eghiazar : 681?–687? (Aghunie) 9
Eghiazar : 1663–1682 [anti-catholicos], 1682–1691 (Armenia) 67
Eghiazar *Adshapahian* : 1780? [coadjutor] (Cilicia—Armenian Apostolic) 100
Eghiazar : 1651–1652 (Constantinople—Armenian) 104
Eghiazar *of Hromkla* : 1664–1665, 1666–1668, 1670–1677 (Jerusalem—Armenian) 181
Eghishê : 1292–1300 [anti-catholicos] (Aght'amar) 5
Eghishê : -79 (Aghunie) 8
Eghishê *Rshtuni* : 941–946 (Armenia) 66
Eghishê : 1504–1505 [coadjutor] (Armenia) 67
Eghishê : 1940–1942 [locum tenens] (Cilicia—Armenian Apostolic) 100
Eghishê *Durian* : 1909–1911 (Constantinople—Armenian) 106
Eghishê I *Durian* : 1921–1930 (Jerusalem—Armenian) 182
Eghishê II *Derderian* : 1954–1955 [locum tenens] (Armenia); 1949–1957 [locum tenens], 1958–1960 [locum tenens], 1960–1990 (Jerusalem—Armenian) 182
Ehremarus : 1105? [anti-patriarch] (Jerusalem—Latin) 188
Eirênaios *Skopelitês* : 2001–2005 (Jerusalem—Greek) 187
Ek'vt'ime I : 1049–1055 (Georgia) 149
Ek'vt'ime II : 1220–1222 (Georgia) 150
Ek'vt'ime III : 1310–1325 (Georgia) 150
Ek'vt'ime I *Sakvarelizde* : 1578–1605 (Georgia—Abkhazia) 153
Ek'vt'ime II *Sakvarelizde* : 1669–1673 (Georgia—Abkhazia) 153
Eleutherios : 1180? (Alexandria—Greek) 25
Eleutherios : 129–136 (Constantinople—Greek) 109
Eleutherius : 175?–189 (Rome) 210
Elia—*see also*: Ilia
Elia I : 390–400 (Georgia) 148
Elias—*see also*: Helias
Êlias I : 963–1000 (Alexandria—Greek) 24

Êlias II *Alphtheras* : 1170? (Alexandria—Greek) 25
Elias : 1246?–1250 (Antioch—Latin) 45
Êlias I : 787? (Crete) 124
Êlias II : 920–961 (Crete) 124
Êlias III : 12th cent. (Crete) 124
Elias I : 1240–1251 (Cyprus—Latin) 129
Elias III : 1460–1463? (Cyprus—Latin) 130
Elias I, Baselios : -1523 (India—Malankara Jacobite) 170
Elias II, Baselios : 1533–1552 (India—Malankara Jacobite) 170
Elias III, Baselios : 1825–1827 (India—Malankara Jacobite) 172
Elias IV, Baselios : 1827–1838 (India—Malankara Jacobite) 172
Êlias I : 494–516 (Jerusalem—Greek) 185
Êlias II : 770–797 (Jerusalem—Greek) 185
Êlias III : 878–907 (Jerusalem—Greek) 185
Elias I : 1279–1287 (Jerusalem—Latin) 189
Elias II *de Nabinallis* : 1342- (Jerusalem—Latin) 189
Elias, Baselios Mar : 1838–1840 (India—Malankara Orthodox) 166
Êlias : 900 (Sinai) 231
Eliozi : 1399–1411 (Georgia) 150
Elisho : 504–536 (India—Malankara Orthodox) 163
Elpidios : 565–567 (Alexandria—Coptic—Gaianite) 18
Emilian *Antal Târgovişteanul* : 1945–1948 [locum tenens] (Austria—Cernovci) 78
Ephraim : 1715 [anti-archbishop] (Cyprus) 128
Ephraim I : unknown (Jerusalem—Greek) 184
Ephraim II : 1766–1771 (Jerusalem—Greek) 187
Epifaniĭ *Abramov* : 1955–1963 (Russia-Novozybkov) 223
Epip'ane : 1210–1220 (Georgia) 150
Epiphanios : 520–535 (Constantinople—Greek) 110
Epiphanios I : 368–403 (Cyprus) 127
Epiphanios II : 681?–685? (Cyprus) 127
Epiphanios III : 870? (Cyprus) 127
Ep'rem : 1809–1830 (Armenia) 68
Ep'rem I : 1771–1784 (Cilicia—Armenian Apostolic) 99
Ep'rem II : 1823–1831 (Cilicia—Armenian Apostolic) 100

Ep'rem : 1684–1686, 1694–1698, 1701–1702 (Constantinople—Armenian) 105
Ep'rem I : 1497–1500 (Georgia) 150
Ep'rem II *Sidamonidze* : 1960–1972 (Georgia) 152
Eraclius : 1180–1191 (Jerusalem—Latin) 189
Eremia I : -552 (Aghunie) 9
Eremia II : 1676–1700 (Aghunie) 10
Eremia *Sahagian* : 1885–1889 [locum tenens] (Jerusalem—Armenian) 182
Eremij : 1761–1763 (Macedonia) 197
Ermenus : 1709–1710 (Macedonia) 196
Esayi : 1701–1727 (Aghunie) 10
Esayi : 775–788 (Armenia) 65
Esayi I : 1133–1152 (Jerusalem—Armenian) 180
Esayi II : 1391–1394 (Jerusalem—Armenian) 180
Esayi III : 1430–1431 (Jerusalem—Armenian) 180
Esayi IV *Karapetian* : 1864–1885 (Jerusalem—Armenian) 182
Euagrios : 379 (Constantinople—Greek) 110
Eudoxios : 360–369 (Constantinople—Greek) 110
Eugenie *Hacman* : 1835–1873 (Austria—Cernovci) 78
Eugenios I : 237–242 (Constantinople—Greek) 109
Eugenios II *apo Pissideias* : 1821–1822 (Constantinople—Greek) 116
Eugenios *Psalidakês* : 1950–1978 (Crete) 125
Eugenios : 1567–1583 (Sinai) 232
Eugenius I : 654–657 (Rome) 212
Eugenius II : 824–827 (Rome) 213
Eugenius III *Pignatelli* : 1145–1153 (Rome) 214
Eugenius IV *Condulmaro* : 1431–1447 (Rome) 216
Eulalius : 418–419 [anti-pope] (Rome) 211
Eulogios I : 581–608 (Alexandria—Greek) 24
Eulogios II : 1110? (Alexandria—Greek) 25
Eumenês : 131–144 (Alexandria—Greek) 23
Eumenios I *Thaumatourgos* : 668? (Crete) 123
Eumenios II *Xêroudakês* : 1897–1920 (Crete) 125
Euphêmios : 490–496 (Constantinople—Greek) 110
Eusebios : 720? (Alexandria—Greek) 24

Eusebios *Nikomēdeias* : 341–342? (Constantinople — Greek) 109
Eusebius : 309 (Rome) 211
Eustathios : 813–817 (Alexandria — Greek) 24
Eustathios *apo Palatiou* : 1019–1025 (Constantinople — Greek) 111
Eustathios : 890? (Cyprus) 128
Eustochios : 552–564 (Jerusalem — Greek) 185
Eustorgius *de Montaigu* : 1217?–1239 (Cyprus — Latin) 129
Eustratios *Garidas* : 1081–1084 (Constantinople — Greek) 112
Euthymios I : 907–912 (Constantinople — Greek) 111
Euthymios II : 1410–1416 (Constantinople — Greek) 113
Euthymios I : -1084 (Jerusalem — Greek) 186
Euthymios II : -1223 (Jerusalem — Greek) 186
Euthymios : 1223–1224 (Sinai) 231
Eutychianus : 275–283 (Rome) 211
Eutychios I : 654 (Alexandria — Greek) 24
Eutychios II : 933–940 (Alexandria — Greek) 24
Eutychios : 552–565, 577–582 (Constantinople — Greek) 110
Euzōïos : 148–154 (Constantinople — Greek) 109
Evagre : 1480–1492, 1500–1503 (Georgia) 150
Evaristus : 97?–105? (Rome) 210
Evdemoz I *Diasamidze* : 1630–1637 (Georgia) 151
Evdemoz II *Diasamidze* : 1701–1705 (Georgia) 151
Evdemoz I *Chk'etidze* : 1557–1578 (Georgia — Abkhazia) 153
Evdemoz II *Sakvarelizde* : 1666–1669 (Georgia — Abkhazia) 153
Evdokim *Meshcherskiĭ* : 1914–1918 (America — Orthodox Church) 31
Everardus : 1215–1219 (Constantinople — Latin) 119
Evgeniĭ *Baganov* : 1834–1844 [exarch] (Georgia) 151
Evghenie *Hacman* : 1835–1873 (Austria — Cernovci) 78
Evlale : 664–668 (Georgia) 149
Evlavi : 533–544 (Georgia) 148
Evlogie : 1623–1627, 1628–1639? (Austria — Cernovci) 78
Evnoni : 640–649 (Georgia) 149
Evseviĭ *Ilinskiĭ* : 1858–1877 [exarch] (Georgia) 151
Evstatiĭ : 1159? (Bulgaria) 92
Evsuk'i : 887–908 (Georgia) 149
Evtimiĭ : 1375–1393 (Bulgaria) 93

Ewostatewos : unknown (Ethiopia — Official) 140
Ezr : 630–641 (Armenia) 65
Ezra : 1215? (Ethiopia — Historical) 143

Fabianus : 236–250 (Rome) 211
Fabius I *Colonna* : 1550–1554 (Constantinople — Latin) 121
Fabius II Maria *Asquini* : 1844–1845 (Constantinople — Latin) 122
Fabiyus : 253–256 (Antioch — Greek), and 250–253 (Antioch — Greek Melkite), and 244–255 (Antioch — Syrian Catholic), and 251–254 (Antioch — Syrian Catholic) 34, 40, 53, 58
Fabricius : 1464- (Cyprus — Latin) 130
Fan *Noli* : 1923–1924 (Albania) 12–13
Felix I : 269–274 (Rome) 211
Felix II : 355–365 [anti-pope] (Rome) 211
Felix III : 483–492 (Rome) 211
Felix IV : 526–530 (Rome) 211
Felix V *di Savoia* : 1439–1449 [anti-pope] (Rome) 216
Feodor : 1462–1467 (Russia — Moscow) 220
Feodor : 1160–1162? (Ukraine) 235
Feodor : 1337–1347 (Ukraine — Halych) 239
Feofil *Pashkovskiĭ* : 1934–1950 (America — Orthodox Church) 32
Feofilakt *Rusanov* : 1817–1821 [exarch] (Georgia) 151
Feognost : 1328–1352 (Russia — Moscow) 220
Feognost I : 1328–1353 (Ukraine) 236
Feognost II *Lebedev* : 1900–1903 (Ukraine) 237
Feopempt : 1039- (Ukraine) 235
Ferdinandus *de Loazes* : 1566? (Alexandria — Latin), and 1566–1568 (Antioch — Latin) 28, 46
Ferdinandus Maria *de Rossi* : 1751–1759 (Constantinople — Latin) 121
Filaqas : 342–346 (Antioch — Syrian Catholic) 53
Filaqilus : 334–344 [anti-patriarch] (Antioch — Syrian Orthodox) 58
Filaret *Vakhromeev* : 1978- (Belarus) 90, 254, 257, 259
Filaret I *Gumilevskiĭ* : 1842–1848 (Latvia) 191
Filaret II *Filaretov* : 1877–1882 (Latvia) 191
Filaret I *Mihalitzis* : 1753–1760 (Romania) 207

Filaret II : 1792–1793 (Romania) 207
Filaret *Romanov* : 1619–1633 (Russia) 218, 220
Filaret *Drozdoz* : 1821–1867 (Russia — Moscow) 221
Filaret *Voznesenskiĭ* : 1964–1985 (Russia — Church Outside Russia) 224
Filaret I *Amfiteatrov* : 1837–1857 (Ukraine) 237
Filaret II *Denysenko* : 1990 [locum tenens] (Russia), and 1966–1992 [metropolitan] (Ukraine), and 1995- [patriarch] (Ukraine — Kievan Patriarchate) 222, 234, 238, 256–257, 259
Filatawos I : unknown (Ethiopia — Official) 140
Filatawos II : unknown (Ethiopia — Official) 141
Filibbus Butrus *al-Jumayyil* : 1795–1796 (Antioch — Maronite) 50
Filibbus *Arkus*, Ighnatiyus : 1866–1874 (Antioch — Syrian Catholic) 56
Filimun *of Aleppo* : 1766–1767 (Antioch — Greek) 38
Filip : 1000?–1015? (Bulgaria), and (Macedonia) 92, 193–194
Filip : 1591–1592 (Serbia) 227
Filipp I : 1467–1472 (Russia — Moscow) 220
Filipp II : 1568–1572 (Russia — Moscow) 220
Filippos *Berhan* : 1991–1998 [as archbishop], 1998–2002 [as patriarch] (Eritrea) 134
Filitus : 218–231 (Antioch — Greek and Antioch — Greek Melkite), and 223–226 (Antioch — Syrian Catholic), and 220–231 (Antioch — Syrian Orthodox) 34, 40, 53, 58
Filofeĭ *Uspens'kyĭ* : 1876–1882 (Ukraine) 237
Filoteĭ : 1714–1718 (Bulgaria) 95
Filotej : 1714–1718 (Macedonia) 197
Filughunus : 314–324 (Antioch — Greek), and 320–325 (Antioch — Greek Melkite) 35, 40
Filujuniyus : 320–323 (Antioch — Syrian Orthodox) 58
Filuksinus *Nimrud*, Ighnatiyus : 1283–1292 (Antioch — Syrian Catholic) 55
Filuksinus I *Nimrud* : 1283–1292 (Antioch — Syrian Orthodox) 60
Filuksinus II *"The Scribe"* : 1387–1421 (Antioch — Syrian Orthodox) 61
Filuthawus : 979–1003 (Alexandria — Coptic) 17

Index of Primates

Fiqtor : 1050?–1077 (Ethiopia — Historical) 142
Fiqtor I : unknown (Ethiopia — Official) 140
Fiqtor II : unknown (Ethiopia — Official) 140
Fitalis : 306–314 (Antioch — Greek Melkite), and 314–320 (Antioch — Syrian Orthodox) 40, 58
Fitaliyus I : 308–314 (Antioch — Greek) 35
Fitaliyus II : 376–384 (Antioch — Greek) 35
Flabiyanus I : 381–404 (Antioch — Syrian Catholic), and (Antioch — Syrian Orthodox) 53, 58
Flabiyanus II : 495–512 (Antioch — Syrian Catholic), and 498–512 (Antioch — Syrian Orthodox) 54, 59
Flafiyanus I : 384–404 (Antioch — Greek), and (Antioch — Greek Melkite) 35, 40
Flafiyanus II : 505–513 (Antioch — Greek), and 498–512 (Antioch — Greek Melkite) 35, 41
Flakentiyus : 334–341 (Antioch — Greek) 35
Flakilus : 334–343 (Antioch — Greek Melkite) 40
Flavian *Gorodetskiĭ* : 1898–1901 [exarch] (Georgia) 152
Flavian *Slesarev* : 1952–1960 (Russia — Belokrinitsia) 223
Flavian *Horodets'kyĭ* : 1903–1915 (Ukraine) 237
Flavianus : 446–449 (Constantinople — Greek) 110
Fławian *Gorodieckij* : 1891–1898 (Poland) 204
Formosus : 891–896 (Rome) 213
Fotiĭ : 1410–1436 (Russia — Moscow), and 1408–1431 (Ukraine) 220, 236
Franciscus de Pauli *Cassetta* : 1895–1899 (Antioch — Latin) 47
Franciscus I *Landus* : 1409 (Constantinople — Latin) 120
Franciscus II *de Conzié* : 1430– (Constantinople — Latin) 120
Franciscus III *Condulmer* : 1438– (Constantinople — Latin) 120
Franciscus IV *de Lorris* : 1503–1506 (Constantinople — Latin) 120
Franciscus V *Pesaro* : 1530–1544 (Constantinople — Latin) 120
Franciscus VI Maria *Machiavelli* : 1640–1641 (Constantinople — Latin) 121
Franciscus VII Antonius *Marcucci* : 1781–1799 (Constantinople — Latin) 121

Fravitas : 489–490 (Constantinople — Greek) 110
Fredericus *Borromée* : 1655? (Alexandria — Latin), and 1670–1673 (Constantinople — Latin) 28, 121
Fulcherus : 1146–1157 (Jerusalem — Latin) 188
Fulin : 332–337 (Antioch — Syrian Catholic) 53

Gabra Krestos : 1344?–1348? (Ethiopia — Historical) 143
Gabr'el *Iyasu* : 1980–1985 (Eritrea) 134
Gabr'el : 1438–1458? (Ethiopia — Historical) 143
Gabr'el I : unknown (Ethiopia — Official) 139
Gabr'el II : unknown (Ethiopia — Official) 139
Gabr'el III : unknown (Ethiopia — Official) 139
Gabr'el IV : unknown (Ethiopia — Official) 140
Gabr'el V : unknown (Ethiopia — Official) 140
Gabr'el VI : unknown (Ethiopia — Official) 140
Gabr'el VII : unknown (Ethiopia — Official) 140
Gabr'el VIII : unknown (Ethiopia — Official) 140
Gabr'el IX : unknown (Ethiopia — Official) 141
Gabr'el X : 1438–1458? (Ethiopia — Official) 141
Gabriêl *Shiroyan* : 1851–1857 (Aght'amar) 7
Gabriêl : 1757–1770 (Cilicia — Armenian Apostolic) 99
Gabriêl I : 1596 (Constantinople — Greek) 114
Gabriêl II *apo Ganou kai Chōras* : 1657 (Constantinople — Greek) 115
Gabriêl III *Smyrnaios apo Chalkēdonos* : 1702–1707 (Constantinople — Greek) 115
Gabriêl IV *apo Palaiōn Patrōn* : 1780–1785 (Constantinople — Greek) 116
Gabriel I : 502–510 (Georgia) 148
Gabriel II : 838–860 (Georgia) 149
Gabriel III : 1065–1080 (Georgia) 149
Gabriēl I : 858–860 (Greece) 155
Gabriēl II : 1781 (Greece) 157
Gabriêl : 1818–1840 (Jerusalem — Armenian) 182
Gabriēl I : 1154–1160 (Sinai) 231
Gabriēl II : 1445? (Sinai) 231
Gagik I : 947–961 (Aghunie) 9
Gagik II : 1139– (Aghunie) 9
Gaïnas : 537 (Alexandria — Greek) 14, 23

Gaïanos : 536–565 (Alexandria — Coptic) 14, 18
Gaïanos : unknown (Jerusalem — Greek) 184
Gaïnos : 536–565 (Alexandria — Coptic) 18
Gaïos I : 2nd cent. (Jerusalem — Greek) 184
Gaïos II : 2nd cent. (Jerusalem — Greek) 184
Gaius : 283–296 (Rome) 211
Galaction *Codrun* : 1955–1957 (Romania — Old Calendarists) 208
Galesius *de Montolif* : 1445–1447 (Cyprus — Latin) 130
Galust *Vayzhavk* : 1703–1704 (Constantinople — Armenian) 105
Galust : 1697–1704 [coadjutor] (Jerusalem — Armenian) 181
Garegin I *Sargisian* : 1995–1999 (Armenia) 68, 98
Garegin II *Nersêsian* : 1999– (Armenia) 68, 254, 258, 260
Garegin I *Hovespian* : 1943–1952 (Cilicia — Armenian Apostolic) 100
Garegin II *Sargisian* : 1977–1983 [coadjutor], 1983–1995 [catholicos-patriarch] (Cilicia — Armenian Apostolic) 98, 100
Garegin I *Khach'aturian* : 1951–1961 (Constantinople — Armenian) 106
Garegin II Petros *Kazanjian* : 1990–1998 (Constantinople — Armenian) 106
Gavriïl : 1572–1587 (Bulgaria) 94
Gavriïl *Bănulescu* : 1808–1812 (Romania) 207
Gavril I : 1572?–1588, 1593 (Macedonia) 195
Gavril II *Miloševski* : 1986–1993 (Macedonia) 194, 197
Gavrilo *Zmajević* : 1908 [unconsecrated] (Austria — Karlovci) 77, 80
Gavrilo *Dožić* : 1920–1938 (Montenegro) 200, 202, 228
Gavrilo I *Rajić* : 1648–1655 (Serbia) 227
Gavrilo II *Mihailović Sarajevac* : 1752 (Serbia) 227
Gavrilo III *Nikolin* : 1752– (Serbia) 227
Gavrilo IV : 1757?–1758 (Serbia) 227
Gavrilo V *Dožić* : 1938–1950 (Serbia) 200, 202, 228
Geevarghese I, Baselios : 1674–1687 (India — Malankara Jacobite) 171
Geevarghese II, Baselios : 1760–1768 (India — Malankara Jacobite) 171

Geevarghese *Kallacheril*, Baselios Mar : 1958–1964 (India — Malankara Jacobite) 172
Geevarghese, Gregorios Mar : 1996–1999 [locum tenens] (India — Malankara Jacobite) 172
Geevarghese I *Karnchira*, Baselios Mar : 1925–1928 (India — Malankara Orthodox) 167
Geevarghese II *Kallacheril*, Baselios Mar : 1929–1964 (India — Malankara Orthodox) 167
Geevarghese Mar Dionysios VI *Vattasseril* : 1908–1909 [suffragan], 1909–1934 (India — Malankara Syrian); 1913–1925 [locum tenens], 1928–1929 [locum tenens] (India — Malankara Orthodox) 161–162, 167
Geevarghese Mar Koorilose II : 1794–1802 [suffragan], 1802–1808 (India — Thozhiyoor) 175
Geevarghese Mar Koorilose III *Koothoor* : 1829–1856 (India — Thozhiyoor) 176
Geevarghese Mar Koorilose V *Pulikottil* : 1892–1898 [suffragan], 1898–1935 (India — Thozhiyoor) 176
Geevarghese Mar Koorilose VII *Kasseesa* : 1948–1967 (India — Thozhiyoor) 176
Geevarghese Mar Phileksinose : 1816–1817, 1825–1829 (India — Malankara Syrian) 162
Geevarghese Mar Phileksinose II : 1811–1829 (India — Thozhiyoor) 176
Gelasios : 325? (Cyprus) 127
Gelasius I : 492–496 (Rome) 211
Gelasius II *Caetani* : 1118–1119 (Rome) 214
Genadiĭ : 1285? (Bulgaria) 93
Genadij : 1289? (Macedonia) 195
Gennadiĭ *Antonov* : 1979–1996 (Russia-Novozybkov) 223
Gennadios I : 458–471 (Constantinople — Greek) 110
Gennadios II *Scholarios Kourtesēs* : 1454–1456, 1462–1463, 1464 (Constantinople — Greek) 107–108, 113
Gennadios : 1973 [anti-archbishop] (Cyprus) 129
Gêorg I *Hailorbuk* : 792–795 (Armenia) 65
Gêorg II : 877–897 (Armenia) 66
Gêorg : 1067–1072 [coadjutor] (Armenia) 66
Gêorg III *Jalalbêgiants'* : 1443–1465 (Armenia) 67
Gêorg IV *K'erest'echian* : 1866–1882 (Armenia) 68

Gêorg V *Surênian* : 1910–1911 [locum tenens], 1911–1930 (Armenia) 68
Gêorg VI *Ch'êôrêk'chian* : 1938–1945 [locum tenens], 1945–1954 (Armenia) 63, 68
Gêorg I : 1751–1752 (Constantinople — Armenian) 105
Gêorg II *K'erest'echian* : 1858–1860 (Constantinople — Armenian) 106
Gêorg *Arslanian* : 1922–1927 [locum tenens], 1944–1950 [locum tenens] (Constantinople — Armenian) 106
Gêorg : 696–708 (Jerusalem — Armenian) 179
Georgi I : 878?–919? (Bulgaria) 92
Georgi II : 1616–1617 (Bulgaria) 94
Georgij : 1627? (Macedonia) 196
Georgije (I) *Hranislav* : 1841–1842 [locum tenens] (Austria — Karlovci) 79
Georgije (II) *Branković* : 1890–1907 (Austria — Karlovci) 80
Georgije (III) *Letić* : 1919–1922 [locum tenens] (Austria — Karlovci) 80
Geōrgios : 357–361 [anti-pope] (Alexandria — Greek) 23
Geōrgios I : 620–630 (Alexandria — Greek) 24
Geōrgios II : 1021–1052 (Alexandria — Greek) 24
Geōrgios : 679–686 (Constantinople — Greek) 110
Geōrgios II *Xiphilinos* : 1191–1198 (Constantinople — Greek) 112
Geōrgios I : 753? (Cyprus) 127
Geōrgios II : 1254? (Cyprus) 128
Geōrgios I : 914–922 (Greece) 155
Geōrgios II : 1145–1160 (Greece) 156
Geōrgios III *Xēros* : 1175–1179 (Greece) 156
Geōrgios IV *Bourtzēs* : 1180 (Greece) 156
Geōrgios : 797–807 (Jerusalem — Greek) 185
Geōrgios I : unknown (Sinai) 230
Geōrgios II : 1130–1149 (Sinai) 231
Geraldus Odo *de Camboulit* : 1342–1348 (Antioch — Latin) 46
Geraldus : 1225–1239 (Jerusalem — Latin) 189
Gerardus *de Crussol* : 1471–1472 (Antioch — Latin) 46
Gerardus *de Langres* : 1295–1312? (Cyprus — Latin) 130
Gerasim : 1575? (Montenegro) 201

Gerasim *Sokolović* : 1575–1586 (Serbia) 227
Gerasimos I *Spartaliōtēs* : 1620–1636 (Alexandria — Greek) 25
Gerasimos II *Palidas* : 1688–1710 (Alexandria — Greek) 25
Gerasimos III *Gēmarēs Kaliklas* : 1783–1788 (Alexandria — Greek) 26
Gerasimos I : 1320–1321 (Constantinople — Greek) 112
Gerasimos II *apo Tornobou* : 1673–1674 (Constantinople — Greek) 115
Gerasimos III *apo Derkōn* : 1794–1797 (Constantinople — Greek) 116
Gerasimos I *apo Kissamou* : 1716–1719 (Crete) 125
Gerasimos II *Letitzēs Gerontas* : 1725–1755 (Crete) 125
Gerasimos III *apo Chiou* : 1756–1769 (Crete) 125
Gerasimos IV *Pardalēs* : 1800–1821 (Crete) 125
Gerasimos : 1127? (Greece) 156
Gerasimos : 1334?–1349 [antipatriarch] (Jerusalem — Greek) 186
Gerasimos *Propapas* : 1891–1896 (Jerusalem — Greek) 187
Gerbasios I : 1432? (Greece) 156
Gerbasios II : 1462? (Greece) 156
Gerillos I : unknown (Ethiopia — Official) 139
Gerlos —*see also*: Gerillos, Qerlos
Gerlos I : unknown (Ethiopia — Official) 139
German *Anđelić* : 1880–1882 [locum tenens], 1882–1888 (Austria — Karlovci) 80
German I : 972?–1000? (Bulgaria) 92
German II : 1688–1690, 1702–1703 (Bulgaria) 94
German I *of Voden* : 1688–1691, 1702–1703 (Macedonia) 196
German II : 1758–1759 (Macedonia) 197
German I : 1245? (Montenegro) 201
German II : 1520- (Montenegro) 201
German : 1563–1565 (Russia — Moscow) 220
German *Đorić* : 1958–1990 (Serbia) 193, 228
Germane : 1541–1547 (Georgia) 150
Germane : 1742–1754 (Georgia — Abkhazia) 153
Germaniōn : 213 (Jerusalem — Greek) 184
Germanos I : 715–730 (Constantinople — Greek) 111
Germanos II : 1223–1240 (Constantinople — Greek) 112

Germanos III : 1265–1266 (Constantinople — Greek) 112
Germanos IV *apo Derkōn* : 1842–1845, 1852–1853 (Constantinople — Greek) 117
Germanos V *Kabakopoulos* : 1913–1918 (Constantinople — Greek) 117
Germanos *Karabangelēs* [refused election] : 1921 (Constantinople — Greek) 117
Germanos I *Pēsimandros* : 1260?–1275? (Cyprus) 126, 128
Germanos II : 1695?–1705 (Cyprus) 128
Germanos I : -841 (Greece) 155
Germanos II *Kalligas* : 1889–1896 (Greece) 157
Germanos (I) : 1935–1937 [locum tenens] (Greece — Old Calendarists) 158–159
Germanos (II) *Barykopoulos* : 1937–1943 [locum tenens] (Greece — Old Calendarists) 159
Germanos *Peloponnesios* : 1537–1579 (Jerusalem — Greek) 187, 252
Germanos *Mamaladēs* : 1980–1981 [locum tenens] (Jerusalem — Greek) 187
Germanos I : 1177? (Sinai) 231
Germanos II : 1228? (Sinai) 231
Germanos III : 1333- (Sinai) 231
Germogen : 1606–1612 (Russia) 220
Germogen : 1942–1945 (Serbia — Croatia) 229
Gerontiĭ : 1472–1491 (Russia — Moscow) 220
Gervasius : 1215–1219 (Constantinople — Latin) 119
Ghazar : 1723? [locum tenens] (Aght'amar) 6
Ghazar : 4th cent. (Aghunie) 9
Ghazar : 1737–1748, 1748–1751 (Armenia) 68
Ghazar : 1545–1547 (Cilicia — Armenian Apostolic) 99
Ghazar : 1660–1663 (Constantinople — Armenian) 104
Ghedeon I : 1588–1591? (Austria — Cernovci) 77
Ghedeon II : 1701?–1708 (Austria — Cernovci) 78
Ghedeon *Nichitic* : 1783–1788 (Austria — Sibiu) 81
Ghelasie : unknown (Austria — Cernovci) 77
Ghelasie : 1376? (Austria — Sibiu) 80
Ghenadie I : 1579–1585 (Austria — Sibiu) 81
Ghenadie II : 1627–1640 (Austria — Sibiu) 81
Ghenadie III : 1659–1660 (Austria — Sibiu) 81

Ghenadie *Petrescu* : 1893–1896 (Romania) 207
Gheorghe I : 1552–1558 (Austria — Cernovci) 77
Gheorghe II *Moghila* : 1577–1588 (Austria — Cernovci) 77
Gheorghe : 1561?–1562 (Austria — Sibiu) 80
Gherasim *Adamovic* : 1789–1796 (Austria — Sibiu) 81
Gherasim *al Buzaului* : 1822 [locum tenens] (Romania) 207
Gherasim *Timus* : 1893, 1896 [locum tenens] (Romania) 207
Ghewond : 545–548 (Armenia) 65
Ghewond *Maksoutian* : 1910?–1914 [locum tenens] (Jerusalem — Armenian) 182
Ghewondios : 172–190 (Armenia) 64
Ghrighuriyus I *al-Sinaïtah* : 571–594 (Antioch — Greek) 36
Ghrighuriyus II : 610–620 (Antioch — Greek) 36
Ghrighuriyus III : 1483–1497 (Antioch — Greek) 37
Ghrighuriyus IV *Haddad* : 1906–1928 (Antioch — Greek) 34, 38
Ghrighuriyus I *al-Sinaïtah* : 570–593 (Antioch — Greek Melkite) 41
Ghrighuriyus II *Yusuf-Sayur* : 1864–1897 (Antioch — Greek Melkite) 44
Ghrighuriyus III *Laham* : 2000- (Antioch — Greek Melkite) 44, 253, 258–259
Ghrighuriyus I : unknown (Antioch — Maronite) 49
Ghrighuriyus II : unknown (Antioch — Maronite) 49
Ghrighuriyus III *of Halat* : 1130?–1141 (Antioch — Maronite) 49
Ghubriyal I : 909–920 (Alexandria — Coptic) 17
Ghubriyal II *ibn Turaik* : 1131–1145 (Alexandria — Coptic) 17
Ghubriyal III : 1268–1271 (Alexandria — Coptic) 17
Ghubriyal IV : 1370–1378 (Alexandria — Coptic) 17
Ghubriyal V : 1409–1427 (Alexandria — Coptic) 17
Ghubriyal VI : 1466–1475 (Alexandria — Coptic) 17
Ghubriyal VII : 1525–1568 (Alexandria — Coptic) 18
Ghubriyal VIII : 1586–1601 (Alexandria — Coptic) 18
Ghukas : 1780–1799 (Armenia) 68
Ghukas : 1733–1737 (Cilicia — Armenian Apostolic) 99

Gibelinus *of Arles* : 1107–1111 (Jerusalem — Latin) 188
Gilbertus *Borromeo* : 1711–1717 (Antioch — Latin) 47
Gillus *Caninio* : 1524–1530 (Constantinople — Latin) 120
Giorgi I : 677–678 (Georgia) 149
Giorgi II : 826–838 (Georgia) 149
Giorgi III : 1055–1065 (Georgia) 149
Giorgi IV : 1225–1230 (Georgia) 150
Giorgi V : 1380–1397 (Georgia) 150
Giorgi : 1681?– (Georgia — Abkhazia) 153
Giroldus : 1225–1239 (Jerusalem — Latin) 189
Giwargis I : 661–680 (Assyria), and 661–681? (Babylon) 73, 85
Giwargis II : 825–832 (Assyria), and 828–831? (Babylon) 73, 86
Giwargis 'Abdishu' V *Khayyat* : 1895–1899 (Babylon) 88
Giwt : 461–478 (Armenia) 65
Giyorgis I : 1102? (Ethiopia — Historical) 142
Giyorgis II : 1225 (Ethiopia — Historical) 143
Glicherie *Tanase* : 1924–1955 [first hierarch], 1957–1985 [metropolitan] (Romania — Old Calendarists) 208
Goctius *Battaglia* : 1335–1339 (Constantinople — Latin) 120
Gorazd II *Pavlík* : 1921–1942 (Czechoslovakia) 132–133
Gordios : 213 (Jerusalem — Greek) 184
Gormundus : 1118–1128 (Jerusalem — Latin) 188
Gotius *Battaglia* : 1335–1339 (Constantinople — Latin) 120
Grēgorios : 339–341 [anti-pope], 344–348 [anti-pope] (Alexandria — Greek) 23
Grēgorios I : 1243–1263 (Alexandria — Greek) 25
Grēgorios II : 1316–1354 (Alexandria — Greek) 25
Grēgorios III : 1354–1366 (Alexandria — Greek) 25
Grēgorios IV : 1398–1412 (Alexandria — Greek) 25
Grēgorios V : 1484–1486 (Alexandria — Greek) 25
Grēgorios I *Nazianzēnos Theologos* : 380–381 (Constantinople — Greek) 110
Grēgorios II *Kyprios* : 1283–1289 (Constantinople — Greek) 112
Grēgorios III *Mammas* : 1443–1451? (Constantinople — Greek) 113
Grēgorios IV *Straboamaseias* :

1623 (Constantinople — Greek) 114
Grēgorios V *Angelopoulos apo Smyrnēs* : 1797–1798, 1806–1808, 1818–1821 (Constantinople — Greek) 116
Grēgorios VI *Phortouniadēs apo Serrōn* : 1835–1840, 1867–1871 (Constantinople — Greek) 117
Grēgorios VII *Zerboudakēs* : 1923–1924 (Constantinople — Greek) 117
Grēgorios I : 570? (Cyprus) 127
Grēgorios II : 1254? (Cyprus) 128
Grēgorios I : 600? (Greece) 155
Grēgorios II : 780? (Greece) 155
Grēgorios III : 860–867 (Greece) 155
Grēgorios IV : 1799–1820 (Greece) 157
Grēgorios V *Argyrokastritēs apo Euripou* : 1827–1828 (Greece) 157
Gregorios I *Yakoub* : 1204–1215 (India — Malankara Orthodox) 165
Gregorios II *Bar Hebraeus* : 1266–1286 (India — Malankara Orthodox) 165
Gregorios III *Bar Sauma* : 1289–1308 (India — Malankara Orthodox) 165
Gregorios IV *Mathai* : 1317–1360 (India — Malankara Orthodox) 165
Gregorios (I), Mar : 1665–1672 (India — Malankara Syrian) 162
Gregorios (II), Mar : 1751–1772 (India — Malankara Syrian) 162
Gregorios bar Ebrayo : 1264–1286 (India — Malankara Jacobite) 169
Gregorios bar Kainaya : 1361? [anti-maphrian] (India — Malankara Jacobite) 169
Gregorios bar Souma : 1288–1308 (India — Malankara Jacobite) 169
Gregorios Lazar III : 1730–1742 (India — Malankara Jacobite) 169
Gregorios Mar Geevarghese : 1996–1999 [locum tenens] (India — Malankara Jacobite) 172
Gregorios Mathai I : 1317–1345 (India — Malankara Jacobite) 169
Gregorios Yakub : 1189–1214 (India — Malankara Jacobite) 169
Grēgorios I : -1298 (Jerusalem — Greek) 186
Grēgorios II : 1332 (Jerusalem — Greek) 186

Grēgorios III : 1468–1493 (Jerusalem — Greek) 187
Grēgorios *Hadgitophēs* : 1988–1993 [locum tenens] (Latvia) 191
Grēgorios : 1969–1973 (Sinai) 232
Gregorius *Mammas* : 1454?–1459 (Constantinople — Latin) 120
Gregorius I *Magnus "The Great"* : 590–604 (Rome) 212
Gregorius II : 715–731 (Rome) 212
Gregorius III : 731–741 (Rome) 212
Gregorius IV : 827–844 (Rome) 213
Gregorius V : 996–999 (Rome) 214
Gregorius VI : 1012 [anti-pope] (Rome) 214
Gregorius VI *Gratianus* : 1045–1046 (Rome) 214
Gregorius VII : 1073–1085 (Rome) 214
Gregorius VIII *Burdinus* : 1118–1121 [anti-pope] (Rome) 214
Gregorius VIII *de Morra* : 1187 (Rome) 215
Gregorius IX *di Segni* : 1227–1241 (Rome) 215
Gregorius X *Visconti* : 1271–1276 (Rome) 215
Gregorius XI *de Beaufort* : 1370–1378 (Rome) 215
Gregorius XII *Correr* : 1406–1415 (Rome) 215
Gregorius XIII *Boncompagni* : 1572–1585 (Rome) 216
Gregorius XIV *Sfondrati* : 1590–1591 (Rome) 216
Gregorius XV *Ludovisi* : 1621–1623 (Rome) 216
Gregorius XVI *Cappellari* : 1831–1846 (Rome) 217
Grigol — *see also*: Grigoli
Grigol I : 433–434 (Georgia) 148
Grigol II : 760–767 (Georgia) 149
Grigol III : 802–814 (Georgia) 149
Grigol I : 1612–1616? (Georgia — Abkhazia) 153
Grigoli — *see also*: Grigol
Grigoli II *Lortk'ifanidze* : 1706–1742 (Georgia — Abkhazia) 153
Grigor — *see also*: Grigoris
Grigor : 1140? (coadjutor) (Aght'amar) 5
Grigor IV *Gawahets'i* : 1707–1711 (Aght'amar) 6
Grigor V *Hizants'i* : 1725 (Aght'amar) 6
Grigor VI : 1751–1761 (Aght'amar) 7

Grigor III : 1441- (Aghunie) 10
Grigor IV : 1556–1563 (Aghunie) 10
Grigor V : 1634–1653 (Aghunie) 10
Grigor I *Lusaworich' "The Illuminator"* : 302–325 (Armenia) 63–64
Grigor II *Vkayasêr* : 1066–1105 (Armenia) 66
Grigor III *Pahlawuni* : 1113–1166 (Armenia) 66, 252
Grigor IV *Tghay* : 1173–1193 (Armenia) 66
Grigor V *K'aravêzh* : 1193–1194 (Armenia) 66
Grigor VI *Apirat* : 1194–1203 (Armenia) 66
Grigor VII : 1293–1307 (Armenia) 66
Grigor VIII *K'antsoghat* : 1411–1418 (Armenia) 67
Grigor IX *Musabêgiants'* : 1439–1441 (Armenia) 67, 98
Grigor X : 1536–1545 (Armenia) 67
Grigor XI : 1552–1576 [coadjutor], 1576–1590 [catholicos], (Armenia) 67
Grigor *Serapion* : 1603–1624 [coadjutor] (Armenia) 67
Grigor I *Musabêgiants'* : 1441–1451 (Cilicia — Armenian Apostolic) 98–99
Grigor II : 1686–1693? (Cilicia — Armenian Apostolic) 99
Grigor III : 1721?–1729 (Cilicia — Armenian Apostolic) 99
Grigor *Aleadjian* : 1895 [locum tenens] (Cilicia — Armenian Apostolic) 100
Grigor I : 1526–1537 (Constantinople — Armenian) 104
Grigor II : 1601–1608, 1611–1621, 1623–1626 (Constantinople — Armenian) 104
Grigor III *Pasmachian* : 1764–1773 (Constantinople — Armenian) 105
Grigor IV *Khamsets'i* : 1801–1802 (Constantinople — Armenian) 105
Grigor I *Ezekielian* : 669–696 (Jerusalem — Armenian) 179
Grigor II : 981–1006 (Jerusalem — Armenian) 180
Grigor III : 1356–1363 (Jerusalem — Armenian) 180
Grigor IV *of Egypt* : 1386–1391 (Jerusalem — Armenian) 180
Grigor V *Baron-Ter* : 1613–1645 (Jerusalem — Armenian) 181
Grigor VI : 1697–1704 [coadjutor] (Jerusalem — Armenian) 181
Grigor VII *"The Chain-Bearer"* : 1715–1749 (Jerusalem — Armenian) 181, 252

Grigor Petros V *Kupelian* : 1788–1812 (Cilicia — Armenian Catholic) 102
Grigor Petros VI *Jeranian* : 1815–1841 (Cilicia — Armenian Catholic) 102
Grigor Petros VIII *Astuatsaturian* : 1844–1866 (Cilicia — Armenian Catholic) 102
Grigor Petros XV *Aghajanian* : 1937–1962 (Cilicia — Armenian Catholic) 101–102
Grigorie : unknown (Austria — Cernovci) 77
Grigorie I : 1629–1636 (Romania) 206
Grigorie II : 1760–1787 (Romania) 207
Grigorie III *Socoteanu* : 1770–1771 [locum tenens] (Romania) 207
Grigorie IV *Dascălul* : 1823–1829, 1833–1834 (Romania) 207
Grigoriĭ I : -927 (Bulgaria) 92
Grigoriĭ II : 1317? (Bulgaria) 93
Grigoriĭ III : 1364?–1378? (Bulgaria) 93
Grigoriĭ IV : 1551- (Bulgaria) 94
Grigoriĭ V : 1675–1676, 1683–1688 (Bulgaria) 94
Grigoriĭ VI : 1691–1693 (Bulgaria) 94
Grigoriĭ *Chukov* : 1946–1947, 1949–1950 (Estonia) 137
Grigorij I : 1316? (Macedonia) 195
Grigorij II : 1348–1378 (Macedonia) 195
Grigorij III : 1553? (Macedonia) 195
Grigorij IV : 1669–1670 (Macedonia) 196
Grigorij V : 1683–1687, 1691–1693 (Macedonia) 196
Grigoris — *see also*: Grigor
Grigoris I : 1512–1544? (Aght'amar) 6
Grigoris II : 1544?–1586? (Aght'amar) 6
Grigoris III : 1586?–1612? (Aght'amar) 6
Grigoris I : 340–342 (Aghunie) 8
Grigoris II : 1139- (Aghunie) 10
Grigur *Partaya* : 605–608 (Assyria), and 605–609 (Babylon) 72, 85
Gualterus : 1214?- (Jerusalem — Latin) 189
Guido *Brunelli* : 1530? (Cyprus — Latin) 130
Guillelmus — *see also*: Willelmus
Guillelmus *de Chanac* : 1342–1348 (Alexandria — Latin) 27
Guillelmus I *de la Tour* : 1457?–1470 (Antioch — Latin) 46
Guillelmus II : 1471 (Antioch — Latin) 46
Guillelmus I *de Castello* : 1346–1361 (Constantinople — Latin) 120
Guillelmus II : 1379 (Constantinople — Latin) 120
Guillelmus *Gonème* : 1467- (Cyprus — Latin) 130
Guillelmus II : 1263–1270 (Jerusalem — Latin) 189
Guillelmus III : 1351- (Jerusalem — Latin) 189
Guillelmus IV : 1369–1374 (Jerusalem — Latin) 189

Habeeb I, Athanasius : 1528–1533 (India — Malankara Jacobite) 170
Habeeb II, Baseliōs : 1665–1674 (India — Malankara Jacobite) 171
Habib *al-Mazziyati*, Ighnatiyus : 1674–1686 [anti-patriarch] (Antioch — Syrian Catholic), and (Antioch — Syrian Orthodox) 56, 61
Hadaya, Pathros : 1597 (India — Malankara Jacobite) 170
Hakob — *see also*: Hakobus
Hakob : 1736 [anti-catholicos] (Aght'amar) 7
Hakob I *Guitnakan* : 1268–1286 (Armenia) 66
Hakob II : 1327–1341, 1355–1359 (Armenia) 66
Hakob III : 1404–1411 (Armenia) 67
Hakob IV : 1655–1680 (Armenia) 67
Hakob V : 1755–1759 [locum tenens], 1759–1763 (Armenia) 68
Hakob I : 1563–1573 (Constantinople — Armenian) 104
Hakob II *Nalian Zmarats'i* : 1741–1748, 1752–1764 (Constantinople — Armenian) 105
Hakob II *Nalian Zmarats'i* : 1749–1752 (Jerusalem — Armenian) 181
Hakob Petros II *Hovsêp'ian* : 1749–1753 (Cilicia — Armenian Catholic) 102
Hakob Petros VII *Holasian* : 1842–1843 (Cilicia — Armenian Catholic) 102
Hakob Petros IX *Bak'darian* : 1870–1880? [anti-catholicos] (Cilicia — Armenian Catholic) 102
Hakobus — *see also*: Hakob
Hakobus III *Serobian* : 1839–1840, 1848–1858 (Constantinople — Armenian) 105–106
Hakobus I : 1254–1281 (Jerusalem — Armenian) 180
Hariton : 1641–1646 (Macedonia) 196
Hariton : 1372–1380? (Romania) 206
Harut'iwn : 1816?–1823 (Aght'amar) 7
Harut'iwn *Vehapetian* : 1885–1888 (Constantinople — Armenian), and 1889–1910 (Jerusalem — Armenian) 106, 182
Havryïl I *Kremenets'kyĭ* : 1770–1783 (Ukraine) 237
Havryïl II *Bodoni-Banulesko* : 1799–1803 (Ukraine) 237
Havryïl : 1331? (Ukraine — Halych) 239
Hayrapet *P'aykhets'i* : 1705–1707 (Aght'amar) 6
Hedeon *Chetvertyns'kyĭ* : 1685–1690 (Ukraine) 237
Hefajst : 1265? (Macedonia) 195
Helias — *see also*: Elias
Helias II *de Nabinaux* : 1332–1342 (Cyprus — Latin) 130
Hemayag Petros XVII *Ghedighian* : 1976–1982 (Cilicia — Armenian Catholic) 102
Henricus *Cajétan* : 1585? (Alexandria — Latin) 28
Heorhiĭ I : 1062?–1073 (Ukraine) 235
Heorhiĭ II *Deliiev* : 1923–1926 (Ukraine) 238
Heraclius : 1180–1191 (Jerusalem — Latin) 189
Hēraklas : 232–247 (Alexandria — Greek) 23
Hērakleidēs : 90? [anti-archbishop] (Cyprus) 127
Herasym : 1433–1435 (Ukraine) 236
Hercules *Tassoni* : 1596–1597 (Constantinople — Latin) 121
Herman *Swaiko* : 2002- (America — Orthodox Church) 32, 253, 258–259
Herman *Aav* : 1922–1925 [assistant bishop], 1925–1960 [metropolitan] (Finland) 146, 252
Herman : 1918–1924 (Ukraine — Canada) 239
Hermōn : 300–314 (Jerusalem — Greek) 184
Hēsaïas : 1323–1332 (Constantinople — Greek) 112
Hēsaïas : 1209?–1218? (Cyprus) 128
Hidayat Allah, Ighnatiyus : 1597–1639 (Antioch — Syrian Orthodox) 61
Hieremias I *apo Sophias* : 1520–1522, 1523–1537, 1537–1546 (Constantinople — Greek) 114
Hieremias II *Tranos apo Larissēs* : 1572–1579, 1580–1584, 1589–1595 (Constantinople — Greek) 114, 218
Hieremias III *apo Kaisareias Kap*-

padokias : 1716–1726, 1732–1733 (Constantinople — Greek) 116
Hieremias IV *apo Mitylēnēs* : 1808 [locum tenens], 1809–1813 (Constantinople — Greek) 116
Hieremias : 983–1005 (Jerusalem — Greek) 185
Hieronymos *Kotsōnēs* : 1967–1973 (Greece) 154, 158
Hieronymus *Crispi* : 1740? (Alexandria — Latin) 28
Hieronymus *Lando* : 1474–1497 (Constantinople — Latin) 120
Hierotheos *Blachos* : 1924–1929 [locum tenens] (Albania) 12–13
Hierotheos I : 1825–1845 (Alexandria — Greek) 26
Hierotheos II *Staphylopatēs* : 1847–1858 (Alexandria — Greek) 26
Hierotheos : 1875–1882 (Jerusalem — Greek) 187
Hilariōn : 1218?–1220 [anti-archbishop] (Cyprus) 128
Hilariōn *Tzigalas* : 1674–1682 (Cyprus) 128
Hilarius : 461–468 (Rome) 211
Hinukh *Inwardaya*, Ighnatiyus : 1421–145 (Antioch — Syrian Orthodox — Tur Abhdin) 62
Hippolytus : 217–235 [anti-pope] (Rome) 210
Hirun : 107?–130? (Antioch — Greek Melkite), and 107–127 (Antioch — Syrian Orthodox) 40, 58
Hirus I : 100–127 (Antioch — Greek) 34
Hirus II : 151–169 (Antioch — Greek) 34
Hirus : 150?–170? (Antioch — Greek Melkite) 40
Honorius I : 625–638 (Rome) 212
Honorius II *Cadalus* : 1061–1072 [anti-pope] (Rome) 214
Honorius II : 1124–1130 (Rome) 214
Honorius III *Savelli* : 1216–1227 (Rome) 215
Honorius IV *Savelli* : 1285–1287 (Rome) 215
Honoriwos : 1315? (Ethiopia — Historical) 143
Hormisdas : 514–523 (Rome) 211
Hovab : 790–791 (Armenia) 65
Hovakim : 1461–1478 (Constantinople — Armenian) 103
Hovakim *of Kanaker* : 1775–1793 (Jerusalem — Armenian) 181
Hovhan — see also: Hovhannês
Hovhan IV : 892–901 (Aghunie) 9
Hovhannês — see also: Hovhan
Hovhannês : 1155? (coadjutor) (Aght'amar) 5

Hovhannês I : 1510–1512 (Aght'amar) 6
Hovhannês II *T'iwt'iwnji* : 1679–1681? (Aght'amar) 6
Hovhannês III *Kêtsuk* : 1699–1704 (Aght'amar) 6
Hovhannês IV *Hayots'-Zobets'i* : 1720 (Aght'amar) 6
Hovhannês V : 1791? [anticatholicos] (Aght'amar) 7
Hovhannês V *Shatakhets'i* : 1823–1843 (Aght'amar) 7
Hovhannês I : 400- (Aghunie) 9
Hovhannês II : 646–670 (Aghunie) 9
Hovhannês III : 797–822 (Aghunie) 9
Hovhannês V : 1103–1130 (Aghunie) 10
Hovhannês VI : 1195–1235 (Aghunie) 10
Hovhannês VII : 14th cent. (Aghunie) 10
Hovhannês VIII : 14th cent. (Aghunie) 10
Hovhannês IX : -1470 (Aghunie) 10
Hovhannês X : -1586 (Aghunie) 10
Hovhannês XI : 1633–1634 (Aghunie) 10
Hovhannês XII : 1763–1786 (Aghunie) 11
Hovhannês I *Mandakuni* : 478–490 (Armenia) 65
Hovhannês II : 557–574 (Armenia) 65
Hovhannês : 590–611 [anticatholicos] (Armenia) 65
Hovhannês III *Imastaser* : 717–728 (Armenia) 65
Hovhannês IV : 833–855 (Armenia) 66
Hovhannês V *Patmaban "The Historian"* : 898–929 (Armenia) 66
Hovhannês VI *Medzabaro* : 1203–1221 (Armenia) 66
Hovhannês VII *Ajakir* : 1474–1484 (Armenia) 67
Hovhannês : 1505–1506 [coadjutor] (Armenia) 67
Hovhannês : 1740- [anti-catholicos] (Armenia) 68
Hovhannês VIII : 1831–1842 (Armenia) 68
Hovhannês I : 1488–1489 (Cilicia — Armenian Apostolic) 99
Hovhannês II : 1489–1525 (Cilicia — Armenian Apostolic) 99
Hovhannês III : 1525–1539 (Cilicia — Armenian Apostolic) 99
Hovhannês IV : 1602–1621 (Cilicia — Armenian Apostolic) 99
Hovhannês V : 1705–1721 (Cilicia — Armenian Apostolic) 99
Hovhannês VI : 1729–1733 (Cilicia — Armenian Apostolic) 99

Hovhannês : 1831–1833 [coadjutor] (Cilicia — Armenian Apostolic) 100
Hovhannês I : 1573–1581 (Constantinople — Armenian) 104
Hovhannês II : 1590–1591 (Constantinople — Armenian) 104
Hovhannês III : 1600–1601, 1609–1611, 1621–1623, 1631–1636 (Constantinople — Armenian) 104
Hovhannês IV : 1652–1655 (Constantinople — Armenian) 104
Hovhannês V : 1663–1664, 1665–1667 (Constantinople — Armenian) 104
Hovhannês VI : 1674–1675 (Constantinople — Armenian) 104
Hovhannês VII : 1707–1708 (Constantinople — Armenian) 105
Hovhannês VIII : 1714–1715 (Constantinople — Armenian) 105
Hovhannês IX *Kolot* : 1715–1741 (Constantinople — Armenian) 105
Hovhannês X : 1781–1782 (Constantinople — Armenian) 105
Hovhannês XI *Zamach'erchian* : 1800–1801, 1802–1813 (Constantinople — Armenian) 105
Hovhannês XII *Arsharuni* : 1912–1913 (Constantinople — Armenian) 106
Hovhannês I : 730–758 (Jerusalem — Armenian) 179
Hovhannês II *of Garin* : 1230–1238 (Jerusalem — Armenian) 180
Hovhannês III *Joslin* : 1332–1341 (Jerusalem — Armenian) 180
Hovhannês IV : 1378–1386 (Jerusalem — Armenian) 180
Hovhannês V : 1431–1441 (Jerusalem — Armenian) 180
Hovhannês VI *of Egypt* : 1485–1491 (Jerusalem — Armenian) 181
Hovhannês VII : 1517–1522 (Jerusalem — Armenian) 181
Hovhannês VIII *of Amasia* : 1680–1681 (Jerusalem — Armenian) 181
Hovhannês IX *of Constantinople* : 1684–1697 (Jerusalem — Armenian) 181
Hovhannês X : 1707–1708 (Jerusalem — Armenian) 181
Hovhannês XI : 1714–1715 (Jerusalem — Armenian) 181
Hovhannês *of Kanaker* : 1775–1793 (Jerusalem — Armenian) 181
Hovhannês XII *Movsêsian of Zmurnia* : 1850–1860 (Jerusalem — Armenian) 182

Index of Primates

Hovhannês Petros XVIII *Gasparian* : 1982–1999 (Cilicia — Armenian Catholic) 102
Hovsêp' I : 745–762 (Aghunie) 9
Hovsêp' II : 849–874 (Aghunie) 9
Hovsêp' III : 1038? (Aghunie) 9
Hovsêp' I : 444–452 (Armenia) 65
Hovsêp' II *Karidj* : 795–806 (Armenia) 66
Hovsêp' : 1430? [anti-catholicos] (Armenia) 67
Hovsêp' *Arghutian* : 1800–1801 [unconsecrated] (Armenia) 68
Hristofor I : 1557–1559? (Austria — Sibiu) 80
Hristofor II : 1574–1579 (Austria — Sibiu) 81
Hrizostom *Vojinović* [locum tenens] : 1958 (Serbia) 228
Hryhoriĭ *Bolharyn* : 1458–1475 (Ukraine) 236
Hugo — *see also*: Ugo
Hugo I *de Pise* : 1251–1260 (Cyprus — Latin) 129
Hugolinus *de Malabranca* : 1371–1375? (Constantinople — Latin) 120
Humbertus *de Vienne* : 1351–1355 (Alexandria — Latin) 27
Humbertus *de Romanis* : 1262? (Jerusalem — Latin) 189
Husik I *Part'e* : 341–347 (Armenia) 64
Husik II : 373–377 (Armenia) 64
Hyginus : 136?–140? (Rome) 210
Hymenaios : 131–144 (Alexandria — Greek) 23
Hymenaios : 260–298 (Jerusalem — Greek) 184
Hypatios : 827? (Greece) 155

Iachint : 1359–1372 (Romania) 206
Iacob *Putneanul* : 1745–1750 (Austria — Cernovci) 78
Iacobus Juvenalis *des Ursins* : 1449–1457 (Antioch — Latin) 46
Iacobus I *d'Itri* : 1376–1378 (Constantinople — Latin) 120
Iacobus II *Sinibaldi* : 1843–1844? (Constantinople — Latin) 121
Iacobus III Gregorius *Gallo* : 1878–1881 (Constantinople — Latin) 122
Iacobus I *Benoît* : 1442 [locum tenens] (Cyprus — Latin) 130
Iacobus II *de Lusignan* : 1459 (Cyprus — Latin) 130
Iacobus I *Pantaléon* : 1255–1261 (Jerusalem — Latin) 189
Iacobus II *Beltritti* : 1965–1970 [coadjutor], 1970–1987 (Jerusalem — Latin) 189

Iakobi : 363–375 (Georgia) 148
Iakōbos I : 954–960 (Alexandria — Greek) 24
Iakōbos II *Pankōstas* : 1861–1865 (Alexandria — Greek) 26
Iakōbos *Kykysēs* : 1958–1996 (America — Greek) 30, 252
Iakōbos *apo Larissēs* : 1679–1682, 1685–1686, 1687–1688 (Constantinople — Greek) 115
Iakōbos I : 1691?–1692? (Cyprus) 128
Iakōbos II : 1709–1718 (Cyprus) 128
Iakōbos I *apo Mytilēnēs* : 1676–1686 (Greece) 157
Iakōbos II : 1713–1734 (Greece) 157
Iakōbos III *Babanatsos* : 1962 (Greece) 158
Iakōbos I *Adelphotheos* : 50?–62 (Jerusalem — Greek) 183
Iakōbos II : 1460? (Jerusalem — Greek) 187
IAkov *Proarkhiĭ* : 1265? (Bulgaria) 93
Ibrahim I : 962–963 (Antioch — Syrian Catholic) 55
Ibrahim II *ibn Gharib*, Ighnatiyus : 1381–1412 (Antioch — Syrian Catholic) 55
Ibrahim : 962–963 (Antioch — Syrian Orthodox) 60
Ibrahim *ibn Gharib*, Ighnatiyus : 1381–1412 [anti-patriarch] (Antioch — Syrian Orthodox) 61
IEfrem : 1055?–1061 (Ukraine) 235
Ieremia : 429–433 (Georgia) 148
Ieremiia : 1762–1763 (Bulgaria) 95
Ieremiia *Matveevich* : 1963–1969 (Russia-Novozybkov) 223
IEvgen *Bolkhovitinov* : 1822–1837 (Ukraine) 237
Ighnatiyus I : 68–100 (Antioch — Greek) 34, 52, 57
Ighnatiyus II : 1342–1353 (Antioch — Greek) 37
Ighnatiyus III *'Atiyah* : 1619–1634 (Antioch — Greek) 38
Ighnatiyus IV *Hazim* : 1979– (Antioch — Greek) 38, 253, 257, 259
Ighnatiyus I : 70?–107 (Antioch — Greek Melkite) 40, 52, 57
Ighnatiyus II : 1344?–1359? (Antioch — Greek Melkite) 43
Ighnatiyus III *'Atiyah* : 1620–1634 (Antioch — Greek Melkite) 43
Ighnatiyus IV *Sarruf* : 1812 (Antioch — Greek Melkite) 44
Ighnatiyus V *Qattan* : 1816–1833 (Antioch — Greek Melkite) 44
Ighnatiyus I : 68–107 (Antioch — Syrian Catholic) 52–53, 57

Ighnatiyus II : 878–883 (Antioch — Syrian Catholic) 54
Ighnatiyus III *Dawud* : 1222–1252 (Antioch — Syrian Catholic) 55
Ighnatiyus IV *Ishu'* : 1264–1283 (Antioch — Syrian Catholic) 55
Ighnatiyus V *ibn Wahib ibn Zakha* : 1293–1333 (Antioch — Syrian Catholic) 55
Ighnatiyus I Nurono : 68–107 (Antioch — Syrian Orthodox) 52, 57–58
Ighnatiyus II : 878–883 (Antioch — Syrian Orthodox) 59
Ighnatiyus III *Dawud* : 1222–1252 (Antioch — Syrian Orthodox) 60
Ighnatiyus IV *Ishu'* : 1264–1282 (Antioch — Syrian Orthodox) 60
Ighnatiyus *ibn Wahib ibn Zakha* : 1313–1333 [anti-patriarch] (Antioch — Syrian Orthodox) 61
Ighnatiyus 'Abd al-Ghani : 1597–1598 (Antioch — Syrian Catholic) 56
Ighnatiyus 'Abd Allah : 1520–1557 (Antioch — Syrian Catholic) 55
Ighnatiyus 'Abd Allah I : 1520–1557 (Antioch — Syrian Orthodox) 61
Ighnatiyus 'Abd Allah II *al-Saddi* : 1906–1915 (Antioch — Syrian Orthodox) 62, 161
Ighnatiyus 'Abd al-Masih I *al-Rawhi* : 1662–1686 (Antioch — Syrian Orthodox) 61
Ighnatiyus 'Abd al-Masih II : 1895–1905 (Antioch — Syrian Orthodox) 62, 161
Ighnatiyus Afram II *Rahmani* : 1898–1929 (Antioch — Syrian Catholic) 56
Ighnatiyus Afram *Barsum* : 1933–1957 (Antioch — Syrian Orthodox) 62, 161
Ighnatiyus Andrawus *Akhijan Murabbi* : 1662–1677 (Antioch — Syrian Catholic) 56
Ighnatiyus Antun I *Samhiri* : 1853–1864 (Antioch — Syrian Catholic) 56
Ighnatiyus Antun II *Huwayyik* : 1968–1998 (Antioch — Syrian Catholic) 56
Ighnatiyus 'Aziz *ibn Shabhta* : 1466–1488 (Antioch — Syrian Orthodox — Tur Abdin) 62
Ighnatiyus Bihnam I *Hajlaya* : 1412–1455 (Antioch — Syrian Catholic) 55, 61, 252
Ighnatiyus Bihnam II *Banni* : 1893–1897 (Antioch — Syrian Catholic) 56

Ighnatiyus Bihnam *Hajlaya* : 1412–1445 [anti-patriarch], 1445–1454 (Antioch — Syrian Orthodox) 55, 61, 252

Ighnatiyus Bilatus : 1591–1597 (Antioch — Syrian Catholic), and (Antioch — Syrian Orthodox) 56, 61

Ighnatiyus Butrus IV *Dawud* : 1577–1591 (Antioch — Syrian Catholic) 56

Ighnatiyus Butrus V : 1598–1639 (Antioch — Syrian Catholic) 56

Ighnatiyus Butrus VI *Shahbadin* : 1677–1702 (Antioch — Syrian Catholic) 56

Ighnatiyus Butrus VII *Jarwah* : 1820–1851 (Antioch — Syrian Catholic) 56

Ighnatiyus Butrus VIII *Abd al-Ahad* : 2001- (Antioch — Syrian Catholic) 56, 253, 258–259

Ighnatiyus Butrus IV *al-Ma'usili* : 1872–1894 (Antioch — Syrian Orthodox) 62, 161

Ighnatiyus Dawud : 1519–1520 (Antioch — Syrian Catholic) 55

Ighnatiyus Dawud I : 1517–1520 (Antioch — Syrian Orthodox) 61

Ighnatiyus Dawud II Shah *Butrus ibn Nur ad-Din* : 1576–1591 (Antioch — Syrian Orthodox) 62

Ighnatiyus Filibbus *Arkus* : 1866–1874 (Antioch — Syrian Catholic) 56

Ighnatiyus Filuksinus *Nimrud* : 1283–1292 (Antioch — Syrian Catholic) 55

Ighnatiyus Habib *al-Mazziyati* : 1674–1686 [anti-patriarch] (Antioch — Syrian Catholic), and (Antioch — Syrian Orthodox) 56, 61

Ighnatiyus Hidayat Allah : 1597–1639 (Antioch — Syrian Orthodox) 61

Ighnatiyus Hinukh *Inwardaya* : 1421–1445 (Antioch — Syrian Orthodox — Tur Abhdin) 62

Ighnatiyus Ibrahim II *ibn Gharib* : 1381–1412 (Antioch — Syrian Catholic), and 1381–1412 [anti-patriarch] (Antioch — Syrian Orthodox) 55, 61

Ighnatiyus Ilyas II *Ankaz* : 1838–1847 (Antioch — Syrian Orthodox) 62

Ighnatiyus Ilyas III *Shakar* : 1917–1932 (Antioch — Syrian Orthodox) 62

Ighnatiyus Ishaq II *Azar* : 1709–1723 (Antioch — Syrian Catholic) 56

Ighnatiyus Ishaq *Azar* : 1709–1723 (Antioch — Syrian Orthodox) 61

Ighnatiyus Ishu' I : 1509–1510 (Antioch — Syrian Catholic), and 1509–1512 (Antioch — Syrian Orthodox) 55, 61

Ighnatiyus Ishu' II *Qamah* : 1655–1661 (Antioch — Syrian Catholic), and 1659–1662 (Antioch — Syrian Orthodox) 56, 61

Ighnatiyus Ishu' I *ibn Muta* : 1390–1418? (Antioch — Syrian Orthodox — Tur Abhdin) 62

Ighnatiyus Ishu' II *Inwardaya* : 1455–1466 (Antioch — Syrian Orthodox — Tur Abhdin) 62

Ighnatiyus Isma'il *Yuhanna* : 1333–1365 [anti-patriarch] (Antioch — Syrian Orthodox) 61

Ighnatiyus Ismil *Yuhanna* : 1333–1366 (Antioch — Syrian Catholic) 55

Ighnatiyus Jibra'il *Tabbuni* : 1929–1968 (Antioch — Syrian Catholic) 56

Ighnatiyus Jirjis II : 1690–1709 (Antioch — Syrian Catholic) 56

Ighnatiyus Jirjis III : 1746–1768 (Antioch — Syrian Catholic) 56

Ighnatiyus Jirjis IV : 1768–1781 (Antioch — Syrian Catholic) 56

Ighnatiyus Jirjis V *Shilhut* : 1874–1891 (Antioch — Syrian Catholic) 56

Ighnatiyus Jirjis II : 1687–1708 (Antioch — Syrian Orthodox) 61

Ighnatiyus Jirjis III : 1745–1768 (Antioch — Syrian Orthodox) 61

Ighnatiyus Jirjis IV : 1768–1781 (Antioch — Syrian Orthodox) 62

Ighnatiyus Jirjis V *Sayyar* : 1819–1837 (Antioch — Syrian Orthodox) 62

Ighnatiyus Khalaf : 1455–1484 (Antioch — Syrian Catholic), and 1455–1483 (Antioch — Syrian Orthodox) 55, 61

Ighnatiyus Mas'ud I *Slakhaya* : 1418–1420 (Antioch — Syrian Orthodox — Tur Abhdin) 62

Ighnatiyus Mas'ud II : 1490?–1495 (Antioch — Syrian Orthodox — Tur Abhdin) 62

Ighnatiyus Matiyus *ibn 'Abd Allah* : 1782–1817 (Antioch — Syrian Orthodox) 62

Ighnatiyus Mikha'il III *Jarwah* : 1782–1800 (Antioch — Syrian Catholic) 52, 56

Ighnatiyus Mikha'il IV *Dahir* : 1802–1810 (Antioch — Syrian Catholic) 56

Ighnatiyus Musa *Dawud* : 1998–2001 (Antioch — Syrian Catholic) 56

Ighnatiyus Ni'mat Allah : 1557–1576 (Antioch — Syrian Catholic) and (Antioch — Syrian Orthodox) 56, 61

Ighnatiyus Nuh : 1494–1509 (Antioch — Syrian Catholic), and 1493–1509 (Antioch — Syrian Orthodox) 55, 61

Ighnatiyus Quma *ibn Gafil* : 1446–1455 (Antioch — Syrian Orthodox — Tur Abhdin) 62

Ighnatiyus Qustantinus (II) : 1312–1313 [anti-patriarch] (Antioch — Syrian Orthodox) 61

Ighnatiyus Sabbas *ibn Wahib* : 1364–1389 (Antioch — Syrian Orthodox — Tur Abhdin) 62

Ighnatiyus Shaba *Arbaya* : 1488- [anti-patriarch] (Antioch — Syrian Orthodox — Tur Abhdin) 62

Ighnatiyus Shihab : 1366–1381 [anti-patriarch] (Antioch — Syrian Catholic), and 1365–1381 (Antioch — Syrian Orthodox) 55, 61

Ighnatiyus Shim'un I *of Tur-Abdin* : 1640–1659 (Antioch — Syrian Catholic) and (Antioch — Syrian Orthodox) 56, 61

Ighnatiyus Shukr Allah I : 1640- (Antioch — Syrian Catholic) 56

Ighnatiyus Shukr Allah II : 1723–1745 (Antioch — Syrian Catholic) 56

Ighnatiyus Shukr Allah : 1722–1745 (Antioch — Syrian Orthodox) 61

Ighnatiyus Sim'an II *Hindi Zora* : 1811–1818 (Antioch — Syrian Catholic) 56

Ighnatiyus Ya'qub : 1510–1519 (Antioch — Syrian Catholic) 55

Ighnatiyus Ya'qub I : 1509–1512 (Antioch — Syrian Orthodox) 61

Ighnatiyus Ya'qub II : 1847–1871 (Antioch — Syrian Orthodox) 62

Ighnatiyus Ya'qub III *Tuma* : 1957–1980 (Antioch — Syrian Orthodox) 62

Ighnatiyus Yuhanna XVIII *Akhsinaya Bar Shilla* : 1484–1494 (Antioch — Syrian Catholic) 55

Ighnatiyus Yuhanna XIII *Akhsi-*

naya Bar Shilla : 1483–1493 (Antioch — Syrian Orthodox) 61

Ighnatiyus Yuhanna *ibn Qufar* : 1488–1493 (Antioch — Syrian Orthodox — Tur Abhdin) 62

Ighnatiyus Yunan : 1818–1819 (Antioch — Syrian Orthodox) 62

Ighnatiyus Zakka *'Iwas* : 1980- (Antioch — Syrian Orthodox) 62, 253, 257, 259

Ignatie I : 1653–1655 (Romania) 206

Ignatie II : 1810–1812 (Romania) 207

Ignatiĭ I : 1272?–1277? (Bulgaria) 93

Ignatiĭ II : 1660–1662 (Bulgaria) 94

Ignatiĭ III : 1673–1675? (Bulgaria) 94

Ignatiĭ IV : 1693–1695 (Bulgaria) 94

Ignatiĭ : 1605–1606 [anti-patriarch] (Russia) 220

Ignatij I : 1659, 1659–1662 (Macedonia) 196

Ignatij II : 1673? (Macedonia) 196

Ignatij III : 1693–1695, 1703?– (Macedonia) 196

Ignatios *Gagmachian* : 1869 (Constantinople — Armenian) 106

Ignatios *Rhangabē* : 847–858, 867–877 (Constantinople — Greek) 107, 111

Ignatios : 1381? [locum tenens] (Crete) 124

Ignatios : 1634- [anti-archbishop] (Cyprus) 128

Ignatios I *Barkiki* : 997–1022 (India — Malankara Orthodox) 164

Ignatios II *Lo Asar* : 1143–1164 (India — Malankara Orthodox) 165

Ignatios III *David* : 1215–1222 (India — Malankara Orthodox) 165

Ignatios IV *Sleeba of Edessa* : 1253–1258 (India — Malankara Orthodox) 165

Ignatios Mar Nuh *of Homs* : 1490–1494 (India — Malankara Orthodox) 166

Ignatios Petros XVI *Batanian* : 1962–1976 (Cilicia — Armenian Catholic) 102

Ignatius bar Keekke : 991–1016 (India — Malankara Jacobite) 169

Ignatius David II : 1215–1222 (India — Malankara Jacobite) 169

Ignatius Lazar I : 1142?–1164 (India — Malankara Jacobite) 169

Ignatius Sleeba III : 1222–1231 (India — Malankara Jacobite) 169

Ihor *Isichenko* : 2000 [locum tenens] (Ukraine — Autocephalous) 238

Iierofei *Malyts'kyĭ* : 1796–1799 (Ukraine) 237

Ijeronim *Ekzemplarskij* : 1898–1905 (Poland) 204

Ilarijon — SEE: Ilarion

Ilarion : -1838 (Bulgaria) 95

Ilarion : 1870–1872 [refused election] (Bulgaria) 91, 95

Ilarion I : 1220–1242 (Montenegro) 201

Ilari(j)on II *Roganović* : 1860–1863 [locum tenens], 1863–1882 [metropolitan] (Montenegro) 202

Ilarion I : 1487?–1502? (Romania) 206

Ilarion II : 1523–1526? (Romania) 206

Ilarion : 1833–1840 [locum tenens] (Romania) 207

Ilarion : 1051–1055? (Ukraine) 235

Ilarion *Ohiĭenko* : 1951–1972 (Ukraine — Canada) 240

Ilia —*see also:* Elia

Ilia II *Shiolashvili* : 1977 [locum tenens], 1977- (Georgia) 148, 152, 255, 257, 259

Ilie *Iorest* : 1640–1643 (Austria — Sibiu) 81

Iliia *Kucha* : 1577–1579 (Ukraine) 236

Ilisha' : 524–538 (Assyria), and 524–537? (Babylon) 72, 85

Iliya I : 1028–1049 (Assyria) 74

Iliya II *bar Mulki* : 1111–1132 (Assyria) 74

Iliya III *Abu Khalim* : 1176–1190 (Assyria) 74

Iliya IV : 1407–1420 (Assyria) 74

Iliya V : 1491–1504 (Assyria) 74

Iliya I : 1028–1049 (Babylon) 87

Iliya II *bar Mulki* : 1111–1132 (Babylon) 87

Iliya III *Abu Khalim* : 1176–1190 (Babylon) 87

Iliya IV : -1437 (Babylon) 87

Iliya V : 1502–1503 (Babylon) 87

Iliya VI *bar Mama* : 1558–1576 (Babylon) 70, 87

Iliya VII *bar Mama*, Shim'un : 1576–1591 (Babylon) 87

Iliya VIII *bar Mama* : 1591–1617 (Babylon) 87

Iliya IX *bar Mama*, Shim'un : 1617–1660 (Babylon) 87

Iliya X *bar Mama*, Yukhannan : 1660–1700 (Babylon) 87

Iliya XI *bar Mama*, Marugin : 1700–1722 (Babylon) 87

Iliya XII *bar Mama*, Dinkha : 1722–1778 (Babylon) 87, 251–252

Iliya XIII *bar Mama*, Ishu'yabh : 1778–1804 (Babylon) 83, 87

Iliya XIV *Abulyunan*, Pitrus : 1879–1894 (Babylon) 88

Iliya Shim'un XII : 1600–1653 (Assyria) 74

Ilyas —*see also*: Ayliya

Ilyas I : 840–852 (Antioch — Greek) 36

Ilyas II : 1003–1010 (Antioch — Greek) 36

Ilyas III : 1182–1184 (Antioch — Greek) 37

Ilyas IV *Muawad* : 1970–1979 (Antioch — Greek) 34, 38

Ilyas *Kurban* : 1979 [locum tenens] (Antioch — Greek) 38

Ilyas I : 907–934 (Antioch — Greek Melkite) 41

Ilyas II : 1031–1032 (Antioch — Greek Melkite) 42

Ilyas Butrus *al-Huwayyik* : 1899–1931 (Antioch — Maronite) 51

Ilyas II *Ankaz*, Ighnatiyus : 1838–1847 (Antioch — Syrian Orthodox) 62

Ilyas III *Shakar*, Ighnatiyus : 1917–1932 (Antioch — Syrian Orthodox) 62

Immih, Mari : 647–650 (Assyria), and 647–650 (Babylon) 72, 85

Indriyas : 1841 (Ethiopia — Historical) 144

Innocentius I : 401–417 (Rome) 211

Innocentius II *Papareschi* : 1130–1143 (Rome) 214

Innocentius III : 1179–1180 [antipope] (Rome) 215

Innocentius III *di Segni* : 1198–1216 (Rome) 27, 215

Innocentius IV *Fieschi* : 1243–1254 (Rome) 215

Innocentius V *de Tarentaise* : 1276 (Rome) 215

Innocentius VI *Aubert* : 1352–1362 (Rome) 215

Innocentius VII *de' Migliorati* : 1404–1406 (Rome) 215

Innocentius VIII *Cibò* : 1484–1492 (Rome) 216

Innocentius IX *Facchinetti* : 1591 (Rome) 216

Innocentius X *Pamphili* : 1644–1655 (Rome) 216

Innocentius XI *Odescalchi* : 1676–1689 (Rome) 83, 216

Innocentius XII *Pignatelli* : 1691–1700 (Rome) 216

Innocentius XIII *dei Conti* : 1721–1724 (Rome) 216

Innokentiĭ *Veniaminov* : 1840–1858 (America — Orthodox Church) 31

Innokentiĭ *Beliaev* : 1909–1913 [exarch] (Georgia) 152

Innokentiĭ *Vasil'ev* : 1999–2000 [locum tenens] (Japan) 178

Innokentiĭ *Veniaminov* : 1868–1879 (Russia — Moscow) 221

Inochentie *Moisiu* : 1886 [locum tenens] (Romania) 207

Inokentije *Pavlović* : 1898–1905 (Serbia — Beograd) 228

Iōakeim I *Panu* : -1567 (Alexandria — Greek) 25, 251

Iōakeim II *Kos* : 1665?–1671 (Alexandria — Greek) 25

Iōakeim I : 1498–1502, 1504 (Constantinople — Greek) 113–114

Iōakeim II *Kokkōdēs apo Kyzikou* : 1860–1863, 1873–1878 (Constantinople — Greek) 117

Iōakeim III *Debetzēs* : 1878–1884, 1901–1912 (Constantinople — Greek) 117

Iōakeim IV *apo Chiou* : 1884–1886 (Constantinople — Greek) 117

Iōakeim : 1821–1824 (Cyprus) 129

Iōakeim : 1431- (Jerusalem — Greek) 186

Ioakim I : 1233?–1246 (Bulgaria) 93

Ioakim II : -1272 (Bulgaria) 93

Ioakim III : 1291–1300 (Bulgaria) 93

Ioakim IV : 1590–1593 (Bulgaria) 94

Ioakim *Savelov* : 1674–1690 (Russia) 221

Ioakime : 1455–1474 (Georgia — Abkhazia) 153

Ioan — *see also*: Ioane

Ioan : 1605–1608 (Austria — Cernovci) 78

Ioan I : 1456? (Austria — Sibiu) 80

Ioan II : 1553–1557? (Austria — Sibiu) 80

Ioan III : 1585–1605? (Austria — Sibiu) 81

Ioan *Tirca* : 1706?–1707 (Austria — Sibiu) 81

Ioan IV *Gheorghievic* : 1768–1769 (Austria — Sibiu) 81

Ioan *Popovic* : 1774–1784, 1788–1789, 1796–1805 [locum tenens] (Austria — Sibiu) 81

Ioan *Popasu* : 1874 [unconsecrated] (Austria — Sibiu) 82

Ioan V *Metianu* : 1898–1916 (Austria — Sibiu) 82

Ioan *Papp* : 1918–1920 [locum tenens] (Austria — Sibiu) 82

Ioan I : 1018–1037 (Bulgaria) 92

Ioan II *Lakapin* : 1065–1078? (Bulgaria) 92

Ioan III *Ainos* : 1079?–1084 (Bulgaria) 92

Ioan IV *Komnin* : 1143?–1157? (Bulgaria) 92

Ioan V *Kamatir* : 1183?–1215? (Bulgaria) 93

Ioan II : 610–619 (Georgia) 149

Ioane — *see also*: Ioan

Ioane I : 335–363 (Georgia) 148

Ioane III : 744–760 (Georgia) 149

Ioane IV : 1100–1142 (Georgia) 150, 252

Ioane V : 1208–1210 (Georgia) 150

Ioane VI *Avaliashvili* : 1610–1613 (Georgia) 151

Ioane VII *Diasamidze* : 1688–1691, 1696–1700 (Georgia) 151

Ioane : 1455–1474 (Georgia — Abkhazia) 153

Ioanichie : 1472–1504 (Austria — Cernovci) 77

Ioanichie : 1479? (Austria — Sibiu) 80

Ioanikiĭ I : 1240? (Bulgaria) 93

Ioanikiĭ II : 1340? (Bulgaria) 93

Ioanikiĭ III : 1370? (Bulgaria) 93

Ioanikiĭ *Rydniev* : 1891–1900 (Ukraine) 237

Ioann *Mitropolskiĭ* : 1870–1877 (America — Orthodox Church) 31

Ioann *Alekseev* : 1958–1961 (Estonia) 137

Ioann *Smirnov* : 1910–1918 (Latvia) 191

Ioann *Kartushin* : 1898–1915 (Russia — Belokrinitsia) 223

Ioann *Vitushkin* : 2004, 2005- [locum tenens] (Russia — Belokrinitsia) 223

Ioann *Kalinin* : 1944–1955 (Russia — Novozybkov) 223

Ioann I : 1008–1038 (Ukraine) 235, 252

Ioann II : 1077?–1089 (Ukraine) 235

Ioann III : 1090–1091 (Ukraine) 235

Ioann IV : 1163–1166 (Ukraine) 235

Ioann V *Sokolov* : 1944–1964 (Ukraine) 238

Ioann *Teodorovych* : 1924–1947 (Ukraine — Canada), and 1924–1971 (Ukraine — Church of the USA) 240

Iōannēs III : 567- (Alexandria — Coptic — Gaianite) 19

Iōannēs I *Talaïas* : 477, 482 (Alexandria — Greek) 23

Iōannēs II : 496–505 (Alexandria — Greek) 23

Iōannēs III : 505–516 (Alexandria — Greek) 23

Iōannēs IV *Theopeithēs* : 570–580 (Alexandria — Greek) 24

Iōannēs V *Eleēmōn* : 610–621 (Alexandria — Greek) 24

Iōannēs VI : 670? (Alexandria — Greek) 24

Iōannēs VII *Kōdōnatos* : 1062–1100 (Alexandria — Greek) 25

Ioannes I *de Aragón* : 1328–1334 (Alexandria — Latin) 27

Ioannes II *de Cardaillac* : 1372- (Alexandria — Latin) 27

Ioannes III *Vitelleschi* : 1435? (Alexandria — Latin) 27

Ioannes IV *d'Harcourt* : 1451? (Alexandria — Latin) 27

Ioannes I *de Maguellone* : 1408- (Antioch — Latin) 46

Ioannes II *de Vico* : 1410? (Antioch — Latin) 46

Ioannes III *de Ribera* : 1568–1611 (Antioch — Latin) 46

Ioannes IV Baptistus *Pamfili* : 1626?–1629 (Antioch — Latin) 46

Ioannes V Franciscus Guidus *di Bagno dei Talenti* : 1795–1796 (Antioch — Latin) 47

Iōannēs I *Chrysostomos* : 398–404 (Constantinople — Greek) 110

Iōannēs II *Kappadokēs* : 518–520 (Constantinople — Greek) 110

Iōannēs III *Scholastikos* : 565–577 (Constantinople — Greek) 110

Iōannēs IV *Nēsteutēs* : 582–595 (Constantinople — Greek) 110

Iōannēs V : 669–675 (Constantinople — Greek) 110

Iōannēs VI : 712–715 (Constantinople — Greek) 111

Iōannēs VII *Grammatikos Pankratiou* : 837?–843 (Constantinople — Greek) 111

Iōannēs VIII *Xiphilinos* : 1064–1075 (Constantinople — Greek) 112

Iōannēs IX *Agapētos Hieromnēmōn* : 1111–1134 (Constantinople — Greek) 112

Iōannēs X *Kamatēros* : 1198–1206 (Constantinople — Greek) 112

Iōannēs XI *Bekkos* : 1275–1282 (Constantinople — Greek) 112

Iōannēs XII *Kosmas* : 1294–1303 (Constantinople — Greek) 112

Iōannēs XIII *Glykys* : 1315–1319 (Constantinople — Greek) 112

Iōannēs XIV *Kalekas* : 1334–1347 (Constantinople — Greek) 112

Ioannes I *Halegrin* : 1226 [unconsecrated] (Constantinople — Latin) 119

Ioannes II *Contarini* : 1409- , 1424- (Constantinople — Latin) 120

Ioannes III *de la Rochetaillée* :

1412–1423 (Constantinople — Latin) 120
Ioannes IV *Michele* : 1497–1503 (Constantinople — Latin) 120
Ioannes V *Borgia* : 1503 (Constantinople — Latin) 120
Ioannes VI Iacobus *Panciroli* : 1641–1643 (Constantinople — Latin) 121
Ioannes VII Baptistus *Spada* : 1643–1658 (Constantinople — Latin) 121
Ioannes VIII *de la Puebla* : 1771–1779 (Constantinople — Latin) 121
Ioannes IX *Soglia-Ceroni* : 1835–1839 (Constantinople — Latin) 121
Ioannes X Ludovicus *Canali* : 1845–1851 (Constantinople — Latin) 122
Ioannes XI Baptistus *Casali del Drago* : 1895–1899 (Constantinople — Latin) 122
Iōannēs I : 597? (Crete) 123
Iōannēs II : 10th cent. (Crete) 124
Iōannēs III : 1106? (Crete) 124
Iōannēs IV : 1166–1177 (Crete) 124
Iōannēs I : 691? (Cyprus) 127
Iōannēs II *Krētikos* : 1151?–1174 (Cyprus) 128
Ioannes I *d'Ancone* : 1288–1295 (Cyprus — Latin) 130
Ioannes II *de Polo* : 1312–1332 (Cyprus — Latin) 130
Ioannes III : 1400? (Cyprus — Latin) 130
Ioannes IV Franciscus *Brusato* : 1464? (Cyprus — Latin) 130
Iōannēs I : 550? (Greece) 155
Iōannēs II : 680? (Greece) 155
Iōannēs III : 704–714 (Greece) 155
Iōannēs IV : 810–819 (Greece) 155
Iōannēs V *Blachernitēs* : 1069–1087 (Greece) 155
Iōannēs VI : 1180–1181 (Greece) 156
Iōannēs I : 2nd cent. (Jerusalem — Greek) 184
Iōannēs II : 386–417 (Jerusalem — Greek) 184
Iōannēs III : 516–524 (Jerusalem — Greek) 185
Iōannēs IV : 575–594 (Jerusalem — Greek) 185
Iōannēs V : 706–735 (Jerusalem — Greek) 185
Iōannēs VI : 838–842 (Jerusalem — Greek) 185
Iōannēs VII : 964–966 (Jerusalem — Greek) 185
Iōannēs VIII *Chrysostomitēs Merkouropōlos* : 1106- (Jerusalem — Greek) 186

Iōannēs IX : 1156–1166 (Jerusalem — Greek) 186
Ioannes *de Vercellis* : 1278- (Jerusalem — Latin) 189
Ioannes I : 523–526 (Rome) 211
Ioannes II : 533–535 (Rome) 212
Ioannes III : 561–574 (Rome) 212
Ioannes IV : 640–642 (Rome) 212
Ioannes V : 685–686 (Rome) 212
Ioannes VI : 701–705 (Rome) 212
Ioannes VII : 705–707 (Rome) 212
Ioannes VIII : 844 [anti-pope] (Rome) 213
Ioannes VIII : 872–882 (Rome) 213
Ioannes IX : 898–900 (Rome) 213
Ioannes X : 914–928 (Rome) 213
Ioannes XI : 931–935 (Rome) 213
Ioannes XII : 955–964 (Rome) 213
Ioannes XIII : 965–972 (Rome) 213
Ioannes XIV *Canepanova* : 983–984 (Rome) 213
Ioannes XV : 985–996 (Rome) 213
Ioannes XVI *Philagathos* : 997–998 [anti-pope] (Rome) 214
Ioannes XVII *Sicco* : 1003 (Rome) 214
Ioannes XVIII *Fasanus* : 1004–1009 (Rome) 214
Ioannes XIX : 1024–1032 (Rome) 214
Ioannes XX [there is no pope of this name] (Rome)
Ioannes XXI *Julião* : 1276–1277 (Rome) 215
Ioannes XXII *Duèse* : 1316–1334 (Rome) 215
Ioannes XXIII *Cossa* : 1410–1415 [anti-pope] (Rome) 216
Ioannes XXIII *Roncalli* : 1958–1963 (Rome) 217, 251
Iōannēs I *Athēnaios* : 1081–1091 (Sinai) 231
Iōannēs II : 1164? (Sinai) 231
Iōannēs III : 1265–1290 (Sinai) 231
Iōannēs IV : 1299?– (Sinai) 231
Ioannes Paulus I *Luciani* : 1978 (Rome) 217
Ioannes Paulus II *Wojtyła* : 1978–2005 (Rome) 70, 217
Ioannikiĭ *Rudnev* : 1877–1882 [exarch] (Georgia), and 1882–1891 (Russia — Moscow) 151, 221
Iōannikios *Diodios Berrhoias* : 1645–1664 (Alexandria — Greek) 25

Iōannikios I *apo Sōzopoleōs* : 1522–1523 (Constantinople — Greek) 114
Iōannikios II *Lindios apo Hērakleias* : 1646–1648, 1651–1652, 1653–1654, 1655–1656 (Constantinople — Greek) 115
Iōannikios III *Karatzas apo Chalkēdonos* : 1761–1763 (Constantinople — Greek) 116
Iōannikios *Xephloudēs Zagorēsios* : 1856–1858 (Crete) 125
Iōannikios : 1783 [anti-archbishop] (Cyprus) 129
Iōannikios : 1840–1849 (Cyprus) 129
Iōannikios : 1020–1040 (Jerusalem — Greek) 186
Iōannikios I *Laskaris* : 1671–1702 (Sinai) 232
Iōannikios II *Lesbios* : 1721–1728 (Sinai) 232
Ioaquim Fernandus *Puerto Carrero* : 1735–1743 (Antioch — Latin) 47
Ioasaf *Bolotov* : 1798–1799 (America — Orthodox Church) 31
Ioasaf : 1682–1683 (Austria — Sibiu) 81
Ioasaf I : 1628? (Bulgaria) 94
Ioasaf II : 1719–1745 (Bulgaria) 95
Ioasaf I : 1634–1641 (Russia) 220
Ioasaf II : 1667–1672 (Russia) 220
Ioasaf I *Krakovs'kyĭ* : 1708–1718 (Ukraine) 237
Ioasaf II *Leliukhin* : 1964–1966 (Ukraine) 238
Iōasaph I *Kokkas* : 1464–1466? (Constantinople — Greek) 113
Iōasaph II *Megaloprepēs apo Adrianoupoleōs* : 1555–1565 (Constantinople — Greek) 114
Iōasaph : 1702–1710? (Crete) 125
Iōasaph *apo Rhodou* : 1617–1660 (Sinai) 232
Iōb : 954–960 (Alexandria — Greek) 24
Iōb : 1395? (Sinai) 231
Iobi : 375–390 (Georgia) 148
Iona : 425–429 (Georgia) 148
Iona *Vasil'evskiĭ* : 1821–1832 [exarch] (Georgia) 151
Iona : 1448–1462 (Russia — Moscow) 220
Iona I *Odnoüshev* : 1442?–1461 (Ukraine) 236
Iona II *Hlezna* : 1492–1494 (Ukraine) 236
Iona III : 1503–1507 (Ukraine) 236
Iona IV *Protachevych-Ostrovs'kiĭ* : 1568–1577 (Ukraine) 236
Ionafan *Kopolovich* : 1972–1986 (Moldova) 198

Iordanus *de' Caetani* : 1485- (Antioch — Latin) 46
Iorest : 1651?–1656 (Austria — Cernovci) 78
Iōrios : 1035- (Sinai) 231
Iosaf *Kałłistow* : 1915–1918 (Poland) 204
Iosebi *Jandieri* : 1755–1764 (Georgia) 151
Iosebi *Bagrationi* : 1767–1776 (Georgia — Abkhazia) 153
Iōsēph I *Galesiōtēs* : 1266–1275, 1282–1283 (Constantinople — Greek) 112
Iōsēph II *apo Ephesou* : 1416–1439 (Constantinople — Greek) 113
Iōsēph I : unknown (Jerusalem — Greek) 184
Iōsēph II : 980–983 (Jerusalem — Greek) 185
Iosephus Antonius *Davanzati* : 1746? (Alexandria — Latin) 28
Iosephus Melchiades *Ferlisi* : 1858–1860 (Antioch — Latin) 47
Iosephus I *della Porta Rodiani* : 1823–1835 (Constantinople — Latin) 121
Iosephus II Melchiades *Ferlisi* : 1860–1865 (Constantinople — Latin) 122
Iosephus III *Capetelli* : 1903–1917 (Constantinople — Latin) 122
Iosephus *Valerga* : 1847–1872 (Jerusalem — Latin) 189
Iosif : unknown (Austria — Cernovci) 77
Iosif *Budal* : 1680–1682 (Austria — Sibiu) 81
Iosif I : 870–878? (Bulgaria) 92
Iosif II : 1746–1751 (Bulgaria) 95
Iosif : 1877–1915 [exarch] (Bulgaria) 91, 95
Iosif I : 1464–1477? (Romania) 206
Iosif *al Argeşului* : 1812 [locum tenens] (Romania) 207
Iosif II *Gheorghian* : 1886–1893, 1896–1908 (Romania) 207
Iosif *Naniescu* : 1896 [locum tenens] (Romania) 207
Iosif : 1642–1652 (Russia) 220
Iosif *Petrovykh* : 1926 [deputy locum tenens] (Russia) 222
Iosif *Morzhakov* : 1961–1970 (Russia — Belokrinitsia) 223
Iosif *Volchanskiĭ* : 1742–1745 (Russia — Moscow) 221
Iosyp I : 1236?–1240? (Ukraine) 236
Iosyp II *Bolharynovych* : 1498–1501 (Ukraine) 236
Iosyp III *Soltan* : 1508–1521 (Ukraine) 236
Iosyp IV : 1522–1534 (Ukraine) 236
Iosyp V *Neliubovych-Tukal's'kyĭ* : 1663–1675 (Ukraine) 237

Iosyp *Zuk* : 1928–1934 (Ukraine — America and Canada) 241
Ioubenalios : 422–458 (Jerusalem — Greek) 185
Ioudas I : 107?–111 (Jerusalem — Greek) 184
Ioudas II : -134 (Jerusalem — Greek) 184
Ioulianos : 179–189 (Alexandria — Greek) 23
Ioulianos I : 2nd cent. (Jerusalem — Greek) 184
Ioulianos II : 2nd cent. (Jerusalem — Greek) 184
Ioustos : 121–131 (Alexandria — Greek) 23
Ioustos I : 107?–111 (Jerusalem — Greek) 184
Ioustos II : 2nd cent. (Jerusalem — Greek) 184
Iov *Tirca* : 1706?–1707 (Austria — Sibiu) 81
Iov : 1587–1589 [metropolitan], 1589–1605 [patriarch] (Russia) 218, 220
Iov *Borisov* : 1871–1912 (Russia?Belokrinitsia) 223
Iov *Bortes'kiĭ* : 1620–1631 (Ukraine) 237
Iovel I : 448–452 (Georgia) 148
Ioveli II : 668–670 (Georgia) 149
Irenaeus, Joseph Mar : [suffragan] (India — Mar Thoma Syrian) 173
Ireney *Bekish* : 1953–1960 (Japan), and 1965 [locum tenens], 1965–1977 [metropolitan] (America — Orthodox Church) 32, 178
Irinarkh *Popov* : 1836–1841 (Latvia) 191
Irinarkh *Parfenov* : 1940–1952 (Russia — Belokrinitsia) 223
Irun : 107–127 (Antioch — Syrian Catholic) 53
Irus : 154–170 (Antioch — Syrian Catholic) 53
Isaak : 941–954 (Alexandria — Greek) 24
Isaak : 1630 (Constantinople — Greek) 114
Isaakios : 601–609 (Jerusalem — Greek) 185
Isaaq : 686–689 (Alexandria — Coptic) 16
Isaaq : 755–756 [anti-patriarch] (Antioch — Syrian Orthodox) 59
Isaia I : 1564?–1577 (Austria — Cernovci) 77
Isaia II *Baloşescu* : 1823–1834 (Austria — Cernovci) 78
Isaiia *Kopyns'kiĭ* : 1631–1640 (Ukraine) 237
Isaija I *Đaković* : 1708 (Austria — Karlovci) 79

Isaija II *Antonović* : 1748–1749 (Austria — Karlovci) 79
Ishai Shim'un XXIII : 1920–1975 (Assyria) 70, 75, 251–252
Ishai Ya'qub *Zaya*, Niqula : 1838–1847 (Babylon) 88
Ishaq *Ghattas* : 1955–1958 [coadjutor] (Alexandria — Coptic Catholic) 21
Ishaq : unknown (Antioch — Maronite) 49
Ishaq I : 755–756 (Antioch — Syrian Catholic) 54
Ishaq II *Azar*, Ighnatiyus : 1709–1723 (Antioch — Syrian Catholic) 56
Ishaq *Azar*, Ighnatiyus : 1709–1723 (Antioch — Syrian Orthodox) 61
Ishaq I : 1210?– (Ethiopia — Historical), and unknown (Ethiopia — Official) 139, 143
Ishaq I : 399–410? (India — Malankara Jacobite) 167
Ishaq II, Baselios : 1687–1709 (India — Malankara Jacobite) 171
Ishaq : 375–386 (India — Malankara Orthodox) 163
Isaya, Baselios : 1626 (India — Malankara Jacobite) 171
Ishu' I : unknown (Antioch — Maronite) 49
Ishu' II : unknown (Antioch — Maronite) 49
Ishu' I, Ighnatiyus : 1509–1510 (Antioch — Syrian Catholic) 55
Ishu' II *Qamah*, Ighnatiyus : 1655–1661 (Antioch — Syrian Catholic) 56
Ishu' I, Ighnatiyus : 1509–1512 (Antioch — Syrian Orthodox) 61
Ishu' II *Qamah*, Ighnatiyus : 1659–1662 (Antioch — Syrian Orthodox) 61
Ishu' I *ibn Muta*, Ighnatiyus : 1390–1418? (Antioch — Syrian Orthodox — Tur Abhdin) 62
Ishu' II *Inwardaya*, Ighnatiyus : 1455–1466 (Antioch — Syrian Orthodox — Tur Abhdin) 62
Ishu' *bar Nun* : 820–824 (Assyria), and 823–828 (Babylon) 73, 86
Ishu'yabh I *Arzunaya* : 581–595 (Assyria) 72
Ishu'yabh II *Gdalaya* : 628–644 (Assyria) 72
Ishu'yabh III *Khdayabaya* : 650–660 (Assyria) 73
Ishu'yabh IV *bar Khazqi'il* : 1023–1027 (Assyria) 74
Ishu'yabh V *Baladaya* : 1148–1175 (Assyria) 74
Ishu'yabh I *Arzunaya* : 582–595 (Babylon) 85

Ishu'yabh II *Gdalaya* : 628–646? (Babylon) 85
Ishu'yabh III *Khdayabaya* : 650–658? (Babylon) 85
Ishu'yabh IV *bar Khazqi'il* : 1020–1025 (Babylon) 86
Ishu'yabh V *Baladaya* : 1149–1175 (Babylon) 87
Ishu'yabh Iliya XIII *bar Mama* : 1778–1804 (Babylon) 83, 87
Ishu'yabh Shim'un VIII *bar Mama* : 1538–1551 (Assyria) 69, 74
Ishu'yabh Shim'un XIII : 1653–1690 (Assyria) 74
Ishu'yabh Shim'un VII *bar Mama* : 1538–1551 (Babylon) 69, 87
Isidor *of Kiev* : 1459–1463 (Constantinople — Latin) 120
Isidor *Bogoiavenskiĭ* : 1947–1949 (Estonia) 137
Isidor *Nikolskiĭ* : 1844–1858 (Georgia) 151
Isidor : 1436–1448 (Russia — Moscow) 220
Isidōros I *Boucheiras apo Monembasias* : 1347–1350 (Constantinople — Greek) 113
Isidōros II *Xanthopoulos* : 1456–1462 (Constantinople — Greek) 113
Isidōros : 1456? (Greece) 156
Isidorus *of Kiev* : 1459–1463 (Constantinople — Latin) 120
Isidorus : 1463?– (Cyprus — Latin) 130
Iskandar : 414–424 (Antioch — Syrian Catholic) 53
Iskhaq : 399–411 (Assyria), and 399–410 (Babylon) 72, 85
Isma'il *Yuhanna*, Ighnatiyus : 1333–1365 [anti-patriarch] (Antioch — Syrian Orthodox) 61
Ismil *Yuhanna*, Ighnatiyus : 1333–1366 (Antioch — Syrian Catholic) 55
Isnardus *Tacconi* : 1311–1329 (Antioch — Latin) 46
Israyêl : 1763–1765 [anti-patriarch] (Aghunie) 11
Israyêl : 667–677 (Armenia) 65
Israyil *Karkaya* : 961–962 [unconsecrated] (Assyria) 73
Israyil I *of Kashkar* : 877 [unconsecrated] (Babylon) 86
Israyil II *Karkaya* : 961 (Babylon) 86
Istifan — *see also*: Istifanus
Istifan I : 346–351 (Antioch — Syrian Catholic) 53
Istifan II : 480–481 (Antioch — Syrian Catholic) 54
Istifan III : 481–482 (Antioch — Syrian Catholic) 54
Istifanus — *see also*: Istifan
Istifanus I *Sidarus* : 1958–1986 (Alexandria — Coptic Catholic) 21
Istifanus II *Ghattas* : 1986– (Alexandria — Coptic Catholic) 21, 253, 257, 259
Istifanus I : 341–345 (Antioch — Greek) 35
Istifanus II : 490–493 (Antioch — Greek) 35
Istifanus III : 493–495 (Antioch — Greek) 35
Istifanus IV : 742–748 (Antioch — Greek) 36
Istifanus V : 871 (Antioch — Greek) 36
Istifanus I : 343–344 (Antioch — Greek Melkite) 40
Istifanus II : 478–481 (Antioch — Greek Melkite) 41
Istifanus III : 742?–745? (Antioch — Greek Melkite) 41
Istifanus IV : 866–870 (Antioch — Greek Melkite) 41
Istifanus I : unknown (Antioch — Maronite) 49
Istifanus II *ibn Mikha'il al-Duwayhi* : 1670–1704 (Antioch — Maronite) 50
Istifanus : 342–344 [anti-patriarch] (Antioch — Syrian Orthodox) 58
Istifanus : 478–481 [anti-patriarch] (Antioch — Syrian Orthodox) 59
Istifanus : 481–482 [anti-patriarch] (Antioch — Syrian Orthodox) 59
Isydor I : 1436–1441 (Ukraine) 236
Isydor II *Nikol's'kyĭ* : 1858–1860 (Ukraine) 237
Iulianus : 1571–1577 (Cyprus — Latin) 131
Iulius Maria *della Somaglia* : 1788–1795 (Antioch — Latin) 47
Iulius *Lenti* : 1887–1894 (Constantinople — Latin) 122
Iulius I : 337–352 (Rome) 211
Iulius II *della Rovere* : 1503–1513 (Rome) 216
Iulius III *Ciocchi del Monte* : 1550–1555 (Rome) 83, 216
Iustin *Moïsescu* : 1956–1957 (Austria — Sibiu), and 1977 [locum tenens], 1977–1986 [patriarch] (Romania) 82, 208
Ivanios, Mar : 1751–1794 (India — Malankara Syrian) 162
Ivanios, Joseph Mar *Kasseesa* : 1807 [suffragan] (India — Thozhiyoor) 176
Iwannis I : 740–754 (Antioch — Syrian Orthodox) 59
Iwannis II : 954–957 (Antioch — Syrian Orthodox) 60
Iwannis III : 1080–1082 (Antioch — Syrian Orthodox) 60
Izid-Bozidi : 683–685 (Georgia) 149

Jakov *Proarhij* : 1275? (Macedonia) 195
Jakov : 1286–1292 (Serbia) 226
Ján *Kuchtin* : 1956–1964 (Czechoslovakia) 133
Jānis I *Pommers* : 1920–1934 (Latvia) 191
Jānis II *Garklavs* : 1943–1944 (Latvia) 191
Jarmanus : 1898–1899 [locum tenens] (Antioch — Greek) 38
Jawrji — *see also*: Jirjis, Jawrjiyus
Jawrji I : 758–790 (Antioch — Syrian Orthodox) 59
Jawrjiyus I : 640–656 (Antioch — Greek) 36
Jawrjiyus II : 690–695 (Antioch — Greek) 36
Jawrjiyus III : 902–917 (Antioch — Greek) 36
Jawrjiyus IV *Laskaris* : 1010–1015 (Antioch — Greek) 36
Jawrjiyus I : 649?–660? (Antioch — Greek Melkite) 41
Jawrjiyus II : 685?–702? (Antioch — Greek Melkite) 41
Jefrem : 1375–1379, 1389–1392 (Serbia) 226
Jelevferij *Voroncov* : 1946–1955 (Czechoslovakia) 132–133
Jeremije *Papazoğlou* : 1766–1784 (Serbia — Beograd) 228
Jerotej : 1589–1591 (Serbia) 227
Jerotheu *Vllaho* : 1924–1929 [locum tenens] (Albania) 12–13
Jerzy *Jaroszewski* : 1921–1923 (Poland) 203–204
Jerzy *Korenistow* : 1962–1965 [locum tenens], 1969–1970 [locum tenens] (Poland) 204
Jevstatij : 1134? (Macedonia) 194
Jevstatije : 1270–1278 (Montenegro) 201
Jevstatije I : 1279–1286 (Serbia) 226
Jevstatije II : 1292–1309 (Serbia) 226
Jevtimije : 1405 (Montenegro) 201
Jibra'il I : unknown (Antioch — Maronite) 49
Jibra'il II *al-Hajjula* : 1357?–1367? (Antioch — Maronite) 50
Jibra'il III *al-Blawzawi* : 1704–1705 (Antioch — Maronite) 50
Jibra'il *Tabbuni*, Ighnatiyus : 1929–1968 (Antioch — Syrian Catholic) 56
Jirasimus *Propapas* : 1885–1891 (Antioch — Greek) 38

Jirjis —see also: Jawrji
Jirjis I *ibn 'Amayrah* : 1633–1644 (Antioch — Maronite) 50
Jirjis II *Habakuk al-Bashalani* : 1657–1670 (Antioch — Maronite) 50
Jirjis I : 758–790 (Antioch — Syrian Catholic) 54
Jirjis II, Ighnatiyus : 1690–1709 (Antioch — Syrian Catholic) 56
Jirjis III, Ighnatiyus : 1746–1768 (Antioch — Syrian Catholic) 56
Jirjis IV, Ighnatiyus : 1768–1781 (Antioch — Syrian Catholic) 56
Jirjis V *Shilhut*, Ighnatiyus : 1874–1891 (Antioch — Syrian Catholic) 56
Jirjis II, Ighnatiyus : 1687–1708 (Antioch — Syrian Orthodox) 61
Jirjis III, Ighnatiyus : 1745–1768 (Antioch — Syrian Orthodox) 61
Jirjis IV, Ighnatiyus : 1768–1781 (Antioch — Syrian Orthodox) 62
Jirjis V *Sayyar*, Ighnatiyus : 1819–1837 (Antioch — Syrian Orthodox) 62
Joahim : 1588?–1593 (Macedonia) 195
Joanikij : 1238? (Macedonia) 195
Joanikije *Lipovac* : 1940–1945 (Montenegro) 202
Joanikije I : 1272–1276 (Serbia) 226
Joanikije II : 1338–1346 [metropolitan], 1346–1354 [patriarch] (Serbia) 226
Joanikije : 1506? [metropolitan] (Serbia) 227
Joanikije III *Karadža* : 1739–1746 (Serbia) 227
Joannikij *Gorskij* : 1860–1875 (Poland) 204
Joasav I : 1628? (Macedonia) 196
Joasav II : 1719–1745 (Macedonia) 197
Johannes *Rinne* : 1987–2001 (Finland), and 1996–1999 [locum tenens] (Estonia) 136, 146
Joseph : 785–786 (India — Malankara Jacobite) 168
Joseph I : 552–556 (India — Malankara Orthodox) 163
Joseph II : 789–793 (India — Malankara Orthodox) 164
Joseph Mar Athanasios I : 1883–1888 [suffragan], 1888–1898 (India — Thozhiyoor) 176
Joseph Mar Dionysios V *Putikkottil* : 1865–1909 (India — Malankara Syrian) 161–162, 173, 252

Joseph Mar Irenaeus : [suffragan] (India — Mar Thoma Syrian) 173
Joseph Mar Ivanios *Kasseesa* : 1807 [suffragan] (India — Thozhiyoor) 176
Joseph Mar Koorilose IV *Kassesa* : 1856–1888 (India — Thozhiyoor) 176
Joseph Mar Koorilose IX *Panakal* : 1981–1986 [suffragan], 1986– (India — Thozhiyoor) 176, 255, 257, 260
Josif *Rajačić* : 1842–1861 (Austria — Karlovci) 76–77, 79
Josif : 1746–1752 (Macedonia) 197
Josif : 1453? (Montenegro) 201
Josif : 1544? (Serbia) 227
Josif *Cvijović* : 1941–1946 [locum tenens] (Serbia) 228
Jovan *Đorđević* : 1768–1769 [locum tenens], 1769–1773 (Austria — Karlovci) 79
Jovan I : 1018–1027 (Macedonia) 194
Jovan II *Lampin* : 1065–1078 (Macedonia) 194
Jovan III *Aoinos "The Sober"* : 1079–1081? (Macedonia) 194
Jovan IV *Komnen* : 1143–1157 (Macedonia) 194
Jovan V *Kamatir* : 1183–1215 (Macedonia) 195, 252
Jovan I *Mladenović* : 1993–1994 (Macedonia — Serbian Archdiocese) 194, 197
Jovan II *Vraniskovski* : 2002– (Macedonia — Serbian Archdiocese) 194, 197
Jovan : 1293–1305 (Montenegro) 201
Jovan : 1508?–1509? (Serbia) 227
Jovan *Kantul* : 1592–1614 (Serbia) 227
Jovan *Pavlović* : 1989–1990 [locum tenens] (Serbia) 228
Juhanon Mar *Thoma* : 1937–1947 [suffragan], 1947–1976 (India — Mar Thoma Syrian) 173
Jüri *Välbe* : 1956–1961 (Estonia) 136
Justinian *Marina* : 1948 [locum tenens], 1948–1977 (Romania), and 1955–1956 [locum tenens] (Austria — Sibiu) 82, 208, 252

Kaladyanu : unknown (Ethiopia — Official) 141
Kalandhiyun : 495 (Antioch — Greek), and 481–485 (Antioch — Greek Melkite) 35, 41
Kalinik I *Skopljanac* : 1691–1710 (Serbia) 227
Kalinik II : 1765–1766 (Serbia) 227

Kalistrate *Tsintsadze* : 1923–1926 [locum tenens], 1932–1952 [catholicos] (Georgia) 152
Kallawtiyanus : 157–167 (Alexandria — Coptic), and 152–166 (Alexandria — Coptic Catholic) 15, 21
Kallinikos *Olympios* : 1858–1861 (Alexandria — Greek) 26
Kallinikos I : 694–706 (Constantinople — Greek) 111
Kallinikos II *Akarnan apo Prousēs* : 1688, 1689–1693, 1694–1702 (Constantinople — Greek) 115
Kallinikos III *apo Hērakleias* : 1726 (Constantinople — Greek) 116, 251
Kallinikos IV *apo Proïlabou* : 1757 (Constantinople — Greek) 116
Kallinikos V *apo Nikaias* : 1801–1806, 1808–1809 (Constantinople — Greek) 116
Kallinikos I : 1683–1685? (Crete) 124
Kallinikos II : 1697–1699 (Crete) 125
Kallinikos III *ex Ankialou* : 1823–1830 (Crete) 125
Kallinikos IV *Gargalados* : 1839–1842 (Crete) 125
Kallinikos V *Chougias* : 1842–1843 (Crete) 125
Kallistos I : 1350–1353, 1355–1363 (Constantinople — Greek) 113
Kallistos II *Xanthopoulos* : 1397 (Constantinople — Greek) 113
Kallistos : 1550–1564 (Greece) 156
Kallistratos : 1867–1884 (Sinai) 232
Kapiōn : 2nd cent. (Jerusalem — Greek) 184
Karapet *Krdshadz* : 1661? [anticatholicos] (Aght'amar) 6
Karapet I : 1677–1679? (Aght'amar) 6
Karapet II : 1783–1787 (Aght'amar) 7
Karapet III : 1810?–1813? (Aght'amar) 7
Karapet IV : 1814?–1816? (Aght'amar) 7
Karapet : 1406–1411 (Aghunie) 10
Karapet I *Bobik* : 1392–1404 (Armenia) 67
Karapet : 1446– [anti-catholicos] (Armenia) 67
Karapet II : 1726–1729 (Armenia) 67
Karapet : 1446–1478 (Cilicia — Armenian Apostolic) 99
Karapet I : 1478–1489 (Constantinople — Armenian) 103
Karapet II : 1676–1679, 1680–1681, 1681–1684, 1686–1687, 1688–1689 (Con-

stantinople — Armenian) 104–105
Karapet III *Palat'ts'i* : 1823–1831 (Constantinople — Armenian) 105
Karapet I *of Jerusalem* : 1238–1254 (Jerusalem — Armenian) 180
Karapet II : 1356 [locum tenens] (Jerusalem — Armenian) 180
Karapet III *of Kantsag* : 1761–1768 (Jerusalem — Armenian) 181
Kassianos : 2nd cent. (Jerusalem — Greek) 184
Kastinos : 230–237 (Constantinople — Greek) 109
Kayanus : 536–565 (Alexandria — Coptic — Gaianite) 18
Keladiōn : 154–167 (Alexandria — Greek) 23
Keladiōn *of Ptolemaïs* : 1931–1934 [locum tenens] (Jerusalem — Greek) 187
Kerdōn : 98–110 (Alexandria — Greek) 23, 23
Khach'atur : 1287? (coadjutor?) (Aght'amar) 5
Khach'atur I : 1813–1814 (Aght'amar) 7
Khach'atur II *Mokats'i* : 1844–1851 (Aght'amar) 7
Khach'atur III *Shiroyan* : 1864–1895 (Aght'amar) 7
Khach'atur I *Chorik* : 1550?–1560 (Cilicia — Armenian Apostolic) 99
Khach'atur II *"The Musician"* : 1560–1584 (Cilicia — Armenian Apostolic) 99
Khach'atur III : 1657–1674 (Cilicia — Armenian Apostolic) 99
Khach'atur I : 1642–1643 (Constantinople — Armenian) 104
Khach'atur II : 1688 (Constantinople — Armenian) 105
Khach'ik I *Arsharuni* : 973–992 (Armenia) 66
Khach'ik II : 1058–1065 (Armenia) 66
Kha'il I : 744–767 (Alexandria — Coptic) 16
Kha'il II : 849–851 (Alexandria — Coptic) 16
Khalaf, Ighnatiyus : 1455–1484 (Antioch — Syrian Catholic), and 1455–1483 (Antioch — Syrian Orthodox) 55, 61
Khameeso : 578–609 (India — Malankara Jacobite) 167
Khariton : 1643–1647?, 1651–1652 (Bulgaria) 94
Khat *Adjapahian* : 1942–1945 [locum tenens], 1952–1955 [locum tenens] (Cilicia — Armenian Apostolic) 100
Khazqi'il : 570–581 (Assyria), and 567–581 (Babylon) 72, 85

Khnanishu' I *"The Lame"* : 686–693 (Assyria), and 685?–700? (Babylon) 73, 85
Khnanishu' II : 774–778 (Assyria), and 773–780 (Babylon) 73, 86
Khnanishu,' Yusip : 1918–1927 [locum tenens] (Assyria) 75
Khorēn *Muradbēgian* : 1930–1932 [locum tenens], 1932–1938 (Armenia) 63, 68
Khorēn *Baroyan* : 1955–1956 [locum tenens], 1963–1983 (Cilicia — Armenian Apostolic) 100
Khorēn *Ashegian* : 1888–1894 (Constantinople — Armenian) 106
Khristufurus I : 960–966 (Antioch — Greek) 36
Khristufurus II : 1184–1185 (Antioch — Greek) 37
Khristufurus : 960–969 (Antioch — Greek Melkite) 42
Kiprian : 1378–1410 (Russia — Moscow) 220
Kirakos : 1441–1443 (Armenia) 67
Kirakos I *"The Great"* : 1797–1822 (Cilicia — Armenian Apostolic) 100
Kirakos II : 1855–1865 (Cilicia — Armenian Apostolic) 100
Kirakos : 1866–1871 [locum tenens] (Cilicia — Armenian Apostolic) 100
Kirakos : 1641–1642 (Constantinople — Armenian) 104
Kirakos I : 1363 [locum tenens] (Jerusalem — Armenian) 180
Kirakos II *Mnats'akanian of Jerusalem* : 1847–1850 (Jerusalem — Armenian) 182
Kiril — *see also*: C'irilo, Kirilo
Kiril : 1759–1762 (Bulgaria), and 1759–1762 (Macedonia) 95, 197
Kiril *Markov* : 1951–1953 [locum tenens], 1953–1971 [patriarch] (Bulgaria) 91, 96
Kirile I : 791–802 (Georgia) 149
Kirile II : 1737–1739 (Georgia) 151
Kirillus I : 412–444 (Alexandria — Coptic) 16
Kirillus II : 1078–1092 (Alexandria — Coptic) 17
Kirillus III *Dawud ibn Laqlaq* : 1235–1243 (Alexandria — Coptic) 17
Kirillus IV *Dawud Tuma Bashut* : 1854–1861 (Alexandria — Coptic) 18
Kirillus V *ibn Ibrahim Sa'ad Matar al-Nasikh* : 1874–1927 (Alexandria — Coptic) 18, 252
Kirillus VI *Azir Yusuf 'Ata* :

1959–1971 (Alexandria — Coptic) 18
Kirillus I : 412–444 (Alexandria — Coptic Catholic) 21
Kirillus II *Makariyus* : 1895–1899 [apostolic administrator], 1899–1908 [patriarch] (Alexandria — Coptic Catholic) 20–21
Kirillus I : 277–299 (Antioch — Greek) 34
Kirillus II : 1287–1308? [anti-patriarch] (Antioch — Greek) 37
Kirillus III *al-Za'im* : 1694–1720 (Antioch — Greek) 38, 43, 252
Kirillus I : 271–306 (Antioch — Greek Melkite) 40
Kirillus II : 1290?–1308? (Antioch — Greek Melkite) 42
Kirillus III : 1316- (Antioch — Greek Melkite) 42
Kirillus IV *al-Dabbas* : 1620–1627 [anti-patriarch] (Antioch — Greek Melkite) 43
Kirillus V *al-Za'im* : 1672, 1682–1720 (Antioch — Greek Melkite) 38, 43, 252
Kirillus VI *al-Tanas* : 1724–1759 (Antioch — Greek Melkite) 33, 39, 44
Kirillus VII *Siyaj* : 1794–1796 (Antioch — Greek Melkite) 44
Kirillus VIII *Jiha* : 1902–1916 (Antioch — Greek Melkite) 44
Kirillus IX *Mughabghab* : 1925–1947 (Antioch — Greek Melkite) 44
Kirilo — *see also*: C'irilo, Kiril
Kirilo I : 1407–1419 (Serbia) 226
Kirilo II : 1758–1763 (Serbia) 227
Kirilo : 1825–1826 (Serbia — Beograd) 228
Kirion I : 595–610 (Georgia) 149
Kirion II : 678–683 (Georgia) 149
Kirion III *Sadzaglishvili* : 1917–1918 (Georgia) 147, 152
Kirioni III *Sadzaglishvili* : 1917–1918 (Georgia) 147, 152
Klēmatios : 400? (Greece) 155
Klēmēs *apo Ikoniou* : 1667 (Constantinople — Greek) 115
Klēmēs : 1514? (Sinai) 232
Klimentos : 908–914 (Georgia) 149
Klyment *Smoliatych* : 1147–1159 (Ukraine) 235
Kodratos : 200? (Greece) 155
Komitas : 615–628 (Armenia) 65
Konstantin I : 1160?–1170? (Bulgaria), and 1157–1166 (Macedonia) 92, 194
Konstantin II *Kavasila* : 1254?–1259? (Bulgaria), and 1250–1261 (Macedonia) 93, 195

Kōnstantinos *Katsarakēs* : 1966–1968 [locum tenens] (Alexandria — Greek) 26
Kōnstantinos I : 675–677 (Constantinople — Greek) 110
Kōnstantinos II : 754–766 (Constantinople — Greek) 111
Kōnstantinos III *Leichoudēs* : 1059–1063 (Constantinople — Greek) 111
Kōnstantinos IV *Chliarēnos* : 1154–1157 (Constantinople — Greek) 112
Kōnstantinos V *Baliadēs* : 1897–1901 (Constantinople — Greek) 117
Kōnstantinos VI *Araboğlu* : 1924–1925 (Constantinople — Greek) 108, 117–118
Kōnstantinos I : 12th cent. (Crete) 124
Kōnstantinos II : 12th cent. (Crete) 124
Kōnstantinos : 783?–787? (Cyprus) 127
Kōnstantinos : 965? (Greece) 155
Kōnstantinos : -869? (Sinai) 231
Kōnstantios I *apo Sinaiou* : 1830–1834 (Constantinople — Greek) 116, 232, 251–252
Kōnstantios II *Asophos apo Tornobou* : 1834–1835 (Constantinople — Greek) 116
Kōnstantios *Chalkiopoulos* : 1711–1716, 1719–1722 (Crete) 125
Kōnstantios I : 1748–1759 (Sinai) 232
Kōnstantios II *apo Sinaiou* : 1804?–1859 (Sinai) 116, 232, 251–252
Konstantyn *Buggan* : 1993–1995 (Ukraine — Orthodox Church of the USA) 240
Konstantyn I : 1155–1159 (Ukraine) 235
Konstantyn II : 1167–1169 (Ukraine) 235
Konstantyn III *D'iakov* : 1934–1937 (Ukraine) 238
Kooriakose : 964–982 (India — Malankara Orthodox) 164
Kooriakose Mar Koorilose VI : 1936–1947 (India — Thozhiyoor) 176
Koorilose, Paulose Mar : 1911–1917 (India — Malankara Jacobite) 161, 172
Koorilose, Yoyakin Mar : 1846–1852 (India — Malankara Syrian) 162
Koorilose I *Kattamangat*, Abraham Mar : 1771–1802 (India — Thozhiyoor) 160, 175
Koorilose II, Geevarghese Mar : 1794–1802 [suffragan], 1802–1808 (India — Thozhiyoor) 175

Koorilose III *Koothoor*, Geevarghese Mar : 1829–1856 (India — Thozhiyoor) 176
Koorilose IV *Kasseesa*, Joseph Mar : 1856–1888 (India — Thozhiyoor) 176
Koorilose V *Pulikottil*, Geevarghese Mar : 1892–1898 [suffragan], 1898–1935 (India — Thozhiyoor) 176
Koorilose VI, Kooriakose Mar : 1936–1947 (India — Thozhiyoor) 176
Koorilose VII *Kasseesa*, Geevarghese Mar : 1948–1967 (India — Thozhiyoor) 176
Koorilose VIII, Mathews Mar : 1978–1986 (India — Thozhiyoor) 176
Koorilose IX *Panakal*, Joseph Mar : 1981–1986 [suffragan], 1986- (India — Thozhiyoor) 176, 255, 257, 260
Korneli? *Jakobs* : 1990- (Estonia) 137
Kornēlios *Rodoussakēs* : 2000–2001, 2005 [locum tenens] (Jerusalem — Greek) 187
Kornelius *Jakobs* : 1990- (Estonia) 137
Kosmas I *"The Needle-Maker"* : 727–768 (Alexandria — Greek) 24
Kosmas II *Byzantios* : 1712–1714, 1723–1736 (Alexandria — Greek) 25
Kosmas III *Kalokagathos* : 1737–1746 (Alexandria — Greek) 25
Kosmas I *Hierosolymitēs* : 1075–1081 (Constantinople — Greek) 112
Kosmas II *Attikos* : 1146–1147 (Constantinople — Greek) 112
Kosmas III *Chalkēdonios* : 1714–1716 (Constantinople — Greek) 116
Kosmas I : 867 (Greece) 155
Kosmas II : 1339 (Greece) 156
Kosmas *Byzantios* : 1703–1706 (Sinai) 232
Kostandin I : 1221–1267 (Armenia) 66
Kostandin II *Pronogordz* : 1286–1289 (Armenia) 66
Kostandin III : 1307–1322 (Armenia) 66
Kostandin IV : 1323–1326 (Armenia) 66
Kostandin V : 1372–1374 (Armenia) 66
Kostandin VI : 1430–1439 (Armenia) 67
Krestodolo I : 1588?- (Ethiopia — Historical), and unknown (Ethiopia — Official) 140, 143

Krestodolo II : 1663?–1671? (Ethiopia — Historical), and (Ethiopia — Official) 141, 143
Krestodolo III : 1720–1735 (Ethiopia — Historical), and (Ethiopia — Official) 141, 144
Kriskēs : 256? (Crete) 123
K'ristap'or *Ardzuni* : 478 [anti-catholicos] (Armenia) 65
K'ristap'or I : 539–545 (Armenia) 65
K'ristap'or II : 628–630 (Armenia) 65
K'ristep'ore I *Amilak'ori* : 1616–1622 (Georgia) 151
K'ristep'ore II : 1638–1660 (Georgia) 151
K'ristep'ore III *Tsitskishvili* : 1927–1932 (Georgia) 147, 152
Kristofor *Kisi* : 1937–1948 (Albania) 12–13
Kupriian : 1375?–1381 (Ukraine) 236
Kurdunus : 98–109 (Alexandria — Coptic), and 95–106 (Alexandria — Coptic Catholic) 15, 20
Kuregh *Israelian* : 1944–1949 (Jerusalem — Armenian) 182
Kuriakose : 962–979 (India — Malankara Jacobite) 169
Kurillos, Baselios *Abd al-Azeez* : 1811–1816 (India — Malankara Jacobite) 172
Kurniliyus : 127–151 (Antioch — Greek), and 130?–150? (Antioch — Greek Melkite) 34, 40
Kurush : 707- (Antioch — Maronite) 49
Kuz'ma : 1156? (Ukraine — Halych) 239
Kyprianos : 1766–1783 (Alexandria — Greek) 26
Kyprianos *apo Kaisareias Kappadokias* : 1707–1709, 1713–1714 (Constantinople — Greek) 115
Kyprianos : 1761 [anti-archbishop] (Cyprus) 129
Kyprianos : 1810–1821 (Cyprus) 126, 129
Kyprianos : 1986- (Greece — Old Calendarists) 158–159, 255, 257, 260
Kyriakos I : 214–230 (Constantinople — Greek) 109
Kyriakos II : 595?–606 (Constantinople — Greek) 110
Kyrillianos : 214–230 (Constantinople — Greek) 109
Kyrillos I : 412–444 (Alexandria — Greek) 23
Kyrillos II : 1115? (Alexandria — Greek) 25
Kyrillos III *Loukaris* : 1601–1620 (Alexandria — Greek) 25
Kyrillos I *Loukaris* : 1612 [locum tenens], 1620–1623,

1623–1630, 1630–1633, 1633–1634, 1634–1635, 1637–1638 (Constantinople — Greek) 114–115
Kyrillos II *Kontarēs apo Borrhoias* : 1633, 1635–1636, 1638–1639 (Constantinople — Greek) 114–115
Kyrillos III *Spanos apo Tornobou* : 1652, 1654 (Constantinople — Greek) 115
Kyrillos IV *apo Kyzikou* : 1711–1713 (Constantinople — Greek) 115
Kyrillos *apo Prousēs* : 1720 [antipatriarch] (Constantinople — Greek) 116
Kyrillos V *Karakalos apo Nikomēdeias* : 1748–1751, 1752–1757 (Constantinople — Greek) 116
Kyrillos VI *Serbetsoglous apo Adrianoupoleōs* : 1813–1818 (Constantinople — Greek) 116
Kyrillos VII *apo Amaseias* : 1855–1860 (Constantinople — Greek) 117
Kyrillos I *Hieromartys* : -304 (Crete) 123
Kyrillos II : 824? (Crete) 124
Kyrillos I : 1849–1854 (Cyprus) 129
Kyrillos II *Papadopoulos* : 1900–1909 [locum tenens], 1909–1916 (Cyprus) 126, 129
Kyrillos III *Basileiou* : 1916–1933 (Cyprus) 126, 129
Kyrillos I : -1611 (Greece) 157
Kyrillos II : 1699–1703 (Greece) 157
Kyrillos I : 350–357, 358–360, 362–367, 378–386? (Jerusalem — Greek) 184
Kyrillos II : 1845–1872 (Jerusalem — Greek) 183, 187
Kyrillos I : 1470? (Sinai) 231
Kyrillos I *Krēs* : 1759–1790 (Sinai) 232
Kyrillos III *Byzantios* : 1859–1867 (Sinai) 232
Kyros *of Phasis* : 630–643? (Alexandria — Greek) 24
Kyros : 706–712 (Constantinople — Greek) 111
Kyrylo I : 1045? (Ukraine) 235
Kyrylo II : 1224–1233 (Ukraine) 235
Kyrylo III : 1243?–1281 (Ukraine) 236

Ladislaus Michael *Zaleski* : 1916–1925 (Antioch — Latin) 47
Lando (or Landus) : 913–914 (Rome) 213
Laurentios : 154–166 (Constantinople — Greek) 109
Laurentios : 1588? (Cyprus) 128
Laurentios : 1528–1550 (Greece) 156
Laurentios : 1592–1617 (Sinai) 232
Laurentius I *Zane* : 1473–1485 (Antioch — Latin) 46
Laurentius II *Mattei* : 1822–1833 (Antioch — Latin) 47
Laurentius III *Passerini* : 1901–1915 (Antioch — Latin) 47
Laurentius : 498, 501–505 [antipope] (Rome) 211
Laurus *Skurla* : 2001- (Russia — Church Outside Russia) 224, 256, 258–259
Lavr *Skurla* : 2001- (Russia — Church Outside Russia) 224, 256, 258–259
Lavrentie I : unknown (Austria — Cernovci) 77
Lavrentie II : 1689–1702 (Austria — Cernovci) 78
Lawndiyus *"The Eunuch"* : 345–350 (Antioch — Greek), and 344–358 (Antioch — Greek Melkite) 35, 40
Lawntiyus *"The Eunuch"* : 344–357 [anti-patriarch] (Antioch — Syrian Orthodox) 58
Lazar I, Ignatius : 1142?–1164 (India — Malankara Jacobite) 169
Lazar II, Baselios : 1713 (India — Malankara Jacobite) 171
Lazar III, Gregorios : 1730–1742 (India — Malankara Jacobite) 171
Lazar Yusip V *Khindi* : 1757–1781 (Babylon) 83, 88
Lazaros *apo Sina* : 1300? (Greece) 156
Lazaros : 1334?–1368 (Jerusalem — Greek) 186
Lazaros : 1491? (Sinai) 232
Leo *Makkonen* : 2001- (Finland) 146, 255, 258, 260
Leo I *Magnus "The Great"* : 440–461 (Rome) 211
Leo II : 682–683 (Rome) 212
Leo III : 795–816 (Rome) 212
Leo IV : 847–855 (Rome) 213
Leo V : 903 (Rome) 213
Leo VI : 928 (Rome) 213
Leo VII : 936–939 (Rome) 213
Leo VIII : 963–965 (Rome) 213
Leo IX *von Egisheim* : 1049–1054 (Rome) 214
Leo X *de' Medici* : 1513–1521 (Rome) 216
Leo XI *de' Medici* : 1605 (Rome) 216
Leo XII *della Genga* : 1823–1829 (Rome) 20, 217
Leo XIII *Pecci* : 1878–1903 (Rome) 217

Leōn *Styppēs* : 1134–1143 (Constantinople — Greek) 112
Leōn : 12th cent. (Crete) 124
Leōn I *Synkellos* : 1054?–1061? (Greece) 155
Leōn II *Synkellos* : 1061?–1069? (Greece) 155
Leonardus *Delfino* : 1401–1402? (Alexandria — Latin) 27
Leonardus *Faliero* : 1302–1305? (Constantinople — Latin) 119
Leonide *Okropiridze* : 1917 [locum tenens], 1918–1921 (Georgia) 152
Leōnidēs : 250? (Greece) 155
Leonids *Poljakov* : 1966–1989 (Latvia) 192
Leontiĭ : 919- (Bulgaria) 91–92
Leontiĭ *Lebedinskiĭ* : 1891–1893 (Russia — Moscow) 221
Leontiĭ : 992–1008 (Ukraine) 235
Leontij *Lebjedinskij* : 1875–1891 (Poland) 204
Leontije *Lambrović* : 1801–1810, 1811–1813 (Serbia — Beograd) 228
Leontios : 1052–1059 (Alexandria — Greek) 24
Leontios *Theotokitēs* : 1189 (Constantinople — Greek) 112
Leontios *Leontiou* : 1933–1947 [locum tenens], 1947 [archbishop] (Cyprus) 126, 129
Leontios I : 912–929 (Jerusalem — Greek) 185
Leontios II : 1170–1190 (Jerusalem — Greek) 186
Leonty *Turkevich* : 1950–1965 (America — Orthodox Church) 32
Leuïs : 2nd cent. (Jerusalem — Greek) 184
Lev I *ek Rōmaiōn* : 1027–1056 (Macedonia) 194
Lev II *Boungos* : -1120 (Macedonia) 194
Liberius : 352–366 (Rome) 211
Linus : 67?–76 (Rome) 210
Livius *Podocator* : 1524- (Cyprus — Latin) 130
Lo Asar : 856–869 (India — Malankara Orthodox) 164
Lotharius : 1214?- (Jerusalem — Latin) 189
Loukas : 365, 375–378 [antipope] (Alexandria — Greek) 23
Loukas *Chrysobergēs* : 1157–1169? (Constantinople — Greek) 112
Luca : 1602–1629 (Romania) 206
Lucas Ermenegildus *Pasetto* : 1950–1954 (Alexandria — Latin) 28
Lucius I : 253–254 (Rome) 211
Lucius II *Caccianemici* : 1144–1145 (Rome) 214
Lucius III *Allucingoli* : 1181–1185 (Rome) 215

Ludovicus I Caetanus *di Sermoneta* : 1622–1626? (Antioch—Latin) 46
Ludovicus II *Calini* : 1751–1766 (Antioch—Latin) 47
Ludovicus I : 1405 (Constantinople—Latin) 120
Ludovicus II *Pic de la Mirandole* : 1706–1712 (Constantinople—Latin) 121
Ludovicus *Pérez Fabrice* : 1471–1483 (Cyprus—Latin) 130
Lukijan *Bogdanović* : 1907–1908 [locum tenens], 1908–1913 [patriarch] (Austria—Karlovci) 77, 80
Luqa : 1137–1155 (Antioch—Greek) 37
Luqa *al-Banhrani* : 1272–1300 (Antioch—Maronite) 50
Luv I *ek Rōmaiōn* : 1037?–1054? (Bulgaria) 92
Luv II *Mung* : 1108?–1120? (Bulgaria) 92

Macarie I : 1477–1487? (Romania) 206
Macarie II : 1512–1521? (Romania) 206
Maghak'ia *Örmanian* : 1896–1908 (Constantinople—Armenian), and 1914–1916 [locum tenens] (Jerusalem—Armenian) 106, 182
Magina : 398–400 (India—Malankara Orthodox) 163
Makar *Ter-Petrosian* : 1885–1891 (Armenia) 68
Makari : 553–569 (Georgia) 149
Makariĭ I : -1291 (Bulgaria) 93
Makariĭ II : 1295?–1299? (Bulgaria) 93
Makariĭ I : 1542–1563 (Russia—Moscow) 220
Makariĭ II *Bulgakov* : 1879–1882 (Russia—Moscow) 221
Makariĭ III *Nevskiĭ* : 1912–1917 (Russia—Moscow) 221
Makariĭ I : 1495–1497 (Ukraine) 236
Makariĭ II : 1534–1555 (Ukraine) 236
Makariĭ III *Karmazin* : 1924–1925 (Ukraine) 238
Makarij : 1294–1299 (Macedonia) 195
Makarije : 1560 (Montenegro) 201
Makarije *Sokolović* : 1557–1571 (Serbia) 227
Makarios : 1376?–1379, 1390–1391 (Constantinople—Greek) 113
Makarios : 1357? (Crete) 124
Makarios I : 1854–1865 (Cyprus) 129

Makarios II *Myriantheus* : 1947–1950 (Cyprus) 129
Makarios III *Mouskos* : 1950–1973, 1973–1977 (Cyprus) 126–127, 129
Makarios I : 1394–1404 (Greece) 156
Makarios II *Pelekanos* : 1689–1693 (Greece) 157
Makarios I : 478–486 (Jerusalem—Greek) 184
Makarios II : 552, 564–575 (Jerusalem—Greek) 185
Makarios I : 454? (Sinai) 230
Makarios II : 967? (Sinai) 231
Makarios III : 1224- (Sinai) 231
Makarios IV : 1486? (Sinai) 232
Makarios V *Kyprios* : 1547- (Sinai) 232
Makariyus I : 932–952 (Alexandria—Coptic) 17
Makariyus II : 1102–1128 (Alexandria—Coptic) 17
Makariyus III : 1944–1945 (Alexandria—Coptic) 18
Makariyus I : 656–681 (Antioch—Greek) 36
Makariyus II "the Virtuous" : 1015–1023 (Antioch—Greek) 36
Makariyus III : 1164–1166 (Antioch—Greek) 37
Makariyus IV *al-Za'im* : 1648–1672 (Antioch—Greek) 38
Makariyus I : 660?–681 (Antioch—Greek Melkite) 41
Makariyus II *ibn Khilal* : 1543?–1550? [anti-patriarch] (Antioch—Greek Melkite) 43
Makariyus III *al-Za'im* : 1647–1672 (Antioch—Greek Melkite) 43
Makariyus IV *Tawil* : 1813–1815 (Antioch—Greek Melkite) 44
Makary *Oksijuk* : 1951–1959 (Poland) 203–204
Makaryos : 1804–1808? (Ethiopia—Historical), and (Ethiopia—Official) 141, 144
Makedonios I : 344–346, 350–360 (Constantinople—Greek) 109
Makedonios II : 496–511 (Constantinople—Greek) 110
Makkikha I *bar Shlimun* : 1092–1109 (Assyria), and 1092–1110 (Babylon) 74, 87
Makkikha II : 1257–1265 (Assyria), and 1257–1265 (Babylon) 74, 87
Maksim *Minkov* : 1971- (Bulgaria) 91–92, 96, 251, 254, 257, 259
Maksim : 1477–1481 (Macedonia) 195
Maksim *Skopljanac* : 1655–1674 (Serbia) 227

Mak'sime I *Machutadze* : 1639–1657 (Georgia—Abkhazia) 153
Mak'sime II *Abashidze* : 1776–1795 (Georgia—Abkhazia) 153
Maksimiyanus : 188–191? (Antioch—Greek), and 182–191 (Antioch—Greek Melkite) 34, 40
Maksimus : 264–282 (Alexandria—Coptic) 15
Maksimus (I) : 264–282 (Alexandria—Coptic Catholic) 21
Maksimus (II) *Jayid* : 1824–1831 (Alexandria—Coptic Catholic) 21
Maksimus (III) *Sidfawi* : 1908–1927 (Alexandria—Coptic Catholic) 21
Maksimus : 450–459 (Antioch—Greek) 35
Maksimus I : 449?–455 (Antioch—Greek Melkite) 40
Maksimus II *Hakim* : 1760–1761 (Antioch—Greek Melkite) 44
Maksimus III *Mazlum* : 1833–1855 (Antioch—Greek Melkite) 39, 44
Maksimus IV *al-Sa'igh* : 1947–1967 (Antioch—Greek Melkite) 39, 44
Maksimus V *Hakim* : 1967–2000 (Antioch—Greek Melkite) 39, 44
Maksimus I : 172–190 (Antioch—Syrian Catholic), and 182–191 (Antioch—Syrian Orthodox) 53, 58
Maksimus II : 449–456 (Antioch—Syrian Catholic), and 449–455 (Antioch—Syrian Orthodox) 53, 58
Maksym *Hrek "The Greek"* : 1283–1305 (Ukraine) 236
Malak'ia : 1528–1538 (Georgia) 150
Malak'ia I *Abashidze* : 1529–1532 (Georgia—Abkhazia) 153
Malak'ia II *Gurieli* : 1616–1639 (Georgia—Abkhazia) 153
Malatiyus I : 354 (Antioch—Greek) 35
Malatiyus II *al-Dumani* : 1899 [locum tenens], 1899–1906 (Antioch—Greek) 33, 38
Malatiyus : 359?–381 (Antioch—Greek Melkite), and 362–381 (Antioch—Syrian Catholic) 40, 53
Malkeesadek : 857–869 (India—Malankara Jacobite) 168
Mamai : 731–744 (Georgia) 149
Ma'na : 420 (Assyria and Babylon) 72, 85
Mana : 420 (India—Malankara Jacobite) 167

Index of Primates

Manouēl I *Sarantēnos Charitopoulos* : 1216?–1222 (Constantinople — Greek) 112
Manouēl II : 1243?–1254 (Constantinople — Greek) 112
Manouēl I : 12th cent. (Crete) 124
Manouēl II : 12th cent. (Crete) 124
Maqares : 1320? (Ethiopia — Historical), and unknown (Ethiopia — Official) 140, 143
Maqiduniyus : 628–631, 632–640 (Antioch — Greek), and 639?–649? (Antioch — Greek Melkite) 36, 41
Marcellinus : 296–304 (Rome) 211
Marcellus I : 308–309 (Rome) 211
Marcellus II *Cervini* : 1555 (Rome) 216
Marcu : 1516- (Austria — Sibiu) 80
Marcus *Condolmer* : 1445? (Alexandria — Latin) 27
Marcus *Cornaro* : 1506–1507, 1522–1524 (Constantinople — Latin) 120
Marcus : 336 (Rome) 211
Mardarie : 1591?–1595 (Austria — Cernovci) 78
Mardarije I *Kornećanin* : 1639?–1649? (Montenegro) 201
Mardarije II *Kornećanin* : 1659? (Montenegro) 201
Mari I : 48–81 (Assyria), and 1st cent. (Babylon) 71, 84
Mari II *bar Tubi At'uraya* : 987–1000 (Assyria), and 987–999 (Babylon) 73, 86
Mari : 152–185 (India — Malankara Orthodox) 163
Mari Aba I *Raba* : 540–552 (Assyria) 72
Mari Aba II : 741–751 (Assyria) 73
Mari Immih : 647–650 (Assyria) and (Babylon) 72, 85
Marinos : 386- [anti-patriarch] (Constantinople — Greek) 110
Marinos : 702–704 (Greece) 155
Marinus *Grimani* : 1545–1546 (Constantinople — Latin) 120
Marinus I : 882–884 (Rome) 213
Marinus II : 942–946 (Rome) 213
Mark *Ksilocarf* : 1466–1467 (Macedonia) 195
Markianos : 144–154 (Alexandria — Greek) 23
Markiyanus : 143–154 (Alexandria — Coptic), and 141–152 (Alexandria — Coptic Catholic) 15, 21
Marko *Ksilokarav* : 1467?– (Bulgaria) 93

Marko : 1524? (Serbia) 227
Markos : 1788–1791 (Aght'amar) 7
Markos I : 997- (Aghunie) 9
Markos II : -1077 (Aghunie) 9
Markos I *Euangelistēs* : 42–62 (Alexandria — Greek) 22
Markos II : 144–154 (Alexandria — Greek) 23
Markos III : 1195? (Alexandria — Greek) 25
Markos IV : 1385–1389 (Alexandria — Greek) 25
Markos V : 1425–1435 (Alexandria — Greek) 25
Markos VI : 1459–1484 (Alexandria — Greek) 25
Markos I : 198–211 (Constantinople — Greek) 109
Markos II *Xylokarabēs Eugenikos* : 1466 (Constantinople — Greek) 113
Markos I : 134?– (Jerusalem — Greek) 184
Markos II : 1191- (Jerusalem — Greek) 186
Markos III : -1503 (Jerusalem — Greek) 187
Markos I : 869- (Sinai) 231
Markos II : 1100? (Sinai) 231
Markos III : 1181? (Sinai) 231
Markos IV : 1375? (Sinai) 231
Markos V : 1496? (Sinai) 232
Markozi : 1460–1466 (Georgia) 150
Marqos I : 1481–1530? (Ethiopia — Historical) 143, 252
Marqos II : 1538–1546? (Ethiopia — Historical) 143
Marqos III : 1576?–1588? (Ethiopia — Historical) 143
Marqos IV : 1634–1648? (Ethiopia — Historical) 143
Marqos V : 1671? (Ethiopia — Historical) 143
Marqos VI : 1693?–1716 (Ethiopia — Historical) 143
Marqos I : unknown (Ethiopia — Official) 139
Marqos II : unknown (Ethiopia — Official) 139
Marqos III : unknown (Ethiopia — Official) 140
Marqos IV : unknown (Ethiopia — Official) 140
Marqos V : unknown (Ethiopia — Official) 140
Marqos VI : unknown (Ethiopia — Official) 140
Marqos VII : 1481–1530? (Ethiopia — Official) 141, 252
Marqos VIII : 1576?–1588? (Ethiopia — Official) 141
Marqos IX : 1634?–1648? (Ethiopia — Official) 141
Marqos X : 1693?–1716 (Ethiopia — Official) 141

Martinus I : 649–655 (Rome) 212
Martinus II [there is no pope with this name] (Rome)
Martinus III [there is no pope with this name] (Rome)
Martinus IV *de Brie* : 1281–1285 (Rome) 215
Martinus V *Colonna* : 1417–1431 (Rome) 216
Martiriyus : 461–465 (Antioch — Greek), and 459–470? (Antioch — Greek Melkite) 35, 41
Martiros *Gurji* : 1660–1662 (Aght'amar) 6
Martiros I : 1509–1526 (Constantinople — Armenian) 104
Martiros II : 1659–1660 (Constantinople — Armenian) 104
Martiros III : 1706 (Constantinople — Armenian) 105
Martiros I : 1399 [coadjutor] (Jerusalem — Armenian) 180
Martiros II *of Egypt* : 1419–1430 (Jerusalem — Armenian) 180
Martiros III *of Broussa* : 1491–1501 (Jerusalem — Armenian) 181
Martiros IV : 1677–1680, 1681–1683 (Jerusalem — Armenian) 181
Martiros V : 1706 (Jerusalem — Armenian) 181
Martur : 460–470, 471–473 (Antioch — Syrian Catholic) 53–54
Marturiyus : 459–468 (Antioch — Syrian Orthodox) 59
Martyrios : 451? (Crete) 123
Martyrios : 478–486 (Jerusalem — Greek) 185
Martyrios : 400? (Sinai) 230
Ma'ruf Yusip III *Sliba* : 1696–1712 (Babylon) 83, 88
Marugin Iliya XI *bar Mama* : 1700–1722 (Babylon) 87
Marun 'Abdishu' IV : 1555–1567 (Babylon) 70, 83, 88
Marutha : 629–649 (India — Malankara Jacobite) 168
Mashtots' : 897–898 (Armenia) 66
Mas'ud I *Slakhaya*, Ighnatiyus : 1418–1420 (Antioch — Syrian Orthodox — Tur Abhdin) 62
Mas'ud II, Ighnatiyus : 1490?–1495 (Antioch — Syrian Orthodox — Tur Abhdin) 62
Mateï : 1408–1411? (Bulgaria) 93
Matej : 1408–1410 (Macedonia) 195
Matewos : 1889–1926 (Ethiopia — Historical) 144, 252
Matewos I : unknown (Ethiopia — Official) 139
Matewos II : unknown (Ethiopia — Official) 139

Matewos III : unknown (Ethiopia — Official) 140
Matewos IV : unknown (Ethiopia — Official) 140
Matewos V : unknown (Ethiopia — Official) 140
Matewos VI : unknown (Ethiopia — Official) 140
Matewos VII : unknown (Ethiopia — Official) 140
Matewos VIII : unknown (Ethiopia — Official) 141
Matewos IX : unknown (Ethiopia — Official) 141
Matewos X : unknown (Ethiopia — Official) 141
Matewos XI : 1889–1926 (Ethiopia — Official) 142, 252
Matfeĭ : 1201–1220 (Ukraine) 235
Mathai — *see also*: Mathew, Mathews
Mathai I, Gregorios : 1317–1345 (India — Malankara Jacobite) 169
Mathai II, Baselios : 1709 (India — Malankara Jacobite) 171
Mathai III, Baselios : 1714- (India — Malankara Jacobite) 171
Mathew — *see also*: Mathai, Mathews
Mathew IV, Baselios : 1820 (India — Malankara Jacobite) 172
Mathew Mar Thoma VII : 1796–1809 (India — Malankara Syrian) 162
Mathews I *Vattakunnel*, Baselios Mar Thoma : 1970–1975 [suffragan], 1975–1991 (India — Malankara Orthodox) 167
Mathews II, Baselios Mar Thoma : 1980–1991 [suffragan], 1991- (India — Malankara Orthodox) 167, 255, 257, 259
Mathews Mar Athanasios *Palakunnath* : 1842–1852 [suffragan], 1852–1875 (India — Malankara Syrian), and 1843–1877 (India — Mar Thoma Syrian) 160–162, 173
Mathews Mar Koorilose VIII : 1978–1986 (India — Thozhiyoor) 176
Matiyus *ibn 'Abd Allah*, Ighnatiyus : 1782–1817 (Antioch — Syrian Orthodox) 62
Matta — *see also*: Mattawus
Matta I : 1378–1409 (Alexandria — Coptic) 17
Mattawus — *see also*: Matta
Mattawus I : 1378–1409 (Alexandria — Coptic) 17
Mattawus II : 1452–1465 (Alexandria — Coptic) 17

Mattawus III : 1634–1649 (Alexandria — Coptic) 18
Mattawus IV *al-Miri* : 1660–1675 (Alexandria — Coptic) 18
Mattawus *Righat* : 1788–1822 (Alexandria — Coptic Catholic) 21
Matt'ê — *see also*: Matt'êos
Matt'ê II : 775–777 (Aghunie) 9
Matt'êos — *see also*: Matt'ê
Matt'êos I : 342- (Aghunie) 8
Matt'êos III : 1412–1440 (Aghunie) 10
Matt'êos IV : 1470- (Aghunie) 10
Matt'êos I *Ch'ukhachian* : 1858–1865 (Armenia) 68
Matt'êos II *Izmirlian* : 1908–1910 (Armenia) 68
Matt'êos : 1694–1705 (Cilicia — Armenian Apostolic) 99
Matt'êos I : 1692–1694, 1706 (Constantinople — Armenian) 105
Matt'êos II *Ch'ukhachian* : 1844–1848 (Constantinople — Armenian) 106
Matt'êos III *Izmirlian* : 1894–1896, 1908–1909 (Constantinople — Armenian) 106
Matt'êos : 1706 (Jerusalem — Armenian) 181
Matthäus : 1221–1226 (Constantinople — Latin) 119
Matthaios *Psaltēs* : 1746–1765 (Alexandria — Greek) 25
Matthaios I *apo Kyzikou* : 1397–1402, 1403–1410 (Constantinople — Greek) 113
Matthaios II *apo Iōanninōn* : 1595, 1598?–1602, 1603 (Constantinople — Greek) 114
Matthaios : 1943–1949 [locum tenens], 1949–1950 [archbishop] (Greece — Old Calendarists) 159
Matthias : 1221–1226 (Constantinople — Latin) 119
Matthias : 2nd cent. (Jerusalem — Greek) 184
Maxim *Brancovici* : 1505–1508 (Romania) 206
Maximianos : 431–434 (Constantinople — Greek) 110
Maximos : 265–282 (Alexandria — Greek) 23
Maximos I *Kynikos* : 381 (Constantinople — Greek) 110
Maximos II *apo Akoimētōn* : 1216 (Constantinople — Greek) 112
Maximos III *Manassēs* : 1476–1482 (Constantinople — Greek) 113
Maximos IV *apo Serrōn* : 1491–1497 (Constantinople — Greek) 113
Maximos V *Baportzēs* : 1946–1948 (Constantinople — Greek) 117

Maximos *Progiannakopoulos* : 1786–1800 (Crete) 125
Maximos I : 2nd cent. (Jerusalem — Greek) 184
Maximos II : 2nd cent. (Jerusalem — Greek) 184
Maximos III : 333–348 (Jerusalem — Greek) 184
Mazabanēs : 251–260 (Jerusalem — Greek) 184
Mefodiĭ *Kudriakov* : 2000- [acting primate] (Ukraine — Autocephalous) 234, 238, 256, 258, 260
Mehruzhan : 240–270 (Armenia) 64
Melchiades : 311–314 (Rome) 211
Melentije I *Stefanović* : 1809–1811 (Serbia — Beograd) 228
Melentije II *Pavlović* : 1815–1816, 1830–1833 (Serbia — Beograd) 228
Meletie : unknown (Austria — Cernovci) 77
Meletiĭ I : 1637–1643 (Bulgaria) 94
Meletiĭ II : 1676–1677 (Bulgaria) 94
Meletiĭ *Kartushin* : 1915–1934 (Russia — Belokrinitsia) 223
Meletij I : 1637–1641 (Macedonia) 196
Meletij II : 1677–1679 (Macedonia) 196
Meletios I *Pēgas* : 1590–1601 (Alexandria — Greek) 25
Meletios *Apostolopoulos* : 1899–1900 [locum tenens] (Alexandria — Greek) 26
Meletios II *Metaxakēs* : 1926–1935 (Alexandria — Greek) 26, 108, 117–118, 135, 145, 157
Meletios I *Pēgas* : 1597–1598? [locum tenens] (Constantinople — Greek) 114
Meletios II *apo Larissēs* : 1768–1769 (Constantinople — Greek) 116
Meletios III *Pankalos apo Kyzikou* : 1845 (Constantinople — Greek) 117
Meletios IV *Metaxakēs* : 1921–1923 (Constantinople — Greek) 26, 108, 117–118, 135, 145, 157
Meletios I *Nikoletakēs* : 1831–1839 (Crete) 125
Meletios II *Kalymnios* : 1868–1874, 1877–1882 (Crete) 125
Meletios I : 1275–1289 (Greece) 156
Meletios II *Mētrou apo Naupaktou kai Artēs* : 1703–1713 (Greece) 157
Meletios III *Metaxakēs* :

Index of Primates

1918–1920 (Greece) 26, 108, 117–118, 135, 145, 157
Meletios *apo Kaisareias* : 1731–1737 (Jerusalem — Greek) 187
Melitōn : 1972 [locum tenens] (Constantinople — Greek) 117
Melitōn *of Madabon* : 1934–1935 [locum tenens] (Jerusalem — Greek) 187
Melhisedek *Paieuskiĭ* : 1922–1925 (Belarus) 89–90
Melitê : 452–456 (Armenia) 65
Melk'isedek : 1593–1603 [coadjutor] (Armenia) 67
Melk'isedek I : 1599–1600 (Constantinople — Armenian) 104
Melk'isedek II: 1698–1699, 1700–1701 (Constantinople — Armenian) 105
Melk'isedek I : 1012–1045 (Georgia) 149
Melk'isedek II *Bagrationi* : 1538–1541 (Georgia) 150
Melk'isedek III *Pk'aladze* : 1952–1960 (Georgia) 152
Melk'iset' : 1593–1596 (Aghunie) 10
Mēnas : 634? (Alexandria — Coptic — Gaianite) 19
Mēnas *Sampsōn* : 536–552 (Constantinople — Greek) 110
Merbukhat : 401–420 (India — Malankara Orthodox) 163
Merkorewos *Fenta* : 1988–1991 (Ethiopia — Historical), and (Ethiopia — Official) 138, 142, 144
Mesrop : 439–440 [locum tenens] (Armenia) 65
Mesrop : 1359–1372 (Armenia) 66
Mesrop I *Naroyan* : 1927–1944 (Constantinople — Armenian) 106
Mesrop II *Mutafian* : 1998 [locum tenens], 1998- [patriarch] (Constantinople — Armenian) 106, 254, 258, 260
Mesrop I : 1008 [coadjutor] (Jerusalem — Armenian) 180
Mesrop II : 1402 [coadjutor] (Jerusalem — Armenian) 180
Mesrop III : 1454–1461 (Jerusalem — Armenian) 181
Mesrop IV *Nishanian* : 1930–1931 [locum tenens], 1939–1944 [patriarch] (Jerusalem — Armenian) 182
Methodios I : 843–847 (Constantinople — Greek) 111
Methodios II : 1240?–1241? (Constantinople — Greek) 112
Methodios III *Mōrōnēs apo Hērakleias* : 1668–1671 (Constantinople — Greek) 115
Methodios *apo Karpathou* : 1823 (Crete) 125

Methodios *Fougas* : 1979–1988 [locum tenens] (Latvia) 191
Metodiĭ I : 1708 (Bulgaria) 95
Metodiĭ II : 1757–1758 (Bulgaria) 95
Metodij I : 1708 (Macedonia) 196
Metodij II : 1757–1758 (Macedonia) 197
Metodije : 1791–1801 (Serbia — Beograd) 228
Mētrophanēs : 1636–1639 (Alexandria — Greek) 25
Mētrophanēs I : 315–325 (Constantinople — Greek) 109
Mētrophanēs II *apo Kyzikou* : 1440–1443 (Constantinople — Greek) 113
Mētrophanēs III *apo Kaisareias* : 1565–1572, 1579–1580 (Constantinople — Greek) 114
Mētrophanēs : -1619 (Greece) 157
Michaēl I : 860–870 (Alexandria — Greek) 24
Michaēl II : 870–903 (Alexandria — Greek) 24
Michael *Bonelli* : 1587? (Alexandria — Latin) 28
Michaēl *Kōnstantinidēs* : 1949–1958 (America — Greek) 30
Michael Angelus *Mattei* : 1693- (Antioch — Latin) 47
Michaēl I *Kēroularios* : 1043–1058 (Constantinople — Greek) 107, 111
Michaēl II *Kourkouas Oxeitēs* : 1143–1146 (Constantinople — Greek) 112
Michaēl III *Anchialou* : 1170–1178 (Constantinople — Greek) 112
Michaēl IV *Autōreianos* : 1208–1214 (Constantinople — Greek) 112
Michael *Zezza di Zapponeta* : 1923–1927 (Constantinople — Latin) 122
Michaēl : 12th cent. (Crete) 124
Michael : 1375? (Cyprus — Latin) 130
Michaēl I : 1007–1030 (Greece) 155
Michaēl II : 1133? (Greece) 156
Michaēl III *Akominatos Chōniatēs* : 1182–1222 (Greece) 156,2 52
Michael *Augustine*, Mar : 1900–1911 [locum tenens] (India — Chaldean) 174
Michael I : 1194 (Jerusalem — Latin) 189
Michael II *Sabbah* : 1987- (Jerusalem — Latin) 188–189, 255, 257, 259
Michaēl : 1455? (Sinai) 231
Mihail I *Maksim* : 1120- (Macedonia) 194
Mihail II *Gogov* : 1993 [locum

tenens], 1993–1999 (Macedonia) 194, 197
Mihail I : 1585?–1589 (Romania) 206
Mihail II : 1592–1594 (Romania) 206
Mihaïlo *Grujić* : 1913–1914 [locum tenens] (Austria — Karlovci) 80
Mihaïlo I : 1280? (Montenegro) 201
Mihaïlo II : 1305–1319 (Montenegro) 201
Mihaïlo III *Dedeić* : 1998- (Montenegro) 202, 256–257, 259
Mihaïlo *Jovanović* : 1859–1881, 1889–1898 (Serbia — Beograd) 228
Mika'el *Wolde Mika'el* : -1980? (Eritrea) 134
Mika'el I *Habib al-Atfihi* : 1105?–1153 or 1130?–1199? (Ethiopia — Historical) 142
Mika'el II *Kilus ibn al-Mulabbas* : 1205–1210? (Ethiopia — Historical) 143
Mika'el III, *Yerda'* : 1220? (Ethiopia — Historical) 143
Mika'el IV : 1438–1455? (Ethiopia — Historical) 143
Mika'el V : 1649? (Ethiopia — Historical) 143
Mika'el I : unknown (Ethiopia — Official) 139
Mika'el II : unknown (Ethiopia — Official) 139
Mika'el III : unknown (Ethiopia — Official) 139
Mika'el IV : unknown (Ethiopia — Official) 139
Mika'el V : unknown (Ethiopia — Official) 140
Mika'el VI : unknown (Ethiopia — Official) 140
Mika'el VII : unknown (Ethiopia — Official) 140
Mika'el VIII : unknown (Ethiopia — Official) 140
Mika'el IX : unknown (Ethiopia — Official) 140
Mika'el X : unknown (Ethiopia — Official) 140
Mika'el XI : 1438–1458? (Ethiopia — Official) 141
Mika'el XII : unknown (Ethiopia — Official) 141
Mika'el XIII : 1648? (Ethiopia — Official) 141
Mikael *Kasanskin* : 1919–1922 [assistant bishop] (Finland) 145
Mik'ayêl : 1796–1810 (Aght'amar) 7
Mik'ayêl : 706–741 (Aghunie) 9
Mik'ayêl : 1545–1567 [coadjutor], 1567–1576 [catholicos] (Armenia) 67

Mik'ayêl I : 1737–1758 (Cilicia — Armenian Apostolic) 99
Mik'ayêl II : 1832–1855 (Cilicia — Armenian Apostolic) 100
Mik'ayêl : 1706–1707 (Constantinople — Armenian), and : 1706–1707 (Jerusalem — Armenian) 105, 181
Mik'ayêl Petros III *Gasparian* : 1753–1780 (Cilicia — Armenian Catholic) 102, 252
Mik'el I : 452–467 (Georgia) 148
Mik'el II : 774–780 (Georgia) 149
Mik'el III : 930–944 (Georgia) 149
Mik'el IV : 1178–1186 (Georgia) 150
Mik'el V : 1325–1330 (Georgia) 150
Mik'el VI : 1411–1426 (Georgia) 150
Mikha'il —*see also*: Khail
Mikha'il III : 880–907 (Alexandria — Coptic) 16
Mikha'il IV : 1092–1102 (Alexandria — Coptic) 17
Mikha'il V : 1145–1146 (Alexandria — Coptic) 17
Mikha'il VI : 1476–1478 (Alexandria — Coptic) 18
Mikha'il I : 879–890 (Antioch — Greek) 36
Mikha'il II : 1353–1376 (Antioch — Greek) 37
Mikha'il III : 1401–1410 (Antioch — Greek) 37
Mikha'il IV *ibn al-Mawardi* : 1454–1462 (Antioch — Greek) 37
Mikha'il V *ibn al-Mawardi* : 1523–1541 (Antioch — Greek) 37
Mikha'il VI *Sabbagh al-Hamawi* : 1577–1581 (Antioch — Greek) 37
Mikha'il I : 1368–1375 (Antioch — Greek Melkite) 43
Mikha'il II : 1395–1412 (Antioch — Greek Melkite) 43
Mikha'il III *ibn al-Mawardi* : 1451?–1456? (Antioch — Greek Melkite) 43
Mikha'il IV : 1470?–1484? (Antioch — Greek Melkite) 43
Mikha'il V *ibn al-Mawardi* : 1523?–1529 (Antioch — Greek Melkite) 43
Mikha'il VI *Sabbagh* : 1534–1543 (Antioch — Greek Melkite) 43
Mikha'il VII *al-Hamawi* : 1576–1593 (Antioch — Greek Melkite) 43
Mikha'il I *ibn Yuhanna al-Ruzzi* : 1567–1581 (Antioch — Maronite) 50
Mikha'il II Butrus *Fadl* : 1793–1795 (Antioch — Maronite) 50
Mikha'il I *al-Kabir* : 1167–1200 (Antioch — Syrian Catholic) 55
Mikha'il II *Ishu' Siftana* : 1207–1208 (Antioch — Syrian Catholic) 55
Mikha'il III *Jarwah*, Ighnatiyus : 1782–1800 (Antioch — Syrian Catholic) 52, 56
Mikha'il IV *Dahir*, Ighnatiyus : 1802–1810 (Antioch — Syrian Catholic) 56
Mikha'il I *al-Kabir* "the Great" : 1166–1199 (Antioch — Syrian Orthodox) 60
Mikha'il II *ibn Sawma* : 1292–1312 (Antioch — Syrian Orthodox) 60
Mikha'il III *Ishu' ibn Shushan* : 1312–1349 (Antioch — Syrian Orthodox) 61
Mikhaïl *Maksim* : 1120?– (Bulgaria) 92
Mikhaïl : 1948–1949 [locum tenens] (Bulgaria) 95
Mikhaïl *Kochetov* : 1938–1944 (Russia-Novozybkov) 223
Mikha'il Shim'un XVII : 1740?–1780? (Assyria) 74
Militus : 360–381 (Antioch — Syrian Orthodox) 58
Miliyus : 83–98 (Alexandria — Coptic) 15
Miltiades : 311–314 (Rome) 211
Mina I : 767–774 (Alexandria — Coptic) 16
Mina II : 956–974 (Alexandria — Coptic) 17
Minas : 1751–1753 (Armenia) 68
Minas : 1621–1632 (Cilicia — Armenian Apostolic) 99
Minas : 1749–1751 (Constantinople — Armenian) 105
Minas I : 270? (Ethiopia — Historical) 142
Minas II : 923? (Ethiopia — Historical) 142
Minas I : unknown (Ethiopia — Official) 139
Minas II : unknown (Ethiopia — Official) 139
Minas III : unknown (Ethiopia — Official) 140
Minas IV : unknown (Ethiopia — Official) 140
Minas V : unknown (Ethiopia — Official) 140
Minas I : 1191–1205 (Jerusalem — Armenian) 180
Minas II : 1426 [coadjutor] (Jerusalem — Armenian) 180
Minas III : 1697–1704 (Jerusalem — Armenian) 181
Miron *Nikolić* : 1913 [locum tenens], 1914–1919 [locum tenens] (Austria — Karlovci) 80

Miron *Romanul* : 1874–1898 (Austria — Sibiu) 82
Miron *Cristea* : 1919–1925 [metropolitan], 1925–1939 [patriarch] (Romania) 208
Misaël *Apostolidēs* : 1862 (Greece) 157
Misail I : 1685?–1689 (Austria — Cernovci) 78
Misail II : 1729–1735 (Austria — Cernovci) 78
Mithudiyus *of Naxos* : 1823–1850 (Antioch — Greek) 38
Mitrofan : 1550?–1552 (Austria — Cernovci) 77
Mitrofan *šević* : 1908 [refused election] (Austria — Karlovci) 80
Mitrofan : 1614–1616 (Bulgaria), and 1610?–1614 (Macedonia) 94
Mitrofan *Ban* : 1884–1885 [locum tenens], 1885–1920 [metropolitan] (Montenegro) 200, 202
Mitrofan I : 1526?–1534? (Romania) 206
Mitrofan II : 1716–1719 (Romania) 206
Mkhit'ar : 1341–1355 (Armenia) 66
Mkhit'ar : 1699–1700 (Constantinople — Armenian) 105
Mkrtich' *Khrimian* : 1892–1907 (Armenia) 68
Mkrtich' *K'êfsizian* : 1871–1894 (Cilicia — Armenian Apostolic) 100
Mkrtich' *Khrimian* : 1869–1873 (Constantinople — Armenian) 106
Mkrtich' I : 708–730 (Jerusalem — Armenian) 179
Mkrtich' II : 1363–1378 (Jerusalem — Armenian) 180
Mkrtich' III : 1476–1479 (Jerusalem — Armenian) 181
Mobidani : 436–448 (Georgia) 148
Modestos : 431? (Greece) 155
Modestos : 632–634 (Jerusalem — Greek) 185
Moiseĭ *Bogdanov-Platonov* : 1832–1834 [exarch] (Georgia) 151
Mojsej I *Petrović* : 1726–1730 (Austria — Karlovci) 79
Mojsej II *Putnik* : 1781–1790 (Austria — Karlovci) 79
Mojsije *Rajović* : 1712–1726 (Serbia) 227
Mojsije *Veresić* [locum tenens] 1881–1883 (Serbia — Beograd) 228
Monachus : 1194– (Jerusalem — Latin) 189
Mondillus *Orsini* : 1729– (Constantinople — Latin) 121

Morooso : 628–649 (India — Malankara Orthodox) 163
Mosa, Dionysius : 1112–1134 (India — Malankara Jacobite) 169
Mose : 410–425 (Georgia) 148
Moudyano, Bar Souma : 1422–1455 (India — Malankara Jacobite) 170
Moüsēs : unknown (Sinai) 230
Movsês I : 4th cent. (Aghunie) 8
Movsês II : 777–779 (Aghunie) 9
Movsês III : 822 (Aghunie) 9
Movsês IV : 992–997 (Aghunie) 9
Movsês I : 456–461 (Armenia) 65
Movsês II : 574–604 (Armenia) 65
Movsês III : 1629–1632 (Armenia) 67
Movsês : 1109–1133 (Jerusalem — Armenian) 180
Mstyslav *Skrypnyk* : 1969–1990 [metropolitan], 1990–1993 [patriarch] (Ukraine — Autocephalous), and 1947–1950 (Ukraine — Canada), and 1971–1993 (Ukraine — Orthodox Church of the USA) 234, 238, 240
Muron : 1436–1437 [coadjutor] (Jerusalem — Armenian) 181
Murqus I : 43?–68 (Alexandria — Coptic) 14–15
Murqus II : 799–819 (Alexandria — Coptic) 16
Murqus III *ibn Zur'a* : 1167–1189 (Alexandria — Coptic) 17
Murqus IV : 1349–1363 (Alexandria — Coptic) 17
Murqus V : 1602–1618 (Alexandria — Coptic) 18
Murqus VI : 1650–1660 (Alexandria — Coptic) 18
Murqus VII : 1745–1769 (Alexandria — Coptic) 18
Murqus VIII : 1796–1809 (Alexandria — Coptic) 18
Murqus : 1870–1874 [locum tenens] (Alexandria — Coptic) 18
Murqus I : 50?–68 (Alexandria — Coptic Catholic) 20
Murqus II *Khuzam* : 1927–1958 (Alexandria — Coptic Catholic) 21
Murqus I : 1308–1342 (Antioch — Greek) 37
Murqus II : 1426–1436 (Antioch — Greek) 37
Murqus III : 1462–1476 (Antioch — Greek) 37
Murqus I : 1377–1378 (Antioch — Greek Melkite) 43
Murqus II : 1425?–1434? (Antioch — Greek Melkite) 43
Murqus III : 1456?–1458? (Antioch — Greek Melkite) 43
Murqus : unknown (Antioch — Maronite) 49
Musa *ibn Sa'adi al-'Aquri* : 1524–1567 (Antioch — Maronite) 50
Musa *Dawud*, Ighnatiyus : 1998–2001 (Antioch — Syrian Catholic) 56
Mushê I : 93–123 (Armenia) 64
Mushê II : 526–534 (Armenia) 65
Musi *ibn Sa'adi al-'Aquri* : 1524–1567 (Antioch — Maronite) 50, 252
Mykhaïl *Horoshyî* : 1972–1975 (Ukraine — Canada) 240
Mykhaïlo I : 988–992 (Ukraine) 235
Mykhaïlo II : 1130–1145? (Ukraine) 235
Mykhaïlo III : 1171 (Ukraine) 235
Mykhaïlo IV : 1378?–1379 (Ukraine) 236
Mykhaïlo V *Rahoza* : 1589–1596 (Ukraine) 237
Mykhaïlo VI *IErmakov* : 1921–1929 (Ukraine) 238
Mykola I : 1097?–1101 (Ukraine) 235
Mykola II *IArushevych* : 1941–1944 (Ukraine) 238
Mykola *Borets'kyĭ* : 1927–1930 (Ukraine — Autocephalous) 233, 238
Mykola *Hrokh* : 1990–1991 [locum tenens] (Ukraine — Autocephalous) 238
Mykyta : 1122–1126 (Ukraine) 235
Myrōn *Thaumatourgos* : -350 (Crete) 123
Mytiaï IV : 1378?–1379 (Ukraine) 236

Nahapet : 1691–1705 (Armenia) 67
Narkissos : 117–138 (Greece) 155
Narkissos : 185–211 (Jerusalem — Greece) 184
Narsai : 524–535 (Assyria), and 524–537? (Babylon) 72, 85
Nasr Allah Butrus *Sfayr* : 1986- (Antioch — Maronite) 51, 253, 257, 259
Natēras : unknown (Sinai) 230
Nathanaël *Emporos* : 1602–1604 (Greece) 157
Nazariĭ *Blynov* : 1919–1921 (Ukraine) 238
Nectarie *Cotlarciuc* : 1924–1935 (Austria — Cernovci) 78
Nectarie : 1812–1819 (Romania) 207
Neilos : 1869–1870 [anti-patriarch] (Alexandria — Greek) 26
Neilos *Kerameus* : 1380–1388 (Constantinople — Greek) 113
Neilos *Kouerinos* : 1555? (Sinai) 232
Nektariĭ I : 1598–1604 (Bulgaria) 94
Nektariĭ II : 1617–1622? (Bulgaria) 94
Nektariĭ III : 1673? (Bulgaria) 94
Nektarij I : 1598- (Macedonia) 196
Nektarij II : 1616–1623? (Macedonia) 196
Nektarij III : 1671–1673 (Macedonia) 196
Nektarios : 381–397 (Constantinople — Greek) 110
Nektarios : 1660–1669 (Jerusalem — Greek) 187
Nektarios : 1660–1661 (Sinai) 232
Nemet Allah, Baselios : 1555–1557 (India — Malankara Jacobite) 170
Neofit *Bozveli* : 1840?–1850?, 1856?–1857? (Bulgaria) 95
Neofit : 1934–1944 [locum tenens] (Bulgaria) 95
Neofit : 1551 (Macedonia) 195
Neofit : 1250–1270 (Montenegro) 201
Neofit I *Cretanul* : 1738–1753 (Romania) 207
Neofit II : 1829–1833, 1833–1840 [locum tenens], 1840–1849 (Romania) 207
Neophytos I *Enkleistos Klaustrarios* : 1153? (Constantinople — Greek) 112
Neophytos II *Karykēs* : 1602–1603, 1607–1612 (Constantinople — Greek) 114
Neophytos III *apo Hērakleias* : 1636–1637 (Constantinople — Greek) 115
Neophytos IV *apo Adrianoupoleōs* : 1688–1689 (Constantinople — Greek) 115
Neophytos V *apo Hērakleias* : 1707 [unconsecrated] (Constantinople — Greek) 115
Neophytos VI *apo Kaisareias Kappadokias* : 1734–1740, 1743–1744 (Constantinople — Greek) 116
Neophytos VII *apo Marōneias* : 1789–1794, 1798–1801 (Constantinople — Greek) 116
Neophytos VIII *Papakōnstantinou* : 1891–1894 (Constantinople — Greek) 117
Neophytos *Patellaros* : 1646–1679 (Crete) 124, 252
Neophytos I : 1222?–1251 (Cyprus) 128
Neophytos II : -1592 (Cyprus) 128

Neophytos : 1745 [anti-archbishop] (Cyprus) 128
Neophytos I : 1366 (Greece) 156
Neophytos II : 1492–1498 (Greece) 156
Neophytos III *Karykēs* : 1597–1602 (Greece) 156
Neophytos IV : 1774–1776 (Greece) 157
Neophytos V *Metaxas apo Talantiou* : 1833–1861 (Greece) 157
Nēphōn : 1366–1385 (Alexandria — Greek) 25
Nēphōn I *apo Kyzikou* : 1310–1314 (Constantinople — Greek) 112
Nēphōn II *apo Thessalonikēs* : 1486–1488, 1497–1498, 1502 (Constantinople — Greek) 113
Nersēs (I) : 1312 (coadjutor) (Aght'amar) 6
Nersēs (II) *Bolat* : 1368?–1369? [anti-catholicos] (Aght'amar) 6
Nersēs (III) : 1393? [anti-catholicos] (Aght'amar) 6
Nersēs (IV) *Kurdjibeguyan* : 1489? [anti-catholicos] (Aght'amar) 6
Nersēs I : 687?–704 (Aghunie) 9
Nersēs II : 1171? (Aghunie) 10
Nersēs III : 1235–1262 (Aghunie) 10
Nersēs IV : 1478–1481 (Aghunie) 10
Nersēs V : 1706–1763 (Aghunie) 11
Nersês I *"The Great"* : 353–373 (Armenia) 64
Nersês II : 548–557 (Armenia) 65
Nersês III *Shinogh* : 641–661 (Armenia) 65
Nersês IV *Shnorhali* : 1166–1173 (Armenia) 66
Nersês : 1506–1507 [coadjutor] (Armenia) 67
Nersês V *Ashtaraketsi* : 1843–1857 (Armenia) 68
Nersês *Vartsapetian* : 1884 [unconsecrated] (Armenia) 68
Nersês *Pozapalian* : 1999 [locum tenens] (Armenia) 68
Nersês : 1648–1654 (Cilicia — Armenian Apostolic) 99
Nersês I : 1704 (Constantinople — Armenian) 105
Nersês II *Vartsapetian* : 1874–1884 (Constantinople — Armenian) 106
Nersês Petros XIX *Tarmouni* : 1999- (Cilicia — Armenian Catholic) 102, 251, 254, 258, 260
Nestor *Zass* : 1878–1882 (America — Orthodox Church) 31
Nestor *Anisimov* : 1945–1948 (China) 97
Nestorios : 428–431 (Constantinople — Greek) 110

Netras : unknown (Sinai) 230
Nichifor : 1589–1592 (Romania) 206
Nicodim *Munteanu* : 1939 [locum tenens], 1939–1948 [patriarch] (Romania) 208
Nicolae : unknown (Austria — Cernovci) 77
Nicolae *Vasilevic* : 1691- [anti-archbishop] (Austria — Cernovci) 78
Nicolae *Hutovic* : 1805–1811 [locum tenens] (Austria — Sibiu) 81
Nicolae I *Balan* : 1920–1955 (Austria — Sibiu) 82
Nicolae II *Colan* : 1957–1967 (Austria — Sibiu) 82
Nicolae *Corneanu* : 1967 [locum tenens] (Austria — Sibiu) 82
Nicolae III *Mladin* : 1967–1981 (Austria — Sibiu) 82
Nicolaus *Tanara* : 1845–1853 (Antioch — Latin) 47
Nicolaus I *de Castro Arquato* : 1234–1251 (Constantinople — Latin) 119
Nicolaus II : 1308–1331? (Constantinople — Latin) 120
Nicolaus *de Hanapis* : 1288–1294 (Jerusalem — Latin) 189
Nicolaus I *Magnus "The Great"* : 858–867 (Rome) 213
Nicolaus II : 1059–1061 (Rome) 214
Nicolaus III *Orsini* : 1277–1280 (Rome) 215
Nicolaus IV *Masci* : 1288–1292 (Rome) 215
Nicolaus V *Rainalducci* : 1328–1330 [anti-pope] (Rome) 215
Nicolaus V *Parentucelli* : 1447–1455 (Rome) 216
Nifon I : 1503?–1505 (Romania) 206
Nifon II : 1849–1850 [locum tenens], 1850–1875 (Romania) 207
Nifont : 1303–1305 (Ukraine — Halych) 239
Nikanōr : 1866–1870 (Alexandria — Greek) 26
Nikanor *Grujić* : 1872–1874 [locum tenens] (Austria — Karlovci) 79
Nikanor : -1557 (Bulgaria), and 1555?–1557 (Macedonia) 94, 195
Nikanōr : 1570–1592 (Greece) 156
Nikanor I : 1591? (Montenegro) 201
Nikanor II *Ivanović-Njeguš* : 1853–1858 [locum tenens], 1858–1860 (Montenegro) 202
Nikanor I *Klemientiewskij* : 1843–1848 (Poland) 204

Nikanor II *Kamienskij* : 1905–1908 (Poland) 204
Nikanor : 1589? (Serbia) 227
Nikanor *Burshak-Abramovych* : 1953–1969 (Ukraine — Autocephalous) 234, 238
Nikēphoros *Klarontzanēs* : 1639–1645 (Alexandria — Greek) 25
Nikēphoros I : 806–815 (Constantinople — Greek) 111
Nikēphoros II *apo Ephesou* : 1260–1261 (Constantinople — Greek) 112
Nikēphoros *Hierodiakonos* : 1586? [locum tenens], 1586?- [locum tenens] (Constantinople — Greek) 114
Nikēphoros I *Moschopoulos* : 1285–1322 (Crete) 124
Nikēphoros II : 1312?–1318? (Crete) 124
Nikēphoros III *Skōtakēs* : 1679–1681? (Crete) 124
Nikēphoros : 1640?–1674 (Cyprus) 128
Nikēphoros : 1103–1121 (Greece) 156
Nikēphoros I : 1020 (Jerusalem — Greek) 186
Nikēphoros II : 1166–1170 (Jerusalem — Greek) 186
Nikēphoros *Marthalēs Glykys* : 1728–1747 (Sinai) 232
Nikētas I : 766–780 (Constantinople — Greek) 111
Nikētas II *Mountanēs* : 1186–1189 (Constantinople — Greek) 112
Nikētas I : 9th cent. (Crete) 124
Nikētas II : 9th cent. (Crete) 124
Nikētas III : 11th cent. (Crete) 124
Nikētas I : 867–877 (Greece) 155
Nikētas II : 922–927 (Greece) 155
Nikētas III *Kourtēs* : 1086–1103 (Greece) 155
Nikētas IV *Hagiotheodōritēs* : 1166–1175 (Greece) 156
Nikifore : 1657 (Georgia — Abkhazia) 153
Nikodēmos : 1371? (Greece) 156
Nikodēmos : 1883–1890 (Jerusalem — Greek) 187
Nikodim *Rotov* : 1963 (Belarus) 90
Nikodim : 1452? (Bulgaria), and (Macedonia) 93, 195
Nikodim : 1540? (Montenegro) 201
Nikodim *Latyshev* : 1971–1986 (Russia — Belokrinitsia) 223
Nikodim I : 1317–1324 (Serbia) 226
Nikodim II : 1446–1453 (Serbia) 227
Nikodimos *Abebe* : 1988–1991 (Eritrea) 134

Nikoghayos : 1736–1751 (Aght'amar) 7
Nikoghayos : 1478–1489 (Constantinople — Armenian) 103
Nikola *Pozdnev* : 1923–1934 (Russia-Novozybkov) 222–223
Nikolaĭ I *Adoratskiĭ* : 1891 (America — Orthodox Church) 31
Nikolaĭ II *Ziorov* : 1891–1898 (America — Orthodox Church) 31
Nikolaĭ I : 1347? (Bulgaria) 93
Nikolaĭ II : 1486–1502? (Bulgaria) 93
Nikolaĭ *Nalimov* : 1898–1905 (Finland); 1905–1906 [exarch] (Georgia) 145, 152
Nikolaĭ I *Kassatkin* : 1880–1912 (Japan) 177, 252
Nikolaĭ II *Ono* : 1941–1967? (Japan) 177–178
Nikolaĭ III *Sayama* : 1967–1970 (Japan) 178
Nikolaj *Dmitrijević* : 1730–1731 [locum tenens] (Austria — Karlovci) 79
Nikolaj *Kocvár* : 1999–2000 [locum tenens], 2000- (Czechoslovakia) 133, 254, 258–259
Nikolaj I : 1345–1348? (Macedonia) 195
Nikolaj II : 1481?–1487? (Macedonia) 195
Nikolaj *Ziorow* : 1908–1915 (Poland) 204
Nikolaos I : 1210?– (Alexandria — Greek) 25
Nikolaos II : 1263–1276 (Alexandria — Greek) 25
Nikolaos III : 1389–1398 (Alexandria — Greek) 25
Nikolaos IV : 1412–1417 (Alexandria — Greek) 25
Nikolaos V *Euangelidēs* : 1936–1939 (Alexandria — Greek) 26
Nikolaos VI *Barelopoulos* : 1968–1986 (Alexandria — Greek) 26
Nikolaos I *Mystikos* : 901–907, 912–925 (Constantinople — Greek) 111
Nikolaos II *Chrysobergios* : 979–991 (Constantinople — Greek) 111
Nikolaos III *Grammatikos Kyrdiniatēs* : 1084–1111 (Constantinople — Greek) 112
Nikolaos IV *Mouzalōn* : 1147–1151 (Constantinople — Greek) 112
Nikolaos *apo Kaisareias* : 1921, 1923 [locum tenens] (Constantinople — Greek) 117
Nikolaos I : 12th cent. (Crete) 124
Nikolaos II : 1195?–1221? (Crete) 124
Nikolaos *Mouzalōn* : 1110? (Cyprus) 128
Nikolaos *Hagiotheodōritēs* : 1166–1175 (Greece) 156
Nikolaos : 1156 (Jerusalem — Greek) 186
Nikoloz I *Gulaberidze* : 1150–1178 (Georgia) 150
Nikoloz II : 1240–1280 (Georgia) 150
Nikoloz III : 1364–1380 (Georgia) 150
Nikoloz IV *Bagrationi* : 1562–1584 (Georgia) 151
Nikoloz V *Bagrationi* : 1584–1591 (Georgia) 151
Nikoloz VI : 1678–1688, 1691–1696 (Georgia) 151
Nikoloz VII *K'erk'evlidze* : 1741–1744 (Georgia) 151
Nikoloz I : 1290? (Georgia — Abkhazia) 152
Nikolozi II : 1703–1710 (Georgia — Abkhazia) 153
Nikon *Sofiĭskiĭ* : 1906–1908 [exarch] (Georgia) 152
Nikon *de Greve* : 1960–1962 (Japan) 178
Nikon *Fomichev* : 1962–1963 [locum tenens], 1963–1966 (Latvia) 192
Nikon : 1652–1658 (Russia) 220, 222
Nikon : 1420–1435 (Serbia) 226
Nilus : 1393–1401 (Antioch — Greek) 37
Ni'mat Allah, Ighnatiyus : 1557–1576 (Antioch — Syrian Catholic), and (Antioch — Syrian Orthodox) 56, 61
Niphōn I *apo Kyzikou* : 1310–1314 (Constantinople — Greek) 112
Niqifurus *"The Black"* : 1084–1088 (Antioch — Greek), and 1090- (Antioch — Greek Melkite) 37, 42
Niqula Ishai Ya'qub *Zaya* : 1838–1847 (Babylon) 88
Niqulawus I : 826–834 (Antioch — Greek) 36
Niqulawus II : 860–871, 871–879 (Antioch — Greek) 36
Niqulawus III *Stouditēs* : 1000–1003 (Antioch — Greek) 36
Niqulawus I : 847–866? (Antioch — Greek Melkite) 41
Niqulawus II *Stouditēs* : 1022–1030 (Antioch — Greek Melkite) 42
Niqun : 1387?–1395 (Antioch — Greek Melkite) 43
Niyufutus *apo Chiou* : 1674–1684 (Antioch — Greek), and 1672–1682 (Antioch — Greek Melkite) 38, 43

Novatianus : 251 [anti-pope] (Rome) 211
Nuh *the Lebanese* : 1489–1493 (India — Malankara Jacobite) 170
Nuh, Ighnatiyus : 1494–1509 (Antioch — Syrian Catholic), and 1493–1509 (Antioch — Syrian Orthodox) 55, 61
Nuh, Ignatios Mar *of Homs* : 1490–1494 (India — Malankara Orthodox) 166
Nykyfor I : 1104–1121 (Ukraine) 235
Nykyfor II : 1183–1198 (Ukraine) 235
Nyphōn II *apo Thessalonikēs* : 1486–1488, 1497–1498, 1502 (Constantinople — Greek) 113

Oah : 386–393 (India — Malankara Orthodox) 163
Odoardus *Cybò* : 1689–1700 (Constantinople — Latin) 121
Oēalēs II : 2nd cent. (Jerusalem — Greek) 184
Ok'ropir Ioane I : 980–1001 (Georgia) 149
Ok'ropir Ioane II : 1045–1049 (Georgia) 149
Oleksandr *Petrovs'kyĭ* : 1937–1940 (Ukraine) 238
Olympianos : 187–198 (Constantinople — Greek) 109
Olympios I : 449?–451? (Cyprus) 127
Olympios II : 490? (Cyprus) 127
Olympios : 300? (Greece) 155
Onēsimos : 54–68 (Constantinople — Greek) 109
Onopsos : 711? (Alexandria — Greek) 24
Onysyfir *Petrovych-Devochka* : 1579–1589 (Ukraine) 237
Opizio I : 1254–1255 (Antioch — Latin) 45
Opizio II *Fieschi* : 1270?–1292 (Antioch — Latin) 46
Orestēs : 983–1005 (Jerusalem — Greek) 185
Otto *de Sala* : 1322–1323 (Alexandria — Latin) 27
Oualēs I : 2nd cent. (Jerusalem — Greek) 184
Oualēs II : 2nd cent. (Jerusalem — Greek) 184
Ougen *Turuthi*, Baselios Mar : 1962–1964 [suffragan], 1964–1975 [catholicos] (India — Malankara Orthodox), and (India — Malankara Jacobite) 161, 167

Paavali *Olmari* : 1960–1987 (Finland) 146
Pachōmios I *apo Zichnōn* : 1503–1504, 1504–1513 (Constantinople — Greek) 113–114

Pachōmios II *Patestos apo Kaisareias* : 1584–1585 (Constantinople — Greek) 114
Pafnutiĭ : 1660 (Bulgaria) 94
Pahomie : 1504–1522 (Austria — Cernovci) 77
Pahomije *Gačić* : 1994–2002? (Macedonia — Serbian Archdiocese) 194, 197
Pahomije I : 1491? (Montenegro) 201
Pahomije II *Komanin* : 1569? (Montenegro) 201
Païsi *Vodica* : 1949–1966 (Albania) 12–13, 252
Païsiĭ (I) : 1558–1566 (Bulgaria) 94
Païsiĭ (II) : 1850?–1856?, 1861- (Bulgaria) 95
Païsiĭ *of Vratsa* : 1949–1951 [locum tenens] (Bulgaria) 96
Païsios : 1671–1678 (Alexandria — Greek) 25
Païsios I *apo Larissēs* : 1652–1653, 1654–1655 (Constantinople — Greek) 115
Païsios II *Kiomourtzoglous apo Nikomēdeias* : 1726–1732, 1740–1743, 1744–1748, 1751–1752 (Constantinople — Greek) 116
Païsios : 1759–1761, 1761–1767 (Cyprus) 128–129
Païsios : 1645–1660 (Jerusalem — Greek) 187
Pajsij : 1565–1566 (Macedonia) 195
Pajsije I *Janjevac* : 1614–1648 (Serbia) 227, 252
Pajsije II : 1757? (Serbia) 227
Palladiĭ *Raev* : 1887–1892 [exarch] (Georgia) 152
Palladiĭ *Vydybida-Rudenko* : 1954–1971 (Ukraine — Autocephalous Church in Exile) 241
Paloungerus : 1370? (Cyprus — Latin) 130
Panaret (I) : 1671 (Bulgaria) 94
Panaret (II) : 1838–1840? (Bulgaria) 95
Panaret : 1671 (Macedonia) 196
Panaretos : 1827–1840 (Cyprus) 129
Pant : 4th cent. (Aghunie) 9
Pantaleon *Giustiniani* : 1253–1286 (Constantinople — Latin) 119
Panteleiman *Rozhnovskiĭ* : 1942–1946 (Belarus) 89–90
Panteleimon *Rudyk* : 1941–1943 (Ukraine) 238
Papa *bar Aggai* : 285–326? (India — Malankara Jacobite) 167
Papa *bar Gaggai* : 247–326 (Assyria), and 300? (Babylon) 69, 71, 84, 251

Paphnytios : 282- [anti-patriarch] (Alexandria — Greek) 23
Pappa : 267–336 (India — Malankara Orthodox) 163
P'arhên *of Ashtishat* : 348–352 (Armenia) 64
Partenie *Clinceni* : 1896 [locum tenens] (Romania) 207
Parteniĭ I : 1566–1567 (Bulgaria) 94
Parteniĭ II : 1677–1683 (Bulgaria) 94
Parteniĭ : 1915–1918 [locum tenens] (Bulgaria) 95
Partenij I : 1566?–1567? (Macedonia) 195
Partenij II : 1679–1683 (Macedonia) 196
Parthenios I *Prochoros* : 1678–1688 (Alexandria — Greek) 25
Parthenios II *Pankōstas* : 1788–1805 (Alexandria — Greek) 26
Parthenios III *Koinidēs* : 1987–1996 (Alexandria — Greek) 26
Parthenios I *Gerōn apo Naupaktou* : 1639–1644 (Constantinople — Greek) 115
Parthenios II *Oxys Keskinēs* : 1644–1646, 1648–1651 (Constantinople — Greek) 115
Parthenios III *Parthenakēs apo Chiou* : 1656–1657 (Constantinople — Greek) 115
Parthenios IV *Mogilalos Koukoumēs* : 1657–1662, 1665–1667, 1671, 1675–1676, 1684–1685 (Constantinople — Greek) 115
Parthenios : 1806 [locum tenens] (Constantinople — Greek) 116
Parthenios : 1737–1766 (Jerusalem — Greek) 187
Paschalis : 687 [anti-pope] (Rome) 212
Paschalis I : 817–824 (Rome) 213
Paschalis II : 1099–1118 (Rome) 214
Paschalis III *da Crema* : 1164–1168 [anti-pope] (Rome) 215
Pathros Hadaya : 1597 (India — Malankara Jacobite) 170
Paul *Menebisoglou* : 1974–1996? [locum tenens] (Estonia) 136
Paulos : 537–540 (Alexandria — Greek) 14, 23
Paulos *Lingrēs* : 1996–1997 [locum tenens] (Alexandria — Greek) 26
Paulos I : 337?–339, 342–344, 346–351 (Constantinople — Greek) 109
Paulos II : 641–653 (Constantinople — Greek) 110
Paulos III : 688–694 (Constantinople — Greek) 111

Paulos IV : 780–784 (Constantinople — Greek) 111
Paulos I : 64? (Crete) 123
Paulos II : 667 (Crete) 123
Paulos *Gebre-Yohannes* : 1992- (Ethiopia — Historical), and (Ethiopia — Official) 138, 142, 144, 255, 257, 259
Paulose I : 728–757 (India — Malankara Jacobite) 168
Paulose II, Baselios Mar : 1975–1996 (India — Malankara Jacobite) 161, 172
Paulose I : 537–539 (India — Malankara Orthodox) 163
Paulose II : 728–757 (India — Malankara Orthodox) 164
Paulose *Kathanar*, Baselios Mar : 1912–1914 (India — Malankara Orthodox) 161, 166
Paulose Mar Athanasios : 1918–1935 [locum tenens], 1935–1953 (India — Malankara Jacobite) 172
Paulose Mar Athanasios II *Panakal* : 1917–1927 [suffragan] (India — Thozhiyoor) 176
Paulose Mar Koorilose : 1911–1917 (India — Malankara Jacobite) 161, 172
Paulose Mar Phileksenose III : 1967 [suffragan], 1967–1977 (India — Thozhiyoor) 175–176
Paulus I Augustus *Foscolo* : 1847–1867 (Alexandria — Latin) 28
Paulus II *Ballerini* : 1867–1897 (Alexandria — Latin) 28
Paulus III *de Huyn* : 1921–1946 (Alexandria — Latin) 28
Paulus *Brunoni* : 1869–1877 (Antioch — Latin) 47
Paulus I *Guillelmus* : 1366–1370 (Constantinople — Latin) 120
Paulus II : 1379?- (Constantinople — Latin) 120
Paulus I : 757–767 (Rome) 212
Paulus II *Barbo* : 1464–1471 (Rome) 216
Paulus III *Farnese* : 1534–1549 (Rome) 216
Paulus IV *Carafa* : 1555–1559 (Rome) 216
Paulus V *Borghese* : 1605–1621 (Rome) 216
Paulus VI *Montini* : 1963–1978 (Rome) 27, 45, 108, 119, 188, 217
Pavel *Popov* : 1866–1870 [locum tenens] (America — Orthodox Church) 31
Pavel *Dimitrovskiĭ* : 1945–1946 (Estonia) 137
Pavel Lebedev : 1882–1887 [exarch] (Georgia) 151
Pavel *Mashinin* : 1969–1979 (Russia-Novozybkov) 223

Index of Primates

Pavle *Nenadović* : 1749–1768 (Austria — Karlovci) 79
Pavle : 1530? (Montenegro) 201
Pavle : 1530?–1541? (Serbia) 227
Pavle *Stojčević* : 1990- (Serbia) 228, 256–257, 259
Pelagius I : 556–561 (Rome) 212
Pelagius II : 579–590 (Rome) 212
Pero *Petrović Njevosh* : 1851–1852 [locum tenens] (Montenegro) 202
Pertinax : 169–187 (Constantinople — Greek) 109
Petar I *Petrović Njegos* : 1782–1830 (Montenegro) 202, 252
Petar II *Petrović Njegos* : 1830–1851 (Montenegro) 202
Petar *Jovanović* : 1833–1858 (Serbia — Beograd) 228
Peter *Arihara* : 2000 [unconsecrated] (Japan) 177–178
Pëtr *Ekaterinovskiĭ* : 1859–1867 [locum tenens] (America — Orthodox Church) 31
Pëtr : 1305–1325 (Russia — Moscow) 219
Pëtr *Polianskiĭ* : 1925 [locum tenens] (Russia) 218, 221
Petre I : 467–474 (Georgia) 147–148
Petre II : 689–720 (Georgia) 149
Petro I : 1308–1326 (Ukraine) 236
Petro II *Mohyla* : 1633–1646 (Ukraine) 237
Petros I : 1662?–1670 (Aght'amar) 6
Petros II *Pilpilian* : 1858–1864 (Aght'amar) 7
Petros I : 974–992 (Aghunie) 9
Petros II : 1323- (Aghunie) 10
Petros III : -1406 (Aghunie) 10
Petros IV : 1653–1675 (Aghunie) 10
Petros I : 300–311 (Alexandria — Greek) 23
Petros II : 373–380 (Alexandria — Greek) 23
Petros III *Mongos* : 482–489 (Alexandria — Greek) 23
Petros IV : 643–651 (Alexandria — Greek) 24
Petros V : 680? (Alexandria — Greek) 24
Petros VI : 690- (Alexandria — Greek) 24
Petros VII *Papapetrou* : 1997–2004 (Alexandria — Greek) 26
Petros *Iakoumelos* [locum tenens] : 2004 (Alexandria — Greek) 26
Petros *Getadardz* : 1019–1058 (Armenia) 66
Petros *Kutur* : 1748 [locum tenens] (Armenia) 68

Petros : 1601–1608 [coadjutor] (Cilicia — Armenian Apostolic) 99
Petros I : 1708–1710 [coadjutor] (Cilicia — Armenian Apostolic) 99
Petros II *Sarachian* : 1939–1940 [vicar general], 1940 [catholicos] (Cilicia — Armenian Apostolic) 100
Petros I *Ardzivian*, Abraham : 1740–1749 (Cilicia — Armenian Catholic) 101–102
Petros II *Hovsêp'ian*, Hakob : 1749–1753 (Cilicia — Armenian Catholic) 102
Petros III *Gasparian*, Mik'ayêl : 1753–1780 (Cilicia — Armenian Catholic) 102, 252
Petros IV *Avkadian*, Barsegh : 1780–1788 (Cilicia — Armenian Catholic) 102
Petros V *Kupelian*, Grigor : 1788–1812 (Cilicia — Armenian Catholic) 102
Petros VI *Jeranian*, Grigor : 1815–1841 (Cilicia — Armenian Catholic) 102
Petros VII *Holasian*, Hakob : 1842–1843 (Cilicia — Armenian Catholic) 102
Petros VIII *Astuatsaturian*, Grigor : 1844–1866 (Cilicia — Armenian Catholic) 102
Petros IX *Hassun*, Anton : 1866–1881 (Cilicia — Armenian Catholic) 101–102
Petros IX *Bak'darian*, Hakob : 1870–1880? [anti-catholicos] (Cilicia — Armenian Catholic) 102
Petros X *Azarian*, Step'anos : 1881–1899 (Cilicia — Armenian Catholic) 102
Petros XI *Emmanuelian*, Poghos : 1899–1904 (Cilicia — Armenian Catholic) 102
Petros XII *Sabbaghian*, Poghos : 1904–1910 (Cilicia — Armenian Catholic) 102
Petros XIII *Terzian*, Poghos : 1910–1931 (Cilicia — Armenian Catholic) 102
Petros XIV *Arpiarian*, Awetis : 1931–1937 (Cilicia — Armenian Catholic) 102
Petros XV *Aghajanian*, Grigor : 1937–1962 (Cilicia — Armenian Catholic) 101–102
Petros XVI *Batanian*, Ignatios : 1962–1976 (Cilicia — Armenian Catholic) 102
Petros XVII *Ghedighian*, Hemayag : 1976–1982 (Cilicia — Armenian Catholic) 102
Petros XVIII *Gasparian*,

Hovhannês : 1982–1999 (Cilicia — Armenian Catholic) 102
Petros XIX *Tarmouni*, Nersês : 1999- (Cilicia — Armenian Catholic) 102, 251, 254, 258, 260
Petros : 654–666 (Constantinople — Greek) 110
Petros I *Ikonios* : 431? (Crete) 123
Petros II *Kolybitēs* : 761? (Crete) 124
Petros I : 923? (Ethiopia — Historical) 142
Petros II : 1559?–1570 (Ethiopia — Historical) 143
Petros III : 1600?–1607 (Ethiopia — Historical) 144
Petros IV : 1881–1889 (Ethiopia — Historical) 144
Petros I : unknown (Ethiopia — Official) 139
Petros II : unknown (Ethiopia — Official) 139
Petros III : unknown (Ethiopia — Official) 139
Petros IV : unknown (Ethiopia — Official) 140
Petros V : unknown (Ethiopia — Official) 141
Petros VI : 1600?–1607 (Ethiopia — Official) 141
Petros VII : 1881–1889 (Ethiopia — Official) 142
Petros I : 1461–1476 (Jerusalem — Armenian) 181
Petros II : 1501–1507 (Jerusalem — Armenian) 181
Petros III : 1794–1800 (Jerusalem — Armenian) 182
Petros : 524–552 (Jerusalem — Greek) 185
Petros : 985? (Sinai) 231
Petru : 1538–1550 (Austria — Sibiu) 80
Petru *Păduraru* : 1992–1995 [locum tenens], 1995- [metropolitan] (Moldova — Bessarabia) 199
Petrus I *Amiel de Brenac* : 1388?- (Alexandria — Latin) 27
Petrus II *Amaury de Lordat* : 1409? (Alexandria — Latin) 27
Petrus I *d'Angoulême* : 1201–1208 (Antioch — Latin) 45
Petrus II *d'Amalfi* : 1209–1217 (Antioch — Latin) 45
Petrus III *de Capoue* : 1219 (Antioch — Latin) 45
Petrus IV *Clasquerin* : 1375- (Antioch — Latin) 46
Petrus V *Villanova Castellacci* : 1879–1881 (Antioch — Latin) 47
Petrus I *Correr* : 1286–1302 (Constantinople — Latin) 119
Petrus II *de Bolonesio* : 1331?- (Constantinople — Latin) 120

Petrus III *Thomas* : 1364–1366 (Constantinople — Latin) 120
Petrus IV *Riario* : 1472–1474 (Constantinople — Latin) 120
Petrus I *de Plana-Cassano* : 1314–1322 (Jerusalem — Latin) 189
Petrus II *Nicosiensis* : 1322–1324 (Jerusalem — Latin) 189
Petrus III *de Palude* : 1329–1342 (Jerusalem — Latin) 189
Petrus : 33?–67? (Rome) 33, 49, 101, 210
Phēlix : 136–141 (Constantinople — Greek) 109
Philadelphos : 211–214 (Constantinople — Greek) 109
Philathose, Baselios : 1576–1591 (India — Malankara Jacobite) 170
Phileksinose, Geevarghese Mar : 1816–1817, 1825–1829 (India — Malankara Syrian) 162
Phileksinose I *Kasseesa*, Skaria Mar : 1807–1808 [suffragan], 1808–1811 (India — Thozhiyoor) 176
Phileksinose II, Geevarghese Mar : 1811–1829 (India — Thozhiyoor) 176
Phileksinose III, Paulose Mar : 1967–1977 (India — Thozhiyoor) 175–176
Philipose Mar Chrysostom : 1999- (India — Mar Thoma Syrian) 173, 255, 258–259
Philippos : 170–190 (Crete) 123
Philippos : 981? (Greece) 155
Philippos : 2nd cent. (Jerusalem — Greek) 184
Philippus *Anastasi* : 1724–1735 (Antioch — Latin) 47
Philippus Ioshua *Caucci* : 1760–1771 (Constantinople — Latin) 121
Philippus I *de Chambarlhac* : 1344–1360 (Cyprus — Latin) 130
Philippus II *Mocenigo* : 1560–1571? (Cyprus — Latin) 131
Philippus I *de Cabassole* : 1361–1368 (Jerusalem — Latin) 189
Philippus II *Camassei* : 1906–1919 (Jerusalem — Latin) 189
Philippus : 768 [anti-pope] (Rome) 212
Philix : 136–141 (Constantinople — Greek) 109
Philotheos I : 1045- (Alexandria — Greek) 24
Philotheos II : 1435–1459 (Alexandria — Greek) 25
Philotheos III : 1523- (Alexandria — Greek) 25
Philotheos *Kokkinos apo Hērakleias* : 1353–1354?, 1364–1376 (Constantinople — Greek) 113
Philotheos : 1734–1745, 1745–1759 (Cyprus) 128
Philoxenos : 510? (Cyprus) 127
Phlabianos : 446–449 (Constantinople — Greek) 110
Phōtios *Peroğlou* : 1900–1925 (Alexandria — Greek) 26
Phōtios I : 858–867, 877–886 (Constantinople — Greek) 107, 111
Phōtios II *Maniatēs* : 1929–1935 (Constantinople — Greek) 29, 117
Phōtios : 1882–1883 [anti-patriarch] (Jerusalem — Greek) 187
Phōtios : 544?–546? (Sinai) 231
Phrabitas : 489–490 (Constantinople — Greek) 110
P'ilippos : 1671? (Aght'amar) 6
P'ilippos : 1563- (Aghunie) 10
P'ilippos : 1632–1655 (Armenia) 67
P'ilippos : 1542–1550 (Jerusalem — Armenian) 181
Pimen *Nedelchev* : 1996–1998 [anti-patriarch] (Bulgaria) 92, 96
Pimen *Izvekov* : 1970–1971 [locum tenens], 1971–1990 [patriarch] (Russia) 219, 222
Pistos : 336–338? [anti-pope] (Alexandria — Greek) 23
Pistos : 325? (Greece) 155
Pitirim *Oknov* : 1914–1915 [exarch] (Georgia) 152
Pitirim : 1672–1673 (Russia) 221
Pit'iun : 731–740 (Assyria), and 731–740 (Babylon) 73, 86
Pitrus Iliya XIV *Abulyunan* : 1879–1894 (Babylon) 88
Pius I : 140?–155? (Rome) 210
Pius II *Piccolomini* : 1458–1464 (Rome) 216
Pius III *Todeschini-Piccolomini* : 1503 (Rome) 216
Pius IV *de' Medici* : 1559–1565 (Rome) 216
Pius V *Ghislieri* : 1566–1572 (Rome) 216
Pius VI *Braschi* : 1775–1799 (Rome) 217
Pius VII *Chiaramonti* : 1800–1823 (Rome) 217
Pius VIII *Castiglione* : 1829–1830 (Rome) 217
Pius IX *Mastai-Ferretti* : 1846–1878 (Rome) 101, 217, 252
Pius X *Sarto* : 1903–1914 (Rome) 217
Pius XI *Ratti* : 1922–1939 (Rome) 217
Pius XII *Pacelli* : 1939–1958 (Rome) 217
Placidus *Ralli* : 1882–1884 (Antioch — Latin) 47
Plato *Kulbusch* : 1917–1919 (Estonia) 135–136
Platon *Rozhdestvenskiĭ* : 1907–1914, 1922–1934 (America — Orthodox Church) 1915–1917 [exarch] (Georgia), 31–32, 152
Platon *Gorodetskiĭ* : 1848–1867 (Latvia) 191
Platon *Ciosu* : 1919 [locum tenens] (Romania) 208
Platon I *Malinovskiĭ* : 1748–1754 (Russia — Moscow) 221
Platon II *Levshin* : 1775–1812 (Russia — Moscow) 221
Platon *Horodets'kyĭ* : 1882–1891 (Ukraine) 237
Ploutarchos : 89–105 (Constantinople — Greek) 109
Ploutarchos : 620?–625? (Cyprus) 127
Poghos : 1086–1087 [anti-catholicos] (Armenia) 66
Poghos I : 1374–1382 (Armenia) 67
Poghos II : 1418–1430 (Armenia) 67
Poghos I *Grigorian* : 1815–1823 (Constantinople — Armenian) 105
Poghos II *T'agt'agian* : 1863–1869 (Constantinople — Armenian) 106
Poghos I : 1321–1323 (Jerusalem — Armenian) 180
Poghos II *of Karni* : 1415–1419 (Jerusalem — Armenian) 180
Poghos III *of Van* : 1768–1775 (Jerusalem — Armenian) 181
Poghos IV : 1824–1847 [vicar general] (Jerusalem — Armenian) 182
Poghos Petros XI *Emmanuelian* : 1899–1904 (Cilicia — Armenian Catholic) 102
Poghos Petros XII *Sabbaghian* : 1904–1910 (Cilicia — Armenian Catholic) 102
Poghos Petros XIII *Terzian* : 1910–1931 (Cilicia — Armenian Catholic) 102
Politianos : 768–813 (Alexandria — Greek) 24
Polyeuktos : 956–970 (Constantinople — Greek) 111
Polykarp *Sikors'kyĭ* : 1942–1953 (Ukraine — Autocephalous Church) 233–234, 238
Polykarpos I : 71–89 (Constantinople — Greek) 109
Polykarpos II : 141–144 (Constantinople — Greek) 109
Polykarpos : 1808–1827 (Jerusalem — Greek) 187
Pontianus : 230–235 (Rome) 210

Porfiriĭ *Paleolog* : 1624? (Bulgaria) 94
Porfiriĭ : 1521–1522 (Russia—Moscow) 220
Porfirij *Paleolog* : 1623–1624 (Macedonia) 196
Porphyrios *Phōtiadēs* : 1839 (Crete) 125
Porphyrios I *apo Zakynthou* : 1885–1904 (Sinai) 232
Porphyrios II *Logothetēs* : 1904–1926 (Sinai) 232
Porphyrios III *Paulinos* : 1926–1968 (Sinai) 232
Poulos *Konikara* : 1945–1952 [locum tenens] (India—Chaldean) 175
Pouplios : 161–180 (Greece) 155
Pouplios : 2nd cent. (Jerusalem—Greek) 184
Praülios : 417–422 (Jerusalem—Greek) 185
Primos : 110–121 (Alexandria—Greek) 23
Probos : 303–315 (Constantinople—Greek) 109
Prochoros : 1410? [locum tenens] (Crete) 124
Procopie *Ivașcovici* : 1873–1874 (Austria—Sibiu) 82
Prohor : 1523–1550 (Macedonia) 195
Prokhor : 1528?–1550 (Bulgaria) 94
Prokhoron : 1749 (Constantinople—Armenian) 105
Proklos : 434–446 (Constantinople—Greek) 110
Prokopije *Ivačković* : 1874–1880 (Austria—Karlovci) 79
Prokopios *apo Smyrnēs* : 1785–1789 (Constantinople—Greek) 116
Prokopios I *Geōrgiadēs* : 1874–1889 (Greece) 157
Prokopios II *Oikonomidēs* : 1896–1901 (Greece) 157
Prokopios I : 1788 (Jerusalem—Greek) 187
Prokopios II : 1873–1875 (Jerusalem—Greek) 187
Prosperus *Rebiba* : 1573–1594 (Constantinople—Latin) 121
Proterios : 451–460 (Alexandria—Greek) 14, 22–23
Publius : 161–180 (Greece) 155
Pulikkottil Mar Dionysios II : 1815–1816 (India—Malankara Syrian) 162
Pulus : 539–540 (Assyria) 72
Pulus I : 537?–539? (Babylon) 85
Pulus II *Shaikhu* : 1958–1989 (Babylon) 88
Pulus : 1295? (India—Chaldean) 174
Pulus Shim'un XXII : 1918–1920 (Assyria) 74

Punnathra Mar Dionysios III *Ittoop* : 1817–1825 (India—Malankara Syrian) 162
Pymin : 1380–1384 (Ukraine) 236
Pyrrhos : 638–641, 654 (Constantinople—Greek) 110

Qalandiyun : 482–485 [anti-patriarch] (Antioch—Syrian Orthodox) 59
Qalandun : 482–483 (Antioch—Syrian Catholic) 54
Qarabukt : 421 (Assyria), and 420 (Babylon) 72, 85
Qayuma : 393–399 (Assyria), and –399 (Babylon), and 372?–380 (India—Malankara Jacobite) 72, 85, 167
Qerillos II : unknown (Ethiopia—Official) 140
Qerlos—*see also*: Gerlos, Qerollos
Qerlos I : 623? (Ethiopia—Historical) 142
Qerlos II *Abdon* : 1077- (Ethiopia—Historical) 142
Qerlos III : 1144? [anti-abuna] (Ethiopia—Historical) 142
Qerlos IV : 1260?–1273 (Ethiopia—Historical) 143
Qerlos V : 1815?–1828? (Ethiopia—Historical) 144
Qerlos VI : 1927–1936, 1945–1950 (Ethiopia—Historical) 138, 144
Qerlos II : unknown (Ethiopia—Official) 140
Qerlos III : unknown (Ethiopia—Official) 140
Qerlos IV : 1815?–1828? (Ethiopia—Official) 141
Qerlos V : 1927–1936, 1945–1950 (Ethiopia—Official) 138, 142
Qozmos I : unknown (Ethiopia—Official) 140
Qozmos II : unknown (Ethiopia—Official) 140
Quadratus : 200? (Greece) 155
Quma *ibn Gafil*, Ighnatiyus : 1446–1455 (Antioch—Syrian Orthodox—Tur Abhdin) 62
Quom Yesu : 578–579 (India—Malankara Orthodox) 163
Quoyumo : 370–375 (India—Malankara Orthodox) 163
Quriakose : 962–979 (India—Malankara Jacobite) 169
Qurillus : 283–299 (Antioch—Syrian Catholic), and 283–303 (Antioch—Syrian Orthodox) 53, 58
Quriyaqus *of Takrit* : 793–817 (Antioch—Syrian Catholic), and (Antioch—Syrian Orthodox) 54, 59
Qurnil : 127–154 (Antioch—Syrian Catholic) 53

Qurniliyus : 127–154 (Antioch—Syrian Orthodox) 58
Qusma(n) I : 730–731 (Alexandria—Coptic) 16
Qusma(n) II : 851–858 (Alexandria—Coptic) 16
Qusma(n) III : 920–932 (Alexandria—Coptic) 17
Qustantinus : 1292- [anti-patriarch] (Antioch—Syrian Orthodox) 60
Qustantinus, Ighnatiyus : 1312–1313 [anti-patriarch] (Antioch—Syrian Orthodox) 61
Quzman—SEE: Qusman

Radulphus I : 1135–1140 (Antioch—Latin) 45
Radulphus II : 1187–1201 (Antioch—Latin) 45
Radulphus I : -1225 (Jerusalem—Latin) 189
Radulphus II : 1294–1304 (Jerusalem—Latin) 189
Rafaïl : 1699–1702 (Bulgaria), and (Macedonia) 95, 196
Rafaïl *Zaborovs'kyĭ* : 1731–1747 (Ukraine) 237
Ralph I : 1135–1140 (Antioch—Latin) 45
Ralph I : -1225 (Jerusalem—Latin) 189
Ranucius *Farnese* : 1546–1549, 1554–1565 (Constantinople—Latin) 120–121
Ranulphus : 1275?–1280 (Cyprus—Latin) 130
Rapa'il *Bidawid* : 1989–2003 (Babylon) 88
Raphaël I *Serbos* : 1475–1476 (Constantinople—Greek) 113
Raphaël II *apo Methymnēs* : 1603–1607 (Constantinople—Greek) 114
Raphael : 1264- (Cyprus—Latin) 130
Raymundus *de Saigues* : 1364–1374 (Antioch—Latin) 46
Raymundus *de la Pradèle* : 1366- (Cyprus—Latin) 130
Raymundus *Bequin* : 1324–1328 (Jerusalem—Latin) 189
Raynerius *de Tuscia* : 1219–1225 (Antioch—Latin) 45
Rezq Allah: 1617?–1633 (Ethiopia—Historical), and 1617?–1633? [anti-abuna] (Ethiopia—Official) 141, 143
Rhēginos : 431- (Cyprus) 127
Rhouphinos : 303 (Constantinople—Greek) 109
Robertus *Vicentini* : 1925–1953 (Antioch—Latin) 47
Robertus : 1240–1254 (Jerusalem—Latin) 189

Rogerus Ludovicus Æmilius *Antici-Mattei* : 1866–1875 (Constantinople — Latin) 122
Rolandus *de Ast* : 1339 (Constantinople — Latin) 120
Roman : 1330? (Bulgaria) 93
Roman *Tang* : 1950–1952 (Estonia) 137
Romanus : 897 (Rome) 213
Romul (or Romil) : 1540–1559 (Montenegro) 201
Rubil Shim'un XX : 1861–1903 (Assyria) 74
Ruvim I : 1561? (Montenegro) 201
Ruvim II *Boljević Njegoš* : 1593–1636 (Montenegro) 201
Ruvim III *Boljević* : 1673–1685 (Montenegro) 201

Saba I : 523–533 (Georgia) 148
Saba II : 1146–1150 (Georgia) 150
Sabas — SEE: Sabbas
Sabastiyanus : 687–690 [antipatriarch] (Antioch — Greek Melkite) 41
Sabbas : 1117? (Alexandria — Greek) 25
Sabbas *ibn Wahib*, Ighnatiyus : 1364–1389 (Antioch — Syrian Orthodox — Tur Abhdin) 62
Sabbas I : 877–880 (Greece) 155
Sabbas II : 889–914 (Greece) 155
Sabbas : 1106? (Jerusalem — Greek) 186
Sabbas : 1429? (Sinai) 231
Sabbazd *Vrabec* : 1925–1951 (Czechoslovakia) 132–133
Sabinianus : 604–606 (Rome) 212
Sabinos I : 403- (Cyprus) 127
Sabinos II : 457?–458? (Cyprus) 127
Sabrishu' I *Garmaqaya* : 596–604 (Assyria), and 596–604 (Babylon) 72, 85
Sabrishu' II : 832–836 (Assyria), and 831–835 (Babylon) 73, 86
Sabrishu' III *bar Zanbur* : 1057–1072 (Assyria), and 1064–1072 (Babylon) 74, 87
Sabrishu' IV *bar Qayyuma* : 1222–1226 (Assyria), and 1222–1224 (Babylon) 74, 87
Sabrishu' V *bar Masikh* : 1226–1256 (Assyria), and 1226–1256 (Babylon) 74, 87
Sabrishu' : 880? (India — Chaldean) 174
Sahak (I) *Artskets'i* : 1698 (Aght'amar) 6
Sahak (II) : 1736 [anti-catholicos] (Aght'amar) 6
Sahak I : 4th cent. (Aghunie) 8
Sahak II : 929–947 (Aghunie) 9
Sahak I *Part'e "The Great"* : 387–436 (Armenia) 65

Sahak II : 534–539 (Armenia) 65
Sahak III : 677–703 (Armenia) 65
Sahak : 1624–1629? [coadjutor] (Armenia) 67
Sahak *Ahagwin* : 1755–1760 [unconsecrated] (Armenia) 68
Sahak I *Mêykhachêchi* : 1674–1686 (Cilicia — Armenian Apostolic) 99
Sahak II *Khapayan* : 1902–1939 (Cilicia — Armenian Apostolic) 100, 252
Sahak : 1707, 1708–1714 (Constantinople — Armenian) 105
Sahak I : 1152–1180 (Jerusalem — Armenian) 180
Sahak II : 1707, 1708–1714 (Jerusalem — Armenian) 181
Sahak *Khapayan* : 1916–1917 [locum tenens] (Jerusalem — Armenian) 182
Sahan *Sivakian* : 1990 [locum tenens], 1998 [anti-locum tenens] (Constantinople — Armenian) 106
Sakralla I, Baselios : 1639–1652 (India — Malankara Jacobite) 171
Sakralla II, Baselios : -1722 (India — Malankara Jacobite) 171
Sakralla III, Baselios : 1748–1764 (India — Malankara Jacobite) 171
Salama I *Fremenatos* : 245? (Ethiopia — Historical) 138, 142
Salama II : 870? (Ethiopia — Historical) 142
Salama III : 1285? (Ethiopia — Historical) 143
Salama IV : 1348–1388 (Ethiopia — Historical) 143, 252
Salama V : 1762–1770? (Ethiopia — Historical) 144
Salama VI : 1841–1867 (Ethiopia — Historical) 144
Salama I *Fremenatos* : 245? (Ethiopia — Official) 138–139
Salama II *Minas* : unknown (Ethiopia — Official) 139
Salama III : unknown (Ethiopia — Official) 140
Salama IV *Andreyas* : 1841–1867 (Ethiopia — Official) 142
Salloustios : 486–494 (Jerusalem — Greek) 185
Samoel I : 474–502 (Georgia) 148
Samoel II : 544–553 (Georgia) 148
Samoel III : 575–582 (Georgia) 149
Samoel IV : 582–591 (Georgia) 149

Samoel V : 634–640 (Georgia) 149
Samoel VI : 670–677 (Georgia) 149
Samoel VII : 780–790 (Georgia) 149
Samoel VIII : 814–826 (Georgia) 149
Samouēl *Kapasoulēs* : 1712, 1714–1723 (Alexandria — Greek) 25
Samouēl *Chantzerēs apo Derkōn* : 1763–1768, 1773–1774 (Constantinople — Greek) 116, 193, 225
Samouēl *Primpetos* : 1602 (Greece) 156
Samuêl : 874–891 (Aghunie) 9
Samuêl : 516–526 (Armenia) 65
Samu'el : 1223? (Ethiopia — Historical) 143
Samuel : 614–624 (India — Malankara Jacobite), and (India — Malankara Orthodox) 163, 168
Samuïl *Myslavs'kyĭ* : 1783–1796 (Ukraine) 237
Samuïlo *Maširević* : 1861–1864 [locum tenens], 1864–1870 (Austria — Karlovci) 79
Sanutiyus — *see also*: Shanudah
Sanutiyus I : 858–880 (Alexandria — Coptic) 16
Sanutiyus II : 1032–1046 (Alexandria — Coptic) 17
Sarbiel : 794–810 (India — Malankara Jacobite) 168
Sargis I : 1521–1555 (Aghunie) 10
Sargis II *Hassan-Jalaliants'* : 1794–1815 (Aghunie) 11
Sargis I : 992–1019 (Armenia) 66
Sargis : 1076–1077 [anti-catholicos] (Armenia) 66
Sargis II *Ajatar* : 1462–1469 [coadjutor], 1469–1474 [catholicos] (Armenia) 67
Sargis III *Miwsayl* : 1474–1484 [coadjutor], 1484–1515 [catholicos] (Armenia) 67
Sargis IV : 1515–1520 [coadjutor], 1520–1536 [catholicos] (Armenia) 67
Sargis *Subaya* : 860–872 (Assyria), and 860–872 (Babylon) 73, 86
Sargis I : 1587–1590 (Constantinople — Armenian) 104
Sargis II : 1592–1596 (Constantinople — Armenian) 104
Sargis III : 1664–1665, 1667–1670 (Constantinople — Armenian) 104
Sargis IV : 1679–1680 (Constantinople — Armenian) 104
Sargis V *Guyumchian* : 1860–1861 (Constantinople — Armenian) 106

Index of Primates

Sargis : 872–883 (India — Malankara Jacobite), and (India — Malankara Orthodox) 164, 168

Sargis I : 1281–1313 (Jerusalem — Armenian) 179–180

Sargis II : 1394–1415 (Jerusalem — Armenian) 180

Sargis III : 1507–1517 (Jerusalem — Armenian) 181

Sarkis *al-Ruzzi* : 1581–1596 (Antioch — Maronite) 50

Sarmeane : 767–774 (Georgia) 149

Sarugoyo, Yuhannan : 1164–1188 (India — Malankara Jacobite) 169

Sava I : unknown (Austria — Cernovci) 77

Sava II : 1656–1658 (Austria — Cernovci) 78

Sava I : 1559- , 1562–1570 (Austria — Sibiu) 80

Sava II *Brancović* : 1656, 1662–1680 (Austria — Sibiu) 81

Sava III : 1684–1685 (Austria — Sibiu) 81

Sava I *Kaluđerović* : 1694–1697 (Montenegro) 202

Sava II *Petrović* : 1719–1735 [coadjutor], 1735–1750, 1766–1767, 1773–1781 (Montenegro) 202

Sava I *Nemanjić* : 1219–1233 (Serbia) 225–226

Sava II *Nemanjić* : 1263–1271 (Serbia) 226

Sava III : 1309–1316 (Serbia) 226

Sava IV : 1354–1375 (Serbia) 226

Sava V : 1398–1406 (Serbia) 226

Savatije I *Kaluđerović* : 1694–1697 (Montenegro) 202

Savatije *Sokolović* : 1587 (Serbia) 227

Savvatiĭ *Levshin* : 1882–1898 (Russia — Belokrinitsia) 223

Savvatij *Vrabec* : 1925–1951 (Czechoslovakia) 133

Sawa *Hrycuniak* : 1998 [locum tenens], 1998- (Poland) 204, 256, 258–259

Sawatij *Vrabec* : 1925–1951 (Czechoslovakia) 133

Sawira I *al-Antakhah* : 512–518 (Antioch — Syrian Catholic) 33, 54, 57

Sawira II *ibn Mashqa* : 667–680 (Antioch — Syrian Catholic) 54

Sawiriyus I *al-Antakhah* "the Great" : 512–538 (Antioch — Syrian Orthodox) 33, 57, 59

Sawiriyus II *ibn Mashqa* : 667–681 (Antioch — Syrian Orthodox) 59

Sawiros : 1078? (Ethiopia — Historical) 142

Scipio *Rebiba* : 1565–1573 (Constantinople — Latin) 121

Sebastian *Rusan* : 1948–1950 [titular] (Austria — Cernovci) 78

Sebastianus : 1495? (Antioch — Latin) 46

Sebastianus *Priuli* : 1496–1498? (Cyprus — Latin) 130

Sedekiōn : 105–114 (Constantinople — Greek) 109

Se'la Krestos : 1617?–1633 (Ethiopia — Historical), and 1617?–1633? [anti-abuna] (Ethiopia — Official) 141, 143

Sem'on : 1600?–1617 (Ethiopia — Historical) 143

Sem'on I : unknown (Ethiopia — Official) 139

Sem'on II : unknown (Ethiopia — Official) 139

Sem'on III : unknown (Ethiopia — Official) 139

Sem'on IV : unknown (Ethiopia — Official) 141

Sem'on V : 1600?–1617 (Ethiopia — Official) 14

Senekas : 2nd cent. (Jerusalem — Greek) 184

Sentyos : unknown (Ethiopia — Official) 141

Serafim : 1667–1669, 1671–1685? (Austria — Cernovci) 78

Serafim *Lukianov* : 1918–1919 [assistant bishop] (Finland) 145

Serafim *Protopopov* : 1874–1877 (Latvia) 191

Serafim : 1576–1585 (Romania) 206

Serafim *Samoĭlovich* : 1926–1927 [deputy locum tenens] (Russia) 222

Serafim *Glagolevskiĭ* : 1819–1821 (Russia — Moscow) 221

Serafin *Cziczagow* : 1918–1921 [unconsecrated] (Poland) 204

Serapheim I *apo Nikomēdeias* : 1733–1734 (Constantinople — Greek) 116

Serapheim II *apo Philippoupoleōs* : 1757–1761 (Constantinople — Greek) 116

Serapheim *Tikas* : 1974–1998 (Greece) 154, 158

Seraphinus Oliverus *Razalio* : 1602? (Alexandria — Latin) 28

Serapion *Fadeev* : 1986–1989 (Moldova) 198

Serapion *Aleksandrovs'kyĭ* : 1803–1822 (Ukraine) 237

Sergei *Stragorodski* : 1906–1917 (Finland) 145

Sergej : 1241? (Macedonia) 195

Sergi *Samon* : 1973–1974 [unconsecrated] (Estonia) 136

Sergiĭ *Petrov* : 1963–1965 (Belarus) 90

Sergiĭ I : 925? (Bulgaria) 92

Sergiĭ II : 1250? (Bulgaria) 93

Sergiĭ *Voskresenskiĭ* : 1941 (Estonia) 137

Sergiĭ *Tykhomirov* : 1912–1940 (Japan) 177

Sergiĭ *Voskresenskiĭ* : 1941–1943 (Latvia) 191

Sergiĭ *Liapidevskiĭ* : 1893–1898 (Russia — Moscow) 221

Sergiĭ *Stragorodskiĭ* : 1925–1926 [deputy locum tenens], 1927–1937 [deputy locum tenens], 1937–1943 [locum tenens], 1943–1944 [patriarch] (Russia) 218–219, 222, 224

Sergiĭ I *Kumyns'kyĭ* : 1925–1930 (Ukraine) 238

Sergiĭ II *Hryshyn* : 1932–1934 (Ukraine) 238

Sergios I : 610–638 (Constantinople — Greek) 110

Sergios II : 1001–1019 (Constantinople — Greek) 111

Sergios : 643? (Cyprus) 127

Sergios I : 842–844 (Jerusalem — Greek) 185

Sergios II : 908–911 (Jerusalem — Greek) 185

Sergius *Samon* : 1973–1974 [unconsecrated] (Estonia) 136

Sergius I : 687–701 (Rome) 212

Sergius II : 844–847 (Rome) 213

Sergius III : 904–911 (Rome) 213

Sergius IV : 1009–1012 (Rome) 214

Severinus : 640 (Rome) 212

Shaba *Arbaya*, Ighnatiyus : 1488- [anti-patriarch] (Antioch — Syrian Orthodox — Tur Abhdin) 62

Shahak : 352–353, 359–363 [locum tenens], 373–377 (Armenia) 64

Shahdost : 344–345 (India — Malankara Jacobite) 167

Shahdust : 345–347 (Assyria), and 341?–342 (Babylon) 71, 84

Shahên : 124–150 (Armenia) 64

Shahluppa : 246–266 (India — Malankara Orthodox) 163

Shahoudoth : 350–352 (India — Malankara Orthodox) 163

Shakhlupa *of Kashkar* : 224–244 (Assyria), and 3rd cent. (Babylon) 71, 84

Shakrulla, Baselios Mar : 1751–1764 (India — Malankara Orthodox) 166

Shanudah —*see also*: Sanutiyus

Shanudah III *Gayid Rafail* : 1971- (Alexandria — Coptic) 15, 18, 253, 257, 259

Sharbeel : 794–810 (India — Malankara Orthodox) 164

Shawarsh : 151–171 (Armenia) 64

Shemavun : 811- (India — Malankara Jacobite) 168

Shihab, Ighnatiyus : 1366–1381 (Antioch — Syrian Catholic), and 1365–1381 [anti-patriarch] (Antioch — Syrian Orthodox) 55, 61
Shila : 505–523 (Assyria), and 505–522? (Babylon) 72, 85
Shilo : 502–504 (India — Malankara Orthodox) 163
Shim'un —*see also*: Sim'an
Shim'un I *of Tur-Abdin*, Ighnatiyus : 1640–1659 (Antioch — Syrian Catholic) 56
Shim'un *of Tur-Abdin*, Ighnatiyus : 1640–1659 (Antioch — Syrian Orthodox) 61
Shim'un I *Kipa* : 33 (Assyria) 70
Shim'un II *bar Sabba'i* : 328–341 (Assyria) 71
Shim'un III : 1369–1392 (Assyria) 74
Shim'un IV : 1403–1407 (Assyria) 74
Shim'un V : 1420–1447 (Assyria) 69, 74
Shim'un VI *d'Bat' Sadi* : 1448–1490 (Assyria) 74
Shim'un VII : 1505–1538 (Assyria) 74
Shim'un VIII *bar Mama*, Ishu'yabh : 1538–1551 (Assyria) 69, 74
Shim'un IX *bar Mama*, Dinkha : 1552–1558 (Assyria) 74
Shim'un X, Yabhalaha : 1558–1580 (Assyria) 70, 74
Shim'un XI, Dinkha : 1580–1600 (Assyria) 70, 74, 83
Shim'un XII, Iliya : 1600–1653 (Assyria) 74
Shim'un XIII, Ishu'yabh : 1653–1690 (Assyria) 74
Shim'un XIV, Yabhalaha : 1690–1692 (Assyria) 74
Shim'un XV, Dinkha : 1692–1700 (Assyria) 74
Shim'un XVI, Shlimun : 1700–1740? (Assyria) 74
Shim'un XVII, Mikha'il *Mukhatas* : 1740?–1780? (Assyria) 74
Shim'un XVIII, Yunan : 1780?–1820? (Assyria) 74
Shim'un XIX, Abraham : 1820?–1861 (Assyria) 74
Shim'un XX, Rubil : 1861–1903 (Assyria) 74
Shim'un XXI, Binyamin : 1903–1918 (Assyria) 74
Shim'un XXII, Pulus : 1918–1920 (Assyria) 74
Shim'un XXIII, Ishai : 1920–1975 (Assyria) 70, 75, 251–252
Shim'un I *bar Sabba'i* : -341 (Babylon) 84
Shim'un II : 1364- (Babylon) 87
Shim'un III : 1400? (Babylon) 87
Shim'un IV *d'Bat' Sadi* : 1437–1497 (Babylon) 59, 87, 251–252
Shim'un V : 1497–1502? (Babylon) 87
Shim'un VI : 1504–1538 (Babylon) 87
Shim'un VII *bar Mama*, Ishu'yabh : 1538–1551 (Babylon) 69, 87
Shim'un VIII *bar Mama*, Dinkha : 1551–1558 (Babylon) 87
Shim'un IX *Sulaqa*, Yukhannan : 1551–1555 [rival patriarch] (Babylon) 69–70, 83, 88
Shimun bar Sabbae : 326?–344 (India — Malankara Jacobite) 167
Shim'un Iliya VII *bar Mama* : 1576–1591 (Babylon) 87
Shim'un Iliya IX *bar Mama* : 1617–1660 (Babylon) 87
Shim'un Yabhalaha IV : 1578–1580 (Babylon) 83, 88
Shio I : 1356–1364 (Georgia) 150
Shio II : 1440–1443 (Georgia) 150
Shlimun Shim'un XVI : 1700–1740? (Assyria) 74
Shlimun *Warduni* : 2003 [apostolic administrator] (Babylon) 88
Shmuel : 432–437 [anti-catholicos] (Armenia) 65
Shnorhk' *Galustian* : 1961–1990 (Constantinople — Armenian) 106, 252
Shukr Allah I, Ighnatiyus : 1640- (Antioch — Syrian Catholic) 56
Shukr Allah II, Ighnatiyus : 1723–1745 (Antioch — Syrian Catholic) 56
Shukr Allah, Ighnatiyus : 1722–1745 (Antioch — Syrian Orthodox) 61
Shup'aghishoy : 500- (Aghunie) 9
Sibastiyanus : 687–690 (Antioch — Greek) 36
Silbestros : 1569–1590 (Alexandria — Greek) 25
Silbestros : 1718–1733 (Cyprus) 128
Silfistrus *of Cyprus* : 1724–1766 (Antioch — Greek) 33, 38–39, 252
Silouanos : 1465? (Sinai) 231
Silverius : 536–537 (Rome) 212
Silvestru *Morariu-Andrievic* : 1880–1895 (Austria — Cernovci) 78
Silvestru *Onofrei* : 1985–1992 (Romania — Old Calendarists) 208
Silvius *Savelli* : 1594–1596 (Constantinople — Latin) 121
Sim'an —*see also*: Shim'un
Sim'an I : 834–840 (Antioch — Greek) 36
Sim'an II *ibn Abu Sa'ib* : 1245–1268 (Antioch — Greek) 37
Sim'an I *ibn Zarnaq* : 892–907 (Antioch — Greek Melkite) 41
Sim'an II *ibn Abu Sa'ib* : 1206?–1235? (Antioch — Greek Melkite) 42
Sim'an I : unknown (Antioch — Maronite) 49
Sim'an II : unknown (Antioch — Maronite) 49
Sim'an III : unknown (Antioch — Maronite) 49
Sim'an IV : 1244?–1268? (Antioch — Maronite) 50
Sim'an V : 1300?–1322? (Antioch — Maronite) 50
Sim'an VI *ibn Dawud al-Hadathi* : 1492–1524 (Antioch — Maronite) 50
Sim'an VII Butrus *Awwad* : 1743–1756 (Antioch — Maronite) 50
Sim'an II *Hindi Zora*, Ighnatiyus : 1811–1818 (Antioch — Syrian Catholic) 56
Simawun I : 689–701 (Alexandria — Coptic) 16
Simawun II : 830 (Alexandria — Coptic) 16
Simêon I : 704–706 (Aghunie) 9
Simêon II : 902–923 (Aghunie) 9
Simêon III : 1596- (Aghunie) 10
Simêon IV : 1675–1701 [anti-patriarch] (Aghunie) 10
Simêon V : 1794–1810 (Aghunie) 11
Simêon : 1763–1780 (Armenia) 68
Simeon I : 1346? (Bulgaria) 93
Simeon II : 1550 (Bulgaria) 94
Simeon *Du* : 1962–1965 [locum tenens] (China) 97
Simêon I : 1539–1545 (Cilicia — Armenian Apostolic) 99
Simêon II : 1633–1648 (Cilicia — Armenian Apostolic) 99
Simêon I : 1090–1109 (Jerusalem — Armenian) 180
Simêon II : 1688–1691 [coadjutor] (Jerusalem — Armenian) 181
Simeon I : 1550 (Macedonia) 195
Simeon II : 1634- (Macedonia) 196
Simeon : 1496–1511 (Russia — Moscow) 220
Simeon : 1528–1532? (Serbia) 227
Simion *Stefan* : 1643–1656 (Austria — Sibiu) 81
Simon *de Cramaud* : 1391? (Alexandria — Latin) 27
Simon : 1227–1232 (Constantinople — Latin) 119

Simun I *Bar Sheba* : 337–350 (India — Malankara Orthodox) 163
Simun II : 812–828 (India — Malankara Orthodox) 164
Simplicius : 468–483 (Rome) 211
Sinoda : 1671?–1693? (Ethiopia — Historical), and (Ethiopia — Official) 141, 143
Sion : 767–775 (Armenia) 65
Sirabiyun : 191–212 (Antioch — Greek), and (Antioch — Greek Melkite), and 190–211 (Antioch — Syrian Catholic), and 191–211 (Antioch — Syrian Orthodox) 34, 40, 53, 58
Sirafim *of Constantinople* : 1813–1823 (Antioch — Greek) 38
Siricius : 384–399 (Rome) 211
Sirjiyus *of Tella* : 544–546 (Antioch — Syrian Orthodox) 57, 59
Sirkis *of Tella* : 539–541 (Antioch — Syrian Catholic) 54, 57
Sisinnios I : 426–427 (Constantinople — Greek) 110
Sisinnios II : 996–998 (Constantinople — Greek) 111
Sisinnius : 708 (Rome) 212
Sixtus I : 115?–125? (Rome) 210
Sixtus II : 257–258 (Rome) 211
Sixtus III : 432–440 (Rome) 211
Sixtus IV *della Rovere* : 1471–1484 (Rome) 216
Sixtus V *Peretti* : 1585–1590 (Rome) 216
Skaria Mar Phileksinose I *Kassesa* : 1807–1808 [suffragan], 1808–1811 (India — Thozhiyoor) 176
Sleeba I, Yuhannan : 1075–1106 (India — Malankara Jacobite) 169
Sleeba II, Dionysius : 1222–1231 (India — Malankara Jacobite) 169
Sleeba III, Ignatius : 1252–1258 (India — Malankara Jacobite) 169
Sleeba IV, Baselios : 1773- (India — Malankara Jacobite) 171
Slibazka : 714–728 (Assyria), and 714–728 (Babylon) 73, 86
Soffredus : 1203- (Jerusalem — Latin) 189
Sofron *Borova* : 1967–1973 [locum tenens] (Albania) 13
Sofronie *Chirilovic* : 1769–1774 (Austria — Sibiu) 81
Sofroniĭ : 1567–1572? (Bulgaria) 94
Sofronij : 1567–1572 (Macedonia) 195
Sofronije *Podgoričanin* : 1710–1711 (Austria — Karlovci) 79

Soghomon I : 782 (Aghunie) 9
Soghomon II : 786–797 (Aghunie) 9
Soghomon : 791–792 (Armenia) 65
Solomon : 853–858 (Babylon) 86
Solomōn : 855–860 (Jerusalem — Greek) 185
Solomōn : 1480? (Sinai) 232
Sōphronios I : 848–860 (Alexandria — Greek) 24
Sōphronios II : 941? (Alexandria — Greek) 24
Sōphronios III : 1166? (Alexandria — Greek) 25
Sōphronios IV *Meidintzoğlou* : 1870–1899 (Alexandria — Greek) 26
Sōphronios I *Syropoulos* : 1463–1464 (Constantinople — Greek) 113
Sōphronios II : 1774–1780 (Constantinople — Greek) 116
Sōphronios III *Meidintzoğlou* : 1863–1866 (Constantinople — Greek) 117
Sōphronios I *apo Ainou* : 1850 (Crete) 125
Sōphronios II *apo Didumoteichou* : 1874–1877 (Crete) 125
Sōphronios I : 550? (Cyprus) 127
Sōphronios II : 1191? (Cyprus) 128
Sōphronios III : 1865–1900 (Cyprus) 129
Sōphronios I : 1565–1570 (Greece) 156
Sōphronios II : 1633–1636 (Greece) 157
Sōphronios I : 634–638 (Jerusalem — Greek) 185
Sōphronios II : 1040–1059 (Jerusalem — Greek) 186
Sōphronios III : 1236- (Jerusalem — Greek) 186
Sōphronios IV : 1579–1608 (Jerusalem — Greek) 187
Sōphronios V : 1771–1775 (Jerusalem — Greek) 187
Sōphronios : 1540?–1545 (Sinai) 232
Soter : 166?–175? (Rome) 210
Spiridon : 1379–1389 (Serbia) 226
Spyridōn *Papageōrgiou* : 1996–1999 (America) 30
Spyridōn *Blachos* : 1949–1956 (Greece) 158
Spyrydon : 1475–1482 (Ukraine) 236
Stachys : 38–54 (Constantinople — Greek) 109
Stefan I : unknown (Austria — Černovci) 77
Stefan II : 1644?–1646? (Austria — Černovci) 78

Stefan : 1516–1534 (Austria — Sibiu) 80
Stefan : 870–878? (Bulgaria) 92
Stefan *Giorgiev* : 1922–1934 [locum tenens], 1944–1945 [locum tenens], 1945–1948 [exarch] (Bulgaria) 91, 95
Stefan *Veljanovski* : 1993 [locum tenens], 1999- (Macedonia) 194, 197, 255, 258, 260
Stefan *Rudyk* : 1965–1969 (Poland) 204
Stefan I : 1648–1653, 1655–1668 (Romania) 206
Stefan II : 1732–1738 (Romania) 207
Stefan *IAvorskiĭ* : 1700–1721 [locum tenens] (Russia) 218, 221
Stefan *Rastorguev* : 1934–1935 [locum tenens], 1935–1937 (Russia-Novozybkov) 223
Stefanus *Charalambidēs* : 1999- (Estonia) 136, 254, 258, 260
Stêp'an —*see also*: Step'anos
Stêp'an *Maghak'ian* : 1861–1863 [locum tenens] (Constantinople — Armenian) 106
Step'ane : 1470–1516 (Georgia — Abkhazia) 153
Step'anos —*see also*: Stêp'an
Step'anos I : 1165?–1185? (Aght'amar) 5
Step'anos II : -1272 (Aght'amar) 5
Step'anos III *Sefedinian* : 1272–1296? (Aght'amar) 5
Step'anos *Tghay* : 1288–1292 [anti-catholicos?] (Aght'amar) 5
Step'anos IV *Ardzruni* : 1336?–1346 (Aght'amar) 6
Step'anos V *Kurdjibeguyan* : 1464–1489 (Aght'amar) 6
Step'anos VI : 1612? [anti-catholicos] (Aght'amar) 6
Step'anos VI : 1671? (Aght'amar) 6
Step'anos I : 1077–1103 (Aghunie) 10
Step'anos II : 1130–1132 (Aghunie) 10
Step'anos III : 1155?–1195 (Aghunie) 10
Step'anos IV : 1262–1323 (Aghunie) 10, 251
Step'anos I : 788–790 (Armenia) 65
Step'anos II *Rshtuni* : 929–930 (Armenia) 66
Step'anos III : 969–972 (Armenia) 66
Step'anos IV : 1290–1293 (Armenia) 66
Step'anos V : 1545–1567 (Armenia) 67
Step'anos : 1567- [coadjutor] (Armenia) 67

Step'anos : 1477?–1483 (Cilicia— Armenian Apostolic) 99
Step'anos I : 1550–1561 (Constantinople—Armenian) 104
Step'anos II : 1670–1674 (Constantinople—Armenian) 104
Step'anos III *Zak'arian* : 1831–1839, 1840–1841 (Constantinople—Armenian) 105
Step'anos : 758–774 (Jerusalem—Armenian) 179
Step'anos Petros X *Azarian* : 1881–1899 (Cilicia—Armenian Catholic) 102
Stephanos I : 886–893 (Constantinople—Greek) 111
Stephanos II *apo Amaseias* : 925–927 (Constantinople—Greek) 111
Stephanos : 1027?–1030? (Crete) 124
Stephanos *Charalambidēs* : 1999- (Estonia) 136
Stephanus I : 1339–1345 (Constantinople—Latin) 120
Stephanus II : 1346 (Constantinople—Latin) 120
Stephanus III *Ugolini* : 1667–1670 (Constantinople—Latin) 121
Stephanus *de Carrare* : 1406–1412 (Cyprus—Latin) 130
Stephanus : 1128–1130 (Jerusalem—Latin) 188
Stephanus I : 254–257 (Rome) 211
Stephanus (II) : 752 [unconsecrated] (Rome) 212
Stephanus II : 752–757 (Rome) 212
Stephanus III : 768–772 (Rome) 212
Stephanus IV : 816–817 (Rome) 213
Stephanus V : 885–891 (Rome) 213
Stephanus VI : 896–897 (Rome) 213
Stephanus VII : 928–931 (Rome) 213
Stephanus VIII : 939–942 (Rome) 213
Stephanus IX : 1057–1058 (Rome) 214
Stevan I *Metohijac* : 1708–1709 (Austria—Karlovci) 79
Stevan II *Stratimirović* : 1790–1836 (Austria—Karlovci) 79, 252
Stevan III *Stanković* : 1837–1841 (Austria—Karlovci) 79
Stevan : 1591? (Montenegro) 201
Subrus *al-Antakhah* : 513–518 (Antioch—Greek), and 512–518 (Antioch—Greek Melkite) 35, 41
Sufruniyus : 1335? (Antioch—Greek Melkite) 43

Suk'ias : 1323- (Aghunie) 10
Sulpitius : 1191- (Jerusalem—Latin) 189
Suntyos : unknown (Ethiopia—Official) 141
Surin : 752–754 (Assyria), and 754 (Babylon) 73, 86
Surmak : 428–429, 437–444 [anti-catholicos] (Armenia) 65
Svimeon —*see also*: Svimon
Svimeon I : 400–410 (Georgia) 148
Svimeon IV *Gulaberidze* : 1142–1146 (Georgia) 150
Svimon —*see also*: Svimeon
Svimon II : 569–575 (Georgia) 149
Svimon III : 1001–1012 (Georgia) 149
Svimon V : 1547–1550 (Georgia) 150
Svimon I *Chk'etidze* : 1660–1666 (Georgia—Abkhazia) 153
Svimon II : 1665–1681 (George—Abkhazia) 153
Svimon Petre : 595–610 (Georgia) 149
Sylvester *Haruns* : 1974–1977 [locum tenens] (America—Orthodox Church) 32
Sylvester I : 314–335 (Rome) 211
Sylvester II : 999–1003 (Rome) 214
Sylvester III *of Sabina* : 1045 (Rome) 214
Sylvester IV : 1105–1111 [antipope] (Rome) 214
Syl'vestr I *Bel'kevych* : 1556–1567 (Ukraine) 236
Syl'vestr II *Kosov* : 1647–1657 (Ukraine) 237
Symeōn *Trapezountios* : 1466?–1467, 1471–1475, 1482–1486 (Constantinople—Greek) 113
Symeōn : 1218?–1220 (Cyprus) 128
Symeōn I *Kleōpa* : 62?–107? (Jerusalem—Greek) 183
Symeōn II : 1084–1106 (Jerusalem—Greek) 186
Symeōn I : 1003–1035 (Sinai) 231
Symeōn II : 1203–1223 (Sinai) 231
Symeōn III : 1258? (Sinai) 231
Symeōn IV : 1306–1324 (Sinai) 231
Symeon : 1481–1488 (Ukraine) 236
Symmachos : 2nd cent. (Jerusalem—Greek) 184
Symmachus : 498–514 (Rome) 211

T'abori : 629–634 (Georgia) 149
T'addai —*see also*: Addai

T'addai I *Shlikha* : 33–45 (Assyria) 71
T'adêos : 43–66 (Armenia) 63–64
T'adêos : 1499–1504 [coadjutor] (Armenia) 67
T'adêos : 1577- [coadjutor] (Armenia) 67
Tadewos *Biwonegin* : 1985–1988 (Eritrea) 134
Takla Haymanot I : 1280 (Ethiopia—Historical), and unknown (Ethiopia—Official) 139, 143
Takla Haymanot II *Wolde Mika'el* : 1976–1988 (Ethiopia—Historical), and (Ethiopia—Official) 138, 142, 144
T'alale : 720–731 (Georgia) 149
Tarasios : 784–806 (Constantinople—Greek) 111
T'avp'ech'agh I : 510–516 (Georgia) 148
T'avp'ech'agh II : 649–664 (Georgia) 149
Telesphorus : 125?–136? (Rome) 210
Teoctist *Blajevic* : 1877–1879 (Austria—Cernovci) 78
Teoctist : 1606–1622 (Austria—Sibiu) 81
Teoctist *Arăpaşu* : 1980–1982 [locum tenens] (Austria—Sibiu), and 1986 [locum tenens], 1986- [patriarch] (Romania) 82, 198, 205, 208, 256–257, 259
Teodor I : 15th cent. (Romania) 206
Teodor II : 1521?–1523 (Romania) 206
T'eodore I : 685–689 (Georgia) 149
T'eodore II : 1186–1206 (Georgia) 150
T'eodore III : 1430–1435 (Georgia) 150
T'êodoros : 1792–1794 (Aght'amar) 7
T'êodoros : 782–786 (Aghunie) 9
T'êodoros I *Rshtuni* : 930–941 (Armenia) 66
T'êodoros *Alakhosik* : 1077–1090 [anti-catholicos] (Armenia) 66
T'êodoros II : 1382–1392 (Armenia) 67
T'êodoros I *of Khorên* : 1752–1761 (Jerusalem—Armenian) 181
T'êodoros II *of Van* : 1800–1818 (Jerusalem—Armenian) 182
Teodosie I : 1530–1550? (Austria—Cernovci) 77
Teodosie II *Barbovschi* : 1598–1600, 1600–1605 (Austria—Cernovci) 78
Teodosie III : 1669?–1671 (Austria—Cernovci) 78

Index of Primates 317

Teodosie : 1668–1672, 1679–1708 (Romania) 206
Teodosie *Aṭanasiu* : 1911–1912 [locum tenens] (Romania) 207
Teodosiĭ I : 1337? (Bulgaria) 93
Teodosiĭ II : 1363? (Bulgaria) 93
Teodosije : 1446? (Montenegro) 201
Teodosije : 1520? (Serbia) 227
Teodosije *Mraović* : 1883–1889 (Serbia — Beograd) 228
Teodul I *apo Mōkiou* : 1056?– 1065 (Bulgaria), and 1056–1065 (Macedonia) 92, 194
Teodul II : 1588–1590 (Bulgaria), and 1588 (Macedonia) 94, 195
Teofan I : 1528–1530 (Austria — Cernovci) 77
Teofan II : 1646?–1651 (Austria — Cernovci) 78
Teofan III : 1658–1666 (Austria — Cernovci) 78
Teofan *Živković* : 1880 [locum tenens], 1881 [unconsecrated] (Austria — Karlovci) 79–80
Teofan : 1676 (Bulgaria), and 1675?–1676 (Macedonia) 94, 196
Teofan (I) : 1446 (Serbia) 226
Teofan (II) : 1544? (Serbia) 227
Teofil *Bendela* : 1873–1875 (Austria — Cernovci) 78
Teofil : 1692–1697 (Austria — Sibiu) 81
Teofil : 1636–1648 (Romania) 206
Teofilakt *ex Euripou* : 1085?–1108? (Bulgaria), and 1081–1112? (Macedonia) 92, 194
Terrius : 1206–1211 (Cyprus — Latin) 129
Tewoflos *Melaktu* : 1971–1976 (Ethiopia — Historical), and (Ethiopia — Official) 138, 142, 144
Thaddaios : 1298 (Jerusalem — Greek) 186
Thawdurus : 731–743 (Alexandria — Coptic) 16
Thawdurus *Abu Karim* : 1832–1854 (Alexandria — Coptic Catholic) 21
Thawdusiyus I : 535–567 (Alexandria — Coptic) 16
Thawdusiyus II : 1294–1300 (Alexandria — Coptic) 17
Thawdusiyus *Rumanus of Takrit* : 887–896 (Antioch — Syrian Orthodox) 60
Thawdutus : 417–428 (Antioch — Syrian Orthodox) 58
Thawfaniyus : 952–956 (Alexandria — Coptic) 17
Thawfilus : 385–412 (Alexandria — Coptic), and 384–412 (Alexandria — Coptic Catholic) 16, 21

Thawfilus : 169–182 (Antioch — Syrian Orthodox) 58
Thawna : 282–300 (Alexandria — Coptic), and (Alexandria — Coptic Catholic) 16, 21
Theocharistos : 694–702 (Greece) 155
Theodēgios : 985–1007 (Greece) 155
Theodoricus : 1100 [anti-pope] (Rome) 214
Theodōros : 695? (Alexandria — Coptic — Gaianite) 19
Theodōros I *Skribōn* : 608–609 (Alexandria — Greek) 24
Theodōros : 655? [not officially recognized] (Alexandria — Greek) 24
Theodōros II *Choreutakēs* : 2004- (Alexandria — Greek) 26, 253, 258, 260
Theodōros I : 677–679, 686–687 (Constantinople — Greek) 110
Theodōros II *Eirēnikos Kōpas* : 1214–1216 (Constantinople — Greek) 112
Theodōros : 553? (Crete) 123
Theodōros : 431? [anti-archbishop] (Cyprus) 127
Theodōros : 1438–1453? (Greece) 156
Theodōros : 735–770 (Jerusalem — Greek) 185
Theodōros : 649?–680? (Sinai) 231
Theodorus I : 642–649 (Rome) 212
Theodorus II : 687 [anti-pope] (Rome) 212
Theodorus II : 897 (Rome) 213
Theodosios I : 537? (Alexandria — Greek) 23
Theodosios II : 1130? (Alexandria — Greek) 25
Theodosios I *Borrhadiotēs* : 1179–1183 (Constantinople — Greek) 112
Theodosios II *Maridakēs apo Thessalonikēs* : 1769–1773 (Constantinople — Greek) 116
Theodosios I : 800? (Greece) 155
Theodosios II : 820? (Greece) 155
Theodosios, Alexios Mar : 1934–1962 [suffragan] (India — Malankara Orthodox, 167
Theodosios : 862–878 (Jerusalem — Greek) 185
Theodosios : 1239? (Sinai) 231
Theodosius *Lazor* : 1977–2002 (America — Orthodox Church) 32
Theodosius *Nagashima* : 1972–1999 (Japan) 177–178
Theodotos I *Kassitēras Melissēnos* : 815–821 (Constantinople — Greek) 111

Theodotos II : 1151?–1153? (Constantinople — Greek) 112
Theofan "Fan" *Noli* : 1923–1924 (Albania) 12–13
Theoklētos I *Mēnopoulos* : 1902–1917, 1920–1922 (Greece) 157–158
Theoklētos II *Panagiōtopoulos* : 1957–1962 (Greece) 158
Theoleptos I *apo Iōanninōn* : 1513–1522 (Constantinople — Greek) 114
Theoleptos II *apo Philippoupoleōs* : 1585–1586? (Constantinople — Greek) 114
Theōnas : 282–300 (Alexandria — Greek) 23
Theophanēs : 1925–1926, 1935–1936, 1939 [locum tenens] (Alexandria — Greek) 26
Theophanēs I *Karykēs* : 1596–1597 (Constantinople — Greek) 114
Theophanēs II *apo Melekinou* : 1657 (Constantinople — Greek) 115
Theophanēs I : 1458? (Greece) 156
Theophanēs II *Karykēs* : 1592–1597 (Greece) 156
Theophanēs III : 1620–1633 (Greece) 157
Theophanēs I : 1424–1431 (Jerusalem — Greek) 186
Theophanēs II : -1450 (Jerusalem — Greek) 186
Theophanēs III : 1608–1644 (Jerusalem — Greek) 187
Theophilos I : 384–412 (Alexandria — Greek) 23
Theophilos II : 1010–1020 (Alexandria — Greek) 24
Theophilos III *Pankōstas* : 1805–1825 (Alexandria — Greek) 26
Theophilos *Blachopapadopoulos* : 1862–1873 (Greece) 157
Theophilos I : 1012–1020 (Jerusalem — Greek) 186
Theophilos II : 1417–1424 (Jerusalem — Greek) 186
Theophilos III *Giannopoulos* : 2005- (Jerusalem — Greek) 187, 255, 258, 260
Theophilus *Pashkovskiĭ* : 1934–1950 (America — Orthodox Church) 32
Theophylaktos : 695? (Alexandria — Greek) 24
Theophylaktos *Lekapēnos* : 933–956 (Constantinople — Greek) 111
Theophylaktos : 1140? (Greece) 156
Thiyudhurus I : 767–797 (Antioch — Greek) 36

Thiyudhurus II : 966–977 (Antioch — Greek) 36
Thiyudhurus III *Laskaris* : 1010–1015 (Antioch — Greek) 36
Thiyudhurus IV *Balsamōn* : 1185–1199 (Antioch — Greek) 37
Thiyudur : 649–667 (Antioch — Syrian Catholic) 54
Thiyuduritus : 787? (Antioch — Greek Melkite) 41
Thiyudurus I : 970–976 (Antioch — Greek Melkite) 42
Thiyudurus II *Laskaris* : 1033–1041 (Antioch — Greek Melkite) 42
Thiyudurus III *Balsamōn* : 1185?–1195? (Antioch — Greek Melkite) 42
Thiyudurus : 649–667 (Antioch — Syrian Orthodox) 59
Thiyudusiyus I : 852–860 (Antioch — Greek) 36
Thiyudusiyus II *Chrysobergēs* : 1075–1084 (Antioch — Greek) 37
Thiyudusiyus III : 1180–1182 (Antioch — Greek) 37
Thiyudusiyus IV : 1269–1276 (Antioch — Greek) 37
Thiyudusiyus V *de Villehardouin* : 1276–1285 (Antioch — Greek) 37
Thiyudusiyus VI *Abu Rajaili* : 1958 [locum tenens], 1958–1970 [patriarch] (Antioch — Greek) 38
Thiyudusiyus I : 870–890 (Antioch — Greek Melkite) 41
Thiyudusiyus II : 936–943 (Antioch — Greek Melkite) 41
Thiyudusiyus III *Chrysobergēs* : 1057?– (Antioch — Greek Melkite) 42
Thiyudusiyus IV *de Villehardouin* : 1275–1284? (Antioch — Greek Melkite) 42
Thiyudusiyus V *Dahan* : 1761–1788 (Antioch — Greek Melkite) 44
Thiyudusiyus : 887–895 (Antioch — Syrian Catholic) 55
Thiyudut : 424–427 (Antioch — Syrian Catholic) 53
Thiyudutus : 418–427 (Antioch — Greek), and 417–429? (Antioch — Greek Melkite) 35, 40
Thiyufanis : 681–687 (Antioch — Greek), and 681–683? (Antioch — Greek Melkite) 36, 41
Thiyufilaktus *ibn Qanbara* : 748–767 (Antioch — Greek), and 745?–768? (Antioch — Greek Melkite) 36, 41
Thiyufilus : 169–182? (Antioch — Greek), and 170?–182 (Antioch — Greek Melkite), and 170–172 (Antioch — Syrian Catholic) 34, 40, 53
Thiyukharistus : 944–948 (Antioch — Greek Melkite) 41
Thoma —*see also*: Thomas, T'uma
Thoma (IV) *Rocos* : 1861–1862 (India — Chaldean) 174
Thoma (V) *Darmo* : 1952–1968 (India — Chaldean) 75, 174–175
Thoma I : 834–847 (India — Malankara Jacobite) 168
Thoma II : 910–911 (India — Malankara Jacobite) 168
Thoma II *of Tigris* : 848–856 (India — Malankara Orthodox) 164
Thoma III *Asthunoro* : 912–913 (India — Malankara Orthodox) 164
Thoma I *Pakalomarram*, Mar : 1652–1670 (India — Malankara Syrian) 160, 162
Thoma II, Mar : 1670–1686 (India — Malankara Syrian) 160, 162
Thoma, Mar : 1674 (India — Malankara Syrian) 162
Thoma III, Mar : 1686–1688 (India — Malankara Syrian) 162
Thoma IV, Mar : 1688–1728 (India — Malankara Syrian) 162
Thoma V, Mar : 1728–1765 (India — Malankara Syrian) 162
Thoma VI, Mar [i.e., Mar Dionysios I] : 1761–1765 [suffragan], 1765–1808 (India — Malankara Syrian) 160, 162, 175
Thoma VII, Mathew Mar : 1796 [suffragan], 1796–1809 (India — Malankara Syrian) 162
Thoma VIII, Mar : 1806–1816 (India — Malankara Syrian) 162
Thoma IX, Mar : 1816 (India — Malankara Syrian) 162
Thomas —*see also*: Thoma
Thōmas I : 607–610 (Constantinople — Greek) 110
Thōmas II : 667–669 (Constantinople — Greek) 110
Thōmas : 1948 [locum tenens] (Constantinople — Greek) 117
Thomas I *Morosini* : 1204–1211 (Constantinople — Latin) 119
Thomas II *Palaiologos Tagaris* : 1379?–1384? (Constantinople — Latin) 120
Thomas III *Bakócz de Erdoed* : 1507–1521 (Constantinople — Latin) 120
Thomas, Dionysios Mar : 1999–2002 [locum tenens] (India — Malankara Jacobite) 173
Thomas I, Baselios Mar : 2002– (India — Malankara Jacobite) 173, 255, 258–259
Thomas I : 35–72 (India — Malankara Orthodox) 160, 162
Thōmas I : 807–820 (Jerusalem — Greek) 185
Thōmas II : 969–978 (Jerusalem — Greek) 185
Thomas *Agni de Lentino* : 1272–1277 (Jerusalem — Latin) 189
Thomas Mar Athanasios : 1877–1893 (India — Mar Thoma Syrian) 173
Thomas Mar Athanasios : 1982– [suffragan] (India — Mar Thoma Syrian) 173
Thomas Mar Timotheos : 1992– [suffragan] (India — Malankara Orthodox) 167
Thomooso : 364?–372? (India — Malankara Jacobite) 167
Thomuso : 360–368 (India — Malankara Orthodox) 163
Tikhon *Belavin* : 1898–1907 (America — Orthodox Church), and 1917–1925 (Russia) 31–32, 135, 190, 218, 221, 223
Timathiyus : 274–283 (Antioch — Syrian Catholic) 53
Timat'ius I : 780–820 (Assyria), and 780–823 (Babylon) 73, 86
Timat'ius II : 1318–1328 (Assyria), and 1318–1332 (Babylon) 74, 87
Timat'ius Yusip IV *Mushi* : 1713–1757 (Babylon) 88
Timayus : 273–277 (Antioch — Greek), and 266–271 (Antioch — Greek Melkite) 34, 40
Timiyus : 273–282 (Antioch — Syrian Orthodox) 58
Timofeĭ *Sacherbatskiĭ* : 1764–1767 (Russia — Moscow) 221
Timotej *Jovanovski* : 1993 [locum tenens] (Macedonia) 197
Timotheos I *Aktēmōn* : 380–384 (Alexandria — Greek) 23
Timotheos II *Ailouros* : 457–460, 475–477 (Alexandria — Greek) 14, 23
Timotheos III *Salophakialos* : 460–475, 477–482 (Alexandria — Greek) 14, 23
Timotheos IV : 517–535 (Alexandria — Greek) 23
Timotheos *Euangelidēs* : 1949 (America — Greek) 30
Timotheus, Mar Abimaleck : 1920s [locum tenens] (Assyria)

1908–1945 (India – Chaldean), 75, 175
Timotheos I *Kēlōn* : 511–518 (Constantinople – Greek) 110
Timotheos II *apo Palaiōn Patrōn* : 1612–1620 (Constantinople – Greek) 114
Timotheos I *Kastrinogiannakēs* : 1882–1897 (Crete) 125
Timotheos II *Benerēs* : 1934–1941 (Crete) 125
Timotheos III *Papoutsakēs* : 1978- (Crete) 125, 254, 257, 259
Timotheos : 1572–1588? (Cyprus) 126, 128
Timotheos : 1622- [anti-archbishop] (Cyprus) 128
Timotheos, Thomas Mar : 1992- [suffragan] (India – Malankara Orthodox) 167
Timotheos *Themelēs* : 1935–1955 (Jerusalem – Greek) 183, 187
Timuthawus I : 380–385 (Alexandria – Coptic) 16
Timuthawus II *Ailouros* : 458–460?, 475–480 (Alexandria – Coptic) 14, 16
Timuthawus *Salophakialos* : 460–475 [anti-pope] (Alexandria – Coptic) 14, 16
Timuthawus III : 517–535 (Alexandria – Coptic) 16
Timuthawus : 378–384 (Alexandria – Coptic Catholic) 21
Tiran *Nersoyan* : 1957–1958 [patriarch-elect] (Jerusalem – Armenian) 179, 182
Tiraniyun : 299–308 (Antioch – Greek) 35
Tiranus : 306–314 (Antioch – Greek Melkite) 40
Tiratur : 1586–1592 [anti-catholicos] (Cilicia – Armenian Apostolic) 99
Tiratur : 1561–1563, 1596–1599 (Constantinople – Armenian) 104
Tit *Simedrea* : 1940–1945 (Austria – Cernovci) 78
Titos : 242–272 (Constantinople – Greek) 109
Titos I *Apostolos* : 64? (Crete) 123
Titos II *Zōgraphidēs* : 1922–1933 (Crete) 125
Titos I *Mar Thoma* : 1894–1910 (India – Mar Thoma Syrian) 173
Titos II *Mar Thoma* : 1899–1910 [suffragan], 1910–1944 (India – Mar Thoma Syrian) 173
T'iyaduris : 850–852 (Assyria) 73
T'iyadusis I : 850–852 (Assyria) 73
T'iyadusis II : 1257–1265 (Assyria) 74
T'iyadusis : 853–858 (Babylon) 86

Tiyufilaqtus : unknown (Antioch – Maronite) 49
Tōbias : 2nd cent. (Jerusalem – Greek) 184
Tomas : 1237 (Ethiopia – Historical) 143
T'orgom *Manugian* : 1994–1995 [locum tenens] (Armenia) 68
T'orgom I *Gushakian* : 1931–1939 (Jerusalem — Armenian) 182
T'orgom II *Manugian* : 1990- (Jerusalem – Armenian) 182, 255, 257, 259
T'oros I : 1548–1550? (Cilicia – Armenian Apostolic) 99
T'oros II : 1654–1657 (Cilicia – Armenian Apostolic) 99
T'oros III *Adshapahian* : 1784–1796 (Cilicia – Armenian Apostolic) 100
T'oros : 1681, 1687–1688 (Constantinople – Armenian) 104–105
T'ovma – *see also*: T'ovmas
T'ovma I *Toghlabeghian* : 1681–1698 (Aght'amar) 6
T'ovma : 1722? [locum tenens] (Aght'amar) 6
T'ovma II : 1761–1783 (Aght'amar) 7
T'ovma : -1495 (Aghunie) 10
T'ovma II : 1644, 1657–1659 (Constantinople – Armenian) 104
T'ovmas – *see also*: T'ovma
T'ovmas I : 1581–1587 (Constantinople – Armenian) 104
Trdat I : 741–764 (Armenia) 65
Trdat II : 764–767 (Armenia) 65
Troïlos : -431 (Cyprus) 127
Tryphōn : 927–931 (Constantinople – Greek) 111
Tubiyya Butrus *al-Khazin* : 1733, 1756–1766 (Antioch – Maronite) 50
Tuma : 683?–685? (Antioch – Greek Melkite) 41
T'uma – *see also*: Thoma
T'uma I *Shlikha* : 33 (Assyria) 71, 160
T'uma II *Darmu* : 1968–1969 (Assyria – Ancient Church of the East) 75, 174–175
T'uma *Shlikha* : -33 (Babylon) 84, 160
T'uma I : 795?–824? (India – Chaldean) 174
T'uma II : 1056? (India – Chaldean) 174
T'uma III : 1490? (India – Chaldean) 174
T'uma IV *Rocos* : 1861–1862 (India – Chaldean) 174
T'uma V *Darmu* : 1952–1968 (India – Chaldean) 75, 174–175
T'umarsa : 383–393 (Assyria), and 388?- (Babylon) 72, 85

Turanus : 299–313 (Antioch – Syrian Catholic), and 304–314 (Antioch – Syrian Orthodox) 53, 58
Tymofiĭ *Shcherbats'kiĭ* : 1748–1757 (Ukraine) 237
Tymoteusz *Szretter* : 1947–1951 [locum tenens], 1959–1961 [locum tenens], 1961–1962 [metropolitan] (Poland) 204

Ugo – *see also*: Hugo
Ugo *de Robertis* : 1402- (Alexandria – Latin) 27
Ugo II *de Lusignan* : 1413–1442 (Cyprus – Latin) 130
Ukhtanês : 670–681? (Aghunie) 9
'Ummanu'il : 937–949 (Assyria) 73
'Ummanu'il I : 937–960 (Babylon) 86
'Ummanu'il II *T'uma*, Yusip : 1900–1947 (Babylon) 88, 252
'Ummanu'il III *Delly* : 2003- (Babylon) 84, 88, 254, 258–259
Urbanus I : 222–230 (Rome) 210
Urbanus II : 1088–1099 (Rome) 214
Urbanus III *Crivelli* : 1185–1187 (Rome) 215
Urbanus IV *Pantaléon* : 1261–1264 (Rome) 215
Urbanus V *de Grimoard* : 1362–1370 (Rome) 215
Urbanus VI *Prignano* : 1378–1389 (Rome) 209, 215
Urbanus VII *Castagna* : 1590 (Rome) 216
Urbanus VIII *Barberini* : 1623–1644 (Rome) 216
Ursinus : 366–367 [anti-pope] (Rome) 211

Vahan *Siuni* : 968–969 (Armenia) 66
Vahan *Kostanian* : 1954 [locum tenens] (Armenia) 68
Valaam : 1596–1598 (Bulgaria), and 1597–1598 (Macedonia) 94, 196
Valentin *Rusantsov* : 1994- (Russia – Autonomous Church) 224
Valentinus : 827 (Rome) 213
Varfolomeĭ *Gondarovskiĭ* : 1969–1972 (Moldova) 198
Varlaam : 1735–1745 (Austria – Cernovci) 78
Varlaam : 1685–1692 (Austria – Sibiu) 81
Varlaam *Eristavi* : 1811–1817 [exarch] (Georgia) 151
Varlaam I : 1534?–1544 (Romania) 206
Varlaam II : 1672–1679 (Romania) 206

Varlaam : 1511–1521 (Russia — Moscow) 220
Varlaam I *IAsyns'kyĭ* : 1690–1707 (Ukraine) 237
Varlaam II *Vanatovych* : 1722–1730 (Ukraine) 237
Varnava *Rosić* : 1930–1937 (Serbia) 228
Vasile I *Moga* : 1810–1845 (Austria — Sibiu) 81
Vasile II *Mangra* : 1916–1918 (Austria — Sibiu) 82
Vasiliĭ I : 1185–1233 (Bulgaria) 93, 252
Vasiliĭ II : 1246- (Bulgaria) 93
Vasiliĭ *of Ruse* : 1918–1922 [locum tenens] (Bulgaria) 95
Vasiliĭ *Shuan* : 1956–1962 (China) 97
Vasilije I : 1532? (Montenegro) 201
Vasilije II *Veljekraĭski* : 1649? (Montenegro) 201
Vasilije III *Petrović* : 1744–1750 [coadjutor], 1750–1766 (Montenegro) 202
Vasilije *Jovanović-Brkić* : 1763–1765, 1772 (Serbia) 227
Vasyl' *Lypkisv'kyĭ* : 1921–1927 (Ukraine — Autocephalous) 233, 238
Vasyliĭ *Fedak* : 1985–1990 (Ukraine — Canada) 240
Vavyla : 1491–1520 (Montenegro) 200–201
Vazgên *Palchian* : 1955–1994 (Armenia) 68, 98
Venceslaus *Králik* : 1397–1416 (Antioch — Latin) 46
Veniamin *Karelin* : 1867–1874 (Latvia) 191
Venijamin : 1582–1591 (Montenegro) 201
Vićentije I *Popović* : 1713–1725 (Austria — Karlovci) 79
Vićentije II *Jovanović* : 1731–1737 (Austria — Karlovci) 79
Vićentije III *Jovanović-Vidak* : 1774–1780 (Austria — Karlovci) 79
Victor *Marcello* : 1477- (Cyprus — Latin) 130
Victor I : 189–199 (Rome) 210
Victor II *von Dollnstein-Hirschberg* : 1055–1057 (Rome) 214
Victor III : 1086–1087 (Rome) 214
Victor IV *Conti* : 1138 [anti-pope] (Rome) 214
Victor IV *de Monticelli* : 1159–1164 [anti-pope] (Rome) 215
Vigilius : 537–555 (Rome) 212
Vikentiĭ *Nikitin* : 1934–1938 [locum tenens] (Russia — Belokrinitsia) 223

Vikentije I *Stefanović* : 1756? (Serbia) 227
Vikentije II *Prodanov* : 1950–1958 (Serbia) 193, 228
Viktor *Sviatin* : 1950–1956 (China) 97
Vincentius *Tizzani* : 1886–1892 (Antioch — Latin) 47
Vincentius *Bracco* : 1873–1889 (Jerusalem — Latin) 189
Viroy : 596–630 (Aghunie) 9
Visarion *Xhuvani* : 1929–1936 (Albania) 12–13
Visarion *Puiu* : 1935–1940 (Austria — Cernovci) 78
Visarion : 1310? (Bulgaria) 93
Visarion I : 1482–1485 (Montenegro) 201
Visarion II *Kolinović* : 1649? (Montenegro) 201
Visarion III *Borilović Bajica* : 1685–1692 (Montenegro) 201
Visarion IV *Ljubiša* : 1882–1884 (Montenegro) 202
Vitalianus : 657–672 (Rome) 212
Vitaliĭ *Ustinov* : 1985–1986 [locum tenens], 1986–2001 (Russia — Church Outside Russia) 2001- (Russia — Church in Exile), 224, 256–257, 259
Vladimir *Sokolovskiĭ-Autonomov* : 1887–1891 (America — Orthodox Church) 31
Vladimir *Repta* : 1902–1924 (Austria — Cernovci) 78
Vladimir *Bogoiavlens'kyĭ* : 1892–1898 [exarch] (Georgia) 152
Vladimir *Nagoskiĭ* : 1962–1972 (Japan) 178
Vladimir *Cantareanu* : 1989- (Moldova) 198, 256–257, 260
Vlasie *Mogârzan* : 1992- (Romania — Old Calendarists) 208, 256–257, 260
Volodymyr I *Bohoiavlens'kyĭ* : 1915–1918 (Ukraine) 238
Volodymyr II *Sabodan* : 1992- (Ukraine) 234, 238, 256–257, 259
Volodymyr *Romaniuk* : 1993–1995 (Ukraine — Kiev Patriarchate) 234, 238
Volunnius *Bandinelli* : 1658–1667 (Constantinople — Latin) 121
Vrt'anēs *Part'ē* : 333–341 (Armenia) 64
Vrt'anēs *Kert'ogh* : 604–607 [locum tenens] (Armenia) 65
Vrt'anēs I : 1323–1332 (Jerusalem — Armenian) 180
Vrt'anēs II : 1860–1864 [locum tenens] (Jerusalem — Armenian) 182
Vsevolod *Kolomiĭchev-Maĭdanskiĭ* : 1987–1997 (Ukraine — America) 241

Willelmus — *see also*: Guillelmus
Willelmus I : 1130–1145 (Jerusalem — Latin) 188

Yaballaha : 414?–420 (India — Malankara Jacobite) 167
Yabhalaha I : 415–420 (Assyria), and (Babylon) 72, 85
Yabhalaha II *bar Qayyuma* : 1191–1222 (Assyria), and 1190–1220 (Babylon) 74, 87
Yabhalaha III *bar Turkaya* : 1281–1318 (Assyria), and 1283–1318 (Babylon) 69, 74, 87
Yabhalaha IV Shim'un X : 1558–1580 (Assyria) 70, 74, 83
Yabhalaha IV, Shim'un : 1578–1580 (Babylon) 88
Yabhalaha I : 1407? (India — Chaldean) 174
Yabhalaha II : 1503? (India — Chaldean) 174
Yabhalaha Shim'un XIV : 1690–1692 (Assyria) 74
Ya'eqob : 2002 [locum tenens], 2002–2003 [patriarch] (Eritrea) 134
Ya'eqob I : 848? (Ethiopia — Historical) 142
Ya'eqob II : 1250? (Ethiopia — Historical) 143
Ya'eqob III *Madhinana Egzie* : 1337–1344 (Ethiopia — Historical) 143
Ya'eqob : unknown (Ethiopia — Official) 140
Yahb Allaho : 393–398 (India — Malankara Orthodox) 163
Yakoub : 213–231 (India — Malankara Orthodox) 163
Yakub, Gregorios : 1189–1214 (India — Malankara Jacobite) 169
Yalda, Baselios Mar : 1634–1685 (India — Malankara Orthodox) 166
Ya'qub : 819–830 (Alexandria — Coptic) 16
Ya'qub I *Butrus of Ramat* : 1141?–1151 (Antioch — Maronite) 49
Ya'qub II : 1268?- (Antioch — Maronite) 50
Ya'qub III *ibn Hid al-Hadathi* : 1445–1458 (Antioch — Maronite) 50
Ya'qub IV Butrus *Awwad* : 1705–1733 (Antioch — Maronite) 50
Ya'qub, Ighnatiyus : 1510–1519 (Antioch — Syrian Catholic) 55
Ya'qub I, Ighnatiyus : 1512–1517 (Antioch — Syrian Orthodox) 61
Ya'qub II, Ighnatiyus : 1847–1871

Index of Primates

(Antioch — Syrian Orthodox) 62
Ya'qub III *Tuma*, Ighnatiyus : 1957–1980 (Antioch — Syrian Orthodox) 62
Ya'qub I : 172–190 (Assyria), and 2nd cent. (Babylon) 71, 84
Ya'qub II : 754–773 (Assyria), and 754–773 (Babylon) 73, 86
Ya'qub I : 1328? (India — Chaldean) 174
Ya'qub II : 1503–1549? (India — Chaldean) 174
Yaraklas : 231–247 (Alexandria — Coptic), and 230–246 (Alexandria — Coptic Catholic) 15, 21
Yavanan, Baselios : 1803 (India — Malankara Jacobite) 172
Yeldho, Baselios : 1678–1685 (India — Malankara Jacobite) 171
Yerda' Mika'el III : 1220? (Ethiopia — Historical) 143
Yes'aq — *see also*: Yeshaq
Yes'aq I : 1210?– (Ethiopia — Historical), and unknown (Ethiopia — Official) 139, 143
Yeshaq — *see also*: Yes'aq
Yeshaq II : 1481–1505? (Ethiopia — Historical), and 1481–1510? (Ethiopia — Official) 141, 143
Yoakim Mar Koorilose : 1846–1852 (India — Malankara Syrian) 162
Yohannes I : 820?–840? (Ethiopia — Historical) 142
Yohannes II : 1310? (Ethiopia — Historical) 143
Yohannes III : 1437? (Ethiopia — Historical) 143
Yohannes IV : 1530? (Ethiopia — Historical) 143
Yohannes V : 1649?– (Ethiopia — Historical) 143
Yohannes VI : 1743–1761 (Ethiopia — Historical) 144
Yohannes VII : 1939–1945 [anti-abuna] (Ethiopia — Historical) 138, 144
Yohannes : 1976 [locum tenens] (Ethiopia — Historical) and (Ethiopia — Official) 142, 144
Yohannes I : unknown (Ethiopia — Official) 139
Yohannes II : unknown (Ethiopia — Official) 139
Yohannes III : unknown (Ethiopia — Official) 139
Yohannes IV : unknown (Ethiopia — Official) 139
Yohannes V : unknown (Ethiopia — Official) 139
Yohannes VI : unknown (Ethiopia — Official) 140
Yohannes VII : unknown (Ethiopia — Official) 140

Yohannes VIII : unknown (Ethiopia — Official) 140
Yohannes IX : unknown (Ethiopia — Official) 140
Yohannes X : unknown (Ethiopia — Official) 140
Yohannes XI : unknown (Ethiopia — Official) 141
Yohannes XII : unknown (Ethiopia — Official) 141
Yohannes XIII : 1648?– (Ethiopia — Official) 141
Yohannes XIV : 1743–1761 (Ethiopia — Official) 141
Yohannes XV : 1939–1945 [anti-abuna] (Ethiopia — Official) 138, 142
Yohannon (V) Elia *Mellus* : 1874–1882 (India — Chaldean) 174
Yosab I : 1547?–1559? (Ethiopia — Historical) 143
Yosab I : unknown (Ethiopia — Official) 140
Yosab II : 1539?–1559? (Ethiopia — Official) 141
Yosab III : 1770–1803 (Ethiopia — Official) 141
Yosef : unknown (Ethiopia — Official) 140
Yostos I : unknown (Ethiopia — Official) 140
Yostos II : unknown (Ethiopia — Official) 140
Youhanon I *Soubo* : 687–688 (India — Malankara Orthodox) 164
Youhanon II *Keeyunoyo* : 758–788 (India — Malankara Orthodox) 164
Youhanon III *of Damascus* : 991–997 (India — Malankara Orthodox) 164
Youhanon IV *Sleeba* : 1075–1106 (India — Malankara Orthodox) 165
Youhanon V *Srugayo* : 1165–1188 (India — Malankara Orthodox) 165
Youhanon VI *Bar Madan* : 1232–1253 (India — Malankara Orthodox) 165
Yoyakin Mar Koorilose : 1846–1852 (India — Malankara Syrian) 162
Yuhanna I : 427–443 (Antioch — Greek) 35
Yuhanna II : 475–490 (Antioch — Greek) 35
Yuhanna III *Kōdōnatos* : 495–497 (Antioch — Greek) 35
Yuhanna IV : 797–811 (Antioch — Greek) 36
Yuhanna V *Politēs* : 995–1000 (Antioch — Greek) 36
Yuhanna VI : 1051–1062 (Antioch — Greek) 36

Yuhanna VII *Oxeitēs* : 1090–1106 (Antioch — Greek) 37
Yuhanna VIII : 1106–1137 (Antioch — Greek) 37
Yuhanna IX : 1155–1159 (Antioch — Greek) 37
Yuhanna I : 429?–442? (Antioch — Greek Melkite) 40
Yuhanna II *Kōdōnatos* : 477?–478? (Antioch — Greek Melkite) 41
Yuhanna III *Politēs* : 997–1022 (Antioch — Greek Melkite) 42
Yuhanna IV *Oxeitēs* : 1098–1100 (Antioch — Greek Melkite) 42
Yuhanna *Haddad* : 2000 [apostolic administrator] (Antioch — Greek Melkite) 44
Yuhanna I *Marun* : 681–707 (Antioch — Maronite) 48–49
Yuhanna II *Marun* : 8th cent. (Antioch — Maronite) 49
Yuhanna III : 8th cent. (Antioch — Maronite) 49
Yuhanna IV : unknown (Antioch — Maronite) 49
Yuhanna V : unknown (Antioch — Maronite) 49
Yuhanna VI : unknown (Antioch — Maronite) 49
Yuhanna VII *of Lahfad* : 1151–1154 (Antioch — Maronite) 49
Yuhanna VIII Butrus *al-Jaji* : 1239?–1244? (Antioch — Maronite) 50
Yuhanna IX : 1322?–1357? (Antioch — Maronite) 50
Yuhanna X *al-Jaji* : 1404–1445 (Antioch — Maronite) 50
Yuhanna XI *ibn Makhluf* : 1608–1633 (Antioch — Maronite) 50
Yuhanna XII *al-Safrawi* : 1648–1656 (Antioch — Maronite) 50
Yuhanna XIII Butrus *al-Hilu* : 1809–1823 (Antioch — Maronite) 50
Yuhanna XIV Butrus *Hajj* : 1890–1898 (Antioch — Maronite) 51
Yuhanna I : 427–440 (Antioch — Syrian Catholic) 53
Yuhanna II *Kōdōnatos* : 480, 484–485 (Antioch — Syrian Catholic) 54
Yuhanna III : 631–649 (Antioch — Syrian Catholic) 54
Yuhanna IV : 740–755 (Antioch — Syrian Catholic) 54
Yuhanna : 758–763? [anti-patriarch] (Antioch — Syrian Catholic) 54
Yuhanna V : 847–874 (Antioch — Syrian Catholic) 54
Yuhanna VI : 910–922 (Antioch — Syrian Catholic) 55

Yuhanna VII : 936–953 (Antioch — Syrian Catholic) 55
Yuhanna VIII : 954–957 (Antioch — Syrian Catholic) 55
Yuhanna IX *Sarighta* : 965–986 (Antioch — Syrian Catholic) 55
Yuhanna X *of Abhdun* : 1004–1030 (Antioch — Syrian Catholic) 55
Yuhanna XI : 1042–1057 (Antioch — Syrian Catholic) 55
Yuhanna XII *Ishu' ibn Shushan* : 1063–1073 (Antioch — Syrian Catholic) 55
Yuhanna XIII *Shinudah* : 1075–1077 (Antioch — Syrian Catholic) 55
Yuhanna XIV : 1079–1087 (Antioch — Syrian Catholic) 55
Yuhanna XV *Mawdyani* : 1129–1137 (Antioch — Syrian Catholic) 55
Yuhanna XVI *Ishu'* : 1208–1220 (Antioch — Syrian Catholic) 55
Yuhanna XVII *ibn Ma'dani* : 1253–1263 (Antioch — Syrian Catholic) 55
Yuhanna XVIII *Akhsinaya Bar Shilla*, Ighnatiyus : 1484–1494 (Antioch — Syrian Catholic) 55
Yuhanna I : 428–442 (Antioch — Syrian Orthodox) 58
Yuhanna *Kōdōnatos* : 476–478 [anti-patriarch] (Antioch — Syrian Orthodox) 59
Yuhanna II *of the Sedre* : 631–648 (Antioch — Syrian Orthodox) 59
Yuhanna : 758–763? [anti-patriarch] (Antioch — Syrian Orthodox) 59
Yuhanna III : 846–873 (Antioch — Syrian Orthodox) 59
Yuhanna IV *Qurzahli* : 910–922 (Antioch — Syrian Orthodox) 60
Yuhanna V : 936–953 (Antioch — Syrian Orthodox) 60
Yuhanna VI *Sarighta al-Ma'tuk* : 965–985 (Antioch — Syrian Orthodox) 60
Yuhanna VII *ibn Abhduni* : 1004–1033 (Antioch — Syrian Orthodox) 60
Yuhanna VIII : 1049–1057 (Antioch — Syrian Orthodox) 60
Yuhanna IX *Ishu' ibn Shushan* : 1063–1073 (Antioch — Syrian Orthodox) 60
Yuhanna *Abdun* : 1075–1091? [anti-patriarch] (Antioch — Syrian Orthodox) 60
Yuhanna X *Mawdyani* : 1129–1137 (Antioch — Syrian Orthodox) 60

Yuhanna XI *Ishu'* : 1208–1220 (Antioch — Syrian Orthodox) 60
Yuhanna XII *ibn al-Ma'dani* : 1252–1263 (Antioch — Syrian Orthodox) 60
Yuhanna XIII *Akhsinaya Bar Shilla*, Ighnatiyus : 1483–1493 (Antioch — Syrian Catholic) 61
Yuhanna *ibn Qufar*, Ighnatiyus : 1488–1493 (Antioch — Syrian Orthodox — Tur Abhdin) 62
Yuhanna, Mar : 1685–1693 (India — Malankara Syrian) 162
Yuhannan I : 686–688 (India — Malankara Jacobite) 168
Yuhannan II : 758–785 (India — Malankara Jacobite) 168
Yuhannan III : 980?–988 (India — Malankara Jacobite) 169
Yuhannan *bar Ma'dani* : 1232–1252 (India — Malankara Jacobite) 169
Yuhannan *Sarugoyo* : 1164–1188 (India — Malankara Jacobite) 169
Yuhannan *Sleeba* I : 1075–1106 (India — Malankara Jacobite) 169
Yuhannis I *Hemula* : 495–503 (Alexandria — Coptic) 16
Yuhannis II *Nikiotēs* : 503–515 (Alexandria — Coptic) 16
Yuhannis III : 677–686 (Alexandria — Coptic) 16
Yuhannis IV : 775–799 (Alexandria — Coptic) 16
Yuhannis V *ibn Abi'l-Fath* : 1147–1167 (Alexandria — Coptic) 17
Yuhannis VI *ibn Abi Ghali* : 1189–1216 (Alexandria — Coptic) 17
Yuhannis VII *ibn Abi Sa'id* : 1262–1268, 1271–1293 (Alexandria — Coptic) 17
Yuhannis VIII : 1300–1320 (Alexandria — Coptic) 17
Yuhannis IX : 1320–1327 (Alexandria — Coptic) 17
Yuhannis X *al-Mu'taman* : 1363–1369 (Alexandria — Coptic) 17
Yuhannis XI *Abu'l-Farag* : 1427–1452 (Alexandria — Coptic) 17
Yuhannis XII : 1479–1482 (Alexandria — Coptic) 18
Yuhannis XIII : 1484–1524 (Alexandria — Coptic) 18
Yuhannis XIV *al-Manfulati* : 1570–1585 (Alexandria — Coptic) 18
Yuhannis XV : 1619–1634 (Alexandria — Coptic) 18

Yuhannis XVI *al-Maghribi* : 1676–1718 (Alexandria — Coptic) 18
Yuhannis XVII *al-Malawi* : 1726–1745 (Alexandria — Coptic) 18
Yuhannis XVIII *al-Fayumi* : 1769–1796 (Alexandria — Coptic) 18
Yuhannis XIX : 1927–1928 [locum tenens], 1928–1942 [patriarch] (Alexandria — Coptic) 18, 138
Yuhannis *Faragi* : 1781–1788 (Alexandria — Coptic Catholic) 21
Yukhannan I *bar Marta* : 680–682 (Assyria) 73
Yukhannan II *Garba "The Leper"* : 693–694 (Assyria) 73
Yukhannan III *bar Narsai* : 884–892 (Assyria) 73
Yukhannan IV *bar Akhiha* : 892–898 (Assyria) 73
Yukhannan V *bar Abgara* : 900–905 (Assyria) 73
Yukhannan VI *bar Ishu'* : 1001–1012 (Assyria) 73
Yukhannan VII *Nazuk* : 1013–1022 (Assyria) 73
Yukhannan VIII *bar Targali* : 1049–1057 (Assyria) 74
Yukhannan I *bar Marta* : 681?–683 (Babylon) 85
Yukhannan *Garba "The Leper"* : 691–693? [anti-patriarch] (Babylon) 85
Yukhannan II *bar Akhiha* : 884–891 (Babylon) 86
Yukhannan III *bar Narsai* : 893–899 (Babylon) 86
Yukhannan IV *bar Abgara* : 900–905 (Babylon) 86
Yukhannan V *bar Ishu'* : 1000–1011 (Babylon) 86
Yukhannan VI *Nazuk* : 1012–1016 (Babylon) 86
Yukhannan VII *bar Tarbali* : 1049–1057 (Babylon) 87
Yukhannan VIII *Khurmiz* : 1804–1830 [locum tenens], 1830–1838 [patriarch] (Babylon) 83, 88
Yukhannan I : 1000? (India — Chaldean) 174
Yukhannan II : 1110? (India — Chaldean) 174
Yukhannan III : 1122?–1129? (India — Chaldean) 174
Yukhannan IV : 1490? (India — Chaldean) 174
Yukhannan V Elia *Mellus* : 1874–1882 (India — Chaldean) 174
Yukhannan *Iliya* X *bar Mama* : 1660–1700 (Babylon) 87
Yukhannan *Shim'un* IX *Sulaqa* :

1551–1555 (Babylon) 69–70, 83, 88
Yuliyanus—*see also*: Yulyan
Yuliyanus : 180–189 (Alexandria—Coptic), and 178–188 (Alexandria—Coptic Catholic) 15, 21
Yuliyanus : 471 (Antioch—Greek), and 471–476? (Antioch—Greek Melkite), and 471–476 [anti-patriarch] (Antioch—Syrian Orthodox) 35, 41, 59
Yulyan—*see also*: Yuliyanus
Yulyan I : 473–477 (Antioch—Syrian Catholic) 54
Yulyan II : 592–595 (Antioch—Syrian Catholic) 54
Yulyan III *"The Roman"* : 688–709 (Antioch—Syrian Catholic) 54
Yulyan I : 591–595 (Antioch—Syrian Orthodox) 59
Yulyan II *"The Roman"* : 686–708 (Antioch—Syrian Orthodox) 59
Yunan, Ighnatiyus : 1818–1819 (Antioch—Syrian Orthodox) 62
Yunan Shim'un XVIII : 1780?–1820? (Assyria) 74
Yusab I : 830–849 (Alexandria—Coptic) 16
Yusab II *Filibbus* : 1942–1944 [locum tenens], 1946–1954 (Alexandria—Coptic) 18
Yusab I : 1547?–1559? (Ethiopia—Historical) 143
Yusab II : 1770–1803 (Ethiopia—Historical) 144
Yusip : 552–567 (Assyria) 72
Yusip Khnanishu' : 1918–1927 [locum tenens] (Assyria) 75
Yusip I : 551–567? (Babylon) 85
Yusip II : 1681–1695 (Babylon) 83, 88
Yusip III *Sliba*, Ma'ruf : 1696–1712 (Babylon) 83, 88
Yusip IV *Mushi*, Timat'ius : 1713–1757 (Babylon) 88
Yusip V *Khindi*, Lazar : 1757–1781 (Babylon) 83, 88
Yusip (VI) *Khindi*, Agustinus : 1804–1828 [unconsecrated] (Babylon) 83, 88
Yusip VI *Audu* : 1848–1878 (Babylon) 84, 88
Yusip VII *Ghanima* : 1947–1958 (Babylon) 88
Yusip I *of Edessa* : 345? (India—Chaldean) 174
Yusip II : 1231 (India—Chaldean) 174
Yusip III : 1556–1569 (India—Chaldean) 174
Yusip Khnanishu' : 1918–1927 [locum tenens] (Assyria) 75

Yusip 'Ummanu'il II *T'uma* : 1900–1947 (Babylon) 88, 252
Yustus : 122–130 (Alexandria—Coptic), and 118–129 (Alexandria—Coptic Catholic) 15, 21
Yusuf I *al-Jirjisi* : 1100? (Antioch—Maronite) 48–49
Yusuf II *ibn Musa al-Ruzzi* : 1599–1608 (Antioch—Maronite) 50
Yusuf III *ibn Halib al-'Aquri* : 1644–1647 (Antioch—Maronite) 50
Yusuf IV Butrus *Dirgham al-Khazin* : 1733–1742 (Antioch—Maronite) 50
Yusuf V Butrus *Istifan* : 1766–1793 (Antioch—Maronite) 50
Yusuf VI Butrus *al-Tiyyan* : 1796–1807 (Antioch—Maronite) 50
Yusuf VII Butrus *Hubaysh* : 1823–1845 (Antioch—Maronite) 50
Yusuf VIII Butrus *al-Khazin* : 1845–1854 (Antioch—Maronite) 51
Yusuf : 790–792 (Antioch—Syrian Catholic), and (Antioch—Syrian Orthodox) 54, 59
Yuwakim I : 1199–1219 (Antioch—Greek) 37
Yuwakim II : 1411–1426 (Antioch—Greek) 37
Yuwakim III : 1476–1483 (Antioch—Greek) 37
Yuwakim IV *ibn Jumma* : 1543–1576 (Antioch—Greek) 37
Yuwakim V *ibn Daww* : 1581–1592 (Antioch—Greek) 37
Yuwakim VI *Ziyada* : 1593–1604 (Antioch—Greek) 38
Yuwakim VII : 1724 [anti-patriarch] (Antioch—Greek) 38
Yuwakim I : 1412?–1425? (Antioch—Greek Melkite) 43
Yuwakim II : 1458?–1459? (Antioch—Greek Melkite) 43
Yuwakim III : 1527 [anti-patriarch], 1531–1534? (Antioch—Greek Melkite) 43
Yuwakim IV *ibn Jumma* : 1540 [anti-patriarch], 1543?–1575 (Antioch—Greek Melkite) 43
Yuwakim V *ibn Daww* : 1581–1592 [anti-patriarch] (Antioch—Greek Melkite) 43
Yuwakim VI *Ziyada* : 1593–1604 (Antioch—Greek Melkite) 43
Yuwakim VII : 1724 [anti-patriarch] (Antioch—Greek Melkite) 44

Zabina : 231–237 (Antioch—Syrian Orthodox) 58

Zacharias *Maridakēs* : 1769–1786 (Crete) 125
Zacharias : 1734–1741 (Greece) 157
Zacharias : 609–632 (Jerusalem—Greek) 185
Zacharias : 741–752 (Rome) 212
Zacharias : 1103–1114 (Sinai) 231
Zaharij : 1487?– (Macedonia) 195
Zak'aria I *Sefedinian* : 1296–1336 (Aght'amar) 6
Zak'aria II *Nahatak* : 1369–1393 (Aght'amar) 6
Zak'aria III : 1434–1464 (Aght'amar) 6
Zak'aria IV : 1489–1496 (Aght'amar) 6
Zak'aria I : 4th cent. (Aghunie) 9
Zak'aria II : 630–646 (Aghunie) 9
Zak'aria : 68–72 (Armenia) 64
Zak'aria I : 855–876 (Armenia) 66
Zak'aria : 1461–1462 [anti-catholicos] (Armenia) 67
Zak'aria II : 1507–1515 [coadjutor], 1515–1520 [catholicos], (Armenia) 67
Zak'aria I : 1626–1631, 1636–1640 (Constantinople—Armenian) 104
Zak'aria II : 1773–1781, 1782–1799 (Constantinople—Armenian) 105
Zak'aria *Jorjadze* : 1623–1630 (Georgia) 151
Zak'aria *K'variani* : 1657–1659 (Georgia—Abkhazia) 153
Zak'aria *Ter-Grigorian of Gop* : 1841–1846 (Jerusalem—Armenian) 182
Zakaryas : unknown (Ethiopia—Official) 140
Zakchaios : 111?– (Jerusalem—Greek) 184
Zakhariĭ : 1515? (Bulgaria) 93
Zakhariya : 890 (Antioch—Greek) 36
Zakhariyas : 1004–1032 (Alexandria—Coptic) 17
Zakka *'Iwas*, Ighnatiyus : 1980– (Antioch—Syrian Orthodox) 62, 253, 257, 259
Zambdas : 298–300 (Jerusalem—Greek) 184
Zareh *Payaslian* : 1956–1963 (Cilicia—Armenian Apostolic) 98, 100
Zawên : 377–381 (Armenia) 64
Zawên *Eghiayan* : 1913–1915, 1919–1922 (Constantinople—Armenian) 106
Zebede I : 1550–1557 (Georgia) 150
Zebede II : 1603–1610 (Georgia) 151
Zementos : 72–76 (Armenia) 64

Zena Marqos *Bogosew* : 1991–1992 [locum tenens] (Ethiopia—Historical), and (Ethiopia—Official) 142, 144
Zephyrinus : 199–217 (Rome) 210
Zibinus : 231–240? (Antioch—Greek) and (Antioch—Greek Melkite) 34, 40
Zoïlos : 541–551 (Alexandria—Greek) 24
Zosim I : 1662–1669 (Macedonia) 196
Zosim II : 1695–1699, 1707?–1708?, 1708–1709 (Macedonia) 196
Zosima I : 1663–1670 (Bulgaria) 94
Zosima II : 1695–1699, 1707–1708, 1708–1709 (Bulgaria) 94–95
Zosima : 1491–1496 (Russia—Moscow) 220
Zosimus : 417–418 (Rome) 211

www.ingramcontent.com/pod-product-compliance
Lightning Source LLC
Chambersburg PA
CBHW080803020526
44114CB00046B/2752